Between Civil and Religious Law

Recent Titles in
Contributions in Legal Studies

Comparative Constitutional Federalism: Europe and America
Mark Tushnet, editor

Church-State Constitutional Issues: Making Sense of the Establishment Clause
Donald L. Drakeman

The Politics of Obscenity: Group Litigation in a Time of Legal Change
Joseph F. Kobylka

An Essential Safeguard: Essays on the United States Supreme Court and Its Justices
D. Grier Stephenson, Jr., editor

A "Representative" Supreme Court? The Impact of Race, Religion, and Gender on Appointments
Barbara A. Perry

State Constitutions and Criminal Justice
Barry Latzer

The Social Dimension of 1992: Europe Faces a New EC
Beverly Springer

The Sixth Amendment in Modern American Jurisprudence: A Critical Perspective
Alfredo Garcia

Positive Neutrality: Letting Religious Freedom Ring
Stephen V. Monsma

Questioning the Law in Corporate America: Agenda for Reform
Gerald L. Houseman

Reason Over Precedents: Origins of American Legal Thought
Craig Evan Klafter

The Iron Horse and the Constitution: The Railroads and the Transformation of the Fourteenth Amendment
Richard C. Cortner

Between Civil and Religious Law

The Plight of the *Agunah* in American Society

Irving A. Breitowitz

Contributions in Legal Studies, Number 70

Greenwood Press
Westport, Connecticut • London

Library of Congress Cataloging-in-Publication Data

Breitowitz, Irving A.
Between civil and religious law : the plight of the *Agunah* in American society / Irving A. Breitowitz.
p. cm.—(Contributions in legal studies, ISSN 0147-1074 ; no. 70)
Includes bibliographical references and index.
ISBN 0-313-28471-7 (alk. paper)
1. Divorce—Law and legislation—United States. 2. Divorce (Jewish law) 3. Agunahs—United States. I. Title. II. Series.
KF536.B74 1993
346.7301'6—dc20
[347.30616] 92-551

British Library Cataloguing in Publication Data is available.

Library of Congress Catalog Card Number: 92-551
ISBN: 0-313-28471-7
ISSN: 0147-1074

First published in 1993

Greenwood Press, 88 Post Road West, Westport, CT 06881
An imprint of Greenwood Publishing Group, Inc.

Printed in the United States of America

The paper used in this book complies with the Permanent Paper Standard issued by the National Information Standards Organization (Z39.48-1984).

10 9 8 7 6 5 4 3 2 1

This book is dedicated to my parents David and Helen Breitowitz who, after escaping the horrors of Nazi persecution and enduring the deprivations of the Siberian wilderness, courageously built a new life in America. Their courage, tenacity, self-sacrifice, and love have been a constant source of strength and inspiration.

Contents

List of Tables and Supplementary Endnotes

---

*For the convenience of the general reader, certain extended discussions of intricate or arcane points of Jewish law have been moved from the main body of text and appear as endnotes following the particular chapters to which such discussions are connected. In addition, some endnotes contain summary material in tabular or outline form.

Preface

The subject of this book concerns a tragedy faced by a significant segment of the Jewish population, the inability of women who are civilly-divorced to remarry because of the refusal of their husbands to grant them a religious divorce. Such women are known as *agunot** (chained or anchored women). While marital breakdown is invariably tragic, it becomes much more so when parties are disabled from rebuilding their lives anew due to the animosity and spite of their former spouses. Finding grounds to enable an *agunah* to remarry is a great spiritual merit tantamount to the "rebuilding of the ruins of Jerusalem"** and generations of eminent Talmudists have labored mightily to achieve that end. If this book does nothing more than raise the consciousness of the Jewish public and help stimulate the great rabbinic and legal minds of our time in devising effective remedies for these unfortunate women, the effort of its composition will be more than amply rewarded.

Portions of this book are somewhat more technical and dense than I would have liked, particularly some of the mini-essays in the footnotes, and may not be "easy reading" for those not schooled in the subtle intricacies of Jewish law. To some degree, this difficulty is inevitable, reflecting both the complexity of the *halachic* process and the additional burdens of having to integrate that process into the constraints and categories of a very different legal order. I have endeavored to be as clear as possible even at the expense of a certain amount of repetition but only the reader can decide if I have succeeded. If not, I beg his or her indulgence. In any event, the main thrust of the argument may be followed without pursuing some of the fascinating and esoteric detours of the notes.

I have the pleasant duty to acknowledge those whose assistance enabled

---

*This is the plural form of *agunah*. Occasionally, the plural is Anglicized as *agunahs*.

**See 8 OTZAR HaPOSKIM, p. 102 (Heb. pagination), quoting TESHUVOT BACH HaCHADASHOT.

the completion of this work. April Cropper typed and retyped endless and often illegible drafts of the manuscript with consummate skill and unfailing good cheer. Mike Kelly, former dean of the University of Maryland School of Law and now vice-president at Georgetown, was ever supportive in his encouragement and in providing summer research stipends. Donald Gifford, Maryland's current dean, has graciously continued this tradition of faculty support. Michael Broyde, assistant professor at Emory's law school and its department of religion, gave an earlier draft of the manuscript a thorough reading and graced it with many perceptive comments, some of which found their way into the book. He also saved me from several embarrassing errors. Professor Sherman Cohn of the Georgetown Law School made a number of valuable suggestions, particularly in the constitutional law area. Nathan Lewin, Esq., eminent attorney and Jewish communal activist, made available his voluminous files concerning the New York *get* law (of which he was the principal drafter). I drew on these files quite heavily, particularly in the preparation of Chapter Six. David Zweibel, Esq., General Counsel of Agudath Israel of America, was kind enough to assemble and send materials regarding other proposed *get* laws in spite of his own busy schedule and provided invaluable insights into the background and meaning of New York's newest legislative initiative in this area, the amendment to Section 236B of its Domestic Relations Law. Special thanks must also be given to David Grahek, Maxine Grosshans, and Dennis Guion, the reference librarians at the University of Maryland School of Law, for their unfailing assistance in locating whatever obscure or hard to find materials I needed to unearth. Much thanks too to Nita Romer and the editorial staff at Greenwood Press for their fine technical assistance.

I also want to acknowledge the pioneering work of Rabbi J. David Bleich of Yeshiva University. Although he was not directly involved in the preparation of this volume, all who study and write in this area, as in numerous other areas of Jewish law, are greatly in his debt. Mention should also be made of the excellent works of Rabbis Irwin Haut and, more recently, Shlomo Riskin, who have made major contributions to this field and from whom I have learned a great deal. Needless to say, all errors that remain are my sole responsibility.

Finally, I want to express my profound gratitude to my wife Sally and son Moshe for the innumerable ways they have enriched my life. Without their love and support, this work, and any other endeavor, could not have been completed.

"Blessed is He who gives strength to the weary." (Morning service, based on Isaiah 40:29)
"As You [G-d] have enabled me to complete this work so may You enable me to begin other works and complete them - to learn and to teach, to observe and to perform all the words of Your Torah with love." (Traditional prayer recited upon completion of a tractate of the Talmud.)

Note on Sources, Terminology, and Abbreviations

A work of this nature is largely based on Jewish law sources. Because these sources are generally in Hebrew or Aramaic and both the books and their authors may be largely unknown to the general reader, I have attempted to provide supplementary information that will, I hope, enable the reader to follow the discussion. An elucidation of the primary literary sources of Jewish law and their relative hierarchy and status may be found in Appendix E. Brief biographical sketches of some of the major personalities mentioned in this work appear in Appendix F. The Selected Bibliography at the end of the book not only lists the primary sources utilized but provides the dates of the authors' lives and their respective countries of residence so that the reader may place these towering figures in both a historical and geographical perspective. All Hebrew and Aramaic terms are defined in the text the first time they appear and the definitions are reiterated and amplified in Appendix D (Glossary).

Just as every lawyer recognizes that an opinion of the New York Family Court is not entitled to the same weight as an opinion of the New York Court of Appeals, so too in Jewish law certain works are recognized as classic, authoritative texts whose pronouncements are more-or-less definitive while other works fall closer to the category of speculative scholarship. It would be ludicrous, for example, to cite some contemporary cleric as being of coequal status with Maimonides or the Talmud. As noted, Appendix E attempts to give the reader some "feel" for this ranking or hierarchy but the presentation offered therein is necessarily abbreviated. It must be emphasized that determining positions in Jewish law is not simply a matter of counting heads; it very much matters which heads are the ones being counted. In recognition of this crucial fact, when conflicting lines of authority are cited in text or notes, these various lines are generally of coequal status or rank, analogous to the differences of opinion among state supreme courts or federal courts of appeals.

In terms of importance, the Talmud occupies the highest rank. The Babylonian Talmud, known in Hebrew as Talmud Bavli, consists of a number of treatises. *Ketubot* is the one cited here most frequently. All *halachic* codes are based on the Talmud. The major codes include *Mishna Torah* authored by Maimonides (known in this work by his Hebrew title Rambam); *Tur* authored by Rabbi Yaakov Ben Asher; and *Shulchan Aruch* authored by Rabbi Yosef Karo. Of particular relevance to this work are the portions of *Tur* and

Shulchan Aruch dealing with family law, both of which are entitled *Even HaEzer*. All of these works are the subject of numerous commentaries. For further information, I again refer the reader to Appendixes E and F.

Transliteration of Hebrew into English poses some difficult problems and scholarly literature does not follow a wholly consistent pattern. The word *ketubah*, for example, may be spelled in several ways - *kesuba*, *kesuva*, *ketuba*, *ketuva*, *ketubah*, *kethuba* etc. I have generally adhered to the Sefardic pronunciation prevalent in the State of Israel today but the reader should be aware that courts and other writers may utilize different spellings. Any quotations from other sources reproduce whatever spelling those sources used.

Finally, the following is a selective list of the most common abbreviations and acronyms employed in the text and notes:

E.H.	=	*Even HaEzer*, volume of *Shulchan Aruch* dealing with family law.
H.M.	=	*Hoshen Mishpat*, volume of *Shulchan Aruch* dealing with commercial law and judicial procedure.
M.T.	=	*Mishna Torah*, monumental code of law, authored by Rambam (Moses Maimonides).
R.	=	Rabbi.
Rambam	=	Hebrew acronym for Rabbi Moshe Ben Maimon (Moses Maimonides, 1135-1204).
Ramban	=	Hebrew acronym for Rabbi Moshe Ben Nachman (Moses Nachmanides, 1194-1270).
Rema	=	Hebrew acronym for Rabbi Moshe Isserles (16th Century Poland), author of major glosses to the *Shulchan Aruch*.
Rosh	=	Hebrew acronym for Rabbi Asher Ben Yechiel (c. 1250-1327).
S.V.	=	*sub verbo* (under the word), indicating the portion of a primary text - Torah or Talmud - that a given commentator is explaining.
T.B.	=	Talmud Bavli (Babylonian Talmud).

Other abbreviations and acronyms are explained in the text or notes as they appear. A complete explanation of the legal abbreviations and citation forms utilized may be found in THE BLUEBOOK: A UNIFORM SYSTEM OF CITATION (15th ed. 1991) published by the Law Review Associations of Columbia, Harvard, University of Pennsylvania, and Yale schools of law.

Between Civil and Religious Law

Introduction

This book deals with the difficult, and often tragic, plight of the *agunah*,[1] a person (usually a woman) who, following a civil divorce, is unable to remarry within her faith because of the unwillingness of the other party (usually the husband) to participate in a religious divorce.[2] The motivation for the other side's refusal is occasionally a sincere desire for reconciliation but more often sheer malice or spite or a desire to obtain valuable concessions in terms of alimony, property settlements, or child custody. In any event, it is not uncommon for abandoned wives to remain in this *agunah* status for many years.[3] Neither civil nor religious authorities can effect a religious dissolution;

---

1. The term "*agunah*," which appears frequently in the Talmud, see, *e.g.*, TALMUD BAVLI [Babylonian Talmud, hereinafter T.B.] GITTIN 3a, is derived from the term "*agun*" or anchor and refers to parties who are literally "chained" to their former spouses. See A. Kohut, ARUCH HaSHALEM, *s.v. Agunah*.

2. In order to dissolve a marriage under Jewish law, the husband must present to his wife a specially prepared document known as a *get*. The requirement of a *get* is found in DEUTERONOMY 24:1: "When a man takes a wife and marries her, if it then comes to pass that she finds no favor in his eyes for he has found something unseemly in her, he shall write her a document of divorce and give it to her hand, and send her out of his house" (free translation).

3. Obviously, a party is an *agunah* only if his or her religious principles prohibit remarriage without a religious divorce. The vast majority of Jews no longer follow Jewish religious law and, as such, the presence or absence of *get* is a matter of indifference for them as individuals though it is a major concern for the Jewish community at large. See *infra* notes 216 and 305. Moreover, the Reform movement has officially abandoned the requirement of a *get* though many encourage its execution to avoid complications later. S. Freehof, REFORM JEWISH PRACTICE, pp. 99-110 (1944). Thus, the parties who are immediately affected are religiously observant and knowledgeable Orthodox or

only the parties themselves can. As a practical matter, then, religious divorces require mutual consent and participation and thus give rise to the possibilities of parties refusing to cooperate in order to obtain pecuniary or nonpecuniary advantages or simply to inflict pain.

The number of women subject to this status is unclear. Some estimates have placed the number as high as 150,000 in the state of New York alone while others contend that there are as few as fifty.[4] Whatever the number, however, each case carries its share of human misery and serves as a sad reminder of how the ennobling teachings of religion can be manipulated and twisted to serve immoral purposes. It also highlights the relative impotence of religious law *qua* law in a secular society, an inevitable by-product of the fundamental concept of the separation of church and state embodied in the First Amendment's establishment clause.

Conservative Jews. For these Jews, however, the lack of a *get* is a true chain and a source of anguish. As one woman, who had to wait three years for a *get*, remarked: "Your life is in limbo. You cannot begin to date, let alone think of marrying. You are at the mercy of another person who can resort to blackmail and other pressures, and your children are privy to the tension. Many women in this legal entanglement speak of feeling like hostages." Quoted in NEW YORK TIMES (July 5, 1982), p.40, column 2 (Style). Indeed, this author knows of one case where a woman has been unable to marry for over 20 years. For a graphic fictional description of the *agunah*'s state, see Chaim Grade, THE AGUNAH (1974). A more recent attempt which explores *agunah* problems through the genre of the murder mystery is Kritch, TILL DEATH DO US PART (1992).

4. The New York Times article of July 5, 1982 quoted an astounding figure of 150,000. Nat Hentoff quoted a figure "of at least 15,000," see VILLAGE VOICE (September 13, 1983), p. 6, which leads one to suspect that the ten-fold increase in the Times report may have been a typographical error. At the other extreme, Rabbi Mendel Epstein, a long-time activist in the area of "agunah-rights," claims that at any one time there are no more than 50 women who meet the basic definition of *agunah*, which he defines as a woman unable to obtain a *get* after exhausting all rabbinical procedures and obtaining a rabbinical order directing the husband to give a *get* which he then refuses to do. See Epstein, A WOMAN'S GUIDE TO THE GET PROCESS, p. 2. As noted earlier, if neither party knows or cares about a *get*, then the absence of a *get* creates no individual hardship. The Times figure of 150,000 may well include all Jewish married couples who have divorced without a *get* but only a tiny fraction of them perceive their status as problematical. While the Hentoff figure claims to comprise "religiously observant Jewish women who have been civilly-divorced" without a Jewish divorce, Epstein is correct that many of these women have not yet invoked the conventional channels and procedures. However, Epstein's own number ignores the very heavy obstacles that women face in securing a rabbinical court order, see discussion *infra* text at notes 54-59, and is therefore much too low. See also *infra* note 59 (respective positions of Agunah, Inc. and Rabbi Leib Landesman concerning the scope of the problem). Ultimately, whether a woman is or is not called an *agunah* is largely irrelevant. Nothing substantive turns on the nomenclature. If her marriage is in fact ended and she doesn't have the freedom to remarry, she has a problem worthy of consideration.

The pattern of this work is, first, to describe the contours of the problem including a description of Jewish divorce procedure, the grounds under which it can be invoked, and the consequences of failing to implement it; second, to sketch out the possible internal *halachic*[5] responses and adjustments to the situation; and finally, to consider the possibilities of utilizing the secular judicial system. I consider the Jewish law approaches first both because these avenues are less familiar to the general public and because, as a matter of principle, it is preferable to devise an effective solution within the contours of the Jewish law's own system of values rather than invoke the long but intrusive arm of the state. Overreliance on the secular system not only raises constitutional problems under the establishment clause but also undermines the autonomy and integrity of religious institutions. In a conceptually-perfect world, such reliance would be an alternative many would rather avoid. Nevertheless, in a perfect world there would also be no *agunah* problem so the options of civil enforcement must and will be carefully considered.

As far back as Biblical times, attempts were instituted to alleviate the plight of a spouse who would otherwise be unable to marry. Historically, the *agunah* problem originated not in the recalcitrance of the husband but in his unexplained absence. Jewish law does not recognize a presumption of death arising from prolonged absence. Accordingly, if a husband were captured in war or his whereabouts were otherwise unknown, his wife would not be permitted to remarry until the husband's death could be definitely established.[6] The burden of proof for establishing death was originally quite high; nothing less than the eyewitness testimony of two observers who actually saw the corpse and could conclusively identify the body as that of the husband would suffice.

According to the Talmud,[7] King David instituted a practice that required all soldiers assigned to combat to execute and deliver *gittin* to their wives so that in the event of any of them being taken prisoner or missing in action, their wives would be able to remarry. If the soldier returned safely, the parties could remarry each other. Although this procedure created the risk that one's wife might abscond with another - upon receipt of a *get*, nothing compelled her to wait for her husband's return[8] - such a step was justified to

---

5. *Halacha* is the entire corpus of Jewish law. A detailed description of *halacha* appears in Appendix D of this work.

6. This proposition appears many times in the Talmud. See, e.g., T.B. GITTIN 28a - 28b.

7. See T.B. SHABBAT 56a and KETUBOT 9b. The Talmud is attempting to explain why David's marriage to Bathsheba, although clearly characterized as an immoral act, was technically not adultery since she had been divorced from her husband Uriah before he went to war. Had David committed adultery, he would not have been permitted to marry Bathsheba even after the death of Uriah. [The analysis in the text follows the interpretation of Rabbeinu Tam, see TOSAFOT, *s.v. Get* but *cf.* RASHI, *s.v. Get* in their respective comments to KETUBOT 9b.]

8. But see the "Divorce of Vienna" controversy as recorded in TESHUVOT MAHARAM LUBLIN, nos. 102-106. A young man had given his wife a divorce anticipating death from a serious illness. He recovered and upon his recovery, sought to remarry her. When she refused, Maharam ruled that the prior get was invalid for it was given with the understanding that if

avoid the anguish of a wife remaining in limbo. Indeed, according to some commentaries, this enactment dated from the Mosaic era.[9]

A second example of concern for the *agunah* dates from the Second Judaean Commonwealth where the rules of evidence establishing death were considerably relaxed. In order to alleviate the burden of proving a spouse's death, the testimony of one, rather than two witnesses, was deemed sufficient and this witness could even be someone who was normally ineligible to testify.[10]

This particular scenario has by no means faded from the scene. In the aftermath of the Holocaust, for example, hundreds of women had no definitive proof of their husbands' deaths and rabbis were faced with the agonizing duty of relieving their plight while remaining faithful to the dictates of the law. A number of eminent *halachic* scholars performed this duty with great distinction.[11] This problem recurs with some regularity in the State of Israel and less frequently, in the United States.[12]

Nevertheless, in recent years we have seen the emergence of a different sort of *agunah* case: one in which the husband is very much alive and present but uses his power to grant or withhold a *get* as a stranglehold to wring out favorable concessions. While the Talmudic precedents cited above are thus not directly in point, they do indicate the concern that classical Jewish law had for the woman's plight and the willingness of the *halachic* system to take concrete steps to alleviate that concern.

---

husband recovered, they would be reunited. A contrary opinion was expressed by R. Shmuel Eidels, known as Maharsha (16th Century Poland) and the bulk of the Polish rabbinate.

9. See comment of Baal HaTurim to NUMBERS 32:21.

10. T.B. YEBAMOT 87b as later codified in SHULCHAN ARUCH EVEN HaEZER (E.H.) 17:3-13. Examples of normally ineligible witnesses include women, minors, relatives of the decedent or wife, or persons guilty of certain religious offenses.

11. Examples include the late Dr. Isadore Grunfeld of the London *Bait Din*, Rabbi Yitzchok I. Weiss of Manchester and Jerusalem, Rabbi T.P. Frank of Jerusalem and Rabbi Moshe Feinstein, for many years the "dean" of *halachic* authorities in the United States. A touching vignette of the personal anguish rabbis felt for the predicament of these "war widows" is recounted by Lord Immanuel Jakobovitz, former Chief Rabbi of Great Britain, in *Preserving the Oneness of the Jewish People: Can a Permanent Schism Be Averted*? 24 TRADITION 78, 91 (Winter 1989).

12. On an individual basis, rabbis would often advise persons going to war or going abroad under hazardous conditions to execute a get, following the venerable precedent instituted by David or even Moses. The Israeli Chief Rabbinate at one time toyed with the idea of imposing this procedure for all of their soldiers going to combat but concluded that mandating even a *pro forma* divorce would adversely affect combat morale. See Bleich, I CONTEMPORARY HALAKHIC PROBLEMS, p. 154.

Chapter One

The Nature of the Problem: Basic Dimensions and Contours

To fully comprehend the nature of the problem and the difficulties in trying to solve it, three Jewish law concepts must be understood: (1) the *get* and Jewish divorce procedure; (2) the role of the *bait din* [rabbinical court]; and (3) the rules governing divorces executed under duress.

WHAT IS A *GET*?

A *halachically*-valid marriage may be terminated in only two ways: (1) through death; or (2) the granting of a *get*.[13] A civil divorce has no effect in the eyes of *halacha* and any subsequent cohabitation or remarriage in the absence of a *get* is regarded as adulterous. A *get* is an Aramaic term meaning "document."[14] The "document" in question refers to a brief written statement containing a legally prescribed text. When the husband or his designated proxy

---

13. See T.B. KIDDUSHIN 2a. See infra text at notes 203-217 for a discussion as to which marriages are *halachically* valid and which may not be.

14. See A. Kohut, ARUCH HaSHALEM, s.v. *Get*. While the term "*get*" can be, and occasionally is, employed in reference to any legal document, its predominant usage is in connection with bills of divorce. See TOSAFOT to T.B. GITTIN 2a, *s.v. Hamevee*, who suggests that the numerical equivalent of the Hebrew letters that make up the word *get* is twelve. (Every letter in the Hebrew alphabet may also function as a number just as the letter "A" can be representative of the number "one.") This in turn corresponds to the custom that the *get* be composed in exactly twelve lines.

Tosafot goes on to note that in a Scroll of the Law used in the synagogue (the Sefer Torah), there are a total of twelve blank lines separating the books of the Pentateuch from each other. Since "twelve" connotes a number symbolic of separation and division and the *get* itself is termed "*sefer keritot*" [a document of separation], it is therefore appropriate to compose the *get* in twelve lines and refer to the document by a name that indicates this fact. See also comments of Rema to SHULCHAN ARUCH E.H. 125:12 (whether after the fact a *get* that is longer or shorter than the customary length may be used).

hands this document to his wife or her designated proxy, the marriage between them is terminated. The *get* itself is written in a combination of Hebrew and Aramaic; a rough translation follows:

> On the _____ day of the week, the ____ day of the month of _ in the year ____ since the creation of the world according to the calendar reckoning we are accustomed to count here in the city ___ situated on the River ____, I ____ the son of ___ have desired of my free will, being under no duress, to release [*alt. trans.* - remove, sever], let go, and expel you my wife _____ daughter of _____ who has been my wife from time past. And thus, I release [*alt. trans.* - remove, sever], let go of, and expel you so that you may have permission and authority over yourself to be married to any man you may desire and no one may raise any protest against your doing so from this day forward and forever more. Behold, you are permitted to all men. This shall be to you from me a book of expulsion, a letter of letting go, and a document of release [*alt. trans.* - removal, severance] in accordance with the law of Moses and Israel.
>
> ____ the son of ___ witness
> ____ the son of ___ witness[15]

The execution of a *get* is a private act; it does not require the participation or even the consent of a rabbinical tribunal, though in view of the fact that the formalities surrounding the writing and transfer of a *get* are numerous and complex, a rabbinical court of at least three is invariably present.[16] Even so, the role of the rabbi is supervisory only. In the eyes of *halacha*, it is the *husband* who *divorces* his wife rather than the state or the judiciary dissolving the marriage. A corollary of this fact is that under Biblical and Talmudic law, any coercion directed towards a husband in the giving of a *get* rendered the divorce a nullity while a wife could be forced to receive a *get*.[17]

The basic ceremony is fairly simple and can normally be accomplished in under an hour.[18] The entire body of the *get* is only a twelve-line document. Husband and wife meet at a prearranged time and place. There will be three rabbis present, one of whom will have primary responsibility for insuring observance of the requisite formalities [the *Mesader HaGet*, the "Arranger of the *Get*"] with the other two serving as witnesses. There will also be a scribe who will compose the text of the *get* by hand. The *get*, although a standardized text except for names or places, may not be printed, Xeroxed, or even prewritten with spaces left blank for names and places. The document in its entirety must be written anew for the specific couple whose marriage is being terminated. Since the writing of the *get* devolves in the first instance upon the

---

15. An extensive commentary to the text of a *get*, as well as some textual variants, appears *infra* Appendix C.

16. See T.B. KIDDUSHIN 6a: "All who are not intimately familiar with the laws of marriage and divorce should take no part in their proceedings." See also gloss of Rema to SHULCHAN ARUCH E.H. 154 (Appendix).

17. See infra text at notes 60-65.

18. The mechanics of the ceremony are spelled out in the Appendix following SHULCHAN ARUCH E.H. 154. English treatments can be found in Haut, DIVORCE IN JEWISH LAW AND LIFE, pp. 31-41, and in Amram, JEWISH LAW OF DIVORCE, Chapter 16.

husband, the husband must formally designate the scribe as his agent before the scribe can begin the composition of the *get*. The *get* must contain proper dates based on the traditional Jewish calculation, location and names of the husband and wife including common nicknames, etc. with the traditional tag "*son* of" or "*daughter* of." (Last names are not used.) These names must be spelled correctly. Indeed, one of the most difficult, albeit tedious, jobs of the *Mesader HaGet* is to determine which names should be included - (What if Robert is sometimes called Rob, Bob, Robby, Bobby, or Skip and in addition has a Jewish name of Rafael which he never uses? The same questions may be raised regarding *his* father, *his* about-to-be-divorced wife, and her father.)- and how to transliterate those names into Hebrew. Upon completion of the writing of the *get*, two witnesses sign at the bottom. The husband and wife are both asked a set of formalized questions as a final assurance that the *get* is not a product of duress, compulsion, extortion, etc. The husband then takes the document, physically deposits it in his wife's hands - again in the presence of witnesses - and, upon the *get's* delivery, the marriage is terminated. As a procedural matter, a divorced woman generally does not keep the *get* but returns it to the custody of the *bait din*, which will issue an official receipt stating that such *get* was properly delivered. If further evidence of her divorced status ever becomes necessary, the *bait din* will produce the original from its archives. If either husband or wife is unable to be present, the entire procedure may be consummated via designated proxy and the *Mesader* must insure that all powers of attorney are in proper form.[19]

A divorced woman is free to marry anyone she chooses including her former spouse[20] except for the following: a) a *Cohen*, a descendant of the priestly class; b) a man with whom she committed adultery; c) persons who served as witnesses for the *get*; d) her former husband if in the interim she marries someone else who then dies or divorces her; or e) her former husband if she was guilty of adultery during the course of a marriage.[21] In addition, she

---

19. The details of the law of agency are quite complex. Appropriate power of attorney forms can be found in the Appendix following SHULCHAN ARUCH E.H. 154.

20. Indeed, unless the husband is a *Cohen* or the wife has remarried in the interim, the reuniting of divorced spouses is considered a meritorious deed, undoing in part the havoc produced by the divorce. See Haut, *supra* note 18, p. 43.

21. The prohibition against a divorcee's marrying a *Cohen* is found in LEVITICUS 21:7 and is nonwaivable, *i.e.*, a person cannot "resign" the priesthood to marry a divorcee, *including his own former wife*. Note, however, that a female descendant of a *Cohen* may marry a divorced man. See comments of Rashi to LEVITICUS 21:7. The law that a woman may not marry the man with whom she committed adultery is based on the Talmudic interpretation of NUMBERS 5:11-13 and is codified in SHULCHAN ARUCH E.H. 11:1. The rule that witnesses on a *get* cannot marry the divorcee stems from the need to remove a possible bias from their testimony and is recorded in the comments of Rema to SHULCHAN ARUCH E.H. 130:31.

The prohibition against remarrying one's own spouse once she has married (not merely cohabited with another) is found in DEUTERONOMY 24:1-4. The basis for this law, not found in any other ancient code, is somewhat obscure. Indeed, the Islamic law of the KORAN, *Sura* II, provides exactly the

must wait ninety days from the delivery of *get* to determine whether or not she is pregnant from her first husband; marrying earlier could cast doubt on the paternity of a later offspring.[22]

The delivery of a *get* also triggers alimony, child support, and custody rights but these are beyond the purview of this book.[23]

Interestingly, just as a civil divorce has no validity in the eyes of religious law, a religious divorce is not recognized civilly. Unlike marriage where virtually all states recognize that a marriage performed by an authorized minister of the faith is accorded validity, the power of dissolution still rests exclusively with the secular judiciary.[24] Thus, the *get* is totally unrelated to either the granting or withholding of a civil dissolution. As a matter of practice, however, many rabbinical tribunals will not supervise the execution of a *get* until all attempts at reconciliation have failed and this may mean

---

opposite: remarriage to a former spouse is not permitted until there has been an interim union with an outsider. One interesting suggestion has been advanced that the Deuteronomic prohibition protects the second marriage of the divorcee from undue interference by a prior spouse who longer stands to gain from a second breakup. See Yaron, *Biblical Law: Prolegomena*, JEWISH LAW IN LEGAL HISTORY AND THE MODERN WORLD (B. Jackson, ed.) 27, 37 (1980). Here too, as in the earlier rule of a *Cohen*, a woman may remarry her former husband after he has gone through a second divorce.

Finally, the rule that a woman guilty of voluntary adultery may not remain with her husband is found in SHULCHAN ARUCH E.H. 11:1, along with the related prohibition of marriage to the paramour.

22. See T.B. YEBAMOT 41a and SHULCHAN ARUCH E.H. 13:1. The stated rationale for this rule is the legal presumption that it normally takes three months until a pregnancy is physically noticeable. Were a woman to marry before that point and a child to be born six to eight months afterwards, it would be uncertain whether the child was a full-term pregnancy from the first husband or a premature birth from the second. As codified, however, this ninety-day period is essentially absolute. Remarriage before the expiration of ninety-days is prohibited even under circumstances where an undetected pregnancy is an impossibility, e.g., the woman is infertile, past menopause, or was physically separated from her husband for far more than three months. *Id.*, 12:2 based on T.B. KETUBOT 60b. For this reason, modern authorities have ruled that the ninety-day period is not waivable by means of a sonogram or other early pregnancy test. See 2 OTZAR HaPOSKIM E.H. 13:5.

23. Jewish law treatment of child custody is sparse. For representative articles, see Schaffer, *Child Custody: Halacha and the Secular Approach*, 6 JOURNAL OF HALACHA AND CONTEMPORARY SOCIETY 33 (1984) and Warburg, *Child Custody: A Comparative Analysis*, 14 ISRAEL LAW REVIEW 480 (1981). See also Shareshevsky, DINAI MISHPACHA (2nd ed. 1967), pp. 376-384. With respect to property rights, see *infra* Appendix B and the excellent, though brief, overview in Engel, *Marital Property Rights in Jewish Law: A Survey and Comparison*, 2 NATIONAL JEWISH LAW REVIEW 97 (1987).

24. This, however, was not always the case. Civil divorce is a comparatively late development. See *infra* text at notes 474-478.

delaying the *get* until a judgment of dissolution has been entered.[25]

THE RIGHT TO INITIATE THE JEWISH DIVORCE PROCESS

The Mishna in *Gittin* discusses the grounds upon which divorce should be pursued and records three opinions.[26] The House of Shammai maintains that one should not divorce one's spouse unless she is guilty of adultery. The House of Hillel permits divorce even on the basis of trivial dissatisfactions such as burning the soup. Finally, R. Akiva asserts that a husband has the right to divorce his wife even in the absence of any basis for dissatisfaction, for example, he is simply attracted to someone else. It is clear from a number of places in the Talmud that these opinions do not pertain to the legal validity of a *get* issued after the fact but merely to the moral advisability or proprietary of instituting the procedure.[27] (The Talmud after all is a mixture of law, morality and spiritual aspiration; it is both a *legal* and *religious* work). In point of fact, a husband has an absolute right, or at least power,[28] to divorce his wife at will for no reason at all and, unlike the case in marriage, her consent is not required.[29] The many laws and regulations concerning the *get meusah* (the

---

25. This is the official practice of the Chief Rabbinate of Great Britain, which has taken the position that such deferral is required by secular law. See Maidment, *The Legal Effect of Religious Divorces*, 37 MOD. L. REV. 611 (1974). Rabbis in the United States do not have a standard practice.

26. T.B. GITTIN 90a.

27. See, for example, T.B. GITTIN 90a (Statement of Rava to R. Papa). The *Shulchan Aruch*, however, does note that it is morally improper to divorce one's first wife for any grounds short of actual or suspected adultery or extreme nastiness of disposition. E.H. 119:34.

28. To use the terminology of Wesley Hohfeld, a person has a "right" to perform a certain act only if others have a "duty" to let him perform it. Since Jewish law may prohibit divorce for less than weighty reasons and the *bait din* is duty-bound to discourage it, the husband does not have a "right" of unqualified divorce in Hohfeldian terms. "Power," on the other hand, refers to a capacity of creating, divesting, or altering rights and does not necessarily imply a duty on others of noninterference. In that sense, the *ex post facto* validity of a *get* executed for any reason at all is indicative of a "power" rather than a "right." See generally Hohfeld, FUNDAMENTAL LEGAL CONCEPTIONS AS APPLIED IN JUDICIAL REASONING (1923, reprinted 1964, 1966), pp. 64-114. Hohfeld's unique terminology has been quite influential in modern jurisprudential thought though his scheme is both incomplete and difficult to fully master. See, *e.g.*, Pound, IV JURISPRUDENCE, pp. 77-106, especially p. 83 note 101 for a bibliography of writings on the subject (through 1954).

29. See T.B. YEBAMOT 112b ("A wife may be divorced either willingly or unwillingly but a husband may divorce only from his free will.") and its codification in SHULCHAN ARUCH E.H. 119:6. It should be noted, however, that the *halachic* right of the husband to effect divorce without the consent of the wife does not permit the divorce of a spouse who is deemed mentally incompetent, though the level of requisite competence for divorce law may be somewhat lower than it is in other areas such as commercial

"compelled get") pertain to compulsion directed to the *husband* not the *wife*.[30]

The absolute right of a husband recognized by Biblical and Talmudic law to institute divorce proceedings underwent a drastic change in the 10th Century. Rabbeinu Gershom,[31] acknowledged leader of East European Jewry, spearheaded the enactment of a decree that prohibited a husband from divorcing his wife against her will except in narrowly defined circumstances. In addition, he instituted a decree banning the Biblically permitted, though discouraged, practice of polygamy.[32] These *takkanot* (legislative enactments) essentially

---

transactions. (The standard merely requires that she perceive that she has been divorced and knows that she is no longer to live with her husband). *Id.*, 119:6-7.

Note should also be taken of two uncommon instances where, under Jewish law, a husband may *not* divorce his wife. According to EXODUS 22:15-17, if a man rapes an unmarried virgin, he is obligated to marry her if she so desires and may not divorce her. If he does give her a *get*, the divorce is valid but he is under a legally-enforceable obligation to remarry her. See T.B. MAKKOT 14b-15a. According to DEUTERONOMY 22:13-19, a man who wrongfully accuses his wife of unchastity during betrothal is permanently enjoined from divorcing her against her will and, as in the case of the rape, is obliged to remarry her in the event of a divorce.

Other than the wife who is: (1) mentally incompetent; (2) the victim of her husband's rape; or (3) wrongfully accused of adultery, there were no other limitations in Biblical or Talmudic law on the husband's absolute right to initiate divorce proceedings though the overly-hasty exercise of this right was subject to considerable moral opprobrium. See *supra* note 27.

30. Despite the availability of "no fault" divorce at least on the part of the husband, the Talmud is replete with references concerning the tragedy of divorce. "When one divorces his wife, even the altar in heaven sheds tears," T.B. GITTIN 90b, and the rabbinic court is enjoined to attempt to bring the parties to an amicable reconciliation. Indeed, even after the divorce, the parties may be encouraged to remarry (unless the husband is a *Cohen*, a member of the priestly class who may not marry a divorcee or if the woman remarries and is then widowed or divorced a second time.)

Divorced women also have substantial property and custody rights. See *infra* Appendix B. In fact, the stated justification for the institution of the *ketubah* imposing alimony obligations is to create a disincentive against divorce. See T.B. KETUBOT 11a and Rambam, MISHNA TORAH, *Hilchot Ishut* 10:10.

31. Rabbeinu Gershom [our Master Gershom], known by his contemporaries as Me'or HaGolah ["The Light of the Diaspora"], lived in Mayence in the latter part of the 10th Century. Historians have debated whether he in fact promulgated the *takkanot* that have been attributed to him. See 7 ENCYCLOPEDIA JUDAICA, "Gershom Ben Yehuda," pp. 511-512 (1971); A. Grossman, THE EARLY SAGES OF ASHKENAZ (Hebrew), p. 1451, notes 135-137 (1981).

32. The ban on polygamy is noted in SHULCHAN ARUCH E.H. 1:10 though the author points out that the ban has not spread to, nor been accepted by, all Jewish communities. Indeed, the Sefardic communities of North Africa, Palestine, and Spain (Moslem countries) never accepted Rabbeinu Gershom's *takkana* and continued the practice of polygamy until very recent times. (I

introduced a spirit of equality in divorce proceedings and for the most part necessitate that all divorce occur through *mutual* consent. As one authority noted:

> When [Rabbeinu Gershom] saw how the generation was abusive of Jewish daughters insofar as divorcing them under compulsion, he enacted that the rights of women be equal to those of men, and just as a man divorces only from his own will, so too a woman might henceforth be divorced only willingly.[33]

Although subsequent to the *takkana* of Rabbeinu Gershom, husbands and wives seem to be on the same footing, this is not entirely true. In the first place, the consequences of adultery on the part of a married woman are considerably more severe than they are for a married man. If a married woman (and that term includes any woman *halachically* married if that marriage has not been terminated by a *get*) cohabits with a man other than her husband (whether that other is married or not), she and her paramour are guilty of a capital offense;[34] any children resulting from such a union bear the stigma

---

believe, however, that even these communities did not permit the divorcing of a woman without her consent.) Interestingly, the BAIT YOSEF, E.H.I., informs us that Rabbeinu Gershom intended his ban to be in effect only until the end of the Fifth Millennium (1240) and continued adherence to the ban is no longer a matter of strict law but simply long-standing community custom. Others maintain that the Ashkenazic communities through their religious leadership renewed the ban before its expiration date without stipulating a time period. See generally Schwartz, *Heter Meah Rabbanim*, 11 JOURNAL OF HALACHA AND CONTEMPORARY SOCIETY 33, 37-38 (Spring 1986).

In any case, even among the communities that did not follow the ban and permitted polygamy (Sefardic), it was fairly common to incorporate contractually the equivalent of an anti-polygamy clause in the *ketubah*, e.g., "in the event H marries another wife, he shall forthwith divorce W and pay" an exorbitant amount of money as alimony or to impose a solemn oath banning the taking of another spouse. See generally Shareshevsky, *supra* note 23, pp. 72-73. Moreover, the religious leadership of the modern State of Israel has essentially banned polygamy even for the immigrants from Sefardic lands not bound by the *takkana* though special dispensations might be granted for preexisting marriages, *e.g.*, someone comes to Israel with several wives. See the enactments of the Israeli Chief Rabbinate (Rabbis Herzog and Uziel, 1950) reprinted as Appendix B in Shareshevsky, *supra* note 23.

A final point regarding this ban: the intriguing suggestion has been advanced that the purpose of Rabbeinu Gershom's ban on polygamy was the protection of *agunot*. Disabling the husband from remarrying until he divorces his first wife would invariably pressure him to execute a *get*. History suggests, however, that while *agunah*-protection may indeed be the *result* of Rabbeinu Gershom's enactment, it is unlikely that it ever was its *purpose*. See *infra* note 144 for a fuller elaboration of this point.

33. TESHUVOT ROSH 42:1.

34. See DEUTERONOMY 23:22-27 (which, however, recognizes the defense of forcible rape). This fact has only theoretical importance today. Under Biblical law, Jewish courts had the authority to impose capital punishment for a variety of offenses including blasphemy, murder, adultery, and desecration of the Sabbath. Interestingly, rape of an unmarried woman was

of *mamzer*;[35] and if the relationship was consensual (*i.e.*, not a rape), the woman forfeits her alimony rights and is not permitted to remain married to her husband even if he is willing to forgive the offense.[36] Moreover, subsequent to a divorce from her husband, she is not permitted to marry her paramour.[37] If a married man commits adultery with an unmarried woman, technically

---

not a capital crime. *Id.*, 28-29. Even when the laws of capital punishment were in effect, the procedural and evidentiary requirements for the imposition of a capital sentence were so difficult to satisfy [eyewitness testimony of two adult males not related to each other or to the defendants; defendants had to be warned not to perform the forbidden act, had to acknowledge the warnings, and had to commit the act immediately subsequent to the warnings; witnesses were cross-examined separately and even minor discrepancies in their recollection of the event would invalidate their testimony] that the Mishna already remarked that any court which executed a defendant once in seventy years was considered unusually violent. See T.B. MAKKOT 7a. The power to impose capital punishment lapsed between 30 and 40 c.e., shortly after the Roman conquest of Judaea, see T.B. SANHEDRIN 41a, and at least insofar as the Biblical offenses are concerned, has not been reinstated by the modern State of Israel. As a matter of religion and conscience, however, "capital offenses" are still deemed more serious transgressions than noncapital sins. See Rambam, MISHNA TORAH, *Hilchot Teshuva* 1:4. See also the classic work by S. Assaf, HaONSHIN ACHAR CHATIMAT HaTALMUD (1922) and the treatment in Schreiber, JEWISH LAW AND DECISION MAKING, pp. 400-424. These authors demonstrate that a number of Jewish communities throughout the Middle Ages continued to impose capital punishment and a variety of other extraordinary sanctions, hundreds of years after their power to do so had supposedly lapsed.

35. The term "*mamzer*" is normally translated as "illegitimate" but has a specialized, technical meaning that is not captured in the translation. In the first place, a child born out of wedlock is not a *mamzer* and is under no disability at all. A *mamzer* is a child born out of incest or born out of an *adulterous* union between a *married* woman and a man whether *married or not*. Second, a *mamzer's* disabilities while quite severe are also limited to one particular sphere: restrictions on the choice of marriage partners. A *mamzer* may not marry another Jew unless that person is also a *mamzer* or a convert. See SHULCHAN ARUCH E.H. 4:1, 13, 22. In all other respects, however, such as inheritance rights and eligibility for community positions of authority, *halacha* does not permit discrimination. See, *e.g.*, SHULCHAN ARUCH H.M. 7:2 (*mamzer* may serve as a judge) and H.M. 176:6 (inheritance rights). Indeed, the Talmud states that a "*mamzer* who is a scholar of the Law is entitled to more respect than a High Priest who is an ignoramus." T.B. HORIYOT 13a.

36. See SHULCHAN ARUCH E.H. 115:5 (forfeiture of *ketubah*) and 178:16 (prohibition of continuing the marriage).

37. See SHULCHAN ARUCH E.H. 11:1 and ARUCH HaSHULCHAN E.H. 178:30.

under Biblical law, no crime has been committed at all[38]; any resulting children are not tainted with the stigma of illegitimacy; he is permitted to remain with his wife if she consents and indeed perhaps if she doesn't; and in the event of marital breakup, he may marry his lover.[39]

Moreover, although Rabbeinu Gershom's *takkana* normally precludes both divorce without consent of the wife and polygamy, this is not always the case. While a married woman can in no instance be permitted to remarry without a *get* (since to do so involves a Biblical infraction not subject to rabbinical annulment or dispensation), the rabbinical ban of R. Gershom may be annulled pursuant to a procedure described as *heter meah rabbanim* ["dispensation of 100 rabbis"]. The first mention of this extraordinary procedure appears in the *Kol Bo*:

> The excommunication ban which Rabbeinu Gershom decreed is not to be lifted except with the approval of one hundred sages from three communities and from three countries such as Aragon, Lombardy, and France. They should not agree to remove it until and unless they see an unquestionable and clearcut reason for such leniency, and also that the particular case be clearly defined.[40]

The grounds for which such dispensation may be granted are many: (1) inability to have children from his present wife; (2) where the first marriage is prohibited by Jewish law; (3) where the present wife refuses to cohabit with her husband; (4) where a wife unjustifiably abandons her home; (5) where the present wife suffers a mental disability that renders her unable to accept a *get*. Sometimes, the effect of the annulment is to lift the ban on polygamy, thereby permitting the husband to marry again but leaving him married to his first spouse. Other times, the *heter* permits the institution of an involuntary divorce.[41] (It should be noted, however, that as a practical matter, many rabbinical authorities were extremely reluctant to participate in this annulment

---

38. The statement in the text that "no crime has been committed" means only that the act is not adulterous. A married man cohabiting with an unmarried woman is, under strict Biblical law, no different than an unmarried man cohabiting with an unmarried woman. The marital status of the male is simply irrelevant. Nevertheless, although the male's marital status does not transform the union into adultery nor does it taint the offspring with the stigma of *mamzeirut*, it is prohibited to the same degree as any out-of-wedlock relationship. The extent of this lesser prohibition is discussed *infra* text at notes 190-201.

39. See Rema, comment to E.H. 154:1 (if husband is a "frequenter of prostitutes" and the wife demands a divorce, "some are of the opinion" that the husband may be forced to grant a *get*). See also the comment of Rabbi Tzvi Ashkenazy (17th Century Germany and Poland), TESHUVOT CHACHAM TZVI, no. 133 who limits the ruling of Rema to the habitual offender, not the one-time adulterer who has repented of his sin. Note, however, that the unfaithful *wife* is not given the luxury of repentance.

40. KOL BO, Ch. 116; 1 OTZAR HaPOSKIM E.H. 1:61.

41. For an extensive discussion, see 1 OTZAR HaPOSKIM E.H. 1:68 and Schwartz, *supra* note 32, pp. 41-49.

procedure.)[42]

The upshot is that, although after the *takkana* neither party can initiate the *get* process without the consent of the other and in theory each party may be held hostage to the recalcitrance of the other (and thus, *agunah* is not exclusively a female problem), the negative consequences of a refusal of the other party to consent to a *get* are both more severe and less avoidable in the case of the wife than in the case of a husband. Thus, the *agunah* issue is perceived correctly as predominantly, though by no means exclusively, a woman's tragedy.

THE ROLE OF THE *BAIT DIN*

General Function

A *bait din* ["house of law"] [plural: *batei din*] is the term for a rabbinical tribunal commonly comprised of three rabbis or even one rabbi and two lay persons assembled to decide matters of Jewish law or resolve disputes. Under classical Biblical and Talmudic law, each community had its own *bait din* that would be empowered to rule on matters of Jewish law and to compel obedience to its ruling.[43] Indeed, even after the destruction of the Judaean state, for hundreds of years Jews were able to maintain the rule of Jewish law and to preserve the functioning of their courts. As one commentator noted, "Among all the institutions of self-government in the Middle Ages, the Jewish court was by far the most distinctive and characteristic."[44] The aftermath of the French Revolution led to a fragmentation of communal cohesiveness, the withdrawal of legal recognition of religious communities as politically-autonomous entities, and the development of the separation of church and state. These developments have created a situation where a *bait din* no longer has coercive power and can decide only those disputes that the parties have voluntarily submitted to its jurisdiction. While it is still true as a religious matter that civil disputes among Jews must be submitted to a *bait din* rather than a secular tribunal[45] and if an individual refuses to respond to the summons

---

42. See Rabbi Shlomo Kluger, HaELEF L'CHA SHLOMO, E.H. 7 and Schwartz, *supra* note 32, p. 46.

43. See generally Rambam, MISHNA TORAH, *Hilchot Sanhedrin* 1:1-10 and Schreiber, JEWISH LAW AND DECISION MAKING: A STUDY THROUGH TIME, pp. 236-280.

44. Comment, *Jewish Divorce and the Civil Law*, 12 DE PAUL LAW REVIEW 295, 300 note 24 (1962).

45. The religious obligation on a Jew to seek resolution of his disputes through the framework of a *bait din* rather than a secular court is codified in SHULCHAN ARUCH H.M. 26:1. See also E. Quint, I A RESTATEMENT OF JEWISH CIVIL LAW, pp. 176-181. For a fascinating discussion whether this prohibition is limited to litigants with attorneys being guilty, if at all, only as secondary facilitators, or applies with equal force to Jewish attorneys appearing in court in representative capacities, see Broyde, *On the Practice of Law According to Halacha*, 20 JOURNAL OF HALACHA AND CONTEMPORARY SOCIETY 5, 10-13 (Fall 1990). Compare also Rabbi Menashe Klein, 7 MISHNE HALACHOT, no. 255 (the attorney is a direct transgressor of the litigation prohibition) with Rabbi Ovadiah Yosef, 4

of a *bait din* or initiates action in a secular tribunal, the court may issue a *k'tav siruv* [a citation declaring him to be in contempt], the *siruv* itself carries with it no legal sanction, and at best may result in no more than a certain degree of community pressure (but often doesn't).[46] Moreover, as a practical matter, many *batei din* are extremely reluctant to issue a *k'tav siruv* and, as a result, even the bit of pressure that could be applied to the recalcitrant party fails to materialize. Thus, the cold reality is that, in the absence of an arbitration agreement, it is extremely difficult to compel an unwilling party to take a dispute of any kind to a *bait din*. If neither party is willing, it becomes impossible.

A second point to consider is the fact that most communities today do not have a standing *bait din*. Taking my own community as an example, there is no officially designated *bait din* of Baltimore whose rulings are accepted by all segments of Baltimore Jewry. Indeed, there is not even an officially-designated Orthodox or Conservative *bait din* on either the local or the national level whose rulings would be (morally) binding on adherents of their respective movements. In the absence of a standing *bait din* which is normally regarded as the preferable alternative, the *Shulchan Aruch* rules that each party may pick one judge of their choice and the two chosen judges choose a third.[47] The vast majority of disputes submitted to a *bait din* are decided under this procedure, which is commonly referred to as *ZABLA* [acronym for "*Ze Boreir Lo Achad*" - "Each chooses one"]. While the paucity of rabbinical judges in the community

---

YECHAVE DA'AT, no. 65 (the attorney is only an aider and abettor, facilitating a primary prohibition only on the part of the actual litigants).

46. The sanctions may include denial of synagogue honors and social ostracism. Technically, once a defendant has been found in contempt, the *bait din* is empowered to impose a form of ban or excommunication known as *shamta* or *nidui*. See SHULCHAN ARUCH H.M. 11:1. Persons placed under such ban may not be counted towards a synagogue quorum and are not permitted to shave or wear freshly-laundered clothing. In addition, others must distance themselves from the banned person and minimize social interaction. The minimum duration of the ban is normally thirty days but this time may be extended or shortened depending on the defendant's compliance. See generally SHULCHAN ARUCH YORE DE'AH 334:11-12. (The possibility of sanctions other than *nidui*, *e.g.*, fines, is discussed *infra* notes 292 and 319 though, as a matter of secular law, a *bait din* has no way to enforce any fines it may impose absent agreement of the parties). The sanction of *nidui* is extremely potent in a *halachically*-observant society where these ostracism norms will be kept. In a *nonhalachic* society, however, a recalcitrant defendant will simply ignore the *nidui* just as he ignored the *bait din* and his friends and colleagues may very well do the same. In any event, a *bait din* is usually reluctant to impose a formal ban and will often content itself with a mere declaration of contempt that is even less efficacious. Indeed, as noted in the text, it will frequently not even issue a *k'tav siruv*.

While the *k'tav siruv* thus exerts relatively little direct pressure on a disobedient defendant, one very important consequence that it does have is the enabling of the other party to proceed in secular court despite the fact that such litigation is ordinarily prohibited. See *supra* note 45 and SHULCHAN ARUCH H.M. 26:2.

47. SHULCHAN ARUCH H.M. 13:1-2.

may make *ZABLA* a necessity, the procedure raises a host of problems.

Giving the defendant the right to choose a judge creates opportunities for indefinite delays and makes it virtually impossible that he could ever be held in contempt since, until he makes his choice, there is no *bait din* that can issue a *siruv*. Second, many have a common misconception that in a *ZABLA*, each of the two judges is supposed to function as an advocate for the side that chose him. This is patently untrue. All three judges are supposed to be unbiased, disinterested adjudicators.[48] Nevertheless, as a consequence of this misconception, litigants may have a fundamental disrespect for the process. Feeling that the process is tainted, they refuse to utilize it and disregard its orders. Moreover, it cannot be denied that in more than a few cases, litigants' contentions have been borne out. This too explains why a *k'tav siruv* is so infrequently issued and, when issued, often ignored. Even litigants acting in bad faith escape the wrath of their communities by alleging bias on the part of one of the *ZABLA* judges, an accusation typically hard to disprove. Third, because the *bait din* is typically *ad hoc* and indeed may contain lay people, its professional expertise in matters of Jewish law may not be as great as it should or there may be a perception to that effect whether true or not. This not only results in erroneous decisions but further contributes to a disrespect for the system. Finally, regardless of the competence or expertise of the *bait din* in an individual case, the fact that each *bait din* is an *ad hoc* group means there is no institutional continuity, no sense of precedent, and few or no standardized procedures regarding admissibility of evidence, use of documentation, participation of attorneys, and the like. Different *batei din* simply do things differently, sometimes based on *halachic* considerations, sometimes based on the curbstone equities of the case, and sometimes based on run-of-the-mill common sense. Under a *ZABLA* system, therefore, there is no real way litigants can know the rules of the game in advance. This too severely undermines confidence in the system, generates considerable though at times unfounded anxiety about its use, gives bad-faith recalcitrants yet another way out in disregarding the decision of the court, and results in attorneys often counselling their clients to stay away from a *bait din* because its processes are too unpredictable and arbitrary.[49]

Many of these problems could be eliminated if community-wide standing *batei din* were established. Such institutions would enjoy community acceptance and as such their orders are more likely to be respected. Unwilling litigants would in turn feel greater pressure to comply. Replacing a system where judges are chosen and compensated by the parties with one that is community-funded minimizes bias or the appearance of bias. Greater expertise in *halachic* rules governing dispute resolution would be fostered. Most important of all, a community-wide *bait din* could establish uniform standards of practice and procedure so that the appearance of instability, inconsistency, and arbitrariness would be dispelled. These standards could be published and circulated among all segments of the Jewish community so that the *bait din*

48. See ROSH, SANHEDRIN 3:2 but see ARUCH HaSHULCHAN H.M. 13:1-2.

49. I address these problems in greater detail in Breitowitz, Review of Quint, A Restatement of Jewish Civil Law, 51 JEWISH ACTION 78 (Summer 1991).

would once again be regarded as a viable alternative to civil remedies.[50]

Assuming both parties do eventually come before a *bait din* of either the standing or the *ZABLA* type, the general procedure of the tribunal is relatively simple and informal.[51] The use of attorneys is normally discouraged although not precluded; the litigants and witnesses are questioned directly by the judges.[52] All evidence including hearsay may be admissible although its weight may be appropriately discounted. Before deciding the case, the *bait din* will normally ask the parties to sign its equivalent of a binding arbitration agreement to insure that its ultimate decision will be civilly enforceable.[53] Thus, while it is extremely difficult to bring a party before a *bait din*, it is far easier to enforce the decision of a *bait din* once made (at least, no more difficult than enforcing an arbitration in general).

The *Bait Din* in Divorce Cases

In the area of divorce, a *bait din* may be involved at two different points. First, in the event both parties have agreed to a divorce, the actual execution and delivery of the *get* will be under the supervision and in the presence of a *bait din*. Here, in universal acknowledgement of the fact that the laws of writing a *get* are extremely complex, *ZABLA* is invariably not used. Rather communities tend to have individual rabbis who are experts in the area. These rabbis handle all *gittin* in the community and choose two other people who will assist them in their task.

However, a *bait din* may be necessary to resolve a contested proceeding. Here, *ZABLA* again raises the potential for serious abuse. Let us assume that a wife wants a *get* and the husband refuses to give it to her. Since a secular court cannot order a religious divorce (at least in the absence of contract), her only recourse is to go to a *bait din* which will determine whether

---

50. A number of communities do have standing *batei din* as do a number of national organizations. Examples are the various Chassidic groups [Lubavitch, Satmar, Belz] and organizations like the Rabbinical Council of America. While these are highly respected and do supply the vital element of procedural regularity, they still fall short of constituting a central authority for a discrete geographical area. As such, their decisions are often flouted and they in turn are reluctant to issue a *k'tav siruv* on the theory that to do so would be a useless act.

51. Much of the information in this paragraph is a product of this author's own experience in sitting on a *bait din*. In addition, see Kirsh, *Conflict Resolution and the Legal Culture: A Study of the Rabbinical Court*, 9 OSGOODE HALL LAW JOURNAL 335 (1971) and Note, *Rabbinical Courts: Modern-Day Solomons*, 6 COLUMBIA JOURNAL OF LAW AND SOCIAL PROBLEMS 49 (1970).

52. See Frimer, The Role of the Lawyer in Jewish Law, 1 JOURNAL OF LAW AND RELIGION 297 (1982) and Kirschenbaum, *Representation in Litigation in Jewish Law*, 6 DINE ISRAEL XV (1975).

53. Indeed, it has been held that a refusal to sign an arbitration agreement is tantamount to a failure to appear, justifying the issuance of a *k'tav siruv* even against a party who is otherwise willing to submit to the jurisdiction of a *bait din*. See Rabbi Y. Henkin, KOL KITVAI Ha'GRIYA (collected writings), pp. 171-179.

grounds exist that would *halachically* justify an order directing the husband to give a *get*.[54] The *bait din* would want to inquire into details concerning physical, mental, emotional abuse; support obligations; and all relevant aspects of marital and family life. Medical and psychiatric testimony would be admissible and welcome to aid the *bait din* in its determination and for the most part, the *bait din* would attempt to be fair and neutral. Nevertheless, for the reasons described above, it is fairly easy for the husband to evade coming to *bait din*. If she obtains a summons from a standing *bait din*, he may invoke *ZABLA* as a delaying mechanism and then not bother to designate his judge. Even if both parties agree on a *bait din*, he may fail to appear. Even if he appears and the *bait din* orders him to give a *get*, he may simply fail to comply. It must be emphasized that there is a fundamental distinction between the procedure of a *bait din* in monetary matters and in *gittin*. As noted, in monetary matters the parties sign an arbitration agreement so that the decision of the *bait din* may be civilly enforced through the courts. This device cannot readily be employed in *get* cases. As a general proposition, *gittin* that are issued pursuant to the order of a civil court and under threat of fine or incarceration for civil contempt are invalid.[55] There are a wide variety of circumstances where the *bait din* might advise or even order the husband to execute the *get* but, as a matter of Jewish law, could not allow the courts to enforce their order.[56]

Thus, not only are women faced with the normal difficulties of getting an adversary to respond to a summons and appear before the *bait din* - difficulties common to any proceeding before a *bait din*- but they face the additional problem of not being able to civilly enforce the *bait din* order even where the husband did appear.

At that point, her only recourse is to capitulate to whatever demands he might be making concerning alimony, child support, custody, or the like,[57]

---

54. These grounds are discussed *infra* text at notes 108-133.

55. See *infra* text following note 60 (discussion of the principle of *get meusah*).

56. See discussion *infra* text at notes 110-120.

57. Withholding a *get* is commonly done as a device to secure concessions in property rights or custody. A recent case in New York may change the picture somewhat though its effect is a bit uncertain. *Perl v. Perl*, 126 A.D. 2d 91, 512 N.Y.S. 2d 372 (N.Y. App. Div. 1987), involved a separation agreement in open court under which, in exchange for a *get*, a wife surrendered her one-half interest in the marital home, vacated the premises, surrendered jewelry and an automobile, and executed a $15,000 promissory note. Reversing the trial court, the Appellate Division permitted the settlement to be avoided on the grounds that it was procured through duress. The pressure of being unable to marry without a *get* left the wife with no reasonable alternative other than acceding to her husband's demands and if the resulting terms are unfair or inequitable, they may later be set aside. (The court remanded the case for trial on the issue of one-sidedness since the husband alleged he had given the wife some stock). The Appellate Division, however, denied any imposition of affirmative liability on the grounds of intentional infliction of emotional distress since the husband's motivations were purely economic in nature with "mental distress a regrettable by-product." This aspect of the case is discussed *infra* note 712. A similar ruling was recently issued in

or to mobilize community support in calling for sanctions such as boycotts, posting the husband's picture in public places, having her husband branded as a disobeyer of *bait din* or depriving him of synagogue honors. Unfortunately, women have often had to organize this pressure by themselves with the *bait din* whose decisions were flouted simply not getting involved.[58] There have been many calls for greater rabbinic and community activism in this area. A word of caution, however, may be in order. Strong-arm tactics sometimes backfire with spiteful husbands simply digging in their heels even deeper.[59]

Golding v. Golding, 581 N.Y.S. 2d 4 (N.Y. App. Div. 1992).

The impact of *Perl* and *Golding* is not clear. On one hand, it may allow women to promise their husbands the world in order to receive their *get* and afterwards, have the agreement set aside. (This is probably already the case with child custody agreements where any prior concession as to custody is reviewable or modifiable under the "best interests of the child" test.) On the other hand, the ability to apply such strategy may backfire. It may mean that, notwithstanding concessions, the husband will refuse to act in the absence of a guarantee that the concessions will not be overturned by a court later. As such, *Perl* may aggravate the *agunah* problem rather than diminish it.

[Cases like *Perl* and *Golding* raise yet another issue of extreme gravity: what is the *halachic* validity of a *get* that is given pursuant to the terms of a settlement in cases where, after the *get* is received, the settlement is overturned on the grounds of duress? It is arguable that, at least in some cases, such reneging may invalidate the *get* since it was given with the understanding that reciprocal benefits be realized. See *infra* text at notes 161-164 (law of conditions). Indeed, this may be true even if no explicit condition was articulated. See, for example, *supra* note 8 (ruling of Maharam in "Divorce of Vienna" controversy). The resolution of this vital issue is beyond the purview of this book. For one permissive approach to the problem, see IGROT MOSHE E.H. III, no. 44 (reneging on settlement will *not* invalidate the *get* unless compliance with settlement was *expressly* made a condition to the *get*'s continuing validity).]

58. In fairness to the *bait din*, there may be *halachic* considerations in their refusal to get involved. See *infra* text at notes 110-120 regarding the limits on what a *bait din* may do to secure a *get*.

A welcome development in this area is the adoption of a recent resolution by rabbis whose synagogues are affiliated with the Agudath Israel movement (the same movement responsible for the drafting of the New York *get* law, see *infra* text at notes 531-532) to the effect that a person against whom a *k'tav siruv* has been issued or who has otherwise violated the order of a *bait din*: (1) forfeits his/her rights to synagogue membership; (2) may not serve as a prayer leader or be called to the Torah; (3) may not utilize synagogue facilities for family celebrations; and (4) will be informed that he/she is generally not welcome to attend services. See COALITION (January 1992), p. 3. While this resolution technically binds only a small number of Orthodox synagogues (those affiliated with Agudath Israel), the influence of its sponsors may convince other rabbis and synagogues to follow suit.

59. In recent years, women themselves have organized support groups to exert pressure on unwilling husbands. One organization known as GET (Getting Equitable Treatment) uses volunteer "caseworkers." "We will do whatever we can without force - we do not use brute strength - to convince the

GET MEUSAH: A BILL OF DIVORCE GRANTED UNDER COMPULSION OR DURESS*

A final introductory concept that needs to be elucidated is that of *get meusah*, the invalidity of a bill of divorce executed under duress or compulsion. In any attempt to deal with the unwilling, recalcitrant spouse, this is a formidable obstacle that must be surmounted. Whether and how the problem of *meusah* can be circumvented is central to any analysis of prenuptial agreements or other possibilities of civil enforcement. As such, some introduction to the term may be useful.

The Parameters of Invalid Compulsion

It is axiomatic that a *get* is effective only if it is executed and delivered with the husband's consent.[60] As a corollary, a *get* that the husband ostensibly authorized, but as a consequence of duress, is invalid for it was not a product of the unfettered exercise of his will.[61] Duress includes use or threats of

---

recalcitrant spouse." Statement of Gloria Greenman, President of GET quoted in *Orthodox Jewish Divorce: The Religious Dilemma*, NEW YORK TIMES (July 5, 1982), p. 40.

Occasionally, this pressure takes a more drastic form. See Greenberg, *Jewish Attitudes Towards Divorce*, JEWISH DIRECTORY AND ALMANAC 106, 111 (1984) (A group of women in a Canadian city announced that none of them would cohabit with their husbands until a friend of theirs received a free *get* from an ex-husband who was holding out for $25,000. She received her *get* in short order.) Reported in JEWISH PRESS (October 26, 1979) (Magazine) at M41 and NEW YORK TIMES (July 5, 1982) (Style) at p. 40. Occasionally, mass demonstrations or picketings either against the recalcitrant spouse or what is perceived as an overly passive rabbinical leadership are organized with moderate success. Conversation with David Farber, a self-styled "*agunah* organizer" November 23, 1990, Union of Orthodox Jewish Congregations National Convention, Washington, D.C. The author appeared on a panel with Mr. Farber.

A more recently established organization is Agunah, Inc., a women's advocacy group headquartered in New York City. For a description of its work authored by three of its directors, see Aronoff, Haut, and Alter, *Agunot: Is the System Working?* JEWISH HOMEMAKER (Oct. 1992), p. 6. See also the interesting response article by Avrohom Goldstein interviewing Rabbi Leib Landesman, an experienced head of a well-respected *bait din* who sharply disputes many of Agunah, Inc.'s criticisms of the present system.

*A simplified outline of the rather intricate *halachic* concepts discussed in this section may be found in Additional Note (III) following Chapter Four, *infra* text at note 453.

60. See, e.g., T.B. YEBAMOT 112b and Rambam, MISHNA TORAH, *Hilchot Ishut* 1:1 and numerous other places.

61. See T.B. GITTIN 88b. The notion that transactions entered under duress are voidable is a familiar one to students of Anglo-American law yet has not yet been entirely incorporated into *halacha* which in general validates conveyances entered under duress unless they are gratuitous. See SHULCHAN

physical force against person or property.[62] One particular issue pertaining to duress involves the impact of contractually-assumed self-imposed penalties. Assume, for example, that a husband agrees to divorce his wife and stipulates payment of a penalty in the event the divorce is not delivered by a certain date. The husband then later declares his unwillingness to execute the *get* but does so in order to avoid payment of the penalty. On one level, such a *get* is a product of duress since the decision to give the *get* was motivated by the desire to avoid the imposition of a penalty. On the other hand, since the creation of the penalty was entirely consensual, the *get* is arguably valid.[63] The authorities are divided over this issue[64] and at least as an initial matter no *get* should be

---

ARUCH H.M. 205:1. This suggests that classical *halacha* was more concerned with the fairness of the resulting exchange rather than the underlying defects in the bargaining process. See generally Herzog, II MAIN INSTITUTIONS OF JEWISH LAW, pp. 130-131. According to many decisors (though not all), the same rule is true for marriage, at least in theory. See SHULCHAN ARUCH E.H. 42:1 and commentary of *Bait Shmuel*. (If a man, under duress, marries a woman, many authorities regard the marriage as valid. If a woman entered into a marriage under duress, the marriage would have been valid but this is one of the rare circumstances where the Talmud authorizes rabbinical annulment, see *infra* text at notes 172-174.) The fact that duress is recognized as a basis for the invalidation of a *get*-such a *get* is void, not merely voidable - underscores the crucial importance of consent and the problematical nature of judicial coercion.

62. What if the duress is directed towards a third person? Contrary to the rule under Anglo-American law, most decisors maintain that this is not duress. See Comments of Rema, SHULCHAN ARUCH E.H. 134:5; PITCHAI TESHUVA E.H. 134:5 (11-12) and ARUCH HaSHULCHAN E.H. 134:24. Cf. RESTATEMENT OF CONTRACTS (Second) §176, Comment *b* ("Where physical violence is threatened, it need not be to the recipient of the threat, nor even to a person related to him if the threat in fact induces the recipient to manifest his assent.") and Illustration 2.

63. Under common law principles, a "threat" to enforce a contractual right against a debtor unless debtor consents to some additional obligation or undertaking would not be grounds for the avoidance of the resulting commitment since to the extent any "threat" was made, its exercise will be entirely lawful. See RESTATEMENT OF CONTRACTS (Second) §176, Comment *d*. The result will of course be different if the one making the threat knows that his claim is without legal foundation. See *infra* note 74.

[While the common law of duress would thus come to the same conclusion as those *halachic* schools that validate the *get*, the theories of validation are distinct. Under common law, the key to negating duress in the case of a self-imposed obligation is the legality or propriety of the "threat." Under *halacha*, the key lies in the consensual nature of the sanction assumed. Indeed, it is arguable that as long as the penalties are self-assumed, the resulting *get* would be valid even if the penalties lack *halachic* enforceability. See *infra* text following note 432.]

64. R. Shlomo Ben Aderet (known by the acronym Rashba)(12th century Spain) took the position that such a *get* was invalid even *ex post facto*, TESHUVOT RASHBA IV, no. 40. *Accord*: R. Menachem Meiri (13th Century France) BAIT HaBECHIRA, Commentary to Gittin 88b. A contrary

issued unless and until there is a prior unconditional forgiveness of indebtedness.[65]

At the same time, however, certain types of pressure are not deemed sufficiently coercive to invalidate a *get* issued in order to escape them. For example, employment of psychological pressure, organization of boycotts (even with economic impact), or posting of signs would apparently not render the *get* a *meusah* even in the absence of a decision of a *bait din* although prior to such a decision, employment of these measures is morally reprehensible. A second category involves what might be termed "coercive circumstances arising from reasons unrelated to the *get* itself." This category was first recognized by the great Spanish authority, Rivash.[66] The case involved a person thrown into debtor's prison for nonpayment of a debt. His wife's relatives offered to

---

position is espoused by R. Shimon Ben Tzemach in TASHBATZ II, no. 68 (one who gives a *get* in order to avoid a penalty which came of his own accord is acting willfully) and in *Teshuvot Ritva* quoted in BAIT YOSEF, TUR E.H. end of Chapter 154 (p. 76b, standard edition). An intermediate position is adopted by a number of authorities who would distinguish between voluntarily-assumed penalty clauses where the promisor retains the freedom of not delivering the *get* and incurring the penalty and cases of solemn oaths which by virtue of their being specifically-enforceable, effectively destroy freedom of choice. See, for example, the view of Rabbeinu Peretz cited by TUR E.H., end of Chapter 154 (p. 76b, standard edition) and that of Rabbi Maimon Nager cited by BAIT YOSEF, TUR E.H., Chapter 134 (p. 36b, standard edition). See also the comments of *Bait Yosef* who notes that even in the case of a *get* issued pursuant to oath, the *get* is valid *ex post facto* although *ab initio* should not be delivered until the oath is *halachically* annulled. See BAIT YOSEF, TUR E.H. 154 (p. 76b of standard edition) and discussion *infra* text at notes 76-86 (reasonable alternative test).

65. The final and generally-accepted compromise ruling is recorded by R. Moshe Isserles [Rema] in SHULCHAN ARUCH, E.H. 134:5. Rema's permissive ruling is subject to one major qualification. Some opinions would validate the *get* after the fact only under circumstances where the husband at the time of the *get*'s execution did not desire to rescind his agreement and did not indicate that he was acting under duress. If the husband indicates that he is desirous of reneging but states that he will not do so out of fear of incurring a financial penalty, some understand that even according to Rema, the *get* is invalid. See ARUCH HaSHULCHAN E.H. 134:26-29. Others maintain that Rema's ruling applies even where husband desires to rescind. See LEVUSH E.H. 134, end of chapter (analyzing predecessor sources upon which Rema relied); CHAZON ISH E.H. 99:5; and the extensive discussion in PITCHAI TESHUVAH E.H. 134:5 (10).

[It should also be noted that many, if not most, of these self-imposed penalties raise an additional *halachic* problem of *asmakhta*. See *infra* text at note 306. Arguably, that fact alone might render the resulting *get* invalid even after the fact notwithstanding Rema's ruling. This in turn depends on how one construes the decision of Tashbatz regarding illegitimate means. See *infra* text at notes 73-74 and 432-452 (where I conclude that *asmakhta* will not have this effect but not all agree).]

66. See TESHUVOT RIVASH, no. 127 and TASHBATZ II, no. 68. See also *infra* Appendix F for some biographical detail.

satisfy the debt and obtain his release from prison on the condition that he would execute a *get* and divorce his wife. He willingly complied. In considering whether the *get* is a product of coercion, Rivash concludes that because the man "was not seized in order to divorce his wife but on account of his debt, the *get* is not coerced but is the product of free will."[67] The theory appears to be that where the compelling event was not generated for the purpose of inducing a *get* although the granting of the *get* will effectively *remove* the source of the compulsion, the *get* retains its validity. A modern example of this distinction might be a separation agreement whereby one spouse agrees to forego property or custody rights in exchange for a *get* (admittedly a reprehensible instance of blackmail). Although the execution of the *get* might in some sense be viewed as a means of escaping the financial burdens that would otherwise fall on the husband's shoulders, because these burdens are not generated as inducements to give a *get* but are independent rights arising out of the marital relationship, the *get* is seen as conferring a benefit rather than removing a compulsion.[68]

An interesting contemporary application of this concept arose in Israel where, by operation of law, religious tribunals still maintain exclusive

---

67. See also TESHUVOT RIVASH, no. 232 (violation of community ordinance prohibiting marriage in the absence of a quorum of ten carried sanction of imprisonment; a commutation of sentence contingent on the execution of a *get* did not constitute duress) and TESHUVOT MAHARIK, no. 123 (where a person is imprisoned for offenses unrelated to the granting of a *get*, a refusal of the community to intervene until such *get* is granted is not coercive but simply a withholding of assistance). Whether this pressure could take the form of affirmative statements requesting a denial of clemency is quite debatable. See *infra* note 93. See also TESHUVOT MABIT I, no. 22 (citizen of Safed imprisoned by civil authorities for criminal activity; the Jewish community offered to secure his release if he would divorce his wife and leave the jurisdiction. Held: *get* valid).

68. Indeed, this same result follows under common law. If I threaten to drown someone unless they agree to a contract, any contract resulting from such a threat is voidable under duress. If, on the other hand, someone is already drowning and I offer to save them if they sign, the resulting contract would not be voidable. The distinction is based on the fact that duress renders a contract voidable only when the threat that induced the assent was "improper." See RESTATEMENT OF CONTRACTS (Second) §175 and §253. A threat is "improper" if what is threatened constitutes a "crime" or a "tort." *Id.* at §176(1)(a). Since Anglo-American law imposes no affirmative duty of rescue, threatening to "let" someone drown unless he consents is not tortious. *A fortiori*, this would be true where the promisor is not faced with loss of life but simply imprisonment or property forfeiture. The common law of contracts would probably come to the same conclusion as Rivash, Maharik, and Mabit cited *supra* note 67. Ironically, these *halachic* authorities came to this conclusion despite the fact that, under Jewish law, there is indeed an affirmative duty of rescue and one who fails in this duty has in fact acted (or omitted to act) in a wrongful manner. See LEVITICUS 19:16 ("Do not stand idly over your friend's blood"), as interpreted in T.B. SANHEDRIN 73a.

jurisdiction over marriage and divorce.[69] A young woman had married a man who was serving a four-year prison sentence in Israel for drug offenses. The wife petitioned for a divorce on the grounds of nonsupport and loss of consortium. The Rabbinical Court of Tel-Aviv (*bait din*) directed the husband to execute the *get* but did *not* find any grounds either under Israeli or Jewish law that would mandate the direct imposition of coercive sanctions such as additional imprisonment or fines. The issue before the court was whether it was *halachically* proper to recommend parole or reduction of sentence in exchange for the husband's executing a *get*. Conversely, could the rabbinic tribunal submit a recommendation against parole unless the *get* is executed? On one hand, the *get* is the mechanism by which the prisoner may obtain his freedom and if a person is told, "Sign the *get* or stay in jail," this resembles duress. Yet because the imprisonment was for completely unrelated offenses, the failure to give a *get* does not in and of itself result in direct coercion but simply removes the extra privileges or benefits of parole that would otherwise ensue. An additional complication arose from the fact that the husband behaved abusively in the presence of the court, spitting and cursing at the judges. The prisoner's behavior clearly constituted contempt of court and could properly be taken into account as a factor bearing on "good moral character" in a parole hearing. Could the *bait din* "forgive" their contempt and agree *not* to report it in exchange for a *get*?

In a 2-1 decision, the *bait din* ruled that it would be improper to threaten the husband with an explicit recommendation for denial of parole. Such a recommendation would be tantamount to the imposition of an additional *punishment* for the failure to give a *get* and indeed, this would be so even if the recommendation would be predicated on the husband's abusive behavior rather than on the grounds of "bad moral character" for noncompliance with a court order.[70] The dissent took the position that even an explicit recommendation

---

69. The case is thoroughly discussed in Bleich, II CONTEMPORARY HALAKHIC PROBLEMS at pp. 94-103, and is reported at 11 PISKE DIN RABANIYIM (Decisions of Rabbinic Tribunals), no. 10, pp. 300-308 (1978). The dissent by Rabbi Shlomo Dichovsky was published as a separate article in I TECHUMIN 248-254 (1980).

70. The *bait din* found possible grounds to distinguish between a recommendation *against* parole and failure to make a positive recommendation for parole. The *bait din* is certainly entitled to condition any positive intervention on the prisoner's compliance with their decree. The basis for this distinction may be found in TESHUVOT MAHARIK, no. 123: "But if a person is imprisoned by gentiles because of taxes or some other matter, we may say to him 'We will not attempt to have you released from prison unless you divorce your wife with a valid *get*.' This is not duress since we are not doing him evil but simply withholding assistance. Withholding assistance of benefit is not considered duress."

The court's ruling, based on Maharik, that the granting of affirmative assistance may be made conditional on the granting of a *get* has been followed by other rabbinical courts as well. For example, under Israeli law contracting marriage with a woman under the age of seventeen is a criminal offense punishable by imprisonment or a fine. The rabbinical courts have routinely informed the violator that they will intercede and recommend a commutation of sentence upon execution of the *get*. Because the imprisonment is for

against parole constitutes only a denial of benefit since the husband's imprisonment was for grounds unrelated to the divorce. (An alternative approach to this case, one adopted by neither the majority nor the dissent, is set out in the note below.)[71]

---

violation of the criminal statute and is totally unrelated to the granting of a *get*, the making or withholding of a clemency recommendation is not an act of compulsion. See also TESHUVOT RIVASH, no. 232 (violation of a local community ordinance forbidding the celebration of marriages without the presence of a quorum of ten; imprisonment subject to release upon execution of a *get* is a valid practice since the imprisonment is a sanction for violation of the ordinance). See generally Rabbinowitz-Teumim, *Self-Imposed Constraints in Divorce* (Heb.), I NOAM 287 (5718/1958-1959). Bleich regards these precedents as inconsistent with the majority's ruling that an explicit recommendation against parole is improper. See II CONTEMPORARY HALAKHIC PROBLEMS, pp. 99-100. Somewhat confusingly, however, his assertion ignores the very distinction the court made, *i.e.*, between the imposition of punishment and the denial of benefit. The court's whole point - and one that is surely debatable - is that a negative recommendation against parole (which would otherwise be granted) is closer to a new punishment than a withholding of a privilege, at least where it is premised on failure to grant a *get*. His point, however, may be cogent with respect to the report concerning courtroom abuse since that indeed is totally unrelated to the *get*.

71. Essentially, the question faced by the rabbinical court was whether a denial of parole for failure to execute a *get* constituted the imposition of additional punishment, thereby rendering a resulting *get* a product of duress or whether the granting or recommendation of parole is merely the extension of a privilege which may legitimately be held out as an inducement to have a *get* executed. This suggests an interesting parallel to American constitutional law concerning the rights of prisoners to a constitutional due process hearing before they are denied parole. See, *e.g.*, *Greenholtz v. Inmates of the Nebraska Penal and Correctional Complex*, 442 U.S. 1 (1979) (in the absence of a statute *requiring* release on parole unless there are grounds for denial, a prisoner has no due process liberty interest merely because the state holds out a generalized possibility of early release. Such a possibility amounts to nothing more than a mere expectation and gives rise to no legally-enforceable substantive or procedural rights). The rule is different where a prisoner has actually been granted parole which the state now seeks to revoke since such a revocation directly impinges on a state-granted currently-enjoyed liberty interest. See *Morrissey v. Brewer*, 408 U.S. 471 (1972) (parole); *Gagnon v. Scarpelli*, 411 U.S. 778 (1973) (probation).

If the due process cases furnish an appropriate analogy - and it is debatable if they do - they suggest a distinction somewhat different from the one drawn by the rabbinical court. To the extent a prisoner has no protected liberty interest in securing his early freedom, the failure of a party to intervene on his behalf can hardly be regarded as a punishment. Moreover, this could very well be the case even if the *bait din* affirmatively recommends that parole be denied since there is nothing that the prisoner presently "has" that the nonissuance of the *get* is taking away. If, on the other hand, probation or parole had actually been granted, and the *bait din* would allege the failure to grant a *get* as a basis for revocation, such a threat could very well constitute improper coercion as

One other major consideration applicable to indirect sanctions is whether the sanctions are themselves legitimate under Jewish law.[72] The execution of a *get* in order to escape payment of a debt that is in any event not actionable (under *halacha*) is regarded as the product of duress even if the compulsion arises from reasons unrelated to the granting or withholding of the *get*.[73] Only forgiveness of a legitimate debt constitutes a proper inducement for divorce.[74]

---

it involves the deprivation of a presently enjoyed liberty.

In short, rather than distinguishing between a negative recommendation and the withholding of a positive one, the due process analogy would distinguish between interventions that arise *before* parole is granted and interventions that seek revocation. Thus, although the dissent does not expressly address this point, it is probable that any negative recommendation for the *revocation* of parole (rather than merely its denial) would clearly constitute invalidating duress even under Rabbi Dichovsky's definition.

72. The impact of this qualification on the earlier discussion of self-imposed penalties, *supra* notes 63-65, is discussed *infra* text at notes 432-452.

73. See TASHBATZ I, no. 1. The exact meaning of this requirement is susceptible to multiple interpretations. See, for example, TESHUVOT RANACH, no. 63; *Torat Gittin* cited in PITCHAI TESHUVA E.H. 134:5 (11); and IGROT MOSHE E.H. I, no. 137. Stated briefly, the issue is whether illegitimacy of the sanction is a separate invalidating factor or whether it is simply indicative of linkage to a *get*. These interpretations are noted and analyzed *infra* text at notes 432-452.

The relationship and apparent contradiction between Tashbatz's "illegitimacy prong" and his validation of a *get* issued in exchange for the forgiveness of a penalty (cited *supra* note 61) - despite the fact that enforcement of penalties may be *halachically* illegitimate - is also addressed *infra* text at notes 432-452.

74. If Tashbatz's distinction is taken at face value, *i.e.*, that the illegitimacy of the sanction employed is sufficient in and of itself to invalidate the resulting *get* on the grounds of duress, it closely parallels a similar rule under common law. A promise to perform *X* in exchange for the forgiveness of debt *Y* may be an invalid product of duress if debt *Y* is a clearly unenforceable claim. (Such a promise would also be lacking in consideration as well.) Nevertheless, in order to enforce the promise, the promisee need not show that he could have succeeded on the merits but merely that the asserted claim that is being forgiven has a reasonable basis and is not entirely frivolous. Moreover, even where the forgiven debt is unactionable, a promise obtained in exchange for its release will not necessarily be voidable if defending against the unenforceable claim constituted a "reasonable alternative." See Dawson, *Duress Through Civil Litigation*, 45 MICHIGAN LAW REVIEW 571 (1947); Farnsworth, CONTRACTS (2nd ed.) §4.17, p. 276; RESTATEMENT OF CONTRACTS (Second) §175, Comment *b* (even where a threat is improper, it will *not* amount to duress if it allows the victim a reasonable alternative); and *supra* note 68. Under common law, the ability to assert a defense against a frivolous claim normally constitutes such an alternative unless particularly oppressive tactics are employed. From a Jewish law perspective, it is not clear whether being put to the burden of litigating constitutes a "reasonable alternative." Nevertheless, the concept of "reasonable alternatives" negating

The Existence of Reasonable Alternatives

The foregoing discussion demonstrates that, in order for sanctions not to run afoul of the strictures of *get meusah*, one of two conditions must be met: either that the sanctions themselves are not sufficiently compelling as to constitute an overpowering of the recalcitrant party's will, *e.g.*, psychological pressure, "jawboning," and the like, or in the alternative, that the pressures are generated from factors extraneous to the failure to execute a *get* although execution of the *get* may furnish a basis to escape from those pressures. We have also seen that even where the pressures are independently generated, there is (according to many authorities) an additional requirement that the imposition of the sanction, whether a monetary fine or incarceration, be legitimate and not constitute an act of extortion, kidnapping, or theft. It has been argued, however, that even where both these prongs are met - formal independence from the *get* and legitimacy - there is yet a third element necessary for validation, that the recalcitrant spouse be left with a "reasonable alternative" to executing the *get*.[75] Whether this proposition is in fact true, at least with

---

get meusah has been recognized by at least some authorities. *See* TESHUVOT MABIT II, no. 138 and *infra* text at notes 92-93.

[The correspondence between Tashbatz's ruling and the common law doctrines of duress through illicit or improper threats will of course break down if illegitimacy is *not* a separate invalidating prong but merely evidence of linkage. See *infra* text at notes 432-452.]

75. See Dichovsky, *supra* note 69, pp. 252-253. The notion of a "reasonable alternative" originates in remarks of Mabit in TESHUVOT MABIT II, no. 138 though the precise application of this concept is subject to considerable uncertainty in light of Mabit's own words in TESHUVOT MABIT I, no. 22. See *infra* note 93 and III SIMCHAT COHEN E.H., no. 9 for suggested resolutions to this contradiction.

On its face, a requirement of a "reasonable alternative" to negate duress appears consistent with American law that similarly provides that duress sufficient to avoid a transaction exists only when there is no reasonable alternative. See, *e.g.*, RESTATEMENT OF CONTRACTS (Second) §175. Yet it is apparent that what Mabit and other authorities mean by "meaningful choice" or "reasonable alternative" (to use modern terminology) has absolutely nothing to do with the common law concept. On one level, *halacha* would regard an alternative as "reasonable" even where common law would not. Thus, Mabit concedes that the ability to pay a sum of money in lieu of a *get* does constitute a "reasonable alternative" as long as such payment is in the realm of possibility. Under American law, if avoidance of contract could be accomplished only by the incurrence of a financial loss, the promisor is not deemed to have a reasonable alternative and the contract is avoidable. Conversely, however, *halacha* is also considerably stricter than the common law. Under the latter, any "threat" inducing contract which is lawful does not constitute duress because it is not improper regardless of its magnitude. By contrast, Rema's ruling regarding direct sanctions for nondelivery of *get*, E.H. 134:5, and Mabit's ruling regarding the need for a "reasonable alternative" even in cases of indirect sanctions clearly indicate that even the prosecution or threat of prosecution of *lawful enforceable* claims raise the cloud of *get meusah*.

respect to independently-generated pressures, is highly debatable and can only be determined by an examination of the contexts in which the concept of "reasonable alternative" makes its appearance.

The preceding section cited a number of authorities who validate a *get* given to escape the imposition of contractually-imposed monetary penalties.[76] The opinions that sustain such a *get* offer two distinct reasons why. Some maintain that self-imposed sanctions, no matter how severe, cannot by definition be regarded as coercive since the promisor had the option not to assume them in the first place.[77] Others argue that the ability of the promisor to avoid the granting of the *get* by paying a sum of money eliminates the problem of *meusah* because of the existence of a "reasonable alternative," *i.e.*, payment.[78]

There are a number of practical differences that flow from one's choice of theory. Assume, for example, that in lieu of a monetary stipulation, a formerly-recalcitrant husband bound himself to give a *get* by a solemn oath which under Biblical law must be kept.[79] Is a *get* given to comply with a binding oath invalid as a *get meusah*?[80] Under the theory that self-imposition negates coercion, the *get* would be valid. Under the theory of "reasonable alternative," it would not be since the husband left himself no out.[81] Similarly,

76. See authorities cited *supra* note 64.

77. TASHBATZ II, no. 68 and Rabbeinu Peretz cited in TUR E.H. 154.

78. TESHUVOT MAHARIK, no. 63 cited in Rema, gloss to SHULCHAN ARUCH E.H. 134:5. It should be noted that many authorities use both reasons more or less interchangeably without clearly indicating which one is primary.

79. The laws governing oaths can be found in SHULCHAN ARUCH YORE DE'AH, Chapters 203-239.

80. See the opinion of the "French scholars" cited by BAIT YOSEF, comment to TUR E.H. 134 (*get* issued pursuant to oath invalid). *Cf. Teshuvot Ritva* cited in BAIT YOSEF, TUR E.H. 154, who argues that while such a *get* should not be executed in the first instance, it is acceptable after the fact. Rema in SHULCHAN ARUCH E.H. 134:5 rules in accordance with Ritva.

81. Although *Bait Yosef* cites opinions that invalidate such a *get*, it is not entirely clear why oaths are treated differently than are monetary sanctions. Jewish law recognizes that oaths can be annulled through a specially-prescribed procedure in the presence of a *bait din*. See SHULCHAN ARUCH YORE DE'AH 228:1-51. Just as monetary penalties offer the choice of granting a *get* or paying the price, the promisor bound by oath has the option of keeping the oath or annulling it. Hence, even if the annulment option is *not* pursued, the *get* should be valid because of the existence of the annulment alternative. (According to the opinions that sustain *gittin* issued pursuant to monetary penalties, the *get* would be valid *ab initio*; according to Rema, at least after the fact).

Moreover, at least in some cases, invalidating a *get* issued pursuant to oath may pose a real dilemma. Certain types of oaths cannot be annulled, YORE DE'AH 228:21; accordingly, a woman whose husband has taken such an oath would literally have no possible way of ever securing a *get* since any *get* that she receives would invariably be tainted as a *meusah*. But *cf.* PITCHAI TESHUVAH E.H. 134:5 (7).

[It should be noted that *meusah* problems in connection with *gittin* issued

if one posits an extremely high financial sanction that the promisor cannot possibly meet, the second theory would once again invalidate the *get* since there is only one possible "choice" the promisor can make, *i.e.*, to execute a *get*.[82]

---

under oath apply only in cases where, under *halacha*, a *get* may not be compelled. See *infra* text at notes 108-120. Where *halacha* requires a *get* to be granted and authorizes the imposition of coercive measures (*kofin*), any additional oath the husband may have taken, even if irrevocable, is of no consequence. See BAIT SHMUEL E.H. 134:5 (6).]

82. This conclusion, intimated by Bleich at III CONTEMPORARY HALAKHIC PROBLEMS, pp. 339-340 and others, does not necessarily follow. In truth, from a purely legal perspective, in any commitment to do X or Y there is invariably a third choice - the consequences of doing neither X nor Y. For example, if one promises to pay a million dollars or grant a *get*, there are three possible courses of action: (1) grant a *get*; (2) pay a million dollars; (3) do neither and face the consequences. In determining whether there exists a "reasonable alternative" to the granting of the *get* (option one) it would appear erroneous to merely look at the possibility of payment (option two). One would also have to consider option three; if doing *nothing* is a "reasonable alternative," an election to execute the *get* should be valid.

At a time and in a society where the consequences of not paying a debt were incarceration, lashes, or involuntary servitude, a debt that was too large to be paid indeed left the promisor with no alternative short of executing a *get*. At least in the United States, this is presently not the case. Virtually all states have abolished imprisonment for nonpayment of debt. If one owes a large amount of money, a creditor may obtain a judgment, have the debtor's assets seized by the sheriff and sold at a judicially-supervised sale, and have writs of garnishment issued to employers and bank accounts directing that monies owed the debtor be paid over to the creditor. For a detailed description of the process, see Crandall, Hagedorn, and Smith, THE LAW OF DEBTORS AND CREDITORS, Chapters 5 and 6, and sources cited *infra* note 360. Federal and state laws exempt a great portion of the debtor's assets and income from seizure and garnishment. See, for example, 15 U.S.C. §§1671-1677 that essentially exempts 75% of a debtor's take- home income from the reach of creditor process. A debt that is "impossible" to pay will either be eventually written off as a loss or will simply be repaid voluntarily or involuntarily over a longer period of time. As such, there is always an alternative short of executing the *get* regardless of the size of the monetary sanction: the alternative of doing nothing, thereby subjecting oneself to the relatively minimal creditors' rights process which at worst results in a partial divestment of assets and income over a prolonged period of time, a sanction that, at least for purposes of *get meusah*, is regarded as "reasonable."

Thus, an argument could certainly be made that the imposition of an *indirect* monetary sanction would not result in a *get meusah* under any circumstances no matter what the size of the debt. Once again, however, considerations of caution may dictate that we evaluate "reasonable alternatives" by exclusive reference to the possibilities explicitly assumed, rather than considering the alternative of breach (the silent option three).

It should also be noted that claims for alimony and child support do have unique mechanisms for enforcement. Nonpayment may result in incarceration. See Melli, Stanton, and Haynes, ALIMONY, CHILD SUPPORT AND

Finally, assume that the self-imposed sanction went beyond the pecuniary. What if, for example, one agreed to a form of involuntary servitude or even imprisonment unless a *get* were to be executed by a date certain and the *get* is then executed for the sole purpose of escaping such draconian sanction? Once again, the first theory would validate the *get* while the second theory would not. (Imprisonment or involuntary servitude are presumably not reasonable alternatives).

Conversely, the "reasonable alternative" approach does not on its face require that the penalty be self-imposed. A statute or court order imposing a fine unless a *get* is granted would not raise problems of *get meusah* as long as payment of the fine was a reasonable alternative.[83] Under the "self-imposition" theory, however, the *get* would be invalid.

In the specific context of direct monetary penalties, the above discussion is largely moot. Rema rules that, in the first instance, no *get* should ever be executed until all monetary penalties are forgiven unconditionally.[84] This definitive ruling rejects both the theory of "self-imposition" and the theory of the "reasonable alternative."[85] The "reasonable alternative" analysis does assume considerable importance where the sanctions are imposed for reasons independent of the nonissuance of a *get* but may be avoided if a *get* is in fact executed. Examples include the prisoner incarcerated for unrelated charges who may receive parole if he grants a *get* or the husband who is subject to an exorbitant support obligation that may be terminated only through a *get* although the obligation did not have its genesis in attempts to secure a *get* but simply arose from the marital relationship itself.[86]

COUNSEL FEES (1991) at §9.08 (nonpayment of alimony enforceable by civil or criminal contempt) and §15.02 (nonpayment of child support subject to criminal prosecution). Thus, to the extent a support obligation is beyond the ability of the husband to meet, there may indeed be no "reasonable alternative" to granting a *get*. Adjusting a prenuptial support obligation to an amount that the husband could reasonably pay may thus be *halachically* essential even if such a step is unnecessary in cases of other indirect monetary sanctions. See *infra* text at note 399. (Query, however, whether the ability to procure a judicial modification of the agreement in itself constitutes a "reasonable alternative." This may not be the case because there is no guarantee that such modification would be forthcoming).

83. Indeed, under the "reasonable alternative" theory, it is arguable that even a clearly illegal or illicit monetary threat, *e.g.*, theft, would not result in a *get meusah* since the husband has the alternative of surrendering the property. See especially *infra* text at notes 446-449.

84. Rema, gloss to SHULCHAN ARUCH E.H. 134:5.

85. Choice of theory will become relevant, however, in determining the "after the fact" validity of such a *get* already executed and delivered.

[But see *infra* text at notes 313 and 432-452 (whether the *asmakhta* defect in penalty clauses raises a problem of *get meusah* even after the fact. The conclusion is that it does not.)]

86. The parole case of course is the one discussed *supra* text at notes 69-71 where the Rabbinical Court of Tel-Aviv rejected the possibility of threatening a negative recommendation against parole as leverage to secure a *get*, in part, on the grounds that offering the prisoner the choice between jail

A number of *halachic* authorities require the existence of a reasonable alternative not only in the context of sanctions that are directly linked to the failure to execute a *get* but even for penalties that are ostensibly unrelated.[87] They would differentiate between the execution of a *get* to avoid unrelated incarceration (where the *get* would be invalid since the husband's only choice is to write the *get* or stay in jail) and execution of a *get* to avoid an unrelated financial liability or to obtain forgiveness of debt (where the *get* would be valid because the husband has the option of payment). Even the latter would be valid only where the alternative obligation is within the ability of the husband to perform.[88] Others maintain that the existence of a reasonable alternative is irrelevant where the sanctions arise from circumstances unrelated to the *get*; provided the compulsion, whether it be fines or imprisonment, arises from an independently-generated cause, its existence will have no impact on the validity of the *get*.[89]

The use of independently-generated compulsions is a promising avenue that may assist many unfortunate *agunot*. This author personally knows of cases where recalcitrant husbands were imprisoned for nonpayment of child support but were informed by judges, sympathetic to the needs of Orthodox women, that the sentence would be commuted upon prompt execution of a *get*. There are fertile possibilities for the structuring of prenuptial agreements predicated on the use of indirect sanctions. While a direct promise to pay a fixed sum if a *get* is not forthcoming upon demand may well raise serious *meusah* problems at least *ab initio*,[90] the same result could be accomplished without these concerns by structuring the sum as a support obligation of the marriage (rather than a fine for breach of duty) with the *get* serving as a mechanism for terminating the marriage and hence terminating the obligation. There are other ways such agreements may be structured as well.[91]

All of these possibilities, however, must be evaluated in light of the "reasonable alternative" test. As a matter of definitive *halacha*, it is difficult to discern whether the existence of "reasonable alternatives" is truly necessary, at least in cases where the sanctions are indirect and ostensibly independent. There are certainly many authorities that would dispense with such a

---

and *get* would have left no reasonable alternative. Antenuptial support agreements are discussed *infra* text following note 379.

87. This was the position of the Tel-Aviv *bait din* and is based on their reading of TESHUVOT MABIT II, no. 138.

88. But see *supra* note 82. As therein argued, while Mabit does appear to impose this requirement, it may not be applicable to the contemporary legal setting.

89. This was Rabbi Dichovsky's position in his dissent reproduced in I TECHUMIN 248 (1980) based largely on the rulings of Rivash, Maharik, Ranach, and indeed another decision by Mabit himself. See sources cited *supra* notes 67, 70, and 73.

90. See also *infra* text at notes 313 and 432-452 (whether defect of *asmakhta* present in penalty clauses would render the *get* invalid after the fact. The conclusion is that it does not.).

91. These options are discussed *infra* text at notes 347-378.

requirement altogether[92] and where the compelling event is truly independent and free-standing (rather than merely formalistically so) it is likely that all authorities would.[93] Nevertheless, as a matter of caution and prudence, such

---

92. Rema, for example, who validates (after the fact) *gittin* executed pursuant to oath by analogy to *gittin* executed pursuant to monetary penalties apparently ignores the element of "reasonable alternative" and simply distinguishes between self-imposed sanctions linked directly to the withholding of *get* (where, in the first instance, the *get* should not be written but if executed and delivered, will be valid) and sanctions arising from independent factors. Similarly, Rivash, Ranach, and Tashbatz do not seem to require that the husband have an "out" where the sanctions are indirect though Tashbatz's language may lend some slight support to that view. See *supra* notes 67, 70, and 73 for a summary of these holdings.

93. It is likely that even the views that require the existence of reasonable alternatives will not do so where the sanction is totally independent, not only in the sense of having an independent cause but also in the sense of not being motivated by a desire to secure a *get*. Consider, for example, the case of a husband imprisoned on a drug charge who refuses to divorce his wife. The *bait din* offers to recommend parole if a *get* is granted. Although the convict has no reasonable alternative - essentially he must stay in jail or grant a *get* - it is extremely difficult to see how promising to intervene to secure a release is any different from promising to give a recalcitrant spouse $10,000. Neither of these constitutes duress since the sanction bears no connection to the *get*. Thus, the Tel-Aviv *bait din* saw no problem in extending the "carrot" of a positive recommendation in exchange for a *get* although they were unwilling to use the "stick" of a negative threat.

The area of controversy seems to arise only in cases of sanctions which are ostensibly independent from the *get* but which are being pursued or enforced with the motive to compel the *get*'s execution. Examples include the husband whose wife files criminal charges for nonpayment of support to coerce him to divorce her; the judge who sentences the husband for nonsupport but clearly indicates that the unrelated sanction is being used as a club to compel a religious divorce; the *bait din* that affirmatively recommends or threatens to recommend a denial of parole, on the independent grounds of contemptuous conduct but whose real motivation is to create the stick that generates pressure to write a *get*; the execution of a prenuptial support agreement with the dominant purpose of making an "end run" around the *meusah* problem; the resurrection of a long-dormant claim or debt that would never have been pursued if *get* hadn't become an issue. In all of these cases, the pressures - be they criminal charges, incarceration, or debt - are ostensibly and formalistically independent and distinct from the *get* but their imposition or threat is motivated almost exclusively by the *get*. At best, they could be regarded only as quasi-independent and hence, according to some, will be allowed only if they present a "reasonable alternative."

Indeed, this distinction is supported by the Mabit himself. TESHUVOT MABIT II, no. 138 is often cited for the proposition that even in the case of indirect sanctions some reasonable alternative to granting a *get* must exist. The case concerned the enforcement of an independent monetary claim that would be dropped in exchange for a *get* where Mabit ruled that if the claim was beyond the husband's ability to meet, the *get* is *meusah*. Yet in TESHUVOT

alternatives should normally be present. To avoid casting aspersions on the validity of the *get*, the recalcitrant spouse should always be afforded a "meaningful choice" to elect not to execute the *get* although the balance of

---

MABIT I, no. 22, where a man was imprisoned for heretical conduct, offers to secure his release upon execution of a *get* did not render the *get meusah* although the husband had no meaningful choice. The distinction appears to be fundamentally one of *motive*; no. 138 dealt with an ostensibly-independent sanction (a debt) that was employed exclusively for purposes of compelling a *get* while no. 22 dealt with a sanction that not only was based on non-*get* factors (as indeed was also the case in no. 138) but was employed for a non-*get* reason. As such, the requirement of a "reasonable alternative" would be inapplicable.

Another way of expressing this distinction, which to a large extent leads to the same result, is to differentiate between active interventions against a party if he doesn't grant a *get* and active intervention for the benefit of a party if he does (the "carrot" v. "stick" approach). Only the former requires the presence of alternatives. Where the parties seeking to induce a *get* offer active intervention to alleviate a financial or legal difficulty having nothing to do with the *get*, and even if the *get* will not be executed, the worst that will happen is the maintenance and continuation of the *status quo*, the magnitude of the *status quo* and the fact that it may constitute a totally intolerable alternative are irrelevant and no problem of *meusah* arises. See, *e.g.*, TESHUVOT MAHARIK, no. 63. Where, however, the parties seeking the *get* threaten active intervention - criminal charges, incarceration, denial of parole, prosecution of monetary claims - that will increase the burdens on a recalcitrant spouse and will change the *status quo* in a negative sense although such actions may be predicated on allegedly-neutral independent grounds, some (not all) would treat the *get* as *meusah* unless a "reasonable alternative" is presented. (Note, however, that the presence of such alternatives suffices only for "indirect" not "direct" sanctions in accordance with Rema's ruling.) See also III SIMCHAT COHEN E.H., no. 9, who seems to allude to a similar distinction.

This explains why the Tel-Aviv *bait din* was willing to induce a *get* by promising an affirmative recommendation *for* parole but was unwilling to induce a *get* by the threat of a negative recommendation although such a recommendation was premised on grounds having nothing to do with the *get*, *i.e.*, contemptuous and disrespectful behavior. See *supra* text at notes 69-71.

[It is also arguable that TESHUVOT MABIT II, no. 138 never intended to impose a requirement of "reasonable alternatives" as an independent condition for the validity of indirect sanctions. In point of fact, it is quite possible that the *only* test for the validity of such sanctions is one of purpose or motive on the part of the persons imposing them. Mabit merely notes that to the extent a recalcitrant spouse is presented with a "choice" of only one possible outcome - and the parties imposing this "choice" are aware of this fact - their intent is inevitably to secure a *get*. Rather than there being a specific requirement of alternatives, Mabit uses the presence or absence of alternatives exclusively in an evidentiary capacity as having bearing on the ultimate issue of intent or motive. This reading too leads to the result that a truly independent sanction raises no problem of *get meusah* even according to Mabit.]

pressure may clearly push him in the direction of doing so.[94] In the case of imprisonment for nonsupport, he must be given an "out" with which he could reasonably comply - an installment payment of arrearages. In the case of antenuptial support agreements, the sum specified must be within the possibilities of payment.[95] While the existence of these alternatives may reduce the efficacy of the sanctions, it also renders them *halachically* more acceptable.

The Paradox of the Obligatory *Get*

Jewish law recognizes a number of discrete circumstances where a husband may be ordered by the *bait din* to execute a *get*.[96] In at least some of these cases (though not all), the order may be enforced by sanctions including fines, incarceration, and corporal punishment.[97] At first blush, allowing a *bait din* to coerce the granting of a *get* seems flatly inconsistent with the law of *get meusah* which necessitates that a *get* be executed exclusively through the voluntary action of the husband without duress of any kind. The Talmud responds laconically that in such cases the person is forced until he declares, "I am willing."[98] There must indeed be a formal expression of consent even where a *get* is *halachically* obligatory but such formal expression may be induced through virtually any form of psychological, financial, or even physical compulsion including threat of bodily injury or even death.[99] Yet this too seems to contradict the law of *get meusah* which normally regards "coerced consent" as an oxymoron.

The classic response to the paradox of "consent obtained via compulsion" is formulated by Rambam[100] who states as follows: It is assumed that every Jew truly desires to comply with the dictates of religious law and any

---

94. Keep in mind as pointed out *supra* note 75 that the *halachic* standards for "meaningful choice" are far broader than those under Anglo-American law.

95. See *infra* text at notes 378 and 399. It should be noted that the ability of the recalcitrant husband to meet this obligation (and thereby have a reasonable alternative to the execution of the *get*) would apparently have to be gauged as of the date of the *get*, rather than as of the date the obligation was assumed. Otherwise, the *get* would presumably be *meusah* (at least according to the restrictive interpretation of TESHUVOT MABIT II, no. 138), notwithstanding the reasonableness of the sum at the time the support agreement was executed.

96. See *infra* text at notes 108-120.

97. *Id.* As therein noted, the technical term utilized when those circumstances exist is *kofin* ("we force").

98. See, *e.g.*, T.B. YEBAMOT 106a.

99. Note that the coercion that is utilized in such cases may be *directly* linked to the failure to grant a *get* and it need not afford the recalcitrant spouse a "reasonable alternative." The doctrines concerning "independently-generated" pressures and the need for "reasonable alternatives," discussed *supra* text at notes 75-95, are applicable only in cases where *halacha* does not mandate direct compulsion.

100. See Rambam, MISHNA TORAH, *Hilchot Gerushin* 2:20. Rambam is the Hebrew acronym of Rabbi Moshe Ben Maimon (Moses Maimonides). See *infra* Appendix E.

refusal to do so is merely the result of an "evil disposition" which temporarily overpowers or vanquishes his "free will." Duress is therefore applied not to overcome the husband's exercise of will but to remove the impediment that prevents that "free will" from emerging. Naturally, this logic holds true only under the specific circumstances where Jewish law *obligates* the husband to execute a *get*.[101] In the absence of obligation, the failure to grant a *get* cannot be attributed to an "evil disposition," and hence attempting to override a refusal through coercion would indeed constitute improper and invalidating duress.[102] To the extent such an obligation does exist, however, there is no *halachic* requirement that coercion be employed directly by the religious court system itself. The Talmud expressly endorses the use of non-Jewish authorities to enforce the mandate of the *bait din*[103] and the victim and her friends or relatives

---

101. Indeed, this is true only when the obligation falls under the category of *kofin*, not *yotzee*. See *infra* text at note 116. (But see at *id.* the contrary view of Rabbi Herzog.).

102. Even where there is no *halachic* obligation to grant a *get* - or at least no obligation that rises to the level of *kofin*, *infra* text at notes 108-120 - the stratagems of indirect sanctions may be available but these are subject to the limitations discussed *supra* text at notes 75-95. The statement in the text refers to direct sanctions imposed specifically for the purpose of securing a *get*.

103. T.B. GITTIN 88b. The Mishna appears to validate the use of non-Jewish coercion only in cases where the coercers specifically indicate that they are acting to enforce the decision of the *bait din* ("do what the Jewish court says"). The consensus of most authorities, however, is that such coercion is *halachically* efficacious whether it is expressed as a demand to comply with a *bait din* or as a direct demand to execute a *get*. See BAIT SHMUEL E.H. 134:9 (15), *cf.* contrary view of R. Meir HaLevi cited in TUR E.H. 134. (It would nevertheless appear that the recalcitrant husband must at least be aware of the *bait din*'s order, see the third paragraph of note 105, but this will almost invariably be the case.)

While *Bait Shmuel*'s ruling establishes that it makes no difference what the coercers *say*, it is still not clear if it makes any difference what the coercers *think*. Must they intend to force compliance with the mandate of a *bait din* or need they even be aware that such an order was ever issued? What if a woman, well in advance of a *bait din*'s decision, hired thugs (whether Jewish or not) to beat up her recalcitrant husband and, unbeknownst to that group, the *bait din*'s decision is rendered in the woman's favor in advance of their beating? Is the *get* invalid as a *get meusah* since, under these facts, the coercers clearly did not intend to act as the surrogate enforcers for the Jewish court?

It is arguable that : (1) as long as the *bait din* issued an order mandating the execution of a *get* (on *kofin* grounds, see *infra* text at notes 111-112); and (2) the recalcitrant husband is aware of such an order (see *infra* note 105), the logic of Rambam's argument - that acquiescence to a *halachic* directive constitutes "true will" - should dictate that the intention, motive, or knowledge of the coercing agents should simply be immaterial. See B'EER YITZCHOK E.H., no. 10 (section 8).

Rambam's own ruling on this matter appears somewhat equivocal. He writes that if non-Jews on their own volition (presumably, this includes any secular authority not acting as a *bait din*) force a husband to give a *get*, the *get*

may invoke self-help remedies as well such as posting the husband's name and picture all over town or, in extreme cases, even hiring a band of thugs to

---

is invalid, at least rabbinically (*pasul*), although the substantive grounds for compulsion exist. See MISHNA TORAH, *Hilchot Gerushin* 2:20. Does Rambam mean that no *bait din* issued an order and only there, is the *get* invalid or does his rule encompass even cases where a *bait din* did issue the order but the secular authorities were either unaware of it or were applying pressure on grounds unrelated to the *bait din*'s decision? *Shulchan Aruch* seems more explicit. In discussing the permissible use of non-Jewish (read: secular) authorities to compel a *get*, the *Shulchan Aruch* appears to condition this use on the Jewish court requesting secular intervention and the authorities acting in response to the request, a significant reformulation of Rambam's words. See SHULCHAN ARUCH E.H. 134:9. While there probably need not be a formal request that enforcement mechanisms be employed (the order itself presumably constitutes the requisite "request" for relief, at least implicitly, for otherwise the self-help route would be unavailable; no *bait din* would openly request the commission of acts that may be tortious under secular law), at the very least this formulation would necessitate, first, that the coercers be aware of the order and second, that they act for the purpose of insuring that the order be obeyed.

(As noted *infra* end of note 105, these additional requirements of knowledge and intent would at most be only rabbinically-mandated and their absence would not affect the validity of the *get* on a Torah level. Nevertheless, as a practical matter, even a *get* that is "only" invalid rabbinically does not enable a woman to remarry though it may avoid the stigma of *mamzeirut*. See, *e.g.*, T.B. GITTIN 86a. It should also be noted that, even according to *Shulchan Aruch*, it is possible that the limitations concerning knowledge and intent apply only to the utilization of secular authorities and not to the use of self-help. See T.B. GITTIN 88b and commentaries there. Thus, in the example presented in the second paragraph of this note, the *get* would be valid even accepting *Shulchan Aruch*'s premises. This last point, however, is far from certain and needs further investigation.)

This additional limitation may create problems that pervade many discrete aspects of the *agunah* issue. Throughout this book, we will be exploring various avenues of judicial and legislative relief available to women who find themselves in the *agunah* predicament. See generally Chapters Three through Eight. Many of these remedies involve elements of coercion or duress that may trigger the law of *get meusah*. See, *e.g.*, text at notes 263-265, 291-299, and 632-639. The consistent assumption in the literature, and indeed throughout this book, is that once a woman has secured a *kofin* order from a *bait din*, the *meusah* problem simply disappears since once such an order is issued, all compulsion becomes *halachically* permissible. In light of the above analysis, this "obvious" conclusion may simply not be true. Many of the secular remedies are not tied to a *bait din*'s determination and predicate their sanctions or directives on considerations having nothing to do with securing compliance with a *bait din*'s order. As such, these avenues raise *get meusah* problems not only where *kofin* grounds do not exist but even when they do. See also *infra* text at note 681 (R. Elyashiv specifically notes this problem). This problem will be noted at appropriate places in the text. See also IGROT MOSHE E.H. IV, no. 106 and *infra* note 392 for one possible approach to an analogous problem.

"teach the husband a lesson."[104]

---

104. To clear up a point of potential confusion, under classical *halacha*, a *bait din* is vested with the powers that all courts have to enforce compliance with their judgments through processes similar to levy and execution on property, incarceration, the imposition of fines, and even corporal punishment. See *infra* notes 292 and 319. Outside of the State of Israel, *batei din* are currently unable to exercise their enforcement powers as a matter of secular local law though Jewish law still accords them the right to render decisions. Accordingly, modern-day enforcement of the decisions of *batei din* is accomplished through moral persuasion, (secular) judicial enforcement, community pressure, or self-help. The point in the text that such self-help may even take the form of violence should not be taken to suggest that such measures are permissible. Obviously, under secular law a *bait din* has no authority to permit acts which are criminal or tortious nor will a responsible *bait din* (if for no other reason than to protect itself from liability) ever explicitly authorize or encourage such acts. Nevertheless, since a determination of *kofin* means that, in a pure *halachic* system, the *bait din* itself or its designated agents would have been empowered to utilize all possible sanctions, any *get* that results from the employment of these sanctions by anyone (provided they act with the intention of enforcing the *bait din*'s decree, see *supra* note 103) will not be viewed as the product of coercion.

Of course, the foregoing analysis begs a fundamental question. Granted that criminal or tortious acts undertaken to enforce a *bait din*'s decision are prohibited under *secular law* but are they permitted *halachically*? What answer would be given to a person unafraid of the risks of apprehension by law enforcement authorities who asks, "May I as a *halachically* committed individual act as a self-deputized surrogate enforcer for the *bait din* and utilize whatever a *bait din* could have done to insure that its decree is upheld?" I believe that, notwithstanding the issuance of a *kofin* order, the answer is at best ambiguous. Even when a *bait din* did possess the full range of its enforcement powers, employment of these powers by persons other than authorized agents of the court could result in liability under Jewish law (except in extremely limited and specific circumstances, see SHULCHAN ARUCH H.M. 4 and commentaries), notwithstanding the fact that the tort feasor was attempting to enforce the judgment of a *bait din*. Is the issuance of a *kofin* order equivalent to a general authorization to the world to function as agents of the *bait din* (although such authorization will not confer immunity under secular law) or is it merely a declaration that since in a pure *halachic* system, the circumstances are such that coercion could have been employed, the use of such coercion now will not result in a *get meusah*? Under the second reading, a *kofin* order does not *permit* coercion even *halachically* but merely validates the *get* that is thereby obtained. In other words, it is entirely possible that vigilante enforcement may not be *halachically* permissible but nonetheless (in cases of *kofin*) *halachically* efficacious. This is a subtle distinction that is often overlooked.

While the distinction may possess conceptual merit, it is apparently rejected by the *Shulchan Aruch*. As noted *supra* note 103, *Shulchan Aruch* attributes the efficacy of non-Jewish coercion (and presumably that of any person who is not an officer of the *bait din*) on its being at the "request of the *bait din*." This suggests that if the employment of self-help coercion does

In short, the strictures against *get meusah* are inapplicable to the cases of *halachically*-compelled divorces where all sanctions may be legitimately employed.[105] It should be emphasized, however, that even in such instances,

---

indeed generate a valid *get*, it could do so only on the theory that the issuance of a *kofin* order constitutes such a "request." Absent such a "request," the historical ability of a *bait din* to utilize force could not validate its use today or, to be more accurate, could not validate the *get* obtained through the use of such force. (This, however, would only be a rabbinic flaw, see *supra* note 103). It would therefore appear that the distinction between "permissibility" and "effectiveness" is *not* a valid distinction at least in the narrow context of utilizing secular enforcement. [But *cf. infra* note 116 (R. Herzog does indeed posit such a distinction in connection with the enforcement powers of a *bait din*).] In order for the coercion to be effective in negating *get meusah*, it would have to be employed in a *halachically* permissible manner. The *Shulchan Aruch* does not resolve whether a *kofin* order is construed as an authorization of otherwise-tortious self-help or not; the one proposition it does establish is that if the order does *not* amount to such an authorization (but merely a declaration of what a *bait din could have* done), the use of such coercion will indeed result in a *get meusah*.

[There is an alternative construction of the "request" requirement. It may not mean that *batei din* must authorize the specific form the compulsion may taken but only that their ruling be communicated to the "enforcers" and the "enforcers" act for the purpose of ensuring compliance with the decree. See *supra* note 103. Thus, the efficacy of a *get* obtained through coercion may not depend on the permissibility and legitimacy of the sanctions as employed in a time or place where *batei din* lack enforcement authority or by persons who are not officers of the *bait din* and would lack such authority in any case but is gauged exclusively by the sanctions that a *bait din* could have imposed in a pure *halachic* system that recognized the full scope of its authority. The "permissibility" v. "efficaciousness" dichotomy would still be valid.

In any event, it is arguable that, even according to *Shulchan Aruch*, the requirements of knowledge and intent apply only to a secular court and not to self-help via "unofficial" channels. See *supra* end of note 103. In the latter category, it is possible that the coercers need not intend to enforce the mandate of the *bait din* nor even be aware that the *bait din* issued a *kofin* order. If indeed such awareness is unnecessary, their exceeding the *bait din*'s authorization will most certainly not raise a *meusah* problem as long as *kofin* grounds exist. This result will also follow according to *B'eer Yitzchok*'s ruling cited in the third paragraph of note 103.]

105. The requirement that coercion may be employed only if very specific *halachic* grounds are met has both a substantive and procedural element. Substantively, the facts justifying compulsion must of course be present. See *infra* text at notes 108-133. In the absence of a finding that those facts exist, the decision by the *bait din* would be nothing more than advisory and could not trigger the *halachic* validation of a *get* executed in response to subsequent coercive measures. There is, however, an additional procedural requirement as well. The strictures of *get meusah* are avoided only if a duly-constituted *bait din* has issued a final judgment directing the husband to give a *get*. The existence of the underlying substantive ground alone (even if verified by a later determination of a *bait din*) would not suffice to validate a coerced *get* unless

the *bait din*'s findings and order predated the *get*'s execution. See T.B. GITTIN 88b. (It is uncertain, however, whether this procedural requirement is necessary only when a spouse seeks enforcement via secular authorities or applies even if a spouse invokes self-help, see *supra* note 103.)

On one level, this procedural requirement is puzzling. If Jewish law substantively requires the granting of a divorce, in theory a recalcitrant spouse is immediately under a religious duty to comply even prior to the determination of a *bait din*. If we accept Rambam's theory of "true will," the existence of this religious duty should in itself be sufficient to validate a coerced *get* without the need for an *a priori* determination and judgment of a *bait din*. (While a *bait din* would at some point in time have to determine whether there were in fact *halachic* grounds, there would be no reason for the *bait din*'s decision to precede the use of coercion.)

One answer might be that the notion that a person's "true will" is to obey the dictates of Jewish law can apply only if the person is conscious of the dictates and obligations of that law. Only then could we conclude that the husband truly desires to execute the *get*. Until the *bait din* rules, the recalcitrant spouse may lack the knowledge that he is obligated and hence could not "truly will" the *get* to be written. "Doing the right thing" is not sufficient unless the spouse is also aware that he is "doing the right thing."

This line of reasoning, however, is hardly compelling. In the first place, at least some husbands may very well be aware of their *halachic* obligations yet the coerced *gittin* obtained from even these persons will be invalid unless there was a preexisting order of the *bait din*. Second, Rambam's concept may rest in part on a metaphysical ideal of the soul which may indeed have *halachic* understandings beyond the conscious knowledge of the physical entity (the person) being coerced. Moreover, given the fact that the person "truly desires" to comply with religious law, would it not follow that, even as the person is being coerced, there is always an implicit conditional acquiescence to the *get* if it is found even later to be *halachically* mandatory? Why then is a *bait din*'s *prior* determination essential?

Interestingly, Rambam's own language suggests a different solution. In *Hilchot Gerushin* 2:20, he rules that if non-Jews force a *get* which the husband is in fact obligated to give but no *bait din* has yet ordered, the *get* is *pasul* (invalid). Earlier in the same chapter, *id.* at 2:7, Rambam defines *pasul* as a term connoting invalidation by reason of rabbinic enactment. (The stronger term "*eino get*" - "it is not a *get*" - is used when the *get* is invalid under Torah law.) In effect, the procedural hurdle is not Biblically-required; under Torah law, the problem of *meusah* is indeed successfully circumvented as long as substantive grounds exist, which is exactly the conclusion one would derive from Rambam's explanation of "true will" in 2:20. The procedural need for an *a priori* determination of a *bait din* was a later rabbinic device to discourage precipitous and violent self-help but in no way impacts on the validity of the *get* (insofar as Torah law is concerned). While Rambam's use of the term *pasul* in this context has been criticized, see KESEF MISHNA on *Gerushin* 2:20, and seemingly contradicts T.B. GITTIN 88b, it is fully consistent with Rambam's own understanding of the whole area. See also *infra* note 682.

[As noted *supra* note 103, in addition to the procedural necessity of a *bait din* issuing a prior mandatory order (rather than relying on an after the fact determination), there may be a further requirement of having the order communicated to the coercing entity (as a request for relief or otherwise) and the *get* must ultimately be authorized by the husband. If his "consent" cannot be obtained even with the application of coercive sanctions, the *bait din* has no power to terminate the marriage.[106]

This chapter has attempted to introduce the reader to the basic Jewish law concepts that must be considered in addressing the social problem of the *agunah*. Equipped with a basic understanding of Jewish divorce procedure, the role of a *bait din*, and the strictures against *get meusah*, we are now in a position to evaluate a variety of proposals that have been advanced to assist *agunot* not only from the standpoint of their legal effectiveness but, more importantly, from the perspective of their *halachic* permissibility, a dimension rarely, if ever, grasped by lawyers and judges.

---

having the coercers act with the intention of insuring compliance. The need for this additional element is a matter of uncertainty and indeed appears inconsistent with the "true will" theory articulated by Rambam. But see *infra* text at note 681 (position of R. Elyashiv). Even if this requirement does exist, it too would at most be only rabbinic, covered by the same term *pasul*.]

106. This is the generally-accepted *halachic* rule. The possibilities of rabbinic annulment without the need for the husband to authorize a *get* are discussed *infra* text at note 135 and notes 171-182 but these options have been flatly rejected by virtually all recognized *halachic* authorities.

Chapter Two

Halachic Responses

There have been a number of proposals advanced to alleviate the plight of the *agunah*. They include: (1) expansion of the powers of *bait din* to compel the granting of a *get*; (2) the institution of a conditional marriage; (3) the invocation of rabbinical annulment; (4) the initiation of a divorce proceeding; (5) the reinstitution of concubinage; (6) attacks on the *halachic* validity of a given marriage; and (7) the utilization of the civil courts to enforce the rabbinical decree. Some of these proposals depend entirely on *halacha*; others require careful consideration and application of other bodies of law. This chapter will consider the first six of these alternatives. The last of these alternatives, the use of the secular judiciary, will be analyzed in Chapters Three through Eight.

EXPANDING ACCESS TO THE PROCESS

With respect to a male spouse who desires to divorce his wife, the notion of "grounds" was essentially superfluous since he had the absolute right to divorce her at will without her consent. At most, the presence of grounds was necessary to effect forfeiture or reduction of property rights. Subsequent to the ban of Rabbeinu Gershom, which generally prohibits unilateral divorce action, the existence of "grounds" may also constitute sufficient basis for the procedure of *heter meah rabbanim* or indeed may even obviate the need for such a *heter*.[107]

Since a woman did not have the unconditional right to initiate divorce proceedings against her husband, the notion of "just cause" assumed great importance. Upon a showing of specified causes, a woman could obtain a court order directing her husband to execute and deliver a *get*. (Note that even here it was ultimately the husband who had to give the *get*; neither the wife nor the rabbinical tribunal had any power to dissolve the marriage).

---

107. See discussion *supra* following note 39.

Classical Grounds

The Mishna enumerates a number of specified grounds that enable a woman to petition for divorce and later authorities have supplemented the list.[108]

1. If her husband becomes afflicted with certain loathsome diseases after marriage or even if such disease predated the marriage but, as of the date of the marriage, its existence was unknown to her.
2. Impotence or sterility.
3. Failure to provide material support.
4. Refusal to cohabit.
5. Physical or verbal abuse.
6. Husband forces wife to violate religious law.
7. Husband is engaged in certain occupations that are physically repulsive such as dung-gathering or tanning hides.
8. Husband becomes an apostate.
9. Habitual infidelity.

With respect to some of these grounds, the woman's right to a divorce carries with it the entitlement to the alimony settlement stipulated in the *ketubah*; with respect to others, she gains her freedom only at the cost of forfeiting those rights.[109]

Assuming that grounds do exist for the issuance of a court order directing divorce, how is that order enforced? What sanctions is the rabbinical court empowered to implement in order to insure compliance with its decree? Many authorities maintain that the coercive power of a *bait din* is virtually unlimited and includes the imposition of monetary fines, imprisonment, corporal punishment, a ban of excommunication, and even threat of death.[110] Other authorities[111] took a much more cautious and limiting view of judicial enforcement and drew a distinction between two Talmudic terms. Any ground for which it is stated "*kofin*" ("we force") is deemed sufficiently grave that physical threats and force may indeed be employed. If, on the other hand, the less emphatic term "*yotzee*" ("he shall [or must] divorce") is used, the court may issue the order but cannot impose any coercive measures other than those that are purely psychological such as moral suasion or public proclamation of disobedience.[112] According to some, it may also be permitted to proclaim a

---

108. See T.B. KETUBOT 77a and SHULCHAN ARUCH E.H. 154.

109. See discussion in Shareshevsky, DINAI MISHPACHA, pp. 285-300.

110. See RIF, ch. 7 KETUBOT quoted in TUR E.H. ch. 154 at end.

111. See discussion in TOSAFOT, *s.v. Yotzee*, T.B. KETUBOT 70a and ROSH, end of 6th Chapter YEBAMOT.

112. For example, the Mishna employs the term "*kofin*" for cases of repulsive occupations and loathsome diseases while the lesser term "*yotzee*" is used for refusals to provide material support or cohabitation. See T.B. KETUBOT 77a and YEBAMOT 64a. Whether impotence is grounds for a full-blown *kofin* order or only the lesser sanctions permitted under *yotzee* is a matter of considerable disagreement. The famed decisor Rabbi Shabtai Cohen (16th Century Poland) ruled that compulsion may not be employed, at least where the condition is treatable. See GEVUROT ANASHIM, ch. 42. Many authorities, however, take a contrary position. See Bleich, II CONTEMPORARY HALAKHIC PROBLEMS, p. 102.

boycott on doing business with the recalcitrant husband until he complies with the decree.[113] (The court cannot, however, take the more drastic step of excommunication which in its extremity is as serious as threatening bodily injury.)[114] According to Rosh,[115] because the propriety of utilizing coercive measures is a matter of dispute, the correct procedure is to abstain from employing such measures except where the term "*kofin*" is employed. He notes that the use of enforcement mechanisms that are excessive or unauthorized may not only be an abuse of judicial power but would render the resulting *get* a *meusah* (product of duress) and invalid, making any subsequent marriage adulterous.[116] Thus, to this very day, a *bait din*'s decree of divorce may take

---

One undisputed instance where physical compulsion can clearly be employed is the case of a prohibited union, *e.g.*, a *Cohen* who married a divorceé. SHULCHAN ARUCH E.H. 154:20 and comment of Rema to 154:21.

113. Rabbeinu Tam, cited in Rema, E.H. 154:21. As indicated, what sanctions can be employed in *yotzee* cases is a matter of considerable controversy. While Rema was willing to allow anything short of corporal punishment, the imposition of fines, or formal excommunication and thus validated the use of the "public boycott" of Rabbeinu Tam, many authorities were far more cautious and, in practice, Rabbeinu Tam's remedy is often not utilized. See GEVUROT ANASHIM, ch. 72; PITCHAI TESHUVA E.H. 154:21 (30). Other eminent *poskim*, however, have quoted the Rema with no equivocation. See ARUCH HaSHULCHAN E.H. 154:63. Perhaps *batei din* should be less reticent in invoking this remedy than they have been in the past. See also CHAZON ISH E.H. 108:12 who suggests that the use of such a boycott would not produce a *get meusah*.

Interestingly, a recent decision of Agudath Israel rabbis supports the use of a more limited social ostracism limited to synagogue honors and the like but even this falls far short of the full boycott permitted by Rabbeinu Tam. See *supra* note 58.

114. A description of excommunication [*nidui*, *shamta*] is found *supra* note 46.

115. Quoted in TUR E.H. 154. Rosh is the Hebrew acronym for Rabbi Asher Ben Yechiel. See *infra* Appendix F. He was also the father of the author of *Tur* and is frequently quoted in that work.

116. Although I found no early source that explicitly differs with Rosh on this point (but *cf.* end of note), Rosh's conclusion appears problematical. The theory of validating a coerced *get* in *kofin* cases rests on the fact that the person's "true will" is desirous of complying with *halachic* obligations; coercion therefore does not overpower such will but simply subjugates the "evil inclination" that prevents such will from emerging. See Rambam, cited *supra* text at note 100. Since the *halachic* obligation to divorce (in the sense of a religion-moral imperative) is identical in both *kofin* and *yotzee* cases, a *get* obtained by coercion should be equally valid in both.

This is not to suggest that no distinction between *kofin* and *yotzee* may exist but rather that such distinctions should pertain only to the scope of the legitimate power a *bait din* may or may not exercise but not to the secondary question of whether a *get* that resulted from even illegitimate pressure would be invalid as a *meusah*. It would be totally logical to conclude, for example,

one of two forms: (1) a directive that the husband *must* divorce his wife; (2) a directive that the husband may be *compelled* to divorce his wife. From the perspective of moral and religious obligations, both are equally binding yet only the latter may be enforced through conventional mechanisms, the former remaining essentially a matter of conscience. The notion of a judicial order *not* subject to enforcement must certainly strike the conventional legal mind as odd. At least since Holmes, it is commonplace to regard the very meaning of a right as the remedy available for its vindication. Thus, one could not state that a woman has a "right" to divorce unless she could call upon the mechanism of the state to get it for her.[117] Yet in a system where legal courts are also

---

that in *yotzee* cases a *bait din* is not authorized or permitted to impose incarceration but if incarceration is in fact imposed, a *get* granted to escape it would not be *meusah* by reason of the moral and religious obligation the prisoner has to grant it.

Indeed, a similar dichotomy exists even within the *kofin* category. Once a finding of *kofin* has been made, any employment of force (even one not authorized by the *bait din* and indeed, considered tortious) will have no impact on the *get*. See *supra* note 104. What compulsion may be permissible and what effect such compulsion has on the *get* are two distinct questions.

Nevertheless, Rosh's ruling that *kofin*-measures applied in *yotzee*-cases result in a *get meusah* appears to be universally conceded, with little or no discussion to the reasons why. See, *e.g.*, language of Rema, gloss to SHULCHAN ARUCH E.H. 154:21; ARUCH HaSHULCHAN 154:63; and CHAZON ISH E.H. 99:11. Most recently, this stance was affirmed in an unpublished responsum by Rabbi Yosef Elyashiv of Jerusalem. See *infra* text at notes 681-682. But *cf.* CHELKAT YOAB, *Dinai Ones*, Chapter 5. (Significantly, Rambam himself makes no distinction between *kofin* and *yotzee* cases, a stance fully consistent with his understanding of why coercion in *halachically*-obligatory divorces does not produce a *get meusah*. See *supra* text at note 100.)

[As this book was going to press, I came across the illuminating comments of Rabbi Isaac Herzog, the late Chief Rabbi of Israel, who indeed suggests that even those opinions which distinguish between *kofin* and *yotzee* do so only with respect to the *bait din*'s authority and not with respect to whether the resulting *get* would be invalid as a *get meusah*. He thus concludes that although the imposition of *kofin* sanctions in *yotzee* cases may well be improper and tortious, the *get* thereby secured would nonetheless be valid. He also posits that, in cases of great necessity, *kofin*-sanctions might be employed in *yotzee*-cases even *ab initio*. See 2 OTZAR HaPOSKIM (Appendix), pp. 11-12. While this is a welcome confirmation for the argument advanced above, the argument itself has not to date been accepted by the majority of *halachic* scholars who continue to assume that *kofin* sanctions without *kofin* grounds produce a *get meusah* even where the husband is under a religious obligation to divorce. This work therefore proceeds under the majority assumption.

Rabbi Herzog's distinction, if accepted, would change a number of conclusions that appear in the text and these shall be noted in the appropriate places.]

117. As Oliver Wendell Holmes remarked in a celebrated 1897 speech: "If you want to know the law and nothing else, you must look at it as a bad man, who cares only for the material consequences which such knowledge

religious and moral educators and where rights and obligations have transcendent bases of authority going beyond human mechanisms of compulsion, such a concept is entirely understandable.

Outside the State of Israel,[118] rabbinical courts have no power of compulsion in any event so the distinction between the two forms of decree may appear at first glance to be merely academic. Such an impression would be erroneous. Even where *batei din* lack their own enforcement powers, the *kofin-yotzee* distinction continues to be critical. *Halacha* generally permits the utilization of the secular court system to insure compliance with the dictates of a *bait din* and the use of this system may be obtained through the drafting of appropriate prenuptial agreements.[119] It would seem, however, that this would be *halachically* acceptable only for a decree of *kofin* and not for a decree of *yotzee* since it is unlikely that *halacha* would allow a secular court to do what its own *bait din* cannot.[120] Thus, both the permissibility and efficacy of *secular* enforcement, an avenue that will be explored in Chapters Three and Four, depend directly on the understanding of this dichotomy.

Divorce on the Grounds of Incompatibility, Irreconcilable Differences: Talmudic Precedent

It can be readily seen that although only the husband or his proxy could actually execute the *get*, women did have access to the rabbinical court to secure an order obligating (*yotzee*) or compelling (*kofin*) their husbands to divorce them. All the categories enumerated above, however, involve clearly defined objective criteria: loathsome diseases, repulsive occupations, nonsupport, abandonment, infidelity, abuse. What if a woman simply no longer wanted to be married to a certain individual? What if she claims *mais alai* ("he is now repulsive to me")? Rabbinical authorities were sharply divided over this issue and their conclusions depend on the interpretation of several key

---

enables him to predict.... One of the many evil effects of the confusion between legal and moral ideas ... is ... to consider the right or the duty as something existing apart from and independent of the consequences of its breach...." Holmes, COLLECTED LEGAL PAPERS (1920), pp. 167, 168-171. Suffice it to say that a system of law predicated on Divine revelation and moral duty would disagree with the above characterization.

118. Under present Israeli law, imprisonment is the severest sanction that rabbinical courts may impose even in a *kofin*-type situation. See Rabbinical Courts Jurisdiction (Marriage & Divorce) Law 1953, §6 and M. Elon (ed.), THE PRINCIPLES OF JEWISH LAW ("Divorce"). See also *infra* text at notes 510-529 for a discussion of the jurisdiction of rabbinical courts in the State of Israel.

119. See *infra* text at notes 291-299.

120. *Id.* This distinction appears to have escaped the attention of Rabbis Haut and Riskin. See *infra* text at notes 151-160.

[Of course, under the Herzog analysis cited at the and of note 116, the *kofin* - *yotzee* distinction assumes considerably less importance since the resulting *get* will in either case not be a *get meusah*. Even Rabbi Herzog, however, recognized that the distinction determines which sanctions are *halachically* permissible (as opposed to being merely efficacious after the fact). In any case, Rabbi Herzog's position has not been widely accepted.]

Talmudic passages dealing with what is called the *moredet* or "rebellious wife."

The Mishna in *Ketubot* speaks of "the rebellious wife," defined as a woman who refuses to cohabit with her husband, and provides that as a way of compelling her to resume the relationship, there is weekly deduction of seven *dinaarim* (*zuz*) from her alimony entitlement.[121] Since the standard alimony entitlement is 200 *dinaarim*, it would take approximately seven months to reduce her claim to zero.[122] Beyond that period, the seven *dinaarim* turn into an affirmative liability chargeable against the wife's property interests.

Within one generation, the punishment/deterrent accorded to the *moredet* took on a different form. In lieu of a gradual depletion, a public proclamation in the synagogue was made for four consecutive Sabbaths urging her to recant. After that point, there was an immediate forfeiture of the entire *ketubah*. The Talmud discusses the particulars of these announcements and various other warnings the *moredet* receives.[123] The Talmud also provides (though this is probably a Saboraic[124] addition) that even after the forfeiture of alimony upon expiration of the four-week period, the husband may continue to exert pressure upon his wife by withholding support for up to one year.[125]

---

121. T.B. KETUBOT 63a.

122. Riskin points out that although the husband was within his rights to divorce the *moredet* at any time - and indeed this is the case even after the *takkana* of Rabbeinu Gershom - upon the depletion of the *ketubah*, a divorce would become mandatory under the rule that husband and wife are prohibited to cohabit without a *ketubah*. Thus, unless husband would be willing to forgive his wife's rebellion and reinstate the *ketubah*, the marriage would invariably have to end in divorce. Indeed, this was part of the incentive pushing the woman to abandon her rebellion. See S. Riskin, WOMEN AND JEWISH DIVORCE, p. 12. Riskin's assertion that after depletion divorce must inevitably follow seems to contradict the opinion in the Mishna that the husband may continue to let the clock run and actually have an affirmative claim against his wife. Moreover, the prohibition on cohabitation would apparently apply not only when the *ketubah* is reduced to "zero" but as soon as it falls below 200 *zuz*. Finally, his analysis seems inconsistent with the twelve-month waiting period recognized by the Talmud, discussed *infra* text at note 125.

123. Actually, Riskin, *supra* note 122, p. 40, convincingly argues that the Talmudic law of *moredet* underwent four distinct changes: (1) gradual reduction of alimony; (2) month-long period of court-initiated private persuasion followed by immediate forfeiture of alimony and divorce; (3) four weeks of public announcement in synagogue followed by alimony forfeiture; (4) combination of four weeks of private warning followed by public announcement followed by private warning. As noted, subsequent changes occurred in the time of the Saboraim and later in the time of Gaonim.

124. See Riskin, *supra* note 122, pp. 44-46. The Saboraim ("persons who reflect or reason") were the religious leaders of Babylonian (and essentially world) Jewry during the 6th Century and are generally credited with the final redaction of the Talmud. See Grayzel, A HISTORY OF THE JEWS, p. 222.

125. The Talmud does not clearly indicate what happens after that year. There are three distinct interpretive possibilities: (1) after the year, the husband may be compelled to grant a *get*; (2) after the year, the *bait din* will urge him to give a *get* but will not impose coercive measures; or (3) the

The Talmud then proceeds to discuss the nature and motivation of the woman's refusal to cohabit with her husband. The relevant passage reads as follows:

> What is to be understood by the term "rebellious wife?" Amemar said: She who says "I want him but want to cause him pain." If she says, however, "He is repulsive to me," we do not force her. Mar Zutra said: She is forced. Such an incident once occurred and Mar Zutra forced and Rabbi Haninah of Sura was born from this relationship. This, however, was not proper. In that case, it was the intervention of Providence.[126]

The Talmud clearly indicates that it inclines to the reading of Amemar that a woman who declares "he is repulsive to me" does not fall within the category of *moredet* and we therefore "do not *force her*." The critical and undefined question is the meaning of that phrase. Rambam offers the following interpretation:

> A woman who refuses to engage in sexual relations with her husband is called a rebellious wife. [The court] asks her why she is rebelling. If she says 'I find him repulsive and I cannot willingly engage in sexual relations with him,' *[the court] forces [kofin] him to divorce her immediately because she is not a captive woman who must have sexual relations with one whom she hates.* She goes out without any *ketubah* [but does receive whatever property she brought into the marriage and must refund all that was given to her by her husband] "even the shoe from her foot or the kerchief from her head."[127] (emphasis added)

The chief protagonist who vigorously disputed Rambam's view was Rabbeinu Tam who argued that it is totally improper to allow a woman to obtain a divorce merely on the grounds of a self-serving declaration of repulsiveness and such an approach substantially undermines family stability.[128] Moreover, the Talmud merely says that in the case of *mais alai*, "we don't force her," and does not state "we force him." Rabbeinu Tam's disagreement is forcefully articulated by Rosh, who states:

> [I]t is very astonishing that Rambam (may his memory be a blessing) wrote that if she said, 'I find him repulsive and I am unwilling to have sexual relations with him,' they force

---

husband is not ordered to give a *get* but if he desires to stay married, must resume support and reinstate the *ketubah*.

126. T.B. KETUBOT 63a.

127. Rambam, MISHNA TORAH, *Hilchot Ishut* 14:8. With respect to the "true *moredet*" who rebels out of spite, Rambam codifies the Talmudic procedure of public announcements for four weeks with private warnings preceding and following the public ones. Upon conclusion of the warnings, she forfeits all her *ketubah* and may claim even the property she brought in to the marriage only to the extent it is in her custody and possession. She may also be kept in a state of limbo for up to one year.

128. See TOSAFOT to T.B. KETUBOT 63a, *s.v. Avel*. Rabbeinu Tam ("our master, the perfect") was the reverential title of Rabbi Yaakov Ben Meir, one of the great Talmudists of Medieval France and a grandson of Rashi. See *infra* Appendix F.

> him to divorce her at that time for she is not a captive woman who must have sexual relations with one who is hateful to her. But what kind of reason has he given for coercing the man to divorce and to permit a married woman to cohabit with another? Rather let her not have sexual relations with her husband and let her remain chained all of her days for after all, *she* is not commanded to be fruitful and multiply! Because she followed the dictates of her heart and cast her eyes upon another and desired him more than the husband of her youth, do we then fulfill her lust and force the man who loves the wife of his youth to divorce her? Heaven forbid, that any judge would judge in such a manner.[129]

In short, there are two fundamental views. According to Rambam, the Talmud is discussing two types of rebellious women. Type one is a married woman who desires to stay married but temporarily refuses to have intercourse with her husband out of anger, spite, or dissention. Here, the Talmud modifies the Mishnaic sanction of gradually depleting the alimony and provides for four weeks of warning followed by immediate forfeiture. Upon such forfeiture, she must return all property received from her husband and may remove even the property she brought in to the marriage only to the extent such property is actually under her physical custody and control. The second type is a woman who refuses to have relations with her husband because she no longer desires to stay married. Here, even without substantiation of her claim, she is immediately entitled to an order compelling the execution and delivery of a *get* without public or private warnings and, while she must return whatever value received from her husband, she may recover *all* property she brought into the marriage whether presently under her physical control or otherwise.

Under the reading of the Rabbeinu Tam and Rosh, both types of women are generally treated the same. That is, regardless of her motives for rebellion, she is subject to the warning and forfeiture sanctions. The statement of Amemar merely meant that if a woman stated that she was so anxious to escape a marriage that she was willing to forego all claim to alimony immediately, such a waiver is valid with the result that the husband *may* (not *must*) divorce his wife immediately at no cost. Thus, the phrase "we do not force her" simply means that upholding the waiver avoids a situation whereby the husband would have a built-in incentive to delay the *get* and this in turn may facilitate expeditious relief. In no case, however, would anyone other than the husband dictate or compel any particular course of action. Indeed, Rabbeinu Tam asserts that if the court did order and compel the execution of such a *get*, the *get* would be invalid as *meusah* and a second marriage would be adulterous.

The definitive ruling of the *Shulchan Aruch* is essentially that of Rabbeinu Tam with some additional qualifications:[130]

First, if a woman claims she finds her husband repulsive and no longer desires to remain married, the husband is nevertheless *not* compelled to divorce

---

129. TESHUVOT ROSH 43:8. Note, however, that in that very same responsum, Rosh was willing to compel a divorce where the woman supported her claim of repulsiveness with objective, verifiable criteria.

130. This ruling is found in SHULCHAN ARUCH E.H. 77:2.

her even if she is willing to forego alimony. If he does so on his own, she receives no alimony and must return all property received from her husband, even gifts of clothing and shoes. With respect to property that she brought into the marriage, the *Shulchan Aruch* grants her an absolute right of reclamation. Other opinions cited would recognize an absolute right only for *melog* and limit her rights in *tzon barzel* to assets already in her possession. Still a third group would deny even her rights to *melog* except to the extent that such property is in her physical custody.[131] Under all three views, there is no *in personam* restitutionary liability. There are no public or private announcements designed to make her recant.

Second, if the woman rebels out of spite, the four-week warning sanction is employed.[132] Upon the expiration of the four-week period, her alimony claim is immediately forfeited. The husband may then keep her in a twelve-month limbo, neither granting her a *get* nor providing spousal support.[133]

---

131. The latter two views are cited *id.* by Rema. The terms *nichsai melog* (*n.m.*) and *nichsai tzon barzel* (*n.t.b.*) are described *infra* Appendix B and in the Glossary. Briefly, both are terms for various types of marital property arrangements. *N.m.* property is brought into the marriage by the wife with the understanding that, during the marriage, the husband has the benefit of use and possession but upon termination of the marriage, the property will be returned *in specie* with the widow or divorcee bearing the risks of loss or the benefit of appreciation. *N.t.b.* property is brought into the marriage pursuant to an agreement that upon termination of the marriage, the widow or divorcee will receive a fixed monetary settlement based on the property's assessed value as of the date it was contributed. The husband or his estate bears the risk of loss and the benefit of appreciation. Whether property is *n.m.* or *n.t.b.* depends entirely on the mutual agreements between the parties. Because *n.m.* property allocates the risks and benefits of ownership to the donor spouse, it is commonly regarded as her property.

As applied to the wife who claims her husband is repulsive, all opinions deny *in personam* restitutionary rights. Opinion no. 1, however, permits the wife at her option to convert the monetary claim of *n.t.b.* into an *in specie* claim for property actually brought in as well as asserting her normal *in specie* claim for *n.m.* Opinion no. 2 maintains that an *in specie* claim is only appropriate for *n.m.* since the donor spouse is deemed the present owner, but would nevertheless accord such an option even for *n.t.b.* to the extent the wife is in possession. Opinion no. 3 adopts an essentially punitive approach, denying not only the woman's right to restitution but even her rights to an *in specie* return of *n.m.* property except to the extent of any possessory entitlement. See also R. Elijah of Vilna, BIUR HaGRA E.H. 77:2 (7), who maintains that these latter two opinions are inconsistent with the Talmudic discussion.

132. There is a dispute whether this means four consecutive weeks or four consecutive sabbaths. *Cf.* language of *Shulchan Aruch* with gloss of Rema.

133. Within that year, if the husband so desires, he may divorce her at any time without the need to pay a *ketubah* and free of the constraints of the ban of Rabbeinu Gershom. Other authorities disagree with the *Shulchan Aruch* and maintain there is no forfeiture of *ketubah* until the expiration of the entire twelve-month period. See BAIT SHMUEL E.H. 77:2 (13). Note, however, that to the extent the woman retracts and effects a reconciliation with her

Divorce on the Grounds of Incompatibility, Irreconcilable Differences: *Takkanat HaGaonim* and *Dina D'Mesivta*

General Scope and Acceptance of the Enactment

Although the Talmudic discussion of the *moredet* seems to provide for a four-week warning period and a twelve-month wait before she receives her *get*, these rules were considerably modified by a post-Talmudic enactment of the Gaonim.[134] The *takkana* has come down to us from a variety of sources and, in essence, provided women with the right to obtain a *get* immediately without the need to suffer the humiliation of public embarrassment or the limbo of being married without support for twelve months.[135] The stated purpose of

---

husband during the twelve-month period or afterwards, a new *ketubah* would be mandatory.

With respect to *n.m.* and *n.t.b.*, her claims are limited to assets actually in her possession even according to the opinions that did not impose this limitation in the first case discussed in note 131. As would be expected, the spiteful *moredet* is treated less favorably than the repulsed one.

134. The Gaonim were the recognized leaders of the major Babylonian academies of Jewish learning for the several centuries after the redaction of the Talmud. These academies were accepted by Jewish communities worldwide as the definitive expositors of Jewish law, second only to the Talmud itself. Our primary source of knowledge concerning the institution of the Gaonate is the famed IGGERET R. SHERIRA GAON, authored by one of the last Gaonim in the 10th Century. A fascinating description of all aspects of the educational, judicial, and administrative activities of the Gaonim and their academies appears in Holder, HISTORY OF THE JEWISH PEOPLE: FROM YAVNEH TO PUMBEDISA, pp. 223-309.

135. The earliest reference to this innovation appears in a responsum authored by R. Yehudai Gaon, head of the Sura Academy in the middle of the 8th Century. See Tykocinski, TAKKANOT HaGAONIM, pp. 11-12. Most historians, however, date the actual *takkana* around 100 years earlier to 650 c.e. See Riskin, *supra* note 122, pp. 47-60; Haut, *supra* note 18, p. 49; and Chapter One in Tykocinski's work.

The legal grounds for validating a *get* issued under this *takkana* is a matter of dispute. Some assert that the legitimacy of judicial coercion pursuant to even a post-Talmudic edict is the same as that for the cases specifically enumerated in the Talmud. See OR ZARUA para. 754. Ultimately, however, the woman may remarry only if her husband gives her a *get*. The *Takkanat HaGaonim* merely permits compulsion directed towards that end. There is also a more radical understanding of the *takkana* which would regard the marriage as terminated pursuant to the power of rabbinic annulment rather than *get*. See TESHUVOT ROSH 43:8. This could arguably have enabled a woman to remarry even if her husband, impervious to all pressure, refuses to grant a *get*. (This conclusion, however, does not inexorably follow. It is entirely possible for there to be an *annulment* conditional on the obtaining of a *get*, albeit a coerced one.) The text here discusses the *Takkanat HaGaonim* from the perspective of the first approach, that a *get* is necessary, since that seems to be

the *takkana* was to prevent Jewish women from enlisting the support of gentiles to coerce their husbands into giving them a *get* or from leaving their religion entirely.[136] Indeed, the solicitude for the unhappy wife was so great that, according to many authorities, albeit not all, not only could the wife demand the immediate execution and delivery of a *get* but was entitled both to her alimony claim and to all property that she had brought into the marriage.[137]

This *takkana*, known as the *Dina D'Mesivta* ("Law of the Academy"), was widely utilized throughout the Jewish communities in Europe, Palestine, and North Africa for almost 500 years. For reasons that are not altogether clear, however, the *takkana* fell out of use from the 12th Century onwards.[138] Rambam argued that the Gaonic *takkana* had no continuing validity because it never achieved widespread community acceptance.[139] R. Zerachyah HaLevi

---

the understanding of the *takkana* maintained by most commentators.

136. This explanation appears in a responsum authored by Rav Natronai Gaon, head of the Sura Academy in the middle of the 9th Century. See 8 OTZAR HaGAONIM, p. 189. Riskin cogently notes that the phrase women "coming to a bad end" may refer to the fact that under Islamic law, a woman who converted to Islam had the right to obtain an immediate divorce from her husband who refused to convert. An unknown number of women may have employed this procedure to obtain the assistance of the Islamic courts. See Riskin, *supra* note 122, p. 75 and Reuben Levy, THE SOCIAL STRUCTURE OF ISLAM, pp. 122-123.

137. This appears to be the decision of Rav Amram Gaon, the head of the Sura Academy in the latter half of the 9th Century and one of the most eminent of the Gaonim. See HAGAHOT MAIMONIYOT on MISHNA TORAH, *Hilchot Ishut* ch. 14 note 30. Riskin, *supra* note 122, in Chapter IV at note 10 points out that this position is often erroneously attributed to R. Natronai Gaon but this would be inconsistent with the responsa cited in the preceding note where Rav Natronai rules that the *moredet* forfeits the *ketubah* (although may reclaim her property).

As noted in the text, many authorities would not allow the wife to collect her *ketubah*. See HALAKHOT GEDOLOT; R. Natronai Gaon, cited in 8 OTZAR HaGAONIM, p. 189. However, R. Amram's decision was followed by R. Sherira Gaon and his son Hai and is the definitive tradition recorded by Rif, KETUBOT 26b-27a although he himself rules that the Gaonic tradition should not be followed. Note that all authorities concede that she must return any property received from her husband and forfeits right to *tosefet*. Conversely, all authorities concede that she may reclaim any property she brought into the marriage whether or not it is presently in her custody. The areas of disagreement focus on her right to *ketubah* and whether she is entitled to restitution of *nichsai tzon barzel* that have been damaged or dissipated.

138. Rif already mentions that "although there is a dispute among the great scholars, it is logical not to follow the [Gaonic] *takkana*." Rif, KETUBOT 27a (Vilna ed.).

139. MISHNA TORAH, *Hilchot Ishut* 14:14. Note, however, that Rambam interpreted *Talmudic* law in a manner that led to a substantially similar result. *Supra* text at note 127.

(*Sefer HaMaor*)[140] and Rashba[141] argued that the *Dina D'Mesivta* was an emergency measure enacted for a particular generation and situation and was never intended to have permanent effect. Rabbeinu Tam argued that the Gaonim had no authority to enact such a *takkana* and a *get* delivered pursuant to such compulsion would be void.[142] Although a number of eminent authorities were perfectly willing to utilize the *Dina D'Mesivta*,[143] as a practical matter it became a dead letter and is not even quoted as a minority opinion in the definitive *Shulchan Aruch*.

The *Takkanat HaGaonim* created an essential equality between men and women in their ability to invoke the dissolution process, the only difference being that the woman must normally proceed by seeking relief in a *bait din* through the obtaining of a court order while the man may initiate the process on his own. Moreover, the woman could actually be somewhat better off since if she initiates the divorce process, many opinions would grant her alimony while if he initiates it against her, he will normally have to pay. It must also be remembered that the 10th Century saw the promulgation of the *takkana* of Rabbeinu Gershom which generally prohibited divorcing one's wife against her will. Were the *Takkanat HaGaonim* combined with the *takkana* of Rabbeinu Gershom, *halacha* would have created a situation where the wife would have an unqualified right to demand a divorce and have the court compel the husband to execute it while the husband could only divorce his wife for cause or with her consent - a 180-degree turn from the original pattern of Mosaic legislation.[144]

---

140. COMMENTARY TO RIF, KETUBOT 27a, but see Ramban's (Nachmanides') comment in MILCHAMOT HaSHEM where he accuses the *Sefer HaMaor* of disingenuousness.

141. TESHUVOT RASHBA I, nos. 1192 and 1238. See also TESHUVOT MEYUCHOSOT L'RAMBAN, no. 138.

142. SEFER HaYASHAR Sect. 599. He also asserted that the Gaonic *takkana* did not include any provision for coercion but simply permitted the husband to waive the twelve-month waiting period if he desired to do so. It appears, however, that Rabbeinu Tam could not have seen the actual texts of the relevant responsa where the term "*kofin*" ("compel") is consistently used. See especially the comments of R. Sherira Gaon, 8 OTZAR HaGAONIM, pp. 191-192.

143. See, for example, TOSAFOT RID to GITTIN 88b and OR ZARUA, para. 754. Ramban (Nachmanides), in theory, was in favor of implementing the Gaonic *takkana*, maintaining that it was intended to be permanent, but concludes that because the application of the *takkana* is a matter of dispute, the court that refuses to implement it has not done anything wrong and in fact may be deserving of credit for its caution. MILCHAMOT HaSHEM, commenting on Rif, KETUBOT 27a.

144. In a personal communication to this author dated December, 1991, Professor Michael Broyde of Emory has pointed out that historically these two *takkanot* did not appear to exist side by side. Indeed, if one considers the *other* aspect of Rabbeinu Gershom's *takkana* (the ban on polygamy), these enactments may represent two opposite responses to an identical problem. The Gaonic response to the plight of a woman unable to remarry because of her husband's recalcitrance was to increase the woman's access to the divorce

As noted, however, this was simply not to be.

The Relationship of Takkanat HaGaonim to Talmudic Precedent

The *Takkanat HaGaonim* was clearly understood both by its promulgators and by later generations of commentators as a legislative departure from the law as laid down in the Talmud in the direction of a greater expansion of women's rights. In order to gauge the extent of this departure, one must ascertain, first, the requirements of Talmudic law and second, the specific aspects of the Gaonic *takkana* that constituted a deviation from this norm. In short, what exactly did the Gaonim change?

In light of the preceding analysis, the following conclusions emerge:

First, to the extent the *Takkanat HaGaonim* rests on principles of annulment,[145] it is a leniency that goes far beyond anything mentioned in the Talmud. At best, the Talmud grants (according to Rambam) the dissatisfied wife the right to petition for an order compelling a *get* while the Gaonim allow remarriage even if a *get* is not obtained.[146] Rif and most other authorities, however, do not understand the Gaonic *takkana* to operate in such a drastic manner.[147]

Second, assuming the *Takkanat HaGaonim* is not as broad and in fact necessitates a *get*, the Gaonic innovation is less clear. According to Rambam's view, the Talmud already enables a dissatisfied wife (with a claim of *mais alai*) to obtain a *get* via compulsion immediately. If so, the sole contribution of the *takkana* was to augment that privilege by granting the wife superior rights to *ketubah* and marital property.[148] Its benefits to the dissatisfied spouse lay not

---

process enabling her to invoke the coercive powers of the *bait din* (or obtain an annulment, see *supra* note 135). Rabbeinu Gershom's response was not to strengthen the hands of the woman but to shackle those of the man prohibiting *him* from remarrying until a *get* is executed. In a religiously-observant society, this *takkana* would in itself be a powerful impetus towards the solution of *agunah* problems though it is less so today. Professor Broyde's suggestion that Rabbeinu Gershom's *takkana* was adopted as a remedy for *agunot* is intriguing but is not borne out by the historical evidence. See Grossman, *supra* note 31, p. 1451 and Shareshevsky, *supra* note 23, pp. 67-68 (stressing economic factors). (This is not to deny, however, that Rabbeinu Gershom's *takkana* cannot have this salutary effect).

145. See *supra* note 135.

146. As indicated *supra* note 135, however, even the annulment theory may in fact have required a *get* albeit a coerced one.

147. See description in Rif, KETUBOT 27a (Vilna ed.). It is not clear how Rambam viewed the *Takkanat HaGaonim*. In 14:14 of *Hilchot Ishut*, he simply notes that the Gaonim of Babylon had distinct rulings and customs in connection with the dissatisfied wife and concludes that these practices should not be followed but never informs us exactly what these practices were. But see *infra* note 148.

148. For example, under the *Takkanat HaGaonim* many authorities would grant a woman with a claim of *mais alai* the right to collect the *ketubah* although, under Talmudic law, it is clear the *ketubah* is forfeited. All

in her enhanced access to the coercive powers of a *bait din* - an access already present under Talmudic law - but in the preservation of economic rights that would otherwise be forfeited.[149]

---

authorities subscribing to the *takkana* would recognize her *in specie* reclamation claims for *nichsai melog* and *nichsai tzon barzel* whether or not the property is physically in her possession even though, under Talmudic law, her rights to marital property may be limited to those assets she physically retains as of the date of the divorce. See *supra* notes 131, 133 and 137. (Under both rules, gifts received by the husband during the marriage must be refunded.)

While Rambam provides no explicit statement as to the nature of the Gaonic *takkanot*, I would suggest that he too understood their innovation in a primarily economic sense. In ruling that Gaonic enactments should not be followed, Rambam writes: "The Gaonim have said that in Babylon they have special practices concerning the rebellious wife. These practices have not spread among most Jews and many as well as great persons in most locales differ with them. It is therefore proper to judge in accordance with the law of the Talmud." MISHNA TORAH, *Hilchot Ishut* 14:14. Rambam's ruling not to follow Gaonic practices is comparatively mild, suggesting that no particularly-catastrophic consequences ensue one way or the other. If Rambam understood the Gaonim to be authorizing annulment, *i.e.*, the remarriage of a woman without a *get*, one would have expected the denunciation to be far more severe since such remarriages are adulterous and would produce *mamzeirim* unable to marry within the Jewish faith. See *supra* text at note 35. Rabbeinu Tam, for example, who denied that the Talmud permitted a compelled *get*, condemned any understanding of the Gaonic *takkana* that authorized such a *get* in precisely such strong denunciatory terms. Rambam's lukewarm reservations suggest, therefore, that he viewed the *takkana* as a relatively-minor adjustment of economic entitlements. (While the *takkana* did in fact allow women to obtain *gittin* via compulsion, Rambam maintains this was no innovation at all since the Talmud already does the same. The *only* Gaonic change was in the sphere of property).

149. An alternative interpretation would be that the *Takkanat HaGaonim* abrogated the Talmudic rule that applied to the "true" *moredet* substituting an immediate right to a *get* in lieu of the twelve-month waiting period. See *supra* text at note 125. This is implausible, however, for a number of reasons. First, the "true" *moredet* is a woman who desires to stay married but withholds marital affection out of spite or for leverage. Why should such a woman be "entitled" to an immediate *get* which, by hypothesis, she doesn't even want? Second, why should such a woman be entitled to *ketubah* and other marital property if her motives are spiteful and she does not assert the claim of *mais alai*? Third, if in fact the *takkana* allows for a compelled *get* under circumstances where the Talmud does not, *i.e.*, the "true" *moredet*, Rambam should have criticized the Gaonic *takkana* in much harsher terms. See *supra* note 148.

For all the above reasons as well as the historical circumstances of the Gaonic enactment, it seems clear that the *Takkanat HaGaonim* was concerned exclusively with the woman claiming *mais alai* and desirous of divorce and did not purport to change the Talmudic law of the "spiteful *moredet*" (which, in any event, is an infrequent case). Once the *takkana* is limited to the former, it is clear that at least according to Rambam its primary focus must be

Third, if, on the other hand, Talmudic law never provided for a compulsory divorce but merely stated that, if the husband elects of his own volition to execute a *get*, there is an immediate forfeiture of *ketubah* (hence, creating no incentives on the part of the husband to procrastinate), the Gaonic *takkana* indeed marks a major innovation in allowing for a compulsory *get*. (As noted, however, Rabbeinu Tam, who adopted this narrower reading of Talmudic precedent, not only rejected the continuing validity of the *Takkanat HaGaonim* but maintained that such an enactment would have been invalid from its inception.)[150]

Modern Proposals

Riskin, Haut, and others have suggested that *halacha* should reinstitute the views of Rambam or the procedure of the Gaonim and thereby allow unhappy wives a virtually unlimited right to seek dissolution of an unsatisfactory marriage.[151] Riskin maintains that Rabbeinu Tam's interpretation of the Talmudic passage as *not* permitting a compulsory divorce was a minority opinion that sharply broke with past understanding and that virtually all earlier authorities upheld the woman's right to obtain a *get* upon the claim of *mais alai*.[152] It was only the immense personal prestige of Rabbeinu Tam that, in the guise of a novel and unique interpretation, single-handedly changed the course of *halachic* development for over 700 years and resulted in the inability of women to initiate divorce proceedings. As such, there is ample *halachic* precedent to follow Rambam, which (Riskin concludes) would greatly alleviate the plight of *agunot*. Others have argued that even if the Talmud did not recognize the unqualified right of a woman to escape an unhappy marriage,

---

economic.

150. Rabbeinu Tam sought to avoid such a harsh critique by positing that such a *takkana* never in fact existed but this is contradicted by history. *Supra* note 142.

151. See Riskin, *supra* note 122, p. 94 and Haut, *supra* note 18, pp. 49, 96-97.

In fairness to Rabbi Riskin, it must be noted that at no point in his work does he explicitly call for a readoption of either the view of Rambam or the *Takkanat HaGaonim*. Indeed, the only solution he openly advocates is a relatively-noncontroversial prenuptial agreement of the type validated by *Avitzur*, see *infra* text at notes 277-282 (though even there, he fails to distinguish between *kofin* and *yotzee* cases, see *infra* text at notes 156-158). Nevertheless, the entire thrust of his work is to demonstrate, through an examination of the primary sources, that Rabbeinu Tam's restrictive view was a sharp break with the past and it was unfortunate that it ever gained the wide acceptance that it did. Curiously (though understandably), in the final pages of his book, he simply abandons the cumulative weight of his arguments and goes off on an entirely-different track, *i.e.*, the use of a prenuptial agreement. All references to the "Riskin approach" should be understood as referring to his general analysis of source material and not his actual conclusion. Rabbi Haut, I believe, is less cautious and has openly called on modern *halachic* authorities to accept the views of Rambam and/or the *Dina D'Mesivta*.

152. Indeed, this thesis is boldly and explicitly stated on the book's jacket although Rabbi Riskin does not espouse this view for practical implementation.

such a right can be recognized by a revival of the long-dormant *Dina D'Mesivta*.[153]

Even accepting Riskin's reading of the earlier sources, it certainly does not follow that, as a matter of normative *halachic* practice, the views of Rambam should be reinstated. Indeed, Rabbi Riskin himself appears to concede this point, albeit with some reluctance. In the first place, neither *Shulchan Aruch* or Rema even quote the Rambam as an acceptable minority opinion and it is a well-established principle in *halachic* decision-making that opinions not recorded in the *Shulchan Aruch* or its standard commentaries may not be relied upon for any purposes whatsoever (including extenuating circumstances, and the like).[154] Thus, arguing for the revival of a long-rejected opinion calls upon rabbinical courts to take a drastic step that they are not only unwilling but unable to take.

Note too that the consequences of error are extremely severe and potentially irreversible. The *get* that Rambam or the Gaonim would *compel* would be an invalid product of coercion according to Rabbeinu Tam, the *Shulchan Aruch*, and virtually every other *halachic* authority for the past 700 years. Any marriage pursuant to such a *get* would be adulterous and the children resulting there from would be tainted with the permanent stigma of *mamzeirut*. In the absence of a centralized rabbinical court that could promulgate uniform directives that would be binding on all rabbinical courts, any court unilaterally ordering a *get* on the basis of Rambam's ruling runs the significant risk that other courts would deny recognition to the divorce. This would introduce an intolerable element of divisiveness in this already highly divisive area and may well preclude segments of even *halachically*-committed Jews from marrying other segments of like-minded Jews. Thus, whatever may have been the state of *halacha* 700 years ago, it may simply be too late to turn back the clock.

Second, it is not entirely true that Rabbeinu Tam's interpretation has shut the door on women's access to the rabbinical courts. Even those authorities who follow Rabbeinu Tam agree that if a woman's claim of *mais alai* is substantiated by objectively verifiable criteria such as nonsupport or physical or verbal abuse, a *get* can be ordered, at least on a *yotzee* level.[155] In most cases where the husband refuses to grant a *get* amicably, one would normally expect that such criteria would not be excessively difficult to meet and indeed in practice they are not though *batei din* have tended to be cautious in this regard.

Third, even a reacceptance of Rambam's viewpoint results only in expanding a wife's right to petition for an order directing her husband to execute a *get*. Outside the State of Israel, the decisions of a rabbinical court, regardless of their "binding" *halachic* nature, are not enforceable either by that court or the secular judiciary. In the absence of some prenuptial agreement submitting the dispute to the tribunal and agreeing to abide by their decision, expanding the *halachic* grounds for ordering the execution of a *get* will have little practical effect.

Finally, even within the State of Israel or even where a prenuptial

---

153. Haut, *supra* note 18, pp. 96-97.

154. For one expression of this idea, see URIM Ve'TUMIM, *Kitzur Takfo Cohen* section 124 (context of monetary litigation).

155. See TESHUVOT ROSH 43:8, cited *supra* note 129.

agreement has been executed giving rise to the possibility of civil enforcement, it must be remembered that not all grounds for divorce give rise to *kofin*; some are only *yotzee*.[156] It would further appear that any "obligatory" *get* for which the *bait din* itself could not impose coercive measures cannot be enforced by a secular court either.[157] Since under no interpretation does the Talmud employ the magic word *kofin* in connection with *mais alay*, adoption of Rambam's view would not necessarily expand the parameters of their *coercive* powers but simply the range of their moral directives.[158] It should also not be forgotten that in any event the court itself does not dissolve the marriage but simply requires the husband to do so and if the husband is stubborn enough, he may be quite willing to languish in prison.

In short, reacceptance of the now-discarded view of Rambam is unwise and impractical. To the degree it would authorize compulsion, it is largely ineffective without secular assistance; to the degree it would merely make divorce mandatory (without compulsion), it is largely superfluous. Either alternative standing alone would not substantially alleviate the *agunah's* plight. While full adoption of Rambam's view *along* with a prenuptial agreement to abide by the *bait din's* decision would in fact effectively respond to *agunah* problems, the present state of *halacha* essentially makes this impossible.[159] The same considerations are largely true for the superseded *Takkanat HaGaonim*, particularly if it is construed in its more radical form of permitting outright annulment.[160]

THE CONDITIONAL MARRIAGE

A second approach to the *agunah* problem would be to structure marriages so that no *get* would be necessary for their dissolution. Scholars looked to the "law of conditions" to achieve this result. Under basic Talmudic

---

156. See discussion *supra* at 110-120.

157. See *supra* text at notes 297-299 where this point is developed at greater length. But *cf. supra* note 116 (view of Rabbi Herzog).

158. I fully recognize the somewhat circular nature of this argument. Rambam himself does not differentiate between *kofin* and *yotzee* and clearly rules that, in cases of *mais alai*, a *get* will be compelled, not merely ordered. Thus, if one *were* to adopt Rambam's view in its entirety, the parameters of the *bait din's* coercive powers would indeed be expanded. (The same is true if one would readopt the *Takkanat HaGaonim.*) The point of the text is that, in order to do so, one must reject the decision of the *Shulchan Aruch* and Rema in two different respects and surmount a double hurdle: first, in construing the law of *mais alai* as a mandatory directive for divorce which the *Shulchan Aruch* and Rema both rule that it is not and second, by classifying this mandatory directive as *kofin* allowing the imposition of coercive sanctions although Rema rules that, even in cases of *gittin* which are clearly mandatory, such coercive measures may not be employed except in fairly-rare circumstances. The understandable, and well-founded, reluctance of rabbinical authorities to depart from the explicit ruling of the codes is magnified greatly when there must be a double or cumulative deviation.

159. See also *infra* text at notes 291-299.

160. See *supra* note 135.

principles derivable from Biblical law, virtually any legal status may be created subject to a condition with the nonoccurrence of the condition effecting a divestment of that status.[161] For example, the Talmud records the case of a man who conveyed his property "on the condition that he move to Palestine." When he was unable to make the move, a necessary condition for the validity of the conveyance had not taken place and so the conveyance was void.[162] According to a number of rulings in the Mishna, marriage and divorce may be subject to a variety of conditions, the nonfulfillment of which will render the marriage or divorce invalid.[163] One may betroth a woman on the condition that she give him a sum of money by a certain day or that her family behave a certain way or possess a certain status. In all of these cases, if the stipulated condition fails to occur, the marriage is simply annulled, *i.e.*, in the eyes of the law, it is deemed to have *never* existed and as a nonexistent marriage void *ab initio*, no *get* is needed for its dissolution. There is literally no relationship to dissolve.[164]

The suggestion has been made that every *halachic* marriage should contain a condition to the effect that if a civil divorce is granted and the husband fails to give a *get* within X number of days, the marriage should be retroactively annulled. Put differently, the validity of *every* marriage could be made subject to the granting of *get* prior or subsequent to the civil dissolution of a marriage. That way, no woman could ever be faced with an inability to remarry for she would either be divorced or technically unmarried.

An early precedent for this interesting innovation may be found as far back as the Second Temple period. According to an early record, the atmosphere of immorality in the Jewish community of Alexandria was such that men would often grab women and rape them in the interim between betrothal and consummation of the marriage. Since in some cases this would mean that the husband would not be permitted to remain married to his wife and any resulting children of the rape would bear the stigma of *mamzeirut*, all betrothals were made conditional on their being consummated by a certain date. In the event of an interim rape, a charge of adultery could be avoided by simply not

---

161. See generally Herzog, II THE MAIN INSTITUTIONS OF JEWISH LAW, pp. 216-227.

162. T.B. KIDDUSHIN 49b.

163. See, for example, T.B. KIDDUSHIN 60a.

164. Note that the typical condition in the Mishna is not a condition precedent, *e.g.*, this marriage shall be effective *when* you give me $100, but rather a condition subsequent, *e.g.*, this marriage is effective from now but in the event the $100 is not paid by the designated time, the marriage shall be null and void. Note, however, that unlike the traditional condition subsequent which terminates the conveyance, transfer, or relation only from the date of the nonfulfillment of the condition, the voidability of the conveyance under Jewish law is in the nature of *nunc pro tunc* (now as of then). Thus, if a spouse in a marriage conditional on payment by Day 30 commits adultery on Day 29, payment of the money by Day 30 effectively validates the marriage retroactively and wife is guilty of a crime. Nonpayment of the sum invalidates the marriage *ab initio* (not only as of Day 30) and effectively exonerates her. It is obvious which way one would want to proceed.

consummating the marriage.[165] This relatively simple procedure was employed throughout Palestine for hundreds of years as a matter of course and became formalized into a prenuptial agreement called a *simphon*[166] ("breaker" of the marriage).

The Alexandrian prenuptial agreement and the Palestinian *simphon* were not designed to protect women from the recalcitrance of an unreasonable spouse though they very well may be adapted to that end. An even more direct precedent may be found in the enactment of Rabbi Israel Bruna (died 1480). The case he was asked to decide involved a man whose brother was an apostate who had converted to Christianity. The man had fears that were he to die without children, his brother would refuse to comply with the necessary religious ceremonies of release, thereby rendering his widow an *agunah*.[167] Nor was he willing to give his wife a *get*. Rabbi Israel ruled that he marry his wife on the condition that if he should die without offspring, the marriage would be retroactively annulled thereby obviating the need for the *chalitza* release.[168]

---

165. See TOSEFTA KETUBOT ch. 4, para. 9; A. H. Freiman, SEDER KIDDUSHIN V'NISUIN ACHAR CHATIMAT HaTALMUD (The Marriage Ceremony in Post-Talmudic Times), p. 11.

166. See JERUSALEM TALMUD, KIDDUSHIN 3:3 and JERUSALEM TALMUD, BABA BATRA 10:1. For a variety of reasons, the *simphon* procedure was not employed in Babylonia, perhaps because there was less of a need. The Babylonian Talmud does make mention of the Palestinian custom in passing. See T.B. KIDDUSHIN 10b and T.B. KETUBOT 57b. Freiman notes that although the Palestinian *simphon* was modelled after the earlier Alexandrian procedure, there were major differences between them. In the Alexandrian stipulation, cohabitation was a condition precedent to the validity of the marriage ceremony; under the Palestinian *simphon*, the failure to cohabit was a condition subsequent albeit one that effected an annulment. See Freiman, *supra* note 165, p. 11.

167. As recorded in DEUTERONOMY 24:7-10, if a man dies without children, it is normally incumbent upon his brother to marry the widow in order to perpetuate the name of the deceased. In the event he refuses to do so, the widow may not marry another unless a specified ceremony of release is performed. The ceremony involves the widow removing the shoe of the brother-in-law, spitting in front of him, and declaring, "So shall be done to the man who refuses to build his brother's house." The *chalitza* ceremony ["removal of shoe"] serves the same function in levirate marriage as a *get* does in ordinary marriage.

168. The ruling of Rabbi Bruna is quoted approvingly by Rema, see DARCHAI MOSHE E.H. 157 para. 3 and in SHULCHAN ARUCH E.H. 157:4; by Rabbi Israel Iserlin, TERUMOT HaDESHEN chapter 223; and by Rabbi Joel Sirkes, BAYIT CHADASH, TUR E.H. ch. 157. The ruling, however, has not been universally accepted. As eminent an authority as Rabbi Yosef Karo ruled that "it is impossible to be lenient in this matter and such an argument should not even be made. We have neither heard nor seen anyone who has ever made such a condition." BAIT YOSEF, TUR E.H. 157.

Generally speaking, the Ashkenazic communities following Rema's lead endorse Rabbi Bruna's permissive ruling and indeed extended this ruling to cover brothers who were deaf or mute, missing, or insane. See, *e.g.*,

A number of proposals were advanced to extend the contours of Rabbi Israel's ruling to cover not only cases of levirate marriage but *agunah* problems as well by having the husband stipulate at the time of the marriage ceremony that the validity of the marriage was subject to a condition that, in the event of a civil dissolution, a *get* would be forthcoming. In the event a *get* was not forthcoming, the marriage would be void *ab initio*.[169] For a variety of

---

TESHUVOT RABBI AKIVA EIGER, no. 93; CHATAM SOFER, E.H. no. 111; NODA B'YEHUDA I, E.H. no. 56; SHVUT YAAKOV I, no. 127; and most recently, ARUCH HaSHULCHAN E.H. 157:15. Indeed, many have allowed such a condition in contexts other than levirate marriage. See comments of Rabbi Chaim Sanzer quoted in IMREI AISH E.H., no. 95.

The Sefardic communities of Spain and North Africa were initially faithful to the ruling of the *Bait Yosef* and refused to allow the leniency of the conditional marriage as a way of avoiding the need for levirate release. See Rabbi Azulai, CHAIM SHE'AL II, ch. 38 para. 68. Later, however, they too eventually accepted the lenient position. See CHIKREI LEV, E.H. ch. 58; CHAIM V'SHALOM II, E.H. no. 103; RAV PO'ALIM II, E.H. no. 6.

Ironically, at the same time the Sefardic communities were moving in the direction of greater acceptance of the *takkana*, the Ashkenazic rabbinate became less enthusiastic about its deployment. See, for example, Rabbi Isaac Meir Alter, SHEEALOT U'TESHUVOT HaRIM E.H., no. 22 and Rabbi A. I. Kook quoted in Rabbi Makovsky, YECHAVE DA'AT, no. 92 ("the use of such condition has been greatly reduced in our day and age and we have practically not heard of any case in which it has been employed.").

169. The history is ably recounted in Freiman, *supra* note 165, pp. 288-294 and Meiselman, JEWISH WOMEN AND JEWISH LAW, pp. 103-115. The bulk of the proposals originated from France, the first European country to recognize civil divorce (which it did on July 29, 1884). Rabbi Michael Weil, an emigre from Algeria whose community had employed the conditional marriage authorized by R. Israel Bruna, sought to institute a procedure whereby all *halachic* marriages were made conditional on a timely *get* following a civil divorce. Rabbi Tzadok HaKohen, the Chief Rabbi of Paris, forwarded the proposal to Rabbi Yitzchok Elchonon Spector of Kovno (Kaunas), Lithuania, the acknowledged leader of the European rabbinate. Rabbi Spector ruled unequivocally against the proposed conditional marriage. After Rabbi Tzadok HaKohen's passing in 1906, the now discredited Weil proposal was revived and once again it was virtually unanimously rejected. For a collection of the newspaper articles, correspondence, and *halachic* responsa detailing these proposals and the arguments against them, see Y. Lubetsky, EIN T'NAI B'NISUIN ("There Are No Conditional Marriages") published in Vilna (Vilnius) in 1930. Without enumerating all of the authorities in opposition, suffice it to say that they constituted the most illustrious, erudite, and respected spiritual and *halachic* leaders of the 19th and early 20th Centuries: Rabbis Chaim Ozer Grodzensky of Vilna, David Friedman of Karlin, David Hoffman of Berlin, Salmon Breuer of Frankfurt, Chaim Soloveitchik of Brest-Litovsk, Meir Cohen of Dvinsk, Yechiel Epstein, and many others.

In 1967 Dr. Eliezer Berkovitz, the dean of the Skokie Rabbinical College, attempted to reopen the issue of conditional marriage but his work elicited virtually no response from the Orthodox rabbinate since in substance it was merely a rehashing of the Paris proposals. See Berkovitz, T'NAI B'NISUIN

technical reasons, primarily the notion that cohabitation subsequent to a conditional marriage constituted a waiver of condition thereby making the marriage absolute (and in need of a *get*),[170] virtually all responsibie members

---

V'GET ("Conditional Marriages and Divorces") and the critical review by Kasher, 11 NOAM 346 (1968). The Conservative movement, however, voted in 1968 to accept Berkovitz's proposal though, to my knowledge, they have not extensively implemented it. See 32 PROCEEDINGS OF THE RABBINICAL ASSEMBLY OF AMERICA (1968), pp. 229-241.

170. The proposition that cohabitation may or does render a conditional marriage absolute is well-accepted in *halacha*, see T. B. KETUBOT 73b; Rambam, MISHNA TORAH, *Hilchot Ishut* 7:23; TUR E.H. ch. 38; SHULCHAN ARUCH E.H. 38:35 but there is considerable disagreement as to the reason why. The Talmud tells us that there is a legal presumption that "no man desires his intercourse to be one of promiscuity." In other words, since in every conditional marriage the nonoccurrence of the condition would render the marriage void *ab initio* and all expressions of marital intimacy would be converted into nonmarital encounters, it is presumed that all conditions are waived so that intercourse is no longer promiscuous or nonmarital. There are two legal theories as to how this is accomplished. Rambam bases this on a theory of implied waiver or excuse of condition: any transaction that was originally made conditional may become absolute by waiver. Indeed, if the parties *expressly* waive their condition, the waiver would be effective even in the absence of cohabitation. The Talmud's mention of cohabitation is to simply highlight the circumstances under which a waiver should be *inferred*. (*Query*: Rambam seems to say that the stipulating party may waive the condition; would this not require mutual consent as does the marriage itself?) Moreover, such a waiver does not require a ceremony or witnesses or the like.

The second theory is that the conditional nature of the initial marriage ceremony cannot in fact be changed but that cohabitation, which in itself may be a method of effecting a valid marriage, see T.B. KIDDUSHIN 2a, creates a *new* marital bond which is unconditional. See discussion in Ran, COMMENTARY TO RIF, KETUBOT 73b. Which theory governs is not merely academic but has significant practical repercussions. Would a waiver be valid in the absence of cohabitation? (Rambam - Yes; second school - No). Would the waiver validate the absolute nature of the marriage as of the date of the ceremony or only as of the date of the consummation -- *e.g.*, what if woman commits adultery between the conditional marriage ceremony and consummation? (According to Rambam, marriage becomes absolute from its inception, see BAIT SHMUEL E.H. 38:35 (57). According to the second theory, the absolute nonconditional nature of the marriage dates only from its consummation.) In order for consummation to effect a waiver, must there be witnesses to their seclusion? (Under Rambam's theory, *no* since it is the prior marriage ceremony that is being validated and that ceremony had the requisite witnesses. Under the second theory, *yes* because to the extent consummation effects a *new* marriage, witnesses must be present (not of course to actually witness the physical consummation but to witness the seclusion for that purpose). But see *infra* text at note 211 where this may not necessarily be the case. As a matter of practice, Rambam's view of waiver has been accepted by all the authoritative codes. See TUR E.H. 38 and SHULCHAN ARUCH E.H. 38:3.

of the world Orthodox rabbinate rejected this approach.

RABBINICAL ANNULMENT

An alternative approach to the *agunah* problem, often advocated concurrently with the conditional marriage, is the invocation of the power of rabbinical annulment. There are a total of five places in the Talmud where a marriage is declared terminated without the need of a *get* based on the concept that "all [Jews] who marry do so with the consent of the rabbis and the rabbis nullified the marriage."[171] An examination of the contexts in which this

---

There are several other points that require clarification. First, while express waiver clearly converts a conditional marriage into an absolute one, it is less clear that this is the case when there is only an implication of waiver arising from cohabitation. Indeed, the *Shulchan Aruch* and Rema both state that if subsequent to cohabitation a woman wrongfully accepts marriage from a third party, she may require two *gittin*. See E.H. 38:35 (Rema) and 39:5 (*Shulchan Aruch*). Thus, the vice of the Weil proposal was only that it would permit a woman who *might* be *halachically* married from remarrying without a *get*. Such a remarriage, however, is only potentially adulterous, not certainly so. Second, to the extent cohabitation constitutes or *may* constitute a waiver of condition, could not the parties override this waiver by simply declaring (preferably in the presence of witnesses) that they intend the conditions to remain? After all, the Talmudic assumption that "no man desires his intercourse to be one of promiscuity" is a *rebuttable* presumption, not a substantive rule of law. As such, could not the Weil-Berkovitz proposal be employed today as a simple solution to the *agunah* crisis? In theory, it could but since the *halachic* presumption of waiver arises anew upon every single instance of cohabitation, it can only be negated by specific reaffirmation of the condition every single time. Suffice it to say, this is essentially an impossible and unverifiable requirement to meet.

A further line of inquiry that might be used to validate the Weil-Berkovitz proposal is the suggestion that in a day and age where premarital relations are commonplace and carry no stigma of immorality and indeed where this very couple may have been together before their marriage, the basis for the Talmudic presumption is no longer present at least in some cases. See, *e.g.*, TESHUVOT RIVASH, no. 6 and *infra* text at note 210. The counterargument is that the presumption rests on considerations of emotional commitment rather than avoidance of sin.

171. See T.B. YEBAMOT 110a, BABA BATRA 48b, GITTIN 33a and 73a, KETUBOT 3a. Interestingly, this concept is nowhere found in the Jerusalem Talmud.

While the Talmud mentions rabbinical annulment in only five contexts, commentators have noted that the principle furnishes the implicit basis for a number of other Talmudic rulings: (1) the eligibility of a single witness to establish husband's death, see TESHUVOT RASHBA I, no. 1162; (2) the rule that a Jewish divorce may be effected by the bill of divorce being placed within the wife's four cubits even without her actually holding the *get*, Ramban, COMMENTARY to T.B. GITTIN 78a; (3) the invalidity of a marriage where the object of value was rabbinically prohibited to use, *e.g.*, leavened bread on the eve of Passover in the hour preceding noon. Rashi, COMMENTARY to

extraordinary power of annulment was invoked is instructive. The earliest instance of its appearance is in the second generation of Babylonian Amoraim. A young woman had been betrothed as a minor and upon attaining adulthood was being led to her marriage ceremony. On the way there, she was kidnapped by someone who then proceeded to marry her himself. (The passage is not entirely clear whether she consented.) As a matter of law, her prior betrothal to the first person was not valid because of her infancy. As such, she would normally be regarded as married to the kidnapper, necessitating a *get* for her release. Nevertheless, "because he acted improperly, we therefore do to him that which is improper and the rabbis annulled his marriage."[172]

The second instance involves marriages under duress. Contrary to common law principles, classical *halacha* occasionally recognized "coerced consent," *e.g.*, "sell me your land or I'll kill you," as effective provided fair consideration was received for the transfer.[173] Put differently, *halacha* did not inquire into the bargaining *process* unless the resulting terms of exchange were substantively unfair. Rabbi Ashi informs us, however, that this is not the case in marriage. Any marriage entered into without the unfettered consent of the woman is a nullity, again due to the rabbinical power of annulment.[174] The first two cases involve elements of fraud, coercion, or duress that were present in the marriage ceremony.

The next three cases involve circumstances pertaining to the granting of a *get*. *Case 1*: Husband designates an agent to deliver a *get* to his wife who is abroad. After the agent leaves, husband rescinds the agency or revokes the *get*. Under *halacha*, which does not recognize agency doctrines such as apparent authority, the agent's status has been terminated and the delivery of the *get* would be invalid. Recognizing the tremendous injustice this would cause to a woman who would remarry in good faith, the rabbis enacted that any revocation of agency not in the presence of the agent is invalid. The

---

T.B. PESACHIM 7a. Nevertheless, the principle has its limits. See discussion *infra* text at notes 180-182.

172. T.B. YEBAMOT 110a (Rav Brona and Rav Chananel annulled; Rav Ashi gave the above-quoted explanation).

173. See T.B. BABA BATRA 47b and comment of RASHBAM *s.v. Zevinai* as codified in SHULCHAN ARUCH H.M. 205:1 (distinction between sales and gifts). Note that the *ex post facto* validity of a nongratuitous transaction entered into under duress did not exonerate the extortionist from *criminal* liability. See T.B. BABA METZIA 5b-6a and Rambam, M.T. *Hilchot Gezeila V'Aveida* 1:9 and comments of MAGID MISHNA.

Mention should also be made of the unusual institution of *moda'ah*, a procedure that allows the seller to avoid the validation of a coerced sale by making a written or oral declaration to witnesses *in advance* of the sale (which will normally be done in secret) that the transaction is under compulsion and that seller has no true intent to part with his ownership. See, generally, SHULCHAN ARUCH H.M. 205:1-12 and Herzog, II MAIN INSTITUTIONS OF JEWISH LAW, pp. 130-132.

174. T.B. BABA BATRA 48b. Note, however, that a coerced marriage on the part of the *man* may in fact be valid under the same principle as a coerced sale. See SHULCHAN ARUCH E.H. 42:1 which cites two views.

mechanism through which this was accomplished was rabbinical annulment.[175]

Case 2: A bill of divorce was delivered on an express condition that it would be effective only if the husband failed to return by a certain date. The husband was willing, able, and ready to return by that date but was prevented from doing so by circumstances beyond his control, *e.g.*, flooding, impassible roads. Under general principles of *halacha*, his readiness to perform was tantamount to his actually arriving. Nevertheless, since a spouse would have no way of knowing the basis for a delay and would normally be entitled to assume that the validating condition ("failure to return") had been met, the rabbis permitted her remarriage on a theory of annulment.[176]

Case 3: A man anticipating imminent death executes and delivers a *get* to his wife to enable her to immediately remarry and escape the confines of levirate marriage. Unbeknownst to his wife, he recovers. Under Biblical law, his recovery would invalidate the *get* since it was understood by both parties that the *get* was delivered on the condition that death would shortly follow. Nevertheless, to protect spouses who in good faith would be unaware of an unforeseeable change in circumstances, the Talmud once again invokes the annulment remedy.[177]

At least insofar as the Talmud is concerned, rabbinical annulment is a fairly-narrow remedy confined to cases where there is either duress or fraud in the marriage process or where women have received *gittin* under circumstances where they formed a good faith belief that the *get* was valid but where in fact it was not because of an unforeseen change of circumstances.[178] The question is whether the annulment remedy could be broadened to encompass areas beyond those specifically enumerated? Could it be used to dissolve marriages where a recalcitrant husband refuses to grant a *get*? In the absence of a centralized Sanhedrin, who in fact are the "rabbis" entitled to grant this annulment?

The exact theory upon which annulment is based is somewhat uncertain. Some suggest it is simply an extension of the law of private conditions. In every *halachic* marriage ceremony, the husband recites the words, "Behold you are betrothed to me with this ring *in accordance with the laws of Moses and Israel.*" These words may in fact be interpreted as tantamount to an express condition that this marriage shall remain intact only as long as rabbinical law deems it proper. Viewed in this light, rabbinical annulment is not a juridical act *per se* but is simply the importation of a condition into what otherwise be an unconditional ceremony. Others view it

---

175. T.B. GITTIN 33a and YEBAMOT 90b. Note the irony: if the agent's status was not revoked, the marriage is terminated because of the *get* and the woman is technically a divorcee and unable to marry a *Cohen*. If on the other hand the agent's authority has been revoked without his knowledge and he proceeds to deliver the *get*, the marriage is technically annulled - the woman was effectively never married at all.

176. T.B. KETUBOT 3a. ("There is no claim of *force majeure* to invalidate a get").

177. T.B. GITTIN 73a.

178. Note, however, that such a good faith belief may justify annulment even in the absence of something like detrimental reliance. For example, even if the wife is notified of her husband's recovery *before* she remarries, she is still permitted to do so.

as an extraordinary vesting of jurisdiction in duly-constituted rabbinical tribunals.[179] In either case, where annulment does apply, it effectively dispenses with the need of a *get* even in cases of cohabitation.

Expanding the annulment power has not been traditionally viewed as a promising approach. The bulk of *halachic* authorities limit the annulment power to either the five specific cases enumerated in the Talmud[180] or to a centralized court whose decisions are universally regarded as binding by all segments of Jewry.[181] In the absence of such an authoritative tribunal, the power to annul marriages has lapsed. Even those few authorities who in theory recognize the right of any communal *bait din* to annul would be reluctant to put their theory into practice. Unless the annulment would be recognized by *all* major rabbinical authorities, it would be irresponsible to allow a remarriage without a *get*. To do so would cast serious, irreparable aspersions on the legitimacy of subsequent children born from such a remarriage and would contribute to a divisive rift among segments of *halachically*-committed Jews. The benefits it produces are simply not worth the costs.[182]

---

179. Freiman, *supra* note 165, pp. 13-14, suggests that the concept actually has two distinct underpinnings. Annulment was originally perceived as a legislative-judicial prerogative and only later was assimilated into the law of private conditions. Thus, the earlier sources simply state, "The rabbis nullified the marriage." The later references add the prefatory phase, "All who marry do so with the consent of the rabbis," a phrase that may mean that the validity of all marriages is conditional on rabbinic assent. Thus, what was originally regarded as a procedure superimposed on the will of the parties was eventually perceived as expressing that will through a shorthand incorporation by reference in the marriage ceremony.

180. As well as those cases where the Talmud implicitly employs the concept. See *supra* note 171. (See, however, *supra* note 135, where some have argued that the post-Talmudic *Takkanat HaGaonim* was predicated on the principles of annulment).

181. See, for example, TESHUVOT RASHBA I, nos. 185, 1163, 1186. A contrary position is espoused by TESHUVOT MAHARAM ALSHAKER no. 48, who writes that if a majority of Jewish communities within a single country (presumably, he means a majority of rabbinical courts in those communities) agree, a marriage may be annulled even for grounds not mentioned in the Talmud. Even his opinion is predicated on majority consent, a situation not presently obtainable in light of the divergent traditions and customs within the *halachic* camp.

182. For a more complete discussion of the scope and limitations of rabbinical annulment, see ENCYCLOPEDIA TALMUDIT, *s.v. Afkinnu*; Ellinson, *Siruv Latet Get*, 69 SINAI 135 (1971); Zaks, *Kiddushin Al T'nai*, 1 NOAM 52 (5718/1958-1959). Freiman, *supra* note 165, in his classic work discusses a number of post-Talmudic communal enactments pertaining to the conduct of the marriage ceremony. Among them are rules prohibiting marriages not conducted in the presence of a quorum of ten or not authorized by the rabbi of the community. These enactments were designed to discourage secretive elopements which might involve elements of fraud, duress, or undue influence. Tracing these enactments to all parts of the Jewish world - France, Germany, Italy, North Africa, Palestine, and Spain - Freiman demonstrates that a surprising number of eminent rabbis were in fact willing to annul marriages

UTILIZATION OF THE *GET* PROCEDURE IN ADVANCE

As previously noted, the execution and delivery of a *get* may be accomplished either by the husband himself or through his duly designated agent. Utilization of the agency concept was yet another means suggested for the protection of women. In 1930, Rabbi Louis Epstein of Boston proposed that subsequent to every marriage (at a time when presumably relations were still amicable), the husband appoint his wife as an agent to execute a divorce on his behalf. Thus, in the event that the husband later disappeared or refused to grant a *get*, the woman would be empowered to write or designate others to write the *get* and would essentially be authorized to divorce herself.[183] Although the Rabbinical Assembly of the Conservative movement voted to implement his proposal in 1935, it was not well received by the majority of accepted *halachic* scholars and even the Conservative movement eventually withdrew its support.[184]

The arguments against the Epstein proposal are fairly simple. First, under Jewish law any agency is revocable until such time as the transaction is consummated.[185] Thus, designating the wife as his agent would ultimately not afford her any substantial protection since, at any point that he desires, he could

---

that were performed in violation of the community rules. Nevertheless, since all of these cases involve irregularities in the marriage ceremony, they furnish no precedent for an annulment due to a husband's failure to give a *get*. Moreover, even in the communal enactment cases, a majority of authorities required a *get* and enforced the rule through the imposition of fines and imprisonment.

183. Epstein's proposal first appeared in a work entitled HATZA'AH L'MAAN TAKKANAT AGUNOT. In response to a number of *halachic* criticisms, he reiterated and amplified his suggestions in a later work L'SHEELAT HaAGUNAH published in 1940. As Epstein himself acknowledges, he was not the first to suggest such an idea. As far back as 1912, R. Ben-Zion Alkali of Algeria proposed that the husband designate a *bait din* as his agents. See L'SHEELAT HaAGUNAH, pp. 205-250. Epstein's particular innovation was in allowing the wife to be the husband's agent, thereby avoiding problems if the designated agents were later unavailable. Although not quoted by Epstein, a similar proposal was advanced by the esteemed R. Yosef E. Henkin in 1928. See PERUSHAI IBRA, pp. 110-117.

184. The contemporaneous literature surrounding the Epstein proposal is fairly voluminous. Besides Epstein's own works, see 4 PROCEEDINGS OF THE RABBINICAL ASSEMBLY OF AMERICA (1932), pp. 83-90; vol. 5 (1938), pp. 227-235; 2 BULLETIN OF THE RABBINICAL ASSEMBLY (1939), No. 3, pp. 7-8. See also the anthology of rabbinic correspondence attacking the Epstein proposal published under the title L'DOR ACHARON (Agudas HaRabbonim 1937). More historical background is provided in Meiselman, *supra* note 169, pp. 103-115 and Freiman, *supra* note 165, pp. 394-395.

185. See T.B. GITTIN 32a.

simply withdraw his authorization and leave her as an *agunah*.[186] Imposing oaths or even financial penalties in the event of a revocation hardly guarantees that he won't go ahead and do it anyway and may even raise questions regarding the validity of the *get*.[187]

A second objection is even more compelling. Rambam rules that any cohabitation subsequent to the designation of an agency for divorce is an *automatic* revocation of that agency.[188] Because marital cohabitation is

---

186. This would be true no matter which scenario was followed. Husband may clearly revoke the agency before the *get* was written and may revoke the agency after it was written before there was formal delivery. Even if the woman were to give herself the *get* in advance and stipulate that the *get* would be effective upon the occurrence of specified conditions, *e.g.*, abandonment or civil dissolution of the marriage, the husband could annul or cancel the *get* at any point before its effective date. Indeed, this would be true even if he had given the *get* to his wife personally. See Rambam, MISHNA TORAH, *Hilchot Gerushin* 8:1. In any event, cohabitation that occurs between the writing of the *get* and its delivery and certainly between the delivery of the *get* and its effective date normally renders the *get* invalid. See *Id.*, 3:5; SHULCHAN ARUCH E.H. 148:1-2. While that case specifically covers cohabitation occurring between the writing of the *get* and its delivery, the same concerns are equally applicable in the period between the delivery of the *get* and its effective date. See *infra* note 188 (problem of *get yashan*) Thus, the Epstein proposal must posit that no *get* will even be written until the triggering conditions of abandonment or civil divorce come into play and in that case, the husband's right of revocation is unquestionable.

187. In response to the original proposal of R. Alkali, it was indeed suggested that the agency be coupled with financial penalties in the event of revocation. See statement of R. Yaakov Meir, Chief Rabbi of Israel (Sefardic) quoted in Epstein, L'SHEELAT HaAGUNAH, pp. 271-272. Besides the fact that the deterrent effect of such penalties on a malicious husband may be minimal, if the husband fails to revoke for fear of incurring such penalties, the *get* could very well be a *meusah*. See *supra* text at notes 63-65.

188. See Rambam, MISHNA TORAH, *Hilchot Gerushin* 9:25. [Query: Rambam's ruling is not quoted in *Shulchan Aruch*. Is it clear that we follow it?] Actually, the logic of Rambam's ruling is highly problematical. We already know from the Talmud that any cohabitation that occurs between the writing of the *get* and its delivery renders the *get* invalid and Rambam so rules in 3:5. (This is called a *get yashan* - an old *get*) He then reasons in 9:25 that if cohabitation can invalidate a *get* already written, *a fortiori* it will preclude the agency from writing the *get*. This argument, however, seems inconsistent with the Talmud itself. Cohabitation between writing and delivery invalidates the *get* to avoid the possible casting of aspersions on a child conceived during that interim time frame. For example, assume the *get* is written and dated the first of the month, cohabitation occurs the tenth of the month, and the *get* is delivered on the twelfth. If exactly nine months from the tenth of the month the wife has a child, people may wrongfully assume that the baby was conceived out of wedlock when in fact it was conceived before the *get* was delivered. Rambam himself gives this explanation in Chapter 3. This consideration has no application at all to cohabitation that preceded the writing and dating of the *get*. See the cogent comments of Ramban (Nachmanides)

presumptively expressive of absolute marital commitment, it is deemed inconsistent with any prior attempts to set into motion the machinery of dissolution and effectively cancels them. For the Epstein proposal to work, the agency would have to be reinstated after each and every cohabitation - a practical impossibility.[189]

REINSTITUTION OF CONCUBINAGE: OUT-OF-WEDLOCK RELATIONSHIPS

Perhaps the most bizarre proposal to alleviate the plight of the *agunah* would be to allow the parties the choice of foregoing *halachic* marriage entirely and to opt instead to structure their relationship along the lines of concubinage. The Bible itself speaks of "wives" [*nashim*] and "concubines" [*pilagshim* - singular: *pilegesh*][190] and there is considerable discussion in the *halachic* literature as to both the meaning of the term "*pilegesh*" and its legal status.[191] Rivash[192] and Abarbanel[193] define "*pilegesh*" as a *halachically*-married woman who has simply waived her statutory alimony rights in advance. The majority of commentaries define "*pilegesh*" as a mistress or concubine who has not been *halachically* married[194] and this will be the sense in which the term will be used here.

With respect to the religious permissibility of an out-of-wedlock relationship, Rambam writes quite explicitly:

> Any person who has intercourse with a woman in a promiscuous manner [*leshem zenut*] without

---

quoted in *Magid Mishna*. While many authorities agree with Rambam's decision, they sharply disagree with his use of the *get yashan* precedent.

189. Epstein attempts to address this concern in L'SHEELAT HaAGUNAH, pp. 151-176, though his arguments are not particularly convincing. Meiselman's statement, *supra* note 169, p. 107, that Epstein ignored the objection raised from this passage of Rambam is incorrect.

190. See, for example, GENESIS 25:6.

191. For an exhaustive, though somewhat dated, collection of the voluminous literature surrounding this subject, see 10 OTZAR HaPOSKIM E.H. 26:1-5.

192. TESHUVOT RIVASH, no. 398.

193. COMMENTARY OF ABARBANEL TO JUDGES, Chapter 20. Isaac Abarbanel (15th Century Spain, Portugal, and Italy) was an eminent Talmudist, Bible commentator, and community leader. He was also for a time the finance minister of Spain until he voluntarily offered to join his fellow Jews in the 1492 expulsion.

194. See the many sources quoted in Ellinson, NISUIN SHELO K'DAT MOSHE V'YISRAEL, pp. 54-55 notes 20-29. Interestingly enough, there is some uncertainty as to Rambam's definition of the term. In *Hilchot Melachim* 4:4, the standard editions of Rambam read that a *pilegesh* has neither marriage nor alimony. The *Magid Mishna*, in his comments to M.T. *Ishut* 1:4, asserts this is a mistake in the text and the true reading should be that the *pilegesh* is married but has no alimony. Ellison, *id.*, p. 55 n. 22, claims that all extant manuscripts of *Mishna Torah* support the text as we have it, thus putting Rambam in the majority camp.

marriage [commits a Biblical transgression].[195]

On its face, this would seem to rule out any *halachic* or rabbinic sanction to out-of-wedlock relationships and yet the Rambam's formulation is not without ambiguity. Some have indeed interpreted the Rambam as ruling that any cohabitation outside of marriage is a violation of Torah law.[196] Others focus on Rambam's use of the term "promiscuous" and posit that a relationship that is stable, committed, and exclusive is not violative of Jewish law although that relationship has not been solemnized through a marriage.[197]

In 1930, Rabbi Yaakov Moshe Toledano, one of the rabbinical leaders of the Moroccan community, proposed that the ancient institution of *pilegesh* be reintroduced and formally legitimized in order to avoid problems that may later arise from a husband's disappearance or refusal to give a *get*.[198] The elements of stability and commitment could be assured by the drafting of prenuptial agreements setting out support obligations, property arrangements and the like. This proposal was strenuously opposed. Whatever *halacha* may or may not permit in individual isolated cases, it would be inconceivable for a religious system to set up the *pilegesh* as a viable and equal or even preferable mode of relationship. Such a proposal, it was said, degrades the sanctity of marriage and family life, promotes promiscuity, denigrates women and would

---

195. MISHNA TORAH, *Hilchot Ishut* 1:4. See also *Hilchot Melachim* 4:4 where the institution of *pilegesh* is permitted for kings as part of their royal prerogatives.

196. This is the reading of TESHUVOT RIVASH, nos. 395, 398; MAGID MISHNA to *Hilchot Ishut* 1:4; gloss of Rema, SHULCHAN ARUCH E.H. 26:1.

197. This surprisingly liberal view may be found in BAIT SHMUEL E.H. 26:1 (2); BIUR HaGRA E.H. 26:1 (8); LECHEM MISHNA, comment to M.T. *Hilchot Melachim* 4:4. This also appears to be the view of Ramban, TESHUVOT MEYUCHOSOT L'RAMBAN, no. 284 (but see Ellinson, *supra* note 194, pp. 72-79) and Rabbi Yaakov Emdin in II SHEEALAT YAAVETZ, no. 15.

198. See 6 OTZAR HaCHAYIM (5690/1930), p. 209. A similar proposal was advanced by Rabbi M. Risikoff in SHAAREI SHAMAYIM E.H., no. 42 as a theoretical possibility to consider though he immediately stated that it was not for practical implementation.

Interestingly, there had been an earlier attempt in Morocco to *halachically* permit a nonmarital relationship but it involved a single individual faced with extenuating circumstances: A man had given his wife a *get* and then converted to Islam. She promptly remarried and was soon divorced again. The man desired to rejoin his faith and remarry his wife. Unfortunately, under Biblical law, one is not allowed to remarry one's divorced spouse if she had remarried someone else and that marriage ended in death or divorce. See *supra* note 21. Under Islamic law, however, the man's reconversion to Judaism was not recognized and it was illegal for him to marry a Jewish woman other than one to whom he had been previously married. Under the circumstances, the authorities ruled he could take his wife as a *pilegesh* and thereby not violate the Biblical directive, which prohibited only remarriage. See SHEEALOT U'TESHUVOT MISHPATIM YESHARIM II, no. 170; NOFET TZUFIM E.H., no. 13 (decision of Rabbis Rafael and Pesachya Birdigo).

be a "cure" considerably worse than the illness it seeks to alleviate.[199] In any case, such a proposal would afford no relief to the women who elected to be *halachically* married (as most would undoubtedly do) and now find themselves in an *agunah* predicament. Rabbi Toledano himself expressed serious reservations about his proposal[200] and it is no longer considered a viable alternative.[201]

ATTACKING THE VALIDITY OF THE MARRIAGE

Since only a *halachically*-valid marriage needs termination through a *get*, occasionally the problems of *agunah* may be solved by finding technical inadequacies in the marriage ceremony. In other words, if the parties were not *halachically* married, they need not be *halachically* divorced. One clear example: marriage between a Jew and a non-Jew who has not undergone a conversion procedure is a religious nullity no matter how statistically-prevalent such intermarriages may be.[202] Even if the non-Jewish partner did undergo some form of conversion ritual, the validity of the conversion may not be recognized by various denominations within Jewry.[203]

---

199. See for the example the comments in 7 OTZAR HaCHAYIM (5691/1930-1931), p. 204 ("It is wrong to even discuss such ideas and certainly wrong to print them") and in Lubetsky (ed.), EIN TENAI B'NISUIN, p. 30 (statement of Rabbi Meir Simcha Cohen).

200. See SHEEALOT U'TESHUVOT YAM HaGADOL, no. 75. For further historical detail, see Ellinson, *supra* note 194, pp. 90-92 and Freiman, *supra* note 165, at p. 396.

201. But see Z. Falk, *Al Nisuin Shel Cohen U'Gerusha*, 27 DAOT 35 (1965), who suggests this idea as a means for permitting a *Cohen* to live with a divorcee. Ellison, *supra* note 194, at p. 89 ably refutes Falk's proposals.

Note that although the resurrection of *pilegesh* as an institution may have been rejected, the underlying concept that, if there is no marriage, there is no need for a *get* is very much alive and has been utilized with great success in cases of civil or *nonhalachic* ceremonies. See *infra* text at notes 202-216.

202. See Rambam, MISHNA TORAH, *Issurai Beeah* 12:1-10 and Bleich, *The Prohibition Against Intermarriage*, 1 JOURNAL OF HALACHA AND CONTEMPORARY SOCIETY 5 (1981).

203. For a discussion of the laws of conversion, see SHULCHAN ARUCH YORE DE'AH 268:1-12. Good treatments in English can be found in Lubling, *Conversion in Jewish Law*, 9 JOURNAL OF HALACHA AND CONTEMPORARY SOCIETY 76 (1985) and Lichtenstein, *On Conversion*, 23 TRADITION 1 (1988). A recent book length treatment is Lamm, BECOMING A JEW (1992). *Halachic* conversion requires: (1) circumcision (for males); (2) ritual immersion; and (3) verbal acceptance of the Torah's laws, all in the presence of a *bait din*. Since the Reform movement has dispensed with the need for immersion and in no event requires full acceptance of the commandments, most Orthodox rabbis will not recognize the validity of a conversion performed under Reform auspices. With respect to Conservative conversions, the matter is less clear since the standards of that movement are less rigidly defined and, in some instances, may be indistinguishable from left-

Two particularly difficult areas have been the *halachic ex post facto* validity of civil marriages, *e.g.*, the obtaining of a marriage license and solemnization in front of a judge, or religious ceremonies which do not fully comport with *halachic* technicalities. According to the Mishna in Kiddushin,[204] a marriage may be legally effected in one of three ways: (1) through the handing over of money, property, or other consideration (services) from the husband to the wife; (2) through the handing over of a written document of betrothal from the husband to the wife; or (3) physical intimacy. In modern times, the latter two methods have fallen into disuse. From a strictly legal standpoint, the "marriage" occurs upon the handing of a ring from husband to wife. Note that although a religious ceremony has many elements - the presence of a member of the clergy, the bridal canopy, a procession, the recitation of special blessings and benedictions over wine, the public reading of the *ketubah* - most of these are not necessary for the validity of the marriage after the fact.[205] What is necessary is: (1) handing over of an object of value (2) from the man to the woman, (3) accompanied with a statement that with this object he intends to betroth the woman, (4) with the woman willingly accepting the object with this understanding (though there is nothing that she must say) (5) in the presence of at least two "kosher" witnesses (neither of whom need be a member of the clergy). In order to be a "kosher" witness, the witness must be a Jewish male who is at least thirteen years old and who is not related

---

wing Orthodoxy. But see Bleich, *The Conversion Crisis: A Halakhic Analysis*, 11 TRADITION 16 (1971) (no distinction between Conservative and Reform). These disagreements came to the forefront in the recent "Who is a Jew?" controversy, concerning the issue of whether *nonhalachic* converts to Judaism should be entitled to Israeli citizenship under the (secular) Law of Return. (It must be noted, however, that, heated rhetoric to the contrary, *halachic* scholars never denied the Judaism of Reform and Conservative *Jews* - they merely denied the validity of their conversions of *non-Jews*).

A related, though not identical, issue pertains to the genealogical definition of a Jew. Classical *halacha* recognizes someone as Jewish only if born from a Jewish mother (including one who converted). The product of a mixed marriage where the mother is non-Jewish is technically a non-Jew until such time as he or she converts, regardless of emotional identification or education. The Reform movement has recently departed from this definition and currently regards a child as Jewish *without the need for conversion* as long as either one of his/her parents is Jewish. See generally Gordis *et al.*, *The Issue of Patrilineal Descent - A Symposium*, 34 JUDAISM (1985). Thus, not only are the conversion procedures of one denomination not acceptable by the other but certain persons are now treated as Jews without the need of conversion who are *halachically* not Jewish.

The silver lining to this otherwise dark cloud of divisiveness and disunity is the fact that marriage between a *halachic* Jew and a *nonhalachic* Jew - either a Reform convert or a product of a mixed marriage where the mother was non-Jewish - is a *halachic* nullity not requiring a *get* and hence posing no possibility of *agunah*.

204. T.B. KIDDUSHIN 2a.

205. For a general overview of the religious requirements of a Jewish marriage ceremony, see Werdyger, EDUT L'YISRAEL; Adler, NISUIN K'HILCHATAM; and Kaplan, MADE IN HEAVEN.

to either the bride or the groom or to his fellow witness. In addition, the witnesses must be generally observant of the law. For example, persons who violate the Sabbath or eat nonkosher food are not competent to serve as *halachic* witnesses to a marriage despite their veracity or truthfulness.[206] There is also a principle in Jewish law that provides that, if any one of the designated witnesses is *halachically*-incompetent, the admissibility of *all* the witnesses in that group is impaired.[207] Thus, if two observant Jews join with a third non-observant witness *all* the witnesses are disqualified and the marriage ceremony is a nullity.

It can be readily seen that a large percentage of marriages in which at least one of the partners is Jewish may be *halachically* invalid for one or more of the following reasons: (1) where one partner is non-Jewish and has not undergone a proper conversion process; (2) where the necessary witnesses or *any one of them* was not Jewish, was not religiously observant (a factor especially prevalent today), was female, or was related to the bride or groom; (3) where the ceremony did not involve the husband handing some consideration over to the wife with the intent of effecting a marriage or, if he did, the transfer was part of a mutual exchange, *i.e.*, a double ring ceremony; (4) where the husband did not make the necessary declaration at all or where the wife did it in lieu of, and possibly even in addition to, the husband. A simple application of these principles would lead to the conclusion that civil ceremonies, ceremonies performed by other faiths, or even ceremonies performed under the auspices of the Conservative and Reform movements would not, in many cases, be recognized by classical *halacha*. While this may be religiously offensive to some, it does have the salutary effect of eliminating the need for a *get* in many cases and in preventing the stigma of *mamzeirut* from attaching to the children of any subsequent remarriage. It has been employed as a positive solution in a great many cases.[208]

Unfortunately, matters are not always that simple. Remember that one of the valid means of creating a marriage may be through physical consummation. Even if the original marriage ceremony was *halachically* invalid due to disqualification of witnesses or noncompliance with other technical requirements, a marriage may nonetheless result from subsequent cohabitation as man and wife. Although consummation effects marriage only when there is mutual intent to do so, the *halachic* presumption that people do

---

206. See Rambam, MISHNA TORAH, *Hilchot Edut* 10:4-5. For further elaboration, see Quint, I A RESTATEMENT OF JEWISH CIVIL LAW (Laws of Evidence). But *cf.* Rambam, *M.T. Hilchot Edut* at 12:1 who rules that witnesses are disqualified only when they violate the law intentionally. Given the widespread ignorance of traditional Jewish law within the modern Jewish community, it is questionable whether many persons fall into the category of the "intentional violator."

207. The rule that disqualification of any one member of the group taints the admissibility of the entire group can be traced to T.B. MAKKOT 5b and is codified by Rambam, MISHNA TORAH, *Hilchot Edut* 5:1.

208. See, generally, Frimer and Frimer, *Reform Marriages in Contemporary Halachic Responsa* 21 TRADITION 7 (1984) and sources cited *infra* at note 212.

not "desire their intercourse to be promiscuous"[209] may furnish such intent.[210] Furthermore, while any marriage ceremony requires the presence of designated witnesses - though in the case of consummation this would only necessitate seclusion witnesses - it may be argued that the common knowledge of members of the community that husband and wife *do cohabit* in the context of a committed marital relationship may in itself meet the requisite evidentiary requirements.[211]

---

209. See T.B. KETUBOT 72b and 74a and T.B. GITTIN 81b and *supra* note 170.

210. The basis that a marriage invalid at its inception may become validated by subsequent cohabitation is borne out by Rambam's ruling that if one betroths a woman with an object worth less than a *perutah* (a small copper coin that represents the minimum level of value acceptable for effecting a marriage) or through the forgiveness of an indebtedness, the marriage is not valid. Nevertheless, if husband and wife subsequently cohabit in the presence of witnesses (*i.e.*, witnesses can testify that H. and W. secluded themselves), the marriage is valid and requires a *get* for its dissolution "for the [parties] relied on this intercourse to create a marriage and did not rely on the prior invalid ceremony. There is a presumption that no upstanding member of Israel would attempt to engage in licentious intercourse where it is within his power to presently make it [marital] intercourse." MISHNA TORAH, *Hilchot Ishut* 7:23.

Note, however, that under Rambam's formulation this presumption does not dispense with the evidentiary requirements of witnesses but merely supplies the requisite element of intent. But *cf.* note 211 (public knowledge may suffice). Rambam also utilizes this presumption as a basis for his earlier ruling that cohabitation effects a waiver of all marital conditions but since waiver has a relation-back effect validating the ceremony as of its inception, there is *no* requirement that such cohabitation occur in the presence of witnesses. See MAGID MISHNA, comments to M.T. *Hilchot Ishut* 7:23.

The key questions that Rambam leaves open are: (1) whether the presumption holds true where the couple do not constitute "upstanding" members of the community of Israel or where the act of intercourse is in violation of the law even if it be deemed marital - for example, wife is experiencing her menstrual flow or the day is Yom Kippur; (2) whether the presumption holds true only when the inadequacy in the first ceremony is patently obvious so that the parties knew that their marriage was invalid. Arguably, only in such cases, do they clearly intend to effect a new marriage via cohabitation. Where, however, the parties believed in good faith that they were *already* married in a civil or *nonhalachic* ceremony, the logic of the presumption that they intend to effect marriage via consummation is simply inapplicable.

211. Whether generalized public knowledge that a couple is living together as husband and wife satisfies the evidentiary requirement of "witnesses" although there is no specific testimony that intercourse occurred at a given time and place is a matter of considerable debate and uncertainty. Compare R. Shimshon Mishantz quoted in TESHUVOT MAIMONIYOT, ISHUT 19; R. Yeshaya the Younger quoted in SHILTAI GIBBORIM, KIDDUSHIN, no. 659; and R. Aaron HaLevi in CHIDUSHAI HaREAH to KETUBOT 73a, all of whom maintain that common knowledge is equivalent to eye-witness

The consensus of most contemporary *halachic* authorities is that persons who did attempt to marry in a ceremonial fashion and believed in good faith that their marriage was valid *do not* intend to *effect* a new marriage by later cohabitation and hence, the "marriage" remains a nullity and needs no *get* for its dissolution.[212] The same is true for those who were married civilly. Conversely, those who simply live together out of wedlock are also not obligated to utilize a *get* but for a totally different reason: the presumption that parties intend their intercourse to be nonlicentious applies only where the parties voiced their intention to be married and not where their clearly stated intention is not to be.[213] Where, however, civil or *nonhalachic* religious

---

testimony with R. Ezekiel Landau, NODA B'YEHUDA II, E.H. no. 52 (eyewitness testimony of at least a particular seclusion is necessary). The consensus of modern-day *halachists* is in accordance with the first view, at least for the limited purpose of requiring a *get* whenever possible. See KNESSET HaGEDOLAH to E.H. 43; MISHKENOT YAAKOV, no. 39; BIUR HaGRA E.H. 26:1 (3); CHELKAT MECHOKEK E.H. 31:9 (20); 33:1 (2) and BAIT SHMUEL E.H. 31:9 (22); 26:1 (1); and 154:17 (32). For extended treatment of this topic, see generally Ellinson, *supra* note 194, especially Chapters 9 and 10.

212. This was view of the leading rabbinical decisor of the post-W.W.II era, Rabbi Moshe Feinstein. See, *e.g.*, IGROT MOSHE E.H. I, nos. 73-76; II, no. 19. See also similar opinions voiced by the former Chief Rabbis of Israel - Rabbi Yitzchok Herzog, HAICHAL YITZCHOK II, no. 31 and Rabbi Meir B.Z. Uziel, MISHPATEI UZIEL II, E.H. no. 54; Rabbi Eliezer Waldenberg, TZITZ ELIEZER II, no. 19; and Rabbi Yaakov Breisch, CHELKAT YAAKOV II, nos. 183, 194. This is also the prevailing practice of the rabbinical courts in Israel. See 7 PISKE DIN RABANIYIM, p. 36. But *cf.* 6 PISKE DIN RABANIYIM, pp. 365, 372.

There are, however, some eminent dissenting opinions. Rabbi Yosef Rosen, TZOFNAT PA'ANEACH nos. 1-4; Rabbi Isser Y. Unterman, SHEVET M'YEHUDA Part IV, no. 13; Rabbi Yosef E. Henkin, PERUSHAI IBRA I, no. 4. (Incidentally, Rabbi Henkin was the father of the distinguished legal scholar, Louis Henkin.)

213. The Talmud mentions this presumption in three areas: (1) the conditional marriage followed by cohabitation, T.B. KETUBOT 72b; (2) one who secludes himself with his former wife following the delivery of her *get*, T.B. GITTIN 81b; (3) one who "married" a minor but cohabited with her subsequent to her reaching the age of majority, T.B. KETUBOT 74a. In the time of the Gaonim, attempts were made to expand this presumption of intent to every instance of intercourse outside of marriage. These attempts were strongly rebuffed by Rambam, who limited the presumption to cases where the parties presently had or once had some type of marital relationship. See MISHNA TORAH, *Hilchot Gerushin* 10:19. Rambam's view was codified in the SHULCHAN ARUCH E.H. 149:5. While Rambam's formulation does not necessarily address the problem of the civil or *nonhalachic* ceremony, it has been regarded as definitive in cases where the parties do not intend to effect a marriage at all. (Note, however, that while Rema does not comment on the *Shulchan Aruch*'s ruling in E.H. 149 which normally indicates acquiescence, he does record the more stringent Gaonic position in E.H. 33:1 as an alternative. See ARUCH HaSHULCHAN E.H. 149:12 and TZITZ ELIEZER

ceremonies were utilized as a result of compulsion or fear of religious persecution and the parties desired a marriage that is valid within the *halachic* system, it has been argued that perhaps the presumption would indeed apply with subsequent cohabitation effecting a valid *halachic* marriage.[214]

A full exploration of the intricacies of the *halachic* validity of civil and *nonhalachic* marriages is beyond the purview of this work.[215] Suffice it to say, however, that at least in some cases the woman's need to receive a *get* may be obviated by finding technical defects in the marriage. If there is no marriage, there is of course nothing that need be dissolved.[216]

II, no. 19.)

214. Thus, a number of authorities have differentiated between couples who were civilly married in free countries where no *get* is required and couples who married in Communist countries where a *get* may be required (but only under circumstances where the couple was conscious and observant of Jewish ritual). See Makovsky, YECHAVE DA'AT, no. 18 and Uziel, MISHPATEI UZIEL II, no. 59. Unfortunately, it was often precisely the situation of the Communist marriage which generated problems of *agunah*. In any case, Rabbi Feinstein failed to make such a distinction though he acknowledged that there was a substantial basis for it. IGROT MOSHE E.H. I, no. 74.

215. For more detailed treatment, see Friedman, *The Status of Non-Halachic Marriages*, 8 JOURNAL OF HALACHA AND CONTEMPORARY SOCIETY 118 (Fall 1984), Ellinson, *supra* note 194, and Freiman, *supra* note 165, especially at pp. 355-384, dealing with the aftermath of European emancipation. To sum up, the basic issues are: (1) The meaning of the presumption that intercourse is undertaken with marital intent: Does it apply when the parties believed they were validly married already? Does it apply at all when parties are unobservant of Jewish law? Does intent to marry mean intent to be "Jewishly" married or just intent to form a permanent bond? Must there be intent to *effect* a marriage via intercourse or is it enough that the intercourse is expressive of marital commitment even if the parties don't view it as the medium of validation? (2) Whether knowledge that the parties do cohabit satisfies the evidentiary need for witnesses?

216. As a point of general information, the various responsa dealing with the *ex post facto* validity of civil and *nonhalachic* ceremonial marriages often attempt to address not the plight of the *agunah* - after all, in many of these cases both husband and wife were totally ignorant of the need for a *get* - but the status of the children from a second marriage who would otherwise bear the stigma of *mamzeirut*. The problems of ignorance are considerably more serious than the relatively few though tragic cases of unreasonable recalcitrance, the former involving thousands of persons annually. As a result, a number of nonsectarian organizations are engaged in a massive educational effort to inform the Jewish public of the need to dissolve marriages via the *get*. See *infra* note 305. Even if the parties are totally indifferent to religion, they are well-advised to execute a *get* in order to preserve their children's marital options. If, however, no *get* is obtained, in many cases the first marriage may simply be declared void.

Chapter Three

The Use of Contract Law (I): Express or Implied Promises to Execute a *Get* or Submit to Rabbinic Jurisdiction

The limited enforcement powers of a *bait din* as well as the inadequacies of the various *halachic* grounds that have been proposed leave enforcement though the secular judiciary as a very attractive alternative. Despite its considerable appeal and notwithstanding the fact that members of the judiciary have been relatively sympathetic to the *agunah's* tragic plight, reliance on the good will of courts is not only legally problematic but, even worse, *halachically* questionable since, in many cases, *gittin* executed pursuant to court orders may be invalid. Often enough, well-meaning courts in their attempts to be solicitous of the needs of women have simply been unaware of the interface of *halacha* and law that needs to be considered. Nevertheless, many of these obstacles are surmountable and it is worthwhile to see exactly what courts have done and how the legal system can be responsive in a manner consistent with both constitutional principle and *halachic* directive.

The obligations imposed by religious law are not directly enforceable in the civil courts of the United States nor could they be under the establishment clause of the First Amendment.[217] Thus, the fact that under Jewish law a marriage may be dissolved only through the execution and delivery of a *get* would not in and of itself furnish any basis for legal action to compel this result. Nevertheless, there are a number of cases where courts were called upon to assist parties in vindicating their rights under Jewish law, usually on some theory of express or implied contract.

This chapter will focus on the two most common forms such a contract may assume: (1) the promise to give or receive a *get*; or (2) the promise to submit all marital disputes to a designated rabbinic tribunal and to abide by that tribunal's decision, and will analyze these alternatives from the perspectives of contract, constitutional law, and *halacha*. Chapter Four will consider

---

217. The First Amendment issues pertaining to the granting of religious divorces are discussed *infra* text at notes 238-262 and at notes 283-285. See also text following note 551 and note 645 dealing with the constitutional problems arising under the New York *get* laws; text at notes 733-738 (constitutional issues arising through use of tort law); and all of Chapter Nine.

additional contractual possibilities, some of which are a bit more exotic but more likely to satisfy the rigorous demands of Jewish law.

EXPRESS OR IMPLIED PROMISES TO GIVE A *GET*

The Case Law

The cases fall into a variety of categories. The simplest group involves express agreements to grant a *get* upon the obtaining of a civil dissolution. Typically, husband fails to comply with his contractual undertaking and wife, alleging the inadequacy of damages, brings an equitable action for specific performance. Courts in Florida, Ohio, and Pennsylvania have refused to enforce such agreements either on the theory that judicially compelling a religious divorce would excessively entangle the state in sectarian matters, thereby offending the establishment clause, or on the narrower ground that such an order was beyond the statutory jurisdiction vested in the court.[218] Some

---

218. See *Turner v. Turner*, 192 So.2d 787 (Fla. App. Ct., Third Dist. 1966) where a divided court held that a provision in a final decree of divorce ordering the husband to cooperate with the wife in obtaining a Jewish divorce was unenforceable. Technically, the court's holding rested on the narrow notion that the chancellor had no statutory authority to impose such a requirement in a divorce decree but arguably, such a requirement could be enforced as a simple contract. Nevertheless, the language of the opinion strongly suggests serious First Amendment concerns.

These concerns formed the explicit basis of the holding in *Steinberg v. Steinberg*, No. 44125 (unreported, decided 6/24/82 by the Ohio Appellate Court for the 8th District). *Steinberg* was somewhat unusual because it involved a recalcitrant wife who refused to *accept* a *get*.

In *Steinberg*, a separation agreement was incorporated into a divorce decree providing for alimony in favor of the wife but conditioning receipt of that benefit on her cooperating in the obtaining of a religious divorce. The wife filed a motion to vacate that part of the order that conditioned her alimony entitlement on compliance with religious law; the trial court granted her motion and ordered the husband to pay alimony arrearages notwithstanding her lack of cooperation; and the court's order was affirmed on appeal. The Appellate Court stated that it was obvious that a court could not enforce through its contempt power any clause *requiring* a party to participate in a religious ceremony and a court may not do indirectly (through the withholding of alimony) what it couldn't accomplish directly. The correctness of that last assertion is open to question, see the *Rubin* case, discussed *infra* note 224, but it is abundantly clear that the Ohio court would not sanction direct enforcement of a promise to give or receive a *get* on the grounds that such an order is violative of the First Amendment.

Finally, a 1931 trial court in Pennsylvania denied, on free exercise grounds, the request of a wife seeking specific performance of a prenuptial agreement to give a *get* in the event of a civil divorce. *Price v. Price*, 16 D. & C. 290 (Court of Common Pleas, Philadelphia 1931). "The civil tribunals are certainly without authority to order one to follow the practices of his faith. This is a matter dependent entirely upon his conscience or upon his religious belief." For other citations, see 29 A.L.R. 4th 736 (1983).

decisions have opined that compelling a religious divorce may be an infringement of the free exercise clause as well.[219]

Cases in other jurisdictions, however, have enforced such provisions.[220] In *Koeppel v. Koeppel*,[221] a wife brought suit to compel her husband to comply with an agreement to execute a *get* upon the grant of a civil divorce. The husband moved for a dismissal on the grounds that enforcement of such a provision contravened his First Amendment freedoms. In denying the motion to dismiss and allowing the case to proceed to a trial on the merits, the court stated:

> Defendant has also contended that a decree of specific performance would interfere with his freedom of religion under the Constitution. Complying with this agreement would not compel the defendant to practice any religion, not even the Jewish faith to which he still admits adherence. His appearance before the Rabbinate...is not a profession of faith. *Specific performance herein would merely require the defendant to do what he voluntarily agreed to do.*[222] (emphasis added).

Thus, the mere fact that a ceremony, procedure, or activity is governed by religious law does not preclude its civil enforceability as a simple contract.[223] Other cases in New York, at least on the trial level, have come to the same result though some of the holdings are wildly inconsistent.[224]

Note should also be taken of a recent Florida case *affirming* an order to grant a *get*, precisely the type of order that *Turner* had earlier set aside. See *Fleischer v. Fleischer*, 586 So. 2d 1253 (Fla. App. Ct., Fourth Dist. 1991). The court rested its holding, however, exclusively on the husband's failure to raise the constitutional issues at the trial level.

219. This was the stated rationale in *Price*, *supra* note 218.

220. Beside the New York cases discussed in the text, see also *Feuerman v. Feuerman*, Civil No. 83-267188 (Mich. 6th Jud. Cir. 8/1/84) where the court ordered specific performance of an agreement to obtain a Jewish divorce, at least where such agreement was embodied in settlement papers. More recently, a Delaware court did the same. *Scholl v. Scholl*, 1992 Del. Chan. LEXIS 171 (Fam. Ct. 1992).

221. 138 N.Y.S. 2d 366 (N.Y. Sup. Ct. 1954).

222. After trial, however, the judge ruled that the agreement was too indefinite and therefore unenforceable. Under the language of the agreement, husband was obligated to grant his wife a religious divorce only if "necessary." Since the wife remarried prior to the obtaining of the *get*, the court found that the requisite showing of "necessity" could not be made.

223. But *cf. Gordon v. Gordon*, 140 N.Y.S. 2d 878 (N.Y. Sup. Ct. 1955) which denied enforcement of a *get* agreement on the non-constitutional ground that such a contract violated a state statute prohibiting private agreements to void marriages.

224. See *Waxstein v. Waxstein*, 395 N.Y.S. 2d 877 (N.Y. Sup. Ct. 1976), *affirmed* 57 A.D. 863, 394 N.Y.S. 2d 253 (N.Y. App. Div. 1977) where court granted specific performance of a promise to give a *get* where such promise was part of an integrated separation agreement calling upon wife to vacate her marital abode and transfer title to the house and some stock to her husband; and wife had complied with her part of the deal. The court noted the

inherent unfairness of the husband's receiving the benefits of the agreement without complying with its relatively-light burdens. While *Waxstein*, unlike *Koeppel*, is an actual decision on the merits and moreover was affirmed on appeal, its holding may be limited to cases where the other side, *i.e.*, the party who desires the *get*, has already completely performed his/her part of the agreement and does not necessarily establish that a *get* agreement is enforceable at a time when it is still totally executory. In other words, what would the court have done if Mrs. Waxstein had not yet vacated and transferred the home? Nevertheless, from the standpoint of constitutional law, this distinction appears to be immaterial.

See also *Rubin v. Rubin*, 348 N.Y.S. 2d 61 (N.Y. Family Court 1973), an opinion authored by a judge who happened to be an ordained rabbi as well. In *Rubin*, the parties had executed a separation agreement which made support and alimony contingent upon the wife's acceptance of a *get*. Refusing to cooperate in the *get* process, the wife nonetheless sued for alimony arrearages. In denying her request, Judge Gartenstein noted that a number of New York cases have enforced a contractual undertaking to give a *get*. However, even under rulings such as the *Margulies* case (discussed below in this note) which denied direct enforcement of a *get* promise, Mrs. Rubin was not entitled to the relief she sought. The court sharply differentiated between a *get* as a *promise* and a *get* as a *condition*: "[T]his Court is not called upon to enforce this religious discipline against a recalcitrant party but rather is being called upon by the defaulting party to enforce other relief in her favor at a time when she refuses to perform a condition precedent thereto, which happens to be an act of religious significance. The condition precedent could well have been anything else made crucial by agreement of the parties. [W]here one party to an agreement calling for a Get declines to perform, the Court will either refuse any relief to the defaulting party or will hold any application for the same in abeyance pending performance of the obligations assumed pertaining to the Get." While the *Rubin* court does not expressly rule on whether promises to execute a *get* are *directly* enforceable, failure to carry out such undertakings may constitute the nonoccurrence of a condition precedent barring the recalcitrant party from asserting benefits under the agreement. Thus, a prenuptial or separation agreement conditioning various benefits on the execution of a *get* may well have the desired effect of indirectly inducing compliance. (Note that the use of the *get* clause as a condition precedent was precisely the form of indirect compulsion that was deemed unconstitutional in the Ohio *Steinberg* case, see *supra* note 218.) *Accord* with *Rubin*: *B. v. B.* (N.Y. Sup. Ct. 1978), reported in New York Law Journal 5/4/78, p. 7, col. 2.

The wild card in the New York series of cases is *Margulies v. Margulies*, 42 A.D. 2d 517, 344 N.Y.S. 2d 482 (N.Y. App. Div. 1973). In *Margulies*, the husband had agreed orally in open court to give a *get* to his wife and the stipulation was entered as a court order. Based on his disregard of the order, the defendant was held in contempt twice and fined subject to the provisions that he could purge himself of the contempt upon payment of the fines and appearance before a rabbinical court to execute a *get*. Upon his continued refusal to comply, defendant was committed to jail for fifteen days. The Appellate Division reversed the imposition of imprisonment but allowed the fines to stand. The case is difficult because on one hand the court agreed with defendant's contention that it was without power under the First Amendment

A second line of cases has gone considerably further. Even in the absence of an express agreement to give or receive a *get*, some courts have been willing to infer such an agreement from the fact that the parties solemnized their marriage in accordance with religious tradition, recited a formula at the ceremony that the marriage was in "accordance with the laws of Moses and Israel," or executed the traditional *ketubah* or marriage contract that provides the same. The first recorded case of a spouse petitioning the court for an order compelling the granting of the *get* on the basis of the *ketubah* alone was the Canadian case of *Morris v. Morris.*[225] The trial court sustained the wife's contention that the *ketubah* constituted a civilly-enforceable contract that, if a marriage is to be terminated, it will be terminated in accordance with Jewish law and entered an order of specific performance. The decision was reversed by the Manitoba Court of Appeals and Mrs. Morris did not pursue further avenues for review. Nevertheless, the argument that the ceremony and/or *ketubah* constitutes an implied contract has been accepted by various trial courts in New York, New Jersey, and Illinois, all of which have entered *get*-orders even in the absence of an express prenuptial agreement to that effect.[226]

---

to order defendant to perform a religious act and yet it allowed the fines to stand. Haut suggests that the sustaining of fines meant that the court was in fact amenable to enforceability through sanctions less drastic than jail time. Haut, *supra* note 18, pp. 73-74. This reading appears to be incorrect. In point of fact, the court would apparently deny any enforceability to contracts to give a *get* and sustained the fines on technical procedural grounds (failure to appeal). It must be said, however, that the reversal of the imprisonment and affirmance of the fines are constitutionally difficult to reconcile. (Indeed, the dissenting opinion of Justice Nunez would reverse all sanctions.) The sorry aftermath of this case may be seen in the fact that, over six years later, Mrs. Margulies' motion for attorney's fees incurred in her still-unsuccessful attempts to obtain a *get* was denied. *Margulies v. Margulies*, 70 A.D. 2d 832, 418 N.Y.S. 2d 550 (N.Y. App. Div. 1979).

225. 36 D.L.R. 3d 447, *reversed* in 42 D.L.R. 3d 550 (Manitoba Court of Appeals 1970).

226. See *Stern v. Stern,* 5 FAMILY LAW REPORTER (BNA) 2810 (N.Y. Sup. Ct. 1979). In that case, the Sterns had been married in a Jewish ceremony during which the groom gave the bride a *ketubah* in which he stated that she was his wife "in accordance with the laws of Moses and Israel." Mrs. Stern later sued her husband for divorce; he countersued alleging adultery. On the basis of expert testimony, the court found that under Jewish law, the husband was obligated to give an adulterous wife a bill of divorce and entered an order to that effect. It found no First Amendment barrier in imposing such an obligation since rules in Jewish law that govern the relationship of human beings to each other are "secular" in nature rather than religious. *Accord: Minkin v. Minkin*, 180 N.J. Super. 260, 434 A.2d 665 (N.J. Super. 1981) (Citing the N.Y. cases of *Koeppel* and *Rubin*, the court held that compelling issuance of a *get* was not a prohibited establishment of religion since such an order has a "clear, secular purpose" of completing the process of dissolution. Moreover, because the *get* does not involve a "profession of faith" and the defendant is simply being required to do what he voluntarily agreed to do, there was no infringement of "free exercise" rights). Note that both *Stern* and *Minkin* may be limited to cases where divorce is *mandatory* under Jewish law,

The most recent case in this area, and especially significant as the first case on the appellate level to construe the *ketubah* as an implied contract to give a *get*, is *In re Goldman*.[227] An examination of the facts reveals some of the problems courts face in this area. Kenneth and Annette Goldman were married in a Reconstructionist Jewish ceremony. During the ceremony, a standard Orthodox *ketubah*, purchased in a Jewish bookstore, was signed. Neither party was an Orthodox Jew at the time of the marriage. (This is an extremely crucial point which the court simply glosses over. The *get* is

---

e.g., allegations of adultery, and most certainly, *do not* stand for the proposition that the terms of the *ketubah* create an implied contractual obligation to grant a *get* whenever there is a civil dissolution. Nevertheless, insofar as the Constitution is concerned, whether a divorce is mandated by Jewish law or not is irrelevant. Thus, the inescapable logic of *Stern* and *Minkin* leads to the conclusion that an *express* agreement to give a *get* would always be enforceable in court whether or not Jewish law made a divorce mandatory.

The *Stern* - *Minkin* decisions were broadened by a later New Jersey case. *Burns v. Burns*, 223 N.J. Super. 219, 538 A.2d 438 (N.J. Super. 1987). After obtaining a judgment for divorce, Michelle Burns filed a postjudgment motion seeking an order compelling her former husband to issue a Jewish bill of divorce. The court, relying on *Minkin v. Minkin*, refused to limit that case to adultery and held that in every case of civil dissolution, the *ketubah* imposes an affirmative obligation on the parties to dissolve the bonds of matrimony in a religiously-appropriate manner. The important points about *Burns*: (1) The court rejected Mr. Burns' free exercise claim in part on the grounds of evidence that Burns was willing to give a *get* in exchange for a $25,000 payment. Noting that a "true religious belief is not compromised as the amount of money demanded is increased" and that such an "offer" is akin to extortion and beyond the pale of the First Amendment, the court concluded that no religious freedoms were infringed. This suggests that recalcitrant parties may be able to invoke the free exercise clause as a basis for refusal notwithstanding the existence of an antecedent express or implied agreement, if, for example, the husband's religious beliefs in fact changed. This is a fundamentally different approach than the court took in *Minkin* when it flatly asserted that the giving of a *get* is not a religious act at all. On the other hand, since *Burns* does cite *Minkin* extensively and approvingly, it may very well be that the *Burns* court would have come out the same way. (2) Unlike *Stern* and *Minkin*, the *Burns* court did not directly order the husband to execute a *get* but ordered him to submit to the jurisdiction of a rabbinical court and initiate the *get* procedure. "The ultimate decision of whether a "get" is to be granted is that of the Beth Din and not of this court." While the *Burns* opinion makes a number of errors concerning Jewish law (*e.g.*, describing a *get* as evidence of a divorce, its interpretation of the *ketubah*), perhaps fortuitously its amended order is much more consistent with the dictates of *halacha* than the *Stern-Minkin* analogue. See discussion *infra* text at notes 267-268.

See also *Roth v. Roth*, Civil No. 79-192709 (Michigan 6th Jud. Cir. 1/23/80) which also compelled the granting of a *get* based on its interpretation of the *ketubah*.

227. 196 Ill. App. 3d 785, 554 N.E. 2d 1016 (Ill. App. Ct. 1990), affirming (2-1) the order of the Circuit Court of Cook County.

required for dissolution only in the Orthodox and Conservative traditions and not in the Reform/Reconstructionist. If the marriage were solemnized pursuant to Reconstructionist rites, how could there be an implied understanding that *halacha* would govern the dissolution?)[228] Annette became Orthodox in the course of her marriage after her father died. In May of 1984, Kenneth petitioned for dissolution of the marriage and custody of their two children. Annette counter-petitioned for divorce, custody, and specific performance of the *ketubah* as a premarital contract stipulating that the existence and dissolution of their marriage would be governed by *Orthodox* Jewish law. Kenneth refused to give her a *get* and some evidence was introduced that he was using the *get* as leverage to obtain joint custody of the children. The circuit court found: (1) that the parties' intention at the time they signed the *ketubah* was to "have the marriage recognized by the Orthodox branch of Judaism"; (2) based on expert testimony, "the *ketubah* clearly and unequivocally obligates the husband to proceed with the *get* procedure"; and (3) Kenneth's extreme dislike for Orthodox Judaism did not rise to the level of a religious belief entitled to free exercise protection. The court ordered that Kenneth comply with his contractual obligation to give Annette an Orthodox *get*.

On appeal, Kenneth raised three arguments: (1) the *ketubah* is not a legally-enforceable contract; (2) its terms were too vague to support a decree of specific performance; (3) the order violates the establishment and free exercise clauses. The Illinois Appellate Court in a 2-1 decision rejected all of these contentions and allowed the ruling of the circuit court to stand.

Cases like *Stern*, *Minkin*, *Burns*, and *Goldman* are highly problematical from a number of perspectives: as a matter of contract, constitutional law, and *halacha*, their reasoning is somewhat deficient. Let us analyze these points separately.

Contract Law Issues

Halacha requires that a *ketubah* be executed at or before a marriage ceremony.[229] To this very day, all Orthodox and Conservative weddings utilize a *ketubah* in substantially the same form while in Reform and Reconstructionist ceremonies it is regarded as optional. (Note that the Goldmans did employ an Orthodox *ketubah* although their ceremony followed the Reconstructionist rite.) The *ketubah* is a document written in the form of a series of promises or commitments that do indeed resemble what would be termed "contracts." These promises, all of which are made by the husband to the wife,[230] include:

(1) a declaration that he has betrothed his wife in accordance with the laws of Moses and Israel;

(2) a promise that he will honor, support, and work for his spouse in accordance with the custom of Jewish husbands;

---

228. The court did note, however, that Kenneth had given his prior wife a *get* and told Annette that Jewish marriage requires Jewish divorce. He had never specifically told his wife that he would give her a *get* in the event of civil dissolution.

229. A translation of the *ketubah* and an explanation of its evolution appears *infra* Appendix A.

230. The *ketubah* does state, however, that the bride has agreed to become the groom's spouse and this may suffice as a recital of consideration.

(3) an obligation to provide food, clothing, and intimacy in accordance "with universal custom";

(4) an agreement to pay an alimony lump sum of 200 silver *zuz* in the event of divorce or death;

(5) an agreement to pay a stipulated monetary value for property that the wife brings into the marriage;

(6) a promise to pay an additional alimony sum in excess of the statutory minimum; and

(7) the creation of a lien on all real or personal property whether presently-owned or after-acquired, to secure payment of all obligations under the *ketubah*.

The *ketubah* is then signed by two witnesses who affirm that the groom agrees to be bound. (There is no requirement that the bride or groom sign although it has become customary in many circles for them to do so.)

Significantly, the *ketubah* is written in a difficult Aramaic, frequently without a translation. Even where some English words do appear, the legal portions of the *ketubah* are rarely reproduced. The "translation" may say, for example, that the parties pledge mutual affection and love or other generalized sentiments (which indeed do not even appear in the text). Among many, if not most couples, there is substantial ignorance as to what the *ketubah* says and even officiating rabbis, particularly if they are of the non-Orthodox persuasion, regard the *ketubah* as part of a religious ceremony but not as something generating legally-enforceable relationships.[231] Thus, although the *ketubah* is in the legal form of a contract (at least a unilateral one), in many cases it could give rise to no civilly-enforceable rights because of a clear absence of contractual intent.[232] While this factor alone would not necessarily preclude the

---

231. In the *Goldman* case, their own officiating rabbi stated that "as a liberal Jew, he viewed the *ketubah* in a symbolic rather than literal sense." Kenneth himself testified that he regarded the *ketubah* as art or poetry. While this may have been a self-serving statement, I believe it accurately reflects the widespread ignorance of the American Jewish community about its religious traditions.

232. Although actual subjective intent to be bound is not an essential element for the enforceability of an otherwise-valid contract if the other party reasonably believed there was contractual intent, where neither party intended to be bound *or* each party was aware that the other party lacked such intent, no contract comes into existence. See RESTATEMENT OF CONTRACTS (Second) §201 and general discussion in Farnsworth, *Meaning in the Law of Contracts*, 76 YALE L.J. 939 (1967) and in §§7.7-7.13 of his treatise.

Note that although the absence of intent to be bound would preclude civil enforcement, it has no bearing on the obligatory nature of the *ketubah* under *halacha*. This is so because although the *ketubah* is phrased in the form of a consensual undertaking, in reality its obligations are largely statutory. Even in the absence of a written *ketubah*, a husband is still obligated to provide spousal support and the designated alimony and property settlements. Thus, for the most part, the *ketubah* as a document is a confirmation or memorial of religious law, rather than a source of consensual obligation. See SHULCHAN ARUCH E.H. 66:9 and Rambam, MISHNA TORAH, *Hilchot Ishut* 12:9 (nonwaivable nature of *ketubah* obligations). Moreover, under Jewish law mental reservations or lack of intent normally can not avoid external expressions of

possibility of enforcement, at the very least it could and should impose a heavy burden of proof on the party seeking such enforcement.[233]

Second, even assuming that in a given case the terms of the *ketubah* can be regarded as giving rise to an enforceable contract, the question becomes: contract for what? Certainly, the *ketubah* contains legally-ascertainable commitments with respect to alimony and property settlements[234] but it mentions nothing with respect to the granting of a divorce. Language to the effect that the husband betroths his wife "in accordance with the laws of Moses and Israel" can hardly mean a blanket agreement that all aspects of their family life shall be conducted in accordance with the dictates of Jewish law. No one would suggest, for example, that if one party failed to observe the Sabbath or ate non-kosher food, the other party could bring an action for damages or even worse, a suit for specific performance.[235] Apparently, cases like *Minkin*, *Burns*, and *Goldman* employ the following syllogism:

---

commitment. See generally T.B. KIDDUSHIN 49b and Rambam, MISHNA TORAH, *Hilchot Ishut* 8:6 (irrelevance of mental reservations in context of marriage) and *Hilchot Mechira* 11:9 (same in context of commercial transactions).

233. In the *Goldman* case, the trial court placed heavy reliance on Annette's recollection of conversations with Kenneth in which the *ketubah* was described as a contract. Kenneth denied these conversations. In affirming the trial court's decision, the Appellate Court simply noted that it was well within the trial court's discretion to determine the credibility and weight of opposing testimony. In most cases, there will be virtually no evidence to support a finding of contractual intent.

234. As early as 1917, the Supreme Court of New Jersey ruled that the property settlement provisions of the *ketubah* were enforceable as separation agreements despite their "unusual terminology." *Goldstein v. Goldstein*, 101 A.249 (N.J. 1917). A more questionable use of the *ketubah* appears in *Wener v. Wener*, 301 N.Y.S. 2d 237 (N.Y. Sup. Ct. 1969). In that case, a wife who had filed for divorce also sought support for a child that had been taken into the home of the parties during marriage but had never been formally adopted. In holding that the husband is liable for the child's support, the court relied in part on the agreement in the *ketubah* to "perform all obligations as are prescribed by [Jewish] religious statutes" and under Jewish law the head of a household who takes a child into his home is liable for his/her support. The *Wener* decision is problematical on two grounds. First, it is not at all clear that Jewish law compels this result in the absence of express contract. See SHULCHAN ARUCH E.H. 114:1. Second, even if Jewish law did impose a religious duty to support stepchildren, it is not predicated on any language contained in the *ketubah*. Indeed, the *ketubah* makes no mention of any child-support obligation. Thus, civil recognition of a *halachic* imperative cannot be based on a "*ketubah*-as-contract" theory. In any event, the *Wener* holding was affirmed in 35 A.D. 2d 50, 312 N.Y.S. 2d 815 (N.Y. App. Div. 1970) but the Appellate Division specifically disapproved of the court's reliance on the *ketubah*. See also *Hurwitz v. Hurwitz*, 216 A.D. 362, 215 N.Y.S. 2d 184 (N.Y. App. Div. 1926) (property settlement enforced based on *ketubah*).

235. Indeed, even an express agreement to this effect could probably not be enforced because of the First Amendment. See *infra* text at notes 249-250 and note 257.

> *Major Premise*: An agreement to marry in accordance with the laws of Moses and Israel, while imposing no obligation on how the parties will live, does mean that the parties will comply with all *halachic* obligations pertaining to the creation and dissolution of their marriage.
>
> *Minor Premise*: In order to dissolve a marriage according to *halacha*, a *get* must be executed and delivered.
>
> *Conclusion*: Therefore, the husband must execute a *get* whenever the marriage is civilly dissolved because that is what he agreed to do.

This syllogism is seriously flawed. First, the basis for the major premise appears incorrect. A "marriage in accordance with the laws of Moses and Israel" is not understood by Jewish law as connoting any type of advance commitment to comply with Jewish divorce procedures. While the requirement of a *get* does indeed apply, it is not because of any agreement to that effect but is simply self-executing. It is difficult to see how a court can construe a clause as requiring compliance with Jewish law if Jewish law itself does not so interpret it.

Second, the minor premise is flawed because of a confusion in the term "obligation." Even if the *ketubah* constitutes an agreement to comply with all *halachic* obligations pertaining to the creation and *dissolution* of the marriage, strictly speaking the execution of a *get* is normally not an obligation. While it is true that no marriage may be *halachically* dissolved unless a *get* is granted and in that particular sense a *get* is an "obligatory" step in the process of dissolution, the *get* itself is not "obligatory" because the husband in many cases is under no obligation to dissolve the marriage.[236] While such obligation does indeed exist in cases where the wife is suspected of adultery as in *Minkin*, in many other cases it may not. Whether it does or not poses extraordinarily difficult issues of Jewish law which would invariably entangle the court in complex religious issues beyond its competence and indeed, its constitutional authority.[237]

In short, the *ketubah* as contract theory appears insufficient because of: (1) lack of contractual intent; (2) failure of the *ketubah* to explicitly incorporate a *get* obligation; and (3) the fact that no such obligation could or should be inferred from general statements regarding the "laws of Moses and Israel" since these statements are not understood by classical Jewish law to refer to the divorce process and, at least in cases like *Burns* and *Goldman*, the granting of a *get* is not an obligatory act.

---

236. See generally *supra* text at notes 108-120.

237. This is particularly so under the prong of *Lemon* v. *Kurtzman*, 403 U.S. 602 (1971) that proscribes "excessive entanglement" with religious doctrines and institutions. See *infra* text at note 239. Although express *get* covenants raise no establishment clause problems, the same cannot be said for the construction of implied agreements to "comply with Jewish law." Judicial construction of such agreements would invariably lead to entanglement. *Infra* text at notes 251-255.

First Amendment Concerns*

The First Amendment provides that "Congress shall make no law respecting an establishment of religion, or prohibiting the free exercise thereof."[238] Since the granting of a *get* is a ceremony whose validity derives from the strictures of Jewish law, recalcitrant parties have argued that judicial intervention in the securing of a *get* is violative of their "free exercise" rights which, above all, require that religion be a private matter or alternatively, constitutes an impermissible establishment of religion.

The Establishment Clause

Under the still-definitive test of *Lemon v. Kurtzman*,[239] the Supreme Court construed the establishment clause to require that any law or judicial order: (1) have a secular purpose; (2) have a primary effect that neither advances nor inhibits religion; and (3) not lead to excessive governmental entanglement with religion. While the application of these standards is at best uncertain and wavering,[240] they do appear to support the enforceability of express agreements to give a *get*. Whether they would similarly permit implication of such an obligation from the terms of the *ketubah* may be another matter.

Courts have already noted that Jewish law is in essence a total legal system rather than a collection of religious dogma.[241] Thus, *halacha* is classically divided into commandments "between man and God" and commandments "between man and man" (not stealing, *etc.*).[242] Some courts have enforced *get* agreements on the somewhat tenuous ground that since the *get* affects the relationship between husband and wife, the rule requiring a *get*

---

*The text in this section applies the traditional constitutional standards that have been employed by the Supreme Court in analyzing establishment and free exercise claims. These standards are in the process of undergoing reexamination. Current developments and speculations as to the future are discussed in Chapter Nine. It is the view of this author that these developments will not affect the conclusions stated herein. *Infra* text at notes 860-863.

238. U.S. CONSTITUTION, Amendment One.

239. *Lemon v. Kurtzman*, 403 U.S. 602, 625 (1971), See also Tribe, AMERICAN CONSTITUTIONAL LAW (2nd ed.) §14-3 (voluntarism and separatism as primary values). But see *infra* text at notes 825-859 whether the *Lemon* test is likely to survive.

240. See, especially, Rehnquist's sharp criticism in *Wallace v. Jaffree*, 472 U.S. 38, 108-112 (1985); Johnson, *Concepts and Compromise in First Amendment Religious Doctrine*, 72 CAL.L.REV. 817 (1984); and Schwartz, *Larkin v. Grendel's Den*: *The Burger Court and the Establishment Problem*, 21 HOUSTON L.REV. 179 (1984).

241. See, *e.g.*, *Minkin v. Minkin*, 434 A.2d 665, 668 (N.J. Super. 1981), discussed *supra* at note 226.

242. See T.B. YOMA 85b.

is in itself nothing more than secular law.[243] Characterizing as secular the presence of impediments on remarriage that arise solely because a spouse subscribes to a certain set of religious beliefs seems forced.[244] In point of fact, from the standpoint of Judaism itself, there is no such distinction between "secular" and "religious" components of the law since the obligatory nature of both ultimately derives from Divine revelation and belief in the authenticity of Mosaic law and rabbinical interpretation. Judaic law is "secular" only in the very limited sense that it deals with many of the subjects that are commonly dealt with under non-religious systems, *e.g.*, contracts, torts, agency, and thus bears aspects of similarity that could facilitate comparative analysis. The real question here is not how Judaism within its own internal value system characterizes a given law or proceeding but whether enforcement of that law serves a legitimate secular purpose *as defined by the secular institutions whose assistance is being enlisted*. In short, whether a law serves a "religious" or "secular" purpose must be answered exclusively by *secular law* standards and definitions.

Based on the above, it would appear that agreements to execute a *get* may indeed be enforceable. The purpose of such enforcement from the perspective of the judicial system is *secular*. Indeed, one may identify three distinct secular purposes. First, the state has a legitimate interest in assuring that persons keep their contracts and in affording remedies to persons who are aggrieved by breach. The fact that the contract itself is concerned with a ceremony that coincidentally has religious significance to one or both of the parties is immaterial. In the absence of unconscionability or other constraints of public policy,[245] the parties may agree to do whatever they want and the state has a legitimate interest in encouraging freedom of contract and providing appropriate mechanisms of enforcement. Indeed, it could be argued that a refusal to enforce such contract on the grounds that its content is "religious" constitutes both a denial of "free exercise" and of "equal protection."

Second, the state has a legitimate *secular* interest in enabling its citizens to remarry following a decree of dissolution and in facilitating the removal of impediments or barriers that prevent the exercise of this fundamental right. Indeed, as will be discussed,[246] this interest has furnished the basis for various legislative attempts to ameliorate the plight of the *agunah*

---

243. This was the stated rationale in *Stern v. Stern*, *supra* note 223. In *Goldman*, the Appellate Court also quoted Rabbis Schwartz and Rackman that "marriage and divorce are secular, contractual undertakings."

244. Another problem is that if the Jewish laws governing marriage and divorce are nothing more than secular laws, they should be totally preempted by the forum state's own laws governing marital dissolution. After all, if parties in Maryland were to contract that the dissolution of their marriage was to governed by the laws of Missouri, it is clear that their agreement would have no legal effect. See Scoles and Hay, CONFLICT OF LAWS §15.4, p. 475. There is no particular reason why the "secular" law of a religious denomination should be accorded any greater deference. If anything, the establishment clause cuts the other way.

245. For a discussion of these constraints on freedom of contract, see Farnsworth, CONTRACTS (2nd ed.) §4.28, pp. 323-339 (unconscionability) and §§5.1-5.6, pp. 345-380 (unenforceability on grounds of public policy).

246. See discussion of the New York *get* law *infra* text at notes 531-550.

even in the absence of a prenuptial agreement. At the very least, this interest should enable such agreements to be enforced. Enforcing such agreements encourages marriage, stabilizes family life, and protects fundamental rights of privacy and association.

Third, a deliberate refusal to deliver a *get* knowing that the other will be unable to marry may often constitute intentional infliction of emotional distress. Whether that factor alone would justify state intervention in the form of a tort remedy will be discussed later.[247] Suffice it to say, however, that the fact that religion happens to be the source of the divorcee's belief that she needs a *get* is irrelevant. It is well established that taking knowing advantage of even the irrational or delusional fears of another may be actionable in tort[248] and religious beliefs should certainly not be on an inferior footing. By the same token, where one party in the context of an intimate, confidential relationship has created legitimate expectations that he will not behave in a manner calculated to cause pain or distress to the other, the state has a legitimate interest in compelling him to keep his promise, essentially the same interest it has in protecting any of its citizens from emotional or dignitary harms.

Coming to the second prong of *Lemon*: Does enforcement of such agreements have the primary effect of advancing or inhibiting religion? Consider the following example[249]: A and B enter into an agreement whereby A agrees to observe the Sabbath in exchange for a payment of $100 by B. A reneges on his deal. Can B bring an action for damages or specific performance? Although the ostensible purpose of state enforcement is secular, *i.e.*, promotion of freedom of contract as a facilitator of social exchange, protection of reasonable expectations, it is fairly certain that awarding damages or specific performance would indeed constitute an impermissible establishment because the invariable *effect* of enforceability (even if not the state's purpose) would be the promotion of a religious ritual or observance, matters which constitutionally must be left to conscience alone.

An agreement to give a *get* stands on a different footing. While it would be untrue to characterize a *get* as "secular" in the same way as a divorce decree from Missouri, it does not require a profession of faith or any act of homage to a Deity nor does it even necessitate the personal participation of the spouses, each of whom may designate an agent. The only "effect" of a *get* is that recipients who were formerly prohibited from marrying within their faiths are now permitted to do so. As such, the effect of enforcing *get* agreements is not a promotion or endorsement[250] of a particular set of beliefs or practices but a removal of the societal disabilities and impediments to remarriage that women who subscribe to such beliefs would otherwise suffer. Equalizing the

---

247. See discussion *infra* text at notes 703-739 and Redman, *Jewish Divorce: What Can Be Done In Secular Courts to Aid the Jewish Woman*, 19 GA. L. REV. 389 (1985).

248. See, *e.g.*, RESTATEMENT OF TORTS (Second) §46, Comment *f*, illust. 9-10 and *Alcorn v. Anbro Engineering, Inc.*, 468 P.2d 216 (Cal. 1970).

249. The example, with some modifications, is borrowed from Friedell, *The First Amendment and Jewish Divorce: A Comment on Stern v. Stern*, 18 JOURNAL OF FAMILY LAW 525, 530 (1980).

250. The term is taken from Justice O'Connor's concurrence in *Lynch v. Donnelly*, 465 U.S. 668, 690 (1984), one of the Christmas crèche cases.

post-dissolution status of women who ascribe to Orthodox Jewish beliefs with the status of women who don't puts all persons on an equal footing and does not appear to have the impermissible effect of favoring, advancing, or endorsing religion.

The third factor, excessive entanglement regardless of purpose or primary effect, poses a bit more difficulty. Often described as the most basic and fundamental element in *Lemon*'s tripartite test,[251] it has been sharply criticized by others including members of the Supreme Court as "superfluous" and its continued validity as an independent criterion is somewhat in doubt.[252] To date, however, the "entanglement" prong has not been formally overruled. The "excessive entanglement" criterion has been used in two types of cases. The first involves legislative or administrative programs that would necessitate continual monitoring and interchange between governmental authorities and religious institutions,[253] the two-fold dangers being governmental meddling with the internal operations of religious institutions and the inadvertent imprimatur of approval that such involvement may suggest to the outsider. The second category involves cases where courts are called upon to decide questions of religious practice or doctrine that are beyond their institutional competence.[254]

Even assuming the continued survival of the entanglement test, a court order directing specific performance of a single act that typically takes less than an hour certainly does not constitute the type of "excessive entanglement" that the Supreme Court has condemned nor, in the abstract, does it require any court to consider complex areas of Jewish law. Here, however, I believe that the second prong of entanglement may lead to a distinction between express agreements and agreements implied from documents such as the *ketubah*. To predicate an obligation to give a *get* as a generalized commitment to effect a marriage in "accordance with the laws of Moses and Israel" would in theory require the court to engage in sustained investigation as to what the "laws of Moses and Israel" are and what they require. Among the questions to be considered would be: what is the *halachic* meaning of the vague incantation, "in accordance with the laws of Moses and Israel?" Is it intended to have any legally-binding significance? What are the grounds under which a husband is *obligated* to divorce his wife? What methods of compulsion are authorized? From the standpoint of Jewish law, what actions may a court taken in inducing a recalcitrant spouse to act in accordance with his/her obligation without producing a *get meusah*? (It would make no sense to order a *get* if a *get* executed pursuant to court order is invalid.[255]) Each of these issues is a subject of controversy within the Orthodox camp and is addressed in a voluminous

---

251. See Tribe, *supra* note 239, p. 65.

252. See *Roemer v. Maryland Public Works Board*, 426 U.S. 736 (1976), concurring opinion of Justice White joined by Justice Rehnquist: "As long as there is a secular legislative purpose, and as long as the primary effect of the legislation is neither to advance nor inhibit religion, I see no reason [to] take the constitutional inquiry further." See also *infra* notes 828 and 835.

253. See, for example, *Lemon v. Kurtzman*, 403 U.S. 602, 620 (1971).

254. See *Jones v. Wolf*, 443 U.S. 595 (1979).

255. For an interesting example of a court painting itself into a corner because of its failure to consider this fact, see *infra* note 607 (discussion of *Weiss v. Weiss*).

halachic literature of hundreds of volumes and thousands of years. When one adds in the input of other denominations, it is apparent that a true resolution of the scope of the obligation of the *ketubah* should be precisely the type of issue that civil courts should not be called upon to resolve. The complexity of this type of determination does not seem to have been appreciated by the courts that summarily decided these matters. While enforcement of a specific nonliturgical undertaking should be allowed even where it is an act of religious significance, courts should avoid inferring and enforcing agreements based on nothing more than generalized commitments to obey Jewish law.

The Free Exercise Clause

Unwilling spouses have also argued that any judgment ordering them to give or receive a *get*, insofar as the ceremony is religious, conflicts with their free exercise rights. While this argument is occasionally accepted,[256] for the most part free exercise guarantees should not preclude enforcement. One can suggest four possible reasons of greater or lesser cogency that support this conclusion:

1. *Consent*: Civil enforcement is predicated on express or implied contract which, by hypothesis, presupposes freely-given consent. Compelling a party to do nothing more than what that party has already promised hardly offends the spirit of voluntarism and individual autonomy which lies at the root of the First Amendment.[257]

2. *Motivation*: In many cases a refusal to participate in the *get* ceremony has nothing to do with either religious belief or moral principle but is motivated by either malice or attempted blackmail (for money, custody, or the like). Thus, the court in *Burns* refused to recognize a "free exercise" claim where the evidence showed that the husband was willing to give a *get* if the price was right.[258] Admittedly, establishing this contention may on occasion necessitate a judicial inquiry into the sincerity of a stated belief and may suck the court into the morass of defining "religion" for purposes of the First Amendment.[259] It cannot be denied, however, that at least in some cases, indeed perhaps most, discerning lack of religious motivation will not pose any great difficulty.[260] Lack of such motivation is

256. See, for example, the cases discussed *supra* note 218.

257. In theory, this might mean that the free exercise clause never bars enforcement of a contract against a consenting party regardless of the religious nature of the undertaking. Insofar as the free exercise clause is concerned, even a contract to pray or to eat kosher food might be enforceable. To the extent, however, that the promised activity is overtly religious, the agreement could not be enforced because of establishment concerns, particularly under the "primary effect" test. As noted earlier, *get*-agreements do not implicate the establishment clause. See *supra* text at notes 249-255.

258. See *supra* note 226.

259. This point is addressed in greater detail *infra* note 593.

260. In *Goldman*, the circuit judge dealt with Kenneth's "free exercise" claim by finding that "his intense dislike for Orthodox Judaism ... did not rise to the level of a religious belief." To the extent the court held that the

transparently obvious where the recalcitrant husband is himself committed to Orthodox Judaism.

3. *Nature of Act That Is Being Compelled*: Because the *get* is not a liturgical activity that involves worship, a profession of faith, or acknowledgement of a Deity, it is secular rather than religious in character and should not by definition constitute an infringement on religion even for those persons who reject the tenets of Orthodox Judaism.[261] It is at least arguable that the free exercise clause is violated only when a person is compelled to do an act that is repugnant to his religious convictions or that is prohibited by his religious law.

---

individual's belief system must somehow constitute a "formal religion" to be protected, the holding appears incorrect. It is well established that honestly-held religious beliefs are entitled to free exercise protections even if the claimant is not a member of an established religion or has views that are at variance with his own church. See, for example, *Thomas v. Review Board*, 450 U.S. 707 (1981) and *Frazee v. Illinois Department of Employment Security*, 489 U.S. 829 (1989). Indeed, it is possible that even an atheist may be able to invoke the free exercise clause though the Supreme Court has never squarely addressed the issue. See the *dicta* in *Wallace v. Jaffree*, 472 U.S. 38 (1985) at 52-54 ("The individual freedom of conscience protected by the First Amendment embraces the right to select any religious faith or none at all"). *Cf. United States v. Seeger*, 380 U.S. 163 (1965) (selective service exemption interpreted to cover nontheistic conscientious objectors as a matter of statutory construction). Indeed, simple logic should dictate that just as a Jew could not be compelled to participate in a Christian ceremony neither should an atheist be compelled to participate in a Jewish one. See also *infra* note 593 (atheists may certainly invoke the establishment clause).

Because of these considerations, I find *Goldman* a much more difficult case than *Burns*, *supra* note 226. In *Burns*, the husband was clearly playing the extortionist while in *Goldman*, there was at least some evidence of ideological opposition to the institution of *get*. While the trial court was free to disbelieve Kenneth's contentions - after all, he had given a *get* to his first wife - it seems problematical that the judge can believe him but nonetheless rule that such ideas do not rise to the level of constitutional protection.

261. A number of courts have in fact characterized the *get* as a secular, rather than religious, document. See, for example, *Stern v. Stern*, *supra* note 226. Admittedly, however, this line of argument standing alone is hardly compelling. I have previously argued that because both the need for, and effectiveness of, a *get* stem from the same unitary *halachic*-religious system that is the source of all religious beliefs of Judaism (*i.e.*, Divine revelation), the execution of a *get* should not be regarded as "secular" for purposes of the establishment clause. The mere fact that the *get* is nondevotional in nature would not in itself be sufficient to sustain *get* agreements from attacks based on establishment unless it could be determined that enforcement of such covenants serves distinct secular purposes (which indeed it does). See *supra* text at notes 242-244. Nevertheless, although the nontheistic nature of the ceremony may be immaterial with respect to establishment clause concerns which focus on state endorsement and entanglement, this factor should be highly relevant on the issue of free exercise which above all is designed to protect infringements on religious conscience.

Yet even parties who don't believe in the institution of *get* merely consider it superfluous. They rarely, if ever, have a theological belief that is offended by their participation in what is essentially the rescission of a contract. Rarely, if ever, does recalcitrance have a principled, religious basis.

4. *Injury to Third Persons*: A final rationale is a bit more complex. The free exercise clause does not exempt a party from undoing the harms caused to another by the very restrictions of religion that the party himself invoked but now repudiates. Agreeing to a religious ceremony imposes from the standpoint of *halacha* certain disabilities and restrictions on remarriage. It would be inequitable to invoke "free exercise" as a protective exonerating shield against the very harms that the party had previously created. Just as the First Amendment cannot be used as a defense to acts that are otherwise criminal or tortious[262] so too it should not be employed as a device for the erection or maintenance of barriers against the exercise of another's fundamental freedoms.

Halachic Problems

Civil enforcement of an agreement to give a *get*, whether express or implied from the terms of the *ketubah*, while undoubtedly motivated by benign intentions, may ultimately be a self-defeating proposition. Under Jewish law, a *get* executed under duress or compulsion which includes the order of a non-rabbinical court is invalid.[263] The recipient of such a document is still

---

262. See, for example, *Reynolds v. United States*, 98 U.S. 145 (1878) and, more recently, *Employment Division v. Smith* (*Smith* II), 494 U.S. 872 (1990). The free exercise analysis presented here is made in passing and is further developed *infra* text at notes 589-597.

It should also be noted that at least *some* constitutional rights may indeed afford a limited privilege to engage in acts that would otherwise be tortious. See, *e.g.*, *New York Times v. Sullivan*, 376 U.S. 254 (1964) (constitutional freedoms of speech prohibit the awarding of damages in actions brought by public officials for libel unless the defamatory statement was made with actual knowledge of falsify or reckless disregard of the truth) and *Curtis Publishing Co. v. Butts*, 388 U.S. 130 (1967) (extending this "actual malice" rule to nongovernmental "public figures"). These immunities are limited, however, to rights arising under "freedom of speech and expression" and to acts regarded as essentially communicative in nature (defamatory statements). It is difficult to envision how a refusal to grant a *get* pursuant to one's own previous agreement could legitimately fall within this rubric. As such, the basic rules of *Reynolds* and *Smith* allow the state's interest in the neutral enforcement of its laws - in this case contract law - to override what at best are attenuated "free exercise" concerns.

263. The anomaly of a *get*'s being invalid precisely *because* a court ordered that it be given is noted by one judge in *Morris v. Morris*, 42 D.L.R. 3rd at 574-575 and by Justice Nunez in his dissent in *Margulies v. Margulies*, 344 N.Y.S. 2d 482 (1973), *supra* note 133. See also Glenn, *Where Heavens Meet: The Compelling of Religious Divorces*, 28 AM. JOURNAL OF COMPARATIVE LAW 1, 21 (1980) who notes that "where it is clear that such

halachically unable to marry and any children born from a subsequent, illicit union will be tainted with the heavy stigma of *mamzeirut*.[264] Even though the basis of enforceability is ultimately traceable to an agreement, the consensus of authority is that even self-imposed duress precludes execution of the *get*, particularly when such self-imposed duress could culminate in high fines and even incarceration, well beyond the scope of the sanction voluntarily chosen.[265]

One way around this problem would be for the court to structure its judgment not as a directive to give a *get* but rather as an order to submit to the jurisdiction of the rabbinical court, leaving to that court the issue of whether or not the *get* should be executed.[266] This was exactly the procedure followed in the *Burns* case[267] and successfully avoids *halachic* questions. The difficulties with this approach are, first, imposing such an obligation does not track with the actual language of the agreement (which promises to give a *get*) nor can it be readily inferred from the terms of the *ketubah* and, second, getting the parties to go to the *bait din* is little guarantee that they will obey the decision of the *bait din* once it is rendered.[268]

The foregoing conclusion, that judicial enforcement of *get* covenants may result in an invalid *get*, is subject to one major qualification. An important distinction must be drawn between judicially-ordering affirmative relief against a recalcitrant spouse based on a promise to grant a *get* and

---

recognition not be forthcoming, civil courts should naturally not engage in a pointless exercise." See also *infra* at note 607.

264. See *supra* note 35.

265. See discussion *supra* text at notes 63-65 and at notes 76-86. The point being made is that even the authorities that assert that a *get* issued pursuant to an agreement imposing financial penalties is valid may very well take a different position when sanctions other than, and in excess of, the stipulated penalty are being levied. In such a case, the *get* may be invalid even *after* the fact.

[Nor could this problem be resolved by stipulating the penalty in the *get* covenant. First, even in the case of self-imposed penalties, Rema rules that no *get* can be given until there is a prior unconditional forgiveness, at least *ab initio*. Second, in many cases, a stipulated penalty would simply be ignored by a common law court so ultimately the remedy would in fact not be the one chosen by the parties but rather one that is dictated by the court. See *infra* note 309. Third, many cases of self-imposed penalties are subject to the rule of *asmakhta*, see *infra* text at notes 306-307, and are *halachically* illegitimate. Consequently, *gittin* executed to escape *halachically* illegitimate claims may be invalid after the fact even where the claims are self-imposed. This point is developed at much greater length *infra* text at notes 323-329. But *cf. infra* text at notes 432-452 (*asmakhta* considerations may be irrelevant for *get meusah* purposes).]

266. Express agreements to submit to rabbinic arbitration are discussed at length in the next section, *infra* text following note 274. The suggestion in the text is that even express covenants to grant a *get* might be "shoehorned" into meaning that the parties will submit to rabbinic jurisdiction.

267. See 538 A.2d at 441, *supra* note 226.

268. See discussion *infra* text following note 291 for an extensive discussion of this point.

denying such spouse relief when he or she seeks benefits under a separation agreement.[269] A negotiated separation agreement designating the allocation of marital assets may provide that a spouse's entitlements are conditional on the execution of a religious divorce. Failure to comply with that condition would certainly bar any attempts on the part of the violator to judicially enforce the terms of the agreement even in those jurisdictions that would not directly order the execution of a *get*. To the extent a spouse is "pressured" to grant a *get* in order to secure additional benefits under a separation agreement, the resulting divorce would not be a *get meusah* for *halacha* recognizes a clear distinction between acting to avoid physical or financial harm (where the rules of *get meusah* apply) and acting to obtain benefits (where they do not).[270]

Note, however, that this is true only if the agreement provides a complying spouse with benefits over and above those to which he or she would be entitled in the absence of agreement under the jurisdiction's law of equitable distribution[271] and, conversely, where failure to grant a *get* leaves the recalcitrant party no worse off. To the extent failure to execute a *get* imposes a detriment on the violator leaving him with *less* than he otherwise would have had under state law, such an agreement appears indistinguishable from any other self-imposed penalty clause and the execution of a *get* under such circumstances would appear to be improper.[272]

---

269. This distinction has already been recognized by courts, see *Rubin v. Rubin*, *supra* note 224. I argue here that it is a distinction of *halachic* significance as well.

270. See *supra* text at notes 66-68 and note 93. It is obvious, for example, that one who executes a *get* in exchange for a payment of $10,000 has not acted under duress although he would not have acted without a financial inducement.

271. For a comprehensive state-by-state survey of the manifold approaches to the equitable division of property following marital dissolution, see Golden, EQUITABLE DISTRIBUTION OF PROPERTY (1983, 1990 Supp.) especially pp. 283-327. But see *infra* notes 656-658 (It is not at all clear if the relevant base for determining forfeiture within the meaning of *get meusah* is the secular law of equitable distribution or *halachic* norms. If the latter, many of these "trading chip" agreements would continue to be tainted by the problem of *get meusah*).

[But see IGROT MOSHE E.H. III, no. 44 (1965) where Rabbi Feinstein validates a *get* that was given under the terms of a negotiated settlement although violation of the settlement would have resulted in severe sanctions, *i.e.*, imprisonment. In that case, however, the husband indicated his willingness to grant the *get* but stated that, in the absence of a settlement, he would have negotiated for more favorable rights concerning the children. Rabbi Feinstein ruled that where such apparent willingness exists, the *get* will not be tainted merely because of the presence of a potential source of pressure. See also *infra* note 695 for an elaboration of Rabbi Feinstein's alternative ground.]

272. See *supra* text at note 66-68. The fact that procedurally the "penalty" (forfeiture of marital property) is essentially self-executing and may not require affirmative judicial action for its enforcement - as would the collection of a fine - is of no significance.

Summary of Critique of the Contract Model

In short, courts are sharply divided over the enforceability of agreements to give *gittin*. Some take the position that such agreements are unenforceable either on constitutional grounds or on the more limited basis that *halachic* dissolution procedures have been preempted by state statutory law. A second group has been willing to enforce express agreements by an order of specific performance. Within this group, a smaller number has even been willing to infer such an agreement from the *ketubah* itself notwithstanding the fact that the *ketubah* makes no mention of a *get*. Yet a third line of authority, while not enforcing a *get* - covenant directly, would deny a recalcitrant spouse any benefits under such an agreement until such time as there is full compliance.

On the merits, a strong case can be made that enforcement of an express covenant offends neither the establishment nor the free exercise clauses. The argument that such agreements are somehow preempted by state domestic relations law is similarly unconvincing since the *get* is not being used to supersede the state law of dissolution or replace the need for a civil divorce but simply represents some additional commitment of the parties no different from any other supplementary agreement embodied in a separation. With respect to the *ketubah* as an implied contract, I tried to show, first, as a matter of Jewish law that this is an erroneous reading of the *ketubah* and second, that judicial attempts to scrutinize the *ketubah* may necessitate the very same "excessive entanglement" in religious affairs that the establishment clause proscribes.

Finally, from the standpoint of *halacha*, civil enforcement of *get* agreements whether express or implied may be of very little value since the resulting *get* is likely to be invalid as a *meusah* at least *ab initio*.[273] While the *halachic* problem may be solved by reformulating the order to simply direct the parties to appear before a rabbinic tribunal, such a step does not guarantee that the decision of the *bait din* will ever be carried out.[274] In short, the key problem in the prenuptial *get* agreement is *halachic* rather than *secular* in nature and there is little the current legal system can do to resolve it.

EXPRESS OR IMPLIED PROMISES TO SUBMIT TO RABBINIC JURISDICTION: *AVITZUR v. AVITZUR*

In 1954, Professor Saul Lieberman of the Jewish Theological Seminary (Conservative) proposed that a new clause be added to the *ketubah*. The clause would provide that in the event of marital difficulty, the couple recognizes the authority of the *bait din* of the Rabbinical Assembly or the Jewish Theological Seminary to "counsel them in the light of Jewish tradition" and to "summon either party at the request of the other" and authorizes the *bait din* to impose such terms of compensation as it may see fit for failure to respond to its

273. See *supra* text at notes 60-65.

274. See also *infra* text at notes 287-299 regarding the *halachic* problems of *bait din* agreements.

summons or to carry out its decision."[275] The Rabbinical Assembly quickly approved this addendum although it has not found favor with the Orthodox rabbinate, particularly in its stipulation of a penalty clause.[276]

The theory behind the clause lies in the fact that even if there were *halachic* or constitutional impediments in judicially compelling parties to give or receive a *get*, those concerns would be inapplicable in ordering parties to submit to the jurisdiction of a freely-chosen rabbinic tribunal. Such an agreement is no different in kind from any other agreement to submit disputes to binding arbitration which, in the absence of fraud or duress, would normally be specifically enforceable. Nor would sanctions imposed in order to force someone to go to a *bait din* constitute compulsion that would invalidate the *get* from the standpoint of *halacha*.

The test of the clause's legal enforceability arose in the celebrated case of *Avitzur v. Avitzur*,[277] the only case to date in which a state supreme court has addressed the validity of prenuptial agreements associated with religious divorces. Boaz and Susan Avitzur were married in a religious ceremony on May 22, 1966. They signed a *ketubah* that contained the Lieberman clause. A civil divorce was granted to Boaz in 1978. In 1980, Susan, not having received a *get*, brought an action for specific performance to compel Boaz to appear before a rabbinical tribunal to initiate the *get* process. Boaz filed a motion to dismiss on the ground that enforcement of such an agreement constituted an impermissible and excessive entanglement in religion and violated his own free exercise rights. Special Term (the trial court) denied the motion but the Appellate Division reversed (though not wholly on Boaz's grounds). In a 4-1 decision, the Appellate Division held that because the agreement was entered into as part of a religious ceremony and was "liturgical" in nature, there was no legitimate secular interest that would warrant its enforcement, especially since as far as the state was concerned, the marital bond was already dissolved. Noting that a number of New York cases have enforced *get*-promises (for example, *Koeppel*, *Waxstein*, and *Rubin*),[278] the court pointed out that in each of these cases the provision was incorporated in a civil agreement

---

275. A good discussion of the proposal from the perspective of the Conservative movement appears in Klein, A GUIDE TO JEWISH RELIGIOUS PRACTICE, p. 293.

276. Criticism of the Lieberman proposal may be found in Lamm, *Recent Additions to the Ketubah*, 2 TRADITION (1959) pp. 93-119 and Levin and Kramer, NEW PROVISIONS IN THE KETUBAH. The penalty aspect of *Avitzur* is discussed *infra* text at notes 315-322.

277. 446 N.E. 2d 136, 29 A.L.R. 4th 736 (N.Y. 1983) reversing 86 A.D. 2d 133 (N.Y. App. Div. 1982). Two excellent articles exploring the implications of *Avitzur* are Kahan, *Jewish Divorce and Secular Courts: The Promise of Avitzur*, 73 GEORGETOWN LAW JOURNAL 193 (1984) and Lieberman, *Avitzur v. Avitzur: The Constitutional Implications of Judicially-Enforcing Religious Agreements*, 33 CATHOLIC UNIVERSITY LAW REVIEW 219 (1983).

278. See *supra* note 224.

with no reliance placed on the *ketubah* itself.[279] The exception was *Stern v. Stern*, a trial judge's opinion, of which the *Avitzur* trial court specifically disapproved.[280]

The Court of Appeals, in a 4-3 decision, reversed the Appellate Division and ruled that the Lieberman clause was indeed enforceable and Susan's action for specific performance should be allowed to proceed. Writing for the court, Judge Wachtler stated that there was nothing in law or public policy to prevent judicial recognition and enforcement of the secular terms of the *ketubah* (though it would be a question of fact whether there was actual contractual intent). Characterizing the Lieberman clause as closely analogous to a typical arbitration agreement, the court concluded that the religious context in which the *ketubah* was executed should not deprive it of the same dignity and deference accorded to any other civil contract as long as its enforcement violates neither the law or public policy of the state. While the establishment clause precludes judicial resolution of questions pertaining to religious law, this type of clause may be enforced "solely upon the application of neutral principles of contract law" without need to be entangled in doctrinal or liturgical questions.

As noted, there was a vigorous three-member dissent although the primary point of the dissenters is not entirely clear. It is uncertain whether their objection was based on the fact that 1) the *ketubah* is a religious, rather than secular document; 2) the obligations of the Lieberman clause are not self-explanatory and would in fact necessitate in-depth examination of Jewish religious law and doctrine; 3) the parties lacked true contractual consent[281]; 4) the very notion of ordering someone to submit to an ecclesiastical authority even under the guise of neutral contract enforcement is offensive to the First Amendment, a proposition that would cast serious doubt on a whole group of New York cases, not just *Stern v. Stern*; or 5) the fact that post-dissolution, the state no longer has a legitimate interest in the defunct marital relationship. (Trying to figure out the position of the dissenters may be of some importance because, in a 4-3 decision, a single change in membership could elevate the dissenting position into the majority one.)

Avitzur is a significant victory for those who seek to utilize the legal system to alleviate the *agunah*'s plight. Indeed, even the Orthodox rabbinate who find the Lieberman clause unacceptable could easily draft a *halachically-*valid substitute that would be equally enforceable.[282]

---

279. Why this should make any difference was never explained. If the nature of the undertaking being enforced is not an impermissible establishment, why does it became so because of the *ketubah*? If the problem is a lack of contractual intent, does that have anything to do with the First Amendment?

280. See *supra* note 227.

281. The dissent makes this observation but it is difficult to see how the absence of contractual intent amounts to a constitutional concern. Moreover, why shouldn't the presence or absence of such intent be a question of fact to be resolved at trial?

282. The two problems with the Lieberman proposal are, first, the designation of a particular *bait din* that the Orthodox movement considers invalid and second, the stipulation of an indeterminate monetary penalty that runs afoul of the principle of *asmakhta*. See discussion *infra* text following note 306. Both of these problems can be eliminated through the drafting of an

The extent of its significance, however, should not be over-exaggerated. First, the analysis is a bit flawed or at least incomplete and, in a 4-3 decision, there are distinct possibilities of future reversal on the state or even the federal level. (Admittedly, however, as the decision approaches its tenth anniversary, the prospects of its reversal are less likely.) Moreover, the court's reliance on the so-called "neutral principles of contract law" proves too much. Could not the same be said about an agreement to pray or observe the Sabbath and yet it is inconceivable that any court of law would compel a person to perform an "act of Divine worship" merely because he promised to do so. A possible demarcation point may lie in the difficulties of enforcement. While ordering someone to pray may indeed not be violative of "free exercise" since the person had agreed to do it, a court would be unable to determine compliance with its order (and impose follow-up sanctions) without extensive involvement in religious doctrine, in questions such as the text and structure of prayer, time, place, denomination *etc*. As such, issuing an order which entails in-depth doctrinal inquiry "excessively entangles" the judiciary in religious law, in violation of the establishment clause. By contrast, the court may have felt that ordering parties to submit their disputes to a *bait din* does not necessitate such an inquiry. Alternatively, the court may have reasoned that while prayer and Sabbath observance are "religious acts," going to a *bait din* is not.

Both of these distinctions are open to serious question. First, it may very well be true that no court should issue an order that it will not be able to subsequently enforce without excessive involvement in the resolution of religious doctrine but such difficulties may be equally present under the Lieberman clause. Assume that the court directs the parties to respond to the summons of the *bait din* by treating the *ketubah* as an arbitration agreement. At a later point in time, Susan files a motion to have Boaz declared in contempt for failure to appear. The trial court will then presumably issue a Notice to Show Cause why Boaz should not be held in contempt. At any later contempt hearing, a number of issues can be raised: the meaning of "responding" to a summons (personal appearance or through writing), the necessary content of such a response, evidentiary standards, allegations of disqualification due to bias, *etc*. Presumably, because the parties agreed to a *bait din*, these matters would be determined by Jewish law and yet the court, in the exercise of its contempt function, would have to consider them. If, in lieu of *halacha*, the court applies secular standards in judging the proprietary of the internal procedures of a rabbinical court, the interference and entanglement with religious institutions are even greater. While ordering the parties to "respond" to the summons of a *bait din* may not in itself be an "establishment of religion," the follow-up enforcement procedures may well raise severe constitutional conflicts. There is little sense in issuing orders that the court may not be able to constitutionally enforce.[283]

---

agreement that designates an Orthodox *bait din* and deletes any reference to financial penalties. An agreement drafted along these lines is presented in Bleich, *A Suggested Antenuptial Agreement: A Proposal in the Wake of Avitzur*, 7 JOURNAL OF HALACHA AND CONTEMPORARY SOCIETY 25, 38-39 (Spring 1984).

283. The notion that at least some arbitration agreements invite excessive entanglements with religion underlies an earlier case, *Pal v. Pal*, 45 A.D. 2d 738, 356 N.Y.S. 2d 672 (N.Y. App. Div. 1974). A husband had obtained a

Second, the assumption that, unlike prayer or Sabbath observance, responding to the summons of an ecclesiastical court is not a "religious" act is equally questionable on "free exercise" grounds. Submitting to the authority of a tribunal is a tacit declaration that the tribunal is empowered to resolve particular matters. If the source of tribunal's empowerment is a religious law, submission is an acknowledgement of the binding force of the religion. At least on one level, then, while no act of overt worship is required, enforcement of rabbinical arbitration clauses does touch at least the periphery of free exercise concerns and implicates the promotion and endorsement prongs of establishment as well.

On balance, I do not disagree with the court's holding. Certainly, the fact that an otherwise enforceable agreement appears in a document commonly associated with a religious ceremony should be of no constitutional significance though it may go to the issue of contractual intent, a question not susceptible to summary resolution. Insofar as the First Amendment is concerned, the substance rather than the form of the undertaking should be controlling. Moreover, as noted earlier in connection with *get* agreements, there are a number of arguments that can be made to sustain the constitutionality of enforcing a Lieberman-type *ketubah*.[284] Nevertheless, by placing primary reliance on "neutral principles of contract law," the court failed to explore and thereby address the establishment and free exercise concerns that are being adversely affected. As is evident from the case of the person who contracts to pray, it is just not true that as long as the court orders you to do no more than you promised, there are no constitutional difficulties. In enforcing undertakings that have some religious overtones, it is not enough to ask whether the parties agreed. A comprehensive approach necessitates the examination of the substance of the agreement; the level of potential entanglement in religious

---

civil divorce from his wife. In an open court stipulation later incorporated into the judgment of divorce, the parties agreed to submit themselves to a rabbinical tribunal on the question of whether husband should initiate the *get* process and to abide by their decision (*i.e.*, a Lieberman-like clause but outside of the framework of the *ketubah* or religious ceremony). The agreement did not specify a particular *bait din*; the tribunal would be chosen by each of the parties designating a rabbi of their choice and the two rabbis then choosing a third - a well-recognized *halachic* alternative, see SHULCHAN ARUCH H.M. 13:1 and *supra* text at note 47. The stipulation further provided that if either of the parties failed to choose a rabbi within one week or if the two rabbis failed to timely choose the third, the court would select a competent rabbi as the missing member. A *bait din* was initially assembled without the aid of a court but husband's designated rabbi later withdrew. Upon application of the wife, the trial court designated the third "neutral" member as husband's representative and directed the two to choose a third. This order was reversed on appeal by a summary holding that the trial court had no authority to convene a rabbinical tribunal. While *Avitzur* makes no reference to *Pal*, in all probability *Pal* will continue to be good law. Allowing a court to enforce a rabbinical arbitration agreement is far cry from giving the court the authority even in cases of deadlock to determine a *bait din*'s composition. Nevertheless, the same entanglement concerns that justify reversal of the trial court's decision in *Pal* apply, at least in some degree, to the *Avitzur* case as well.

284. See *supra* text at notes 238-262.

doctrine both in the formulation of the order and in follow-up enforcement measures; possible intrusions into religious autonomy and self-governance; the appearance of according religious institutions or law favorable, preferred status; and infringements of religious liberty. While contractarian analysis is one useful strand in formulating criteria for enforcement, the other factors must be considered as well. As noted, compelling submission of disputes to a *bait din* implicates concerns of both entanglement and autonomy, neither of which the *Avitzur* court fully addresses. As an exposition of constitutional law, the opinion leaves much to be desired.[285]

A second, and less important, observation is that the case fails to address the "monetary penalties" aspect of the Conservative *ketubah*. Assume, for example, that one party refuses to appear after being summoned and the *bait din* imposes a monetary fine. Would this fine be recoverable in a court of law? Assuming the analogy to arbitration agreements, in all probability the answer would be no. Arbitrators are normally not authorized to impose their own penalties for failure to submit or to obey. Nor can the parties agree in advance to the payment of such penalties under basic principles of contract law. The exclusive remedy for breach of a contract to arbitrate is an action for specific performance, which in turn would be enforceable by imprisonment or fines to be determined by the court.[286] It is the judiciary, rather than the *bait din*, that determines the ultimate penalties for non-compliance.

A third point is most crucial of all: Where do we go from here? Technically, the only thing *Avitzur* does is require the parties to respond to the summons of a *bait din*. Presumably, if a party fails to respond, the court may then impose sanctions for civil contempt. Responding to a summons, however, is not the same as carrying out the *bait din*'s order. If the *bait din* later orders the execution of a *get* and the husband refuses, may the wife go back to court and compel compliance with the *bait din*'s decree? *Avitzur* pointedly left the question open. A number of commentators take the view that *Avitzur* would not enforce either an express agreement to give a *get* or the order of a *bait din* to give a *get* entered after submission of a dispute, and permits nothing more than forcing the parties to appear.[287] They argue that the execution of a *get* is a ceremony of religious significance that no court can directly order. This is probably an overly narrow reading of the court's holding. In the first place, there is considerable lower court authority, particularly in New York, that even agreements to execute a *get* may be specifically enforceable,[288] at least when such agreements are explicit although admittedly *Avitzur* did not directly address this question one way or another. Second, under the court's own

---

285. The court was preoccupied with dispelling the notion that the *ketubah* was a "liturgical" document whose terms were not enforceable in civil court, the basis for the decision of the Appellate Division. This, however, is a "red herring" argument based on form rather than substance and is the least significant of the constitutional issues that could be raised. Unfortunately, the terms of debate were largely set by the Appellate Division's reliance on this formality and that determined the direction of Judge Wachtler's opinion as well.

286. See Domke, COMMERCIAL ARBITRATION §37.00, p. 493.

287. See, for example, the analysis offered in an unsigned article appearing in the NEWSLETTER OF THE AMERICAN JEWISH COMMITTEE, Vol. 3, No. 4 at pp. 1-2 (Fall 1983).

288. See *supra* notes 220-226.

contract analysis ("reliance on neutral principles of common law"), as incomplete as it may be, there is no relevant distinction between agreements to give a *get* and agreements to submit to rabbinic arbitration. In both cases, a party is simply being forced to do what he agreed to do. Indeed, mandating appearance before a *bait din* for purposes of dispute resolution on the issue of a *get* may be considerably more invasive than directly ordering execution of a *get*. A *get* can typically be executed in less than an hour while a contested proceeding before a *bait din* may take several days and involve numerous inquiries into intimate details of marital life.[289] Third, since the court characterizes the *bait din* clause as akin to an arbitration agreement, it is well established under New York law as well as elsewhere that not only will specific performance be granted to compel the parties to submit their dispute to the arbitrator but the arbitration order may be specifically enforced as well.[290] Thus, insofar as state law is concerned, the same mechanisms that can be employed to bring the parties before the *bait din* may then be utilized to secure the *get*.

Once again, however, as was true with direct agreements to give *gittin*, we run into serious *halachic* concerns. As noted repeatedly, a *get* issued pursuant to the order of a secular court which provides sanctions for non-compliance is invalid as a *get meusah*.[291] There is one major exception to this rule. If a secular court does nothing more than compel obedience to the preexisting decision of a rabbinic tribunal, the *get* is valid. On its face, this renders the *Avitzur* approach a seemingly-perfect solution to the problem. Compelling the parties to go to a *bait din* certainly raises no *meusah* problem

---

289. For a good informal description of how a *bait din* conducts its examination of the parties, see Epstein, A WOMAN'S GUIDE TO THE GET PROCESS, pp. 39-46.

290. See Domke, COMMERCIAL ARBITRATION §30.01, p. 441. (Technically, the court reduces the arbitration order to a judgment which may then be specifically enforced.) Indeed, a recent New York case specifically applied this rule to the decision of a *bait din* in a domestic relations dispute. See *Lieberman v. Lieberman*, 566 N.Y.S. 2d 190 (N.Y. Sup. Ct. 1991). The case did not involve an order to grant a *get* but was concerned with issues of custody, visitation, child support, and use of the marital abode. Although the court expressly ruled that the decision of a *bait din* is as enforceable as any other arbitration, it did set aside the *bait din's* award of joint custody on the grounds that such an award was not in the children's best interest. Noting that the court's supervisory power over the welfare of minors supersedes the state's policy of otherwise deferring to the will of the parties, the court ruled that it must be free to make its own *de novo* determination on the merits.

While *Lieberman* does indicate that the child custody determinations of a *bait din* will not be accorded special recognition by a secular court, this has nothing to do with the religious nature of the *bait din* or the constitutional constraints of the First Amendment. The lack of deference would have been identical had the joint custody determination been made by a secular arbitration panel. What *Lieberman* does indicate, however, is that while the decision of a *bait din* on the merits is no better than an arbitral award, it is also no worse.

291. See generally *supra* discussion at notes 60-74 (basic parameters of *get meusah*) and text at notes 96-106 (*gittin* issued pursuant to the obligatory order of a *bait din* are not invalid).

and enforcing the *bait din's* order to give a *get* is similarly acceptable under the rule cited above. This makes the *Avitzur* approach far more preferable than the expedient of direct agreement.

Unfortunately, the matter is a bit more complicated and can only be understood in the context of the overall powers of a *bait din* as defined by *halacha*. In an ideal *halachic* system (which today does not exist anywhere in the world), a *bait din* is able to compel compliance with its orders through a variety of sanctions including fines, excommunication, imprisonment, corporal punishment, and even execution.[292] The Mishna makes abundantly clear that these general enforcement powers apply to *get*-orders as well.[293] The early rabbinic commentators noted that permitting a *bait din* to compel the granting of a *get* is ostensibly inconsistent with the principle that a *get* must be given willingly and provided a variety of answers, the best known of which is suggested by Rambam.[294] However this inconsistency be resolved, it is clear that compulsion pursuant to a valid order of a *bait din* does not constitute invalidating cause.

Second, the grounds upon which a *bait din* can order the execution of a *get* is a matter of great dispute and considerable uncertainty. Certain cases are described as *kofin* ("we force") and certain cases are described as *yotzee* ("he must divorce").[295] According to many authoritative decisors, the extensive enforcement powers of a *bait din*, including corporal punishment and incarceration, may be employed only in the comparatively few circumstances which are described as *kofin*-type cases; with respect to *yotzee* cases, while the husband is indeed under a religious and moral obligation to give his wife a *get* and the *bait din* may issue an order directing him to do so, such an order may not be enforced by physical or financial sanctions but only by moral suasion and appeals to conscience (which, in a *halachic* society, may be considerably more potent than they are today). According to these opinions, any use of force or coercion *even for the purpose of enforcing the order of the bait din* will still render the *get* invalid if the order was only on the level of *yotzee*.[296]

---

292. See, *e.g.*, SHULCHAN ARUCH H.M. 97:15 (Rema) who rules that even a willful refusal to pay a simple money judgment may result in physical punishment *ad shetaitzai nafsho* (until, and including, the point of death). See also SHULCHAN ARUCH YORE DE'AH 334:43 (disobedience of a *bait din*'s order may result in severe sanctions of excommunication) and *supra* note 46.

While the specific reference cited deals with sanctions to compel obedience to a final judgment, it is probable (though not certain) that these sanctions are equally available to compel a defendant to appear. See *infra* note 319. In any event, excommunication (*nidui*) is explicitly mentioned as a sanction for nonappearance. SHULCHAN ARUCH H.M. 11:1 and *supra* note 46.

293. T.B. GITTIN 88b.

294. See discussion *supra* at note 100.

295. See discussion *supra* text at notes 110-120.

296. See *supra* note 116 where the logic of this conclusion is questioned. Nevertheless, the conclusion itself seems to be accepted by virtually all *halachic* authorities. This position was recently reaffirmed by Rabbi Y. Elyashiv, a leading *halachic* scholar. See *infra* text at note 681. [But *cf.* note 116 (view of Rabbi Herzog that *kofin* sanctions employed in *yotzee* cases do not result in a *get meusah*).]

The notion of a court issuing an order that cannot be effectively enforced may strike us as strange but makes perfect sense if we remember that *halachic* judges were also the religious and spiritual leaders of their communities and, as such, could issue directives reflective of moral commitment and aspiration although unenforceable on legal grounds.

Third, there is indeed a principle that states that a non-Jewish court may enforce the decision of a Jewish court without invalidating the *get*.[297] I would suggest, however, that this last principle must be read in light of the preceding rules. Where a secular judicial system is acting as the surrogate enforcer for the *bait din*, it would seem clear that the scope of permissible coercion that may be employed could not exceed that degree which is permitted to be exercised by the *bait din* itself in an ideal *halachic* world. Assume, for example, that a *bait din* issues an order directing husband to divorce his wife but the grounds established are such that would only justify a decree of *yotzee* rather than *kofin*. In such a case, according to the opinions cited above, were the *bait din* themselves to fine or imprison the person to compel his compliance, the *get* would be rendered invalid.[298] Would it not be obvious that resort to secular enforcement would produce the same result?[299]

In short, *Avitzur* is a very imperfect solution. Assuming its constitutional validity, it does assure that the parties may be forced to go to a *bait din*. For parties who were religiously indifferent, once they are brought

---

297. See T.B. GITTIN 88b, Rambam, MISHNA TORAH, *Hilchot Gerushin* 2:20, and the discussion *supra* text at notes 103-104.

298. But *cf. supra* note 116 (view of Rabbi Herzog).

299. In fairness, this conclusion may not be as obvious as the text states. It is arguable that the order of a secular court directing compliance with the decision of a *bait din* to grant a *get* can never result in a *get meusah* since compulsion is not directed to the procurement of a *get per se* but to obedience to the order of a *bait din*. As such, secular court enforcement would be a *halachically* permissible option irrespective of whether the *bait din's* order is premised on *kofin* or *yotzee* grounds. If this conclusion is accepted, *Avitzur* becomes a much more valuable weapon in the *agunah*'s arsenal since not only could the court compel the recalcitrant spouse to appear before the *bait din* but could enforce the ultimate decision of the *bait din* as well.

While this reading finds some support in the Talmud, see T.B. GITTIN 88b, I believe it is incorrect. The validation of *gittin* issued pursuant to non-Jewish compulsion is expressly predicated on their being the surrogate agents for the Jewish *bait din*. See SHULCHAN ARUCH E.H. 134:9 ("if the Jewish court forced the *get* through the employment of non-Jews" - in a sense, the enforcing party is the Jewish *bait din*). As such, the legitimacy of the sanctions employed by a secular court acting in a surrogate capacity must be gauged exclusively by reference to those that a Jewish *bait din* (in a *halachic* society) could have imposed directly. See also BAIT SHMUEL E.H. 134:9 (15) who notes that once a *bait din* has issued such an order, it is immaterial whether the non-Jews enforce the order by a direct demand that a *get* be executed or by the more indirect mechanism of demanding that the recalcitrant party comply with the order of the *bait din*. This further indicates that the validity of non-Jewish coercion does *not* depend on the compulsion being one step removed from the *get* but on the fact that the *get* itself is one for which direct compulsion is appropriate.

in front of a *bait din*, the *bait din* may in fact be able to exercise moral suasion, generate community pressure, *etc.* The determined *get*-resister, however, may simply refuse to obey the *bait din*'s order and, unless the circumstances are such that would permit the entry of a *kofin* directive,[300] specific performance would be *halachically* impossible.[301]

The *Avitzur* case can appreciably aid the plight of women only in tandem with a *halachic* re-examination of the grounds that permit judicially-ordered divorces. A number of studies have appeared suggesting the possibility of expansion[302] though the authors rarely make clear if they are expanding the *kofin* category or only the *yotzee* category.[303] If the latter, their proposals accomplish very little.[304] Note that this is an area that demands rabbinical consensus; individual courage, resourcefulness, and ingenuity play little or no role. If individual rabbis or *batei din* were to execute *gittin* that were unacceptable to other segments of the religious community, this would create a catastrophe of divisiveness - where Jews who have been divorced in accordance with views of one *bait din* are still deemed *halachically* married according to the views of another *bait din* with the result that their children and all future issue from a second union would be tainted irrevocably with the status of *mamzer*. Whole segments of religiously-observant Jews would be unable to

---

300. Where *kofin* grounds do exist, however, the *Avitzur* approach fits "like a glove." In enforcing the arbitration order, the secular court is quite literally declaring, "Do what the Jewish court has ordered" and acting as the surrogates of the *bait din*. See *supra* text at note 103. This may not be true of other mechanisms of judicial enforcement which remain *halachically* problematical *even* in cases of *kofin*. See *infra* text at notes 638 and 681 (DRL §236B).

301. Note too that *Avitzur* works only if the parties have executed an agreement to that effect. There has been a widespread reluctance to execute this type of prenuptial agreement based on the feeling that discussing divorce mars the joys of the wedding. See, *e.g.*, comments of Rabbi Feinstein in IGROT MOSHE E.H. IV, no. 107, discussed *infra* at notes 425-431. Suffice it to say, however, that the *ketubah* itself contains alimony provisions and as *Ethics of the Fathers* reminds us, "Who is wise? He who anticipates the future." MISHNA ABOT 4:1. Couples should be encouraged to sign such agreements; it may avoid much grief later. Nevertheless, *Avitzur* is not a panacea and a determined *get*-resister can always find a way out.

302. The best of these are Riskin, *supra* note 122, cited frequently in this work and Haut, *supra* note 18. Riskin's conclusions are criticized in two articles by Gartner, *Problems of a Forced Get*, 9 JOURNAL OF HALACHA AND CONTEMPORARY SOCIETY 118 (1985) and in Book Review, 50 JEWISH ACTION 70 (Spring 1990). See also Schwartz, *Book Review*, 25 TRADITION 94 (Winter 1990).

303. Riskin fails to address this issue at all. None of his arguments support expansion of *kofin* orders.

304. Unless, of course, one were to adopt the view of Rabbi Herzog, discussed *supra* note 116, a view that unfortunately has not gained wide acceptance.

intermarry with each other.[305] As a matter of common sense, no questionable procedure in the execution of a *get* or in the seeking of civil enforcement should ever be employed until it achieves broad-based consensus within all segments of the knowledgeable *halachic* community.

305. To some extent, this has already occurred in the Reform movement which no longer requires a *get*. See *supra* note 3. As a result, the ability of Reform and Orthodox Jews to marry one another has been curtailed because some earlier marriage, perhaps of a great-grandparent long ago, was not terminated with a *get*, thereby resulting in the children of a second union being labelled illegitimate. This result is especially heartbreaking when a descendant from this union is desirous of joining Orthodoxy and then discovers to his/her chagrin that they bear the stigma of *mamzer* through no fault of their own. To their credit, a number of members of the Reform rabbinate counsel their congregants to obtain *gittin* to avoid complications for offspring later. There is also a national organization *Kayama* based in New York whose goal is to educate the general Jewish public about the need for a *get* (even for irreligious non-believers) and to arrange *gittin* at low cost. See Katz, *Jewish Divorce and Jewish Unity*, AMIT WOMEN (Jan-Feb 1989). Indeed, I am personally aware of *Kayama* arranging a *get* within two hours. (*Kayama* does not primarily concern itself with the recalcitrant spouse but the ignorant one.)

As serious as this problem is, the specter of Orthodox rabbis issuing *gittin* not accepted by their counterparts would be far worse. In many cases, Reform marriage ceremonies may be *halachically* invalid. If there was no marriage to begin with, there may be no need for a *get*. See discussion *supra* at notes 202-216. By contrast, where the initial ceremony was a *halachic* one, the lack of a *get* would be fatal.

Chapter Four

The Use of Contract Law (II): Conditional Releases and Support Obligations

This chapter will continue to explore the use of contract law to aid the plight of spouses in need of a *get* by examining two additional proposals: the conditional release and antenuptial support agreements. The chapter will conclude with a discussion of the draft prenuptial agreement prepared by the Rabbinical Council of America (that was later withdrawn) and with a summary table outlining all the contractual alternatives considered in Chapters Three and Four.

PROMISE TO PAY SUMS OF MONEY UNLESS A *GET* IS EXECUTED - *ASMAKHTA* AND CONDITIONAL RELEASES

Concept of *Asmakhta*

One formidable obstacle to the drafting of *halachically* valid prenuptial agreements is the *halachic* concept of *asmakhta*. The exact scope and meaning of the concept is subject to a great variety of conflicting interpretations and only the barest outline can be given here.[306] The term indicates a variety of

306. For a superb though extremely technical treatment of the concept, see Herzog, II MAIN INSTITUTIONS OF JEWISH LAW, pp. 70-106. The term is derived from the verb "*samakh*," "reliance." Contractual obligations are binding under Jewish law only if there is *gemirat daat*, *i.e.*, intention on the part of the person to be legally bound, as well as *semikhat daat*, *i.e.*, a reasonable belief on the part of the beneficiary that such intent is in fact present (though there is no requirement of financial reliance or the like). Agreements subject to various contingencies are said not to be undertaken with serious contractual intent and hence cannot be the basis for *semikhat daat*. What these agreements or contingencies are is subject to a variety of opinions. Ramban (Nachmanides) asserts that at most *asmakhta* could apply only to conditions which are within the party's control or at least which he believed to be within his control. Thus, a typical gambling bet, *e.g.*, "I'll pay $100 if the Orioles win the Series," is not an *asmakhta* since the occurrence or non-occurrence of

agreements that involve certain elements of uncertainty, indecisiveness, contingency, or lack of resolution whereby a party obligating himself subject to a condition does so in the belief that such condition would never materialize. What types of commitments fall within the scope of the rule is highly problematical.[307] At a minimum, however, contractual penalty clauses in the event of non-performance are commonly not enforceable under Jewish law. A contractor who enters into an agreement promising to complete a project by a

---

the condition is beyond the control of the obligor and thus, the obligor knew that he was assuming the risk. By contrast, a stipulation in a contract that if a debt is not paid on time, property in excess of the debt will be forfeited is indeed unenforceable since the obligor, believing that he would pay, never intended to create the obligation. Rashba qualifies the principle further by limiting it to self-imposed penalty clauses upon a failure to perform primary duties and would validate such clauses if they represent a reasonable approximation of actual damage suffered. See also SHULCHAN ARUCH H.M. 61:5 and comments of SEFER MEIRAT AINAYIM [SEMA] (agreement to pay litigation expenses is not an *asmakhta* although the undertaking is both contingent and indeterminate since the obligation is *compensatory* rather than *penal* in nature). *Contra*: R. Shlomo Luria, YAM SHEL SHLOMO, *Baba Kama* 10:14 (recovery of litigation expenses *not* permitted).

Rambam (Maimonides), on the other hand, adopts a far broader view of the nonenforceability of *asmakhta*. First of all, he does not limit the concept to penalty clauses. In *Hilchot Mechira* 11:3, Rambam writes that a person who states, "If you will go with me to Jerusalem on a certain day or if you will bring me a certain object, I will give you this house or I will sell it to you for such and such a price" is not contractually bound to his undertaking. Although such a promise cannot be regarded as a self-imposed penalty for non-performance but is instead an inducement towards another to perform, it is nonetheless unenforceable under the principle of *asmakhta*. At the same time, Rambam maintains that the taint of *asmakhta* may be easily removed by stipulating that the conveyance is effective from today with the condition constituting a condition subsequent, rather than a condition precedent. Thus, "I will sell you the house if you go to Jerusalem by next week" is an invalid indeterminate commitment; "I hereby sell the house to you effective immediately (*me'achshav*) but if you don't go to Jerusalem by Day X, the conveyance shall be void" is a valid transfer. The distinction, originally propounded by R. Hai Gaon in the 10th Century, has not been without problems of its own and there is disagreement about whether it is predicated on possession or the effective date of vesting of title, possessory or not. See SHULCHAN ARUCH H.M. 207:14-15 and commentaries.

For purposes of the analysis in the text, these subtleties are largely immaterial. Under *any* definition of *asmakhta*, an unreasonably large stipulated penalty would be unenforceable under Jewish law though such a clause could pass muster if it represents a reasonable approximation of foreseeable damage, at least according to Rashba.

307. Indeed, the commitment of the *ketubah* itself, *i.e.*, payment of a sum of money upon death or divorce, would have constituted an *asmakhta* at least according to some authorities if not for the fact that it is statutorily mandated, rather than consensual. For one possible reason why the voluntarily-assumed *tosefet* is not an *asmakhta*, see *infra* note 395.

certain time and stipulates that upon failure to complete the project, it will pay a designated amount for every day of delay, cannot be compelled to honor the commitment. Since the contractor presumably assumed the commitment believing it would complete the job, there was no true *gemirat daat* to assume the obligation and hence, no *semikhat daat* that could constitute justified reliance.

One common proposal to alleviate the *agunah* problem calls for a prenuptial agreement to give a *get* in the event of a civil dissolution coupled with financial penalties in the event of non-compliance, perhaps in the form of a specific monetary amount for every day of delay.[308] Wholly apart from the question whether such a penalty clause would be enforceable in secular court,[309]

---

308. For example, the Conservative *ketubah* approved by the Rabbinical Assembly in 1954 contained a prenuptial agreement to submit marital disputes to a designated *bait din* and to abide by their decision. In addition, the clause provided, "We authorize the [*bait din*] to impose such terms of compensation as it may see fit for failure to respond to its summons or to carry out its decision." The Orthodox rabbinate did not approve the widespread use of the clause on the theory that the provision for penalties constituted an *asmakhta*. See, *e.g.*, Lamm, *Recent Additions to the Ketubah*, 2 TRADITION, 93-119 (no. 1, 1959), Meiselman, JEWISH WOMEN AND JEWISH LAW, p. 111, and Rabbinowitz-Teumim, *Self-Imposed Constraints in Divorce* (Hebrew), 1 NOAM 287 (5719/1958-1959). While a number of commentators have stressed the fact that the additional clause stipulates an indeterminate penalty ("such terms as it sees fit"), the identical defect of *asmakhta* would exist even if a specific dollar amount were indicated. The problem of *asmakhta* lies not in the lack of specificity but in the fact that the stipulated undertaking is conditional on non-performance. See Rambam, MISHNA TORAH, *Hilchot Mechira* 11:3. This point has led some later writers astray. See Riskin, WOMEN AND JEWISH DIVORCE, pp. 139-140 where the author erroneously suggests that the designation of a *specified* sum of money avoids *asmakhta*.

Interestingly, without considering the legal enforceability of the penalty clauses *per se*, the New York Court of Appeals did uphold the overall validity of the Conservative *ketubah* by treating it as an arbitration agreement and ordering a recalcitrant husband to submit to the jurisdiction of the *bait din*. See *Avitzur v. Avitzur*, 446 N.E. 2d 136 (N.Y. 1982). See also *supra* text following note 277.

309. Penalty clauses are generally unenforceable by the civil courts and this would similarly apply to penalties arising from the failure to give a *get*. See Levin and Kramer, NEW PROVISIONS IN THE KETUBAH. Nevertheless, under traditional Anglo-American law, parties retained the freedom to designate a sum payable in the event of default ("liquidated damages") if: (1) the sum was not designated as a penalty; (2) the sum represented a good faith and reasonable attempt to estimate damages suffered; and (3) actual damages were difficult to determine. Courts were divided whether the issues of uncertainty and reasonableness were to be determined as of the time the contract was executed or as of the time enforcement of the clause was being sought. See generally Farnsworth, CONTRACTS (2nd ed.) §12.18, pp. 895-904. The traditional view was that uncertainty, difficulty, and apparent reasonableness were to be determined as of the time the contract was made, not at the time of the breach or the trial. See, *e.g.*, *Banta v. Stamford*

such a clause would clearly not be enforceable under Jewish law and indeed, any attempt to enforce such a claim would amount to theft.

It may be contended, however, that *asmakhta* concerns are largely irrelevant. The purpose of such a clause lies primarily in its deterrent effect; otherwise recalcitrant husbands would rather give a *get* than suffer a potential financial penalty. The fact that the penalty is *halachically* void is simply beside the point since the deterrent effect lies in the potential for civil liability, not *halachic* recognition. Unless the victimized spouse is herself committed to *halachic* norms and her husband is fully aware of the fact, even a *halachically* nonenforceable penalty has an *in terrorem* effect.

Unfortunately, matters are not that simple. As noted, a *get* executed under duress is normally invalid.[310] While authorities are in disagreement whether self-imposed monetary penalties constitute the sort of duress that would render a *get* invalid,[311] virtually all agree that a *get* that was executed to escape

---

Motor Co., 92 A. 665 at 667 (Conn. 1914), where the court stated, "The standard of measure here is not furnished by plaintiff's actual loss or injury, as the event proved, but by the loss or injury which might reasonably have been anticipated at the time the contract was made ... It is the look forward and not backward that we are called upon to make." Thus, the extent of loss actually materializing and indeed the absence of any loss at all was irrelevant to the validity of a liquidated damages clause. See, *e.g.*, *Southwest Engr. Co. v. United States*, 341 F. 2d 998 (8th Cir. 1965); *Blackwood v. Liebke*, 113 S.W. 210 (Ark. 1908); *McCarthy v. Tally*, 297 P.2d 981 (Cal. 1956), all of which held that a liquidated damages clause that was reasonable in light of anticipated harm may be enforced even if the aggrieved party suffered no loss at all. Other courts have treated such clauses as penalties. *Massman Constr. Co. v. City Council of Greenville*, 147 F.2d 925 (5th Cir. 1945).

Note that under §2-718 of the UNIFORM COMMERCIAL CODE [UCC], a liquidated damages clause is valid if it is reasonable in "light of the anticipated or actual harm caused by the breach." Thus, even unreasonable forecasts may be upheld in the light of subsequent events. Conversely, a reasonable forecast will be validated even if the anticipated losses fail to materialize, as is already true under common law. Moreover, the UCC abandons the requirement of uncertainty or difficulty of proof. RESTATEMENT OF CONTRACTS (Second) §356 essentially adopts the UCC view in favoring the enforcement of such clauses.

[Commentators have long advocated that the "reasonableness" of the forecast in light of actual or anticipated harm should be the sole test for enforceability and the difficulty of proving damages should be immaterial. See McCormick, LAW OF DAMAGES §148 (1935) ("If the agreement reasonably approximates the probable damages which a court would give, why forbid the parties thus to agree, even if the damage could be readily and exactly foreseen?") and MacNeil, *Power of Contract and Agreed Remedies*, 47 CORNELL L. Q. 495 (1962) ("There seems to be no sound objection to the parties' relieving the judge or jury of the task of fixing damages even where that task would be an easy one.")].

310. See *supra* text at notes 72-74 (*get meusah*).

311. See, *e.g.*, BAIT YOSEF, TUR E.H. 134 citing *Teshuvot Rashba*; Rema, gloss to SHULCHAN ARUCH E.H. 134:5 and *supra* text at notes 63-65.

prosecution of an *illicit* or *invalid* claim is a *get meusah*.[312] Thus, the invalidity of an *asmakhta*-type agreement not only becomes relevant at the collection stage but may in fact taint the *get* that is granted to escape the operation of its provisions.[313]

The Impact of *Asmakhta* Concerns on *Get* or Arbitration Agreements*

The law of *asmakhta* deals with the *halachic* enforceability of privately-assumed monetary obligations, typically those in the nature of a penalty for the nonperformance of a primary duty. Concerns of *asmakhta* thus become relevant only where such an agreement exists and only where the enforceability of the undertaking is predicated on such agreement. The doctrine of *asmakhta* has no bearing, for example, on the powers of a *bait din* to impose sanctions compelling obedience to its orders, powers that exist independently of the parties' agreement. Moreover, even where *asmakhta* unquestionably applies, it does not always taint the resulting *get*. It may therefore be useful to spell out with some specificity exactly which agreements raise *asmakhta* issues and which do not and to what degree those concerns potentially affect the validity of a *get*.

Penalties for Nonappearance

Consider first a standard *Avitzur*-type agreement that obligates the parties to submit to the jurisdiction of the *bait din* and imposes penalties for failure to appear. Conceivably, such a penalty may take one of two forms: 1) a specified dollar amount for each day of nonappearance; or 2) an indeterminate amount to be imposed by the *bait din*. (The latter was the form of the Conservative *ketubah*.)[314] As a simple matter of American contract law, neither alternative is likely to be enforceable. The stipulation would probably be regarded as a penalty clause regardless of any "liquidated damage" label the parties may attach.[315] It is also well established that the exclusive remedy for the breach of a contract to submit disputes to arbitration - which from the standpoint of the secular legal system is all this agreement is - is specific performance, not damages.[316] Thus, as a practical matter, *Avitzur* agreements with penalty clauses are essentially identical to *Avitzur* agreements without them

---

312. See TASHBATZ I, no. 1 and TESHUVOT MABIT I, no. 22 and II, no. 138. See also *supra* text at notes 73-74. But see next note.

313. This seems to be the common assumption of the literature discussing the problem, see, *e.g.*, Bleich, III CONTEMPORARY HALAKHIC PROBLEMS, p. 331 and will be the assumption in the remainder of this chapter. In point of fact, a compelling argument can be made that *asmakhta* has no impact on the *get meusah* problem. The considerations supporting this conclusion are set out at length *infra* text at notes 432-452.

*It may be helpful at this point for the reader to refer to the outline of *get meusah* law that appears *infra* text at notes 453-473.

314. See *supra* note 275.

315. See *supra* text at note 309.

316. See *supra* text at note 286.

since the penalty clauses have no legal effect.[317]

Assuming, however, for purposes of argument that such penalties are legally enforceable, would their enforcement run afoul of the rule of *asmakhta*? From a *halachic* standpoint, an agreement to pay a sum of money upon failure to perform a primary duty is clearly an *asmakhta* whether the amount of the penalty is fixed or indeterminate.[318] Nevertheless, given the fact that *halacha* recognizes the inherent authority of a *bait din* to compel response to its summons by the imposition of sanctions ranging from fines to imprisonment or worse,[319] any agreement to pay the fine imposed by a *bait din* for failure to appear will be *halachically* enforceable not *because* of the agreement (which, after all, remains a classic *asmakhta*) but *in spite* of it. In other words, a sanction which a *bait din* could legitimately impose even in the absence of an agreement will not be vitiated because of the presence of an agreement that contains elements of *asmakhta*.[320] Thus, insofar as *asmakhta* is concerned, this analysis leads to a distinction directly contrary to the one drawn by other commentators.[321] An agreement to pay penalties to be assessed by a *bait din* is more likely to be *halachically* recognized than a fixed, determinate penalty not dependent on the *bait din*'s action.

The first alternative outlined above, the designation of a specified monetary penalty, may indeed constitute an *asmakhta* as commonly understood. Nevertheless, even the stipulation of a penalty clause that is clearly an *asmakhta* and *halachically* unenforceable will not taint a resulting *get* as long as the penalty is limited to coercing *appearance* before the tribunal rather than forcing compliance with its ultimate directive. Only where the *get* itself is the product of compulsion will it be invalid as a *get meusah*; compulsion limited to merely securing a party's appearance before the court will normally have no effect on

---

317. The problems of the *Avitzur* agreement without the inclusion of penalty clauses are discussed *supra* text at notes 277-305.

318. See *supra* notes 306-308. Admittedly, Rabbi Riskin has taken a contrary position limiting *asmakhta* to indeterminate amounts but, for the reasons stated in note 308, this author respectfully differs.

319. Although SHULCHAN ARUCH H.M. 11:1 specifies only excommunication (*nidui*) as the sanction for contemptuous nonappearance, see *supra* note 46, it is clear from earlier authorities that alternative methods of coercion may be employed as well. See comments of BAYIT CHADASH to TUR H.M. 11 (quoting Rabbeinu Yerucham and Rashba). This result would also follow from the general principle empowering *bait din* to compel obedience to the Divine law (*kofin al hamitzvot*). See generally T.B. KETUBOT 86a.

The point being made here regarding sanctions for nonappearance should not be confused with the discussion *supra* at note 292 which focused on sanctions to compel compliance with a final judgment once a litigant has already appeared.

320. Note, too, that the inherent power of a *bait din* to compel response to its summons exists even under circumstances where it could not enforce compliance with its final judgment (*yotzee* rather than *kofin* cases). See *supra* text at notes 110-120 (definition of *kofin* and *yotzee*). Indeed, for the most part, appearance sanctions will be imposed prior to any final judgment being rendered.

321. See the position of Rabbi Riskin, cited *supra* note 308.

the validity of the *get* that is later delivered.

In short, there appears to be relatively little harm or little benefit in utilizing stipulated penalties for failure to appear. At worst, such penalties are superfluous due to their (secular) nonenforceability. At best, they may serve the moderately useful function of getting a recalcitrant spouse in front of a *bait din* who may then exercise moral pressure in getting the spouse to behave in a religiously appropriate way. Any potential *asmakhta* issues arise only to the extent a spouse seeks enforcement of the penalty. Such enforcement may very well be a violation of religious law but will have no impact on the validity of *gittin* issued by spouses as a result of their compelled appearance.[322] In any case, even this *asmakhta* problem could be avoided by leaving the penalty to be fixed by the *bait din*. Ultimately, however, penalties tied to nonappearance alone are likely to be ineffectual since they provide no guarantee that the *bait din*'s judgment will ever be carried out. Any effective penalty clause would have to cover penalties for noncompliance with the court's order as well. It is to that aspect that we now turn.

Penalties for Noncompliance/Failure to Give Get

A clause in a prenuptial or separation agreement that obligates the parties to submit to the jurisdiction of a *bait din* and in addition stipulates monetary penalties for failure to comply with the *bait din*'s decision (in lieu of or in addition to sanctions for failure to appear) may also take two forms: the designation of either a specific dollar amount, *e.g.*, $100 a day per day of noncompliance, or an indeterminate amount to be imposed by the *bait din*. As was the case with nonappearance penalties, from a secular legal perspective either version is likely to be unenforceable, the former because of common law abhorrence of penalties and forfeitures and the latter because arbitration panels - rabbinic or otherwise - are normally not empowered to impose damages on parties that fail to comply with their directives. It is the (secular) court rather than the arbitration panel which enforces the order.

From the standpoint of *halacha*, a penalty clause that is triggered as a result of noncompliance with the decision of a *bait din* will not result in an invalid *get meusah* where the decision of a *bait din* is based on *kofin*.[323] This is certainly true when the penalty is determined and imposed by the *bait din* since a *kofin* order allows the *bait din* to employ any form of coercion it desires even in the absence of an agreement to that effect. As noted above, the fact that an agreement to pay a penalty may constitute an *asmakhta* and thus, a *halachically* invalid commitment is irrelevant where this type of sanction may

322. This is not always going to be the case. Assume, for example, that a recalcitrant husband has refused to appear and becomes obligated (under secular law) to pay significant monetary penalties for his nonappearance. He then offers to execute the *get* in exchange for his wife's releasing her claim against him. Since the wife's claim is arguably *halachically* invalid under the rule of *asmakhta*, it is arguable that executing a *get* to escape its collection constitutes a *get meusah*. The point in the text is simply this: assuming the parties *do* appear in response to the *in terrorem* effect of the penalties and then issue the *get*, the *get* will not be affected by the compulsory nature of their appearance.

323. See *supra* text at notes 110-120.

be imposed by a *bait din* independently.[324] Even where the extent and nature of the penalty are self-imposed, a *get* executed to avoid its imposition would still not be a *get meusah* for, once there is an order of *kofin*, there is no *halachic* requirement that would limit coercive sanctions to those specifically authorized by the *bait din*.[325]

Such sanctions may, however, result in a *get meusah* where the order of the *bait din* is limited to the *yotzee* category.[326] Under those circumstances, the *bait din* does not have an autonomous, independent right to impose penalties. Its ability to do so, from both a secular and *halachic* standpoint, would depend entirely on the binding force of the parties' contractual undertaking. Since *halacha* does not regard those undertakings as having binding force due to the rule of *asmakhta*, any *get* that is executed to escape the imposition of such a liability would be the invalid product of duress.[327]

Thus, while penalty clauses limited to nonappearance will normally have no impact on the validity of a *get*,[328] the same benign assumption cannot be made for those penalties triggered by failure of compliance with the *bait din*'s order. These may indeed implicate the rules of *get meusah* and *asmakhta* and greatly exacerbate the *agunah*'s difficulties rather than alleviate them. Such clauses could be acceptable only if they track the *halachic* justifications for compulsion. For example, the prenuptial or separation agreement could state that the penalties are to apply "only in the event the *bait din* issues a finding warranting compulsion within the meaning of *Shulchan Aruch* E.H. 154." Given, however, the comparative paucity of such grounds as compared to the more expansive *yotzee* category,[329] the attractiveness and utility of the *Avitzur* agreement is correspondingly diminished.

---

324. *Supra* text at notes 319-320.

325. *Supra* notes 103-104. [But *cf. supra* note 103. It may still be essential that secular enforcement be predicated on an attempt to enforce compliance with the *bait din*'s directive rather than on some legal theory independent of the *bait din*'s decision. See *infra* text at note 681.]

326. See *supra* text at notes 110-120.

327. But see *supra* note 116 (view of Rabbi Herzog). If one accepts Rabbi Herzog's view, the employment of *kofin* sanctions in *yotzee* cases will not result in a *get meusah.* While Rabbi Herzog would concede that the employment of such sanctions (including the exaction of money by pressing *halachically* illegitimate *asmakhta* claims) is normally a *halachically* improper practice, he would permit the use of these sanctions in cases of grave necessity which many cases of *agunah* are. Unfortunately, Rabbi Herzog's far-reaching views have not been widely accepted and, as far as I can determine, even he never employed them in practice. Keep in mind too that in many cases, a woman may be entitled to neither a *kofin* nor a *yotzee* order. See, *e.g.*, *supra* text following note 121 (*mais alai* according to most views). Employment of an *asmakhta* sanction to obtain a *get* where no grounds exist for either order will clearly produce a *get meusah* even under the Herzog analysis.

[Note too that under the alternative analysis presented *infra* text at notes 432-452, even an illicit use of *asmakhta* will not taint a *get*.]

328. Except under the circumstances outlined in note 322.

329. See *supra* text at notes 110-120.

Once again, however, let me emphasize that the "real world" impact of *asmakhta* on *Avitzur*-type agreements will probably be minimal for the simple reason that secular courts are likely to ignore stipulated penalties in arbitration agreements and will continue to issue their own decrees of specific performance backed-up with contempt of court sanctions of fines or imprisonment. Thus, whether the agreement contains penalties or not, the mechanisms of its enforcement will be identical. In the case of a naked *get* covenant coupled with a damage remedy, the possibilities for judicial enforcement of the penalty (more accurately "liquidated damage clause") are somewhat greater but here too, to the extent the agreement is enforceable at all, the court will probably retain the freedom to formulate its own remedies. Given the state of Anglo-American law on contractual penalties, the drafters of these prenuptials have been overconfident in their ability to dictate the remedial consequences of breach and, based on that overconfidence, have compelled an examination of the law of *asmakhta*. In reality, it will be the secular court that will dictate the remedies for noncompliance, thereby making the law of *asmakhta* largely moot.

The Relationship of *Asmakhta* and *Get Meusah*

The relationship between these two concepts is fundamental and basic but often poorly understood.[330] Where the taint of *asmakhta* exists, the execution of a *get* to escape its enforcement will inevitably be a *get meusah*.[331] This is so because *asmakhta* is a *halachically* illegitimate and unenforceable claim tantamount to extortion or theft and a *get* issued under threat of extortion or theft is clearly the product of duress.[332] It is sometimes assumed, however, that since *asmakhta* leads to *get meusah*, the removal of *asmakhta* eliminates the problem of *meusah*.[333] This is absolutely not the case. The correlation of these concepts moves in one direction only. While the presence of *asmakhta* invariably means a *get meusah*, its absence affords no guarantee of validation.

To take two illustrations of this fallacy: Some have argued that the rule of *asmakhta* applies only where the amount of the penalty is indeterminate and not where there is a specific dollar amount.[334] They have accordingly recommended the adoption of a penalty clause calling for the payment of X number of dollars for every day a *get* is wrongfully withheld.[335] I have previously argued that this is a mistaken view of *asmakhta*, which applies whether or not a dollar amount is specified.[336] Nevertheless, even granting

---

330. It bears repeating that the analysis here follows the prevailing assumption in the literature. See *supra* note 313. An alternative approach is presented *infra* text at notes 432-452 in which *asmakhta* concerns are irrelevant.

331. Unless, of course, *kofin* grounds exist. See *supra* text at note 112.

332. See *supra* text at notes 73-74.

333. This is the explicit assumption of Rabbi Riskin, *supra* note 122, p. 139 and may be the implicit premise of the RCA proposal discussed *infra* text at notes 408-422.

334. *Id.*

335. The following two paragraphs specifically refer to the RCA proposal discussed *infra* text at notes 408-422.

336. *Supra* text at notes 306-308.

their premise, the *halachic* permissibility of their proposal does not follow. It is true that removal of *asmakhta* converts an illegitimate claim into an enforceable one. But it must be remembered that many authorities invalidate *gittin* issued for the purpose of avoiding monetary sanctions even where those sanctions are valid and enforceable and Rema rules that, at least in the first instance, normative practice will not allow such *gittin* to be written.[337] Making the sanction enforceable is simply not enough to overcome the Rema's directive.

A second ground often advanced for the validity of such penalty clauses misses the mark for much the same reason. It is argued that monetary sanctions for failure to execute a *get* represent reasonable compensation for pain, suffering, and emotional distress which are otherwise difficult to quantify and as such do not constitute the type of punitive penalty that the law of *asmakhta* condemns.[338] Insofar as *asmakhta* is concerned, this argument has considerable validity. Many, though not all, authorities do indeed limit *asmakhta* to noncompensatory penalties.[339] Yet, once again, the conversion of an illegitimate monetary claim to a legitimate one does not negate or obviate the ruling of Rema that no *get* should be issued in exchange for the release of monetary sanctions that are tied directly to the granting or withholding of a *get*.[340] The problem of *meusah* continues to exist unless and until circumstances exist that would justify a *bait din*'s decree of *kofin*.

Devices to Avoid *Asmakhta*

In days when marriages represented major financial commitments on the part of the families being joined, it was common to conclude an engagement with the execution of a document called *Tenayim* ("Conditions" or "Stipulations") obligating the bride and the groom to marry by a specified date and providing for a financial penalty in the event the engagement was cancelled. Enforcing such penalty clauses is on its face inconsistent with the principle of *asmakhta*. In their attempts to uphold the validity of the *Tenayim* - a device that was both widespread and perceived to be socially useful - from attack as an *asmakhta*, the great medieval authorities offered a number of solutions. Some maintain that the "penalty" is nothing more than compensation for the shame and humiliation caused to the rejected party, a very real injury

---

337. See *supra* text at note 65.

338. See *infra* text at note 408 (statement of the RCA).

339. *Supra* note 306. Note, however, that a number of authorities disagree. *Id.* Moreover, it is far from certain that a fixed dollar amount would qualify as a compensatory "liquidated damages" clause under either secular law or *halacha*. See *infra* text at notes 410-412. The point in the text, however, is that even if we *accept* the *asmakhta* argument, we still confront the Rema's ruling of *get meusah*.

340. Note, however, that to the extent a *legitimate* debt had arisen from circumstances unrelated to the granting or withholding of a *get*, the execution of a *get* in exchange for its release is not a *get meusah*. See *supra* text at notes 66-74.

that would otherwise be difficult to quantify.[341] Rambam, apparently rejecting the penalty-compensation distinction suggested by Tosafot,[342] offers as an alternative the long-standing practice of the "sages of Spain":

> When the sages of Spain wished to convey by means of *asmakhta*, they did the following: They entered into a *kinyan*[343] with [one party] that he owes his friend one hundred *dinar*. After he obligated himself they entered into a *kinyan* with his creditor that "whenever such-and-such occur or he shall do a certain act, the debt is forgiven retroactively, but if the event shall not occur or the party not perform, I will claim the money to which he has obligated himself." We acted this way in all engagement contracts between a man and his wife and in all similar matters.[344]

Put differently, the scheme works the following way. Although the rule of *asmakhta* renders conditional promissory undertakings invalid - whether those undertakings constitute penalties for non-performance or inducements to the other party to perform - the doctrine imposes no bar to a conditional release or forgiveness. *Asmakhta* precludes the creation of affirmative liability; it does not preclude the wholly-defensive use of a conditional waiver or release on the part of a beneficiary who has complied with the condition. *Asmakhta* agreements may not be swords but they may be shields.[345]

---

341. See TOSAFOT, B.M. 66a, *s.v. U'minyumi*. This, of course, corresponds almost exactly to the common law notion of upholding liquidated damages clauses if, *inter alia*, they are intended to be compensatory and actual damages are difficult to ascertain.

342. While Rambam provides no reason why he rejects Tosafot's formulation nor does he even quote it, it may be surmised that since Rambam includes all conditional monetary undertakings under the rubric of *asmakhta*, see *supra* note 306, the non-punitive nature of the sanction would simply be irrelevant.

343. "*Kinyan*" ("acquisition") means, in this context, the assumption of an obligation in accordance with the formalities of *halacha*. This is commonly done by the obligor receiving something of value, often a handkerchief, from the person to whom the promise is being made or from witnesses who are acting on that person's behalf. The obligation is incurred in exchange for the value received. The requirement of *kinyan* thus bears a close resemblance to the common law doctrine of consideration. See *infra* note 351 and generally Elon (ed.), THE PRINCIPLES OF JEWISH LAW ("Law of Obligations"). See also *infra* note 348 (*kinyan* unnecessary in promissory notes signed by promisor at least where the obligation is unconditional.)

344. Rambam, MISHNA TORAH, *Hilchot Mechira* 11:18. Rambam's device is codified in SHULCHAN ARUCH H.M. 207:16 and E.H. 50:6.

345. This distinction, implicit in Rambam's view, is expressly articulated by Ran, COMMENTARY TO T.B. NEDARIM 27b, who notes that, in any case of release, the beneficiary is already in possession of the property or funds. As such, possessory entitlements may not be subject to the defects of inadequate *gemirat* or *semikhat daat*. Indeed, as noted above, this may in fact be the reason for the validation of *me'achshav* clauses where the stipulated condition is subsequent, rather than precedent. See *supra* note 306.

This distinction, however, is not universally accepted. *Magid Mishna*

As such, conditional undertakings that would not be enforceable were they explicitly stated as such may be validated through a two-step process. Going back to the engagement contract, assume the parties want to stipulate that in the event the engagement is broken, the withdrawing party will pay the other $1000. A clause expressly providing for such a contingency would not be enforceable. But what if each party would execute an unconditional promissory note of $1000 to the other and the other would execute a release that provides in substance that in the event the marriage is consummated or the obligor was willing, ready, and able to perform, the note would be cancelled or forgiven? Each party would be in possession of two documents - a promissory note drawn on the other and a conditional release executed by the other. As such, if both parties withdraw by mutual consent, their respective claims simply cancel each other out. If party A repudiates and party B desires to go forward, party B may assert his claim based on the unconditional promissory note that A executed and A will be unable to invoke the conditional release for his benefit since he has not complied with the condition precedent to its effectiveness. Conversely, if A attempts to recover or even use as a set-off to B's claim the note executed by B, B may counter with the release executed by A since, in his readiness to perform, B has complied with the necessary conditions to the release's becoming effective. The net result is the enforceability of the penalty against the recalcitrant or repudiating party. Fascinatingly, the device developed by these sages corresponds almost exactly with a common-law mechanism that was widely employed for hundreds of years, the now-defunct penal bond.[346]

---

already notes that the device of the sages of Spain is effective only according to the "majority of opinions" and not all, and Rashi, comment to B.M. 47b expressly maintains that *asmakhta* considerations apply to releases as well as obligations. Nevertheless, it does appear to be the generally accepted rule, codified without disagreement in the authoritative codes. See SHULCHAN ARUCH H.M. 207:16 and E.H. 50:6.

346. A penal bond was an instrument under seal that took the form of a promise to pay a stated sum coupled with a provision that this obligation was null and void in the event a promised performance was rendered. Common-law courts routinely enforced the terms of penal bonds. By the 18th Century, courts of equity would enjoin collection of the bond and send the case to the law courts for a determination of actual damages. Under the rubric of "equity abhors a forfeiture" emerged the famous but still somewhat nebulous distinction between valid liquidated damages clauses and invalid penalties. See, generally, Lloyd, *Penalties and Forfeitures*, 29 HARVARD L.R. 117 (1915) for a detailed history of this development.

The distinction between the penal bond and the mechanism quoted by Rambam is formalistic. While both involve an obligation coupled with a release, the penal bond couples the obligation and the release in the same document making the punitive character of the obligation apparent on its face. In Rambam's device, the obligation and the release are separated so that the obligation does not appear on its face to be a direct penalty for breach or repudiation though, in light of the accompanying release, that is exactly what it turns out to be. Whether this conceptual distinction would be recognized by a common law court is highly questionable. See *infra* text following note 352.

Application of the Devices to the *Agunah* Problem

The Conditional Release

A number of scholars have recently suggested that Rambam's device may provide a framework for the drafting of civilly-enforceable and *halachically* valid prenuptial agreements that could effectively pressure recalcitrant spouses to give or accept a *get* without compromising the validity of a *get* so executed.[347] In its simplest form, since the *agunah* problem primarily involves recalcitrant husbands, this would call on the husband to execute an unconditional promissory note to his wife (in consideration of marriage).[348] The wife in turn would execute a release providing that the obligation should be discharged in the event the husband executes or is willing, able, and ready to execute a religious divorce. Since the promissory note is *halachically* binding and presumably legally enforceable as well, any dissatisfied wife would have substantial leverage in exacting a *get* from her unwilling husband by her ability to collect a sizable sum of money if he refuses. Conversely, no woman desirous of remaining married would attempt to sue on the note since the husband could always trigger the release by executing a *get* or (in the event she refuses to accept) by asserting his willingness to execute one.[349] To the extent significant civil liability does have

---

347. See, especially, Dick, *Is An Agreement to Deliver or Accept a Get in the Event of a Civil Divorce Halachically Feasible*? 21 TRADITION 91 (Summer 1983) and in I SEFER HAYOVEL LIKHAVOD HAGRID SOLOVEITCHIK, p. 226 and Bleich, III CONTEMPORARY HALAKHIC PROBLEMS, pp. 329-344. A critique of the Dick proposal, authored by R. Shaul Yisraeli, appears in an addendum to the Hebrew version of the Dick article.

348. There are no particular formalities that must be observed to insure that the notes are *halachically* binding. Indeed, as long as the document is signed by the promisor, it need not contain any recital of consideration nor need there be any formal *kinyan* (defined in note 343) though consideration will of course be necessary for its enforcement under common law. See generally SHULCHAN ARUCH H.M. 40:1. The same is true for releases. *Id.*, 12:8 (even *oral* releases do not require *kinyan*). But *cf. infra* note 398.

349. One minor point must be clarified. It is a well-established principle in Jewish law that any procedure that would render a *get* invalid even according to a minority opinion should not be employed *ab initio* though after the fact the recipient of such a *get* would be permitted to remarry. Some contend that since Rambam's device is not unanimously accepted, it is therefore an unacceptable way to structure prenuptial agreements to give *gittin*. This criticism is totally misplaced. Those whose opinions differ with Rambam would apply the defect of *asmakhta* to the *release*; the promissory note, on the other hand, is clearly enforceable according to all authorities. Thus, a husband who executes a *get* in order to escape enforcement of a promissory note is not responding to *illicit* pressure which would render the *get* invalid but rather to the prosecution of a wholly-legitimate claim. Nor need the husband be afraid that, because of a minority view, he may be liable even after a *get* is executed. First, insofar as civil enforcement is concerned, there is no doubt that the release would be recognized in accordance with its terms. Second, insofar as Jewish law is

a deterrent or channelling effect,[350] this proposal is quite promising.

There are a number of points that need to be considered. First, would such a promissory note be civilly enforceable? If not, then it provides little or no inducement to execute a *get*. On its face, such an undertaking lacks consideration.[351] Moreover, analysis of the transaction as a whole - a promissory note coupled with a release - suggests that the note is nothing more than a variant of the penal bond, a disguised penalty for the non-execution of a *get* and hence may be unenforceable on that ground alone. Theoretically, some of these problems could be avoided by the use of a negotiable instrument but unless the instrument is transferred to a holder in due course, the obligor [the husband] is perfectly free to raise the issues of lack of consideration and penalty as matters of affirmative defense.[352]

---

concerned, it is obvious that a plaintiff on a claim can have no cause of action based on a minority view that is not even codified in the *Shulchan Aruch* nor can a defendant even raise such a claim by way of defense. See URIM Ve'TUMIM, *Kitzur Takfo Cohen*, section 124. Thus, after the *get*, husband clearly is not subject to any liability. Since the *get* is being executed to escape the imposition of a liability that is *unquestionably valid in accordance with all opinions* - the disagreement concerning only the release - the *get* would be unquestionably valid, at least insofar as *asmakhta* is concerned though there may be other problems. See *infra* text at notes 363-369.

350. In the author's experience, the animosity and recalcitrance of many spouses is such that they would abide by a refusal to grant a *get* irrespective of the monetary or even penal sanctions that could ensue from that refusal. Indeed, even in the State of Israel where husbands are subject to imprisonment for failure to grant a *get*, there are husbands who may prefer to languish in prison. See *infra* text at note 529. The efficacy of monetary sanctions is further diminished when we consider exemption laws, bankruptcy, concealment of assets, and other techniques that could render husbands judgment-proof. See *infra* text at notes 358-360.

351. The doctrine of consideration, as traditionally formulated, requires as a condition to legal enforceability that a promise be made as part of a bargain exchange, *i.e.*, that the person to whom the promise is made confer a reciprocal benefit, incur a legal detriment, or make a return promise. As such, gift promises lacking this element of exchange are generally unenforceable. See Farnsworth, CONTRACTS (2nd ed.) §2.2, pp.43-44.

352. Depending on the particular form an instrument takes, it may be either negotiable or nonnegotiable. See UNIFORM COMMERCIAL CODE [UCC] §§3-104 through 3-113 (1990 Official Text). The principal distinction between negotiable instruments and nonnegotiable ones lies in the fact that in the former certain good-faith purchasers for value (known as holders in due course) are enabled to enforce the instrument free and clear of most, though not all, defenses that could have been asserted against their predecessors in interest. UCC §3-305(a)(1) and (b)(1990 Official Text). Thus, although a promissory note executed gratuitously is initially unenforceable since the commitment lacks consideration, if the note holder sells the note to the holder in due course, the holder acquires rights that are superior to those of his transferor. This marked exception to the rule that a transferee cannot acquire more rights than his transferor had (often referred to as the "derivative title" principle) is justified as a means of enhancing the marketability of such notes, facilitating the

Arguably, the beneficiary may argue: (1) that the obligation is executed in consideration of marriage; and (2) that it is at least formally independent of any release conditioned on the execution of a *get*. This may be especially cogent if the agreement and the release are executed at different times rather than at one sitting.[353] Alternatively (with respect to the penalty aspect), even if the agreement coupled with the release does in fact constitute a monetary sanction for non-execution of the *get*, a court may very well accept the argument that it represents reasonable compensation for the pain and suffering withholding of a *get* undoubtedly causes, the magnitude of which is difficult to calculate. Since courts have generally become more receptive to liquidated damages clauses in recent years,[354] this argument may well be accepted.[355] Moreover, the beneficiary may be able to argue that instead of construing the documents as calling for a primary performance, *i.e.*, delivery of *get*, with a backup penalty for default, *i.e.*, the note, the documents read together create two alternative methods of performance. When a contract stipulates alternative modes of performance, neither one is deemed a penalty for the non-performance of the other.[356] Finally, whether or not the clause is ultimately civilly enforceable may be somewhat beside the point. The purpose of such an agreement is not the financial benefits it confers but the pressure that it places on husbands to grant a *get* in lieu of being subject to a significant penalty. The agreement serves its primary purpose precisely when its terms are not invoked. As long as there is a substantial chance that the clause *may* be enforceable, reasonable husbands may well conclude that it is in their rational best interests to avoid the risk of a judgment.[357]

---

expansion of credit, and augmenting the currency supply. Note should also be taken of a rule promulgated by the Federal Trade Commission [FTC] that essentially bars the use of negotiable instruments in consumer transactions. See Federal Trade Commission, *Holder in Due Course Regulations*, 16 CODE OF FEDERAL REGULATIONS §§433.1-433.3. This is designed to prevent the untoward result of a consumer buying some merchandise on credit, executing a negotiable note which the merchant then transfers to a bank, and having to pay the bank as holder in due course although the goods are defective. Outside of the purview of the FTC Rule, however, negotiability is very much alive and, as indicated in the text, could conceivably be employed in the marital context.

353. See *infra* text following note 369.

354. Farnsworth, CONTRACTS (2nd ed.) §12.18, p. 938.

355. Nevertheless, the prospects for its success remain questionable. See *supra* note 308 and *infra* text at notes 410-412.

356. Essentially, this construction posits a difference between a statement that "I promise to do A and if I don't do A, I'll pay B" and "I promise to do either A or B." Admittedly, however, a jury may be highly reluctant to accept this largely semantic distinction, since regardless of the clause's phrasing, its purpose is the prevention of women languishing as *agunot*.

357. Of course, husband may call wife's bluff in which case wife may be compelled to initiate legal action on the note. In the event wife does secure a judgment, she may then offer to release the judgment in exchange for a *get*. It would appear that if executing a *get* to avoid a potential civil liability under a note is not a *meusah*, the same should be true where the judgment was already rendered. Once the judgment is rendered, it represents an absolute,

A second problem lies in the inevitable fact that even a civilly enforceable penalty does not necessarily protect the women most in need of protection. It is far from always the case that an otherwise-recalcitrant husband will grant the *get* in order to avoid a potential liability. In the first place, it costs money to bring a lawsuit and since attorney's fees are commonly not recoverable in contract actions, the husband's attitude might just be, "So sue me!"[358] (This problem can, and should be, easily solved by inserting a clause in the note obligating husband to pay costs of collection including attorney's fees.)[359] Moreover, obtaining a judgment is not the same as collecting it. All states have exemption laws, assets may be concealed or transferred, the debtor's whereabouts may be difficult to track down, *etc.*[360] Aware of the many roadblocks his spouse may face, the husband may feel he can decline to execute the *get* with relative impunity. Finally, the peculiar psychological dynamic at work in marital breakdowns, particularly among husbands who withhold *gittin* out of malice or spite, generates a kind of *kamikaze* mentality where a party might in fact be willing to incur even a devastating financial liability rather than concede the justification of the other party's request for the *get*. Nevertheless, the mere fact that a solution isn't perfect doesn't mean it isn't useful; especially in cases where a *get* is being withheld in exchange for money, such a prenuptial agreement is likely to significantly change the terms of the bargaining process.

Another problem relates to the issue of timing and manipulation. As noted earlier, it would be clearly imprudent on the husband's part to have his release conditioned on actual execution of the *get*, for that could give rise to a situation where a woman could then refuse the *get* and elect to sue on the note. Obviously, the agreement must condition release on the husband's willingness to execute a *get*, *whether or not* his wife desires dissolution. This creates the

---

unconditional debt. It is well established that any agreement to forgive an already existing debt in exchange for a *get* does not render the *get* invalid. But see *infra* text at note 399.

358. The standard rule in the United States is that, in the absence of statute or agreement, each party bears its own litigation costs and even a successful plaintiff is unable to recover attorneys' fees from a defendant in breach of contract. See A. Corbin, CONTRACTS §1037 (1950, 1991 Supp.). [This so-called "English rule" is cited and explained in *Fleischmann Distilling Corp. v. Maier Brewing Co.*, 386 U.S. 714, 717 (1967).] The rule is quite different in other countries where successful parties (plaintiffs and defendants) may often recover litigation costs. Even within the United States, there are over 100 federal statutes in areas such as civil rights, consumer protection, and antitrust where attorneys' fees will be awarded to a prevailing party. An excellent survey of this area appears in Newberg, ATTORNEY FEE AWARDS (1986, 1991 Supp.).

359. While the matter is not without dispute, most authorities would regard such a clause as enforceable under Jewish law. See *supra* note 306 (opinion of *Sefer Meirat Ainayim*).

360. A good, though somewhat dated, survey of representative exemption statutes appears in Vukowich, *Debtors' Exemption Rights*, 62 GEORGETOWN L.J. 779 (1974). The full text of the exemption laws of all fifty states and the District of Columbia appears in the Appendix to COLLIER ON BANKRUPTCY (15th ed., 1981, 1991 Supp.).

potential for husband's escaping liability by continually asserting his willingness to give a *get* but then failing to come through. Assume, for example, that husband initially refuses to give a *get*. As a result, wife initiates an action on the note. Husband alleges as a defense his present willingness to execute a *get*. Assume that the court then dismisses the action and husband refuses again. This pattern could continue indefinitely. Undoubtedly, a court could avoid this untoward result by treating the husband's refusal as irrevocable as soon as a lawsuit is commenced. A close analogy would be the area of anticipatory repudiation.[361] Although an anticipatory repudiation constitutes a present breach of contract entitling the aggrieved party to terminate and bring an action for damages, the repudiator may retract his repudiation and reinstate the contract until such time as the aggrieved party materially changes its position in reliance on the repudiation or has given notice that it considers the repudiation as final.[362] Commencement of a lawsuit seeking total damages would normally constitute such notice. While the husband's initial refusal to give a *get* does not constitute a repudiation since he is under no contractual obligation to deliver a *get*, a court by analogy could impose the same restriction on retraction once a lawsuit has been commenced. As an alternative, the court's dismissal order could be made conditional on a *get* being executed within X number of days. Under either possibility, once the wife's claim becomes absolute, her willingness to forego enforcement of the judgment is a matter of negotiation between the parties.

In any event, this particular avenue of abuse could be addressed by careful drafting of the release. The release could state, for example, that husband's obligation terminates in the event a *get* is actually executed or the husband appears before a *bait din* ready, willing, and able to execute such a *get* within X number of days after spouse formally requests either a *get* or payment on the note. That way, wife is assured that if she demands a *get*, husband must comply promptly or risk civil liability with no guarantee that he can get the case dismissed through a later promise. Husband is assured that if wife demands payment on the note, husband can escape liability by a willingness to grant a *get* even if she refuses to accept it. Once the time periods pass the obligation of the note does indeed become absolute but the incentive to execute a *get* is still present since the *get* could be offered as an inducement to forgive or compromise the judgment.

The addition of a time period coupled with a "ready, willing, and able"

---

361. The doctrine of breach through anticipatory repudiation entered the common law through the celebrated case of *Hochster v. De la Tour*, 118 Eng. Rep. 922 (Queen's Bench 1853). While its underlying reasoning has been criticized as a *non sequitur* (the court reasoned that unless aggrieved party had immediate recourse to the courts, he could take no productive steps to mitigate his damages), see Corbin, 4 CONTRACTS §960, its holding has been nearly universally accepted, the sole exception being Massachusetts, *Daniels v. Newton*, 114 Mass. 530 (1874). Note, however, that where the aggrieved party has fully performed his part of the bargain, he must await the time of performance before resorting to damages. See RESTATEMENT OF CONTRACTS (Second) §253(1) and Corbin, 4 CONTRACTS §963. *Contra*: *Pitts v. Wetzel*, 498 S.W. 2d 27 (Tex. Civ. App. 1973).

362. See RESTATEMENT OF CONTRACTS (Second) §256 and UCC §2-611.

proviso carefully defined to mean actual appearance before a *bait din* would also address the problem of the husband who does not expressly refuse to grant a *get* but simply delays implementation of the process.

A final concern is the most important of all: granted that an obligation coupled with a release creates both a *halachically* valid and probably legally-enforceable debt but a *halachically* valid penalty does not necessarily result in a *halachically* valid *get*.[363] It will be recalled that, under Jewish law, a *get* granted under compulsion or duress is generally invalid.[364] Most authorities maintain that duress is not limited to threats of death or bodily injury but includes monetary sanctions as well. At least some opinions extend this rule even to self-imposed monetary sanctions and indeed at least *ab initio* a *get* should not be executed under such circumstances.[365] Thus, Rashba rules that a *get* that is executed pursuant to an agreement imposing financial penalties in the event of its non-execution is invalid. In the proposal described above, a very similar situation exists. Husband commits himself to a monetary obligation which can only be eliminated by the execution of a *get* or at least the readiness to do so. Would not such a *get* be a *meusah*?

Professor Bleich convincingly argues that the strictures of *meusah* may be inapplicable in this type of case even according to Rashba.[366] In any marriage, Jewish law imposes financial responsibilities on a husband towards a wife that terminate upon a divorce, *i.e.*, the obligation of support. Every *get* secures the benefit of exoneration from these marital obligations. Certainly even Rashba would not taint the "run of the mill" *get* with the stigma of *meusah* since the husband retains the option of staying in the marriage with all the rights and obligations that the status implies or getting out. It is equally clear that if a husband already owes money to his wife or to a third party and the wife or her family agree to pay off or forgive the debt in exchange for a *get*, the *get* is valid although executed to escape financial sanctions.[367] The distinction between the latter cases and that of Rashba lies in the fact that in one case the obligation arose for reasons unrelated to a *get* although the *get* is now the mechanism through which the obligation can be escaped, while in Rashba's case the source of the obligation, pressure, or duress is the desire of the obligee

---

363. This point was addressed in greater detail *supra* text at notes 332-340.

364. See *supra* text at note 60.

365. See TESHUVOT RASHBA IV, no. 40; BAIT YOSEF to TUR E.H. 134:4. Those who differ with Rashba do so either on the theory that self-imposed duress cannot be defined as compulsion or that the "mere" pressure of financial penalties leaves the recalcitrant spouse with a reasonable alterative to compliance and hence cannot be regarded as "duress." *Cf.* Farnsworth, CONTRACTS (2nd ed.) §4.18, pp. 279-282 and RESTATEMENT OF CONTRACTS (Second) §175(1) ("duress must leave the victim no reasonable alternative"). See also *supra* text at notes 60-65 (self-imposed penalties) and 75-95 ("reasonable alternative" test).

366. Bleich, III CONTEMPORARY HALAKHIC PROBLEMS, pp. 337-338.

367. TASHBATZ II, no. 68 and authorities cited *supra* notes 67-68.

to secure a *get*.[368]

In determining which types of financial incentives render a *get* a product of compulsion and which do not, *halacha* distinguishes between two sorts of agreements. The release or satisfaction of an obligation arising out of matters unrelated to the execution of a *get* - and that at its inception was enforceable whether or not there was a *get* - clearly would not constitute invalidating duress since the pressure from which the *get* constitutes an escape was not generated by attempts to compel a *get*. Conversely, an obligation that is expressly conditioned on not granting a *get* is clearly in the nature of a coercive penalty for non-performance and as such not only raises the specter of *asmakhta* but renders the *get* a product of a compulsion specifically directed towards its procurement.

The obligation coupled with a conditional release falls somewhere in the middle between these two extremes. To be sure, the obligation in form is not expressly conditional. Yet both its purpose and the fact that the obligation is inextricably linked with the release from its inception may mandate that both documents be read in tandem. Viewing the transactions as an integrated whole, the promissory note is in substance, if not form, a stipulated penalty for non-performance rendering the *get* a *meusah*.[369]

One obvious solution would be to execute an unconditional obligation first, either before or after the marriage, and secure the release later rather than execute both documents simultaneously. This would indeed solve the *meusah* problem but there is no assurance that wife will ever execute the release. This creates the unacceptable risk of a wife or even fiancee (depending on when the agreement is signed) being able to sue her husband for a large sum of money whether or not he complies with a *get* demand or indeed, even if no such demand is ever made.

Professor Bleich has suggested that the parties execute two reciprocal obligations of equivalent amount with neither making mention of a *get* or a release.[370] That way, (1) the obligations that arise at their inception are indeed independent from any future decision to grant or withhold a get and (2) neither party at that point could recover from the other because the obligations cancel each other out. At a later point in time, a second pair of documents would be executed providing each party with a conditional release of the obligation held by the other.

The releases must be worded with care and precision. A properly-drafted series of agreements should achieve the following results:

1. During the marriage, neither party should be able to assert a claim against the other.
2. If both parties cooperate in granting or receiving of a *get*, the claims should be extinguished.

---

368. See *supra* note 68 for an example illustrating a similar distinction under the common law of contracts.

369. See TORAT GITTIN E.H. 134:4, who in fact takes the position that the arrangements sanctioned by the sages of Spain are adequate to surmount the *asmakhta* problem but the resulting *get* is still *meusah*.

370. Bleich, III CONTEMPORARY HALAKHIC PROBLEMS, pp. 334-35. The insight of two reciprocal notes followed by two releases is Professor Bleich's. The discussion of proper wording and potential pitfalls in the drafting of these documents is mine.

3. If the husband refuses to accede to the demand of his wife to grant a *get* within X number of days after her demand (or decision of a *bait din*, however the triggering event be defined), the husband should be liable on his note and the wife's liability extinguished.
4. If wife refuses to receive a *get* within X number of days after the husband has issued a demand (or the *bait din* has rendered its decision), the wife should be liable on her note and husband's liability extinguished.

Goals 1 and 2 may be achieved by wording that triggers both releases or neither, since in the event neither release is triggered, the mutual cross-claims are set-offs for each other. Goal 3 necessitates that where the husband is the non-cooperating party, he loses the benefit of his release while his wife gets the benefit of hers. Goal 4 requires the opposite.

While there are various ways of wording the releases to attain these results, I would suggest the following:

W's Release:

In the event W formally[371] demands that her husband give her a *get* and no *get* is executed and delivered to her, her designated agent, or a *bait din* within X number of days from the demand, her obligation is extinguished.

In determining whether X number of days have passed from the demand, any periods in which the husband is *halachically* incapable of executing or authorizing delivery of a *get* or the wife *halachically* incapable of receiving or authorizing the receipt of the *get* are excluded.

H's Release:

In the event H formally demands that his wife receive a *get* and provides her with no less than X dates to appear over a period of not less than X number of days, upon expiration of that time and her failure to appear, his obligation is extinguished. "Failure to appear" means: (1) actual nonappearance; (2) appearance with a refusal to cooperate with the proceedings; or (3) failure to notify her husband within thirty-six hours of a specified date of her intent to appear.

"Failure to appear" shall not include any failure by reason of the *halachic* incompetence of husband to execute or authorize a *get* or of wife to receive or authorize the receipt of a *get*.

I believe that reciprocal obligations coupled with these conditional releases will cover all contingencies.[372] Consider the following six possibilities:

---

371. The manner and content of the demand should be spelled out in the release.

372. The foregoing is one way of drafting the clauses. The releases make reference only to the beneficiary's demands being unmet. Thus, the husband's release is triggered upon the husband's demand being unsatisfied and the wife's release is triggered upon her demand being unsatisfied. Cases where the beneficiary meets a demand produce exoneration not by virtue of the release but by virtue of the set-off of mutual claims.

Case 1: Neither party initiates the demand for a religious divorce. The conditions for the release have not been triggered. The cross-claims in the notes effect mutual set-offs.

Case 2: Both parties consent to a *get* without invoking the formal demand mechanism. Neither release is effective; the mutual claims again cancel each other out.

Case 3: The wife makes a formal demand that her husband give her a *get* and the husband has the *get* executed and delivered to her, her agent, or the *bait din* before expiration of the time limit. Here again, neither release is effective; the claims cancel each other out.

Case 4: The wife makes a formal demand that her husband give her a *get* and the husband does not execute the *get* within the necessary time frame. At that point, the wife's release becomes effective. She automatically has the right to sue her husband on his note (for the condition to his release was not met) and he has no corresponding claim to assert as a set-off.

Case 5: Husband makes a formal demand that wife accept a *get* and designates a choice of dates for her to appear. Assuming she appears, neither release is activated; the mutual claims cancel each other out.

Case 6: Husband makes a formal demand, wife fails to appear at any of the designated dates. Here, husband's release becomes effective and the activating condition for the wife's release has not occurred. Husband may, therefore, assert recovery against wife.

It would be just as easy to draft the clauses in reverse:

W's release:

If H requests a *get* ... and W agrees within X number of days of request, she is released.

H's release:

If W requests a *get* and the husband executes within X number of days and does not rescind by X number of days, he is released.

(It will be recalled that this parallels the release that was utilized when there was only one, see *supra* text at note 347.)

While the language is sufficient for a note executed by H with a single release, this language does not work when two obligations are involved. Here, too, if neither party makes a demand, the claims cancel each other out. This language, however, is deficient for it leads to the following results:

1. If W fails to respond to H's demand, her release is ineffective and H may sue W; yet because H's release is also not effective, W has no liability because of set-off.
2. In the more important case, W demands that H execute a *get*. If H complies within time frame, he obtains a release yet ironically this could expose W to financial liability. Conversely, assume H fails to comply. While he loses the benefit of his release, W has not yet obtained the benefit of hers, with the result that the cross-claims cancel each other out.

It is not enough to grant the husband a release if he complies with the demand. The wife must obtain a release if he doesn't. As noted, however, once this latter language is included, there is in fact no need to include the release upon compliance; reliance can be placed on the cross-claims.

Problem Areas

The efficacy of the proposed language is best tested by some hypothetical problems.

Problem 1 - Retention of Incentives After Expiration of Time

Assume W issues a demand for a *get* and her demand is not met within the requisite number of days. At that point, her release is triggered extinguishing her obligation under the promissory note to H. H in turn is now unconditionally liable to W with no right of set-off. Indeed, H cannot escape his liability even if he were to execute a *get*. What incentive does H have to grant a *get* once the designated time has passed?

Answer: Although H's monetary liability to W is absolute and unconditional, W can certainly agree to release it in exchange for a *get*. Indeed, W can do so even after obtaining a judgment and receiving payment. A *get* executed in exchange for the forgiveness of an unconditional debt is clearly not a *get meusah*. Thus, although the clause creates a primary incentive to grant a *get within* the requisite time in order to avoid validation of W's release, at least a secondary incentive continues to exist afterwards. The same analysis holds true for a demand made on W when she has failed to appear.

Problem 2 - Timely Delivery to *Bait Din* with Subsequent Rescission

Assume W issues a demand for a *get*. H complies by having the *get* executed and delivered to the *bait din* within the requisite time. W is unable to receive it. H then rescinds his authorization. Under the terms of the agreement, the delivery of the *get* to the *bait din* pursuant to W's demand prevented the activation of W's release. As a result, neither party can bring any action against the other because their mutual claims cancel out. If so, what would stop H from rescinding the *get* in the event W had not yet picked it up?

Answer: The possibility of this occurring is quite rare. Even if the woman herself is unable to attend on the scheduled date, she is perfectly free to designate an agent to receive the *get* on her behalf and indeed, a member of the *bait din* could serve as her agent. Nevertheless, if it is deemed desirable to eliminate this remote possibility, language could be added to W's release providing that it will be triggered not only if a *get* is not executed within *X* number of days but also if "H rescinds or revokes a *get* so executed before it is delivered into her possession or that of her duly appointed agent." This insures that subsequent rescission will activate her release and enable a monetary recovery against H.

Problem 3 - Timely Appearance at *Bait Din*/ Later No-Show

A similar problem can arise in the less common "male *agunah*" situation. Assume H issues a demand for his wife's appearance at the *bait din* for the purpose of receiving a *get*. She appears at a designated date but H is unable to be present. She then changes her mind and refuses to come back. A literal reading of the releases appears to suggest that her initial timely appearance prevented the activation of H's release. As a result, H no longer has leverage against W; any action he could bring against her could be set off by her claim against him.

Answer: First, the "male *agunah*" problem is inherently less serious for if W consistently refuses to come to a *bait din*, the *heter meah rabbanim* may well be appropriate.[373] Second, as is the case for the wife, the inability of H to attend can be easily remedied by the designation of an agent who will insure W's receipt of the *get* the first time she shows up. Moreover, the thirty-six hour advance warning proviso, *i.e.*, the clause that states that W is deemed to "appear" only if she gives H thirty-six hours notice, insures that H will have adequate time to either free his schedule or make alternative arrangements (proxy).

Problem 4 - Incompetence of One or Both Parties

During the course of the marriage, one or both of the parties may become *halachically* incompetent to give or receive a *get*.[374] This could result in a situation where H or W issues a demand that the other could not possibly meet, obtain the benefit of a release, and then be able to bring an action on the note against the incompetent party.

Answer: As indicated in paragraph two of the releases, specific language has been added to cover this contingency. This language insures that neither release can be activated during the incompetence of either one of the parties. Both claims accordingly survive as mutual set-offs and neither party gains rights against the other.

Problem 5 - The Demand That Can't Be Met

Assume W issued a demand for a *get* that must now be forthcoming in X number of days. H is ready, willing, and able to comply but W then refuses to accept the *get* in order to retain her claim against H. Can she unilaterally prevent H from complying, thereby enabling her to trigger her release and assert a monetary claim against H?

Answer: No. W's release is effective only if the *get* is *not* delivered to the *bait din*. Since in this case it was, she remains liable on the note and any claim against her husband will be subject to set-off. (Whether in this case H could then rescind or revoke the *get* leaving W an *agunah* is identical to the question posed in Problem 2 and can be dealt with by the language therein suggested.)

Similarly, if H issued a demand to W, he cannot prevent her from compliance since her only obligation is to appear before the *bait din* and be *willing* to receive a *get*, whether or not a *get* is actually offered. Whether she could then refuse to come back is a variant of Problem 3.

Problem 6 - The Change of Heart

Sometimes, a party who gives notice may have a change of heart and

---

373. See *supra* text following note 39.

374. For the definition of incompetency in *get* proceedings, see *supra* note 29.

may later decide not to grant or receive a *get*. This may disadvantage the recipient of a notice who has either appeared when the notifying party did not or who initially failed to comply but is now desirous of granting or receiving a *get*. Many of these problems may be solved by the recipient of the initial notice invoking the notice procedure against the other party.[375]

Example One: H gives notice to W. Shortly after giving notice, H changes his mind. W appears at the *bait din* but no *get* is executed due to H's failure to appear. As indicated in Problem 5, H has not obtained his release. That alone, however, provides no protection for W since her timely appearance merely leaves both claims intact. How will W be able to secure a *get* from a now-unwilling H?

Answer: By simply sending her own notice. If H complies with the dictates of notice 2, neither party has any claim against the other. If H doesn't comply, W's release becomes activated, enabling her to pursue H free of any set-off or counterclaim. H obviously has an incentive to grant a *get*. While it is true that W can derive no advantage from H's noncompliance with *his* notice, there is nothing that precludes her from invoking *her own notice* against him.

The same analysis would hold true if W initially gave notice, change her mind before the designated appearance date, and the husband appeared. Here, too, H's protection would lie in his right to send a second notice.

Example Two: H gives notice to W. W fails to appear. At this point, H's release has been triggered. He has an absolute monetary claim against W whether or not he divorces her. She has no claim against H. If W later desires a divorce, what leverage can she bring to bear on H since H already received the benefit of his release?

Answer: W may send her own notice to H requiring him to execute a *get* within X number of days. If H complies, W's release is not triggered and she remains liable to H under the promissory note. If H fails to comply, W's release becomes activated, leaving H with nothing. Thus, the incentive to H to comply is the preservation of his monetary claim.

Example Three: W gives notice to H. H fails to respond. At this point, W's release has been triggered. She has an absolute monetary claim against H, whether he grants her a *get* or not. She continues to have leverage to obtain a *get* by the possibility of waiving her claim in exchange for a *get* (as indicated in Problem 1). H, however, has no monetary claim against W. If H later desires a divorce but W refuses to receive one (the so-called "male *agunah*" problem), what leverage does H have since W already received the benefit of her release?

Answer: As in Example Two, H is perfectly free to reinvoke the notice provisions against W. In the event W appears, she retains her monetary

---

375. The "change of heart" problems here are different from those discussed in Problems 2 and 3. There, the change of heart problem focused on the *recipient* of a notice who initially complied but then sought to prevent the granting of a *get*. Those issues were addressed by revision of the release forms to insure that subsequent non-cooperation would trigger the *notifier's* release, thereby putting pressure on the recipient to cooperate. In this section, the focus is on the change of mind on the part of the *notice sender* and the extent to which such a change could leave the *recipient* without protection. Here the solution is considerably simpler and necessitates no revision at all of the release forms; all that is required is that the recipient send a notice of his/her own.

claim against H. In the event she fails to appear, H's release is activated and W's claim is extinguished. The incentive for cooperation continues to be present.

Problem 7 - The Double Failure

Assume that either W or H initiates notice and the other party fails to appear. Assume further that both parties later have a reversal of heart and the previously-recalcitrant spouse now desires a *get* while the spouse previously willing has now become recalcitrant. The now-willing spouse sends notice to the other party, as indicated in the preceding two examples. What if, however, the recipient of the *second* notice fails to comply? At this point, all incentives for future cooperation have broken down.

For simplicity, let us assume H sent notice 1 to which W failed to respond. At that point, H's release is triggered giving him a claim against W. If W is later desirous of a *get* from H, she too can send H notice. H's failure to respond to notice 2 triggers W's release. At the point of double failure, both releases have been activated. Neither party has any claim against the other. There is no longer any continuing mechanism to enable one party to obtain a *get* over the recalcitrance of the other.

One response to this problem might be that it is so remote that the risk of its occurrence could be safely ignored. Another approach might be the drafting of a clause to the effect that in the event both releases would otherwise become activated, they are rendered null and void with the result that the reciprocal note obligations become reinstated. This effectively allows the game of notice and counternotice to be played indefinitely and maintains the pressure of compliance on both parties.

****

As complicated as all this may sound, keep in mind the essential simplicity of the proposal. A total of four documents must be executed: two reciprocal promissory notes[376] and two reciprocal releases. The notes can be as simple as signed IOU's and the releases need only contain the two short paragraphs suggested above. While four documents may appear to be cumbersome, the advantage of this procedure lies in its ability to create financial incentives to grant a *get* upon demand that, first, do not run afoul of the twin principles of *get meusah* and *asmakhta* and, second, do not require the prior determination of a *bait din* that circumstances exist that warrant compulsion (*kofin*).[377] As such, even a slightly cumbersome expedient is worthy of serious consideration.

Whatever the precise wording, the notion of duplicate promissory notes to be followed by the later execution of conditional releases not only avoids the defect of *meusah* by separating any linkage that would otherwise exist between the imposition of a financial penalty and the granting of a *get* but also affords a modicum of protection for those husbands who desire to grant a *get* but are unable to remarry because of the refusal of their wives to cooperate (the small

---

376. See *supra* note 348 (formalities unnecessary).

377. See *supra* text at notes 60-74 (discussion of *get meusah*) and notes 110-120 (definition of *kofin* and *yotzee*). This is so because the incentive to give or receive a *get* derives from a desire to escape a technically-unrelated, independently-generated financial obligation.

but significant "male *agunah*" problem). To the extent monetary sanctions influence conduct, this arrangement effectively facilitates the obtaining of a divorce at will by either party.[378]

THE USE OF PRENUPTIAL SUPPORT AGREEMENTS*

Another relatively-simple device of indirectly encouraging the granting of a *get* is the drafting of a prenuptial support agreement. Under Jewish law, a husband is obligated to provide his wife with support either in kind (food, clothing, lodging) or in money.[379] Although this general obligation is spelled out in the *ketubah*, it is *halachically* mandated and exists independently of any written document.[380] Claims for spousal support were enforceable during the life of the marriage based on the *bait din*'s determination of custom, the standards to which the particular woman is accustomed (both pre- and post-

---

378. One further qualification should also be noted. For the reasons developed at length *supra* text at notes 87-95, it may be important that even commitments that are not directly linked to a *get* and are ostensibly independent leave the recalcitrant party with at least the possibility of complying with the sanction instead of granting the *get*. This would mean that the stipulated sum should be an amount that the husband would be able to pay albeit with extreme hardship. (See also *supra* note 82 where I argue that, as a matter of logic, this should not be strictly necessary but may be an appropriate precaution to insure validity of the *get*.)

*Once again, it may be helpful at this point for the reader to refer to the outline of *get meusah* law that appears *infra* text at notes 453-473.

379. See SHULCHAN ARUCH E.H. 70. The Talmud discusses whether such obligation was Biblical in nature (derived from EXODUS 21:10) or was a later rabbinic enactment, see T.B. KETUBOT 47b, and the later authorities are in disagreement. See CHELKAT MECHOKEK and BAIT SHMUEL to E.H. 69:1-2.

380. It should be noted that the husband's obligation to support his wife is not absolute. If a wife unjustifiably deserts or abandons her household, she forfeits her right to support even prior to receiving a *get*. See SHULCHAN ARUCH E.H. 70:12 (Rema) and *supra* text following note 121 (discussion of *moredet*). Indeed, even if the husband was the one who abandoned the household, he may be absolved of support duties if his leaving was triggered by her unjustifiable misconduct. See Shareshevsky, DINAI MISHPACHA, p. 139. [This is similar to the American doctrine of "constructive desertion," see Clark, 2 THE LAW OF DOMESTIC RELATIONS IN THE UNITED STATES §14.3, pp. 16-17 (Practitioner's ed. 1987).] Conversely, however, if the wife abandoned the household for "reasonable cause," she does not forfeit her right to support. Moreover, the "cause" need not rise to the level of *kofin*; even grounds that could not compel a *get* might warrant temporary abandonment. See Shareshevsky, p. 139 (example of husband's parents or other relatives living in the couple's home). Interestingly, while the husband must support his wife in such cases, he need not bear the extra expenses of a dual residence. See TESHUVOT MAHARIT I, no. 113.

marriage), and the cost of living in that particular locale.[381] Once a marriage has been terminated by divorce, however, *halacha* recognizes no continuing support obligations outside of the relatively-paltry one time *ketubah* payment of 200 *zuz* and any other additional sums voluntarily assumed. Alimony in the sense of continuing support is an institution unknown to the *halacha*.[382]

In the State of Israel, as part of their broad authority over questions of personal status, rabbinic courts have jurisdiction to adjudicate support claims to this very day.[383] A common practice employed by these courts when faced with the specter of a recalcitrant husband refusing to give a *get* is to enter a money judgment for an unusually high level of support, *e.g.*, $250 a day.[384] Since the only way the support obligation can be terminated is through dissolution of the marital bond, this judgment creates significant pressure to execute a *get*.[385]

This approach appears questionable for a number of reasons. First, it is unclear that the imposition of a money judgment has a significant deterrent or channelling effect because of exemption laws, concealment of assets, and the like.[386] Especially if the judgment is clearly beyond the husband's capacity to pay, it may not carry any weight.[387] Second, since only husbands are *halachically* responsible for the support of their wives and not vice-versa, the proposal does nothing to alleviate the plight of the small, but significant, number of men who are unable to remarry because of their wives' refusal to accept a *get*.

Most critical of all, there is a distinct possibility that a *get* executed in order to escape an unreasonably exorbitant support obligation would be *halachically* invalid as a *get meusah*. An inordinately-high support obligation not based on need, prevailing custom, or prior standard of living appears to be

---

381. See Shareshevsky, DINAI MISHPACHA, pp. 117-125. In addition to, or in lieu of, her ability to obtain a judgment ordering payment of support, a wife could also petition the *bait din* to order the husband to execute a *get*, at least on a *yotzee* level. See *supra* text at note 108.

382. A widow, however, does have a right to be supported from the property of her late husband's estate until such time as she either remarries or elects to collect her *ketubah*. See T.B. KETUBOT 52b and SHULCHAN ARUCH E.H. 93:3.

383. See Shareshevsky, DINAI MISHPACHA, pp. 10-15.

384. Note, however, that the Israeli *secular* courts have not always been supportive of this approach. See *infra* text at note 526.

385. For a discussion of these precedents, see Ellinson, *Siruv Latet Get* 69 SINAI 135 (Tammuz-Sivan 5731). For earlier precedents utilizing the imposition of support obligations as a mechanism to indirectly compel a *get*, see BAIT MEIR E.H. 154:1 and NACHALAT SHIVA 9:14. A more recent endorsement of this approach appears in 2 OTZAR HaPOSKIM (Appendix), pp. 8-16 [Opinions of Chief Rabbis Herzog and Uziel] and in Gartner, *L'Takkanat Agunot* (Heb.), *For the Benefit of Agunahs*, 16 MORIAH 79 (Iyar 5748/1988.)

386. See *supra* note 360.

387. In any event, it would not be proper for the agreement to stipulate a sum beyond the husband's ability to pay because of the reasons stated *infra* text at note 399 (reasonable alternative test).

nothing more than a disguised penalty for the non-execution of a *get*.[388] Although *batei din* do have the authority to impose coercive sanctions including incarceration and corporal punishment, this is true only in specially-defined circumstances.[389] Without those conditions, even court-imposed penalties could render the *get* invalid.[390] While there is considerable disagreement over what

---

388. It is true that executing a *get* in order to escape a support obligation should normally pose no problem of *get meusah*; such obligations are independent duties arising from the marital relationship and have no direct connection with the withholding of a *get* although the granting of a *get* operates to terminate these duties. See *supra* notes 66-68 (discussion of independently-generated sanctions). Indeed, if the contrary were the case, all *gittin* could be tainted as *meusah* since every *get* has the effect of relieving the husband of his duty of support. Nevertheless, the same benign assumption cannot be made where the support order is clearly in excess of support needs and functions in the nature of a disguised penalty. Technically, the *halachic* defect in such cases may be identified in two distinct ways: (1) a support order in excess of support needs is a *halachically* illegitimate claim and a *get* that is executed to escape the imposition of a *halachically* illegitimate sanction is a *get meusah* even if the sanction is independently generated; (2) alternatively, the fact that the order is in excess of support needs makes it transparently obvious that it is being employed with the intention of procuring a *get* and is therefore not an independently generated sanction.

Which alternative more accurately describes the *halachic* defect depends on how one construes the ruling of Tashbatz, the source of the distinction between legitimate and illegitimate claims. See *infra* text at notes 432-452. For purposes of the case in the text, however, the characterization chosen is irrelevant since the *get* would be invalid under either alternative. Note too that even Ranach who rejects the legitimate-illegitimate distinction, *infra* note 437, would apparently invalidate *gittin* where the imposition of the sanction was expressly for the purpose of securing a *get*.

In spite of the above analysis which, to this author at least, appears quite convincing, it cannot be denied that there is indeed recent and eminent *halachic* authority that seems to uphold the validity of such sanctions even where exorbitant. See *infra* note 392 (responsa of R. Moshe Feinstein).

389. See *supra* text at notes 110-120 (*kofin* and *yotzee* distinction).

390. Although Rema rules that a *get* executed to avoid self-imposed monetary sanctions is valid after the fact, this may be true only where the penalty is self-imposed. Where the penalty is ordered by a court or *bait din* (and the circumstances do not justify *kofin*), even Rema might concede that the *get* is a *meusah* even after the fact. See *supra* text at note 65. In any case, even if Rema's view is taken to mean that threat of monetary sanctions never produces an invalid *get meusah* (because the ability to pay money in lieu of a *get* is regarded as a "reasonable alternative"), it is still true that such *gittin* should not be written or procured in the first instance. See generally the discussion *supra* notes 76-86.

Of course, nothing would prevent the *bait din* from using support obligations to coerce the husband to come to *bait din*, *i.e.*, as an appearance sanction, but this is not the same as a penalty that can be avoided only by an execution of the *get*. *Cf. infra* text at notes 642-644 (how a penalty could be structured to avoid *get meusah* problems).

those circumstances might be, by hypothesis the "support obligation" theory is utilized when coercion is no longer a *halachically* acceptable option. By taking into account factors that are extraneous to the general determination of support, however, the support order itself becomes a *de facto* penalty, thereby rendering it ineffective.[391] This is especially true where the order conditions the amount payable on compliance with a *bait din* or makes specific reference to a *get*, *e.g.*, the amount increases for every week husband refuses to give a *get*.[392]

---

391. Yet another "problem" with this approach is the fact that the "support obligation" theory could not be employed at all under circumstances where a woman is not *halachically* entitled to support. See *supra* note 379. In such cases, the "support obligation" is even more obviously a penalty to coerce a *get*. The problem, however, is largely illusory since the rabbinical courts in Israel do not purport to impose "support obligations" in cases where they do not *halachically* exist. Indeed, in cases of unjustifiable abandonment of household, *halacha* tends not to favor the right of a woman to obtain a divorce. See *supra* text at notes 127-130 (majority view of Rabbeinu Tam; *contra*, view of Rambam). Thus, the inability to utilize this mechanism in cases where no support obligation exists is not necessarily regarded as a problem.

Whether this "problem" could be addressed by contract is discussed *infra* text at note 402.

392. Thus, judgments that impose a two-tiered alimony award, see *Brett v. Brett*, *infra* note 491, are *halachically* problematical even apart from the fact that those awards are promulgated by secular tribunals rather than *batei din*. See also *infra* text at notes 665-668 (discussion of DRL §236B).

The argument in the text asserts that "support obligations" not tied to actual support needs should be treated as penalties for purposes of *get meusah* regardless of their formal designation. There are two important responsa of Rabbi Moshe Feinstein that bear on this issue and that may suggest a contrary approach.

A. The 1959 Letter: In a responsum dated 5719 (1959), Rabbi Feinstein dealt with the following situation: a husband and wife were civilly divorced and the husband was ordered by a court to pay alimony. Failing to meet those obligations, the husband was imprisoned. The wife then agreed to drop her alimony claim (for arrearages) and procure his release if he would execute a *get* which he did. Was this a *get meusah*? Rabbi Feinstein ruled that it was not and such a *get* could be executed even *ab initio*. See IGROT MOSHE E.H. I, no. 137.

Although the responsum validates a *get* given in exchange for a support obligation, its holding does not undercut the analysis in the text and indeed supports it. In validating the *get*, Rabbi Feinstein made two primary points: (1) the sanction of imprisonment was not imposed for the purpose of procuring a *get* but rather to compel payment of a support claim (indeed insofar as the court was concerned, the granting or withholding of a *get* was simply irrelevant); and (2) under the facts of the case (husband effectively refused to cohabit with his wife), the wife was *halachically* entitled to support so that the claim being asserted (from which the *get* effected a release) was legitimate. Thus, both the "legitimacy" prong and the "intention" or "independence" prong were satisfied, neither of which is true where a *bait din* orders exorbitant support for the very purpose of compelling a *get*. See *supra* note 388. The basic ruling is thus relatively non-controversial. See also *infra* text at notes

432-452 (it is questionable whether legitimacy is in fact a separate prong).

Nevertheless, the responsum does make a number of innovative points. First, it recognizes the *halachic* legitimacy of a support order (at least for the secondary purposes of *get meusah*) even though the order was not issued, nor the amount determined, by a *bait din*. Rabbi Feinstein rejected the argument that, because the secular court may have imposed a higher level of support than *halacha* requires, the debt (or at least the excess) becomes illegitimate. He argued that, generally speaking, the sums awarded by a secular court would be no more than a *bait din* would impose and if there is a differential, it would in most cases be so minor that it could not constitute a source of duress or compulsion. (But *cf. Teshuvot Maharit*, *supra* note 380, which seems to undercut this point; under secular law, expenses of dual residence are commonly recoverable.) While R. Feinstein's ruling permitting the bypass of a *bait din* appears highly problematical, his analysis confirms by implication that a truly exorbitant level of support would indeed be an illegitimate claim, as stated in the text. (There is also a suggestion at the beginning of the responsum, though it is not developed, that *halacha* may recognize the legitimacy of support orders issued by secular courts even if the amounts would differ significantly from those ordered by a *bait din* under the principle of *dina d'malchuta dina* ["the law of the land is the law"], see *infra* note 637. Ironically, however, while this rubric might validate *nonhalachic* orders of secular tribunals, it would not sustain the validity of an exorbitant support order issued by a *bait din* in the State of Israel which is bound *both by Israeli and Jewish law* to follow *halacha* in support matters. See *infra* text following note 511. Thus, the point in the text remains unaffected.)

Another interesting, and more troubling, point is the fact that the husband granted the *get* not merely for the purpose of escaping a monetary obligation but in order to secure his release from prison. By focusing exclusively on the legitimacy of the monetary order, the responsum fails to address whether imprisonment - which, after all, is not a *halachically* recognized sanction - may render the *get meusah* even when the underlying monetary claim is valid. See *supra* text at notes 72-74. (It is possible, however, that, on the basis of the principle *kofin al hamitzvot*, see *supra* note 319, imprisonment may in fact be *halachically* legitimate as well. It is also possible that the imprisonment may be legitimized under *dina d'malchuta dina*.)

These reservations should not obscure the limited scope of R. Moshe's ruling. To reiterate, the decision validating the *get* is limited to women who are *halachically* entitled to support, to amounts that are not greatly in excess of those that a *bait din* (considering only support-related factors) would order, and to circumstances where neither the payment nor the imprisonment were imposed for the purpose of procuring a *get*. These qualifications are fully consistent with the views expressed in the text.

B. The 1979 Letter: A second responsum poses somewhat greater difficulty. In a 1979 letter sent to a rabbi in Johannesburg, South Africa, Rabbi Feinstein ruled that if a secular court orders the payment of a certain level of support until a *get* is executed and the husband grants a *get* to escape this higher monetary sanction, the *get* is not a *get meusah*. Moreover, this is true even in circumstances where, *under halacha*, he has no support obligation because of her retention of her earnings. See IGROT MOSHE E.H. IV, no. 106. Unfortunately, the responsum contains no explanation of its reasoning but seems to depart from the 1959 letter in two major respects. First, it apparently validates the use of support orders even when they are imposed for the purpose of compelling a *get* (*e.g.*, a two-tiered support order such as 2 X dollars before *get*, only X dollars afterwards). Second, it allows the utilization of such sanctions even where women have no *halachic* entitlement to support.

It is not at all clear why the *get* should be valid under these circumstances. Such an arrangement fails both the prong of "intent" and the prong of "legitimacy" (unless *dina d'malchuta dina* somehow enters here as well). Even if one adopts the position that where the sanctions are merely monetary, the *get* is valid after the fact on the theory that payment always constitutes a "reasonable alternative," see discussion *supra* text at notes 76-83, at the very least Rema prohibits the writing of such a *get ab initio*. *Supra* text at note 84-85. Yet Rabbi Feinstein validates such a *get* even in the first instance.

A number of alternative possibilities suggest themselves:

(1) Rabbi Feinstein may be adopting a formalist position, *i.e.*, as long as a sanction is designated in the nature of marital support it is *halachically* deemed independent regardless of actual intent or motivation.

(2) The judgment in question must be tied to the decision of a *bait din* ordering the granting of a *get* on a *kofin* level in which case compulsion poses no problem. (There is, however, absolutely no hint of such a qualification in the letter.)

(3) The judgment in question must be tied to the decision of a *bait din* ordering the granting of a *get* even on a *yotzee* level but, for purposes of *get meusah*, the two categories (*kofin* and *yotzee*) may be treated equivalently. See *supra* note 116 (opinion of Rabbi Herzog). (Once again, there is no indication that the judge's order must be connected to any type of decision of a *bait din*.)

(4) Given the presumption that whatever a secular court orders will normally not be substantially higher than what *halacha* would impose - an assumption already made in the 1959 letter - the support obligation imposed by the court is treated equivalently to a (need- related) support obligation imposed by a *bait din*. Since it is undisputed that granting a *get* to escape a (need-related) support obligation of a *bait din* does not produce a *get meusah*, responding to the court's order will produce the same result. In other words, the subjective intention of the coercer to procure a *get* is irrelevant where the same (or substantially the same) pressure would or could legitimately exist without any attempt to procure a *get*. (Unfortunately, this analysis does not cover the case where the wife has no *halachic* claim for support and yet R. Moshe validates the use of support orders even there.)

(5) The judge's order stipulates higher support until the husband submits to the jurisdiction of the *bait din*. In other words, the support order functions as a penalty to compel appearance, rather than the actual execution of a *get*. As noted previously, appearance penalties raise no problems of *get meusah* even under circumstances where direct coercion on a *get* would be prohibited. See *supra* notes 314-322. Unfortunately, that is not the type of order R. Moshe describes; in order to convert the court's order into the equivalent of an appearance penalty, the wife would have to execute an unconditional release of arrearages prior to the *get* even being written. See *infra* text at note 640. This is a qualification at which the responsum does not even hint.

In sum, we lamentably lack clear guidance as to the precise meaning of this ruling. The first interpretation is the only one that fits the wording of

A final consideration is the fact that under *halacha*, in exchange for supporting his wife, the husband is entitled to his wife's earnings.[393] While the wife has the exclusive option to forego support and elect to keep her earnings,[394] she cannot press a support claim and at the same time hold on to her own money. In effect, then, any support claim she asserts would have to be reduced by the amount of earnings she collected that rightfully belonged to her husband, *i.e.*, the husband would assert his rights by way of set-off or counterclaim. In the event her earnings exceeded her support claim, she would have no claim at all though in that case she would simply forego support.

The basic structure of this proposal, however, can be easily modified to satisfy at least some of these objections. First, while *halacha* mandates a certain minimum level of support, there is nothing that prevents the parties from agreeing to a higher level.[395] Second, *halacha* recognizes the power of

---

the letter but it is precisely its elevation of form over substance that is the most problematical from a *halachic* standpoint. The other interpretations are consistent with the majority of *halachic* authorities but depend on conditions and qualifications not present in the responsum.

With respect to the issue of exorbitant support orders issued by rabbinical courts - the problem raised in the text - the first interpretation would support their use, contrary to the conclusion therein stated. The other interpretations would not. At best, then, R. Moshe's rulings are equivocal. The conclusion that the practice is at least "questionable" remains a reasonable supposition.

393. SHULCHAN ARUCH E.H. 80:1 codifying the rule of T.B. KETUBOT 59b.

394. SHULCHAN ARUCH E.H. 69:3.

395. The ability of a husband to obligate himself to a higher level of support than a *bait din* would otherwise impose seems well-established. Support obligations during a marriage are generally treated the same as the post-dissolution obligation of *ketubah*. See, e.g., T.B. KETUBOT 54b (*t'nai ketubah k'ketubah*). It would therefore follow that just as a husband may obligate himself to pay a *tosefet* over and above the statutory minimum of 200 *zuz* so too may he obligate himself to support his wife at a level higher than that required by *halacha*. See also SHULCHAN ARUCH E.H. 114:1 (husband may voluntarily assume the support of his wife's children from a prior marriage). Indeed, according to the vast majority of *halachic* authorities, one may assume support obligations even towards unrelated persons, at least if the monetary amount is fixed and determinate. See SHULCHAN ARUCH H.M. 60:2 and comments of SIFTAI COHEN [SHACH] and SEFER MEIRAT AINAYIM [SEMA] (discussing view of Rambam who would deny the enforceability of an indeterminate support obligation towards an unrelated person but who would concede the enforceability of a promise to pay a fixed amount, *e.g.*, $150 a day, even over an indeterminate period of time).

This relatively straightforward conclusion, however, is complicated by one additional problem. As structured in the text, the support obligation is not absolute but conditional: "I will pay $150 a day only for the days that we do not share bed and board." Any undertakings that are not absolute in form raise the problem of *asmakhta*. Once again, to the extent an agreement is tainted with *asmakhta*, not only is its enforcement tantamount to theft but the execution of a *get* to escape such enforcement results is a *get meusah*. See *supra* text at

the husband to renounce all claim to his wife's earnings.[396] Putting these two

---

notes 72-74 and 313. [But *cf. infra* text at notes 432-452 (alternative analysis under which *asmakhta* does not produce a *get meusah*)]. According to the opinions which limit *asmakhta* to penalty clauses, there is of course no problem. See *supra* note 306. Yet there are other opinions that apply *asmakhta* to virtually any type of conditional undertaking. Why then should support obligations be treated any differently? Indeed, the same question may be raised regarding the *tosefet* of a *ketubah* which, despite its conditional nature, is obviously not subject to the taint of *asmakhta* for otherwise, it could never be enforceable.

Perhaps one may suggest the following: it is clear that *asmakhta*, a doctrine that imposes limits on the enforceability of voluntary undertakings, has no application to duties that are mandated by *halacha* irrespective of agreement. Thus, the statutory duty of 200 *zuz*, although contingent on the death of the husband or his divorcing his wife, cannot be invalidated by reason of *asmakhta* since its enforceability is not predicated on *gemirat daat*. See *supra* note 306. By the same token, the enlargement, expansion, or liquidation of preexisting *halachic* duties may in a sense not be regarded as the creation of new duties under contract but as an amplification of an existing statutory duty that is already in place. Thus, even though the expanded scope of the obligation is indeed voluntarily assumed, it is subject to the same immunity from *asmakhta* as the underlying obligation to which it is being assimilated. (Admittedly, this analysis does not address the issue of *gemirat daat* and how such "assimilation" provides it.)

The characterization of self-assumed support obligations as an extension of an existing duty rather than the creation of a new one appears particularly appropriate where the commitment merely specifies a dollar amount (or waives the right to earnings) for a spouse to whom an obligation of support already exists. It can also be stretched to include support for spousal dependents on the theory that, on some level, such support is essentially an increase of maintenance for one's own spouse. Whether such an analysis could embrace a support obligation under circumstances where *halacha* does not impose any support obligation at all, *e.g.*, a deserting wife, appears questionable. While such a duty could indeed be assumed, it would apparently remain subject to the laws of *asmakhta* to the extent of its conditionality. The implications of this conclusion are spelled out *infra* note 402.

The notion of new obligations being extensions of preexisting ones is not foreign to the common law though the issue arises in a different context. Thus, promises to pay a debt, the collection of which was barred by the statute of limitations or a discharge in bankruptcy, were historically enforceable notwithstanding the lack of new consideration on the theory that the promise merely revived the old debt and did not create a new one. See, *e.g.*, *Little v. Blunt*, 26 Mass. 488 (1830) (statute of limitations) and *Stanek v. White*, 215 N.W. 784 (Minn. 1927) (discharge in bankruptcy). But *cf.* RESTATEMENT OF CONTRACTS (Second) § 82, Comment *c* (criticizing the use of "revival" language and suggesting that the better approach is to simply enforce the new promise as an exception to the consideration doctrine). See also 11 U.S.C. § 524 (c)-(d) (limitations on the enforceability of promises to pay a debt discharged in bankruptcy).

396. SHULCHAN ARUCH E.H. 80:18.

ideas together, the parties could enter into a prenuptial agreement stipulating a high level of marital support for the periods of time that they don't share "bed and board," perhaps a figure of $500 a week coupled with a waiver of the husband's claim to earnings.[397] The agreement should further stipulate that it remains in effect only as long as the parties are *halachically* married; the designated amount is not designed to function as post-dissolution alimony but as spousal support. Because the agreement would be limited to *marital* support, it automatically ceases to be operative upon the granting of a *get* and therein lies its effectiveness as an incentive.[398]

Additional points to keep in mind:

1. The amount stipulated should not be unreasonably high or totally beyond the ability of the husband to pay. If the husband is left with no possible alternative but the granting of a *get*, some authorities would consider the *get* coerced. If, on the other hand, the stipulated sum is capable of being paid, the husband's decision to give a *get* in lieu of payment is considered to be a voluntary act.[399]

---

397. The text articulates a shift from a court [*bait din*] - imposed support obligation to a contractual one. In both, the efficacy of the sanction does not depend on the existence of grounds that would justify a *kofin* order. The superiority of the contract approach is three-fold: (1) it avoids the problem of the apparent penalty, *i.e.*, support amounts not truly pegged to support, since there are no limits as to how high one may obligate himself contractually; (2) it precludes the reduction of a support claim by the wife's earnings; and (3) it operates as an effective device even in settings where court-ordered support will typically not generate *get* incentives, *e.g.*, the United States where spousal support after a civil divorce generally does not vary before or after a *get* [but *cf. infra* text at note 613 (discussion of DRL § 236B)]. Conceivably, a contract approach may have yet another advantage in protecting women who *halachically* are no longer entitled to support but for the reasons stated *infra* note 402, this may not be an available option.

398. Needless to say, the agreement must be executed with all requisite *halachic* formalities including *kinyan*, *i.e.*, the handing over of some object of symbolic barter to the promisor, to insure the agreement's *halachic* validity. See *supra* note 343 (definition of *kinyan*). If a support agreement is *halachically* invalid, a *get* given to escape its secular enforcement may be tainted as *meusah*. See *supra* text at notes 72-74. [But see *supra* text at note 392 (validation of support orders issued by secular tribunals) and *infra* 432-452.]

Although *kinyan* is normally not necessary for obligations incurred by a promissory note, see *supra* note 348, because the obligation here is conditional rather than absolute (covering only times of separation) a *kinyan* should be employed. See SHULCHAN ARUCH H.M. 40:1 and comment of SIFTAI COHEN [SHACH] at subparagraph 4. See also *infra* Appendix A, note 12.

399. Technically, since separation agreements are specifically enforceable, the husband has three options: payment, *get* or imprisonment. To the extent payment is a reasonable alternative, execution of a *get* to escape incarceration is not a *get* executed under duress. To the extent payment is not a reasonable alternative, the *get* is. The concept of "genuine choice" is developed by

2. The amount stipulated should bear some reasonable relationship to support, albeit pegged at a higher standard than that to which the spouse may be accustomed. The agreement should contain a recital that it is designed to afford the spouse the option to pursue a comfortable lifestyle including travel, hotels, restaurants, and entertainment.
3. The amount stipulated should not be conditional on compliance with a *bait din* or the granting of a *get*. It should not provide, for example, that if the husband complies with the directive of the court within two weeks, the support claim is X and for every week of delay, it increases to 2X.[400] Linkage of the support obligation to compliance with a *bait din*'s order makes it strongly resemble a penalty for non-compliance which affects the validity of the *get*. By contrast, where it is a straight, unvarying lump-sum, the obligation is nothing more than a liquidation of a generalized statutory duty of support. Since every *get* terminates this duty, giving a *get* to escape a support obligation raises no problem of *meusah*.
4. The agreement should cover not only periods following a civil divorce before a *get* is granted but any period of time that the parties are separated for reasons of marital discord whether or not pursuant to legal separation or even for prolonged separate vacations. Having the agreement apply to a whole range of circumstances other than the *agunah* case underscores the fact that the clause does not exclusively function as a penalty for the failure to execute a religious divorce.[401]
5. The agreement should contain a clause providing that husband waives his right to his wife's earnings for any period of time that the obligations of the agreement are triggered. This insures that husband cannot reduce or eliminate his liability through set-off.
6. For the husband's own protection, the agreement should specify that his obligation ceases upon execution and delivery of a *get* to a *bait din*. This insures that the wife will not be able to "keep the meter running" by refusing to accept a *get*.
7. The agreement should further provide that the obligation shall

---

TESHUVOT MABIT II, no. 138. But *cf.* TESHUVOT MABIT I, no. 22. See also *supra* text at notes 75-95, especially note 82 which points out that the "reasonable alternative" test may be of greater significance in support obligations than in other monetary commitments.

400. But see *Brett v. Brett*, a British case discussed *infra* text at note 491. In light of the above, the approach adopted by *Brett* raises *halachic* questions. See also *infra* text at notes 665-666 (discussion of DRL §236B). But see *supra* note 392 (responsa of R. Moshe Feinstein).

401. But *cf. supra* note 392 (possibility that, in view of R. Moshe Feinstein's 1979 ruling, such a qualification may be unnecessary but since the meaning of the ruling is in itself unclear, inclusion of such a limitation is highly desirable).

> not apply for any period of time that the wife has forfeited her *halachic* right to support due to unjustifiable misconduct, *e.g.*, desertion, with the existence of this misconduct to be defined and determined by a specifically-designated *bait din* whose determination shall be conclusive.[402]

The foregoing insures that the agreement is *halachically* acceptable and removes the taint of coercion from any resulting *get*. Not all men will respond to indirect monetary sanctions but undoubtedly some will. Moreover, on some level, utilization of support agreements may be more effective than other type of penalties since the benefits flow directly to the aggrieved spouse. While a truly spiteful husband might well prefer incarceration or a large fine to granting his wife a *get*, it is doubtful that he would regard paying his wife a large sum of money in the same favorable light. Admittedly, this type of agreement does not assist the victimized husband whose wife refuses to accept a *get*. At best, he is relieved of his contractual support obligation but has no affirmative claim against his wife. Nevertheless, victimized husbands are a minuscule part of the problem and in many cases have alternatives not available to women.[403]

This proposal is as easily adaptable in the United States as it is in Israel. Anglo-American law, however, poses two unique difficulties. First, in

---

402. In theory, such an agreement could even extend to circumstances where, under *halacha*, a wife has forfeited her right to support. See *supra* note 380. Nevertheless, because the agreement as structured is not absolute but rather conditional or contingent on the parties having separate "bed and board," it arguably raises an *asmakhta* problem at least according to some authorities. While this poses no difficulty with respect to spouses to whom there is a *halachic* obligation of support, see *supra* note 395, *asmakhta* might taint that portion of the agreement that extends to women who have no such right. A *get* that is given to escape the operation of the clause under those circumstances may thus constitute a *get meusah*. The suggested language in the text avoids this risk. (There is an irony in negating *asmakhta* by making the agreement *more conditional* than it would otherwise be but this appears to be a necessary consequence of the distinction drawn in note 395.)

Unfortunately, by introducing considerations of fault, justifiable conduct *etc.*, the support obligation loses some of its force and potential effectiveness as a spur for action. To insure that husband does not utilize the "abandonment" clause as an excuse for indeterminable delay, the text recommends that the agreement designate a *bait din* whose determination on that issue will be conclusive.

Another "problem" with the additional language is that women who are not entitled to support lose their leverage to demand a *get*. The short answer is to that is that *halacha* does not necessarily regard that as a "problem," see *supra* note 391, and it would be fairly easy for a woman to reestablish her claim to support and thereby retrigger the agreement.

[Note too that under the alternative analysis advanced *infra* text at notes 432-452, *asmakhta* concerns will *not* have an impact on the validity of a resulting *get*. As a result, the insertion of the language in the text would be unnecessary. Nevertheless, since there clearly are views that regard the presence of *asmakhta* as fatal, prudence would dictate drafting the agreement to avoid the problem.]

403. See *supra* text at notes 40-42 (discussion of *heter meah rabbanim*.)

most states, divorced spouses may obtain judgments for alimony.[404] To the extent a recalcitrant husband would have to pay his wife alimony even after he grants her a *get*, the contractually-assumed support obligation in effect prior to the *get* would have little effect on his decision. In order to generate incentives for the granting of a *get*, the stipulated sum applicable for the period prior to the granting of a *get* must be considerably larger than any anticipated alimony award, if any. This may create difficulties. As noted, if the sum is too large it may constitute a disguised penalty affecting the validity of a *get*; if no larger than the alimony (which in itself is based on support needs), it no longer serves as an incentive. Presumably, however, some amount in the middle could satisfy all requisite criteria, particularly in jurisdictions where alimony awards are parsimonious; where the wife's economic situation is favorable enough so that her alimony award would be low; or where alimony would be awarded in favor of the husband.[405]

A second problem is a bit more difficult to resolve. Essentially, the agreement is tantamount to a prenuptial separation agreement specifying a fixed sum for spousal support for a designated period until the execution of a religious divorce. The period in question may cover time before the granting of the civil divorce as well as afterwards, in which case the agreement also covers alimony. Separation and support agreements are always reviewable by the court to determine fairness, changed circumstances, and the like, particularly where children are involved.[406] The net result is that the stipulated amount may be regarded by a common law court as a penalty and not enforceable. The factors enumerated above to negate *get meusah*[407] may be equally convincing to a court but this is not certain. If a financial obligation turns out to be unenforceable, it of course can no longer operate as an inducement to act. Nevertheless, such an agreement may still serve a useful purpose. An otherwise-recalcitrant party may well prefer to grant a *get* immediately rather than face the prospect of a large civil liability which he may or may not be able to challenge successfully. Thus, the very existence of the

---

404. Texas remains the only state whose statutes do not permit the award of alimony but *cf. Myrick v. Myrick*, 601 S.W. 2d 152 (Tex. Civ. App. 1980) (although court may not award spousal support, it may approve and enforce an agreement for such support executed by the parties).

405. For a general discussion of the factors courts use in setting alimony awards, see Rutkin (ed.), 3 FAMILY LAW AND PRACTICE §§35.01-35.06.

406. See Clark, *supra* note 379, §19.13, pp. 460-467. Technically, whether the terms of a separation agreement are modifiable by the court depends on whether or not it has been incorporated into the judgment of dissolution. If it has not, it is the same as any other contract and is nonmodifiable except by mutual consent. If, as is common, the agreement is merged into the divorce judgment, it then becomes subject to court modification to the same degree as any alimony judgment even if the agreement contained a "no modification" clause (though a respectable minority of courts would disagree and prohibit modification where the agreement so indicates). This distinction between merged and nonmerged agreements has no application to agreements concerned with custody and child support which are always subject to judicial scrutiny. See also Rutkin (ed.), 4 FAMILY LAW AND PRACTICE §52.01 [3][c], p. 52-11 and §59.07, p. 59-46.

407. See *supra* text at notes 393-403.

agreement, whether or not it ultimately proves enforceable in the secular courts, may be sufficient to produce the desired result.

ADDITIONAL NOTE TO CHAPTER FOUR (I)
AN ABORTED RESPONSE TO *AVITZUR*: THE RCA PROPOSAL

In December 1983 shortly after the decision in *Avitzur*, the Rabbinical Council of America (RCA), the largest association of Orthodox rabbis in the United States, introduced a prenuptial agreement designed to alleviate the problem of the *agunah*.[408] Reputedly four years in the making, the document obligated the bridegroom to issue, and the bride to receive, a *get* within thirty days of the granting of a civil divorce and authorized the RCA to impose "liquidated damages" in the sum of $250 a day for failure to comply. Rabbis were advised to encourage couples to execute the agreement prior to their marriage. In a letter sent to its membership on June 20, 1984, the RCA requested that all Orthodox rabbis suspend use of the document "until further notice." No reason was given and, while the RCA leadership indicated that a revised prenuptial form would be sent out in "about five months," no replacement was ever issued.

While personal and political factors may have played a role in the withdrawal of the proposal and while some rabbis had indicated that they would continue to employ the form even after the RCA disowned it, it cannot be denied that the RCA model form was highly questionable in terms of both its legal enforceability and more importantly, its *halachic* validity. From the legal standpoint, requiring the granting of a *get* within thirty days of a civil divorce was largely inconsistent with the recently-enacted New York *get* law which generally required, at least where the husband petitioned for divorce, that the *get* be issued first.[409] Second, common law rules precluding the enforcement of penalty clauses could render the stipulated sanction illusory.[410] The RCA document tried to address this concern by labelling the penalty a "liquidated damages" clause and stating that the pain and suffering caused by the distress of being an *agunah* were difficult to quantify. Where such uncertainty exists, it is well established that courts will accept contractual stipulations of damage as a "reasonable approximation."[411] Suffice it to say, however, that the difficulty of ascertaining damages for what is essentially a breach of contract action for failure to give a *get* is not substantially greater than in any other contract or tort action involving pain, suffering, or emotional distress, the type of bread and butter case in which courts routinely determine the amount of damages recoverable. As Professor Bleich noted, "Calling something liquidated damages does not make it so."[412]

These factors alone would not argue against the use of the proposal. After all, even a penalty clause of questionable enforceability may induce a recalcitrant husband to grant a *get*. In cases where the husband obtained a civil divorce by the filing of a false affidavit or where the wife was the divorce plaintiff so that the New York *get* law was inapplicable, the RCA document

---

408. The basic information concerning the RCA proposal was obtained from a story in the LONG ISLAND JEWISH WORLD (November 23-29, 1987), p. 12.

409. See *infra* text following note 531.

410. See *supra* text at note 309.

411. See authorities cited in note 309.

412. LONG ISLAND JEWISH WORLD, *supra* note 408, p. 12.

could have served as a useful backup compelling husbands to release their wives from their otherwise-dead marriages. The key problem with the RCA proposal was the distinct possibility that it could have resulted in bills of divorce that were invalid under the principles of *get meusah*. This is so for two distinct reasons. First, the giving of a *get* to avoid the imposition of monetary sanctions that would otherwise attach results in a *get meusah* even where those sanctions are enforceable claims. Many opinions maintain this is true even where the contractual penalties are self-imposed. While there is considerable disagreement over the *meusah* status of self-imposed penalties, the ruling of Rema is that such a *get* should not be written in the first instance though it may be valid after the fact.[413] Moreover, to the extent a dissatisfied spouse would seek enforcement of the contract, damages or specific performance might take quite a different form than the penalty that was self-imposed.

Second, even the opinions that maintain that execution of a *get* to avoid a self-imposed monetary penalty does not result in a *get meusah* take this position only in cases where the "monetary threat" constitutes a legitimate and enforceable claim.[414] Where the claim is unenforceable and a *get* is executed to avoid the imposition of a liability that *halacha* deems improper, virtually all opinions would treat the *get* as a product of duress.[415] Many stipulated penalty clauses are not only unenforceable under common law but also invalid from the standpoint of *halacha* as *asmakhta*.[416] Giving a *get* to escape the threat of an *asmakhta* is tantamount to giving the *get* in exchange for a promise to refrain from theft. The lack of contractual intent in incurring the penalty - the underlying vice of *asmakhta*[417] - is especially manifest in the fact that the parties sign the agreement at a time when divorce is the furthest thing from their minds.[418]

---

413. These matters are discussed *supra* text at notes 60-65.

414. See *supra* text at notes 73-74.

415. But see *supra* note 313 and *infra* text at notes 432-452 for an alternative approach in which *asmakhta* concerns are largely irrelevant.

416. The RCA's unspoken premise may have been that designation of a specific, fixed dollar amount insulates the agreement from the taint of *asmakhta* which invalidates only indeterminate commitments. This seems to be the *halachic* position of at least one eminent member of the RCA, see Riskin, *supra* note 122, pp. 139-140. For the reasons stated in notes 306-308, I believe this assumption is incorrect.

417. See *supra* note 306.

418. The difference between the prenuptial support agreement, see *supra* text at notes 395-407, and the RCA proposal addressed here is two-fold. First, the prenuptial support agreement described above is not expressly linked to the withholding of a *get* but applies whenever the parties are residing separately; at least on its face, it is an obligation that arises out of the marital relationship rather than out of the failure to grant a religious divorce. By contrast, the RCA proposal is linked to the *get* in two ways: (1) the agreement contains an express covenant to give a *get*; and (2) the damages are calculated based on the number of days a *get* is withheld.

Second, prenuptial support agreements, at least where a wife is *halachically* entitled to support, did not suffer from the taint of *asmakhta* and are thus legitimate sanctions. See *supra* note 395. The RCA proposal, on the

While coercion of any type will not invalidate the *get* when it is employed to enforce the order of a *bait din* directing the parties to divorce at least if it is of the *kofin* variety,[419] not every case in which a civil divorce is granted qualifies for such an order.

---

other hand, clearly constituted an *asmakhta* according to the views of at least some authorities, see *supra* note 306, and the granting of a *get* to escape the secular enforcement of a *halachically* illegitimate *asmakhta* claim may produce a *get meusah*. Thus, the RCA proposal lacked the elements of both formal independence from the *get* and *halachic* legitimacy, the two conditions normally needed to avoid the problem of *meusah*. See *supra* note 395 and *infra* text at notes 431-451 (whether legitimacy is in fact a separate prong).

One might assume that support for the proposal may be adduced from Rabbi Moshe Feinstein's 1979 Johannesburg letter where he sustained the *halachic* validity of a *get* issued in response to a (secular) court order providing for a higher level of support before a *get* is granted and a lower level afterwards. See *supra* note 392. This conclusion, however, would be incorrect. While the responsum may indeed suggest that even support claims which on their face are designed to compel a *get* do not render the resulting *get* invalid (but see *id.* for possible alternative readings), this would not validate the RCA proposal. The RCA agreement contained no indication that the stipulated sum was designed for marital support. Indeed, the stipulated sum bears no relationship at all to support needs; insofar as the agreement was concerned, it would have been entirely possible for a wife to recover X amount of dollars a day *in addition* to whatever support was awardable under contract or court order. This also meant that X amount of dollars could never have been regarded as a reasonable estimation of support needs for anyone since there would never be any way of knowing at the time of such agreement how much additional money would be included as support. Moreover, while even exorbitant support orders may be ostensibly justified as providing a necessary economic cushion for women unable to marry, the stipulated sum did not purport to provide this cushion but rather to provide damages for breach of an express promise. In other words, the clause did not attempt to deal with economic hardship *per se* (which could have made it akin to support) - a hardship that is identical whether or not there was any promise to give a *get* - but only to provide redress for failure to keep a promise. As such, the RCA proposal was tantamount to any other self-imposed penalty for breach of a *get* covenant which raises the specter of *get meusah* at least *ab initio* (as per Rema's ruling) even if the technical objection of *asmakhta* could be overcome. Indeed, it would be much easier to construe the RCA document as a support agreement if the *get* covenant were totally eliminated.

In short, of the three defects in the RCA proposal: (1) the *get* covenant; (2) the calculation of damages based on the number of days a *get* was withheld and; (3) the fact that the sum was not in lieu of other support, R. Moshe's responsum would at most validate the second element (allowing a linkage between support and *get*) but furnishes no authority that would resolve the other two problems. The RCA agreement could indeed be *halachically* salvageable by elimination of the *get* covenant and inclusion of a provision that all stipulated sums are to be deemed support but, at that point, it would simply become the prenuptial support agreement discussed in the earlier section.

419. *Supra* text at notes 108-120.

This is not to say that the RCA form was clearly invalid. To the extent one accepts the liquidated damages argument, the same premise that would make the clause enforceable under common law would similarly remove the vice of *asmakhta*, at least according to some opinions.[420] Once the clause is not an *asmakhta* and simply falls under the rubric of self-imposed monetary constraints (in which case, a *get* executed in exchange for a release of those constraints is *ex post facto* valid), it could be argued that in cases of *agunot*, it may very well be appropriate to execute *ab initio* a *get* which is unquestionably valid after the fact.[421] Moreover, since the imposition of the fine was not automatic but required the affirmative decision of the *bait din*, perhaps one could assume that the *bait din* would not assess a monetary penalty except under the circumstances where *kofin* would be appropriate. On balance, however, the proposal did raise enough questions that its withdrawal was appropriate.[422]

A far more acceptable alternative than a direct promise to give a *get* would be the prenuptial agreement to submit disputes to a designated rabbinic tribunal. This was precisely the type of arrangement that *Avitzur* upheld. Judicial enforcement of a promise to go to a *bait din* raises no *halachic* issue whatsoever; indeed, even the designation of a liquidated damage clause, although possibly an *asmakhta*, would have no bearing on the validity of the *get*.[423] As noted earlier, in all probability the decision of the *bait din* could similarly be judicially enforced. Whether the *bait din* acting in their capacity as arbitrators could impose their own penalties remains legally questionable, though at least in some cases (those of *kofin*) *halachically* sound.[424]

---

420. See SHULCHAN ARUCH H.M. 61:5 and comment of the SEFER MEIRAT AINAYIM [SEMA], paragraph 12 (contractual stipulation to pay litigation expenses not invalid as an *asmakhta* because it is compensatory in nature). This position, however, is not universally held. See *supra* note 306 (contrary view of R. Shlomo Luria).

421. This alone would have been a major and controversial step since it would have meant departing from an explicit and authoritative ruling of Rema. Nevertheless, such a departure would not have been without precedent. See, *e.g.*, the suggestion of R. Herzog that, in spite of Rema's ruling that *kofin* sanctions may not be employed in *yotzee* cases, in situations of grave necessity this ruling may be overturned. See *supra* note 116. To my knowledge, however, even R. Herzog never applied this suggestion in practice.

422. Since a *get* issued under threat of *asmakhta* is invalid and any subsequent marriage would be adulterous, prudence would dictate that no agreement be approved by a mainline rabbinical organization unless it eliminates *asmakhta* according to all major views. The RCA proposal failed to do so. The penalty would clearly be an *asmakhta* according to the view of Rambam, cited *supra* note 306, and might be an *asmakhta* even according to Rashba, since the specified amount does not necessarily represent a reasonable approximation of damages. Finally, even accepting the RCA's *asmakhta* arguments, their proposal contravenes the ruling of Rema concerning a *get meusah*, *supra* text at note 65, except in the comparatively-rare situations of *kofin*.

423. See *supra* text at notes 315-322.

424. See *supra* text following notes 323-329.

In 1980, Rabbi Moshe Feinstein,[425] responding to a query of Rabbi Y. Perr of Far Rockaway, wrote that a prenuptial agreement to submit to and abide by the decision of the *bait din* is permissible and constructive in assisting women out of the "chains of *Igun.*" The specter of later civil enforcement would not render the *get meusah*. Rabbi Feinstein's only hesitation was his fear that requiring a couple to contemplate the possibility of a future divorce could in itself be a divisive experience that would potentially undermine marital harmony. He therefore recommended that the officiating rabbi not use the agreement unless he personally knows the bride and groom and judges that the execution of such an agreement will not have this detrimental effect.

The foregoing was the substance of the 1980 letter as it appeared in the 1985 first edition of *Igrot Moshe* E.H. IV.[426] In the second edition, a number of changes were made in the letter (!) without indicating that there were additions.[427] First, Rabbi Feinstein was far less enthusiastic in advocating widespread use of the document, explicitly stating that "in the first instance, it is not proper to impose such a condition as a matter of course"; and rather than merely recommending first-hand knowledge of the couple, he required it. Second, and this is far more significant as well as perplexing, in indicating the legal effect of such a prenuptial document, Rabbi Feinstein wrote that "the purpose of the condition is that the civil courts can force the parties to appear before, and obey the decision of, the *bait din* ***by withholding the grant of a civil divorce***" (emphasis added). The highlighted words did not appear in the earlier version of the responsum. It is difficult to know the meaning of the addition. Under the New York *get* law, the granting of a civil divorce will be withheld until a *get* is executed *whether or not* there is a prenuptial agreement to that effect.[428] The "coercion" that is exercised by the state's withholding its imprimatur to remarry in no way depends on the existence of an *Avitzur*-type agreement. The sole purpose of such an agreement is to be able to seek direct civil enforcement of the promise through mandatory injunction and contempt of court sanctions. If Rabbi Feinstein was intimating that such coercive sanctions implicate the rule of *get meusah* even where they are sought in the context of forcing the parties to either go to a *bait din* or obey the decision rendered by a *bait din*, then the prospects for a viable prenuptial agreement are dim, if not impossible. Such a reading would also contradict well-established principles of Jewish law.[429] It is likely, however, that Rabbi Feinstein was concerned with the use of compulsory mechanisms to enforce the order of a *bait din* when that order is predicated on the noncoercive grounds of *yotzee*

---

425. The leading rabbinic decisor of the post-World War II era, Rabbi Feinstein was born in Russia in 1895. After a distinguished and courageous career in the rabbinate in the face of Stalinist persecution, he emigrated to the United States in 1936 and for the next fifty years provided *halachic* leadership and guidance to generations of world Jewry. His funeral in May 1986 was attended by an unprecedented 250,000 persons. For a biographical treatment, see Finkelman, REB MOSHE: THE LIFE AND IDEALS OF HAGAON RABBI MOSHE FEINSTEIN (Mesorah Publications, 1986).

426. IGROT MOSHE E.H. IV, no. 107 (large volume edition).

427. *Id.* (small volume edition).

428. See *infra* text following note 531.

429. See *supra* text at notes 96-106.

rather than *kofin*.[430] If so, his hesitations confirm my earlier reservations concerning the *Avitzur* approach.[431]

430. If this reading is correct, Rabbi Feinstein necessarily rejected the alternative analysis of Rabbi Herzog cited *supra* note 116.

431. See *supra* text at notes 291-299. Of course, one perplexing problem that Rabbi Feinstein fails to address is that once an *Avitzur*-type agreement is executed, its enforcement cannot be limited to a denial of civil divorce. If there is a *halachic* problem in utilizing the agreement for direct civil enforcement of the *bait din*'s decision, then the logical response is not to execute the document at all, rather than make the unfounded assumption that it can only be used to prevent the granting of a civil divorce.

ADDITIONAL NOTE TO CHAPTER FOUR (II) THE RELEVANCE OF *ASMAKHTA* TO *GET MEUSAH*

The analysis in the text, and throughout most of this book, assumes that a *get* that is executed to escape the enforcement of a *halachically* illegitimate sanction (such as *asmakhta*)is, for that reason alone, an invalid *get meusah*.[432] This assumption is based on the distinction propounded by Tashbatz between "legitimate" and "illegitimate" means, as that distinction is commonly understood.[433] A closer reading of Tashbatz's responsum reveals that this is not necessarily the case and the *asmakhta* component of the *get* covenant may in fact be *halachically* irrelevant, at least insofar as the validity of the *get* is concerned.

Tashbatz articulates his distinction in the context of nominally - independent pressures where the wife or the members of her family offer to release the sanction if a *get* is executed but threaten to enforce the monetary sanction if the *get* is not. An example would be an unrelated debt that husband owes. Consistent with other authorities, Tashbatz rules that because the compulsion that forces the husband to act was not created for the purpose of obtaining a *get*, a *get* executed to escape it is not deemed a product of duress.[434] He then states that if the "debt" whose enforcement is being threatened is a *halachically* unenforceable debt, a *get* executed in exchange for its "forgiveness" "may" be a *get meusah*.[435]

In this limited context, the distinction between legitimate and illegitimate sanctions can be understood in two significantly different ways: (1) illegitimate pressure, in and of itself, constitutes invalidating duress regardless of whether the pressure was generated out of a desire to procure a *get* or arose independently;[436] (2) alternatively, illegitimacy *per se* is not an invalidating cause but merely establishes a linkage between the penalty and the *get* that would otherwise not exist.[437] In other words, where a claim is otherwise unenforceable its resurrection in the context of a *get* indicates that it is being asserted solely as a means of obtaining a *get*, notwithstanding its formal independence. The key is therefore not illegitimacy but linkage and purpose. Illegitimacy is simply a factor that converts that which would otherwise be independent into a pressure that exists for the express purpose of compelling a *get*.

Which reading is correct has important practical consequences. For

---

432. See *supra* text at notes 72-74 and 313.

433. See *supra* note 73.

434. See *supra* note 68 for a common law parallel.

435. Note that even Tashbatz does not say that it is *definitely* invalid but only possibly so.

436. See *supra* note 74 (illegitimacy is of major importance in defining duress under common law).

437. This alternative interpretation of Tashbatz's position is suggested by TESHUVOT RANACH, no. 63 as a possibility and seems to be the understanding of *Torat Gittin* cited in PITCHAI TESHUVAH E.H. 134:5 (11). See also IGROT MOSHE E.H. I, no. 137 who explains *Torah Gittin* in precisely this manner, *i.e.*, that the vice of illegitimacy is the fact that it establishes linkage. See also *infra* note 438.

one thing, does illegitimacy as such have any relevance where the sanction and the *get* are already inextricably linked? Under the first reading, the answer would be yes; under the second reading, the answer would be no. If illegitimacy merely establishes linkage, its existence is immaterial where the linkage already exists; the *get* will either be valid or invalid depending on the nature and magnitude of the coercion but the presence of the additional factor of illegitimacy will play no role in that determination. A second practical difference arises in cases where the sanctions are clearly independent of the *get* but are nonetheless illegitimate. Assuming a sanction or threat were found to be truly independent, would its illegitimacy nevertheless taint the *get*? Once again, under the first reading it would; under the second reading it would not. If illegitimacy creates at best nothing more than a rebuttable presumption of linkage, illegitimacy ceases to be a factor once that linkage clearly does not exist.[438] In this author's view, there is strong evidence to support the second reading.[439]

As noted earlier, there is a disagreement among authorities whether a *get* that is executed pursuant to self-imposed monetary penalties is valid or not.[440] Those that validate the *get* do so on two alternative theories, either on

---

438. A good example of this second application may be drawn from the discussions in TESHUVOT RANACH, no. 63. (Bleich, II CONTEMPORARY HALACHIC PROBLEMS, p. 97 cites this responsum as no. 43 but this is a typographical error.) In the Middle Ages, a number of Jewish communities had promulgated an ordinance prohibiting marriages without a minimum quorum of ten persons present at the ceremony. This rule was intended to prevent elopements, coercion *etc*. A man had married a woman privately in violation of the ordinance and as a result, was imprisoned. His wife offered to secure his release if he executed a *get*. He did so but later claimed that the *get* was invalid since it was executed in order to secure his release from prison. An earlier ruling by the great Spanish authority, Rivash validated the *get* on the theory that the coercive event, *i.e.*, imprisonment, was not imposed for the purpose of securing a *get* but was independently generated. See TESHUVOT RIVASH, no. 232. In commenting on this ruling, Ranach at no. 63 notes that the violation of a community ban did not, as a matter of *halacha*, justify the imposition of a prison sentence and detention on such grounds was illicit and tortious. In view of the illegitimate nature of this pressure, how then could Rivash's ruling be sustained? Ranach suggests one of two possible approaches: (1) Rivash disagrees with Tashbatz's distinction and maintains that illegitimacy is simply an irrelevant factor; (2) alternatively, even Tashbatz articulated his distinction only in cases where the illegitimacy of the sanction indicates that it is being employed solely for the purpose of obtaining a *get*. Where an illegal sanction is clearly imposed for a non*get* - related purpose, even Tashbatz might concede that illegitimacy plays no role. Thus, Ranach concludes, whether or not Tashbatz agrees with Rivash's ruling depends directly on how one construes the illegitimacy prong.

[It should also be noted that, contrary to Ranach's assertion, it is possible that Rivash regarded incarceration as a *legitimate* communal sanction for violation of the ordinance in which case, the meaning of the illegitimacy prong becomes moot.]

439. This evidence is *in addition* to the sources already cited in note 437.

440. See *supra* text at notes 63-65.

the ground that self-imposed restraints are definitionally not coercive or that the ability to pay in lieu of writing a *get* constitutes a "reasonable alternative."[441] Rema rules that while such *gittin* should not be written, they are not invalid after the fact.[442] Given the undeniable reality that many, if not most, self-imposed contractual penalties run afoul of *asmakhta* and are therefore *halachically* illegitimate claims,[443] one may question how these rulings could possibly be true. If illegitimacy is truly a separate invalidating prong, its presence should invariably taint the *get*. All of the opinions sustaining the *get* would have to be limited to monetary sanctions that are carefully structured to avoid *asmakhta* concerns and yet there is no hint in any of the validating views that such intricate restructuring is necessary, at least for purposes of *get meusah*. Why doesn't Rema, for example, qualify his ruling regarding *ex post facto* validation to cases where there is no *halachic* defect of *asmakhta*?[444] Indeed, even Tashbatz, the author of the legitimate-illegitimate distinction, fails to allude to the need to surmount *asmakhta* when he validates *gittin* granted to escape a self-assumed penalty.[445] All of this suggests that to the extent a given penalty does not result in a *get meusah* even where it is explicitly linked to a *get*, the additional factor of illegitimacy will make matters no worse.

If this analysis is correct and illegitimacy *per se* is not an autonomous invalidating factor, some interesting practical conclusions emerge. Consider the following example: A man refuses to grant his wife a *get*. Her family threatens that unless he grants a *get*, they will steal or damage property that he owns. He accedes to the threat and executes a *get*. Assuming the threat was

---

441. See *supra* text at notes 76-78.

442. See *supra* note 65.

443. See *supra* text at notes 306-308.

444. It would have been possible for Rema to limit validation of the *get* to cases where the stipulated penalty was already paid or at least put in escrow with the *get* serving as a mechanism for release and not in cases where assumption of the penalty was a future undertaking. Prepaid penalties subject to refund upon performance do not raise *asmakhta* problems according to many authorities and thus constitute *halachically* legitimate sanctions. See *supra* note 306 (views of Ramban and R. Hai Gaon). Where the penalty has not been paid in advance, however, its contractual assumption is unequivocally an *asmakhta*. Since neither Tashbatz nor Rema differentiate between fines payable in advance and those not payable until default, the inescapable conclusion is that *asmakhta* characterization is *halachically* irrelevant.

445. See TASHBATZ II, no. 68. Tashbatz rejects the "reasonable alternative" theory and sustains the *get* solely on the theory that the penalty was self-generated. Accordingly, in TASHBATZ I, no. 1 (where the legitimacy-illegitimacy distinction is advanced), he indeed rules that : (1) a *get* given to escape (nonself-imposed) monetary duress is invalid; (2) ostensibly independent monetary threats that are *halachically* unenforceable "may" render the *get* invalid as well. Those authorities that subscribe to the "reasonable alternative" theory would differ with both of those conclusions as noted further in the text. See also *infra* note 418 for further textual evidence that Tashbatz's use of legitimacy was exclusively for purposes of linkage.

credible[446] or was actually carried out, is the *get* a *get meusah*? Here, the pressure is: (1) illegitimate; (2) linked to the *get*; and (3) nonself-imposed. Virtually all authorities would regard this as a *get meusah*, invalid even after the fact.[447] Even here, however, to the extent one subscribes to the "reasonable alternative" theory,[448] the *get* may well be valid, notwithstanding the clear illegitimacy of the threat. Once the premise is accepted that illegitimacy is not an autonomous invalidating factor but simply establishes linkage (which, in this example, is already present), the "reasonable alternative" test works just as well in cases of extortion and theft as it does in "threats" to enforce contractual rights.[449]

Consider another example: Assume that a member of wife's family embezzled substantial sums of money from the husband's business. Assume further that such wrongful appropriation was not for the purpose of securing a *get* but simply as an act of theft. Wife desires to be released from her marriage and informs her husband that if he will give her a *get*, she will convince her brother to make restitution. In an attempt to recover his losses and regain property that is rightfully his own, husband grants his wife a *get*.[450] Would this be a *get meusah*?

The difference between this case and the preceding one is that here, the pressure that is pushing the husband to write a *get* (the loss of his property) was not generated for the purpose of securing a *get* but had its genesis as an independent act. Nevertheless, while the tort or crime generating the pressure is technically independent, the act is also illegitimate. Would the illegitimacy

---

446. See TESHUVOT RANACH, no. 43 who makes the interesting observation that some illegitimate threats are so lacking in credibility as not to constitute a source of duress. He thus posits the irony that legitimate pressures may create more *meusah* problems than illegitimate ones. See also RESTATEMENT OF CONTRACTS (Second) §175, Comment *c*.

447. Those authorities, *e.g.*, Rashba, who invalidate *gittin* given under self-imposed monetary duress would certainly do so here. Others who validate such *gittin* - and Rema who validates the *get ex post facto* - do so only where the compulsion is self-assumed. Where it is not, the *get* would be invalid even after the fact.

448. See *supra* text at notes 79-83.

449. Indeed, by virtue of *asmakhta*, many "threats" to enforce contractual rights *will* amount to extortion or theft.

The application of the "reasonable alternative" test depends, of course, on there being a reasonable alternative. The threatened forfeiture must not be so severe as to preclude husband's choosing the financial loss in lieu of the *get*. See *supra* text at notes 82 and 399. Once again, however, whether this is or is not the case in no way depends on the legitimacy of the threat.

450. For purposes of this example, it is assumed that no restitution was made until the *get* was delivered. If such restitution was made in reliance on the husband's promise, the compulsion to write a *get* has effectively been terminated and the *get* would not be a *get meusah*. See TESHUVOT RANACH, no. 43.

of even a clearly independent sanction invalidate the *get*?[451]

Once again, the preceding analysis suggests that the answer is no. Were illegitimacy a separate invalidating factor, the *get* would indeed be invalid. If, on the other hand, illegitimacy is simply evidence of linkage, as long as the illegitimate pressure preceded the issue of *get* and arose from factors clearly independent of, and unrelated to, the *get*, the *get* will be valid notwithstanding the fact that it was executed to recover stolen property. Indeed, Tashbatz, in the very same responsum articulating the legitimate-illegitimate distinction, rules (with some expressions of doubt) that the *get* is valid.[452] This further confirms my conclusion that even illegitimate sanctions, if they are truly independent, will not invalidate the *get*.

The upshot of this analysis is the following: there is no question that *get* covenants coupled with financial penalties raise *halachic* problems of *get meusah*, according to some even after the fact, according to others only *ab initio*. It is also true that such penalties are generally *halachically* unenforceable because of *asmakhta*. Insofar as the *get* is concerned, however, the legality or illegality of the sanction is irrelevant. A *get* that is executed to escape a *halachically* invalid penalty is as valid (or invalid) as a *get* that is executed to escape a *halachically* valid one. While the presence or absence of *asmakhta* will of course become relevant if the wife would ever attempt to *enforce* the penalty (since any attempts to do would be a violation of religious law) and while it might be a matter of "public policy" not to structure prenuptial agreements in a way that is *halachically* improper, as long as the agreement is (arguably) civilly enforceable and serves (by virtue of that fact alone) as an effective pressuring device, the additional factor of its illegitimacy raises no additional question regarding the validity of the resulting *get*. As such, the specter of *asmakhta* is far less threatening than many scholars assume.

---

451. It goes without saying that those authorities who apply the "reasonable alternative" test to validate *gittin* issued under monetary duress even where the threats are explicitly for the purpose of securing a *get* as in the preceding example would certainly do so here. The question is whether the views who invalidate the *get* in *example one* (as the vast majority do) would similarly do so in *example two*.

452. Actually, Tashbatz's case involved a theft by the wife herself who later agreed to return the stolen property if her husband were to give her a *get*. Tashbatz was inclined to rule that the *get* was valid notwithstanding the fact that it was executed under monetary duress though he conceded that the matter was not without doubt. According to *Torat Gittin* cited in PITCHAI TESHUVA E.H. 134:5 (11), Tashbatz would sustain the validity of the *get* only where the husband brought up the *get* issue as an inducement first and not where the wife was the initiator. As explained by IGROT MOSHE E.H. I, no. 137, the distinction is based not on formalism but on probable intent. Where the wife steals money and then initiates a *get* demand, it is probable that the purpose of her theft was to secure a *get*. Where the wife, however, never requests a *get* but the husband merely offers it in an attempt to recover his money, the "pressuring sanction" retains its independence. The example in the text involving a third party theft is a simpler way of making the same point.

ADDITIONAL NOTE TO CHAPTER FOUR (III) *GET MEUSAH* REVISITED: A RECAPITULATION AND PRIMER

Chapters One through Four have analyzed various proposals designed to secure relief for *agunot* and found a number of them questionable on the basis of the rules against *get meusah*. In view of the vast literature covering the subject as well as some of the extensive discussions in the footnotes of this work, it may be helpful to set out in summary fashion the major considerations governing the law of *get meusah* and some of the significant disagreements among *halachic* authorities. This outline will not attempt to resolve among conflicting views but simply to indicate where the problem areas are. While summarization inescapably involves oversimplification, the basic structure of the law can be discerned by focusing on two issues: first, the nature of the pressure involved - monetary or physical, imposed by others or by self, legitimate or illegitimate, and most fundamental of all, whether the sanctions are directly linked to the *get* or formally independent; second, the scope of the "obligatory *get*" exception which negates the application of *get meusah* even where the nature of the coercion is such that the *get* would ordinarily be invalid. Under this second heading would fall questions like the identification of the substantive grounds under which a *bait din* could order a *get*, whether all such grounds qualify for the exception or only some, the procedural requisites for the exception to be triggered, and the unique problems in enlisting secular authorities to secure a *get*, problems that do not necessarily arise when a *bait din* is able to enforce its order on its own. The following outline sets out the multiplicity of considerations that must be understood and addressed and the footnotes provide the references in the text where these considerations are amplified.

I. *Sanctions Directly Linked to Get*

A. *Imposed by Others*: *get* invalid whether sanction is monetary or physical.[453]

Exception: A minority view would validate *gittin* issued under threat of monetary penalty if payment of fine constitutes a "reasonable alternative."[454]

B. *Imposed by Self*: *get* valid after the fact at least where sanction is monetary but *get* should not be written in the first instance without unconditional forgiveness of penalty.[455]

Exceptions: 1. Some limit validation to cases where the husband does not indicate at the time of the *get* that he is acting under compulsion.[456]

2. Some limit this validation to cases where the self-imposed penalty is *halachically* enforceable. Since many self-imposed penalties are not *halachically* enforceable because of *asmakhta*, Rema's ruling (according to this view)

453. *Supra* text at notes 60-65.
454. *Supra* text at note 78.
455. *Supra* text at note 65 (ruling of Rema).
456. *Id.*

will rarely apply.[457]

3. From the opposite perspective, some opinions would allow the *get* to be written even in the first instance either because self-imposed penalties are a product of free will or because payment of any monetary penalty - regardless of who imposes it - constitutes a "reasonable alternative" to execution of the *get*.[458]

II. *Sanctions Independently Generated*

Whether penalties are imposed by others or self, the resulting *get* is valid.[459]

Exceptions: 1. A minority view would validate even the use of independent sanctions only in cases where the husband had a reasonable alternative to executing the *get* and not where the penalty is so exorbitant that the only possible choice is to grant the *get*.[460]

2. A number of authorities would limit the use of these sanctions to cases where they are *halachically* enforceable. (Other do not regard legitimacy of sanction as a necessary prerequisite as long as the sanction is truly independent.)[461]

3. A sanction will not be regarded as independent where it is patently obvious that its sole purpose is to secure a *get*. *In such cases, the rules of Section I will apply*.[462]

III. *Obligatory Get Exception*

No need to consider this exception unless the *get* would otherwise be invalid based on the rulings in Sections I and II. Three elements trigger this exception: (1) grounds; (2) procedural requisites; (3) nature of the enforcement body.

---

457. See the extensive discussion *supra* text at notes 432-452 (highly questionable whether illegitimacy is relevant in the context of self-imposed penalties that are already linked to the *get*).

458. *Supra* text at notes 76-78.

459. *Supra* text at notes 66-71.

460. *Supra* text at notes 75-95 (questionable whether the existence of reasonable alternative is a necessary condition for the *get*'s validity).

461. See *supra* text at notes 432-452 for the development of this point.

462. Some explain that this is precisely what the illegitimacy criterion attempts to establish. See *supra* notes 437-438. Note, however, that even when such linkage is established, the *get* will not necessarily be invalid after the fact since under Rema's ruling, even monetary penalties *expressly* linked to the *get* will not produce an invalid *get meusah* after the fact. Linkage merely "moves" the situation from Section II to Section I.

A. *Grounds*: 1. Some opinions validate compulsion in any case where the Talmud rules that divorce is mandatory.[463]

2. Others validate compulsion only in the very small group of cases where the term *kofin* is used.[464]

3. A third view adopts an intermediate position: while compulsion should not employed except where the Talmud states *kofin*, the resulting *get* will be valid in any case of mandatory divorce.[465]

B. *Procedural Requisites*: A competent *bait din* must have already determined the existence of grounds *prior* to the compulsion being employed. Otherwise, the *get* is invalid notwithstanding the existence of grounds.[466] (At least according to Rambam, the need for this *a priori* determination is only rabbinic.)[467]

C. *Nature of the Enforcement Body*: To the extent enforcement is effected by a secular court system rather than by the officials of a *bait din*, the enforcers must act as surrogates for, and extensions of, the *bait din* rather than as autonomous agents. This carries a number of implications:

1. At a minimum, not only would the *bait din* have to make an *a priori* determination but such determination would have to be known by the enforcing agents.[468]

2. According to a *minority* view, the secular authority must specifically direct the recalcitrant husband to obey the *bait din* rather than direct him to give a *get*.[469]

---

463. This is the apparent view of Rambam and Rif cited respectively *supra* notes 100 and 110.

464. See views cited *supra* note 113.

465. See view of Rabbi Herzog cited *supra* note 116. See also *infra* note 640 (opinion of R. Liebes).

466. But see *infra* note 682 for a possible exception (view of R. Elyashiv).

467. See *supra* note 105 (use of term *pasul* which connotes only rabbinic disqualification although by and large, a *get* that is invalid rabbinically is no better than one that is invalid under Torah law). But see B'EER YITZCHOK E.H., no. 10 (section 8) who argues that as long as the *kofin* decision is rendered and communicated to the husband prior to the *get*'s execution, the *get* will be valid although the coercion *per se* predated the establishment of *kofin* grounds. While this is quite consistent with Rambam's "true will" theory, it seems to contradict the definitive formulation of the *Shulchan Aruch*. See *supra* note 103.

468. Although this conclusion is debatable, it seems to follow from the language of the *Shulchan Aruch*. See *supra* note 103. At worst, however, the *get* would only be rabbinically invalid since even if no decision at all was rendered by a *bait din*, the *get* would still be valid under Torah law as long as the substantive grounds for divorce in fact existed. See also *infra* note 681 (view of R. Elyashiv) and note 472.

469. See view of R. Meir HaLevi cited *supra* note 103. *Contra*: BAIT SHMUEL E.H. 134:9 (15) cited *supra* notes 103 and 299.

3. According to some opinions, while the form in which the secular authority communicates its directive is immaterial, it must nonetheless intend to enforce the decision of the *bait din* rather than predicate its enforcement on some alternative ground having nothing to do with the *bait din*'s decision.[470]

4. Resort to secular authorities must not be in violation of general principles of religious law which prohibit utilization of secular courts without the authorization of a *bait din*.[471]

5. The absence of any of the requirements set out above in nos. 1-4 will at worst render the *get* invalid only rabbinically and not under Torah law.[472]

6. It is unclear to what extent any of these limitations (including the need for an *a priori* determination) would apply where the aggrieved spouse utilizes self-help in lieu of enlisting the secular judicial process.[473]

---

470. This was a major qualification imposed by R. Yosef Elyashiv in a recent communication concerning the just enacted New York *get* law, see *infra* note 681. I have not found this ruling explicitly articulated by earlier authorities though it is a supportable inference from the language of Rambam and especially *Shulchan Aruch*. *Supra* note 103. Note that R. Elyashiv requires that the enforcers not only be *aware* of the *bait din*'s decision but also act for the *purpose* of enforcing it. But see *infra* notes 471-472.

471. The general prohibition of resorting to secular tribunals is discussed *supra* note 45. R. Elyashiv's recent letter, *infra* note 682, suggests that it is the existence of this prohibition which requires that the enforcers act with the intention of enforcing the decision of the *bait din*. Accordingly, he rules that where the prohibition is inapplicable, *e.g.*, husband refuses to submit to a *bait din* and a *k'tav siruv* has been issued to that effect, such intent is not necessary nor must the *bait din* have even issued a prior ruling, provided that requisite grounds for mandatory divorce do in fact exist.

472. See *supra* notes 103 and 105 (use of term *pasul*). It should be reiterated that according to the view of *B'eer Yitzchok*, *none* of the procedural elements of 1-4 need to be met even rabbinically. As long as a *kofin* order was issued and communicated to the husband prior to the execution of the *get*, the intent, motivation, or knowledge of the coercing agents is immaterial. B'EER YITZCHOK E.H., no. 10 (section 8). His ruling, however, appears to be contradict the language of *Shulchan Aruch*. See *supra* note 103.

473. It is indisputable that the need for specific grounds to overcome the strictures of *meusah* is applicable both to cases where pressures are generated by the secular court system and where the pressures are imposed by the utilization of self-help, *e.g.*, hiring thugs. It is less certain that the procedural requisites - *a priori* ruling, knowledge of ruling, and intent - apply in self-help situations since the need for such requirements may stem from the special prohibition of resorting to secular (non-Jewish) tribunals that would otherwise apply - see *supra* note 471 - a consideration that may not be applicable to self-help cases.

TABLE OF CONTRACTUAL OPTIONS AND THEIR LEGAL AND *HALACHIC* VIABILITY

At the conclusion of this chapter, it may be helpful to summarize in tabular form the various options presented and the legal and *halachic* impediments to their use.

Drafting Option	*Enforceability Under Contract Law*
1. *Get* Agreements	
a) without stipulated penalties	a) Some (but not all) jurisdictions will grant specific performance due to inadequacy of damages remedy.
b) with stipulated penalties	b) Probably unenforceable. Penalty clause will be ignored and the court will enforce the agreement as in (a).
2. Arbitration Agreements	
a) without stipulated penalties	a) Specific performance in all jurisdictions.
b) with penalties for failure to appear	b) Penalties generally unenforceable, whether imposed by the parties or by the arbitrators. Specific performance by court order is exclusive remedy.
c) with penalties for failure to comply with order	c) same as (b).
3. Reciprocal Obligations and Releases	Enforceable in accordance with their terms unless treated as disguised penalties by reading all documents as an integrated whole.
4. Antenuptial Support Agreements	Enforceable but may be subject to court modification in the light of changed circumstances, particularly if child support is involved.
5. "Trading Chip" Agreements: The Granting of a *Get* As a Condition to Entitlement, Rather than a Direct Promise.	Enforceable. Even those courts which have not permitted the direct enforcement of *get* agreements have validated the use of a *get* as a condition. A non-cooperating party will be unable to secure benefits under a separation agreement until all conditions precedent have been fulfilled and the granting of a *get* may be designated as one of those conditions.

*Effect on Resulting Get if Particular Drafting Option Is Utilized:**

1. a) Invalid as a *get meusah*. The *get* was executed to either avoid or comply with a court order of specific performance carrying a sanction of civil contempt.

1. b) Invalid as a *get meusah*. The self-imposed nature of the monetary sanction is not the one that in all probability a court will impose. Second, Rema's ruling prohibits the issuance of a *get* even to avoid self-imposed monetary penalties.[1] Third, because penalty clauses are not *halachically* binding under the rule of *asmakhta*, a *get* issued to avoid the imposition of an *illegitimate* claim is invalid even according to the authorities who differ with Rema.[2]

2. a) Valid, to the extent judicial compulsion is limited to having the parties appear. The *get* may be invalid if the court orders the parties to comply with the decision of *bait din* and the decision was not predicated on *halachic* coercive grounds, *i.e.*, only a *yotzee* order.[3] Since courts commonly do enforce arbitration orders, this option very well may produce a *get meusah*.

2. b) Penalties whose coercive effect is limited to having the parties appear have no effect on the validity of a *get*.[4] As noted, however, in all likelihood, these penalties would be analyzed under 2(a).

2. c) Self-imposed penalties for failure to obey the decision of a *bait din* will result in a *get meusah* if the order of the *bait din* is one in which coercion is inappropriate. See 1(b). As noted, in all likelihood, these penalties would be ignored and the agreement would be analyzed under 2(a).

3. Arguably valid, since the obligation is not tied directly to the granting or withholding of a *get*.

4. Arguably valid, unless the support claim is so excessive that it obviously constitutes a disguised penalty to coerce the granting of a *get*. This is likely to be the case where the support obligations after the civil divorce are substantially higher than the support obligations before.

5. Valid. A *get* executed to obtain benefits and concessions over and above those the party is already entitled to under law is not a *get meusah*.[5]
While this option is unquestionably valid, it leaves a spouse open to extortionate demands. It also permits the truly spiteful spouse to refuse to give a *get* and simply forego the benefits.

---

*Numbers and letters correspond to the drafting options enumerated on the preceding page. Footnotes to chart appear on next page.

1. See *supra* text at note 65.
2. See *supra* text at notes 73-74. But *cf. supra* text at notes 432-452.
3. See *supra* text at notes 108-120. But *cf. supra* 116 (view of Rabbi Herzog).
4. This is true irrespective of the *asmakhta* limitations. Self-imposed penalties upon failure to appear before a *bait din* may indeed be *halachically* unenforceable because of *asmakhta* but because avoidance of the *asmakhta* is accomplished by merely appearing in the *bait din*, the subsequent execution of the *get* is not a product of duress. The *asmakhta* aspect of "appearance penalties" has no bearing on the validity of the *get* and is sharply differentiated from the *asmakhta* aspects of either *get*-covenants or "compliance penalties" in arbitration agreements, both of which could result in a *halachically* invalid *get meusah*.
5. It is important to note, however, that the agreement must be structured so that the granting of the *get* gives the recalcitrant party benefits or privileges that would not be enjoyed in the absence of agreement. If the granting of the *get* merely secures privileges that the spouse would have received anyway under the jurisdiction's law of equitable distribution, the withholding of a *get* would effect a penalty. Granting a *get* to avoid such a forfeiture of entitlement (rather than a receipt of benefit) results in a *get meusah*. See *supra* text at notes 270-272. But see *infra* notes 656-568 (uncertainty whether secular or religious law controls).

Chapter Five

Interjurisdictional and Comparative Law Aspects of Civil Enforcement

This chapter briefly discusses a miscellany of themes which focus on the civil courts having to consider the requirements of religious divorce law and enforce or at least accord recognition to those requirements. The first deals with what might be termed the "secular" *agunah* predicament where a spouse did obtain a religious divorce but is unable to obtain a secular one. To what degree will secular courts accord recognition to religious ceremonies? That aspect of church-state law has, of course, only limited relevance to the *agunah* of this book. The second theme, on the other hand - United States recognition and enforcement of foreign judgments to grant a *get* - may be a remedial avenue of considerable importance, albeit for a relatively small category of women, *i.e.*, Israeli women who have obtained judgments from state-sanctioned rabbinical courts. The chapter concludes with a brief look at how courts in other countries have responded.

UNITED STATES RECOGNITION OF RELIGIOUS DIVORCES

Divorces Obtained Abroad

While the bulk of this book deals with the utilization of the judicial system to secure a *get*, occasionally courts are called upon to determine the *secular* effect of a *get* already given. For hundreds of years, religious communities in Europe were given exclusive jurisdiction over matters of personal status pertaining to their membership. Indeed, one's very membership in a faith community was not totally voluntary. By the *secular* law of the land, if one was born into a given religion and did not undergo a formal conversion process, he or she would automatically be subject to the jurisdiction of the ecclesiastical courts, at least with respect to areas such as marriage and divorce.[474] In Great Britain, for example, although prior to 1857 one could obtain a civil divorce only through a special Act of Parliament, a *get* issued by a recognized rabbinical court was accorded presumptive validity. With the introduction of judicial dissolution in 1857, however, there began to be movement away from the recognition of ecclesiastical divorces so that in 1866 the Registrar-General decided as a matter of law that a Jewish divorce could no longer be recognized as valid.[475] Since that time, it has been the invariable practice of the London *Bait Din* and the Chief Rabbinate of Great Britain not to execute a *get* until a civil divorce has been finalized.[476] A similar development took place in France and other European countries.[477]

In the United States, while all states recognize the civil validity of a clerical marriage,[478] no state accords recognition to a Jewish religious divorce. A typical example of non-recognition appears in *Chertok v. Chertok.*[479] That case involved an action for annulment of a marriage on the grounds that at the time the marriage was contracted, defendant was still legally married to his previous wife. Defendant contended that his former wife had already received a religious divorce. The *get* was executed in New York and forwarded through the mails to his first wife in Russia. Assuming that the Russian government would have recognized the *get* as effecting a valid dissolution, a highly questionable proposition at best,[480] the court nonetheless held that because the proceedings were initiated in New York and under New York non-judicial divorces are void, defendant was still married to his first wife and the second

---

474. During much of the Middle Ages, Jewish communities were given almost total judicial autonomy with respect to their membership. While this autonomy was gradually lessened after the French Revolution and the so-called "civil emancipation," control over marriage and divorce was the last to be ceded. See Kisch, *Relations Between Jewish and Christian Courts in the Middle Ages*, LOUIS GINSBERG JUBILEE VOLUME, p. 201 (1945).

475. See Maidment, *The Legal Effect of Religious Divorces*, 37 MOD. L. REV. 611, 619-620 (1974). Professor Maidment notes that despite this nonrecognition, courts have regarded the existence of *get* as an agreement to separate, thereby negating any claim of involuntary desertion. See, *e.g.*, *Joseph v. Joseph*, [1953] 2 All Eng. Rep. 710 (Court of Appeal 1953).

476. See 161 LAW TIMES 244 (March 20, 1876).

477. France was the first European nation to institute civil divorce; in the aftermath of the Revolution, the jurisdiction of ecclesiastical courts was sharply curtailed. Civil divorce, however, was abolished in 1816 and was not finally reinstituted until 1884. Thus, in those interim years, recognition was accorded to religious divorces and on occasion such divorces were even judicially compelled. See Hertzberg, THE FRENCH ENLIGHTENMENT AND THE JEWS, pp. 191-193, 239-247. With respect to Italy, an 1806 concordat between Napoleon I and the Jews similarly limited ecclesiastical authority. See Glenn, *Where Heavens Meet: The Compelling of Religious Divorces*, 28 AMERICAN JOURNAL OF COMPARATIVE LAW 1 at 5,13 (1980).

478. This has been true at least as far back as the mid-18th Century and, for New England, even further. See survey in Blake, THE ROAD TO RENO: A HISTORY OF DIVORCE IN THE UNITED STATES, pp. 34-62.

479. 208 A.D. 161, 203 N.Y.S. 2d 163 (N.Y. App. Div. 1924).

480. See *infra* note 483.

marriage was therefore annulled.[481]

Nevertheless, under general principles of conflict of laws, considerations of comity allow or even mandate civil recognition of ecclesiastical divorces to the extent they are recognized by the jurisdiction in which they were rendered. Thus, in *Leshinsky v. Leshinsky*,[482] where an emigrating woman had received a *get* in Russia before coming to the United States, the court held that her first marriage was validly dissolved and her second husband had no grounds to petition for an annulment. (This again proceeds on the dubious assumption that Russia at the time would have accorded full recognition to religious divorces).[483]

In short, the validity and recognition of a divorce depend on the civil law of the jurisdiction in which it was issued.[484] If a Jewish religious divorce

---

481. *Accord: In re Goldman's Estate*, 282 N.Y.S. 787 (N.Y. Surrogate's Court 1935), where a putative spouse petitioned for letters of administration alleging that she was a widow of the decedent. The children of the decedent from a former marriage claimed that she was still legally married to a prior spouse. While she had still lived in Russia, her first husband, who had come to America some years later, had sent her through the mails a *get* which she received. Several years later, she herself came to the United States and established a relationship with the decedent that could have constituted a common-law marriage. In holding that the *get* was of no legal effect (and hence, the woman could not be the surviving common-law spouse of the decedent), the court once again relied on the fact that the *get* was written in the State of New York and therefore New York governs its validity. Interestingly, both *Chertok* and *Goldman* misconstrue Jewish law. A religious divorce is not effective when the *get* is written but only upon delivery of the document to the wife or her designated agent. As such, the act of divorce technically took place in Russia, not in the United States and its validity here should be coextensive with whatever validity it would have in the jurisdiction where the ceremony took place. The courts were apparently led astray by viewing the writing of a *get* in a *bait din* as equivalent to a judgment of dissolution and mailing of the *get* as simply notice to the other party of that judgment. In point of fact, receipt by that party is the very thing that makes the dissolution effective.

482. 25 N.Y.S. 841 (Super. Ct. of New York City 1893).

483. *Accord: Machransky v. Machransky*, 166 N.E. 423 (Court of Appeals for Cuyahoga County 1927). Courts are not always careful in their determinations of what foreign law actually provides. In *Goldman's Estate*, *supra* note 480, the *get* in question was executed in 1924. In determining that the *get* would have been valid under Russian law, the court relied on the testimony of a rabbi who stated that when he had left Russia twenty-one years previously (in 1903!), local law provided that in matters of divorce Jews were governed by Jewish law. The court seems to have forgotten about the Russian Revolution of 1917, after which Czarist law (as well as deference to any type of religious accommodation) was certainly superseded. A *get* that would have been recognized had it been executed in 1903 would certainly not have passed muster in 1924.

484. This will at least be true where both parties were domiciled in the jurisdiction granting the divorce or where the nondomiciliary submitted to the court's authority even if the marriage were solemnized elsewhere. Whether this rule would also apply in the case of an *ex parte* divorce where only one

is recognized as valid under the secular laws of the jurisdiction where the divorce took place, it will be regarded as valid even in those jurisdictions that normally refuse to recognize nonjudicial or ecclesiastical dissolutions.[485] Conversely, a divorce that is invalid at the place of its execution will not be valid anywhere.[486]

---

party was domiciled in the jurisdiction granting the divorce is open to question. See Scoles and Hay, CONFLICT OF LAWS §15.25, p. 504. Given the fact that in any religious divorce the husband or his delegate must by necessity have participated in the execution of the *get*, the need for an appearance will always be satisfied.

485. Until 1974, England had a peculiar twist in the application of these common law principles. Under *Qureshi v. Qureshi*, [1971] 1 All Eng. Rep. 325 (Probate, Divorce and Admiralty Div. 1970) [dealing with the Islam *talaq*] and the earlier case of *Har-Shefi v. Har-Shefi*, [1953] 1 All Eng. Rep. 783 (Court of Appeal 1953) [dealing with a *get*], even a religious or "nonjudicial" divorce effected in England would be recognized if such a divorce was valid under the civil law of the parties' domicile. Thus, where both husband and wife were domiciled in Israel, England would recognize the validity of their *get* even if it were executed and delivered while the parties were physically present on British soil. (The case law never clarified what the result would be if only one party were domiciled in a recognizing jurisdiction). In any case, *Qureshi* was overruled by the Domicile and Matrimonial Proceedings Act of 1973 which provides that *any* nonjudicial divorce obtained in the British Isles after January 1, 1974 is void. See [1973] 2 STAT. OF ELIZABETH II, Ch. 45 at 1309. My understanding is that this has always been the American rule.

486. See *Sokel v. People*, 72 N.E. 382 (Ill. 1927) (upholding of criminal prosecution for bigamy notwithstanding the fact that first wife received a *get* in Palestine since, under British mandatory law, a *get* was not recognized as a valid means of dissolution. This result would of course be different today because in the present State of Israel the *get* is the exclusive method for dissolving Jewish marriages and hence an Israeli *get* would have full recognition in the United States.

The well-established rule that a divorce that is valid in the place of its issuance will be accorded recognition elsewhere poses special problems in secular court systems that follow private international law norms but incorporate within their structure ecclesiastical tribunals. This gives rise to the anomaly of one part of the system upholding the validity of an act which the other part declares to be invalid. Thus, while the *secular* courts of the State of Israel will accord recognition to a civil divorce valid under the laws of the jurisdiction in which it was issued, its very own rabbinical courts will not. Conversely, the rabbinical courts will recognize a *get* as effecting a valid termination of marriage although the *get* has no such effect in the place where it was issued and will therefore be given no recognition by the Israeli secular court system. For a general discussion of these conflicts, see *Skornik v. Skornik*, 8 Piske Din 141 (Israeli Supreme Court 1954).

The potential for judicial conflict is somewhat minimized by the fact that the statutory jurisdiction of the rabbinical courts in Israel is limited to marriages and divorce *within* Israel's borders. Thus, for the most part, rabbinic courts will have no occasion to determine the validity of an American civil divorce. As *Skornik* indicates, however, the possibilities of conflict have not been

Divorces Obtained Domestically

Although it is true that a religious divorce executed in the United States has no legal effect, it is not true that it is totally ignored. Courts have taken judicial notice that a *get* is at least regarded by the immediate parties as a dissolution mechanism and this has affected their rulings in a variety of contexts. *Shilman v. Shilman*[487] is a good example. In that case, the parties were married in Russia. After receiving a *get* in New York, the wife went back to Russia to remarry. In order to dissolve the marriage under New York law so that he could remarry, the husband sued for divorce on grounds of desertion. In denying the husband's petition, the court found that executing the *get* was an expression of consent to the desertion and hence the necessary grounds for relief could not be established. This result seems excessively harsh, effectively creating a reverse-*agunah* situation: the wife back in Russia is perfectly free to marry on the strength of her religious divorce while the husband is disabled from establishing the grounds that would warrant civil dissolution. With the advent of no-fault divorce, one would hope cases of this nature would be quite infrequent.[488]

Another interesting example of quasi-recognition of a *get* occurred in the immigration context. In *Petition of Schlau*,[489] a man had married his present wife in a civil ceremony in New York after giving his first wife a religious divorce. The government denied his application for citizenship on the grounds that: (1) religious divorces were invalid under New York law; (2) as a result the petitioner's second marriage was a bigamous relationship; (3) the petitioner was therefore of bad moral character. The district court took the quite sensible position that the legal invalidity of a *get* is not enough to show bad moral character. When a person acts morally under Jewish law, particularly where that law was followed in his country of origin, the requisite good moral character has been established. On appeal, the Second Circuit qualified Judge Rifkind's ruling by imposing the additional element that the

---

eliminated.

It should also be emphasized that regardless of the degree of judicial recognition a civil divorce is accorded, the *religious* duty to execute a *get* is never abrogated.

487. 174 N.Y.S. 385 (N.Y. Sup. Ct. 1918).

488. British courts have taken the same position. See *Joseph v. Joseph*, [1953] 2 All Eng. Rep. 710 (Court of Appeal 1953) (A woman who requested and received a *get* from her estranged husband could not then petition the courts for divorce on the grounds of desertion). But *cf. Corbett v. Corbett*, [1957] 1 W.L.R. 486, [1957] All Eng. Rep. 621 (Probate, Divorce, and Admiralty Div. 1957) (Where wife merely acceded to husband's demand that she receive a *get*, she is not barred from alleging desertion). See also *Preger v. Preger*, [1926] All Eng. Rep. 302 (Probate, Divorce and Admiralty Div. 1926) and *Leeser v. Leeser*, reported in the Times 2/5/1955, both of which held that acquiescence in a *get* did not constitute consenting to the other's committing adultery and did not bar the obtaining of a civil divorce on those grounds. Those cases did suggest, in dicta, that if the wife knew that her husband was contemplating marrying another woman at the time of the *get*, the result would be different.

489. 41 F.Supp. 161 (S.D.N.Y. 1941).

petitioner must have a good faith belief in the validity of the *get* and remanded the case for a trial on that issue.[490]

Courts have also utilized the presence or absence of a *get* as a factor in the setting of alimony, one method that can at least indirectly induce recalcitrant husbands to provide their wives with a religious divorce.[491]

Suffice it to say that these peripheral aspects of quasi-recognition have little or no bearing on the *agunah*-problem. Insofar as a couple domiciled in the United States is concerned, in the absence of contract a United States court will neither order the execution of a *get* nor will it recognize a *get* as valid for purposes of civil dissolution.

CIVIL ENFORCEMENT OF FOREIGN JUDGMENTS TO GIVE A *GET*

Another aspect of recognition, however, carries a glimmer of promise at least in a small category of cases. Under the present laws of the State of

---

490. 136 F.2d 480 (2nd Cir. 1943). Somewhat disturbingly, three earlier cases in New York came to the opposite conclusion. See *In re Spiegel*, 24 F.2d 605 (S.D.N.Y. 1928) and *Petition of Horwitz*, 48 F.2d 652 (E.D.N.Y. 1931), both of which held that remarriage after a religious divorce constituted bigamy and evidence of poor moral character that would justify a denial of citizenship. *United States v. Zaltsman*, 19 F. Supp. 305 (W.D.N.Y. 1937), used this rationale to revoke citizenship. It is submitted these were in error. Not only do they fail to take into account the good faith of parties who honestly and even reasonably believed, or may have believed, that a *get* was all that was necessary to enable them to remarry, but even more basically, failed to recognize that a religious divorce that is valid by the civil law of the jurisdiction in which it was executed and delivered will be given extraterritorial effect even in the United States. See *Leshinsky v. Leshinsky*, 25 N.Y.S. 841 (Super. Ct. of New York City 1893) and discussion *supra* note 482. In at least some of these cases, the *get* in question was executed in European countries where there was at least the possibility of validation under local law. The failure of the courts to consider this fact was erroneous. In any event, the Second Circuit's ruling in *Schlau* presumably overrules this trilogy *sub silentio*.

491. See *Brett v. Brett*, [1969] 1 W.L.R. 487, [1969] 1 All Eng. Rep. 1007 (Court of Appeal 1968), where the court imposed an annual alimony obligation of 250 pounds effective as of the date the wife receives a *get* and increased the award ten-fold for the period of time that she does not. It has been suggested that for an American court to take this approach would be a violation of the First Amendment since the husband would be indirectly compelled to execute a *get*. See Friedell, *The First Amendment and Jewish Divorce: A Comment on Stern v. Stern*, 18 JOURNAL OF FAMILY LAW 525, 526 (1979-1980). As *Brett* itself noted, however, the differential alimony award may be justified on purely secular considerations, *i.e.*, a woman with no prospect of remarrying is in greater economic need than one who can. But see *supra* note 392 and *infra* text at notes 660-668 (*Brett* approach may be *halachically* problematical as well as empirically incorrect).

Israel,[492] all matters of marriage and divorce of Jews who are "nationals" or "residents" of the State of Israel are under the exclusive jurisdiction of the rabbinical tribunals of the State. As a matter of substantive law, all marriages and divorces between Jews must be performed in accordance with Jewish law. The *bait din*'s jurisdiction includes issues pertaining to alimony and child support. Most uniquely, Israeli law provides:

> Where a rabbinical court, by final judgment, has ordered that a husband be compelled to grant his wife a *get* or that a wife be compelled to accept a *get* from her husband, a district court [*i.e.*, a non-Rabbinic tribunal] may, upon expiration of six months from the day of the making of the order and upon application of the attorney-general, compel compliance with the order by imprisonment.[493]

Rabbinical courts are thus not only given jurisdiction to oversee the dissolution process but are given the power to issue binding orders directing the execution of a *get*, orders that are ultimately enforceable by imprisonment or fines.[494] While in the absence of an express or implied agreement to give a *get*, no American court could issue a direct order to that effect,[495] it is well established under principles of comity and recognition of foreign judgments that a domestic court will enforce a decree of an authorized rabbinical tribunal ordering execution of a *get* to the same degree that it would enforce a civil judgment touching on any other matter.[496] Assuming the rabbinical courts themselves properly exercised jurisdiction, a victimized spouse would be able to follow her husband to the United States and obtain the assistance of the courts.[497]

---

492. Laws of the State of Israel, Rabbinical Courts Jurisdiction (Marriage and Divorce) Law 5713-1953 (No. 83).

493. *Id.*, section 6.

494. Naturally, however, such orders can be issued only under circumstances where Jewish law permits compulsion to be employed. For a discussion of these circumstances, see *supra* text at notes 108-160.

495. Indeed, even with an express agreement to that effect, a number of courts have refused enforcement. See *supra* text at notes 218-219.

496. See *Shapiro v. Shapiro*, 442 N.Y.S. 2d 928, *aff'd*, 449 N.Y.S. 2d 806 (N.Y. App. Div. 1982), mtn. for leave to appeal to Court of Appeals denied. United States courts will also defer to prior determinations of alimony and child support but retain the freedom to reopen those judgments in the light of changed circumstances just as it could in the case of a sister-state judgment. *Sandra S. v. Glenn M.S.*, 506 N.Y.S. 2d 259 (N.Y. Fam. Ct. 1986).

497. While the rule in the text is well-recognized, one might well question why. Don't First Amendment concerns enter the picture even in the context of a foreign judgment? A simple response might be that First Amendment concerns are never implicated in the enforcement of foreign judgments even where those judgments are based in some degree on religious principles. This is so because the United States is not according recognition to religious law as such but is merely upholding the secular judgments of the tribunals of a sovereign state. Surely, however, that is an incomplete response. No United States court would ever order a party to pray or perform a devotional or liturgical act regardless of the legal authority of the court that issued the edict. It is not immediately obvious why an order to execute a *get* is any different. Presumably, the distinction would lie in the nondevotional nature of the *get-*

In many of these types of cases (spouses who have left the country), the severe jurisdictional limitations placed on rabbinical courts under their own local law often preclude their ability to issue *get* orders in the first place and hence eliminate the possibilities for United States backup enforcement.[498] Nevertheless, in at least some documented instances of *agunah*, United States recognition may be a partial avenue of considerable relief.[499]

THE EUROPEAN EXPERIENCE: A COMPARATIVE PERSPECTIVE*

The problem of a secular society having to deal with religious family law is not of course uniquely American and indeed was confronted by a number of European and North African states as early as the 19th Century.

In the French colonies of North Africa - Algeria, Tunisia, and Morocco - the personal status of the parties was historically governed by religious law.[500] For example, the Court of Appeal of Algier in 1868 applied Jewish divorce rules in recognizing the validity of a Jewish divorce although divorce was not even permitted under French law at the time.[501] This remained true in Tunisia and Morocco throughout the period of French rule. In Algeria, however, the *Décret Cremieux*[502] of October 24, 1870 secularized Jewish family relations by making them subject to French Civil Law. The displacing of religious law by secular gave rise to the difficult issue of the extent to which civil tribunals could compel the execution and delivery of a *get*, an issue that was squarely posed in the celebrated *Darienté* case. Darienté had married a woman in a religious ceremony in 1871, had refused a civil celebration, eventually married another woman civilly and refused to deliver a *get* to his first wife. Under the literal wording of the *Décret Cremieux*, Darienté had committed no wrong. Not being legally married to his first wife, he was

---

ceremony and the fact that it necessitates no profession of faith but the cited cases fail to clarify this crucial point.

498. See discussion *infra* text at notes 511-530.

499. Note, however, that secular enforcement of the decision of a *bait din* may result in a *halachically*-invalid *get meusah*. If compulsion is appropriate, *halacha* validates even non-Jewish coercion if it is being employed to induce compliance with the decision of the *bait din*. However, this may pose problems in cases of *yotzee* rather than *kofin*, a distinction that American courts might find difficult to grasp. See *supra* text at notes 108-120 and at 291-299. [But *cf.* *supra* note 116 (view of R. Herzog)].

*An excellent and comprehensive treatment of comparative and international aspects of the *agunah* problem (received as this book was going to press) appears in a recent publication of the South African Law Commission, WORKING PAPER 45: JEWISH DIVORCE (1992).

500. The information in this paragraph is based largely on the description in Glenn, *supra* note 477, at 13-16.

501. Algier, 3 February 1868, *Jurisprudence algérienne de 1830 à 1876*, publiée par Estoublon IV 1868-1876 at 5 (1891). Civil divorce was first instituted in 1792, abolished in 1816, and not reinstituted until 1884. Glenn, *supra* note 477, at 13 n.60.

502. S.1871.3.11, *Code de L'Algérie Annoté* at 373 (1896-1907).

perfectly free to marry another. Nevertheless, the Cour de Cassation, affirming the Court of Appeal of Algier, granted the first wife's request for an order compelling the husband to deliver the *get* on the theory that his refusal to do so was an unjustifiable deprivation of her liberty to marry and an infringement of her freedom of conscience.[503] This was true even though French law did not even recognize the institution of civil divorce. The *Darienté* decision was widely followed, and, although binding only on cases arising from the French colonies, was applied in cases arising from the interior of France as well.[504] Thus, notwithstanding concepts of separation of church and state analogous to those mandated by the First Amendment,[505] French courts have little trouble in ordering the execution of a *get*. Moreover, such compulsion does not require the existence of an express or implied contract but is based on unjustifiable infringement of another's freedom - a generalized notion of *prima facie* tort, a theory to which American courts have not been particularly receptive.[506]

Germany and Great Britain have had considerably less experience with this issue although there too the precedents are suggestive. As early as 1904, the Imperial German *Reichsgericht* refused to enforce an interspousal agreement to effect a religious divorce on the grounds that enforcing such an agreement would be an impermissible blurring of church and state.[507] This holding was

---

503. *Darienté v. Lelouch*, reported in [1877] DES LOIS ET DES ARRÊTS at 27 (Court of Cassation 1876).

504. See cases cited in Glenn, *supra* note 477, at 14 notes 59-70. The leading modern case reached the Court of Cassation in 1972. A husband had refused to give his wife a *get* and claimed that, under the principles mandating separation of church and state of 9 December 1705, he could not be compelled to do so. The court held that the action of giving a *get* was nonreligious in nature and civil enforcement was therefore an appropriate remedy to protect a woman's interest in remarrying. See *G. v. K.*, Civ. 13 December 1972, reported in GAZETTE DU PALAIS (G.P.) 1973, at page 416.

505. The constitutional principle of separation of church and state is affirmed by Title One, Article Two of the Constitution of France. See Blaustein and Flanz (ed.), 5 CONSTITUTIONS OF THE COUNTRIES OF THE WORLD at p. 22 (1988).

506. See RESTATEMENT OF TORTS (Second) §766B and *infra* text at notes 724-727.

507. B. v. B., 57 R.G.Z. 250 (German Sup. Ct. 1904). Excerpts from this opinion are cited in Note, *Civil Enforceability of Religious Antenuptial Agreements*, 23 UNIV. OF CHICAGO L. REV. 122 at 131 (1955). Significantly, the court did *not* base its decision on the equivalent of a "free exercise" claim. To the contrary, it accepted the finding of the lower court that the granting of a *get* was not a liturgical act, did not involve a profession of faith, and could be accomplished through an agent. Rather the problem was one of excessive entanglement of the state into areas governed by ecclesiastical law; to use analogous, American terms, the issue was one of establishment, rather than one of free exercise.

reaffirmed in a 1973 case although on different grounds.[508]

Note must also be taken of the creative approaches employed by British courts. Although courts will not directly order the parties to comply with religious law, the inability of a spouse to remarry in accordance with the dictates of his/her faith may be a factor in determining the size of an alimony award. Reasoning that spouses with no prospect of remarriage face greater need than spouses who have no such disability, courts have entered two-tier alimony decrees imposing higher levels of payment until such time as a *get* is granted.[509] Such decrees indirectly compel the granting of a *get* without doing violence to freedom of conscience concerns. Linking alimony with a *get*, however, may raise serious *halachic* concerns of *meusah*.[510]

AGUNOT IN THE STATE OF ISRAEL*

As noted, the State of Israel is unique in allowing civil enforcement of the decisions of its rabbinical courts, at least in the limited areas of family law.[511] One would assume that this alone would greatly minimize the *agunah* problem. A closer look at Israeli law will reveal that this is not the case.

Paragraph 6 of the Rabbinical Courts Jurisdiction (Marriage and Divorce) Law of 1953 provides:

> Where a rabbinical court, by final judgment, has ordered that a husband be compelled to grant his wife a *get* or that a wife be compelled to accept a *get* from her husband, a district court may, upon the expiration of six months from the day of the making of the order, and upon application of the attorney-general, compel compliance with

---

508. OLG Koln, 19 March 1973 (decision of Koln *Oberlandesgericht*) reported in 9 MONATSSCHRIFT FÜR DEUTSCHES RECHT 768 (1973). Interestingly, the case involved a husband petitioning the court for an order directing his wife to receive a *get*. The court denied relief on the ground that compelling a party to participate in a religious ceremony violates guarantees of religious freedom.

509. *Brett v. Brett* [1969] 1 W.L.R. 487, [1969] 1 All Eng. Rep. 1007 (Court of Appeal 1968). See also *supra* notes 392 and *infra* notes 660-669 (*halachic* problems with the *Brett* approach).

510. See *supra* text at notes 60-65 and note 392 and *infra* notes 660-669.

*This section will cite and discuss a number of decisions in the name of the Israeli Supreme Court. Technically, the highest court in the State of Israel is called *Bait HaMishpat Ha'Elyon*, a title normally translated as the High Court of Justice. For the convenience of the general reader more familiar with the American judicial system, I will refer to this tribunal by the more colloquial name Israeli Supreme Court.

511. *Supra* text at notes 492-493. It should be noted that, within the panoramic diversity of the Jewish communities in Israel, there are many types of rabbinical courts, most of which are not affiliated with the state judicial structure. Only the decisions of the rabbinical courts under the auspices of the state, however, are accorded secular recognition and civil enforcement. The decisions of other *batei din* are enforced exclusively through the religious norms of the community (which may indeed be extremely potent and effective, see *supra* note 46).

the order by imprisonment.[512]

Note the steps that must be taken before imprisonment may be imposed. First, the rabbinical court must make a finding that compulsion is warranted under the principles of Jewish law. Because of the vital distinction between *kofin* and *yotzee* orders,[513] rabbinical courts are willing to issue "compulsion orders" only in a relatively small number of cases. According to one study, between 1953 and 1977, rabbinical courts issued only twelve *kofin* orders that could ultimately justify imprisonment.[514] Because this difficulty is *halachic* rather than secular in nature, there is little or nothing the Knesset could do to rectify it.

There are, however, unnecessary procedural hurdles built into the statute which make it less helpful or protective than it otherwise could be even given the *halachic* constraints.[515] The six- month waiting period may in many cases be excessive, particularly when the husband has already declared his refusal to obey the decision of the *bait din*. It must be remembered that, before the *bait din* ever issues its *kofin* order, it has already come to the conclusion that the husband should in good conscience divorce his wife and has endeavored to convince him to comply. A "compulsion order" is the last step in a protracted process that takes months or even years and is issued with great reluctance only after all other attempts have failed. Tacking on another six months to a process that has already taken so much time is simply prolonging a spouse's agony.

A second problem lies in the fact that the complaint seeking enforcement must be lodged by the attorney-general. Neither the rabbinical court nor the aggrieved spouse has standing to initiate enforcement. The attorney-general has absolute discretion in deciding whether and when to file or not to file and there are instances of delays of up to three years before a

---

512. For a good discussion of the background of the 1953 law and the tangled history of the jurisdiction of the Israeli rabbinical courts during the period of British mandatory rule, see Chigier, ISH V'ISHA B'DINAI YISRAEL, pp. 1-22 and 72-89. (In the English edition, this material appears on pages 6-109.) A more detailed, technical analysis appears in Chigier, *Rabbinical Courts in Israel*, 2 ISRAEL LAW REV. 147 (1967).

Dr. Chigier points out that the 1953 act is one of the few laws that has not been amended since its enactment, not because the law is perfect but because the conflicts between the religious parties who would like to expand the authority of these courts and the secularists who would like to curtail them have resulted in an uneasy truce or stalemate. See English edition, p. 60, note 1. Nevertheless, while the wording of the statute has not been changed, its scope has been considerably narrowed by restrictive (secular) judicial interpretation as the remainder of this section will discuss.

513. *Supra* text at notes 108-120.

514. Chigier, *supra* note 512, p. 271 (Eng. ed.) quoting Zerach Warhaftig.

515. It must be emphasized as a point of clarification that these procedural and jurisdictional hurdles are not imposed by the *halachic* system but by the secular laws of the State of Israel which condition *secular* recognition and enforcement on these steps being followed.

request was lodged with the district court.[516] While aggrieved spouses may in rare cases obtain the equivalent of a mandamus order against the attorney-general for an abuse of discretion, such petitions for mandamus are commonly denied in summary fashion.[517] At a minimum, the power to seek enforcement should be vested in the person whose interests are adversely affected by willful noncompliance.

A more serious problem lies in the general trend of the Israeli secular judiciary to curtail the authority of its own rabbinic tribunals. First, these courts are given no jurisdiction unless *both* parties to the marriage are either citizens or permanent residents (domiciliaries) of the State of Israel.[518] If one of the parties is a nonresident, the rabbinical courts have no jurisdiction to order the granting of a *get* even if the marriage was itself solemnized within the confines of the state. Indeed, this rule has been applied not only for the protection of a nonresident spouse but even where the petitioner is the nonresident and is perfectly willing to have the *bait din* hear the case and order relief against the resident.[519] The courts have also ruled that domicile or citizenship for purposes of rabbinic jurisdiction is to be determined as of the commencement of the divorce proceeding, rather than as of the time of the marriage.[520] Thus, even where two Israeli citizens were married, the subsequent emigration of one of them would deprive the *bait din* of its authority over the divorce.

---

516. Chigier, *supra* note 512, p. 266 (Eng. ed.) quoting Ze'ev Falk.

517. Indeed, Chigier notes (as of 1985), there was only one attempt to appeal to the High Court of Justice (the Israeli Supreme Court) against the attorney-general's decision not to lodge a petition and the appeal was dismissed summarily. *Id.*

518. See, *e.g.*, *Matlon v. Rabbinical Court*, 17 Piske Din 1640 (Israeli Supreme Court 1964); *X v. Rabbinical Court*, 17 Piske Din 2222 (Israeli Supreme Court 1964). These cases also rejected the old common law rule of "constructive domicile" which assigned a wife the same domicile as her husband irrespective of where she actually lived. Thus, where an Israeli domiciliary petitioned the rabbinical court for a divorce against his wife who was living in Italy, the Israeli Supreme Court ruled that the rabbinical courts were without statutory jurisdiction.

519. See *Genfell v. Rabbinical Court*, 25 Piske Din 471 (Israeli Supreme Court 1971). (A foreign national lodged a petition for divorce against his wife, an Israeli national, in the rabbinical court. The Israeli Supreme Court ruled that rabbinical courts have no jurisdiction over petitions filed by nondomiciliaries even where the respondent is an Israeli national). While the logic of this holding has been soundly criticized, see Chigier (Eng. ed.), *supra* note 512, p. 87, it remains the law. Indeed, based on the well-known legal principle that a court which lacks jurisdiction cannot be empowered to decide by virtue of the parties' consent, it is probable that, if one of the parties is a nondomiciliary, the rabbinical courts would have to dismiss the petition on its own motion even if neither party objects. (In the narrow context of *agunah*, however, if both parties are agreeable to a *get*, there is of course no impediment to their having one executed since there is no *halachic* requirement that a *get* be authorized by the government-sponsored *batei din*.)

520. See analysis in Chigier (Heb. ed.), *supra* note 512, p. 75.

Second, even where both parties are Israeli citizens or domiciliaries, the rabbinic courts cannot assert jurisdiction if one party is physically absent from the state.[521] If an Israeli citizen simply leaves the country on a tourist visa prior to the commencement of a divorce proceeding, that alone would suffice to deprive the *bait din* of its authority to proceed unless and until the absent spouse could be physically served with a summons within the territorial confines of the State of Israel. Conversely, and, somewhat inexplicably, even where the absent party is the party seeking relief (through a local attorney) rather than the one being served, jurisdiction will still not be present despite the petitioner's expressed willingness to seek relief in a *bait din*.[522]

These judicially-imposed constraints of mutual domicile and actual physical presence deprive the rabbinical courts of their authority to handle a large number of *agunah* matters, particularly those that involve spouses of different nationalities or spouses who have simply left Israel, even with the retention of their citizenship.[523] These rules also severely limit the possibility of United States recognition and enforcement of *get* judgments. While it is true that American courts will indeed recognize and enforce foreign judgments that are valid at the place of their rendition,[524] such judgments must be rendered by courts that have jurisdiction to do so under their own local law. The emasculation of rabbinic jurisdiction by the decisions of the Israeli Supreme Court has direct repercussions on the possibilities of interstate enforcement.[525]

---

521. See *Matlon v. Rabbinical Court*, *supra* note 518; *Reiss v. Rabbinical Court*, 27 Piske Din 25 (Israeli Supreme Court 1974); *Chen v. Rabbinical Court*, 31 Piske Din 679 (Israeli Supreme Court 1977). (See, however, the strong dissent in *Chen* by Justice Landau who argues that physical presence should be unnecessary in the case of a citizen or domiciliary.)

522. This was in fact the case in *Reiss*, *supra* note 521, where the *petitioner* was the absent party.

523. Some commentators have asserted yet a third limitation on the jurisdiction of rabbinical courts. Even where both parties are citizens or domiciliaries and even where both are physically present at the time of the commencement of the suit, the rabbinical courts are empowered to order a *get* only where the marriage itself was solemnized in Israel. This further limitation appears to have been flatly rejected in *Kahanof v. Rabbinical Court*, 29 Piske Din 449 (Israeli Supreme Court 1975).

Somewhat inexplicably, Chigier (Eng. ed.), p. 269, cites *Kahanof* for the proposition that if the marriage did not take place in Israel, the husband "will probably have nothing to worry about." My understanding of the case is exactly the opposite: while the place of solemnization may indeed be relevant on a variety of issues pertaining to support and maintenance, it does not appear to be material on the narrow issue of whether the *bait din* may order the execution of a *get*. My reading of *Kahanof* is borne out by Chigier's discussion of the case at pp. 77-79 of the Hebrew edition.

524. See *supra* text at notes 482-485 and at 496-499.

525. It should be understood, however, that once the rabbinic court has acquired jurisdiction based on the twin factors of domicile and physical presence, a subsequent absconding of one of the parties cannot divest it of its authority. Thus, assuming the husband was a citizen of Israel and physically present within the state when his wife commenced an action seeking a *get*, his

The Israeli secular courts have also been hostile to the indirect means of persuasion that rabbinical courts attempt to employ. As noted earlier, it is a fairly-common practice among *batei din* in Israel to pressure a recalcitrant husband into granting a *get* by imposing a high support obligation.[526] For the reasons stated above, the advantage of this mechanism is that it obviates the need to establish the narrow grounds that would warrant compulsion. Yet the Israeli Supreme Court has ruled that the issuance of a support order for the purpose of indirectly inducing a *get* (rather than for purely need-related factors) is beyond the jurisdiction of the rabbinical courts and invalid.[527]

In short, the prevalent attitude of the Israeli Supreme Court towards the assertion of jurisdiction by *batei din* can best be summed up in the words of its own pronouncement:

> Because the rabbinical courts are outside of the ordinary framework of the judiciary, the statutes granting such courts jurisdiction should be construed as narrowly as possible. Where the [jurisdictional] statute is susceptible to two interpretations, preference will be given to the narrower, rather than broader, one.[528]

Unfortunately, however, the lesser the authority of the *bait din*, the greater will be the prevalence of women unable to secure religious divorces.

It must also be kept in mind that even where the system does work optimally, it does not guarantee a woman's freedom. First, some husbands may not be apprehended and will be able to avoid arrest. If they escape to another jurisdiction, there may not be an extradition treaty in effect covering such a contingency. Some husbands may be perfectly willing to languish in jail (where, after all, they receive food, clothing, and shelter) rather than execute a *get* and if that is the case, the hands of the *bait din* are simply tied. (As noted repeatedly, the *bait din* can never dissolve the marriage; it can only order the husband to do so.) Finally, some husbands literally have nothing to lose. In a number of *agunah* cases, husbands are already incarcerated, often for drug-related offenses or violent crimes - indeed, that is why their wives are seeking a divorce. If the maximum sanction available is imprisonment, these men obviously have no incentive to comply. It has occasionally been suggested that rabbinical courts in Israel be revested with their *halachic* authority to impose corporal punishment[529] (*e.g.*, lashes) at least in these exceptional cases, but this proposal has not found favor among the largely-secular Knesset and,

---

later emigration to the United States will not affect the jurisdiction of the rabbinical court and indeed, any judgment it renders will be accorded recognition in the United States.

526. See *supra* text at notes 383-385.

527. See *Rosensweig v. Rabbinical Court*, 9 Piske Din 1541 (Israeli Supreme Court 1955). (Actually, the court in that case affirmed the support order issued by the rabbinical court because it found that the order was not employed as an *in terrorem* mechanism to secure a *get*. The court stated emphatically, however, that to the extent the order was employed as a mechanism of indirect coercion, it would be invalid.)

528. See *Kahanof*, *supra* note 523.

529. I cannot recall the exact source of this argument but it was advanced in the context of a recalcitrant husband who was already serving a lengthy prison sentence.

in view of the trend towards curtailment of the *bait din*'s powers, is unlikely to ever be enacted.

To sum up: delicate *halachic* restrictions, time-consuming procedures, standing limitations, limited penal sanctions, spousal intransigence, and severe jurisdictional constraints all conspire to render the Israeli system far less protective of the rights of abandoned spouses (usually women) than one might have thought. Some of these pitfalls are correctable through legislation (standing, jurisdiction); others are not (spousal intransigence). In essence, however, the bottom line is clear: a woman in Israel may not fare appreciably better than her counterpart in the United States.[530]

530. This somewhat gloomy conclusion is true only insofar as judicial enforcement is concerned. Israel, however, employs other avenues that afford abandoned women a greater degree of protection than they would receive in the United States. The Chief Rabbinate, for example, has representatives that will travel worldwide at government expense to track down missing husbands and attempt to convince them to grant a *get*. While these efforts are noncoercive in nature, they have been fairly successful. For an interesting account of the Rabbinate's detective work, see Kretzmer, *Stalking Runaway Husbands*, THE JERUSALEM REPORT (July 11, 1991), p. 19.

Chapter Six

The New York *Get* Law: Permissible Accommodation or Unconstitutional Establishment

GENERAL OPERATION OF THE STATUTE

In 1983, responding to the strong urgings of the Orthodox Jewish community, New York added §253 to its Domestic Relations Law (DRL).[531] Popularly

---

*The bulk of this chapter focuses on DRL §253, a law that has been in effect since 1983. In July 1992, New York passed an additional piece of *get* legislation amending DRL §236B. This new law is discussed in Chapter Seven.

531. N.Y. DOM. REL. LAW §253 (McKinney 1988). §253 was extensively amended by Laws 1984, Ch. 945 §1. The present version of the statute reads as follows: §253. Removal of barriers to remarriage

> 1. This section applies only to a marriage solemnized in this state or in any other jurisdiction by a person specified in subdivision one of section eleven of this chapter.
>
> 2. Any party to a marriage defined in subdivision one of this section who commences a proceeding to annul the marriage or for a divorce must allege, in his or her verified complaint: (i) that, to the best of his or her knowledge, that he or she has taken or that he or she will take, prior to the entry of final judgment, all steps solely within his or her power to remove any barrier to the defendant's remarriage following the annulment or divorce; or (ii) that the defendant has waived in writing the requirements of this subdivision.
>
> 3. No final judgment of annulment or divorce shall thereafter be entered unless the plaintiff shall have filed and served a sworn statement: (i) that, to the best of his knowledge, he or she has, prior to the entry of such final judgment, taken all steps solely within his or her power to remove all barriers to the defendant's remarriage following the annulment or divorce; or (ii) that the defendant has waived in writing the requirements of this subdivision.

---

4. In any action for divorce based on subdivisions five and six of section one hundred seventy of this chapter in which the defendant enters a general appearance and does not contest the requested relief, no final judgment of annulment or divorce shall be entered unless both parties shall have filed and served sworn statements: (i) that he or she has, to the best of his or her knowledge, taken all steps solely within his or her power to remove all barriers to the other party's remarriage following the annulment or divorce; or (ii) that the other party has waived in writing the requirements of this subdivision.

5. The writing attesting to any waiver of the requirements of subdivision two, three or four of this section shall be filed with the court prior to the entry of a final judgment of annulment or divorce.

6. As used in the sworn statements prescribed by this section "barrier to remarriage" includes, without limitation, any religious or conscientious restraint or inhibition, of which the party required to make the verified statement is aware, that is imposed on a party to a marriage, under the principles held by the clergyman or minister who has solemnized the marriage, by reason of the other party's commission or withholding of any voluntary act. Nothing in this section shall be construed to require any party to consult with any clergyman or minister to determine whether there exists any such religious or conscientious restraint or inhibition. It shall not be deemed a "barrier to remarriage" within the meaning of this section if the restraint or inhibition cannot be removed by the party's voluntary act. Nor shall it be deemed a "barrier to remarriage" if the party must incur expenses in connection with removal of the restraint or inhibition and the other party refuses to provide reasonable reimbursement for such expenses. "All steps solely within his or her power" shall not be construed to include application to a marriage tribunal or other similar organization or agency of a religious denomination which has authority to annul or dissolve a marriage under the rules of such denomination.

7. No final judgment of annulment or divorce shall be entered, notwithstanding the filing of the plaintiff's sworn statement prescribed by this section, if the clergyman or minister who has solemnized the marriage certifies, in a sworn statement, that he or she has solemnized the marriage and that, to his or her knowledge, the plaintiff has failed to take all steps solely within his or her power to remove all barriers to the defendant's remarriage following the annulment or divorce, provided that the said clergyman or minister is alive and available and competent to testify at the time when final judgment would be entered.

8. Any person who knowingly submits a false sworn statement under this section shall be guilty of making an apparently sworn false statement in the first degree and shall be punished in accordance with section 210.40 of the penal law.

9. Nothing in this section shall be construed to authorize any court to inquire into or determine any ecclesiastical or religious issue.

known as the *get* law, it is designed to insure that persons who don't give or receive *gittin* will be unable to receive the benefits of a civil divorce.[532]

The truth of any statement submitted pursuant to this section shall not be the subject of any judicial inquiry, except as provided in subdivision eight of this section.

The enactment of the statute aroused considerable furor in both the legal community and the media. Representative articles in a somewhat polemical vein include a three-part series by Nat Hentoff in THE VILLAGE VOICE: *The Day Mario Cuomo Shortened the First Amendment* (Sept. 6, 1983), p. 6, col. 1; *Who Will Rescue the Jewish Women Chained in Limbo?* (Sept. 13, 1983), p. 6; and *Mario Cuomo Flunks Introductory Constitutional Law* (Sept. 20, 1983), p. 5; Kochen, *Constitutional Implications of New York's Get Statute*, NEW YORK LAW JOURNAL (Oct. 27, 1983), p. 1, col. 3 and the drafter's rejoinder, Lewin, *The Constitutional Validity of New York's Get Statute*, NEW YORK LAW JOURNAL (Nov. 16, 1983), p. 1, col. 3. See also Schick, *Get Law: More Harm Than Good for Religious Jews*, LONG ISLAND JEWISH WORLD (Sept. 2-8, 1983), p. 12 for a rare critical view of the statute from within the Orthodox camp.

532. The dominant force in getting this legislation passed was the Agudath Israel organization, a political action and social service group under the auspices of the Orthodox movement. Aware of the so-called *agunah* crisis for a number of years, Agudath Israel sponsored an all-day conference in 1980 at which rabbis, attorneys, and legal academics discussed ways in which the problem could be addressed in a manner that was both *halachically* and constitutionally sound. The central concept that emerged from this meeting was the notion that the removal of barriers to remarriage following the granting of a secular divorce was a legitimate secular interest worthy of governmental protection. An earlier draft of the bill authored by Professor Alan Dershowitz of Harvard Law School, containing provisions for compulsory arbitration on the issue of compliance, was introduced in 1981. The bill was overwhelmingly approved by both houses of the New York State Legislature. Nevertheless, Governor Carey expressed strong reservations regarding the constitutionality of the bill and, to avoid an anticipated veto, the sponsors withdrew their bill for further study.

A revised bill authored by Nathan Lewin, Esq., eliminating the arbitration panels and relying instead on a verified affidavit, was introduced in 1983. It again sailed through both houses of the legislature and was signed by Governor Cuomo in August. Well aware of the constitutional objections raised by the New York Civil Liberties Union, the Union of American Hebrew Congregations (Reform), and the American Jewish Congress, the Governor stated that he found "no impelling precedent" to indicate that the bill was unconstitutional. "If there was such a precedent, I would defer to it. [But] given the clarity of the need, the efficiency of this statutory solution, and the uncertainty of the constitutional objection, I approve the measure." He then concluded somewhat disingenuously that if there was a constitutional impediment he was sure "that our excellent courts will make that clear in due time," an approach that some critics maintained was an abdication of the executive's legal responsibility to uphold the constitution. See NEW YORK LAW JOURNAL (August 10, 1983), p. 1, column 4.

Since 1983, model *get* bills have been introduced in the legislatures of

Applicable only to marriages solemnized by a religious ceremony,[533] the statute provides that no party to a marriage may obtain a judgment of annulment or divorce unless they allege in their verified complaint that, to the best of his or her knowledge, they have taken or will take prior to entry of judgment all "steps solely within his or her power to remove any barrier to the defendant's remarriage following the annulment or divorce" or that the defendant has waived in writing the need for such steps to be taken.[534] In the event the verified complaint merely contains a statement of intention concerning future compliance, the court must defer entering final judgment until plaintiff files with the court and serves on the other party a sworn statement of actual compliance.[535] The court rendering the divorce judgment has no authority to inquire into the truth of any declaration made in the sworn statement or complaint[536] but the submission of a knowingly-false declaration may give rise to a criminal prosecution for perjury.[537]

Because the operation of the statute is somewhat complex, it may be helpful to illustrate its workings through the very situation it was designed to address. Assume a husband desires to obtain a civil divorce from his wife but out of spite or blackmail refuses to give her a *get*. She may or may not have

---

California, Connecticut, New Jersey, and Pennsylvania but have been voted down. Preliminary drafting of bills was also done in Maryland and Michigan but the bills were never formally introduced. The then-Attorney General of Maryland, Stephen Sachs, reputedly expressed the view that such a bill would be an unconstitutional establishment of religion but issued no formal written opinion to that effect.

The one concrete legislative initiative apart from the New York law is a statute enacted by Canada. The central concept of the statute - that failure to remove barriers to remarriage constitutes a secular wrong - parallels the New York approach but unlike the New York statute which is applicable only where the recalcitrant husband is the divorce plaintiff, the Canadian law provides a modicum of protection even where the victimized spouse is the petitioner. See Act of June 12, 1990, Ch. 18, I STATUTES OF CANADA (1990). A similar statute on the provincial level had previously been adopted by the province of Ontario. See Act of March 1, 1986, §§ 2(4) and 56(5)-(7), Ch. 4, STATUTES OF ONTARIO (1986). (Interestingly, the Canada approach is quite similar to what New York did in a later *get* law enacted in 1992, see *infra* Chapter Seven).

(Much of the information concerning the convoluted history of the New York law was obtained through personal conversations with Nathan Lewin, Esq., the principal draftsman of the bill. Mr. Lewin was also kind enough to make available his voluminous correspondence concerning the bill, which provided useful and enlightening background material. Information gleaned from this source is cited as LEWIN FILE).

533. §253(1).

534. §253(3).

535. *Id.*

536. §253(9).

537. §253(8). Under New York law, making a sworn "apparently false statement" is a class E felony punishable by a prison term not to exceed four years. NEW YORK PENAL LAW §§70.02(e), 210.40.

resorted to the rabbinical courts - that is not a condition under the statute - but, under her beliefs as a Jew, will be unable to marry. Husband will not be able to obtain the benefits of a civil divorce without filing a sworn statement that he has already removed any "barriers to remarriage" the other spouse faces. Since "barrier to remarriage" includes "religious or conscientious restraints or inhibitions," the failure to execute a *get* clearly qualifies as such a "barrier" and the husband cannot truthfully file such an affidavit until a *get* is granted.

It is important to see how limited this statute is. It covers a fairly narrow category of cases and provides a fairly limited protective remedy. First, the court never directly orders the husband to comply with religious law. It merely tells the husband that he will be unable to obtain a civil divorce until he complies or at least alleges under oath that he complies. If the husband is willing to forego the option of civil divorce, he is perfectly free to leave his wife stranded. Indeed, even if the wife were to seek a civil divorce against a recalcitrant husband, the affidavit requirement would not be triggered because the obligation is imposed only on the plaintiff, not the defendant. Assuming a stranded wife would eventually want to take some steps to protect her legal rights, the dictates of §253 could be avoided by a recalcitrant husband simply biding his time.

Second, even where the husband is the divorce plaintiff, he will still be able to obtain relief through the filing of a false affidavit. Under §9 of the law, the court may not inquire into the truthfulness of the allegations contained in the affidavit except in the context of a perjury prosection under §8. While the relationship of §§8 and 9 is not clear, the apparent meaning is that the court may not withhold the granting of a divorce on the grounds of evidence that the affidavit is fraudulent. Its only response is to forward such evidence to the district attorney for criminal prosection. While it is difficult to imagine a court permitting an obvious fraud, it is clear that defendant cannot seek an evidentiary hearing on the merits. Thus, whatever protective force the statute has depends on the *in terrorem* effect of the criminal justice system and the vigilance of victimized spouses in invoking the system.

Third, the statute only applies where the original marriage was solemnized through a religious ceremony.[538] It has no application to marriages which were effected civilly. Moreover, by defining "barriers to remarriage" as those barriers that exist "under the principles of the clergyman or minister who has solemnized the marriage,"[539] the statute requires plaintiff to allege granting of a *get* only when the original marriage ceremony was performed by an Orthodox or Conservative rabbi and not where the clergyman was Reform or of a Christian denomination. In most cases, this poses no problem since if the wife is still an adherent of Reform, the absence of a *get* imposes no disability. It is not uncommon, however, for there to be a change of religious affiliation or commitment in the course of a marriage - often in the direction of greater adherence to traditional beliefs - and women who do change their positions and now find themselves unable to marry without a *get* are simply

538. §253(1).
539. §253(6).

unprotected.[540] Thus, for example, the New York law would have afforded no protection to Annette Goldman.[541]

In the event husband does file a false affidavit, the victimized spouse may invoke what is popularly termed the "clergyman's veto."[542] Even if plaintiff files a sworn affidavit which states that to the best of his knowledge all "barriers to remarriage" have been removed, the court may still not enter a final judgment of divorce if the clergyman or minister who solemnized the marriage certifies in a sworn statement that plaintiff has not.[543] This "clergyman veto" is a back-up guarantee to the veracity of an affidavit in addition to the threat of a perjury prosection. In the event plaintiff seeks to obtain a divorce via a false affidavit, defendant may defeat his petition by submitting an opposing one from the officiating minister.

What is supposed to happen if this opposing affidavit is submitted is not at all clear. It is possible that at that point the court would hold an evidentiary hearing as to what the clergyman's beliefs were and whether the requirements of those beliefs were met. This would be difficult to envision since it would involve the court in a direct inquiry concerning compliance with religious law, an entanglement with religion that the statute carefully tries to avoid. What would probably happen, and the statute should be amended to make this explicit, is that the court could not enter a judgment of divorce until that very same clergyman files a second sworn statement that plaintiff has now complied.[544] In the event that the clergyman is no longer alive or competent to testify, the "veto" power of his earlier affidavit is cancelled and the court would issue a judgment of divorce based on plaintiff's affidavit alone. Allowing the clergyman's affidavit to control even after he becomes unavailable to testify would place plaintiff in an untenable position by permanently disabling him from obtaining a divorce even if he later complied with religious dictates. The only alternative to cancellation would be permitting plaintiff to rebut or show compliance by submitting the affidavit of some other clergyman but such a procedure could embroil the court in inquiries concerning clergy competence and affiliation, denominational belief, *etc.*, all of which are avoided when only

540. Another limitation, though one easily surmounted, is the fact that the affidavit need only allege that "to the best of plaintiff's knowledge" such barriers have been removed. Theoretically, even parties married by the Orthodox clergy may not always know their clergyman's principles, specifically that a *get* is required to dissolve marriage. The statute also emphasizes that the plaintiff is under no duty of investigation or inquiry. Nevertheless, this defect can be easily remedied by having the defendant contact the officiating clergyman who can send a letter to plaintiff informing him or her of his religious beliefs or through invocation of the clergyman's veto discussed in the next paragraph.

541. See *supra* text at note 226.

542. This is a misnomer with potential constitutional overtones. The clergyman is not vetoing governmental action but simply informing the court of a fact. See §253(7).

543. §253(7).

544. An earlier proposal would have made this explicit but this version was never enacted into law. LEWIN FILE, *supra* note 532.

the officiating clergyman is allowed to speak.[545] (Input from other clergy may, however, be highly material in a later criminal prosection.) Admittedly, however, it would make more sense to require plaintiff to file a *new* verified affidavit, rather than being able to rely on the old discredited one.

Some other peculiarities in the statute are also worthy of note. "Barrier to remarriage" does not include restraints or inhibitions that cannot be removed by plaintiff's voluntary act.[546] Thus, if a Catholic husband files for divorce, he will be entitled to civil relief even though his spouse (as well as himself) is unable to remarry since the barrier is one that is not removable by action of the parties. The law further makes it clear that there is no requirement on the part of the plaintiff to remove barriers to remarriage by application to ecclesiastical tribunals such as the initiation of an annulment proceeding.[547] Presumably, a Jewish divorce proceeding does not constitute "application to a tribunal" for although a *bait din* is required, the function of the *bait din* is supervisory rather than judicial, with the actual divorce effected by the acts of the spouses rather than the declaration of the court.[548] To the extent that removal of barriers can be accompanied only by the incurring of expenses, the plaintiff need not remove such barriers unless and until the other party reimburses or agrees to reimburse those expenses.[549]

Finally, in theory the statute is self-executing. Where "barriers to remarriage" exist under the principles of the officiating clergyman, plaintiff may not obtain a civil divorce even if neither party desires a *get*. Read literally, the statute imposes the need for a *get* even in cases of divorce by mutual consent of a Reform couple who happened to have been married by an Orthodox rabbi. As currently worded, however, this should no longer be a problem. If neither party wants a *get*, the requirement of a complying affidavit by plaintiff can be waived by defendant.[550]

CONSTITUTIONAL ISSUES: THE TRADITIONAL TESTS*

It was well understood by the drafters of the bill, its sponsors, and the Governor Cuomo himself that the *get* law posed serious constitutional problems

---

545. An earlier proposal would have allowed another clergyman who certifies that he maintains the same religious principles as the officiator to testify if the officiator is not available, but for the concerns stated in the text, this was dropped. LEWIN FILE, *supra* note 532.

546. §253(6).

547. *Id.*

548. See *supra* text at notes 16-17.

549. §253(6).

550. §253(3)(ii).

*The reader should be alerted that the text in this section applies the traditional constitutional standards that have been employed by the Supreme Court in analyzing establishment and free exercise claims and that were in effect when the *get* law was first enacted. These standards are in the process of undergoing reexamination. Current developments and speculations as to the future are discussed in Chapter Nine. It is the view of this author that these developments will not affect the basic conclusions stated herein. *Infra* text at notes 860-863.

under the First Amendment, though the precedents were not definitive one way or the other.[551] To date, however, no successful constitutional attack has been launched against the main features of the law.[552]

The Inescapable Conflict Between Establishment and Free Exercise

As is frequently the case, the constitutional problem the *get* law poses is whether it can be characterized as a permissible accommodation of free exercise or an impermissible establishment of religion. On one level, the affidavit requirement is a reasonable accommodation to the religious needs of those who would otherwise be unable to remarry. At the same time, however, conditioning the receipt of a civil remedy on the performance of a act prescribed exclusively by religious law seems to be equivalent to state-compelled religious obedience. Where recalcitrance is not based on religious commitment, compelling a *get* albeit indirectly is presumably not a violation of free exercise; nevertheless, it seems to closely approach those concerns of neutrality that are mirrored in the establishment clause.

In a pluralistic society, persons with religious beliefs may suffer various disabilities, disadvantages, or restrictions as compared to persons not sharing those beliefs. Facially-neutral laws of general, across-the-board applicability may have a significant, differential impact on the adherents of certain religions, imposing special costs or burdens on their practitioners. Sometimes these burdens may be generated by societal conditions. What government may or must do about this situation has long been a perplexing

---

551. See *supra* note 532.

552. New York opinions, to date, have generally been supportive of the law's provisions. See, *e.g.*, *Friedenberg v. Friedenberg*, 136 A.D. 2d 593, 523 N.Y.S. 2d 578 (N.Y. App. Div. 1988), where the court stated that until a plaintiff complies with the affidavit requirement, he may not receive any benefits under the divorce judgment. As such, not only will the entry of a divorce be deferred but all transfers of money or property pursuant to the final decree are stayed. The only issue of controversy, an issue now rendered moot with the passage of time, was the application of §253 to actions already pending at the time of its enactment. Compare *Chambers v. Chambers*, 471 N.Y.S. 2d 952 (N.Y. Sup. Ct. 1983) (§253 cannot be constitutionally applied to a pending action pursuant to a written separation agreement; to do so would be an unconstitutional impairment of contract) with *Pinkesz v. Pinkesz* (N.Y. Sup. Ct. 1984), reported in NEW YORK LAW JOURNAL (December 4, 1984), p. 13, col. 3. (§253 does apply to pending actions at least to the extent there is no antecedent separation agreement). Another area of potential conflict arose under an earlier version of the statute that required both parties to submit affidavits in uncontested proceedings. This meant that there were cases where a *plaintiff* could not obtain a civil divorce unless a *defendant* filed an affidavit. The *Chambers* court intimated in dicta that conditioning a *plaintiff's* relief on the responses of a *defendant* may well be a denial of due process. Under the present version of the law, while there is still a double affidavit requirement in uncontested proceedings, plaintiff would be able to waive the defendant's duty to file and would thus be able to secure a divorce on a single affidavit, namely his own. The *Chambers* issue is not likely to arise again.

conundrum of constitutional law, a problem arising from the conflicting messages of two portions of the First Amendment. The establishment clause seems to require an impenetrable "wall of separation" between Church and State necessitating a strictly "hands-off" attitude.[553] The dictates of free exercise, on the other hand, seem to compel the government to structure its programs in a manner that will not adversely affect or inhibit religious practice. The inescapable conflict between the prohibition of establishment and the necessity, or at least permissibility, of reasonable accommodation - the most difficult issue of church-state law - has never been definitively resolved.[554]

Scholars have attempted to propose their own analytic frameworks in reconciling the two clauses though none of their approaches has been consistently applied by the Supreme Court. At one extreme, Professor Kurland has argued that the First Amendment compels a government stance of strict neutrality. The government may not use religious criteria to either confer a benefit or impose a burden.[555] Under Kurland's approach, it would be constitutionally impermissible to grant religious exemptions from otherwise valid general legislation. At the other extreme are commentators like Choper and McConnell who basically take the position that governmental action to remove barriers or costs associated with religious exercise is a permissible accommodation.[556] Yet a third school of thought would differentiate between the types of barrier the government is trying to remove: while the free exercise clause may indeed compel the removal or mitigation of barriers that are the

---

553. See *Everson* v. *Board of Education*, 330 U.S. 1 (1947), at 16 (quoting Thomas Jefferson). Whether Jefferson himself meant for the wall of separation to be absolutely impregnable is open to question. See, *e.g.*, *McCollum v. Board of Education*, 333 U.S. 203 (1948), especially Justice Reed's dissent at 238-256, demonstrating that both Jefferson and Madison were in favor of allowing prayers and religious education on the publicly-funded campus of the University of Virginia as long as no activities were compulsory.

554. The recent case of *Employment Division, Department of Human Resources v. Smith*, 494 U.S. 872 (1990), discussed at length *infra* text at notes 751-825, does resolve part of this historic dilemma. It is no longer constitutionally necessary for federal or state legislation of general applicability to carve out a religious exemption or accommodation. Nevertheless, even after *Smith*, such accommodations may be permissible. See *Smith* at 891. It therefore still becomes necessary to determine at what point reasonable accommodation turns into impermissible establishment. *Smith* partially reformulates the question but does not dispel it entirely.

555. See Kurland, *Of Church and State and The Supreme Court*, 29 UNIV. CHIC. L. REV. 1, 96 (1961) and *The Irrelevance of the Constitution: The Religion Clauses of the First Amendment and the Supreme Court*, 24 VILL. L. REV. 3 (1978). This has long been the position of Paul Freund as well. Freund, *Public Aid to Parochial Schools*, 82 HARV. L. REV. 1680 (1969).

556. See Choper, *The Religion Clauses of the First Amendment: Reconciling the Conflict*, 41 U. PITT. L. REV. 673 (1980) and McConnell, *Accommodation of Religion* 1985 SUP. CT. REV. 1. See also two earlier articles by Professor Choper, *The Establishment Clause and Aid to Parochial Schools*, 56 CAL. L. REV. 260 (1969) and its update at 75 CAL. L. REV. 5 (1977) where he expounds his views at greater length.

products of the government's own laws,[557] the establishment clause prohibits attempts to alleviate religious burdens arising from societal disadvantage since such alleviation would impermissibly elevate religion to a preferred position vis-à-vis the state.[558] The Supreme Court at various times has vacillated between these positions, often in 5-4 decisions. Nevertheless, with the exception of some individual justices, no majority opinion of the Court has ever adopted an absolute stance of neutrality. Virtually all would acknowledge that, at least in some cases, "free exercise" compels, or at least permits,[559] some sort of religious accommodation either in the form of exemption or even through affirmative action. When it does, it overrides *sub silentio* establishment clause concerns. Moreover, the Court has intimated that even accommodations *not* constitutionally required by the free exercise clause may nevertheless not be violative of establishment.[560] As one moves further away from an absolutist position, however, line-drawing becomes progressively more difficult - a difficulty well-reflected in the tortuous history of church-state law, a history of 5-4 opinions and multiple concurrences. To make matters even more confusing, the "establishment" and "free exercise" cases have been analyzed by the Supreme Court under two different tests with little recognition of the fact that both issues are simply mirror images of each other.[561]

In *Lemon v. Kurtzman*,[562] the Supreme Court announced a tripartite test

---

557. At least this was thought to be the case prior to *Smith*, *infra* text at note 751.

558. This is suggested in Rostain, *Permissible Accommodation of Religion: Reconsidering the New York Get Statute*, 96 YALE L. REV. 1147 (1987).

559. It should again be reiterated that after *Smith*, discussed *infra* text following note 751, the issue of religious accommodation becomes one of permissibility rather than necessity. As noted, however, this section describes the constitutional standards that were historically applied in analyzing First Amendment claims and that were in effect at the time of the *get* law's enactment. These standards were indeed thought to necessitate religious exemptions, at least under certain conditions. See *infra* text at notes 567-571. The impact of more recent case law developments is traced in Chapter Nine.

560. Indeed, this is still the case. See, for example, *Smith* at 890.

561. A notable exception has been Justice O'Connor who has pointed out that in evaluating whether legislation that benefits religion is violative of the "establishment clause," a key question should be the extent to which it furthers "free exercise" by removing government imposed burdens on religion. The establishment clause cannot be properly applied without taking into account the concerns and values of free exercise. See *Wallace v. Jaffree*, 472 U.S. 38, 82-83 (1985) (Justice O'Connor concurring) (invalidated moment of silence statute for public schools in Alabama).

562. 403 U.S. 602 (1971). This case marked a pivotal turning away from a more permissive stance in the area of aid to parochial schools. Prior to *Lemon*, the Court had upheld state statutes that provided reimbursement of transportation costs for parents of students attending public and private schools, *Everson v. Board of Education*, 330 U.S. 1 (1947), as well as programs providing parochial schools with textbooks for secular studies, *Board of Education v. Allen*, 392 U.S. 236 (1968) on the grounds that the funds were for a nonreligious purpose. *Lemon*, on the other hand, invalidated a state program

for determining an impermissible establishment, a test that it still applies today.[563] A law accommodating or benefitting religious practice is valid only if it has a secular purpose, if its primary effect neither advances nor inhibits religion, and if its operation does not lead to excessive government entanglement with religious doctrine or the internal administration of religious affairs. The *Lemon* formulation has been sharply criticized on and off the Court as essentially meaningless and infinitely malleable[564] and, in its

---

that provided salary supplements for teachers in parochial schools although the supplements were limited to hours spent teaching secular subjects. According to the majority opinion, teaching supplements were different from textbooks because instructors may advance religious doctrines even in the course of teaching secular subjects and, through salary subsidies, the state would effectively be funding the religious part of the curriculum. The only way to insure that this is not the case would be to institute an on-going surveillance program which in turn would constitute excessive entanglement.

Since *Lemon*, the Court has invalidated virtually any type of public aid to private schools other than transportation and textbooks, which it grudgingly permits more for reasons of precedent than principle. See, *e.g.*, *Levitt v. Committee for Public Education*, 413 U.S. 472 (1973) (invalidated N.Y. program granting private schools reimbursement for services mandated by state law such as record-keeping, testing); *Committee for Public Education v. Nyquist*, 413 U.S. 756 (1973) and *Sloan v. Lemon* (*Lemon* II), 413 U.S. 825 (1973) (invalidated parental tuition reimbursement programs in the forms of tax credits); *Meek v. Pittenger*, 421 U.S. 349 (1975) (invalidated lending of instructional materials to nonpublic schools and the provision of auxiliary testing services to be administered by public school personnel. Recognizing that instructional materials were fundamentally the same as textbooks, it allowed *Allen* to stand on the basis of *stare decisis* but refused to extend it any further); *Grand Rapids School District v. Ball*, 473 U.S. 373 (1985) (invalidated "shared time" programs where public schools employees would come to private schools to teach secular subjects); and *Aguilar v. Felton*, 473 U.S. 402 (1985) (prohibited use of federal funds to pay salaries of public school teachers who provided nonreligious instruction on premises of private schools).

The Court has been more sympathetic to programs extending aid to universities on the theory that the potential for indoctrination is considerably reduced. See, *e.g.*, *Tilton v. Richardson*, 403 U.S. 672 (1971) and *Hunt v. McNair*, 413 U.S. 734 (1973).

563. But see *infra* text following note 826 whether *Lemon* is likely to survive.

564. For in-court criticism, see Justice Rehnquist's dissent in *Wallace v. Jaffree*, 472 U.S. 38, 108-112 (1985). Critical commentary can be found in Johnson, *Concepts and Compromise in First Amendment Religious Doctrine*, 72 CAL. L. REV. 817 (1984); Schwartz, *Larkin v. Grendel's Den, Inc.: The Burger Court and the Establishment Problem*, 21 HOUSTON L. REV. 178 (1984); Note, *Lynch v. Donnelly: Has the Lemon Test Soured?* 19 LOYOLA L.A.L.REV. 133 (1985) (an especially useful review of inconsistent lower court opinions struggling to apply *Lemon* to various situations); Note, *Civil Religion and the Establishment Clause*, 95 YALE L.J. 1237 (1986) as well as the articles, cited *supra* notes 555-556.

application, has yielded sharply inconsistent results, often in 5-4 decisions.[565] Taken literally, it would invalidate nearly any statutory accommodation of religion since the primary purpose and effect of any religious proviso is the benefitting of that religious group. Justice O'Connor has advocated a very useful restatement of the *Lemon* test, substituting the term "endorsing" in place of "advancing";[566] the fact that a given piece of legislation proves "beneficial" to a religious group would not otherwise invalidate it as long as such an accommodation does not carry with it the implication or appearance of endorsement of one religion at the expense of another or the endorsement of religion over nonbelief. Although a majority of the Court has never accepted her precise verbal formulation, the cases do in fact suggest that the concept of "endorsement" may be a useful touchstone to differentiate those accommodations that are prohibited and those that are permitted to stand.

In legislation challenged on free exercise grounds, normally the opposite question is presented; legislation or regulation of general applicability makes no provision or exclusion for religion, and the objection is raised that the failure to provide such an exemption is an infringement of religious liberty. While a number of justices, particularly Justice Stevens,[567] had always rejected this contention outright (as would Professor Kurland[568]), the prevailing test had been, at least until quite recently, that religious exemptions must be recognized unless there was a compelling state interest that could not be adequately served by less restrictive means.[569] Thus, in responding to a free exercise challenge,

---

565. Compare, for example, *Meek v. Pittenger*, 421 U.S. 349 (1975) which invalidated the provision of auxiliary testing services to private schools with *Committee for Public Education and Religious Liberty v. Regan*, 444 U.S. 646 (1980) which upheld state financing of achievement tests. See also the wavering lines of distinction drawn in cases like *Wolman v. Walter*, 433 U.S. 229 (1977) where the Court differentiated between diagnostic or therapeutic tests and those designed to promote or improve educational achievement.

566. See especially her concurrences in *Lynch v. Donnelly*, 465 U.S. 668, 690 (1984) and in *Wallace v. Jaffree*, 472 U.S. 38, 83 (1985).

567. See his concurrence in *Goldman v. Weinberger*, 475 U.S. 503 510 (1986)("yarmulke" case) and in *United States v. Lee*, 455 U.S. 252, 263 (1981).

568. See Kurland, *supra* note 555.

569. The basic standard is set down in *Braunfeld v. Brown*, 366 U.S. 599 (1961). Ironically, over a spirited dissent by Justice Stewart, the Court upheld the constitutionality of Sunday closing laws as applied to Sabbath-observing Jews who would have to lose an extra day of business. The need for a uniform day of rest was an "overriding" secular goal that justified the indirect burden on free exercise. The term "compelling" was introduced in *Sherbert v. Verner*, 374 U.S. 398 (1963) (state unemployment compensation could not be denied to a Seventh-Day Adventist who lost her job for refusing to work on Saturdays. The state interest in not paying persons who voluntarily terminate their employment can be adequately served through less restrictive means). *Sherbert's* holding was recently affirmed in *Hobbie v. Unemployment Appeals Comm'n of Florida*, 480 U.S. 136 (1987).

The *Smith* case, discussed *infra* text following note 751, may have sounded the "death-knell" for the type of strict scrutiny envisioned under

a court had to analyze both the importance of the governmental end and the reasonableness of the means employed to attain that end. While the magnitude of the state's interest did not necessarily have to be as significant as was required for other areas where the term "compelling" was used and while the Court's application of its own test often appeared flawed or questionable,[570] the familiar "ends-means" analysis was still the vehicle most commonly employed, at least until the advent of *Employment Division v. Smith*.[571]

Like ships passing in the night, however, the "establishment" and "free exercise" tests had never been brought together. Under *Lemon*, any explicit religious exemption seemed to constitute an impermissible establishment since its purpose and effect was to aid religious observance and yet, in the absence of a compelling state interest, the very thing the establishment clause prohibited the free exercise clause required. The Court's tacit assumption was that free exercise concerns predominated in cases of conflict but offered no principled explanation for that position.[572] Once again, however, Justice O'Connor's insight was particularly helpful in resolving this apparent dilemma. If the accommodation in question did not constitute an endorsement placing the state's imprimatur on religious activity or conveying a message to the populace favoring religion over nonreligion, it was not an establishment at all. As such, the conflict between free exercise and establishment was largely illusory. Put in the language of *Lemon*, the facilitation of free exercise was in itself a legitimate *secular* purpose that justified governmental intervention.[573] (Primary

---

Sherbert v. Verner. I nevertheless discuss the application of *Sherbert* to the *get* law because first, that was the test in effect when the law was enacted and second, even after *Smith* there may be discrete contexts in which the "compelling state interest" test survives. See *infra* text at notes 782-797.

570. In cases involving racial discrimination, requiring an interest to be "compelling" spells the kiss of death for that legislative program. No interest is ever important enough to allow such discrimination to proceed. In free exercise cases, however, the Court has been quite willing to declare relatively trivial interests "compelling." See *Braunfeld v. Brown*, 366 U.S. 599 (1961) (Sunday closing laws further an "overriding secular goal) and the 5-4 opinion in *Goldman v. Weinberger*, 475 U.S. 503 (1986) (denial of right of air force officer to wear yarmulke).

571. 494 U.S. 872 (1990), discussed *infra* text following note 751. *Smith* essentially abrogated any constitutional need to accommodate religious observance, at least in the context of criminal prosecution, and severely curtails the scope of free exercise claims. But see *infra* text at notes 782-787 (possibilities of strict scrutiny even after *Smith*).

572. See *Abington School District v. Schempp*, 374 U.S. 203, 247 (1963)(Justice Brennan concurring)("[T]he logical interrelationship between the Establishment and Free Exercise Clauses may produce situations where an injunction against an apparent establishment must be withheld in order to avoid the infringement of rights of free exercise.").

573. Indeed, O'Connor's analysis provides a useful analytical framework even after *Smith*, discussed *infra* text following note 761. Although accommodation of free exercise is no longer a constitutional requirement, it is nevertheless a permissible step and legislation attempting such facilitation should be deemed to have a secular purpose. See generally *infra* text at note

effect should also be measured in this manner.)

Applying the Establishment Test to the *Get* Law

The application of the tripartite standard of *Lemon* supports the proposition that a legislative initiative like the New York statute is not an impermissible establishment.[574] First, the purpose of the legislation can clearly be defined in secular terms as a viable means of attaining legitimate state interests. These interests include the following:

1. The state has a legitimate secular interest in insuring the integrity and efficacy of its judgments. The policy of the divorce law is that a marriage that is dead in fact should no longer exist and that the parties should have the freedom to rebuild their lives anew. Maintaining barriers to remarriage following a judgment of divorce frustrates the policy behind divorce statutes and the integrity of the judicial system.
2. Without such a law, women practicing the Orthodox faith would be under additional burdens or disadvantages following a civil divorce vis-à-vis other women not having such beliefs. In its attempts to equalize the status of all women following the granting of a civil divorce, the state is merely accommodating the practice of religion by removing its disadvantages, rather than establishing it in a preferred position. As Justice O'Connor notes, the facilitation of free exercise is in itself a legitimate *secular* state interest which the legislature may address.
3. The state has a legitimate interest in facilitating marriage and a stable family life. To the extent a sizable number of persons for whatever reason are unable to enter into marriages, the state should be entitled to take some step to improve the situation. As a related matter, the inability of women to remarry may increase the incidence of single parent households, increase demands on the social service-welfare system, and exacerbate housing shortages. There is thus not merely an abstract desire to promote a stable long-term family life but a concern that could be translated into dollars and cents.
4. Because the ability to marry and raise a family is an aspect of the fundamental constitutional right to

---

823.

574. Whether the *Lemon* test is likely to survive and what alternatives may take its place are discussed *infra* text at notes 826-859.

> privacy protected and recognized by *Roe v. Wade*,[575] the state has a legitimate state interest in facilitating the ability of its citizens to exercise and enjoy their constitutional rights. Although the deprivation in question arises from private rather than public or governmental action, states should as a matter of principle have the authority, if not the obligation, to affirmatively protect those rights even from private infringement.[576]

---

575. 410 U.S. 113 (1973) and *Zablocki v. Redhail*, 434 U.S. 374 (1978) (statute conditioning freedom to marry on showing that support obligations to minor children have been met violates due process). Indeed, the right to marry has been regarded as fundamental even prior to the recognition of a general constitutional right of privacy. See *Loving v. Virginia*, 388 U.S. 1 (1967) (miscegenation status struck down because it interferes with the fundamental right to marry protected by the due process clause).

576. As a general proposition, constitutional rights are assertable only against the government or its agents and do not directly prohibit private, nongovernmental infringements of rights nor does the Constitution provide any remedy for such infringements. See *In re Civil Rights Cases*, 109 U.S. 3 (1883). (This limitation is commonly termed the "state action" doctrine though it should more properly be called the "governmental action" requirement since its standards are met by federal as well as state activity.) The notable exception is the Thirteenth Amendment which prohibits involuntary servitude of any nature whether public or private. *Id.* See also *Jones v. Alfred H. Mayer Co.*, 392 U.S. 409 (1968) (42 U.S.C. §1982 guaranteeing citizens the right to purchase and convey property was held to prohibit even private discrimination in housing and such prohibition was constitutional because private discrimination was a "badge of slavery" which Congress was empowered to eradicate under the Thirteenth Amendment, an amendment that was not limited to state action). It remains somewhat of an open question whether Congress, in its attempts to protect constitutional freedoms other than those arising under the Thirteenth Amendment, could outlaw purely private discrimination without relying on some plenary power like the Commerce Clause, though in many cases expansive interpretation of the Thirteenth Amendment and the concept of "badges of slavery" may furnish the requisite peg. See generally *United States v. Guest*, 383 U.S. 745 (1966) (where six justices expressed in dicta that Congress could indeed prohibit private infringements of constitutional rights). See also *Westberry v. Gilman Paper Co.*, 507 F.2d 206, (5th Cir. 1975) (42 U.S.C. §1985 (3) applicable to private acts of violence; a conspiracy to kill constituted a deprivation of rights of due process and equal protection). *Cf. Bellamy v. Mason's Store, Inc.*, 508 F.2d 504 (4th Cir. 1974) (while §1985(3) does not apply to private acts, Congress would be fully within its power to enact a statute that did). For an excellent discussion of this very complex area, see Nowak, Rotunda, and Young, CONSTITUTIONAL LAW (3rd ed. 1986) at Chapter 19.

Whether or not Congress possesses inherent authority to protect constitutional rights from private infringement has no bearing on the point in the text. Marriage and family life, indeed the whole area of domestic relations, are matters that traditionally have been left to the states. Facilitating the ability

5. To the extent withholding of a *get* is done out of malice or spite or for reasons of extortion, the state has an interest in protecting its citizens from being victimized by unfair, coercive practices. Many states have recognized intentional infliction of emotional distress as an independent tort.[577] The alleviation of human suffering caused by another is a proper goal of state legislation.

In short, insofar as purpose is concerned, the justifications for the New York law appear to be secular: the furtherance of the state's divorce policy, the validation of the integrity of the judicial system, the facilitation of religious liberty, the encouraging of remarriage and a more stable family life, the protection of fundamental rights of privacy, and the curbing of victimization and extortion all appear to fall within the traditional ambit of general legislative competence. On balance, the "secular purpose" prong of *Lemon* can be easily satisfied.

Coming to the second of *Lemon*'s criteria: is the primary effect of the law the "advancement" of religion? Undoubtedly, in a literal sense the statute advances religion in two distinct ways: one, by making the observance of Orthodox Judaism less burdensome to some of its adherents by eliminating the peculiar disabilities they would otherwise suffer; and two, by indirectly encouraging persons to comply with religious law who otherwise would not, *i.e.*, recalcitrant spouses who seek a civil divorce. As noted, the "effect" of making the practice of Judaism less burdensome on its willing practitioners is probably nothing more than a permissible accommodation of "free exercise" and does not offend *Lemon's* "primary effect" criterion. The second aspect is more problematical; a law that indirectly compels an unwilling party to perform a religious act even if there are legitimate secular purposes for doing so does seem to have the "effect" of advancing religious observance. Yet the mere fact that the law has such an "effect" is not yet sufficient for its invalidation; the impermissible effect must be "primary." What is a "primary" effect and how it is to be distinguished from a "purpose" are difficult definitional questions that have never been clearly addressed. One possibility emerging from the cases is that "primary" is synonymous with "direct and immediate" as opposed to "indirect and attenuated."[578] Thus, to take one example,[579] secular textbook loans by school boards to parochial schools are constitutionally permissible although they indirectly advance the cause of religion by freeing additional resources for religious study because the purpose of the program is secular and the benefit is indirect. By contrast, teacher-salary supplements even to cover the salary for the teaching of secular subjects are not since all teaching may contain religious elements and government money cannot be used to directly

---

to remarry is already within the ambit of a state's legitimate interest. The enshrinement of this right as being so fundamental that it rises to constitutional dimension is a further argument to expand state legislative competence in this area, not curtail it.

577. See *infra* text following note 703.

578. See, for example, the language of the Supreme Court in *Bowen v. Kendrick*, 487 U.S. 589 (1988).

579. The example is taken from *Board of Education v. Allen*, 392 U.S. 236 (1968).

fund religious education.[580]

If "primary" is defined as "direct and immediate," one would have to conclude that the New York *get* law's "primary effect" is indeed the advancement of religion for the granting of the *get* is precisely the result that the operation of the statute produces. The law, albeit for secular purposes, directly provides that no civil divorce can be obtained until the remarriage barrier is removed. The performance of the religious act is not an incidental byproduct of the operation of the statute but the very consequence that is intended to be produced although for nonreligious reasons.

If, however, the notion of "advancing" religion is equated with affirmative promotion or endorsement, the analysis takes a different turn. The statute carries no implication that Orthodox Judaism is a preferred way of life that should be encouraged or that a *get* is a preferred method of marital dissolution. In the first place, the language of the statute is facially neutral, speaking of removal of any barriers whether religious or conscientious. Second, the statute does not require that barriers to remarriage be removed unless the other party feels constrained by them. Thus, the statute is not promoting compliance with religious divorce law as an *intrinsic* desideratum but only as a means of releasing someone else's bind, a bind that was generated by the recalcitrant party's own choice of solemnization. Third, while the delivery of a *get* is a *religious* act in the sense of being mandated by *religious* law, it is a nonliturgical act that requires no profession of faith or overt expression of belief. It is not really clear that encouraging the performance of a Jewish law ceremony, which under Jewish law itself is akin to the dissolution of a partnership and largely devoid of theological significance, constitutes an endorsement or promotion of Jewish values. After all, parties who are nonobservant or non-Jewish already have the rights and benefits that the statute attempts to secure for the Orthodox woman. The statute hardly places her or her beliefs on a pedestal. Indeed, this last point is the most crucial of all. Because the statute does no more than assure that Orthodox women following a civil divorce will enjoy the same rights and privileges as anyone else - and no more - such an equalization effort is far more likely to be perceived by the citizenry as an accommodation of the "free exercise" beliefs of the wife rather than an endorsement or promotion of the wife's beliefs.[581]

The final element of the test is whether the law in question necessitates "excessive entanglement" in religious affairs. As noted earlier,[582] entanglement exists if the legislative scheme necessitates continual monitoring or administrative supervision over religious institutions or programs or else requires the court to resolve doctrinal matters. At least under the present version of the statute, neither of these factors seems to be present. While the statute does require that plaintiff submit an affidavit that he/she has removed

---

580. *Lemon v. Kurtzman*, 403 U.S. 602 (1971).

581. The perception that the public has regarding the nature of a particular legislative program is highly material to an establishment clause analysis. See, *e.g.*, *Lemon v. Kurtzman*, 403 U.S. 602, 622 (1971) (emphasizing political divisiveness and polarization as an evil that the establishment clause attempts to minimize). *Cf.* Nowak, Rotunda, Young, CONSTITUTIONAL LAW (3rd ed. 1986), pp. 1039, 1054-1060, who criticize the "political divisiveness" test as largely superfluous but acknowledge that the Court continues to invoke it.

582. See *supra* text at notes 252-254.

all religious barriers to remarriage, the court holds no evidentiary hearings and makes no particular finding that this is in fact the case. Upon receipt of the affidavit, the court *must* enter a judgment of divorce and may not inquire into the truthfulness of the allegations. Issues concerning the technical validity of the *get*, the qualifications of the executing rabbis, whether the principles of the officiating clergyman have or have not been met and what those principles are - questions that could indeed entangle the court in complex doctrinal matters - pose matters that the court simply does not and may not address.

Insofar as a divorce judgment is concerned, the only way plaintiff's affidavit can be contested is by the officiating clergyman's filing an opposing affidavit. In the event this occurs, the statute is not very clear as to what happens. If the court is then supposed to hold an evidentiary hearing to determine whether there has been compliance with religious law, there may indeed be entanglement problems in at least some cases though not all. If, for example, plaintiff has given a *get* under the supervision of a left-wing Orthodox group and the officiating clergyman alleges that such a group is not truly Orthodox, we would certainly not want the court to determine the scope of a denomination. Where, on the other hand, the contested issue boils down to a simple question of fact - was there any *get* given at all - there would certainly be no objection to a judicial resolution of a nondoctrinal issue.

It is plausible, however, that in the event of an opposing clergy affidavit, the statute does not contemplate a judicial hearing at all. Rather the clergyman's affidavit must be accepted as conclusive until that very clergyman can file a supplemental affidavit of compliance. Thus, at no times does the court ever examine any question of Jewish law or doctrine but simply responds automatically to the verified statements submitted. Moreover, since the only clergyman authorized to contest plaintiff's affidavit is the one who actually officiated, tricky definitional questions regarding denominational affiliation are avoided.

A number of commentators have objected to what they term the "clergyman veto" provision.[583] Granted that the court never makes its own findings on the existence of barriers to remarriage, the very fact that the judicial power to issue a civil divorce is conditioned on the consent (or at least failure to object) of a member of the clergy is in itself an impermissible entanglement with religion, giving religious authorities a veto on the exercise of governmental authority. In *Larkin v. Grendel's Den*,[584] the Supreme Court invalidated a zoning law that granted schools or churches a veto power over the issuance of a liquor license for any premises within a 500 foot radius. Because such a law "enmeshes churches in the exercise of substantial government power," it violates the strictures against establishment.

Reliance on *Grendel's Den* appears misplaced. That case dealt with a state procedure that conferred an unbridled discretion on ecclesiastical authorities to dictate the operations of government. In effect, zoning decisions became a shared responsibility of church and state, at least under the conditions specified in the zoning ordinance. Such a sharing of authority is clearly inimical to the ideals of the First Amendment whether it is condemned under the rubric of "entanglement" or that of "endorsement." By contrast, despite its description as a "clergy veto" - a phrase that invites superficial comparison to

---

583. LEWIN FILE, *supra* note 532.

584. 459 U.S. 116 (1982).

Grendel's Den - the provision in the *get* law for an opposing affidavit does not confer any element of judgment, discretion, or decision-making authority on religious functionaries. They are called upon only to attest to the existence of a fact: whether or not a *get* was executed. The only element upon which they can prevent the issuance of a civil divorce is the allegation of a fact that is already legislatively defined and specific: the failure to remove barriers to remarriage. Assuming the state could designate that fact as a relevant criterion for the withholding of a divorce - and for the reasons stated above, it appears that it could - using the clergy as mere conduits of information may in fact be the only constitutionally- permissible way to proceed.

A final potential entanglement problem may arise in the event a plaintiff is criminally prosecuted for filing a false affidavit. Theoretically, one could imagine situations where some form of dissolution ceremony occurred that allegedly was not in consonance with the principles of the solemnizing clergyman. Where that clergyman is no longer available, it will be necessary to establish those principles through expert testimony. There may be doctrinal disagreements between denominations and within a denomination which the court might have to resolve.[585] Even in these marginal cases, however, the court is not really called upon to resolve doctrinal issues but simply to determine as a matter of fact what the beliefs of the officiating clergyman were regardless of their ultimate truth or validity. Because the inquiry is phrased not in terms of the beliefs of the denomination but those of the actual clergyman, the potential for doctrinal embroilment is slight. If the clergyman is available, he/she should simply be taken at their word. If the clergyman is not available, the court should be able to take testimony concerning a disputed state of mind. What religious beliefs a person in fact entertained (as opposed to whether those beliefs are valid) is fundamentally no different from any other question of fact a judge or jury is called upon to resolve and should fall within the ambit of judicial competence.

Finally, in the run-of-the-mill criminal prosecution there will be no serious entanglement question at all. In most cases of prosecution, one could safely surmise that no *get* was given. Since the basic meanings of affiliations are well understood, establishing the Conservative or Orthodox credentials of

---

585. Consider the following example: The officiating rabbi was ordained in an Orthodox seminary, took a position in a Conservative temple but retained his membership in Orthodox rabbinical associations. The couple in question were divorced through the delivery of a *get* prepared by the Conservative rabbinate. Husband obtained a civil divorce by filing the affidavit. In a criminal prosecution alleging that the affidavit was false for failure to execute an Orthodox *get*, the court would have to make findings concerning the denominational affiliation of the officiating rabbi and whether, based on his hybrid status, he would subscribe to the Conservative method of *get* or the Orthodox. (This presupposes the officiating clergyman is not available to testify.)

Another example: Many Orthodox rabbis invalidate a *get* if one of the witnesses attends a Conservative synagogue even if he otherwise fully committed to the Orthodox tradition. Other Orthodox rabbis consider the *get* valid. Even if the officiating rabbi is Orthodox, in the event he is unavailable a criminal prosecution based on the delivery of this type of *get* would require the court to "choose" between the different schools within a single movement.

the officiating rabbi would automatically mean that the affidavit was false without the need to proceed any further in fine analytical distinctions. The ability of a fertile imagination to conjure up cases where the court will have to choose between the competing readings of the *Shulchan Aruch* on the basis of conflicting rabbinical opinion should not obscure the fact that this event will be so rare as to be practically nonexistent. If in rare cases such entanglement is present, the solution would be to stay a particular prosecution in a given case rather than strike down the law in its entirety.[586]

To sum up: While, as Governor Cuomo remarked, the matter is not free of doubt, §253 appears to meet all three of the *Lemon* criteria for validity. The purpose of the law is the advancement of purely secular interests which includes the facilitation of free exercise by those who would otherwise be burdened because of their religious beliefs. The primary effect of the law is not the endorsement or promotion of religion since it simply equalizes the rights of women holding certain beliefs with those of women who do not. Nor does the law invite excessive entanglements into religious affairs since the court is prohibited from inquiring into the truth of any matters alleged in the affidavit. While rare instances of criminal prosecution may implicate establishment concerns, the potential for constitutional infringement is so insignificant that it should have no effect on the overall validity of the law. As such, §253 is sustainable against attacks based on the establishment clause.

One final point: The foregoing analysis, building on Justice O'Connor's insight, assumes that legislation designed to remove disadvantages suffered by religious adherents does not "advance" religion (in the sense of "endorsement") because it simply equalizes the benefits enjoyed by all - in this case, the ability to remarry following a divorce. As noted earlier, this assumption is not universally shared. Some construe the second prong of *Lemon* as validating religious exemptions or "removal-of-barrier" legislation only where the disability or restriction is state-imposed.[587] Where, however, the disadvantage arises from the religious practice itself, governmental attempts to alleviate it constitute impermissible efforts to advance religion. The inability of Orthodox Jewish women to marry without a *get* may be a serious disability but it is one that has nothing to do with any rule of the state. Not being a *state-imposed burden*, the argument goes, it cannot be ameliorated by legislative action.

I believe this argument is fundamentally incorrect as a matter of law and policy. Nevertheless, even accepting its premises which concededly reflect the thinking of at least *some* justices on the Supreme Court, a respectable argument can still be made for the constitutionality of §253. It all depends on how one defines the burden. While it is true that the inability of a spouse to

---

586. In any event, these constitutional objections apply only to the criminal prosection and not to the affidavit requirements *per se*. (Although eliminating the threat of prosecution removes the disincentives for lying, the women's rights are still protected by the clergy affidavit.) A version of the bill prepared by Agudath Israel contained a severability clause, perhaps for the concerns expressed in the text. For some unknown reason, however, such a clause was deleted from the enacted legislation. Even in the absence of a severability clause, the impermissibility of state prosecution which, after all, is under the *general* penal law, would presumably *not* taint the *get* legislation.

587. See *supra* text at note 556.

marry without a *get* is not a state-imposed burden, the particular problem the statute addresses - the post-dissolution *agunah* - is. The ability of a recalcitrant spouse to obtain a civil divorce exacerbates and magnifies a problem that already exists under Jewish law for, without the ability to obtain a civil divorce, spouses would have to give *gittin* to acquire their own freedom. Since the ability to obtain dissolution of a marriage is a right granted by the state and it is the existence of that right that adds to the cost of religious observance, even a narrow reading of the *Lemon* criteria would justify legislative assistance.[588]

The *Get* Law and Free Exercise

Section 253 does raise problems from the opposite side. By conditioning the grant of a civil remedy on the performance of a religious ceremony, the statute arguably infringes the free exercise rights of the otherwise unwilling spouse. Here, a number of points should be made:

First, the court does not directly order the plaintiff to do anything; it simply conditions the obtaining of relief on the removal of barriers. Conceptually, noncompliance with religious law imposes no additional burdens but simply leaves the parties where they were by continuing the *status quo*.

Second, since the statute requires the giving of a *get* only in cases where a marriage was solemnized by a clergyman whose principles mandate utilization of a *get* and the designation of such a clergyman was a choice that the parties themselves made, it is arguable that the acquiescence in the performance of a religious ceremony carries with it an implied understanding that the existence of the marriage and its dissolution will be governed by religious law, or at least that whatever steps are needed to dissolve the type of bond that was chosen to be forged would be taken. Even if this implication cannot rise to the level of an independently-enforceable contract,[589] the existence of such tacit consent certainly dilutes the presence of coercion that the First Amendment proscribes.

Third, even legislation that burdens religious observance may nevertheless be sustainable if it serves a compelling state interest that could not be adequately protected through less restrictive means.[590] While the facilitation

---

588. Moreover, a woman following a divorce may have many legal disadvantages in terms of securing credit, filing a joint return, obtaining economic support, *etc.* The burdens on a woman who cannot remarry following a *civil* divorce are or may be considerably greater than the burdens on the woman before the civil divorce is granted. The state law of divorce is thus a contributing factor to the overall burden.

589. See *supra* text at notes 227-237 (discussion of *Goldman's* theory of implied contract).

590. Whether the "compelling state interest" test survives the recent case of *Employment Division v. Smith*, 494 U.S. 872 (1990), is discussed *infra* text at notes 788-796. *Smith*, however, does not undercut the essential point in the text. Prior to *Smith*, general legislation that adversely impacted on religious observance could be sustained only if it served a "compelling state interest." *Smith* seems to have abrogated this requirement, at least in the narrow context of criminal law. The New York *get* law, because of its neutrally-worded requirement of removal of "barriers to remarriage," may qualify as a "generally applicable law" within the meaning of *Smith*. If it does so qualify, it is

of the wife's free exercise rights would probably *not* constitute a sufficiently important state interest in and of itself (since it makes no sense to infringe the free exercise rights of A in order to enhance the free exercise rights of B), there are a number of other vital interests that §253 serves: insuring the integrity of its divorce procedure, facilitating marriage and family life, protecting rights of privacy, and curbing extortion and victimization. These policies may constitute precisely the type of vital state interest that overrides a free exercise claim. When we take into account that the affidavit requirement also has the effect of enhancing the religious liberty of the victimized spouse, this further tips the balance in the statute's favor.[591]

An additional point to keep in mind is that in the vast majority of cases, a refusal to give a *get* is not motivated by religious beliefs but out of spite or as a means of obtaining valuable concessions. Indeed, it is precisely because the husband knows that a *get* is needed that he is able to use it as a bargaining chip. Remember that if a couple were married in a Reform ceremony, the husband could obtain his civil divorce without a §253 affidavit regardless of any change in religious commitment the wife may have undergone.[592] By definition, then, the statute is dealing with persons who did invoke a religious system that required a *get* for marital dissolution and presumably were in accord with the requirements of that system.

In any event, the withholding of a civil divorce where the failure to give a *get* is *not* religiously based is certainly not a First Amendment violation.[593] Moreover, even if plaintiff claims that his refusal to grant a *get*

---

sustainable even in the absence of interests that are deemed "compelling." At worst, therefore, the enumeration of such interests may be superfluous. Conversely, if one were to argue that because of its intended focus the statute is specifically targeted towards directing the performance of a religious act, *i.e.*, the execution of a *get*, the "compelling state interest" standard should nevertheless be available as a validating mechanism. The fact that *Smith* no longer necessitates this test for generally-applicable law should not preclude its utilization to validate statutes that do not directly fall under *Smith's* rubric. But see *infra* note 591.

591. It must be conceded, however, that application of a "compelling state interest" standard to something like the New York *get* law goes somewhat beyond Supreme Court precedent. Prior to *Smith*, the test was used to uphold legislation of general applicability that had a negative impact on religious observance. See *supra* text at notes 567-571. Here, on the other hand, the State of New York has enacted a law that directly requires a *halachic* ceremony to be performed. The giving of a *get* is the very purpose the law is trying to achieve. It is not entirely clear that even the existence of compelling interests would suffice.

592. See *supra* text at notes 538-541.

593. As its language suggests, the constitutional privilege of the free exercise clause is limited to belief or conduct that is predicated on religious rather than secular considerations. See *Thomas v. Review Board*, 450 U.S. 707 (1981) and *Frazee v. Illinois Department of Employment Security*, 489 U.S. 829 (1989). It seems obvious that otherwise-Orthodox individuals who withhold a *get* out of financial considerations are not acting out of religious convictions. See also *Burns v. Burns*, discussed *supra* note 226.

Interestingly, the Supreme Court has never given us a definitive

is based on a religious belief, *e.g.*, subsequent to an Orthodox ceremony, he

---

definition of "religion" under the First Amendment. Must beliefs be based on the existence of a Deity or do nontheistic beliefs qualify? Are atheists entitled to invoke the protections of the free exercise clause? *Cf.* *Frazee*, cited above (person need not be a member of an established denomination or church). See also *supra* note 260.

The closest parallel we have is in the selective service area where, by statute, persons having conscientious objection to war are exempt from military service. Under an earlier version of the statute that made specific reference to a Supreme Being, the Supreme Court nonetheless held that *as a matter of statutory construction* (not constitutional law), the exemption applied equally to persons who were opposed to all war on the basis of moral beliefs that were nontheistic. *United States v. Seeger*, 380 U.S. 163 (1965) (construing the original version of 50 U.S.C. App. §456(j)). Subsequent to *Seeger*, the selective service statute was amended to delete any reference to a Supreme Being. P.L. 90-40, §1(7) amending 50 U.S.C. App. §456(j). See also *Gillette v. United States*, 401 U.S. 437 (1971) (the failure of the statute to accommodate the religious beliefs of those opposed not to all war but only to "unjust" ones was not an infringement of free exercise). Since *Gillette* seems to indicate that there is no constitutional entitlement to even a religiously-based opposition to war (and this would certainly be even more true after the *Smith* case, see *infra* text following note 735), *Seeger*'s extension of a statutory exemption to even nontheistic beliefs carries no intimation as to the parameters of the constitutional entitlement. *Seeger*, however, does furnish useful precedent in helping to distinguish between views that are merely political and social and those beliefs that are so central to the person's life and identity that they can be regarded as substitutes or surrogates for religion.

It should be noted that the truly-perplexing issue of defining "religion" under the First Amendment is likely to be less important than it formerly was. Prior to the *Smith* case, even legislation of general applicability had to recognize religious exemptions unless there was a "compelling state interest" that justified not doing so. See *supra* text at note 569. Accordingly, any claims for a "religious" exemption necessitated a preliminary determination of what beliefs were deemed "religious" in nature. After *Smith*, however, even admittedly religious beliefs are no longer entitled to accommodation as long as the statute or regulation is one of general applicability so the "religious-secular" dichotomy assumes far less importance.

A second point to note: even if nontheistic beliefs are not covered by the free exercise clause, any governmental attempts to coerce atheists or agnostics to profess religious belief or engage in religious practices would easily run afoul of *Lemon v. Kurtzman*, *supra* note 562 or any of the alternatives that may replace *Lemon*. See *infra* text at notes 826-859. Thus, denying atheists rights under free exercise most assuredly does not mean they could be forced to attend church! At worst, it would merely mean that they could not seek exemption from general law. Since after *Smith*, even religious beliefs can no longer claim such exemption, the whole issue of free exercise protection for nontheistic beliefs becomes largely moot.

In any event, the fundamental point of the text must be reiterated: whatever the parameters of the free exercise clause, it does not protect conduct that is motivated by greed, spite, or malice.

converted to a different religion, at most he would be entitled to an evidentiary hearing where the veracity of his claim would be examined. While no court may determine the ultimate truth or validity of a religious belief,[594] the court may certainly conduct an inquiry into whether the alleged "religious" objections are sincerely held, as is routinely done in cases of conscientious objectors to military service.[595] Even if a religious objection could in fact be established, it may well be overridden by the compelling state interests enumerated above.

As repeatedly noted, the nondevotional nature of the *get* ceremony and the fact that in the eyes of Jewish law it is nothing more than a legalistic dissolving mechanism[596] may mean that indirectly compelling its execution is not a significant curtailment of religious liberty. Even Reform Jews who don't require a *get* as a matter of religious law do not regard the granting of a *get* as a violation of religious conscience; indeed, for various reasons they are often encouraged by their rabbinate to grant *gittin*.[597] At worst, the granting of a *get* is a superfluous, useless act. Thus, just because a husband asserts he no longer believes that a *get* is necessary should not be enough to justify a free exercise claim unless he can show that it is *offensive* to his sincerely-held religious principles, a showing that would be quite difficult.

HALACHIC CONSIDERATIONS

Unless *kofin* grounds exist, any *get* executed under the compulsion of the order of a secular court is *halachically* invalid.[598] Enlisting the assistance of the legislative and the judiciary in confronting the *agunah* problem would be of no avail unless the resulting *gittin* would be acceptable.

Before submission of its draft proposal to the legislature, Agudath Israel circulated the bill among leading Talmudic scholars for their views as to its *halachic* acceptability. While none of them authored a detailed analysis, the

---

594. The proposition that a court or any governmental authority may not inquire into the ultimate truth or falsify of a religious belief has been affirmed many times by the Supreme Court. See, for example, *United States v. Ballard*, 322 U.S. 78 (1944) (mail fraud conviction of religious cult leaders could not stand unless the government could show not only that the representations were false but also that they were not honestly held; to hold otherwise, would essentially be subjecting religious beliefs to heresy trials) and *Thomas v. Review Board*, 450 U.S. 707 (1981) (state could not deny unemployment compensation to a person who refused to work on Saturday for religious reasons although he was not a member of a church; the sole touchstone for free exercise claims is an honest conviction that such work was forbidden by his religion).

595. While the guarantees of the free exercise clause preclude judicial inquiry into the ultimate truth or falsity of a religious belief, see *supra* note 594, it does not prevent a court or government agency from ascertaining whether the asserted religious belief is honestly held. See *Ballard* and *Thomas*, *supra* note 594. See also *supra* note 260 concerning the selective service issue.

596. See *supra* text at note 261.

597. See *supra* note 305.

598. See *supra* text at notes 60-65. [But see *supra* note 116 (opinion of Rabbi Herzog)].

unanimous consensus was that §253 posed no *halachic* problems.[599] The court never orders the execution of a *get* nor is any sanction, punishment, or fine levied on a recalcitrant husband. The only "sanction" is the fact that a failure to grant a *get* precludes the truthful filing of an affidavit and the obtaining of a civil divorce. At least in *halachic* terms, it is well established that, for purposes of *get meusah*, a denial of a benefit - a civil divorce - is not the same as the imposition of a cost.[600] A law that in effect tells the husband "If you give your wife a *get*, you'll get a civil divorce" is identical to his wife's stating, "If you give me a *get*, I'll give you $100" and both are distinguishable from cases where the husband is told that if he doesn't give a *get*, he will suffer financial loss.

599. See letters of R. Moshe Feinstein dated 9 Tammuz 5743 (Summer 1983); R. Yaakov Kaminecki dated 5741 (1981); R. Shimon Schwab dated 5741 (1981); Rabbi Moshe Stern dated Iyar 5741 (Summer 1981); Rabbi J. Roth, Iyar 5741 (Summer 1981); Rabbi D. Cohen dated 5741 (1981), copies of which are in the possession of the author. See also IGROT MOSHE E.H. IV, nos. 106-107, the latter of which is discussed *supra* at notes 425-431.

600. See *supra* discussion at notes 66-68.

ADDITIONAL NOTE TO CHAPTER SIX JUDICIAL MISHANDLING OF DRL §253 AND THE JEWISH LAW CONSEQUENCES

One troublesome development in New York, particularly from the standpoint of *halacha*, is the occasional judicial departure from §253's sequencing. Rather than withholding a civil divorce until the granting of a *get* (or the removal of barriers to remarriage) as DRL §253 contemplates, some courts have granted the divorce immediately but coupled it with a supplementary order, by stipulation or otherwise, directing the husband to execute a *get* within a certain number of days.[601] Violation of such an order results in contempt of court sanctions ranging from the imposition of fines to incarceration. Courts may find this option attractive because it expedites the implementation of the financial and custodial arrangements between the parties. From the perspective of a judge, it may make little difference whether the *get* is delivered prior to the divorce or shortly afterwards pursuant to order. Indeed, issuing such an order may be an even more efficacious mechanism to enable the prompt securing of a *get* since the recalcitrant spouse faces severe sanctions upon noncompliance.

The degree to which this alternative practice is utilized is unknown but it presents grave problems. Wholly apart from the fact that granting the civil divorce prior to the *get* flatly contradicts the explicit directive of the statute, this departure may very well produce religious divorces that are *halachically* invalid. The whole theory behind the *halachic* validity of the *get* law lies in the fact that it does not force the husband to give a *get* but simply withholds additional benefits, *i.e.*, the privilege of remarrying, until he grants one. One who grants a *get* in order to secure a benefit is not acting under compulsion within the meaning of Jewish law just as one who enters into a sales contract to receive money is not acting under duress within the meaning of common law.[602]

On the other hand, one who is ordered to execute a *get* upon pain of imprisonment or fine and, in order to escape that sanction, delivers a *get*, has indeed acted under compulsion. Even if the order were entered pursuant to stipulation and in a sense the penalties may be regarded as self-imposed, many authorities invalidate *gittin* even where they arise out of self-imposed contractual sanctions and the definitive ruling of Rema was that such *gittin* should not be written.[603] Moreover, as noted previously, it is possible that *all* authorities would invalidate a *get* executed pursuant to a risk of imprisonment whether self-imposed or not.[604] While such threats do not invalidate the *get* if made pursuant to the enforcement of a decision of the *bait din*,[605] the mere

---

601. See *Weiss v. Weiss* (N.Y. Sup. Ct. 1989), reported in the NEW YORK JEWISH WEEK (May 26, 1989), p. 4 and *Kaplinsky v. Kaplinsky*, No. 19437/87. (N.Y. Sup. Ct. [King's County] November 20, 1990), discussed *infra* note 608.

602. See *supra* text at notes 66-68.

603. *Supra* text at note 65.

604. *Supra* text at notes 75-84.

605. At least where the decision is based on *kofin* grounds, *supra* text at notes 110-120 and 291-305.

granting of a civil divorce would certainly not suffice. A direct order to give a *get* is far more troublesome than an *Avitzur*-type agreement where the court is merely directing the parties to submit to the jurisdiction of the *bait din* and raises greater constitutional problems as well, especially when the *get* order was not entered by stipulation.[606]

Ironically, then, there is no possible way the husband can comply with the court's directive. If he doesn't grant a *get*, he goes to jail. If he grants the *get* to stay out of jail, the *get* is invalid and the victimized spouse is still not permitted to remarry. The catch-22 of this situation has not escaped the notice of *batei din*.[607] Unfortunately, members of the secular judiciary, not fully versed in the intricacies of the Jewish law of *get meusah*, have not always been as perceptive and continue to order futile acts that exacerbate the *agunah*'s predicament rather than resolve it.[608] In the absence of a *bait din*'s determination of *kofin*,[609] withholding of a civil divorce is essentially as far as the courts can go and that is precisely the sanction §253 recognizes. Hopefully, courts will confine themselves to the strictures of the statute.[610]

---

606. *Supra* text at notes 263-268 and at 291-299.

607. See, for example, the fascinating saga of *Weiss v. Weiss*, *supra* note 601, where the court granted a civil divorce and then ordered husband to remove the barriers to remarriage imposed on his spouse. Upon husband's failure to execute a *get* within the time ordered by the court, the judge found the husband in contempt and ordered his imprisonment. Husband argued that he was perfectly willing to execute a *get* but the *bait din* refused to authorize it on the grounds that a *get* granted under threat of imprisonment was invalid. The court, understandably confused, granted extensions to the parties to find a *bait din* that would authorize the *get* (there were apparently no takers) and reserved the right to imprison the husband for a separate failure to fulfill his financial obligations.

608. In *Kaplinsky v. Kaplinsky*, *supra* note 601, a judicial hearing officer directed a husband to deliver a *get* to his wife upon pain of imprisonment. The husband raised various issues, among them the spurious contention that a *get* is not universally required within the Orthodox tradition as a condition to remarriage. The hearing officer quite properly rejected this patently false statement. The court, however, did not consider the potential invalidity of a *get* issued under threat of imprisonment.

(I have not found any further published decisions in this case but have been informed that the hearing officer eventually dropped the threat of imprisonment and a proper *get* was then executed.)

609. The grounds for such an order are discussed *supra* text at notes 110-120.

610. The foregoing should not be taken to mean that imprisonment or fines may never be utilized as an effective sanction but merely that these sanctions cannot be employed directly for failure to give a *get*. If, for example, a spouse is being criminally prosecuted for filing a false affidavit or is subject to a contempt sanction of a fine or imprisonment for violation of a court order *other than one compelling the granting of a get*, a dropping of charges or a commutation or reduction of sentence in exchange for the *get* would arguably be perfectly appropriate. (There are, however, some authorities who would possibly disagree with this point.) Although here too the choice is between

giving the *get* and going to jail, the "threatening event" arises from circumstances unrelated to the *get*. See *supra* notes 92-95 for an extensive discussion of this issue and see IGROT MOSHE E.H. IV, no. 106.

(Parenthetically, dropping perjury charges in exchange for the granting of a *get* is probably a bad idea and may seriously undermine the integrity of the New York statute. After all, why shouldn't a recalcitrant husband file a false affidavit if the only adverse consequence of getting caught is that he will be made to do the very thing that he should have done before, *i.e.* grant a *get*? Nevertheless, a *get* that is issued in exchange for the dismissal of a perjury charge is *not* a *get meusah*.)

Chapter Seven

A Second New York *Get* Law: DRL §236B

GENERAL OPERATION OF THE STATUTE

In July 1992, just as this book was going to press, New York State enacted an additional law pertaining to *get* which, to some degree, alleviates the problems of the earlier statute.[611] The new law provides that, in determining equitable distribution of marital property, the court may consider "where appropriate" the refusal of a husband to remove "barriers to remarriage" (such as a refusal to grant a *get*) and condition or limit his entitlements accordingly.[612] The same

---

611. 1992 N.Y. Laws, Ch. 415 amending NEW YORK DOMESTIC RELATIONS LAW §236B. The law originated as a bill introduced by Assemblyman Sheldon Silver and cosponsored by State Senator Steve Saland. It received the strong support of a number of Jewish organizations including the Orthodox Union, the National Council of Young Israel, and the National Jewish Commission on Law and Public Affairs (COLPA) and was signed into law by Governor Cuomo on July 17, 1992. See *Historic Get Bill Signed*, JEWISH PRESS (week of July 24 to July 31, 1992), p. 1. Significantly, Agudath Israel, an organization that spearheaded the enactment of the 1983 *get* bill, see *supra* text at note 532, refrained from taking a position on the desirability of the amendment to §236, pending definitive resolution of the *halachic* concerns detailed below. *Telephone Conversation with David Zweibel, Director of Government Affairs and General Counsel of Agudath Israel of America* (July 29, 1992). See also *infra* text at notes 675-686 (responses of Rabbis Auerbach and Elyashiv).

612. DRL §236B(5), as amended by the addition of new paragraph (h) which states:

> In any decision made pursuant to this subdivision the court shall, where appropriate, consider the effect of a barrier to remarriage, as defined in subsection six of section two hundred fifty-three of this article, on the factors enumerated in paragraph (d) of this subdivision.

Paragraph (d) of section 236(5) enumerates thirteen factors the court must consider in determining "equitable distribution" of marital property. For

factor may be taken into account in setting maintenance (alimony).[613] Thus, for the first time, the statute allows a judge to set a higher level of alimony until a *get* is executed, subject to reduction afterwards.[614] While none of these

---

the most part, these factors are economic in nature focusing both on comparative need and extent of contribution. They include, *inter alia*, the age and health of the parties, the need of a custodial parent to own or occupy the marital abode, the probable future financial circumstances of each party, the loss of inheritance and pension rights upon dissolution of the marriage, and each party's contributions towards the acquisition of assets and the realization of career potential by the other including contributions in the form of services as a parent and homemaker. The last factor, however, is open-ended allowing the court to take into account "any other factor which [it] shall expressly find to be just and proper." Despite this language, the New York Court of Appeals has refused to construe §236(5)(d)(13) as giving judges unlimited discretion in awarding property rights. Specifically, marital fault including adultery, abandonment, and mental cruelty will normally not be a relevant factor in equitable distribution unless the misconduct is so egregious that it shocks the conscience of the court. See *O'Brien v. O'Brien*, 66 N.Y. 2d 576, 489 N.E. 2d 712 (N.Y. 1985). But *cf. Brancoveanu v. Brancoveanu*, 535 N.Y.S. 2d 86 (N.Y. App. Div. 1988) (husband's attempt to murder his wife supported the court's refusal to award a portion of the value of wife's dental practice). As despicable as withholding a *get* may be, it is unlikely that it rises to the level of egregiousness required by *O'Brien*, particularly if the withholding of the *get* is part of a strategy of hard bargaining rather than an act of pure malice or spite. As such, prior to the 1992 amendment, the husband's refusal to grant a *get* would apparently not have been a relevant or even permissible factor in determining his "equitable distribution" rights. At least one judge, however, disagreed. See *Schwartz v. Schwartz*, 583 N.Y.S. 2d 716 (N.Y. Sup. Ct. 1992) (husband's recalcitrance was a relevant factor in "equitable distribution" under DRL §236). Recognizing that Justice Rigler's dictum in the *Schwartz* case was a departure from precedent, would not necessarily be followed by other judges, and was possibly subject to reversal, Assemblyman Silver wanted to insure that the decision be codified and that its benefits be available to litigants statewide. JEWISH PRESS (week of July 24 to July 31, 1992), p. 1.

613. DRL §236B(6), as amended by the addition of new paragraph (d) which states:

> In any decision made pursuant to this subdivision the court shall, where appropriate, consider the effect of a barrier to remarriage as defined in subdivision six of section two hundred fifty-three of this article, on the factors enumerated in paragraph (a) of this subdivision.

Paragraph (a) of section 236B(6) contains a list of eleven factors governing the award of maintenance (alimony) that is substantially similar to the one contained in §236B(5) for equitable distribution including the open-ended authorization to take into account "any other factor" found to be "just and proper." Newly-added paragraph (d) insures that failure to grant a *get* is now a proper factor to be considered.

614. It will be recalled that a differential alimony award was precisely the mechanism utilized by a British court to compel the execution of a *get*. See *Brett v. Brett*, discussed *supra* text at notes 491 and 509. See also *supra* note 532 (similar approach taken by Canada through statutory amendment).

provisions are mandatory, they do provide the sympathetic judge with the tools that can pressure an otherwise-recalcitrant husband to fulfill his religious and moral duties.[615]

Section 236B augments rather than replaces Section 253 and is a marked improvement over the earlier statute in two critical respects. First, the only "sanction" that DRL §253 imposes for failure to grant a *get* is the withholding of a civil divorce,[616] the denial of which may not be especially detrimental in an era of out-of-wedlock relationships and the total disappearance of adultery prosecutions.[617] The new statute, by contrast, carries a real bite in the form of increased alimony liabilities and forfeiture or reduction of claims to marital assets.[618] Second, DRL §253 protects women only in those cases where their husbands were the plaintiffs in the divorce action; it afforded them no relief where they initiated the suit.[619] The new statute makes no such distinction.[620]

---

615. Assume, for example, that the court would enter an order providing that, if a *get* is not executed within thirty days, the husband's one-half interest in marital assets shall be forfeited. Such an order certainly creates an incentive on the part of the husband to grant a *get* within thirty days to avoid forfeiture of his interest. Even after the expiration of the thirty days, the aggrieved wife can now use her superior property rights as bargaining chips, offering for example a one-half interest in exchange for a *get*. While she may continue to be a victim of extortion, §236B gives her more assets with which to negotiate and enables her to bargain from a position of strength.

616. See *supra* text following note 537.

617. From a religious perspective, the presence or absence of a civil divorce is simply irrelevant. See *supra* text at notes 13-17. Not granting the Orthodox Jew a civil divorce until he executes a *get* places no additional marital disability on him beyond the one that already exists by virtue of his not giving the *get*, *i.e.*, the *takkana* of R. Gershom that bans polygamy. See *supra* text at notes 31-42. A man who is willing to marry in violation of this religious ban would hardly be dissuaded from doing so because of the lack of a secular dissolution.

618. Indeed, it is precisely the greater sanctions that §236B employs that create the *halachic* problems of *get meusah*. See *infra* text at notes 626-634.

619. See *supra* text following note 537.

620. This conclusion is somewhat debatable. Both §236B(5)(h) and §236B(6)(d) define "barrier to remarriage" by reference to DRL §253(6). That section in turn provides that barrier to remarriage includes "any religious or conscientious restraint *of which the party required to make the verified statement is aware.....*" (emphasis added; see *supra* note 531 where the language of §253 is quoted in full.) Since a husband is under no obligation to file a verified affidavit where he is not the divorce plaintiff, technically his failure to grant a *get* is not a "barrier to remarriage" within the meaning of §253 and would therefore not constitute such a barrier under §236B. Admittedly, this is indeed the result that a literal reading of the statute compels. Nevertheless, given the clear statements of its sponsors (that the statute is intended to codify Justice Rigler's dicta in the *Schwartz* case, see *supra* note 612) and the fact that the victimization that statute purports to address applies equally in cases where the wife is the divorce plaintiff, it is likely, though

Like §253[621], however, §236B is limited to those "barriers to remarriage" that exist under the principles of the clergyman who solemnized the marriage.[622] Neither statute protects women who were initially married under the auspices of a Reform or Reconstructionist rabbi (neither of whom require a *get* for marital dissolution)[623] but now desire a *get* either because they have become religiously more observant or because they simply want to prevent the stigmatization of their future offspring.[624] This is a serious deficiency in the statute, possibly inadvertent, that should be rectified by corrective legislation.[625]

HALACHIC PROBLEMS

As laudable as the motivations of its drafters may have been, it cannot be denied that §236B, unlike §253, is a *halachically* problematical statute. Any time the withholding of a *get* results in monetary sanctions or forfeiture of property rights that would otherwise accrue, the specter of *get meusah*[626] must be carefully examined. By virtue of the strictures against *get meusah*, the statute in many instances may give rise to the incongruous and inequitable situation of a court's pressuring a person to perform an act which, because of that very pressure, he is disabled from doing.[627] Under the definitive ruling of Rema cited in this work a number of times,[628] if a husband is subject to a monetary penalty unless he grants a *get*, such a *get* may not be written until

---

hardly certain, that courts will ignore the statute's literal reading in favor of a more equitable approach. But see *infra* note 622 (There are limits to how far a court can go in ignoring the language of a statute).

621. See *supra* text at note 538.

622. This result follows from §236B's incorporation of the definition of "barrier to remarriage" contained in §253(b) which expressly provides that the barriers must exist under the principles of the solemnizing clergyman. See *supra* note 538. This qualification, unlike the reference to affidavit (see *supra* note 620), is much more difficult for a court to ignore. Such a qualification is central to the definition of barrier in a way that the peripheral reference to a verified statement is not, covers the classes of women who are most commonly *agunot* (women married in Orthodox or Conservative ceremonies), and is not inconsistent with Justice Rigler's ruling in *Schwartz* which also involved a couple married under Orthodox auspices. It is likely, therefore, that §236B will be subject to the same clerical restriction contained in §253.

623. See *supra* note 3.

624. See *supra* notes 35 and 305 (problem of *mamzeirut* means that often even non-religious women are advised to secure *gittin*).

625. But see *infra* note 649 (such an amendment may create occasional free exercise problems).

626. See *supra* text at notes 60-65.

627. As noted earlier, this paradox has not escaped the attention of *batei din* though courts have sometimes been unaware of the problem. *Supra* notes 607-608 (discussion of *Weiss* and *Kaplinsky*).

628. See *supra* text at note 65.

there is a prior unconditional forgiveness of the penalty.[629] Otherwise, the husband is acting under duress and the *get* may be deemed a *get meusah*. Even those authorities who differ with Rema may do so only where the penalty is self-imposed via contract; where the penalty is imposed by operation of law it is possible that all authorities would prohibit the execution of the *get*.[630] Moreover, such a *get* may be invalid even after the fact, not just *ab initio*.[631]

The procedure contemplated by §236B appears on its face to fall squarely within these proscriptions (although a plausible case can be made to the contrary).[632] Under DRL §236B, a judge may in effect tell a recalcitrant husband the following: "Although you own your home jointly with your wife and would normally be entitled to receive a one-half interest, you are a reprehensible individual because you have spitefully refused to grant your wife a religious divorce. Under §236B, I may consider the reprehensible nature of your conduct in determining your entitlement to marital assets and may order a division that is calculated to insure that you mend your ways. Accordingly, I will enter an order terminating your interest in the marital abode unless you execute a *get* within thirty days." If the husband then executes a *get* on Day 28 to avoid forfeiture of his one-half interest in his home, is that not equivalent to any other case of executing a *get* to escape a monetary sanction? Indeed, the fact that the "penalty" in question is imposed by a judge instead of voluntarily being assumed by the husband makes it considerably worse.[633]

---

629. If such a *get* has already been written and delivered, however, it is valid after the fact and the woman is permitted to remarry. *Id.*

630. See the discussion *supra* at notes 75-86.

631. *Id.* Moreover, to the extent the monetary sanction of property forfeiture and increased alimony are not *halachically* proper, the sanction would be deemed illegitimate. This is yet another reason for invalidating the *get* as a *meusah*. See *supra* text at notes 73-74 and *infra* notes 667. [But *cf.* *supra* text at notes 432-452 (whether illegitimacy is a separate invalidating prong).]

632. See *infra* text at notes 656-674 for a *halachic* defense of the statute.

633. Indeed, it can be persuasively argued that a *meusah* problem exists not only where the husband executes a *get* in order to escape the impact of an outstanding court order but even where a *get* is executed prior to the initiation of court proceedings pertaining to alimony and property rights. The theory is that, after the fact, the husband could always claim that the *get* was executed for the sole purpose of escaping the imposition of a monetary penalty that the wife would otherwise be free to seek. (This argument assumes that the *meusah* problem in this context may invalidate the *get* even *ex post facto* because of the nonconsensual nature of the sanction, see *supra* text at note 630). The problem is only exacerbated if he makes such a declaration *prior* to the *get* being written.

This argument is somewhat questionable, however. The mere possibility of being subject to litigation which the other side may or may not be successful in prosecuting may be too remote and attenuated to be considered a present source of duress, at least in cases where the wife has not indicated prior to the *get* that she plans to raise the withholding of the *get* in the context of an equitable distribution or alimony proceeding. It must be remembered that although the statute as amended provides that the judge "shall" take into

Presumably, a *bait din* would simply refuse to execute a *get* under these circumstances but this places the husband in the untenable and inequitable situation of being unable to comply with the court's directive and nevertheless forfeiting his one-half interest in marital property. Surely it makes no sense to penalize persons for nonperformance of acts which are impossible for them to perform, particularly where it is the very imposition of the penalty that gives rise to this impossibility.[634]

---

account "the effect of a barrier to remarriage," it does not dictate a specific result. At least in theory, depending on the circumstances a judge could find the withholding of a *get* as excusable and not impose any sanction. Thus, one who grants a *get* out of a fear that if he does not, (1) his wife *may* raise the issue in court and (2) the judge *may* take away marital assets to which he is otherwise entitled has probably not acted out of compulsion within the meaning of *get meusah*.

As the threat becomes more probable and imminent, however, the line of *meusah* may be crossed. There is clearly going to be a *meusah* problem where the husband is already under an outstanding court order of forfeiture or diminution unless he grants a *get* (the example in the text) or where the judge has already indicated that he will enter such an order unless a *get* is granted and there could very well be a problem where the wife has already communicated her intention to invoke her rights under the statute. At that time, the "threat" may no longer be attenuated and remote but actual.

In any case, to the extent there is a *get meusah* problem even prior to the court's issuing an order, the procedures outlined in the text may be employed to obviate it. See also *infra* note 637 (*meusah* problem may actually be less pronounced once the court's order becomes operative).

634. Some advocates of the law have suggested that since §236B limits consideration of "barriers to remarriage" to cases where such consideration is "appropriate," a judge will be precluded from invoking the husband's failure to grant a *get* as a factor in equitable distribution or maintenance unless there is a prior order of a *bait din* (presumably of a *kofin* type) directing that a *get* be given. *Zweibel Interview*, *supra* note 611 (quoting various sources in the Jewish community but disagreeing with them as I do). While this construction of the statute avoids the dilemma stated in the text and would eliminate the problem of *get meusah*, it is highly unconvincing. In the first place, it is unlikely that such open-ended, vague language would ever be read to circumscribe the court's discretion to such a great extent and it is virtually inconceivable that a judge *not* waiting for the decision of a *bait din* would ever be reversed on appeal. It must be remembered that judges in New York have already exhibited a propensity to order *gittin* without reference to the decision of a *bait din* in contravention of a much clearer statutory directive than the nonspecific "where appropriate" language of §236B. See *supra* notes 607-608. Second, in the overall context of the statute which lists a variety of economic and need-related factors, the reference to "where appropriate" does not appear to be intended to incorporate *halachic* norms but rather to compel the court to evaluate the "barrier to remarriage" in terms of its prospective economic disadvantage to the disabled spouse. See *infra* text following note 661. Finally, tying the court's jurisdiction to the prior decision of a *bait din* that a *get* is mandatory raises serious constitutional problems under the establishment clause. See *infra* note 655 (excessive entanglement and promotion). It is

At this point, the reader may reach the alarming conclusion that not only will §236B not help *agunot* but will actually have the effect of *keeping* them in their unfortunate state by creating the impossibility of a woman ever receiving a *get* as long as a forfeiture order is in effect. Fortunately, this would normally not be the case. Whether a statute like §236B does in fact result in a *get meusah* is an extraordinarily complex *halachic* question, the parameters of which are best addressed in a separate section,[635] and may in large part depend on what stage in the divorce proceedings the *get* is obtained.[636] Even conceding the existence of a *meusah* problem, however, is not necessarily a cause for concern.[637]

First, a §236B forfeiture order is entirely appropriate, and indeed quite helpful, in those cases where the *bait din* has issued a *kofin*-order since all

---

unlikely that a phrase which is at best ambiguous will be construed in a manner that is constitutionally suspect. See also *infra* note 678 and text at notes 687-702.

635. See *infra* text following note 655.

636. Compare notes 633 and 637. As therein indicated, the *meusah* problem is greatest when the *get* is obtained after the issuance of a judgment but before its terms have gone into effect (the example in the text); the *meusah* problem is less pronounced when the *get* is issued prior to judgment or the initiation of litigation; and the *meusah* problem may be nonexistent if the *get* is issued after a forfeiture has taken place and the husband is seeking to regain property rights which he has already lost.

637. It should also be noted that at least one eminent *halachic* authority has suggested that, although a *get* executed to avoid forfeiture of marital assets may be invalid as a *meusah*, there is no impediment to writing a *get* once a terminating order has already gone into effect and the husband is seeking to regain property already lost. Once the property belongs to the woman unconditionally, if she then bargains her rights away in exchange for a *get* such action clearly constitutes the conferral of a new benefit on the husband. *Rabbi Zalman Goldberg, quoted in Letter of R. Tzvi Gartner to R.Y. Elyashiv* (July 1992), copies on file with this author.

Rabbi Goldberg's point is surely well-taken but can be sustained only if *halacha* recognizes the allocation of marital property in accordance with the judge's order as legitimate and binding. To the extent *halacha* does not recognize the legitimacy of property rights that do not follow *halachic* rules, the woman's continued retention of those assets is technically a matter of theft (from a religious perspective). A *get* that is obtained through the coercion of theft is presumably invalid as a *get meusah* whether the thief receives the *get* by threatening to steal or whether, after the theft, she threatens not to return property already stolen. See also Appendix B for a discussion of the *halachic* rules governing marital property rights.

Thus, a full analysis of this problem would have to focus on the *halachic* recognition of secular property rights that go beyond those embodied within the internal workings of the *halachic* system. See generally Shilo, DINA D'MALCHUTA DINA ("The Law of the Land is the Law").

In any case, Rabbi Goldberg's analysis (a *get* that is granted to regain property already forfeited is not a *get meusah*) would not serve to validate the alimony portion of the statute since the *get* would be given under those circumstances to avoid the imposition of a future liability.

means of compulsion are then *halachically* permissible.[638] Unfortunately, the category of cases falling under *kofin* is relatively small and, according to the vast majority of authorities and standard *halachic* practice, does not include common no-fault grounds such as irreconcilable differences.[639] In the absence of *kofin*-grounds, the only way a *get* could be executed consistent with Rema's ruling is either by the court's rescinding its earlier order (upon advice of the *bait din* that, under the facts of the case, *halacha* does not permit compulsion) or by having the wife execute an unconditional release of her claims under the order (*i.e.*, the claims to which she is entitled by virtue of the withholding of *get*) prior to the *get* being written.[640] Under either alternative, the initial issuance of the order *per se* would not prevent the *get* from being written. Thus, in cases other than *kofin*, §236B at the very least will not exacerbate the

---

638. See *supra* text at notes 110-120 (discussion of *kofin* and *yotzee*). Indeed, according to most authorities, non-Jewish coercion may be employed in *kofin* cases not only where the secular courts direct the recalcitrant husband to obey the *bait din* but even where they directly order him to give a *get* without reference to the *bait din*'s decision (as long as such a decision was in fact issued). See *supra* note 299.

It is arguable, however, that the legitimation of secular enforcement in *kofin* cases may be limited to instances where the intent of the coercive device is to secure compliance with the *bait din* even though the *bait din*'s order need not explicitly be mentioned. See *supra* note 103. If that is the case, the New York statute is *halachically* problematical even in *kofin* cases since the coercive sanction employed by the courts in the determination of equitable distribution and alimony in no way depends on the decision of a *bait din* and is not attempting to ensure compliance with that decision. This appears to be the position of Rabbi Elyashiv cited *infra* text at note 681. It is possible, therefore, that the expedient of a release, described *infra* text at notes 640-643, may even be necessary in *kofin* cases. (Naturally, this is a problem only if the pressures under the statute constitute the type of coercion that results in a *get meusah*. See *infra* text at notes 656-662 for an analysis why they may not.)

639. See *supra* text following note 126 (discussion of *mais alai* and minority view of Rambam).

640. Such a release could take the form of either a property settlement (including maintenance) containing no mention of *get* or one that, in exchange for a *get*, provides the husband with more benefits than he otherwise would be entitled to by virtue of his preexisting marital property interests (so-called "trading chip" agreements, see *supra* text at notes 270-272). [The use of "trading chip" agreements, however, may be problematical because it is unclear whether the husband's preexisting marital property interests are to be defined by *halacha* or *secular law*, see *supra* note 636. Absent such a determination, it would be impossible to know whether withholding the *get* results in a forfeiture or granting the *get* produces a gain. Thus, a *halachically* simpler solution would be the execution of a separation agreement omitting any mention of a *get*.]

Apart from the *Golding* problem discussed *infra* note 643, such agreements would appear to successfully circumvent the directives of §236B. Both (5) and (6) apply only if there is no agreement to the contrary and §236B(3) explicitly allows agreements covering both marital property and maintenance.

agunah's predicament. Yet if §236B does no harm, it also produces little or no benefit since by definition any sanction propelling the husband to grant a *get* must be unconditionally removed before the *get* can be written. Of course, once the sanction is removed, the husband and his unfortunate wife are in exactly the same situation they were in before §236B was ever amended. In essence, then, the real "problem" of §236B is not that it will produce *halachically* invalid *gittin* - that is a problem easily resolvable by responsible *batei din* - but that it is simply ineffectual outside of a narrow range of cases. Since within that narrow (*kofin*) range the statute does indeed produce real benefits, perhaps one shouldn't complain of its limited effectiveness elsewhere.[641]

As a practical matter, §236B may aid the victimized spouse even in cases which do not qualify as *kofin*. While it is true that an unconditional release would have to be executed prior to the writing of the *get*, there is no reason why the release could not be deferred until the husband shows up at the *bait din* and indicates that he is ready, willing, and able to cooperate. The court's order can effectively function as an appearance penalty - a mechanism to compel the husband to come - even where it is phrased as a *get* penalty.[642] Although in theory once the husband gets his release he is free to walk away, once he is in a room with a *bait din* prepared to write a *get* and once he has indicated his readiness to cooperate it is somewhat unlikely that he would have the nerve to back off.[643] Indeed, there is no particular reason why under the

---

641. At least one contemporary authority seems to argue that a *get* may be executed pursuant to a "threat" under §236B not only in the rare cases of *kofin* but in cases of *yotzee* as well. See R. Yitzchok Liebes, BAIT AVI, E.H. no. 169. His failure to distinguish between the two categories of mandatory divorce appears inconsistent with the rulings of earlier *halachic* authorities. See *supra* notes 110-119. But see *supra* note 116 (view of Rabbi Herzog). In any case, Rabbi Elyashiv has taken a diametrically opposite position: the application of the statute produces a *get meusah* even in *kofin* cases. See *supra* note 638 and *infra* text at note 681.

642. As discussed *supra* text at notes 319-322, penalties designed to coerce appearance at a *bait din* raise no issues of *get meusah*.

643. Unfortunately, the recent case of *Golding v. Golding*, 581 N.Y.S. 2d 4 (N.Y. App. Div. 1992), discussed *supra* note 57, may put a crimp into the relative simplicity of this procedure. In *Golding*, the court ruled that a separation agreement, under which a wife gave up valuable property rights in exchange for a *get*, was voidable on the grounds of duress. See also *Perl v. Perl*, *supra* note 57. The procedure suggested above in dealing with §236B involves an analogous problem. We start off with a court entering an order that states, for example, that until husband gives a *get*, he will receive nothing and if he gives a *get*, will receive 50% of marital assets. As a result, husband is now ready, willing, and able to cooperate. To avoid the problem of *meusah*, however, wife must then execute a release which provides that, whether or not husband executes a *get*, he will be entitled to that 50%. Giving husband the freedom to walk away creates the risk that he will but enables the *get* to be written free of any supposed compulsion.

The problem is this: if under cases like *Golding*, the wife's foregoing of her rights in order to secure a *get* is invalid and if husband would in fact walk away she would be free to reinstate her rights under the judge's original

statute the court itself could not draft an order compelling appearance, rather

---

order, the *get* is still a *get meusah*. The execution of a release that is invalid is equivalent to having no release at all. To guarantee the validity of the release, it would be necessary to have the release approved by the court and incorporated into a decree by stipulation before the *get* could even be written. Unfortunately, this gives the husband a much longer period of time to simply welch on his commitment unless the *bait din* literally assembles at the courtroom ready to supervise the *get* immediately after entry of the decree. Even in such an uncommon case, it is somewhat easier for the husband to walk away from the *bait din* in a public building like a courthouse than it would be if the release could simply be executed at the *bait din*'s offices.

[Some additional clarification of the *Golding* point may be helpful: The standard *Golding* scenario will arise where husband agreed to give a *get* as part of an overall marital settlement, the *get* was actually granted, and the wife now in possession of her *get* seeks to overturn her obligations under the settlement on the grounds of duress. *Golding* suggests she may very well be successful (but *cf. supra* note 57 where questions are raised regarding the validity of the *get*). Although a *Golding* claim of duress could be raised by a dissatisfied wife prior to her receiving the *get* as well, this will normally not be the case since then, she will remain in her *agunah* predicament.

In the hypothetical presented in the text, the *Golding* problem will tend to surface in the opposite manner: in terms of how a wife may behave before she receives a *get*, rather than afterwards. In the example of the text, the judge enters an order terminating husband's interest in marital assets unless he executes a *get* by Day 30. In order to avoid the problem of *meusah*, wife effectively renounces her rights under that order on Day 29, thereby providing that husband gets his one-half interest whether or not he grants a *get*. In this scenario, there is no *Golding* argument that a wife can raise *after* the *get* since husband's rights after the *get* in no way depend on the terms of her release. Once the *get* is received (assuming it was timely), husband retains his one-half interest by virtue of the court's original order irrespective of the validity of her prior release. Setting aside her release under those circumstances would simply be an irrelevancy.

Where *Golding* could come into play, however, is in defining the wife's rights *prior* to her receiving a *get*. Although she may have executed an unconditional release reinstating her husband's one-half interest whether or not he grants her a *get*, *Golding* gives her the apparent right to rescind that release and reinstate the court's order which in turn generates a compulsion on the husband to write a *get*, a compulsion that is a possible violation of the rules against *get meusah* (but see *infra* text at notes 656-661). While it may be highly unlikely that the wife will attempt to set aside the settlement prior to her receiving a *get* (since, if she does, a *bait din* may refuse to execute a *get*), even her theoretical ability to do may mean that the husband is acting under compulsion. In effect, even with a release in hand, he knows that if he fails to act he may be subject to monetary penalties.

Thus, while the typical *Golding* problem focuses on arguments that will be normally raised after a *get* has been delivered, the interface of *Golding* with the law of *get meusah* contemplates the possibilities of settlement avoidance prior to the *get* with the result that the husband who executes a *get* is still bound by an external duress.]

than the execution of a *get*. Regardless of what the judge does, however, a *bait din* can effectively use the order to at least get the husband through the door.

On balance, therefore, §236B may be characterized as a marginally beneficial statute, hardly a panacea but at the same time not a blatant violation of religious doctrine. Its use of the law of equitable distribution and alimony is entirely proper in *kofin* cases; the *halachic* problem that it poses in non-*kofin* cases can be circumvented by having the wife execute an unconditional release prior to the writing of the *get*; and the deferral of such release until such time as the husband appears before the *bait din* creates effective and *halachically* legitimate pressures on the husband to appear even where *halacha* would not sanction direct compulsion on the *get*. While §236B is not without *halachic* problems, there is truly less here than meets the eye.[644]

CONSTITUTIONAL ISSUES

The constitutional issues that the new law raises are substantially similar to those arising under the 1983 legislation and one would expect that the New York courts would be equally accommodating.[645] There are, however, some pertinent distinctions which should be noted though, in the judgment of this author, they will ultimately prove to be immaterial.

With respect to free exercise, it is arguable that the new statute is a greater infringement on religious freedom than is the withholding of a civil divorce under DRL §253. Under §253, the only sanction for not granting a *get* is the denial of a civil divorce (where the recalcitrant party is the divorce plaintiff) and the maintenance of the *status quo*. By contrast, under amended §236, the magnitude of the coercion to comply with *halachic* dictates is significantly greater, involving forfeiture of property rights and the imposition of monetary sanctions.[646]

---

644. In effect, the worst accusation that can be levied against §236B is that, in many cases, it will prove ineffectual since no *get* will be executed until the wife gives up the rights that §236B enables her to have. As such, the *halachic* problems of *meusah*, easily surmountable by a *bait din*, should be no reason to call for the statute's repeal. It produces some good and relatively little harm.

[Of course, to the extent some rabbinical authorities would allow *gittin* to be written without obtaining a release (on the theory that the sanctions of §236B do not produce a *get meusah*), the statute does indeed create the potential for devastating mischief. By generating *gittin* that according to other authorities are invalid as *meusah*, the statute would produce the specter of *halachic* adultery and taint offspring of remarriages with the stigma of *mamzeirut*, see *supra* notes 35 and 305. It is hoped, however, that rabbinical authorities regardless of their personal opinion would be responsible enough not to invoke a procedure that would produce *mamzeirut* according to any respectable view. See *supra* note 349 (procedures that render a *get* invalid even according to a minority opinion should not be employed).]

645. See *supra* note 552 (New York case law) and the earlier discussion at notes 553-597 (constitutional issues under §253).

646. Indeed, it is precisely the greater "bite" of §236 that gives rise to the serious *halachic* problem of *get meusah*. See *supra* text following note 626.

Nevertheless, while this distinction is quite important for purposes of Jewish law, it is probably irrelevant for constitutional analysis. It is unlikely that a reallocation of property rights would be deemed a significantly greater intrusion than the denial of access to the civil courts for a remedy that only those courts can grant, *i.e.*, dissolution of the marriage. Indeed, in the eyes of the American judiciary, the opposite may very well be the case.[647] Even if the burden under §236B would be deemed "weightier," American courts, unlike *halachic* authorities, have not tended to distinguish between different categories of burdens in analyzing free exercise claims, at least where those burdens were imposed with the specific intention of compelling the performance of a religious act.[648] Thus, for purposes of free exercise, even the ostensibly greater monetary "burden" of §236B would probably be considered constitutionally equivalent to the lesser "burden" of §253. In any case, the free exercise claims raised by *get*-resisters are typically spurious and relatively trivial and normally

647. The Supreme Court has continually emphasized that the state's exclusive control over the dissolution process and the fact that marriage (and by extension divorce) constitutes a fundamental right impose special responsibilities on the state to provide equal access to the process for all its citizens. See *Boddie v. Connecticut*, 401 U.S. 371 (1971) (filing fees for divorce actions cannot bar indigents; denial of access to the court system where relief cannot be secured in nonjudicial forums is a denial of due process). But *cf. United States v. Kras*, 409 U.S. 434 (1973) (filing fees *can* preclude an indigent's filing for bankruptcy since bankruptcy protection is not a fundamental right and in any event its protections can be secured by consensual arrangements with creditors). See also *Ortwein v. Schwab*, 410 U.S. 656 (1973) (filing fees for appealing welfare terminations upheld against constitutional attack). In light of these cases, a court could properly conclude that the deprivation of a right to remarry (via the withholding of a civil divorce) is a far greater disability than the "mere" forfeiture of property rights. See also *supra* note 499 (marriage and procreation as fundamental rights). (Obviously, these holdings are irrelevant insofar as Jewish law is concerned; §236 clearly raises a more serious problem of *get meusah* than does §253).

648. See, for example, *Torcaso v. Watkins*, 367 U.S. 488 (1961) (A state may not require a declaration of belief in a Deity as condition to assuming public office. Denial of office to nonbelievers is a burden on the free exercise of religion although it does not "take" anything away). [See also U.S. CONSTITUTION, Art. VI which prohibits religious oaths for *federal* employees.] The distinction between burdens that involve forfeitures and burdens that are simply denials of benefit has generally been disregarded in American constitutional jurisprudence, at least where such burdens infringe on constitutionally protected freedoms such as speech, assembly, and religion. Thus, as a general proposition, the state cannot make the gaining or keeping of government benefits conditional upon the recipient foregoing the exercise of constitutional rights even where the government has no obligation to provide the service or benefit at all. See generally Lupu, *Where Rights Begin: The Problem of Burdens on the Free Exercise of Religion*, 102 HARVARD L. REV. 933 (1989) and Sullivan, *Unconstitutional Conditions*, 102 HARVARD L. REV. 1413 (1989).

should not be given credence under either statutory provision.[649]

Looking at the establishment clause, the arguments seem to cut the other way. To the extent that the clause proscribes excessive entanglement with, and promotion of, religion,[650] §236 seems to raise fewer problems. Unlike §253 which singles out a discrete factor of religious importance that a secular court must consider, §236 merely enumerates the maintenance of barriers to remarriage as one of many factors the court looks at in determining equitable distribution and support. Treating religious barriers as one among many factors, rather then the only factor, carries less of a signification of imprimatur, promotion, or endorsement.[651] Moreover, §253's directive is mandatory; if barriers to remarriage are found to exist, the statute compels the court to respond in a certain way, *i.e.*, not granting a civil dissolution. Section 236B, on the other hand, although requiring that the court *consider* certain factors, does not mandate a specific result. In other words, obedience or nonobedience to religious law (or a clergyman's certification to that effect) does not exercise an unconditional and unchecked veto power on governmental functions.[652] This feature minimizes both the appearance of endorsement and the existence of excessive entanglement between religious and secular

---

649. See *supra* text at notes 589-597. Interestingly, the free exercise clause may be an argument against amending the statute to cover all barriers to remarriage. See *supra* text at note 625. As it stands, §236 is applicable only to cases where, under the principles of the solemnizing clergyman, a *get* would be required and does not cover cases of Reform marriages where the wife subsequently becomes Orthodox and is now desirous of a *get*. Were the statute to be amended to apply to the latter cases as well, it would in effect be authorizing judicial compulsion even in the rare instance of the principled *get*-resister whose religious convictions are somehow offended by a *get* and who has never acquiesced in a religious ceremony performed by an Orthodox or Conservative clergyman. As drafted, the statute avoids this sticky free exercise problem by limiting itself to those persons who have effectively consented in some form to be bound by religious law. See *supra* text at note 589.

In fact, however, this argument against statutory amendment is fairly unconvincing. Cases of principled *get*-resisters are extremely rare even among Reform Jews who regard a *get* as superfluous and would furnish no reason to invalidate the statute as a whole. At most, such persons, if they exist at all, would merely be entitled to show that the statute should not be applied to them.

650. See the earlier discussion at notes 578-588 and *infra* notes 857-858 (current definition of "establishment").

651. This is especially true if the statute permits the court to consider the absence of a *get* only in terms of its economic impact on the wife and her increased support needs because of her prospective inability to remarry. See *infra* text at note 662 (Zweibel and Silberman readings). As such, the statute does not promote the granting of a religious divorce as an inherent desideratum but simply considers a marriage barrier as a neutral factor that bears upon the wife's future economic prospects. In this respect §236B is less of a promotion of religion than is §253 in which "barriers to remarriage" stands as a separate impediment to the granting of divorce irrespective of the wife's particular support needs.

652. See *supra* text at note 583 (discussion of *Grendel's Den*).

authorities.[653]

This is not to suggest that §253 is constitutionally suspect - I have already argued before that it is not[654] - but merely that §236B is even less

---

653. There is, however, one particular respect in which § 236B raises a more serious establishment clause concern than does § 253. Under § 253, if the divorce plaintiff files a verified affidavit alleging that all barriers to remarriage have been removed, the court is precluded from inquiring into the truth of those allegations. See DRL § 253(a) and *supra* text at note 582. By contrast, under § 236B the husband's affidavit has no such preclusive effect. If, for example, the husband claims that all barriers to remarriage have been removed while the wife claims they have not, the court would have to hold an evidentiary hearing on issues such as whether a *get* was given, whether it complied with *halachic* dictates, whether the *bait din* supervising the execution of the *get* was valid, and the like. Conceivably, the court could find itself embroiled in the resolution of *halachic* and doctrinal matters in a way that it could not under § 253. Using the formulation of *Lemon*, the potential for "excessive entanglement" with religious doctrine and religious authorities is markedly greater under § 236B than it is under the 1983 law. (I am indebted to David Zweibel, General Counsel of Agudath Israel of America, for this insight.)

Mr. Zweibel's point is a good one. Nevertheless, given the relatively straightforward and uncontroversial nature of a *get* ceremony and the fact that § 236B's definition of "barrier to remarriage" will depend on the religious principles of the solemnizing clergyman, the potential for intensive and extensive entanglement appears slight. (But *cf. infra* note 655.) If, for example, the marriage were solemnized by an Orthodox rabbi, it is highly unlikely that the court will ever be faced with having to resolve conflicting expert testimony *within the Orthodox camp* that a particular *get* is valid or invalid or with having to discern fine points of Jewish laws. In 99 out of 100 cases, the issue before the court will boil down to a simple and mechanical question of fact: was there or was there not a *get* - the resolution of which does not entail any significant degree of entanglement simply because there is virtually no possibility of a good faith doctrinal dispute. (But *cf. Kaplinsky*, *supra* note 608, where a supposedly Orthodox attorney tried to argue that a *get* was *halachically* unnecessary for dissolution. While frivolous or spurious claims can always be advanced, they can also be speedily weeded out and their possible assertion should not be a trigger of the entanglement prong.)

If, in a rare case, such entanglement does exist, the solution would be to enjoin the application of the statute in that particular instance and not to invalidate the statute for the 99% of cases in which no problem arises. In any event, the "excessive entanglement" prong may go the same way as the rest of the *Lemon* test. See *infra* text at notes 826-859. Indeed, even Justice O'Connor, the principal exponent of the "promotion" and "endorsement" prong and one who on the whole advocates the retention of *Lemon*, has questioned the wisdom of the "entanglement" criterion. See *infra* note at 835.

With respect to the remaining prongs of secular purpose and primary effect (as defined by the appearance of "promotion" and "endorsement"), § 236B appears less problematical for the reasons stated in the text.

654. See *supra* text at notes 574-597.

problematical and its constitutionality should therefore be sustained.[655]

655. Ironically, some of the proposals advanced to alleviate the *halachic* problems with the law would actually create constitutional ones. Some have suggested that the statute be redrafted to limit sanctions to cases where a *bait din* has ordered that a *get* be given (*kofin*) or where the husband has ignored its summons. See *Gartner letter*, *supra* note 637. Yet necessitating that a secular court respond in accordance with the decisions and doctrines of a specific religious tribunal may in itself constitute the excessive entanglement with religion that the Constitution proscribes. But see *infra* text at note 701 for an alternative amendment that may pass constitutional muster.

[The entanglement present here would be far greater than that which is involved when the court merely has to determine whether a *get* was given. The latter issue is a straightforward question of fact, normally not subject to good faith disagreement. By contrast, whether grounds exist for a *kofin* - order or whether a husband should be subject to a *k'tav siruv* for a refusal to submit to a particular *bait din* are matters in which even eminent Orthodox rabbis commonly disagree. This author personally knows of a number of cases where husbands were told by one *bait din* that they need not respond to the summons of the other and that they could safely ignore the resulting *k'tav siruv*. The court would be inundated with conflicting testimony and readings of Jewish law in a manner that is far more intrusive than whatever involvement may exist under the statute as currently worded. Note, too, that tying the court's decision to the specific rulings of an ecclesiastical body may create constitutional problems under the "endorsement" or "promotion" prong as well, an aspect of *Lemon* that may survive the demise of the "entanglement" test. See *infra* text at notes 857-858.]

ADDITIONAL NOTE TO CHAPTER SEVEN (I) THE *HALACHIC* VALIDITY OF §236B*

Section 236B authorizes the court to consider the withholding of a *get* (or the maintenance of a barrier to remarriage) as a relevant factor both in the determination of equitable distribution of marital assets and in the setting of alimony. Because the *halachic* considerations pertaining to each category are somewhat distinct, each will be addressed separately.

A. *Equitable Distribution*: It is arguable that an equitable distribution order that diminishes the husband's rights by reason of his failure to grant a *get* does not result in *get meusah*. As repeatedly noted, the problem of *meusah* arises only if nonexecution of the *get* results in forfeiture, not if execution of the *get* results in benefit. A judicial order, or agreement, that says, "If you grant a *get*, you'll pay $100" is fundamentally different than one that says, "If you don't grant a *get*, you'll pay $100."[656] While the distinction is fairly clear, it is difficult to apply in the context of equitable distribution since definitionally it is hard to know whether the husband's reduced entitlement because of his failure to grant a *get* should be characterized as a forfeiture or a mere denial of benefit. If the rule of thumb would have been that marital assets are divided in half unless there are countervailing factors such as a refusal to grant a *get*, it would indeed be clear that such a refusal effects forfeiture. Equitable distribution statutes, including New York's, are not, however, phrased in that manner; they are inherently indeterminate, granting to each spouse only what is equitably theirs upon a consideration of all relevant circumstances. There is no predetermined assignment of property rights or even operating presumption which the court's order would be disturbing. As such, any "forfeiture" or "diminution" resulting from the withholding of a *get* is not the imposition of a penalty - the court is not taking away from the husband something he already "has" - but is the mere denial of benefit.

This line of reasoning, however, is hardly conclusive. In the first place, in determining whether husband is giving something up or simply being denied a benefit, the appropriate definitional base may well be not the state's indeterminate law of equitable distribution but *halacha* itself. The husband's rights in marital property under *halacha* are generally much more expansive than those arising under equitable distribution laws.[657] Essentially, therefore, virtually any diminution of his interest would be taking away something that, *by virtue of halacha*, the husband is entitled to retain. As such, the law of *get meusah* will continue to be implicated. (This would also mean that the pressure of forfeiture would be classified as an "illegitimate pressure," rendering the *get* invalid even after the fact according to virtually all authorities.[658])

Second, even if the baseline for determining the existence of a forfeiture would be secular law, the appropriate secular law may not necessarily be the indeterminate law of equitable distribution but rather the law governing

---

*At this point, it may be beneficial to the reader to review the outline of *get meusah* concepts presented *supra* text at notes 453-473.

656. See *supra* notes 599-600.

657. See generally *infra* Appendix B.

658. See *supra* note 73-74 but see *supra* text at notes 432-452 (whether illegitimacy is in fact a separate basis for invalidation). See also *infra* text at note 669.

the preexisting property interests as they existed within the marriage. If, for example, a home was owned by husband and wife in joint tenancy or in a tenancy by the entireties and now, pursuant to DRL §236B, a court decrees that the husband's interest is to be forfeited by reason of his failure to grant a *get*, such a decree appears to effect a real forfeiture (not just a denial of benefit) under any definition.

B. *Differential Alimony Awards*: The "no forfeiture" argument, advanced above to avoid the problems of *get meusah*, is sustainable only in connection with a property decree and would not *halachically* justify a two-tiered alimony award. It is clear that any order to pay alimony is calling on the obligor to part with assets that indisputably are his own. Such an order is therefore equivalent to the "If you don't give a *get*, you will pay " type, rather than to a mere denial of benefit.

Nevertheless, while the benefit-detriment argument may not apply, there is an alternative theory under which even a two-tiered alimony award may be *halachically* justified. (This would also be an argument equally applicable to the equitable distribution portion of the statute since it too is related at least in part to anticipated support needs.) *Halacha* recognizes that if the source of compulsion arises from factors extraneous to the granting of the *get*, *e.g.*, imprisonment for an unrelated debt, removal of the compulsion in exchange for a *get* does not result in a *get meusah*.[659] It is arguable that the basis for a higher alimony award is not the absence of a *get per se* but the additional economic burdens a woman faces due to her inability to remarry.[660] In essence, what the statute does is authorize the court to set a higher level of support by reason of wife's financial predicament. The function of the higher award is not to compel or direct the husband towards the granting of a *get* nor to punish the husband for failure to grant a *get* but merely to provide an economic cushion for the additional hardships a woman faces due to her inability to obtain support from a particular source, *i.e.*, another husband. Seen in this light, DRL §236B is simply a variant of the support order that has the indirect and salutary effect of encouraging the execution of a religious divorces.[661]

Such an interpretation is quite plausible and indeed finds strong support in the language of the statute. As noted, §236B lists thirteen factors the courts must consider in determining "equitable distribution" of marital property and eleven factors governing the setting of maintenance. Failure to remove barriers to remarriage is *not* listed as a fourteenth (or twelfth) factor but rather as a piece of information the court is to take into account only in applying the thirteen (or eleven) other factors. In justifying a higher alimony award (or in granting wife a greater portion of marital assets), the court could not simply state that husband didn't grant a *get*. The court would have to make a specific finding that the failure to give a *get* implicates one of the enumerated factors, the bulk of which focus on the need for support.[662]

---

659. See *supra* text at notes 66-71.

660. See *Brett v. Brett*, discussed *supra* note 491.

661. See *supra* text following note 379.

662. Once again, I am indebted to David Zweibel of Agudath Israel for this insight; he has also informed me that this interpretation is shared by Linda Silberman, Professor of Law at New York University and a recognized authority on family law.

A further support for this interpretation may be the fact that the statute

Unfortunately, this interpretation does not fully resolve the *halachic* quandary. In the first place, it is not all clear that the purpose of the statute is not to directly compel a *get*. The statute was enacted to codify Justice Rigler's dictum in the *Schwartz* case where he apparently was prepared to consider the withholding of a *get* as a relevant factor in determining support and property rights without regard to economic impact or support needs.[663] Moreover, it must be remembered that not all the factors enumerated in the "equitable distribution" and "maintenance" lists are need-related; both lists contain a catch-all proviso authorizing the court to take into account "any other factors that are just and proper." It is at least arguable that while maintenance of a barrier to remarriage is not specifically enumerated as a separate factor, the court may effectively consider it as such by simply tying it to the catch-all.[664] If so, the statute could in fact be interpreted as penalizing the recalcitrant husband for his "evil" behavior.

Second, predicating a higher support award on the fact that a woman is unable to remarry rests on the dubious assumption that the economic needs of a woman unable to marry are greater than the needs of a woman who is able to marry but currently single. At any given point in time, however, there is no reason why this should be true. Assume that a woman's monthly expenses total $600. A woman unable to marry may need that monthly sum over a longer period of time but what she will need per month does not appear to depend on her prospective ability or inability to remarry. (Ironically, the "greater need" argument makes much more sense in the context of "equitable distribution" where a spouse is awarded a lump sum of property to cover both present and anticipated future needs than it does in the case of periodic payment of alimony.) Thus, regardless of what the statute or judge entering an order pursuant to the statute may say, the underlying reality is that the purpose and effect of the award are coercive.

Third, even if in form the award is structured as a support order, because it is linked directly and explicitly to the granting of a *get*, the sanction lacks the formal independence from *get* that would permit it to be employed.[665] The situation is certainly not comparable to a person imprisoned for an unrelated debt who executes a *get* in exchange for a release[666] since here, the source of the compulsion is the *get* itself.

Fourth, to the extent the alimony obligation exceeds the amount that Jewish law deems necessary for spousal support (which will undoubtedly be the

---

directs the court to consider not the barrier to remarriage alone but rather the *effect* of the barrier to remarriage. While the former language would indicate concern with the reprehensible nature of the husband's conduct in refusing to grant a *get* (which, to Justice Rigler, appeared crucial), the latter suggests that the court is not to be concerned with the impropriety of the husband's conduct but rather with the economic dislocations that arise from such impropriety. (I am indebted to Marvin Jacob, Esq., for calling this insight to my attention.)

663. See *supra* note 612.

664. This of course would mean that the amendment overrules the earlier cases that preclude consideration of non-support related factors, see *supra* note 612.

665. See *supra* text at notes 388-392.

666. See *supra* notes 66-68.

case where the judge is using the award to compel the granting of a *get*), its characterization as an "unrelated debt" would be irrelevant. Where the underlying debt or sanction is *halachically* unenforceable, its forgiveness in exchange for a *get* results in a *get meusah* even where the debt was generated by factors extraneous to the *get*.[667] Yet another reason why the sanctions might be illegitimate (even if they are no higher than what a *bait din* would impose for support) is the fact that these are orders entered by a secular court rather than a *bait din* and that factor alone may deprive them of *halachic* validity.[668]

[There is a counterargument on the illegitimacy point. As noted earlier,[669] illegitimacy *per se* may not be a separate invalidating factor but may simply be probative of the fact that he sanction or pressure is not truly independent of the *get* but rather is designed to compel a *get*. Under this reading, as long as a sanction is truly independent, its illegitimacy would be irrelevant. Thus, if in fact the court's order would be based on a *bona fide* determination of support needs - a proposition that in any event is questionable - its generally illegitimacy from the standpoint of *halacha* (and *a fortiori* the impropriety of the forum) will not be invalidating factors.]

In this regard, Rabbi Moshe Feinstein's 1979 letter is highly instructive.[670] In that responsum, R. Feinstein apparently validates two-tiered alimony orders issued by a secular court without regard to the fact that the order was not issued by a *bait din* or that the sum may not correspond to that which would be ordered by a *bait din* and even though the order is explicitly linked to the granting or withholding of a *get*. The situation that R. Feinstein describes in South Africa seems indistinguishable from the situation contemplated by the New York statute. Indeed, if one accepts Professor Silberman's reading, the New York statute should fare even better as a truly independent support sanction. Unfortunately, Rabbi Feinstein's ruling itself is *halachically* quite difficult to understand and, absent a detailed statement of

---

667. See discussion *supra* text at notes 73-74, but *cf.* contrary opinion of Ranach who apparently rejects the legitimate-illegitimate distinction. [Note, however, that it would be incorrect to assume that any pre-*get* alimony obligation is illegitimate. While it is true that *halacha* does not recognize a support obligation towards divorced spouses beyond the paltry sums specified in the *ketubah*, see *supra* text at notes 27 and 381-382, it must be remembered that, until a *get* is granted, *halacha* regards the persons as still married, with all marital support obligations remaining intact. The imposition of alimony subsequent to the granting of a *get* may in fact be *halachically* improper (except to the extent the sum was the product of mutual agreement) but this is a problem having no bearing on the validity of a *get*. The problem of the illegitimate sanction giving rise to a *get meusah* applies only to: (1) a pre-*get* alimony award; (2) that is higher than the alimony payable after a *get*; and (3) is in excess of support needs as established by Jewish law.]

668. Once again, while this problem exists in connection with any support order issued by a secular court, the issue of *get meusah* arises only if the alimony is set at a higher level prior to the *get* and subject to reduction afterwards.

669. See *supra* notes 73-74 and 432-452.

670. See *supra* note 392.

reasons, uncertain of application.[671]

In short, the *halachic* issues boil down to the questions of independence of sanction from the *get* ("support" v. "punishment" or "coercion") and legitimacy.[672] While respectable arguments can certainly be made that a *get* issued in response to a §236B order may not be a *get meusah* and venerable authority to that effect (Rabbi Feinstein) may be cited, the question is far from settled.[673] Further definitive rabbinic opinion pertaining to this specific statutory scheme must be obtained.[674]

---

671. See the multiple meanings advanced *supra* note 392. It should also be noted that at best Rabbi Feinstein's responsa may only validate the "maintenance" portion of the statute and not the portion dealing with "equitable distribution." See *Letter of Rabbi David Morgenstern quoting Rabbi Yosef Elyashiv* (19 Elul 5752), copies in possession of author.

672. See *supra* text at notes 66-74 and 432-452.

673. See *infra* text at notes 675-686 (recent responses of Rabbis Auerbach and Elyashiv).

674. See also *infra* note 637 regarding the *meusah* problem once a judgment goes into effect.

ADDITIONAL NOTE TO CHAPTER SEVEN (II) LETTERS OF RABBI SHLOMO ZALMAN AUERBACH AND RABBI YOSEF SHALOM ELYASHIV

Shortly after the passage of the amendment to DRL §236B, representatives of Agudath Israel of America submitted a request to Rabbi Shlomo Zalman Auerbach and Rabbi Yosef Shalom Elyashiv, two leading *halachic* authorities residing in Jerusalem, asking them to consider the *halachic* issues raised by the amendment to DRL §236B and to author a formal response expressing their views.[675]

Rabbi Auerbach's response dated 28 Av 5752 (August 27, 1992) is quite brief and conclusory.[676] Noting that a *get* that is executed out of fear of imprisonment or monetary sanction is invalid, he regards the New York law as "dangerous" and something that may cause great trouble. Persons who believe that it may extricate women from their predicament as *agunot* are "mistaken" and overall (from a purely *halachic* standpoint) it would be preferable for such a law not to be on the books.

Rabbi Elyashiv's separate response is a bit more detailed but arrives at essentially the same conclusion.[677] He makes four points:

> 1. The statute may permit coercion for the purpose of securing a *get* even in the absence of a finding of a *bait din* that the granting of a *get* is mandatory. Absent a *halachic* obligation to grant a *get*, such coercion will clearly result in a *get meusah*.[678]
>
> 2. Even if the court would impose its sanctions only in conjunction with the order of the *bait din*, it is highly unlikely that a secular court would distinguish between *kofin* and *yotzee* orders.[679] The employment of sanctions such as monetary penalties even in *yotzee* cases despite the husband's religious obligation to divorce his

---

675. See *Letters of Rabbi Moshe Sherer, President of Agudath Israel of America, to Rabbis Auerbach and Elyashiv* (July 23, 1992), copies on file with this author.

676. A copy of his letter was furnished to me by David Zweibel, Esq.

677. An undated copy of this response was again furnished by Mr. Zweibel. An amplified version was issued 1 Elul 5752 (August 29, 1992).

678. Rabbi Elyashiv alludes to the argument that the "where appropriate" language may limit the court to cases where a *bait din* has ruled, see *supra* note 634, but concludes that the practical dynamics of the adversary system will always enable the wife's attorney to find some *bait din* that would issue a *kofin* ruling even on spurious grounds and the secular court will certainly not inquire into the *halachic* basis of the decision.

[While I express no opinion on R. Elyashiv's view of the *bait din* situation in the United States, there are additional solid arguments to rejecting the "where appropriate" language as covering the *get meusah* problem, among them the constitutional requirement of separation of church and state, a concern that even Rabbi Elyashiv noted. See generally *supra* note 634.]

679. See generally *supra* text at notes 110-120.

wife raises the problem of *get meusah* on a Biblical level.[680]

3. The employment of the statutory sanctions of §236B is *halachically* problematical even in *kofin* cases. Since the judge imposing the sanction is not doing so for the purpose of enforcing the *bait din*'s decision (indeed insofar as the statute is concerned the existence or absence of such a decision is irrelevant) but for the purpose of protecting the wife's right to remarry, the secular court cannot be regarded as the surrogate enforcers of the *bait din* or as acting at the request or authorization of the *bait din*. Hence, an essential prerequisite for the "obligatory *get*" exception to the law of *get meusah* is lacking.[681]

4. Rabbi Elyashiv also suggests, but does not definitely rule, that if a husband has refused his wife's summons to go to *bait din* and the *bait din* has issued a *k'tav siruv*, her resort to the process of §236B may not produce a *get meusah* if in fact her entitlement to a *get* falls under the *kofin* rather than *yotzee* category.[682] Since the New York

---

680. This portion of the responsum makes two important points: (1) the employment of *kofin* sanctions in *yotzee* cases renders the resulting *get* invalid after the fact - this is directly contrary to the position of R. Herzog cited *supra* note 116 and also rejects the ruling of R. Liebes cited *supra* note 641 but is consistent with the majority of authorities; (2) the invalidity of the *get* is a matter of Biblical, not merely rabbinic law. *Accord*: CHAZON ISH E.H. 99:11. This last point is not always made explicit by the earlier authorities.

681. Rabbi Elyashiv thus takes the position discussed *supra* note 638. As therein noted, it is not entirely clear why the coercers' intention should be relevant and why it is necessary that they act at the behest or authorization of the *bait din* as long as a *kofin* order was in fact issued but such a requirement finds solid support in the language of *Shulchan Aruch*. Note, however, that the defect here would be only of a rabbinic, rather than Torah, magnitude (unlike the employment of *kofin* sanctions in *yotzee* cases, *cf.* preceding note).

Rabbi Elyashiv also notes that his ruling apparently contradicts the position found in B'EER YITZCHOK E.H., no. 10 (section 8), cited *supra* note 103, but maintains that *B'eer Yitzchok*'s position is highly problematical and inconsistent with the views of earlier *halachic* authorities.

682. The basis for this ruling lies in the fact that as long as *kofin* grounds exist, *halacha* permits any form of compulsion to force the husband to act. Under Torah law, this would even permit immediate resort to non-Jewish entities without the need of a prior determination or authorization of *bait din*. Since, however, it is a general violation of religious law to bring an action in a secular tribunal, see *supra* note 45, and the rabbis of the Talmud wanted to discourage resort to the secular process, they declared that *gittin* obtained by the coercion of secular authorities to be invalid even where *halacha* required a divorce unless those authorities were acting as surrogate enforcers for the *bait din* or at the *bait din*'s behest. See *supra* notes 103-105. Where the husband refuses to submit to the jurisdiction of a *bait din*, however, resort to non-Jewish courts is generally *halachically* proper. See SHULCHAN ARUCH H.M. 26:2. A plaintiff who resorts to such a forum has committed no religious wrong. While it would still be necessary that the substantive grounds allowing for compulsion exist, the procedural prerequisites of *a priori* determination by a *bait din* and having the coercers act as agents for the *bait din* would at that

statute is neither limited to *kofin* cases or to cases where the husband has been issued a *k'tav siruv*, the statute as written remains problematical.

Neither Rabbi Auerbach or Rabbi Elyashiv explains whether the *meusah* problem exists only when an order is already outstanding or even when a *get* is issued to avoid the wife seeking relief under the statute.[683] Nor do they discuss the possibilities of a release as a negation of the *get meusah* problem.[684] Indeed, they provide no practical guidance at all beyond arguing that the statute be repealed, something that is hardly within the unilateral power of the Jewish community even if it was organized on this matter which it is not.[685] Does their decision mean that every *get* executed in the state of New York is subject to an infirmity, being granted under the cloud of DRL §236 or would the analysis suggested above[686] successfully solve this problem? Hopefully, they and other great *halachic* authorities will continue to ponder these problems and provide us with needed clarification.

---

stage be superfluous. In short, *kofin* circumstances coupled with *k'tav siruv* may replace *kofin* circumstances coupled with secular enforcers acting as authorized agents of the *bait din*. Either prong, however, requires *kofin* circumstances, a condition not mandated by the New York statute.

683. See *supra* text at note 633.

684. See *supra* text at note 640.

685. See *supra* note 611.

686. See *supra* text at notes 656-660.

ADDITIONAL NOTE TO CHAPTER SEVEN (III) DOES THE STATUTORY DEFINITION OF BARRIER TO REMARRIAGE OBVIATE *HALACHIC* CONCERNS?

Some advocates of the law have suggested that a closer reading of the operative statutory term "barrier to remarriage" along with a consideration of the probable sequence of events following the issuance of an order under §236B indicate that the *halachic* concerns are minimal and that the operation of the statute will not in the ordinary course produce invalid *gittin*.[687] Assume, for example, that a judge issues an order directing the husband to take whatever steps he can to remove "barriers to remarriage" within X number of days upon pain of forfeiture of marital assets. Assume further that in response to the judge's order, an otherwise recalcitrant husband appears before a *bait din* expressing his willingness to execute a *get*. Under standard *halachic* procedure, no *bait din* will authorize the writing of a *get* unless the husband declares that he is executing the *get* of his own free will without duress or compulsion of any kind.[688] If he cannot make such a declaration or even if he does where it is apparent that he is doing so solely to avoid forfeiture of marital assets or the imposition of higher alimony, the *bait din* would simply not allow the *get* to be written.[689] If the *bait din* does indeed refuse to proceed, the judge's forfeiture order will not take effect since the barrier to the other spouse's ability to remarry is not one that is presently within the power of the husband to remove, an element built into the very definition of the statutory term.[690] Thus, it is argued, the practical application of the statute will do nothing more than compel the husband to appear before a *bait din*; once he does appear, the issue of *meusah* can be determined by a *bait din* whose findings will be conclusive in the secular context as well.

At first blush, this is a powerful argument in favor of the law's *halachic* acceptability; closer scrutiny, however, will find it wanting. It is

---

687. This argument has been presented by a number of reputable attorneys familiar with both New York law and *halacha* and indeed, has been advanced by Assemblyman Sheldon Silver, the sponsor of §236B. *Conversation with Marvin Jacob, Esq.* (February 1, 1993).

688. See Appendix, SHULCHAN ARUCH E.H. 154.

689. While mental reservations normally do not affect the validity of an external act, see *supra* note 232, where the circumstances make it clear that no true consent exists (*umdenah d'muchach*) an external acquiescence to the contrary will have no *halachic* validity. Note, however, that in *kofin* cases, such "coerced consent" is indeed *halachically* acceptable but only a small percentage of *gittin* full within this category. See *supra* text at notes 108-120.

690. Section 236B incorporates the definition of "barrier to remarriage" that is found in §253. See *supra* text at notes 538-541 and 621-624. While this language was designed to insure that a Catholic husband who failed to obtain an annulment would not be subject to the sanctions of §§236B and 253, there is no reason why it could not also encompass the case of a husband willing to grant a *get* (at least under the pressure of monetary sanctions) who is disabled from doing so by reasons of the strictures of *get meusah*. This avoids the apparent injustice of penalizing the husband for a situation he is unable to change. *Cf.* the *Weiss* and *Kaplinsky* cases, *supra* notes 607 and 608.

undoubtedly true that, after the enactment of §236B (as before), a *bait din* may legitimately refuse to write a *get* (thus avoiding the issuance of a *get meusah*). It is also probable that, in the event of that occurrence, the judge's order would not take effect because of the "barrier to remarriage" definition. Conversely, even after §236B, it is entirely possible for a *bait din* to conclude that, notwithstanding the sanctions of the statute, the husband has granted full voluntary consent to the execution of the *get*. Even the Kollel HaRabonim of Monsey which has openly called for the statute's repeal recognizes that *gittin* can continue to be written if the *bait din* determines that no coercion exists.[691]

Yet what are the circumstances where such a finding would be made? (The Kollel's guidelines on this point are deliberately vague.) Obviously, a husband who would be willing to grant a *get* even if §236B didn't exist can grant a *get* after the statute's enactment but by definition there would be no need to have a statute directed to such a person. At the other extreme, those persons who execute a *get* for the sole purpose of avoiding monetary sanctions and are thus induced to act by operation of the statute's directive are precisely those persons who are *halachically* disabled from complying (unless the circumstances are such that would justify *kofin*).[692] The question is: who is left? Section 236B cannot produce *gittin* from truly recalcitrant husbands (who do however respond to the pressure of monetary forfeiture) but only from those husbands who are willing to obey a *bait din* (even without the pressure of forfeiture) but had been unwilling to appear before it in the absence of threat, a fairly unusual class of men. At best, therefore, if §236B is not *halachically* problematical, it is largely *halachically* useless.[693]

The statute's limited effectiveness would not be by itself a sufficient argument to call for its repeal. If the only response to §236B is that *batei din*

---

691. Kollel HaRabonim, a well-respected *bait din* under the leadership of Rabbi Leib Landesman, has played an especially prominent role in publicizing the *halachic* difficulties that §236B engenders and in calling for its repeal or amendment. See, for example, the lengthy Hebrew responsum authored by Rabbi Chaim Malinowitz on behalf of the Kollel HaRabonim dated 28 Av 5752 (August 27, 1992), copies in possession of this author. The practical guidelines of executing a *get* subsequent to the enactment of the statute were issued several months later in October after the more authoritative decisions of Rabbis Auerbach and Elyashiv were received. See Kollel HaRabonim, *Guidelines for Mesadrei HaGet*, 25 Tishrei 5753 (October 22, 1992). Since the Kollel's pronouncements are not officially binding, whether or not a particular *bait din* will follow them is a matter for that *bait din* to decide.

692. See *supra* note text at notes 638-639 but see *supra* text at note 681 (position of Rabbi Elyashiv that the sanctions of the statute cannot be applied even to *kofin* cases).

693. I recognize that this point is a bit overstated. Getting husbands to appear before a *bait din* is certainly a laudable function and may in fact enable the *bait din* to convince a husband to grant a *get*. Indeed, if the ultimate decision of the *bait din* is *kofin*, the statute could even be used to pressure him into writing a *get*. See *supra* text at 638-641 but see decision of Rabbi Elyashiv, *supra* text at 681. To the extent, however, that §236B functions as merely an appearance penalty, it is hardly the panacea that is proponents envisioned and at best would be, as I have stated before, a "marginally beneficial statute." *Supra* text at note 644.

will not issue improper *gittin*, perhaps the statute would be of little concern (though of negligible impact on the *agunah* problem). What its proponents fail to recognize, however, is that this will not be its sole consequence. These supporters are overly sanguine about the ability of even competent *batei din* to deal with this statute in a uniform and consistent manner. And therein lies the problem. As long as the coercive pressure of §236B is on the books (or has been concertized in a court order),[694] it will be extremely difficult at least in some cases to gauge true consent. A *bait din*, particularly in an *agunah* situation, may erroneously place excessive reliance on external manifestations of consent even where the circumstances are clear that the husband's "agreement" was based on threat of forfeiture. At the very least, some of these cases will generate *gittin* of questionable validity that may not be universally accepted. Indeed, it is precisely the woman most in need of the protection of the statute (*i.e.*, married to a totally recalcitrant spouse) whose *get* may be most seriously compromised.

Moreover, the parameters of true consent are not precisely defined. What if a husband agrees to execute a *get* because of pressures that would normally render the *get* a *get meusah* but states (and indeed sincerely means) that in the absence of such pressures, he would have demanded additional concessions, *i.e.*, he would have given the *get* but on different terms? At least some *batei din* apparently take the position that because there is an underlying will to divorce, the fact that some external pressure caused the husband to forego the making of additional demands does not generate a *get meusah*.[695]

---

694. See *supra* note 633 (whether *meusah* problem exists only where a judgment was entered or even where no proceedings have been commenced in civil court).

695. In the course of sitting on a number of *batei din*, I have heard this contention advanced several times. The theory behind such a ruling rests on the fact that if the husband is truly desirous of terminating the marriage but would otherwise have held out for additional concessions, the coercion is directed not to the granting of the *get* but to the waiver of concessions. This is to be distinguished from the husband who totally refuses to grant a *get* but whose will is broken because of coercion. This position (at least as a matter of *halachic* theory) finds strong support in a responsum of Rabbi Moshe Feinstein. See IGROT MOSHE E.H. III, no. 44. That responsum involved a husband who entered into a divorce settlement that was approved by the courts. As part of the settlement, he agreed to grant a *get* to his wife. Because the settlement was merged into a judgment, violation of its terms would subject the husband to serious penalties including imprisonment. When asked by the *bait din* whether he was giving the *get* of his own "free will," the husband responded that eventually he would have given his wife a *get* even without the settlement but that he would have negotiated certain arrangements concerning the education of his children, arrangements that he now had to forego because of the settlement. In sustaining the validity of the *get*, Rabbi Feinstein noted that the husband intrinsically was amenable to granting a *get*. The coercive effect of the settlement/judgment was not to overpower his will concerning divorce but simply to prevent the use of a *get* as a bargaining chip. (I am indebted to Marvin Jacob, Esq., for calling the relevance of this responsum to my attention). Rabbi Feinstein concludes, however, that *while he finds this line of reasoning persuasive, it should not be relied upon alone unless there are*

Other rabbinical authorities vociferously take issue with this position.[696] Or what about the *get* that is issued before the initiation of any court proceeding but where the husband is aware of the possible impact of §236B if he fails to deliver? This too is a matter of controversy.[697] It can surely be anticipated that many *gittin* that will be executed pursuant to §236B will raise precisely these *halachic* dilemmas and, since there is no rabbinic consensus in this area, the specter of questionable *gittin* continues to loom.

Finally, to the extent there are *batei din* that do not regard the sanctions of the statute as coercive (viewing the liability as simply an increase in spousal support)[698] or that allow such sanctions to be employed even in *yotzee* cases,[699] these authorities will continue to issue *gittin* even where it is absolutely clear that the *sole* reason for the husband's consent is his response to monetary pressure and that otherwise he would not execute the *get* at all - a scenario that will clearly result in an invalid *get meusah* according to other authorities.

Unless and until *halachic* authorities achieve broad-based consensus as to: (1) whether §236B constitutes invalid coercion; (2) if it does, whether such coercion exists only when an order is actually outstanding or even if it is only a possibility; and (3) how true consent can be gauged or even defined when coercive pressures exist, §236B will indeed generate *gittin* that are *halachically* problematical. As noted earlier,[700] these concerns may be alleviated by the execution of a release. In the alternative, the statute itself could be amended to expressly provide that the only barrier to remarriage that a court may consider in equitable distribution or maintenance is the failure of a party to

---

other extenuating or mitigating circumstances present in a specific case. Indeed, in that very case, Rabbi Feinstein found that the husband was not acting under the legal pressure of the settlement at all but was simply desirous of keeping his word, a factor that has never been regarded as compulsion in the absence of an oath or vow. See *supra* notes 64, 80-81. (Note too that the husband in that case was described as a habitual wife beater and as such, his conduct would justify a *kofin* order not subject to the rules of *get meusah*. Somewhat confusingly, however, other than noting the fact of the husband's abusive behavior, Rabbi Feinstein does not take this into account in his analysis, perhaps because the *bait din* that had administered the *get* never entered a *kofin* order, see *supra* note 105).

696. Rabbi Yaakov Weinberg, Dean of the Ner Israel Rabbinical College in Baltimore, Maryland, took strong issue with this approach arguing that whenever a husband is coerced into executing a *get* whether he did not want to grant one at all or whether he was holding out for additional concessions, the resulting *get* should be invalid (unless of course the circumstances warrant *kofin*, see *supra* text at note 108). *Conversation with Rabbi Yaakov Weinberg* (January 1993). It should be noted that Rabbi Weinberg did not comment directly on Rabbi Feinstein's ruling.

697. See *supra* note 633.

698. See *supra* text at notes 659-671. See also IGROT MOSHE E.H. IV, no. 106 and the extensive discussion at note 392.

699. See *supra* text at notes 112-113 (definition of *yotzee*) and note 641 (ruling of Rabbi Yitzchok Liebes).

700. See *supra* text at notes 640-644.

appear before a necessary tribunal, thereby removing any source of secular compulsion once an appearance is secured.[701] Failing these steps, however, it is a gross oversimplification to conclude that nothing need be done and simply let the *bait din* rule.[702]

---

701. Indeed, much of the problem surrounding §236B lies precisely in the fact that it directly incorporates the definition of "barrier to remarriage" found in §253. See *supra* text at notes 620-625. For purposes of *halacha*, however, this wholesale incorporation ignores the essential distinction between the statutes. It is entirely appropriate for a judge to condition the granting of a civil divorce on the divorce plaintiff's executing a *get*. Even if the *get* is executed for the sole purpose of obtaining a civil divorce, the resulting *get* would not be *meusah* since the obtaining of such a divorce is regarded as a benefit. See *supra* text at notes 598-600. By contrast, where a court conditions equitable distribution or maintenance on husband's granting a *get*, the resulting *get* may indeed be a *meusah* and, for the reasons stated above, at least some *batei din* may continue to allow such *gittin* to be written.

If, on the other hand, the "barrier" under §236B would be defined exclusively in terms of a refusal to appear before a tribunal qualified (under the principles of the clergyman who solemnized the union) to determine the existence of a marriage impediment and to supervise its removal, the coercive element of the statute raises no *halachic* problem. Merely getting persons to a *bait din* even by force does not taint the resulting *get* as a *get meusah*. See *supra* text at notes 318-322. Once the husband appears, any decisions he then makes to execute a *get* will unquestionably be a product of his unfettered free will.

Admittedly, converting §236B to a "mere" appearance penalty renders the statute less effective in obtaining *gittin* from recalcitrant husbands but at least insures that whatever *gittin* are obtained are *halachically* valid. Note too that, even under the current version of the law, it is entirely possible for a judge to draft an order conditioning equitable distribution rights on appearance before a *bait din* rather than actual execution of a *get* but, until §236B is amended, there is nothing that requires that the court's order be so limited.

[Query, however, whether such an amendment raises constitutional problems. See *supra* note 655.]

702. A final point that some have raised: if the ability of a judge to condition marital entitlements on removal of barriers to remarriage raises *halachic* concerns, these concerns are not eliminated by the repeal of §236B. After all, Justice Rigler was prepared to issue a forfeiture order even prior to the additional language expressly recognizing this power. If this could have been done before §236B, it could equally be done afterwards. Indeed, since virtually any judge in the United States could do what Justice Rigler did without benefit of express statutory authorization, the problem is not even confined to the State of New York. (In fact, it could even be argued that the problem is *less* pronounced in New York than elsewhere since §236B allows courts to consider only the *effect* of a barrier to remarriage, arguably economic deprivation, rather than the barrier to remarriage itself, see *supra* note 662).

My response would be two-fold. First, in the absence of the statute, courts have not in fact shown any great propensity for utilizing equitable distribution law to generate *gittin*. Rigler's ruling was fairly unique. If such orders are eventually issued, there may indeed be *halachic* problems in New

York (and elsewhere) but with language such as that contained in §236B, the incidence of such orders is likely to rise dramatically. Second, to the extent the *get meusah* problem exists even in the absence of an actual judgment on the theory that the mere possibility of recourse to the courts taints the *get* as a product of coercion, see *supra* note 633, this concern is more likely to exist where a law clearly sets out in advance what a court can do than it does in cases where there is merely a generalized speculative fear of what a creative judge might do. (If Rigler-type rulings become common throughout the United States, this distinction may no longer continue to be valid). Thus, while a court may in fact follow the Rigler approach whether or not §236B remains on the books, explicit statutory warrant for such an approach not only increases the probability of such orders being issued but, by virtue of that probabilistic increase, extends the *meusah* problem (at least potentially) even to those *gittin* - and they are the majority - that are not subject to judicial proceedings. See *infra* note 739-745 for a similar point concerning a tort statute.

In any event, if the statute is amended to function as an appearance penalty rather than repealed outright, those concerns would disappear as well.

Chapter Eight

Tort Law Theories

THE POSSIBILITY OF RECOVERY IN TORT

The occasional suggestion has been made that a woman unable to marry because her husband refuses to give her a religious divorce may have a remedy under tort law.[703] Short of recognizing a new sort of tort for interference with a right to remarry, the most likely basis for potential recovery would be the tort of intentional infliction of emotional distress. Traditionally, tort law was concerned with the protection of a fairly narrow range of interests: bodily integrity, security of property, and protection of reputation. While it was true that if any of those interests were invaded, damages could include compensation for nonpecuniary elements such as shame, embarrassment, or fright - one could, for example, recover damages for the emotional distress incident to a battery (unauthorized physical invasion) - the common law was slow to recognize that the causing of emotional distress without personal or property injury could by itself be tortious. Today, however, virtually every state

703. See Redman, *Jewish Divorce: What Can be Done in Secular Courts to Aid the Jewish Woman?* 19 GA. L. REV. 389 (1984-1985); Cobin, *Jewish Divorce and the Recalcitrant Husband-Refusal to Give a Get As Intentional Infliction of Emotional Distress*, 4 JOURNAL OF LAW AND RELIGION 405 (1986); Friedell, *supra* note 246, at 532. Judicial acknowledgement of potential tort remedies is sparse. The one case in which a tort remedy was specifically sought denied it. *Perl v. Perl*, 126 A.D. 2d 91, 512 N.Y.S. 2d 372 (N.Y. App. Div. 1987). See *supra* note 57 and *infra* note 712. One unreported decision does suggest in dicta that tort recovery may sometimes be available. See *Roth v. Roth*, Civ. No. 79-192709 (Mich. 6th Jud. Cir. 1/23/80), where the court stated: "[A] refusal to give his wife a *get*, knowing she would not be able to remarry without the distress of violating her deep beliefs, constitutes the intentional infliction of emotional harm. Under some circumstances, the law allows damages for such an injury if the defendant's conduct was outrageous."

recognizes the existence of such a tort.[704]

As formulated in the *Second Restatement*,[705] the tort applies when a person "by extreme and outrageous conduct intentionally or recklessly causes severe emotional distress to another."[706] As is evident, the focus is both on the extremity of the defendant's conduct and the severity of the emotional impact on the plaintiff. With respect to the defendant's conduct, the comments inform us somewhat graphically that it must be "so outrageous in character and so extreme in degree as to go beyond all possible bounds of decency and to be regarded as atrocious and utterly intolerable in a civilized community. [A] recitation of the facts to an average member of the community would lead him to exclaim 'Outrageous'!"[707] We are also told that conduct may become outrageous by an abuse of a position of power and control or through special knowledge that a given plaintiff is peculiarly susceptible to being severely distressed, even if such conduct would not elicit this reaction if done to someone else.[708]

With respect to the magnitude of the distress, once again the comments use a picturesque stream of nouns: the distress may be "fright, grief, shame, humiliation, embarrassment, anger, chagrin, disappointment or worry" but must be more than mere "inconvenience, annoyance, regret, vexation, emotional suspense,[709] trivial insults, and hurt feelings." Reminding us that we still live in a world with many rough edges, the comments note that it would be an intolerable burden on the legal system and a clog on human interaction to allow routine social slights to be legally actionable. Finally, the comments emphasize the necessary elements of "intent" or "recklessness"; in order to be liable, defendant must either desire to inflict this magnitude of distress or know that such distress is certain or substantially certain to result from his conduct.

It is entirely possible that in some cases of *agunah*, a tort remedy may

---

704. See generally, Keeton, *et al.*, PROSSER AND KEETON ON THE LAW OF TORTS §122, pp. 901-905 (5th ed. 1984) (hereafter cited as TORTS). The classic article arguing for the recognition of such a cause of action is Magruder, *Mental and Emotional Disturbance in the Law of Torts*, 49 HARV. L. REV. 1033 (1936).

705. See RESTATEMENT OF TORTS (Second) §46 and the extensive annotations following it.

706. Whether this tort should apply where the defendant's conduct is merely negligent (careless) rather than intentional or reckless is a matter of considerable controversy and is far from settled. See the numerous cases cited and discussed in Annotation, *Right to Recover Damages in Negligence for Fear of Injury to Another or Shock or Mental Anguish at Witnessing Such Injury*, 29 A.L.R. 3d 1337 (1970, 1990 Supplement). The *Restatement* in fact rejects the proposition that negligent conduct is actionable if it merely results in emotional distress though if such conduct results in physical injury or illness, "emotional distress" damages may be recoverable as "parasitic" to the physical invasion. Compare RESTATEMENT OF TORTS (Second) §312 with §436A. (Of course, the boundary between "severe emotional distress" and "illness" may be quite difficult to determine.)

707. Comment *d*.

708. Comments *e* and *f*.

709. Whatever that is!

be appropriate. While the failure to give a *get* is omission rather than commission, there is authority that even a failure to act may give rise to tortious liability at least when there was a preexisting intimate or confidential relationship that generated special understandings and expectations.[710] The magnitude of emotional distress a woman undergoes will naturally vary from case to case; the feelings of an intensely Orthodox woman approaching the end of her childbearing years and held in a state of limbo are obviously more intense and deserving of legal protection than those of a Reform divorcee who wants a *get* "just to be on the safe side." Undoubtedly, in some cases, if not most, the anxiety, pain and humiliation will be considerable. Moreover, even if the withholding of a *get* would be of no concern to the average married woman, the husband's knowledge of the particular sensitivities and susceptibilities of his former spouse charges him with a duty to be responsive.[711] Finally, the element of "intent" is normally fairly easy to meet; if the husband's motives are spiteful or malicious, the requisite intent is present by definition.

The more difficult case arises where the husband's motives are not malicious *per se* but are economic. What if the husband is using the *get* as a trading chip to obtain concessions, reduction in alimony, joint custody, extra visitation, *etc.*? As unfair and coercive as this practice might strike many of us, others might defend it as legitimate. In any event, it is not clear that driving a hard bargain or even an unconscionable bargain is conduct of such outrageous or extreme character as to "go beyond all possible bounds of decency" and that it therefore should be regarded as tortious. Indeed, the one case where this contention was raised rejected it, albeit on a different ground.[712] Thus, while the tort theory might be available in the "spite" cases, it is less clear that it precludes a threatened withholding of the *get* in the context of settlement negotiations, even where the demands being made are in themselves unreasonable.[713]

---

710. See, for example, *United States Automobile Ass'n v. Glens Falls Insurance Co.*, 350 F.Supp. 869 (D. Conn. 1972) (failure of an insurer to settle within policy limits may constitute the intentional infliction of emotional distress).

711. See Comment *f* to the Restatement provision.

712. In *Perl v. Perl*, 126 A.D. 2nd 91, 512 N.Y.S. 2d 372 (1987), the Appellate Division ruled that a one-sided inequitable property settlement granted to secure a *get* may be invalidated on the grounds of duress. The court dismissed the wife's claim for damages on the grounds of intentional infliction of emotional distress on the somewhat dubious ground that the husband's motives were purely economic with the component of mental distress only a "the regrettable by-product." Technically, the court is incorrect. As the comments to the *Restatement* (Second) note, intent to inflict emotional distress exists not only when defendant desires to inflict harm but also when he knows that such harm is certain to result from his actions. RESTATEMENT OF TORTS (Second), §46, Comment *i*. Nevertheless, while the economic context of the refusal does not negate intent, it does diminish the "outrageous" and "extreme" character of the recalcitrance at least to the extent that it no longer may be regarded as tortious. For further discussion of *Perl*, see *supra* note 57.

713. This distinction is also suggested by RESTATEMENT OF TORTS (Second) §46, Comment *g* (insisting on legal rights is not tortious).

There may be other impediments to this action as well. As a minor point, not all states recognize this tort though the overwhelming majority do.[714] Second, although interspousal immunities have largely been abolished at least in the context of intentional torts,[715] a number of states have been reluctant to allow suits between spouses based on emotional distress fearing this would flood the courts with excessive litigation.[716] One might assume this obstacle could be surmounted by simply deferring the filing of a complaint until after the grant of a civil divorce,[717] yet case law suggests that courts will refrain from entertaining such suits even where the alleged tortious acts took place after divorce as long as their genesis lies in the marital relationship.[718]

A close examination of the cases denying recovery shows, however, that all of them involve either the potential for repetitive, harassing litigation[719] or the presence of a third party interfering in the marriage,[720] making the complaint tantamount to an action based on alienation of affection.[721] Since

---

714. See generally Annotation, *Modern Status of Intentional Infliction of Mental Distress As Independent Tort: "Outrage,"* 38 A.L.R. 4th 998 (1985, 1990 Supp.). A perusal of the annotation suggests that not more than three to five jurisdictions (depending on how certain cases are construed) have explicitly rejected the doctrine.

715. See Keeton, *et al.* TORTS §122, p. 903.

716. See, *e.g.*, *Browning v. Browning*, 584 S.W. 2d 406 (Ky. Ct. of App. 1979) (court disallowed husband's claim for intentional infliction of emotional harm based on wife's openly consorting with another); *Weicker v. Weicker*, 237 N.E. 2d 876 (N.Y. 1968) (denied relief to ex-wife who claimed that a Mexican divorce was invalid and sued for emotional harm caused by former husband and new wife holding themselves out as validly married); *Haldane v. Bogy*, 25 Cal. Rptr. 392 (Cal. Dist. Ct. App. 1962) (denied relief to husband who sues defendant for harboring plaintiff's wife and paying an attorney to file a groundless divorce action); *Hafner v. Hafner*, 343 A.2d 166 (N.J. Super. 1975) (denied recovery to widow who was prevented from seeing her husband during his last illness by husband's son from a previous marriage); *Friedman v. Friedman*, 361 N.Y.S. 2d 108 (N.Y. App. Div. 1974) (denied recovery of damages by one parent against another for conduct in the course of a child custody battle).

717. Ironically, in New York that would be difficult to do because under DRL §253, at least where husband is a plaintiff, there will be no judgment for civil divorce until the *get* is granted.

718. Thus, for example, in *Friedman*, the court denied recovery for emotional distress incident to a custody battle even though the parties were already divorced. See *Friedman*, 361 N.Y.S. 2d at 110.

719. *Friedman* involved a scenario that was likely to repeat itself often and where hard feelings and animosity were to be expected. *Browning*, *Weicker*, *Haldane*, and *Hafner* all involved third parties who were allegedly interfering with a spousal relationship.

720. See *supra* note 716.

721. The common law tort of "alienation of affection," first recognized in New York in 1866, consists in a third party's depriving one spouse of the affection, love, and companionship of the other. It does not require the commission of an act of adultery or that the influenced spouse abandon the

alienation of affection actions have been either abolished or severely curtailed throughout most of the United States,[722] it stands to reason that courts will not allow their resurrection under the guise of "infliction of emotional distress." Neither of these factors is present in an action predicated on failure to give a *get*. These cases do not involve the presence of an officious third party and they are not actions to restore or compensate for the impairment of a marriage but to insure that a marriage that is legally dead no longer poses any marital disabilities. Moreover, the potential for repetitive litigation appears slight since unlike child custody cases where by definition the feuding parents must remain in frequent contact, the *get* controversy could be resolved by a single act done in less than an hour. The precedents denying recovery for interspousal claims of distress in general do not rule out recovery here. (As noted,[723] however, the one case where the issue was squarely presented did in fact deny recovery at least in the "economic bargaining scenario.")

It might be noted in passing that within the fertile soil of the common law system there is the potential for development of additional tort theories as well. Given that marriage is a fundamental right[724] and without a religious divorce a spouse is disabled from exercising that right, the maintenance of barriers to the exercise of a civil liberty may in itself be tortious, irrespective of the magnitude of emotional distress. Alternatively, a court may invoke the occasionally cited theory of *prima facie* tort, where any significant harm caused

---

household or even cease cohabitation, though it does require some external act or omission evidencing a diminution of marital affection. Indeed, the most common defendant in such an action was the meddling in-law rather than the wicked lover. One who "interferes" with the marital relationship by adultery (either through rape or consent) has committed the separate tort of "criminal conversation" and is civilly liable in damages as well as being subject to state prosecution for the commission of a crime. While the right to bring such an action was originally limited to husbands, virtually all states that allow the action at all currently grant wives the same protections. See RESTATEMENT OF TORTS (Second) §§683-685 and Keeton, *et al.*, TORTS §124, pp. 915-931. Note too the interesting provisions in §686 of the *Second Restatement* which create a privilege for parental intermeddling and those in §698 which deny any relief for the alienation of affection or sexual intercourse with a "betrothed" or "significant other."

722. Because of their great potential for abuse and harassment, these actions have been abolished or at least severely curtailed in the great majority of the states, either by statute or by judicial decision. Indeed, in some jurisdictions, bringing such an action is a criminal offense. For a listing of statutes abrogating this tort, see Keeton *et al.*, TORTS §124, p. 930 at n. 93. The policies behind these statutes, often called "heart-balm laws" are analyzed in two articles by Feinsinger, *Legislative Attack on Heart Balm*, 33 MICH. L. REV. 979 (1935) and *Current Legislation Affecting Breach of Promise to Marry, Alienation of Affection, and Related Actions*, 10 WIS. L. REV. 417 (1935).

723. *Supra* note 712.

724. See *supra* note 575.

to another imposes liability in the absence of reasonable justification.[725] While such theories have been favorably received by European courts,[726] the American judiciary has been less enthusiastic in applying them.[727]

PURPOSES SERVED

In formulating responses to the *agunah* problem, the principal purpose should be to create mechanisms that maximize the chances that otherwise victimized spouses will receive their *gittin*. Since a tort claim is nothing more than the right to obtain a money judgment, tort law in and of itself does not accomplish this goal. The true value of a common law remedy is the extent to which it will never have to be used, that parties who would otherwise be unwilling to give *gittin* will in effect be forced to do so to escape the imposition of civil liability. As a secondary form of inducement, in the event a judgment is obtained, the wife now has a bargaining chip of her own in agreeing to release or reduce the debt in exchange for the execution of the *get*. Yet another incentive on the part of the defendant-husband to execute a *get*, even after being held liable on a judgment, is the possibility of being subject to successive lawsuits. Since each withholding of a *get* is arguably a new "act" of harassment, plaintiff can continue to bring successive actions even after recovering in an earlier suit.[728]

If the principal utility of a tort remedy lies primarily in its deterrent effect, its usefulness may be somewhat limited. The uncertain contours of the common law remedy, its questionable application to interspousal suits, possible difficulties in proving malevolent intent, the uncertain measure of damages, and the high cost of litigation, particularly unreimbursed attorney's fees, combine to make a significant tort recovery so difficult that a recalcitrant husband may well be willing to take his chances. If his wife loses her case, he would be free of any restraint whatsoever.

---

725. The *prima facie* tort doctrine has been employed by a number of New York cases, particularly in the area of interference with prospective advantage, *e.g.*, A induces B not to enter into a contract with C. See, for example, *Rager v. McCloskey*, 305 N.Y. 75, 111 N.E. 2d 214 (N.Y. 1953). See also Forkosch, *An Analysis of the 'Prima Facie' Tort Action*, 42 CORNELL L.Q. 415 (1957) and Brown, *The Rise and Threatened Demise of the Prima Facie Tort Principle*, 54 NORTHWESTERN UNIV. L. REV. 563 (1959). The doctrine is sharply criticized in Dobbs, *Tortious Interference with Contractual Relations*, 34 ARK. L. REV. 335, 363 (1980).

726. See, *e.g.*, the 1972 opinion of the Court of Cassation, cited *supra* note 504.

727. New York is essentially a minority of one and RESTATEMENT OF TORTS (Second) §766B expressly repudiates the *prima facie* tort theory in the context of economic relations.

728. This last proposition may be somewhat debatable in light of the rule of *res judicata* which precludes "splitting" causes of action. See RESTATEMENT OF JUDGMENTS (Second) §§24-26 and James and Hazard, CIVIL PROCEDURE (2nd ed.) §§11.6-11.13, pp. 536-556.

At least one commentator[729] has suggested that a statute be enacted specifically providing that the maintenance of a barrier to remarriage subsequent to the grant of a civil divorce and after receiving notice of such barrier from the other spouse constitutes the intentional infliction of emotional distress; specifying that damages are to be calculated at a specified dollar figure for every day of delay; and providing for the award of attorney's fees and costs. By eliminating troublesome, difficult-to-prove issues such as malice and the amount of damages suffered and by reducing plaintiff's ultimate costs in pursuing the action, the likelihood of an unwilling husband's giving in to his wife's demand is greatly enhanced. To date, no state has acted on this proposal.

Assuming such a tort remedy could be statutorily codified, thereby providing the certainty and the specificity that make it an effective deterrent, it would be superior to the alternative statutory approach of DRL §253 in four respects:

1. While the New York law insures that a plaintiff will not be able to obtain a civil divorce without giving a *get*, it provides no protection to spouses who have already been divorced (prior to 1983, pursuant to wife's complaint, or where wife for some reason waived husband's affidavit requirement).
2. The law applies only where the plaintiff is the party maintaining the barrier. If, for example, a woman whose husband refuses to give her a *get* is the divorce plaintiff, there is no pressure on the husband to come forward and give a *get*. The tort remedy would allow recovery against the recalcitrant party regardless of the identity of the divorce plaintiff.
3. Tort recovery would afford some women relief irrespective of the principles under which the original marriage was solemnized. If, for example, the couples were married by Reform clergy but in the course of the marriage the woman embraced Orthodoxy and is now unable to marry without a *get*, DRL §253 would not apply; the tort action would.[730]
4. One of the constitutional objections to DRL §253 is the fact that it links the power of the state to issue a civil divorce with compliance with a religious ceremony and the concurrence of the officiating clergyman. Giving clergy a veto in the exercise of governmental functions excessively entangles the church and state in violation of the establishment clause.[731] Whatever the merits of this criticism, and I have argued before that there is none, it has no application to tort liability,

729. *Letters from Nathan Lewin, Esq. to David Zweibel, Esq., Director of Government Affairs and General Counsel of Agudath Israel* (July 24, 1985 and August 2, 1985), copies on file with the author.

730. The draft statute prepared by Nathan Lewin, however, does track the New York statute by limiting tort liability to cases where barriers exist "under the religious or conscientious principles under which the former spouses solemnized their marriage."

731. See *Larkin v. Grendel's Den*, 459 U.S. 116 (1982) discussed *supra* text following note 583.

a theory that is totally independent of the granting of a civil divorce. Indeed, such liability would not even be triggered until after a civil divorce was granted. Thus, even the states that have been reluctant to enact an analogue of §253 might consider a tort statute instead.[732]

CONSTITUTIONAL PROBLEMS*

As noted, at least with respect to the *Grendel's Den* problem of intermingling clergy in the exercise of government functions, recognition of a statutory or common law action for damages poses fewer constitutional objections than a procedure which compels the state to delay the entry of a divorce judgment. On the other hand, because the imposition of a monetary sanction might be regarded as substantially more coercive than a mere denial of benefit (nonentry of a divorce judgment), allowing recovery in tort may constitute a greater infringement of religious liberty in the event husband has a "free exercise" claim. In any case, however, the possibility of a legitimate "free exercise" claim is slight and would likely be overcome by a variety of compelling state interests.[733]

With respect to the establishment clause, to the extent recovery is based on judicial application of neutral principles of tort law by pigeonholing a refusal to give a *get* into the recognized category of "intentional infliction of emotional distress,"it is difficult to see any particular "endorsement," "promotion," or "advancement" of religion. Victims of emotional distress or turmoil arising from their religious beliefs should be entitled to at least the same protection as those whose distress arises out of any other sensitivity,

---

732. See *supra* note 532 for a listing of states in which a *get* bill was introduced.

*This section presupposes the continued validity of the tripartite standard of *Lemon v. Kurtzman*. There is a distinct possibility, however, that the test will be replaced. Probable alternatives are discussed *infra* text at notes 826-859.

733. See *supra* text following note 588. Interestingly, because a common law theory would afford recovery irrespective of the principles under which the marriage was solemnized, the "free exercise" problem may be a bit more pronounced since even a committed Reform Jew who *never* believed in the institution of a *get* could find himself liable in damages for failure to give one. This would not occur under DRL §253. Nevertheless, as noted earlier in connection with the *get* law, affording women relief in these circumstances may be justified by the state's interest in insuring the integrity of its divorce procedure, facilitating marriage and family life, protecting rights of privacy, curbing extortion and victimization, and enhancing the religious liberty of the victimized spouse. Moreover, as therein noted, a refusal to give a *get* is rarely motivated by religious beliefs; even a Reform Jew has no principled objection *against* the giving of a *get* and at worst, would regard it as an unnecessary, superfluous act.

In any event, after *Smith*, the possibility of a "free exercise" attack is greatly diminished. See *infra* text following note 751.

proclivity, or even eccentricity of which the defendant is aware.[734] In both cases, the court is protecting the freedom of the plaintiff from unjustifiable emotional invasion, not upholding or affirming the principles of religion.

If, on the other hand, a state were to enact a special statute focused exclusively on the "barrier to remarriage" problem and specifying a unique and large liquidated damages penalty irrespective of actual injury suffered, the constitutional issue would be less clear. Here, the failure to perform a religious act gives rise to sanctions that might be considerably greater than those for causing other forms of emotional distress. The state is in effect passing judgment that noncompliance with religious law is a more heinous violation of personal integrity then other forms of invasion. Elevating religious sensibilities to that preferred position seems to raise establishment problems. While it is true that a tort statute may be neutrally worded (as is DRL §253) speaking of "religious or conscientious" constraints, any court would quickly see that the purpose of the tort remedy is to protect the rights of Jewish women to receive a *get*. Tort law may well be an appropriate, though cumbersome, vehicle in their efforts to secure justice but only a tort law that is even-handed and neutral in its application can do so in a constitutionally-permitted way.

In this respect, I see a "removal of barrier" tort statute as considerably more problematical than the "get" statute.[735] Singling out "removal of barriers to remarriage" in the context of a divorce proceeding makes perfect sense. The state has a specialized, unique, and *secular* interest to insure the efficacy of its divorce laws and withholding the grant of a divorce until its effectiveness can be guaranteed is a narrowly tailored mechanism that achieves that end. By contrast, the state does not have a specialized, unique, *secular* interest in singling out in its tort law one particular vice that impinges on religious practice to the exclusion of other vices that do not. Thus, while many of the secular purposes that justify the *get* statute apply with equal force to the tort remedy,[736] and while the potential for entanglement is in fact significantly reduced,[737] the utilization of a specially-drafted law whose exclusive purpose is the protection of uniquely-religious sensibilities carries with it at least the appearance of the state's giving its imprimatur on religion. As such, the constitutionality of such a statute is highly suspect.[738]

---

734. See RESTATEMENT OF TORTS (Second) §46, Comment *f* (conduct may be extreme and outrageous where defendant has knowledge that a plaintiff is peculiarly susceptible).

735. Although, insofar as the *Grendel's Den* problem is concerned, it is less so. See *supra* text at notes 583-584.

736. These would include furtherance of the state's divorce policy, facilitation of religious liberty, the encouragement of remarriage and a more stable family life, the protection of fundamental rights of privacy, and the curbing of victimization. See *supra* text at notes 574-577.

737. See *supra* text following note 733.

738. Technically, the statute fails the *second* prong of the *Lemon* test as restated by Justice O'Connor (primary effect is the promotion or endorsement of religion). See *supra* text at note 566. But see *infra* text at notes 826-859 (whether "endorsement test" is likely to survive).

HALACHIC CONCERNS

A final point to consider is whether recognition of a tort remedy, either by statute or common law, raises *halachic* problems. As repeatedly noted, any *get* executed under compulsion including the order of a secular court is invalid unless the compulsion was authorized pursuant to the order of the *bait din*.[739] Such compulsion may be authorized only in specially-defined circumstances.[740] According to the authoritative view of Rashba[741] as codified by Rema,[742] invalidating coercion exists not only when there are threats to person or property but also when the alternative to the *get* would be the imposition of financial penalties. Thus, Rashba rules that any *get* executed pursuant to the husband's prior commitment to either pay or divorce is invalid. Moreover, those who differ with Rashba do so only because the self-imposed nature of the undertaking negates the element of compulsion.[743] Where the imposition of financial constraints is non-consensual but arises by operation of (secular) law, it is possible that all authorities would regard the resulting execution of a *get* as invalid.[744]

It would appear, therefore, that any *get* issued under a potential cloud of civil liability may well constitute a *get meusah*. While it may very well be that a generalized fear of a possible common-law exposure in a tort suit may be too remote and attenuated to rise to the level of "actual duress," particularly since the magnitude of the consequences is not spelled out in advance, a statute clearly setting out husband's liability irrespective of his intent and specifying a named sum to be imposed for each day of delay seems indistinguishable from the penalty clause condemned by Rashba. If anything, the fact that the statutory penalties are not voluntarily self-imposed makes them even worse.[745] Theoretically, a *halachically* valid statute could be crafted providing for damages only in cases where the recalcitrant spouse either refuses to appear before a *bait din* or disobeys the decision of a *bait din*. However, any statute that clearly tracked the specific requirements of religious doctrine would even be more vulnerable to an establishment clause challenge and not be likely to survive.

To sum up: While the Jewish community does not have control over the development of common law tort doctrine, it would not be in their interests to lobby for a statute that would make failure to give a *get* an actionable tort. Besides the questionable constitutionality of such an attempt - an issue one

---

739. See *supra* text at notes 60-65.

740. See *supra* text at notes 110-120.

741. TESHUVOT RASHBA IV, no. 40.

742. Rema, gloss to SHULCHAN ARUCH E.H. 134:5. Technically, Rema cites both views but rules that such a *get* should not be executed. If, however, it was, the divorce is valid after the fact.

743. See TESHUVOT MAHARIK, no. 63.

744. This is not entirely clear. Some authorities may take the position that because the penalty is a reasonable alternative, the decision not to pay but to execute the *get* instead becomes a matter of choice. See the responsum of R. Maimon Nager cited in BAIT YOSEF to TUR E.H. 134 and *supra* text at notes 64-65 and at 76-78.

745. See *supra* text at notes 76-86.

could safely leave to the courts - there is the distinct possibility that any resulting *gittin* will be invalid. The proposed "solution" would be far worse than the problem that it was supposed to solve.

Chapter Nine

Current Developments in Church-State Law and Their Impact on the *Agunah* Problem

The foregoing analysis in Chapters Six and Seven has attempted to demonstrate the constitutionality of the two New York *get* laws both in terms of concerns based on establishment and in terms of their possible infringements on free exercise. As therein noted, the legitimacy of governmental action that is alleged to constitute an "establishment of religion" has historically been assessed against the tripartite test developed in *Lemon v. Kurtzman*[746] while infringements on free exercise have been justified only if there is a "compelling governmental interest" that could not be achieved through less burdensome or restrictive means.[747] Absent such an interest, government was constitutionally obliged to accommodate religious observance by some form of exemption. Under both the establishment and free exercise tests as they have been traditionally formulated, the two New York *get* laws as well as judicial enforcement of rabbinical arbitration agreements or indeed even specific performance of *get* covenants would appear to pass constitutional muster.[748] Chapter Eight applied a similar standard in arguing for the constitutional validity of a tort-based action though questions were raised concerning the constitutionality of a statute that would specifically single out "failure to remove barriers to remarriage" for unique treatment.[749] Recent court decisions, however, are changing some of the basic and long-standing ground rules in this area and, in the interest of completeness and accuracy, the impact of these decisions must be assessed.[750] Unfortunately, at the time of this writing, the

---

746. 403 U.S. 602 (1971). See discussion *supra* text following note 562.

747. *Supra* text at notes 567-571.

748. *Supra* text at notes 240-262 (*get*-covenants); 282-285 (*Avitzur*-agreements); 550-597 (*get*-law); and 645-655 (alimony and equitable distribution).

749. See *supra* text at notes 734-737.

750. The reader should be warned, however, that in the judgment of the author these changes will have very little impact on the conclusions stated herein regarding the constitutionality of *get* covenants, *Avitzur*-agreements, and the New York *get* laws. See *infra* text at notes 860-863. I discuss them

law is still in a state of evolutionary flux and any conclusions regarding the probable trends of the future are necessarily tentative.

THE *SMITH* CASE AND THE FIRST AMENDMENT

The Decision

The major recent development in free exercise law was the 1990 decision of the Supreme Court of the United States in *Employment Division, Department of Human Resources v. Smith* (*Smith* II).[751] *Smith* involved two drug counsellors who were fired from their jobs for using peyote as part of a Native American religious ritual. It was assumed that they were sincere practitioners of their religious beliefs.[752] They applied for unemployment compensation, which the state denied on the grounds that the use of a controlled substance constituted job-related "misconduct" which barred the collection of compensation. In an earlier case,[753] the Court ruled that the propriety of the denial depended squarely on whether the use of peyote was proscribed under the state's criminal law and, if it was, whether such a proscription constituted an impermissible infringement of free exercise.[754] Since neither question had been addressed by the Oregon Supreme Court,[755] the case was remanded to the state level for necessary findings.[756] In *Smith* II, the Supreme Court held, in

---

because they are indeed highly significant in the larger picture of the intersection of law and religion and I would be remiss not to at least address these issues in passing. The reader who is less interested in the constitutional questions could safely jump ahead to *infra* text at notes 860-863 where my conclusions are briefly stated.

751. 494 U.S. 872 (1990).

752. *Id.* at 872.

753. 485 U.S. 660 (1988).

754. Although *Smith* did not involve a criminal prosecution, the Court reasoned that any conduct that the state has made criminal can certainly be the basis for the lesser sanction of denial of benefits. Thus, once it is established that the ingestion of peyote even for religious purposes was proscribed by state law and constitutionally could be, the propriety of denial of benefits would automatically follow.

755. The Oregon Supreme Court, 721 P.2d 445, 449-450 (1986) had no reason to address the criminality of sacramental peyote use since it took the position that benefits could not be denied even if the underlying misconduct was criminal as long as it was religiously motivated. The Supreme Court disagreed and remanded the case to the state courts for a determination of criminality.

756. *Smith* I at 673. Note that the Oregon Supreme Court was asked to consider two distinct questions: (1) the scope of Oregon's criminal law; (2) whether that law was valid under the Federal Constitution. Upon remand, the Oregon Supreme Court ruled that the state criminal law did indeed encompass even sacramental use but that such a prohibition was an unconstitutional violation of the First Amendment. 763 P.2d 146, 148 (Oregon 1988). The Supreme Court's review was of course limited only to the constitutional question since a state supreme court's interpretation of its state's law is normally deemed conclusive. *Smith* II reversed the Oregon Supreme Court on

a 6-3 decision,[757] that the state may indeed constitutionally prohibit the use of narcotics even for purposes of religious ceremonies. Although the state could have adopted a religious exemption if it so desired,[758] the adoption of such an exemption was not constitutionally necessary. In its absence, the use of peyote constituted proscribable criminal conduct that would justify the lesser sanction of a denial of unemployment benefits.

The Impact of *Smith* on Free Exercise Analysis

On one level, *Smith* is not particularly shocking. The notion that parties may not invoke religious freedom as a shield to criminal prosection is not new and dates at least as far back as the polygamy cases.[759] What is new and disturbing is the fact that at least five members of the Court took the position that the general, nondiscriminatory scope of the law was in and of itself adequate justification to prosecute religious violators without the need to establish a "compelling state interest" in doing so.[760] The result in *Smith* could easily have been assimilated into the existing test of *Sherbert v. Verner*.[761] The Court could have held, for example, that the pressing societal need to curtail drug use constitutes a compelling state interest of a far greater magnitude than the need for a uniform day of rest recognized in *Braunfeld*.[762] Moreover, the potential for fraud and abuse necessitates that the curtailment be absolute with less restrictive means insufficient to accomplish this goal. The pointed refusal of the Court to predicate its holding on the existence of a compelling state

---

the constitutional question.

757. The opinion of the Court was written by Justice Scalia and was joined by Chief Justice Rehnquist, and Justices Kennedy, Stevens, and White. Justice O'Connor concurred in the judgment but wrote a separate opinion affirming traditional free exercise analysis. A dissenting opinion was authored by Justice Blackmun and was joined by Justices Brennan and Marshall.

758. The opinion of the Court makes clear that although religious accommodations are not constitutionally required, they are permitted. See *Smith* II, at 890. Indeed, a number of states do in fact exempt the sacramental use of peyote from their drug laws. See, *e.g.*, NEW MEXICO STATUTES §30-31-6; COLORADO REV. STATUTES §12-22-317(3). See also *Peyote Way Church v. Thornburgh*, 922 F.2d 1210 (5th Cir. 1991) (a religious exemption limited to the members of the Native American Church is not violative of either the establishment clause or equal protection even where other religious groups are not exempted).

In view of the Court's apparent solicitude for permissible accommodation, a number of groups are urging the enactment of a statute that would effectively restore the "compelling state interest" test, at least on a statutory if not constitutional basis. See *infra* text at notes 811-818 (discussion of Religious Freedom Restoration Act).

759. See, *e.g.*, *Reynolds v. United States*, 98 U.S. 145 (1879) (upholding the enforcement of antipolygamy statutes against Mormons).

760. *Smith* II at 884-886. Justice O'Connor who concurred in the judgment did not agree with this analysis. *Id.*, 897-903.

761. 374 U.S. 398 (1963), discussed *supra* following note 569.

762. *Braunfeld v. Brown*, 366 U.S. 599 (1961), discussed *supra* note 569.

interest, which it could easily have done, augurs poorly for the cause of religious freedom.

What then survives of the free exercise clause and the constitutional recognition of religion as a fundamental right? Outside of the realm of noninterference with belief and affirmation, apparently very little. Justice Scalia, writing for the Court, does indeed indicate that the government may not constitutionally compel affirmation of belief, punish or penalize the expression of religious doctrine it believes to be false, impose special disabilities on the basis of religious views or religious status, or lend its power to one or the other side in controversies over religious authority and dogma.[763] Nor can a state prohibit a given act *only* when it is performed for a religious reason.[764] Nevertheless, the "right of free exercise does not relieve an individual of the obligation to comply with a 'valid and neutral law of general applicability [merely] on the ground that the law proscribes (or prescribes) conduct that his religion prescribes (or proscribes)'[765]. . . . .To make an individual's obligation to obey such a law contingent upon the law's coincidence with his religious beliefs, except where the State's interest is compelling - permitting him by virtue of his beliefs to become a law unto himself - contradicts both constitutional tradition and common sense."[766]

Conceding that the Court had indeed applied the "compelling state interest" test in evaluating free exercise claims in the past,[767] Scalia's opinion for the Court makes the following points:

1. Most of the cases requiring that generally applicable laws accommodate religious observance involved laws which infringed on additional rights besides religion, notably freedom of speech and association, and were not pure "free exercise" claims.[768]
2. Outside of these "hybrid" or "religion-plus" cases, the "compelling state interest" test has been applied to invalidate nondiscriminatory state law impinging on religious freedom in only three instances, each of which involved state regulations concerning unemployment compensation.[769]

---

763. *Smith* II at 877.

764. "It would doubtless be unconstitutional, for example, to ban the casting of 'statues that are to be used for worship purposes' or to prohibit bowing down before a golden calf." *Id.* at 877-878.

765. *Id.* at 879 quoting in part from *United States v. Lee*, 455 U.S. 252, 263 n.3 (1982) (Justice Stevens concurring).

766. *Smith* II at 885.

767. *Id.* at 882-884.

768. *Smith* II at 879-882 citing, *inter alia*, *West Virginia Board of Education v. Barnette*, 319 U.S. 624 (1943)(invalidating compulsory flag statute as applied to religious objectors); *Wisconsin v. Yoder*, 406 U.S. 205 (1972) (invalidating compulsory school attendance laws as applied to Amish parents who refused on religious grounds to send their children to school).

769. *Smith* II at 883-884, citing *Sherbert v. Verner*, 374 U.S. 398 (1963); *Thomas v. Review Board of Indiana Employment Security Division*, 450 U.S. 707 (1981); and *Hobbie v. Unemployment Appeals Comm'n of California*, 480 U.S. 136 (1987). See *supra* note 569.

3. If one factors out the "hybrid religion-plus" cases and the narrow context of unemployment compensation, the "compelling state interest" test has never been employed by the Court to invalidate under the free exercise clause a general law that adversely affects religious freedom, nor has it ever necessitated the recognition of a religious exemption to such law even where the Court ostensibly paid lip service to the test. A standard that is always met is obviously not one intended to provide meaningful scrutiny.[770]
4. Finally, the opinion cites a number of cases where the Court sustained a general law or governmental practice without even making reference to the *Sherbert* test.[771] This too indicates the essential irrelevance of *Sherbert* scrutiny beyond a very narrow range of cases.

As a historical reconstruction of Court precedent, the *Smith* opinion is not quite accurate. While it is true that a number of recent cases failed to apply the *Sherbert* test,[772] those cases do not support the proposition that *Sherbert* was routinely rejected outside of the unemployment benefits context, but rather deal with unique situations where strict scrutiny of governmental action is less appropriate - cases such as government management of its own public lands, prisoners' rights, and the rights of persons in the military.[773] Insofar as the freedom of a private individual was concerned, *Sherbert* was very much the prevailing standard until it was erased by *Smith*.

---

770. *Smith* II at 883 citing, *inter alia*, *United States v. Lee*, 455 U.S. 252 (1982) (upholding the legality of a tax over the religious objections of Amish taxpayers).

771. *Smith* II at 883 citing, *inter alia*, *Goldman v. Weinberger*, 475 U.S. 503 (1986) (validating military regulations that prohibited the wearing of a *yarmulke*; refusal to apply *Sherbert* standards); *Bowen v. Roy*, 476 U.S. 693 (1986) (upholding a federal statute requiring persons to provide social security numbers and making no exception for religious objectors); *O'Lone v. Estate of Shabazz*, 482 U.S. 342 (1987) (validating a prison regulation that did not provide excuses from work detail to accommodate religious service); and *Lyng v. Northwest Indian Cemetery Protective Ass'n*, 483 U.S. 439 (1988) (validating government logging and road construction projects over Native American religious objections).

772. See cases cited in *supra* note 771.

773. See *Smith* II (concurrence of Justice O'Connor) 891, 900-903. Her analysis is especially pertinent since she was the author of *Lyng*, *supra* note 771, a case that supposedly "rejected" the *Sherbert* test. The one exception to the statement in the text is *Bowen v. Roy*, *supra* note 771, where the Court failed to apply the *Sherbert* standard to social security entitlements. But *cf.* *Bowen* (Justice O'Connor, concurring in part and dissenting in part) 476 U.S. at 731-732. In truth, however, *Bowen* cannot even be reconciled with Scalia's opinion for the Court in *Smith* since, even under *Smith*, employment benefits appear to be the one residual category where strict scrutiny will still be applied. See *infra* text at notes 791-795.

Nor is its underlying logic beyond reproach. Justice Scalia tells us, for example, that cases like *Wisconsin v. Yoder*[774] invalidating a compulsory school attendance law as applied to the Amish was not based exclusively on the fact that it infringed on their religious beliefs but on the additional ground that it interfered with the rights of parents to direct the education of their children.[775] Yet it seems clear that the general right of parents to direct the upbringing of their children, if divorced from a religious context, would be a constitutionally-inadequate reason to exempt them from the requirements of compulsory education. Even the 1925 case of *Pierce*[776] merely sustained the rights of parents to send their children to private schools but not, as the Amish do, to dispense with formal schooling altogether beyond the eighth grade. Indeed, the *Pierce* case acknowledged the state's interest in educating its citizenry but merely held that such interest could be fully met outside the confines of the public school system.[777] If *Yoder* recognizes rights beyond those of sending one's child to private schools, those rights must be predicated on unique considerations arising under the free exercise clause as indeed the language of *Yoder* so states.[778] Yet *Smith* tells us that no such free exercise entitlement exists. If the rights of parents to direct the rearing of their children are a constitutionally-insufficient reason to overcome the state's legitimate interest in the education of its citizenry and the free exercise clause raises no entitlement to be exempt, it is difficult to see how their "hybridization" gives rise to rights that neither prong could provide alone.

Moreover, it is not at all clear if there is a meaningful distinction between infringements on religion that suppress speech and association rights and those infringements that "only" suppress religion.[779] Could not Native American groups claim that the state's prohibiting the sacramental use of peyote impairs their ability to achieve a level of communal spiritual discourse, thereby infringing on their associational as well as religious freedoms?

In any case, whether or not the Court's reading of its own precedents is correct, *Smith* radically alters the nature of "free exercise" analysis and, for those concerned for the preservation of religious liberty, not necessarily for the better.[780] It is widely regarded as sounding the "death knell" for free exercise

774. 406 U.S. 205 (1972).

775. *Smith* II at 881-882.

776. *Pierce v. Society of Sisters*, 268 U.S. 510 (1925) (parents have a constitutional right to educate their children outside of the public schools).

777. *Pierce* at 534.

778. See, for example, *Yoder*, 406 U.S. at 215 ("A way of life, however virtuous and admirable, may not be interposed as a barrier to reasonable state regulation of education if it is based on purely secular considerations.") (Chief Justice Burger for the Court).

779. This distinction appears several times in the *Smith* II opinion. See, *e.g.*, *Smith* II at 881-882.

780. Indeed, serious concerns in the aftermath of *Smith* have prompted the introduction of federal legislation specifically designed to overturn it. See *infra* text at notes 811-818.

claims against generally-applicable laws or regulations[781] and this is probably an accurate assessment. Nevertheless, a number of observations should be made:

First, while six justices of the Court concurred in the judgment, only five rested their decision on the abandonment of the "compelling state interest" standard.[782] Justice O'Connor, who concurred with the ruling, did so exclusively on the "compelling state interest" theory rather than relying solely on the law's nondiscriminatory application.[783] Thus, only five justices have expressly indicated their willingness to repudiate the *Sherbert* test; four justices would leave the basic test intact (though within that group, there was a 3-1 disagreement as to how the test should be applied in a particular case). The existence of what amounts to a 5-4 split on the Court indicates that the matter is far from settled and the *Sherbert* test could conceivably be resurrected. It must be noted, however, that of the four justices who would have retained the "compelling state interest" standard (Justices Blackmun, Brennan, Marshall, and O'Connor), two (Brennan and Marshall) are no longer on the Court while all five of the justices who joined in the Scalia opinion (Justices Kennedy, Rehnquist, Scalia, Stevens, and White) still are.[784]

Second, the Court's acknowledgement of the "hybrid" or "religion-plus" category of cases may furnish a basis for the revival of *Sherbert* in another guise. The Court appears to concede that to the extent a religious infringement also affects communicative and associational rights under the First Amendment, strict scrutiny under the "compelling state interest" standard will continue to be appropriate.[785] Many religious liberty claims can be fairly easily reformulated into claims based on state infringement of rights of association, parenting, *etc.* For example, one of the common fears expressed in the wake of *Smith* is that parents could be prosecuted for allowing minors to partake of wine during the Sabbath meals or at the Passover *seder*.[786] Yet could not any Jewish parent raise the argument that the failure to accommodate religious observance not only impacts on free exercise rights of religion but on the rights of parents to direct the upbringing of their children by training them in the precepts of their faith? Indeed, as noted earlier, a similar associational argument could have been raised in *Smith* itself.[787] It remains to be seen whether "religion-plus" arguments will be sympathetically received by the

---

781. See, for example, Raskas, *The Court's Smith Decision Threatens Religious Freedom*, THE DAILY RECORD (June 5, 1991), p. 13 and the various views quoted in Marcus, *Reins on Religious Freedom? Broad Coalition Protests Impact of High Court Ruling*, THE WASHINGTON POST (March 9, 1991, Final Ed.), p. A-1.

782. These include Justice Scalia who wrote the opinion, Chief Justice Rehnquist, and Justices Kennedy, Stevens, and White.

783. *Smith* II at 891, 903-907 (Justice O'Connor, concurring in judgment).

784. Justices Brennan and Marshall were replaced by Justices Souter and Thomas respectively. Their views on the scope of the free exercise clause are unknown yet there is little reason to believe they would be advocates for *Smith*'s overruling.

785. *Smith* II at 881-882.

786. See Raskas, *supra* note 781.

787. See *supra* text at note 779.

courts or whether they will be regarded as transparent attempts to circumvent *Smith*, but the avenue of at least making the argument has been left open.

Third, the opinion itself is a bit vague as to whether the strict scrutiny necessitated by the "compelling state interest" test is totally discarded (at least in "pure" religion cases) or whether it may still survive in contexts outside of criminal prosecution. There is language in the opinion that suggests that *Smith* is limited to a denial of religious exemption for *criminal misconduct*.[788] Where the religious practice in question is not criminal but simply results in a denial of governmental benefits, as in *Sherbert*,[789] the opinion apparently agrees that it is still the law that religious exemptions must be granted unless the "compelling state interest" test is met.[790] Thus, regardless of Scalia's personal views on the matter, *Smith* seems to reaffirm, albeit in a somewhat grudging tone, *Sherbert*, *Thomas*, and *Hobbie*,[791] all of which invalidated state unemployment compensation rules that conditioned the availability of benefits on an applicant's willingness to work under conditions forbidden by his religion.[792] Nor is there anything unique or talismanic about unemployment compensation programs. The critical feature of such programs is that they are already set up to take into account an applicant's individualized circumstances.[793] Once the state "has in place a system of individual exemptions, it may not refuse to extend that system to cases of religious hardship without compelling reason."[794] Such a feature may exist under a wide variety of state statutes and programs and indeed even criminal laws and where it does, strict scrutiny will arguably continue to be employed.[795]

---

788. See, *e.g.*, *Smith* II at 884 ("Even if we were inclined to breathe into *Sherbert* some life beyond the unemployment compensation field, we would not apply it to require exemptions from a generally applicable criminal law."); *id.* ("Whether or not the decisions are that limited, they at least have nothing to do with an across-the-board criminal prohibition on a particular form of conduct."); *id.* at 885 ("The government's ability to enforce generally applicable prohibitions of socially harmful conduct, like its ability to carry out other aspects of public policy, cannot depend on measuring the effects of a governmental action on a religious objector's spiritual development.").

789. *Supra* note 569.

790. *Smith* II at 884-885.

791. These cases are cited *supra* note 769.

792. *Smith*'s affirmance of *Sherbert et al.* appears at 883.

793. The statutes at issue in *Sherbert* and *Thomas* provided that a person was not eligible for unemployment benefits if he had quit work or refused available work "without good cause," thereby allowing for individualized determinations to be made. *Smith* II at 884.

794. *Id.* at 884.

795. Why the existence of such a statutory or regulatory scheme should be of constitutional magnitude is not entirely clear. The theory of the Court seems to be that once a legal program admits of individualized exemptions, it must accord religion such an exemption unless there is a compelling state interest not to. Yet what if, instead of an amorphous "good cause" exemption, the state would have specified in detail twenty cases of refusals to work that were justifiable and did not specify religious observance? Would the religious observer, subject to the general law and uncovered by its exemptions, have a

This conclusion, however, is not inescapable. In distinguishing *Sherbert et al.* from the facts in *Smith*, the Court might simply have been limiting the scope of earlier inconsistent precedent without necessarily suggesting that such precedent, even as narrowly defined, should still be regarded as binding law. At this juncture, it is hard to know what the Court has in mind and perhaps the justices themselves are somewhat uncertain.

In short, the survivability of strict scrutiny after *Smith* (at least in "pure" religion cases) admits of three possible alternatives: (1) state law challenged under the free exercise clause must always be justified under the "compelling state interest" standard except in the narrow context of criminal prosecution; (2) as long as the law under attack is nondiscriminatory, a "compelling state interest" need never be shown except in the context of employment benefits or other programs which take into account individualized circumstances; (3) the "compelling state interest" standard need not be met for anything and essentially even the employment benefit trilogy of *Sherbert*, *Thomas*, and *Hobbie*[796] is no longer the law. As of the date of this writing (January 1993), the Supreme Court has given us no further guidance on this matter. All lower courts that have construed and applied *Smith*, however, have refused to limit the case to criminal prosecution and have upheld a variety of noncriminal laws that negatively impact on religious observance and that do not afford any religious accommodation or exemption.[797] (Note, however, that

---

case? Is the Court's analysis based on the idea that once the door is open to *any* exemptions (even if specified), it must (absent a compelling state interest) be open to religious claims as well, or is the Court's fear that where exemptions are vague, open-ended, and highly dependent on administrative discretion ("good cause"), strict scrutiny is essential as a prophylactic to insure that applicants are not victims of religious discrimination? This latter consideration would be less applicable where the exemption grounds are specifically spelled out in statute or regulation rather than applied on a case by case basis.

No decision has squarely analyzed this point. *Peyote Way Church v. Thornburgh*, 922 F.2d 1210 (5th Cir. 1991), however, addressed the issue implicitly. The Fifth Circuit sustained the constitutionality of a criminal drug statute that exempted sacramental use by the members of the Native American Church but not by other religious groups. The underlying assumption must have been that *Smith*'s rule of triggering strict scrutiny when individualized exemptions are present was limited to amorphous, discretionary exemptions of the "good cause" variety and not those that are specific and nondiscretionary. (*Peyote* also raises difficult issues of equal protection but those are beyond the purview of this work).

796. Cited *supra* note 769.

797. See *Munn v. Algee*, 924 F.2d 568 (5th Cir. 1991) (A tort plaintiff's religiously-motivated refusal to receive a blood transfusion does not automatically negate the duty of avoidable consequences; after *Smith*, there is no longer an absolute right to be free of the constraints applicable to other tort plaintiffs.); *Vandiver v. Hardin County Board of Education*, 925 F.2d 927 (6th Cir. 1991) (*Smith* not limited to criminal laws; applicable to educational testing, equivalency exams.); *Intercommunity Center for Justice and Peace v. INS*, 910 F.2d 42 (2nd Cir. 1990) (*Smith* not limited to criminal law; applicable to civil penalties imposed on employer whose religious beliefs compelled the

none of these cases involved governmental benefits or other programs that consider "individualized circumstances" where *Sherbert* may arguably continue to be the law.)

It should further be noted that even if *Smith* is read as abandoning *Sherbert* entirely, this would not mean that laws impacting on free exercise rights are subject to no judicial scrutiny. Even prior to *Smith*, *Sherbert* was not the only standard applied in responding to free exercise challenges. In the past twenty or so years, prisoners have challenged under the free exercise clause a wide array of prison regulations that impact on their religious observances.[798] The standard for evaluating the constitutionality of these rules is set down in *Turner v. Safley*.[799] Recognizing that the exigencies of prison systems dictate that "we cannot allow a romantic view of constitutional rights of religion"[800] to interfere with the needs of discipline, protection of the public and other inmates, and conservation of public resources, *Turner* adopts a "reasonableness" standard that is considerably less restrictive than that

---

employment of illegal aliens.); *Salvation Army v. New Jersey Department of Community Affairs*, 919 F.2d 183 (3rd Cir. 1990) (Religious group sought exemption from the requirements of a state statute regulating boarding houses. The court held that, under *Smith*, no exemption need be granted. The Third Circuit's opinion contains the most detailed discussion of the issue). See also the disheartening cases of *Yang v. Sturner*, 750 F.Supp. 558 (D.RI 1990), *aff'd without opinion*, 940 F.2d 661 (6th Cir. 1991) and *Montgomery v. County of Clinton*, 743 F.Supp. 1253 (W.D. Mich. 1990), both of which held that a state statute requiring autopsies for victims of violent death need not provide a religious exemption for those people whose religious beliefs prohibit desecration of the dead.

In the aftermath of *Smith*, the Occupational Health and Safety Administration (OSHA) took the position that it would no longer provide religious exemptions for mandatory headgear at construction sites. *OSHA Notice CPL 2* (Nov. 5, 1990) cited in 20 BUREAU OF NATIONAL AFFAIRS OCCUPATIONAL SAFETY AND HEALTH REPORTER 1018 (November 14, 1990). Prior to *Smith*, persons such as the Amish or Sikhs were routinely excused from such requirements on the grounds that the wearing of hard hats conflicted with their religious practices. This permissive policy had been in effect for over twelve years. See *Exemption from Wearing Hard Hats, Old Order Amish and Sikh Dharma Brotherhood*, OSHA INSTRUCTION STD 1-6.3 (October 1978). After *Smith*, however, such an exemption was no longer constitutionally compelled and was therefore unjustified. As a result of public clamor against this decision, OSHA essentially reinstated the exemption as a matter of prosecutorial discretion. see *OSHA Memorandum for Regional Administrators* (July 24, 1991).

798. For a good overview of this area, see Note, *Prisoner's Religious Free Exercise Rights*, 37 AMERICAN UNIVERSITY LAW REVIEW 453 (1988). (Unfortunately, the article predated *Smith* and thus fails to address the potential impact of *Smith* on *Turner* review). See also Gobert and Cohen, RIGHTS OF PRISONERS, pp. 143-165 (1981) and in 1991 SUPPLEMENT, pp. 154-183 (also failing to explicitly address the impact of *Smith*.)

799. 482 U.S. 78 (1987).

800. The quoted language is taken from *Young v. Lane*, 922 F.2d 370, 375 n.14 (7th Cir. 1991), a recent case applying *Turner*.

ordinarily applied to alleged infringements of fundamental constitutional rights. Prison regulations will be sustained if they are "reasonably related to legitimate penological interests."[801] In making this determination, *Turner* directs that four factors be considered: (1) whether the governmental objective underlying the regulation is legitimate and religiously neutral; (2) whether the regulation has a logical connection to the legitimate interest advanced to justify it; (3) whether inmates have alternative means of exercising the religious rights upon which the regulation allegedly impinges; and (4) the impact in terms of cost and security that religious accommodation would have on guards, other inmates, and the allocation of prison resources.[802] Significantly, the justification need not be "compelling" but only "legitimate." Moreover, even if less restrictive alternatives exist, the state need not pursue them.[803]

Nevertheless, the test in *Turner* is not entirely toothless. While regulations need not satisfy a "least restrictive alternative" test, the existence of "obvious, easy alternatives" that impose an essentially *de minimis* cost on prison authorities may be strong evidence that the regulation is not in fact reasonable "but is an exaggerated response to prison concerns."[804] Nor do these alternatives have to be entirely cost-free; "costs that are insubstantial in light of the overall maintenance of the prison" may be equally probative in establishing unreasonableness.[805]

While *Smith* may have displaced the strict scrutiny of *Sherbert*, it does not necessarily preclude the application and extension of *Turner* to both prison and nonprison cases.[806] To the extent *Turner* scrutiny is meaningfully

---

801. *Turner* at 89.

802. *Id.*, listed at 89-91.

803. This last point was made explicit in a later Supreme Court opinion. *Thornburgh v. Abbott*, 490 U.S. 401 (1989).

804. *Turner* at 89.

805. The quoted language is from *Salaam v. Lockhart*, 905 F.2d 1168 (8th Cir. 1990), discussed *infra* note 806.

806. This is at least true in the Eighth Circuit. See *Salaam v. Lockhart*, 905 F.2d 1168 (8th Cir. 1990). That case involved the legality of a prison rule barring inmate changes of name as applied to a prisoner who converted to Islam and assumed an Arabic name. The court struck down the regulation finding that it failed the *Turner* test of "reasonableness." The court further observed that *Smith* does not displace *Turner* scrutiny but rather brings the rights of nonprisoners closer to those of prisoners. *Id.* at 1171, n.7. The Ninth Circuit seems to take a similar position. See *Friend v. Kolodzieczak*, 923 F.2d 126 (9th Cir. 1991) (Although the court upheld a rule banning possession of rosaries, it noted that *Smith* did not replace *Turner*). But *cf. Friedman v. State of Arizona*, 912 F.2d 328 (9th Cir. 1990) (In sustaining a prison ban on facial hair, the court noted that it did not have to decide whether *Smith* narrowed prisoner's rights since the regulations were valid even under the more rigorous review of *Turner*. *Id.* at 331 n.1). The Seventh Circuit, on the other hand, apparently rules that *Smith* eliminates even the relatively-minimal scrutiny of *Turner*. See *Hunafa v. Murphy*, 907 F.2d 46 (7th Cir. 1990) (*Smith* "cut back to minute dimensions the doctrine that requires government to accommodate, at some cost, minority religious preferences, the doctrine on which all the prison reform cases are founded." *Hunafa* at 48). Once again, however, the

conducted, a proposition that is admittedly questionable, there may yet be a role for mandatory religious accommodation even after *Smith*.[807]

Nor should the possibilities of redress under state constitutional law be ignored. *Smith* is a binding interpretation of the First Amendment of the United States Constitution but does not, and indeed could not, purport to tell the states what their own constitutional provisions protect. Many state constitutions contain guarantees of religious freedom[808] and state courts are perfectly free to give these guarantees a more expansive interpretative than *Smith* gives the First Amendment even if the wordings of the state and federal provisions are identical.[809] Moreover, a decision by a state's highest court

---

opinions are inconsistent. See, *e.g.*, *Young v. Lane*, 922 F.2d 370 (7th Cir. 1991) (court applies *Turner* test in validating prison regulation).

807. The *Turner* standard has not been difficult to meet; prison regulations are almost never struck down because they are unreasonable. Of the five cases cited in the preceding note, only *Salaam* invalidated a regulation on the grounds that it failed *Turner* scrutiny. Nevertheless, as minimal as it may be, *Turner* remains a partial bulwark of protection in free exercise cases.

808. For a state-by-state survey, see Legislative Drafting Research Fund, CONSTITUTIONS OF THE UNITED STATES: NATIONAL AND STATE (1982, revised annually). According to the Index, forty-nine states have explicit guarantees of religious liberty. Arizona appears to be the only state that does not guarantee freedom of worship although Article II, §12 of its Constitution does prohibit a religious test as a condition to holding public office or employment or as adversely affecting one's eligibility as a juror.

809. The most eloquent, as well as prestigious, exponent of the notion that state constitutional provisions can, and should, be expanded to fill in the gaps resulting from restrictive Supreme Court opinions curtailing federal rights is former Justice William Brennan. See Brennan, *State Constitutions and the Protection of Individual Rights*, 90 HARVARD LAW REVIEW 489 (Jan. 1977) and his update in *The Bill of Rights and the States: The Revival of State Constitutions As Guardians of Individual Rights*, 61 NEW YORK UNIV. L. REV. 535 (Oct. 1986). Brennan has not limited his remarks to speeches or articles. In a dissent from what he regarded as an unwarranted erosion of a suspect's *Miranda* rights, Brennan openly invited state courts to effectively circumvent Supreme Court restrictions by generously construing their own law. See *Michigan v. Mosley*, 423 U.S. 96, 120-121 (1975) (Justice Brennan, dissenting). See also Pollock, *State Courts As Separate Sources of Fundamental Rights*, 35 RUTGERS LAW REV. 707, 736 (Summer 1983) (referring to Brennan's 1977 article as the "Magna Carta" of state constitutional law). Mr. Pollock is himself a Justice of the New Jersey Supreme Court and was so at the time of his article.

Over the past twenty or so years as the Supreme Court has become more conservative, a number of state courts have in fact become more activist in recognizing fundamental rights under their own constitutions even where such rights do not, or no longer, exist under the federal Bill of Rights. See, for example, *People v. Anderson*, 493 P.2d 880 (Cal. 1972) (California Supreme Court declared the death penalty unconstitutional under its state constitution; interestingly, the California voters overturned the decision by constitutional amendment, see CAL. CONST. Article 1, §27.); *People v. Brisendine*, 531 P.2d 1099 (Cal. 1975) (The search-and-seizure provisions of

construing its own constitution to grant citizens a greater degree of religious liberty than that enjoyed under the free exercise clause is not subject to Supreme Court review.[810]

Finally, note must be taken of the attempts in Congress to enact a piece of legislation entitled the Religious Freedom Restoration Act (1993 H.R. 1308).[811] That bill would require that no state or federal law of even general applicability can burden religious observance unless the governmental unit can show both a compelling governmental interest and that no less burdensome alternative could equally serve that interest.[812] The purpose of the bill, as expressed in its own preamble, is to overrule *Smith* and require the use of the *Sherbert* test, albeit on a statutory rather than constitutional basis.[813] It applies

---

the state constitution afforded suspects greater protections than the Fourth Amendment of the Bill of Rights although the wording of both was identical.); *Right to Choose v. Byrne*, 450 A.2d 925 (N.J. 1982) (Under the New Jersey Constitution, pregnant women had a right to obtain public funding for their abortions).

For an excellent discussion of the methodological approaches utilized by state courts in effectively undercutting otherwise binding Supreme Court precedent, see Williams, *In the Supreme Court's Shadow: Legitimacy of State Rejection of Supreme Court Reasoning and Result*, 35 SOUTH CAROLINA LAW REV. 353 (Spring 1984).

810. See sources cited in preceding note. See also 28 U.S.C. §1257(a) (Supreme Court may review the final decision of a state supreme court only where that decision rests on a question of federal law or federal constitutional right).

811. The Religious Freedom Restoration Act was originally introduced in the summer of 1990 by (now former) Representative Stephen Solarz (D-N.Y.). After failing to reach a floor vote by the end of the 101th Congress, the bill was reintroduced as H.R. 2797 on June 26, 1991. Remarks by Solarz upon introduction of the bill appear at 137 CONG. REC. E 244 (6/27/91) (actually, a revision and extension of remarks). Hearings on the bill were held by the House Subcommittee on Civil and Constitutional Rights on May 13 and 14, 1992. See 138 CONG. REC. D 561 (May 13, 1992) and D 563 (May 14, 1992). In October 1992, the House Judiciary Committee approved the bill for a floor vote with some amendments. 138 CONG. REC. D 1261 (October 1, 1992). Despite the Committee's favorable recommendation and the fact that the bill was cosponsored by almost two hundred members of Congress, it failed to reach the floor for a vote, primarily due to the strong opposition of the Catholic Church and the National Right to Life Committee. See *infra* note 818. On March 11, 1993, the bill was reintroduced as H.R. 1308 by Representative Charles Schumer (D-N.Y.) and as S. 578 by the unlikely combination of Senators Hatch (R-Utah) and Kennedy (D-Mass). See 139 CONG. REC. H 1143 (March 10, 1993) and S 2822 (March 11, 1993).

812. 1993 H.R. 1308, §3.

813. 1993 H.R. 1308, §2(a)(1)-(5). Interestingly, because the bill applies to all federal and state law, it would arguably require strict scrutiny under the "compelling state interest" test even in cases where *Sherbert* itself would have allowed a lesser standard. For example, it would appear that even prison regulations that burden religious observance would now have to be justified by

to both existing and future legislation or regulations.[814] States are bound by its provisions as they are under all provisions of federal law by virtue of the supremacy clause of the Constitution.[815] While a subsequent Congress would of course not be bound by laws passed by an earlier Congress, the bill does provide as a rule of construction that all subsequent federal law is subject to the Act unless such law makes a specific exclusionary reference.[816] Cosponsored by almost two hundred members of Congress, the bill was reported favorably out of the House Judiciary Committee but did not reach the floor for a vote before the expiration of the 102nd Congress at the end of 1992.[817] The bill was recently reintroduced as H.R. 1308 (March 11, 1993) and the chances for its passage are considered quite good.[818]

---

adherence to a more rigorous standard. The proposed statute overrules not only *Smith* but even *Turner*. See *supra* text at notes 798-807.

814. *Id.*, §6(a).

815. U.S. CONSTITUTION, Article VI ("This Constitution, and the Laws of the United States, which shall be made in pursuance thereof; and all Treaties made, or which shall be made, under the Authority of the United States, shall be the supreme Law of the Land; and the Judges in every State shall be bound thereby, any thing in the Constitution or laws of any State to the Contrary notwithstanding.") (original capitalization retained).

816. 1993 H.R. 1308, §6(b).

817. See note 811.

818. In addition to wide support in Congress, the bill, has also received the endorsement of the Clinton administration. See text of letter from President Clinton to Senator Kennedy, reprinted in 139 CONG. REC. S 2823 (March 11, 1993).

Note should also be taken of an almost identical bill, 1991 H.R. 4040, somewhat confusingly named the Religious Freedom Act of 1991. Introduced by Rep. Chris Smith (R- N. J.), it too would require that federal or state laws that burden religious observance be justified under a "compelling governmental interest" standard but would carve out an exception for "any limitation or restriction on abortion, on access to abortion services or on abortion funding." 1991 H.R. 4040, §3(c)(2). Various pro-life groups were concerned that the Solarz bill could mandate governmental funding of abortion where a woman could show that her religious beliefs required abortion under certain circumstances. H.R. 4040 was designed to respond to their concerns. See Besser, *Religious Freedom Bill Facing Obstacles*, BALTIMORE JEWISH TIMES (March 6, 1992), p. 41. H.R. 4040 was also designed to insure that the tax exempt status of churches could not be challenged by positing a free exercise burden. 1991 H.R. 4040, §3(c)(2).

This latter concern (though not the abortion issue) was addressed by the insertion of additional language to §7 of the Schumer bill, see H.R. 1308, §7. Shortly thereafter, the United States Catholic Conference (the social policy arm of the National Conference of Catholic Bishops) dropped its longstanding opposition to the bill, thus paving the way for its virtually certain passage. See LOS ANGELES TIMES (March 13, 1993), p. B-4. It is not anticipated that the alternative Smith bill will be reintroduced.

The Impact of *Smith* on Establishment

Smith involved the validation of a statute that was challenged under the free exercise clause as an infringement of religious freedom. It has no direct impact on *Lemon*'s[819] tripartite analysis under the establishment clause. Indeed, the lower federal courts have continued to apply *Lemon* in cases decided after *Smith*.[820] The close mirror-image relationship between the clauses, however, invariably suggests that changes on one side of the religion equation have some repercussions on the other.

The precise identification of these repercussions is somewhat difficult to determine. One possible approach might be that as fewer cases of religious accommodation become constitutionally compelled, fewer will be constitutionally permitted. After all, virtually any religious accommodation or exemption has as one of its principal effects, if not purposes, the advancement of religion and thus may be said to be violative of establishment. As long as free exercise, however, compelled such accommodation, the fundamental right of religious freedom overrode the competing proscription against establishment.[821] Free exercise no longer compels such accommodation; arguably, then, the establishment clause has a corresponding larger arena within which it may stake its claim.

While this approach has a certain conceptual symmetry, in all likelihood it is *not* the wave of the future. In the first place, as noted, at least the lower courts have not regarded *Smith* as affecting *Lemon* in any way.[822] Second, and more important, Justice Scalia's opinion in *Smith* is replete with ringing endorsements of religious accommodation, consistently emphasizing that while *Smith* does not compel such accommodations, it certainly does not prohibit them and, as a matter of good policy, states would be wise to follow suit.[823] Conceptually, *Smith* reflects a fundamental trust in, and deference to, the political process in safeguarding the rights of religious minorities; such trust would seem to warrant an equally deferential stance in validating the products of such process from attacks based on establishment.[824] Third, within the

---

819. *Supra* note 562.

820. See, for example, *Roberts v. Madigan*, 921 F.2d 1047 (10th Cir. 1990); *Cammack v. Waihee*, 932 F.2d 765 (9th Cir. 1991); *Weisman v. Lee*, 908 F.2d 1090 (1st Cir. 1990) *affirmed sub nom. Lee v. Weisman*, 60 U.S. L.W. 4723 (1992); and *Harris v. City of Zion*, 927 F.2d 1401 (7th Cir. 1991), all of which applied the tripartite test of *Lemon* to alleged establishment clause violations without suggesting that *Smith* changed the test in any way. See also *infra* text at notes 857-859.

821. See *supra* text at note 572.

822. See cases cited *supra* note 818.

823. *Smith* II at 890.

824. "Values that are protected against government interference through enshrinement in the Bill of Rights are not thereby banished from the political process. Just as a society that believes in the negative protection accorded to the press by the First Amendment is likely to enact laws that affirmatively foster the printed word, so also a society that believes in the negative protection accorded to religious belief can be expected to be solicitous of that value in its legislation as well. ..... It may fairly be said that leaving accommodation to

Supreme Court itself, there have been numerous rumblings of dissatisfaction with the *Lemon* test, all in the direction of a *less* rigorous standard that will sustain a greater range of legislative and regulatory initiatives.[825] It is unlikely that *Smith* was intended, or will be read, to impose greater restraints under the establishment clause.

THE FUTURE OF THE *LEMON* TEST UNDER THE ESTABLISHMENT CLAUSE: *ALLEGHENY* AND *LEE*

Indeed, there are strong indications on the Court that the *Lemon* test may undergo a complete overhaul or at least a radical redefinition in the direction of less scrutiny of establishment claims. A harbinger of such an imminent change was the 1989 decision of *County of Allegheny v. American Civil Liberties Union*,[826] a complex, interlocking array of concurrences and dissents,[827] which indicated that at least four justices of the Court are willing

---

democratic government must be preferred to a system in which each conscience is a law unto itself or in which judges weigh the social importance of all laws against the centrality of all religious beliefs." *Id.* at 890 (Justice Scalia for the Court).

Justice O'Connor sharply contested the propriety of leaving the protection of religious rights to majority whim: "In my view, however, the First Amendment was enacted precisely to protect the rights of those whose religious practices are not shared by the majority and may be viewed with hostility." *Id.* at 902 (Justice O'Connor, concurring). Indeed, over half a century ago, in the famous flag-salute case, the Court observed that "the very purpose of a Bill of Rights was to withdraw certain subjects from the vicissitudes of political controversy, to place them beyond the reach of majorities and officials and to establish them as legal principles to be applied by the courts. One's right to life, liberty, and property, to free speech, a free press, freedom of worship and assembly, and other fundamental rights may not be submitted to vote; they depend on the outcome of no elections." *West Virginia State Bd. of Education v. Barnette*, 319 U.S. 624, 638 (1943) (invalidating compulsory flag salute challenged by religious objectors).

In light of the fact that the very purpose of the Bill of Rights was the insulation of certain issues from the political process, the Court's reliance on that process seems problematical.

825. See *supra* text at note 564 and *infra* text at notes 844-859.

826. 492 U.S. 573 (1989).

827. Justice Blackmun's opinion consists of seven parts, only some of which were joined by a requisite majority of the Court. Part I (579-587) contains the factual background of the case including a lengthy disquisition on the historical and religious background of Chanukah. This portion of the opinion was joined only by Justices O'Connor and Stevens. Since, however, Part I contains no rulings, one can only surmise that perhaps a majority of the Court felt that extensive descriptions of religious ceremonies were in themselves a form of endorsement that courts should attempt to avoid. Part II (587-589) simply recounts the procedural history of the case. For reasons that I cannot fathom, this unexceptionable recapitulation was again only joined by Justices O'Connor and Stevens and did not represent part of the opinion of the Court.

to do to the establishment clause exactly what five justices of the Court did to the free exercise guarantees in *Smith*. *Allegheny* involved the constitutionality of two recurring holiday displays located on public property in downtown Pittsburgh: a crèche (nativity scene) placed inside of a courthouse and a Christmas tree-*menorah* combination just outside the City-County Building together with a sign saluting religious liberty. The Court of Appeals for the Third Circuit, applying the *Lemon* test, ruled that both displays violated the establishment clause because their "primary effect" was the advancement of religion.[828] The Supreme Court affirmed in part and reversed in part, ruling that

---

Part III-A (589-594) of the opinion reaffirms the tripartite analysis of *Lemon v. Kurtzman* and emphasizes that the single most important aspect of the inquiry is the question of whether the challenged governmental action has the effect of "endorsing," "promoting,"or "favoring" religion or a particular religious group. This formulation was supported by Justices O'Connor, Brennan, Marshall, and Stevens, making a majority of five. Part III-B (594-597) is a fairly sharp criticism of the Court's opinion in *Lynch v. Donnelly*, 465 U.S. 668 (1984), an earlier 5-4 decision allowing a crèche, essentially stating that the majority's analysis provided no principled basis for decision and only O'Connor's "endorsement" test, as expressed in her *Lynch* concurrence, "provides a sound analytical framework for evaluating governmental use of religious symbols." *Allegheny*, 492 U.S. at 573. This portion of the opinion was joined only by Justice Stevens. For some reason, despite its fulsome praise for her *Lynch* concurrence, even Justice O'Connor did not join Part III-A. See *infra* note 838 for a possible explanation.

Part IV (598-602) strikes down the courtroom crèche as an impermissible establishment of religion under the "endorsement test." It was joined by Justices Brennan, Marshall, Stevens, and O'Connor and thus represented the opinion of the Court. Part V (602-613) contains an unusually rancorous attack on the substitute "proselytization" test advocated by Justice Kennedy and the three justices who joined him, lambasting Kennedy's opinion as "gutting the core of the Establishment Clause" (at 604); and "transparently [lacking] a principled basis" (at 610, n. 57). This too represented the opinion of the Court, being joined by Brennan, Marshall, Stevens, and O'Connor.

Part VI (613-621) expressed Blackmun's view that the *menorah*-Christmas tree display was constitutionally permitted because, in overall context, the symbols are secular in nature and the city had no reasonable alternatives that were less religious in nature. Although O'Connor concurred in the distinction, she did not concur in Blackmun's reasoning and thus Part VI was the opinion of only a single justice. Part VII (621) is the announcement of the judgment of the Court, a judgment that in fact only two justices supported. See *infra* text at notes 831-832.

Thus, in sum, only Parts III-A, IV, and V represented the opinion of the Court and even those portions only garnered the support of a mere five votes.

828. 842 F.2d 655 (1987). As is commonly the case, the Court of Appeals had no need to consider purpose or entanglement since, in its judgment, the displays failed the "primary effect" criterion. [*Cf.* remarks of Judge Easterbrook in a dissenting opinion to *Harris v. City of Zion*, 927 F.2d 1401, 1424 (7th Cir. 1991). After noting that the "effect" prong of *Lemon* has become the dominant focus of inquiry, he observes: "Everything collapses to

the crèche was unconstitutional but the *menorah*-Christmas tree combination could be allowed to stand.[829] Ironically, however, the judgment of the Court was fully supported by only two justices. Four justices would have upheld both displays[830]; three justices would have prohibited both displays.[831] Only Justices Blackmun and O'Connor actually took the position that there was a constitutionally-significant distinction between the crèche and the *menorah*-Christmas tree and they themselves were in disagreement over the reasons why.[832] Thus, although seven out of nine justices felt the actual decision of the Court was erroneous, the crèche was struck down by a vote of 5-4[833] while the *menorah* display was sustained by a vote of 6-3.[834] Since the actual holding of the Court reflects no one's view of the establishment clause other than that of Justices Blackmun and O'Connor, looking at the Court's holding might be less important than focusing on the particular approaches to establishment law that each of the justices advocated in his or her concurrence or dissent.

A careful analysis of the opinions reveals that five justices are willing to retain the tripartite test of *Lemon v. Kurtzman* or at least that part of the test that focuses on "effects."[835] In determining whether a governmental practice has the "primary effect" of advancing religion, these justices strongly support the view, expressed by Justice O'Connor in a number of concurrences, that the touchstone of the inquiry is not merely whether religion is benefitted but whether it is "endorsed," "promoted," or "favored."[836] Specifically, as this test was fleshed out by Justices Blackmun and O'Connor in greater detail, the

---

the no-endorsement rule, one more compelling if divorced from the three-part test (or as advanced thinkers call it these days, 'tri-partite inquiry'). Why use three parts when only one matters?"].

829. *Allegheny*, 492 U.S. at 621.

830. This group includes Kennedy who authored an opinion, concurring in part and dissenting in part, that was joined by Chief Justice Rehnquist and Justices Scalia and White. *Allegheny*, 492 U.S. at 655-679.

831. These include Justice Brennan and Stevens, each of whom authored a separate concurring and dissenting opinion in which the other joined, and Justice Marshall who joined both opinions. *Allegheny*, 492 U.S. at 637 (opinion of Justice Brennan) and 646 (opinion of Justice Stevens).

832. Compare 492 U.S. at 613-621 (Blackmun's analysis) with *id.*, 632-637 (O'Connor's approach).

833. The five were Blackmun and O'Connor together with Brennan, Marshall, and Stevens.

834. The six were Blackmun and O'Connor together with Kennedy, Rehnquist, Scalia, and White.

835. In point of fact, the "effects" prong of *Lemon* is usually the primary basis of decision in most establishment clause cases. See *supra* note 828 (quote of Judge Easterbrook). Indeed, Justice O'Connor herself, who clearly advocates the "endorsement" test in applying the "effects" prong, has openly questioned the wisdom of the "excessive entanglement" criterion. See *Aguilar v. Felton*, 473 U.S. 402, 429 (1985) (dissenting opinion of Justice O'Connor).

836. See *Allegheny*, 492 U.S. at 592-594, citing Justice O'Connor's concurring opinions in *Wallace v. Jaffree*, 472 U.S. 38 at 70 (1985) and *Lynch v. Donnelly*, 465 U.S. 668 at 691 (1984).

question in every instance is whether the challenged practice "sends a message to nonadherents that they are outsiders, not full members of the political community, and an accompanying message to adherents that they are insiders, favored members of the political community."[837] Whether a given display has this effect depends on a consideration of its overall placement and context and how "viewers would fairly understand [its] purpose."[838] It appears that Justices Brennan, Marshall, and Stevens conceded the basic formulation of this standard but simply disagreed as to its application to the specific facts of the case.[839] These justices maintained that the state's imprimatur exists whether Jewish and Christian symbols are combined or only Christian ones are shown. In either case, the nonbeliever is essentially excluded.[840] Blackmun argued, on the other hand, that both the *menorah* and the Christmas tree have become largely secular symbols of historical and seasonal impact and carry no such religious signification.[841] Justice O'Connor, agreeing with Blackmun's result, preferred

---

837. *Allegheny* at 595 quoting *Lynch*, 465 U.S. at 690 (concurring opinion of Justice O'Connor).

838. *Allegheny* at 595 quoting *Lynch* at 692 (concurring opinion of Justice O'Connor).

839. The opinion is a bit confusing on this score. Although five justices joined in Part III-A of Blackmun's opinion which affirmed both the *Lemon* test and the focus on "promotion" and "endorsement," Part III-B which contains the quoted language from *Lynch* regarding the message conveyed to adherents and nonadherents and the need to focus on context was joined only by Stevens. Nevertheless, the basic underlying concept that the vice of establishment is the message that it conveys regarding an adherent's standing in the political community seems to be accepted by Brennan and Marshall as well. See, *e.g.*, *Lynch v. Donnelly*, 465 U.S. 668, 694 (1983) (dissenting opinion of Justice Brennan joined by Marshall, Blackmun, and Stevens). Indeed, the quoted language from III-B of the *Allegheny* opinion is merely an amplification of that which was implicit in Part III-A of the opinion. Presumably, Justices Brennan and Marshall refused to join Part III-B of the opinion because, first, it relies on *Lynch v. Donnelly*, a crèche case with which Brennan and Marshall disagreed and second, it suggests distinctions based on context and proximity to other symbols, distinctions that Brennan and Marshall were not prepared to make. (Ironically, however, Stevens joined III-B, subscribing to its general principles of viewing symbols in context though not applying those principles to validate the *menorah*-Christmas tree display. Why O'Connor did not join Part III-A is a mystery unless she simply did not want to personally attack a prior opinion of the Court as lacking a "sound analytical framework.")

840. See *Allegheny*, at 637-646 (concurring and dissenting opinion of Justice Brennan) and 646-655 (concurring and dissenting opinion of Justice Stevens).

841. *Allegheny* at 613-621. Technically, while the *menorah* itself may indeed be a predominantly religious symbol, its placement next to a Christmas tree, a symbol that is secular and seasonal has the effect of diminishing the religious message of the *menorah* as well, especially when the symbols are accompanied by a sign saluting liberty. *Id.*, 616-618. Moreover, the absence of a secular alternative symbol of the Chanukah season minimizes the inference that the choice of a religious symbol implies endorsement of religion. *Id.*, 618,

not to ignore the religious nature of the symbols employed (at least in the case of the *menorah*) but, in the overall context of the display, felt the message of pluralism and liberty was dominant.[842] In principle, therefore, there does not appear to be a significant disagreement within this group of five although Blackmun and O'Connor are obviously more willing to make finer contextual distinctions than were Brennan, Marshall, and Stevens.[843]

The second group, however, represents a sharp break with past *Lemon* analysis. Justice Kennedy, joined by Rehnquist, Scalia, and White, begins his opinion with an open invitation to reconsider and revamp the *Lemon* test:

> In keeping with the usual fashion of recent years, the majority applies the *Lemon* test to judge the constitutionality of the holiday displays here in question. I am content for present purposes to remain within the *Lemon* framework but do not wish to be seen as advocating, let alone adopting, that test as our primary guide in this difficult area. Persuasive criticism of *Lemon* has emerged ..... Substantial revision of our Establishment Clause doctrine may be in order.[844]

Ultimately, however, this group does apply *Lemon* but, with heavy reliance on the historical sanction given to practices such as prayers at the opening of legislative and judicial proceedings and references to G-d in coinage,[845] they

---

note 1. Justice Brennan criticizes this conclusion by asserting that, rather than the tree's redefining the significance of the *menorah*, it may be just as likely that the *menorah* redefines the nature of the tree. *Id.* at 641.

842. *Allegheny* at 632-637. O'Connor specifically disclaims any reliance on the lack of a more secular alternative. Here too, Brennan makes a trenchant observation in noting that a celebration of religious pluralism that appropriates Jewish and Christian symbols hardly conveys a "neutral" message. He notes that the dictates of the establishment clause mandate neutrality not only among religions but between religion and nonreligion. *Id.* at 644.

843. Indeed, Brennan criticizes Blackmun's preoccupation with the relative size or placement of symbols as being more appropriate to "an exam in Art 101" than to constitutional analysis. *Allegheny* at 643.

844. *Allegheny* at 655-656. It should be noted that even prior to *Allegheny*, a number of the justices who joined Kennedy had already expressed in no uncertain terms their belief that *Lemon* should be discarded. See *Edwards v. Aguillard*, 482 U.S. 578, 636 (1987) (dissenting opinion of Justice Scalia); *Wallace v. Jaffree*, 472 U.S. 38, 112 (1985) (dissenting opinion of Chief Justice Rehnquist) and *Roemer v. Board of Public Works*, 426 U.S. 736, 768 (1976) (concurring opinion of Justice White). See also *supra* note 833 (position of Justice O'Connor).

845. Justice Kennedy's concurrence relies heavily on *Marsh v. Chambers*, 463 U.S. 783 (1983) which sustained the practice of opening legislative sessions with prayer and on the presence of long-standing practices such as the proclamation of a National Day of Prayer, 36 U.S.C. §169h; a religious reference in the Pledge of Allegiance, 36 U.S.C. §172; the national motto of "In G-d We Trust," 36 U.S.C. §186; and the use of that motto on all currency, 31 U.S.C. §5112(d)(1). Conceding that historical patterns alone cannot "justify contemporary violations of constitutional guarantees" (*Allegheny* at 670), Justice Kennedy posited that historically-sanctioned patterns and traditions are highly probative in ascertaining the intended meaning of those guarantees and any

would replace O'Connor's "promotion" test with one that would focus on elements of "coercion," "intimidation," or "proselytization" and would therefore permit state recognition of the religious symbols adopted by its citizenry.[846] Civic acknowledgement of the role religion plays in the lives of its citizens should be regarded as a "reasonable accommodation" to the feelings and sensibilities of its populace rather than an "impermissible establishment."[847]

Notwithstanding the somewhat heated rhetoric in the Court's denunciation of the Kennedy reformulation,[848] the differences between the two tests should not be exaggerated. On a practical level, there may not be that much of a significant distinction between the "endorsement" test under *Lemon* and the "coercion" test advocated by the four-judge plurality. Indeed, there is a substantial overlap. Even the advocates of a "coercion" test recognize that coercion may take subtle forms and may be indirect as well as direct.[849] For example, it is highly unlikely that any justice would permit daily school prayer in an elementary classroom on the grounds that any fifth-grader who elects not to participate could leave the room.[850] Justice Kennedy himself notes that a

---

interpretation of the clause that would prohibit such long-standing traditions "cannot be a proper reading." *Id.*

846. See, for example, *Allegheny* at 659-660, 664-665. It should also be noted that although Kennedy technically articulated his "coercion" standard in the context of applying the *Lemon* test, a test of which he specifically disapproved (see quote in text), in all likelihood the standard he employed within the formal constraints of *Lemon* is identical to the one he would adopt if *Lemon* were overruled or at least limited to the school-funding area. The probable meaning of his reference to reconsidering *Lemon* is the abandonment of a tripartite inquiry focusing on purpose, effect, and entanglement in favor of a single factor focusing exclusively on coercion and proselytization. See also *supra* note 714 (Easterbrook comment). With respect to the single factor of gauging impermissible effect, however, his pre-*Lemon* and post-*Lemon* tests are identical, *i.e.*, "coercion" in lieu of "endorsement."

While the Court's decision in *Lee v. Weisman*, discussed *infra* notes 857-858, muddied the waters somewhat, the "coercion" test seems to be the new emerging standard favored by a current majority of the Supreme Court. *Id.*

847. "In my view, the principles of the Establishment Clause and our Nation's historic traditions of diversity and pluralism allow communities to make reasonable judgments respecting the accommodation or acknowledgement of holidays with both cultural and religious aspects. No constitutional violation occurs when they do so by displaying a symbol of the holiday's religious origins." *Allegheny* at 679.

848. See, *e.g.*, *Allegheny* at 609 n.57 and 611.

849. See *Allegheny*, 492 U.S. at 660-662 (Justice Kennedy concurring and dissenting opinion).

850. Indeed, Kennedy specifically cites with approval *Engel v. Vitale*, 370 U.S. 421 (1962), the case which invalidated prayer in the classroom, as an example of indirect coercion. *Allegheny* at 661, n.1. But see *Lee v. Weisman*, 60 U.S.L.W. 4723, 4739-40 (Justice Scalia, dissenting). Scalia apparently rejects a standard of coercion based solely on psychological factors. See also *infra* text at notes 857-858.

municipally-sponsored year-round display of a prominent cross could very well have an intimidating effect on non-Christians although no one would be openly demanding adherence to the tenets of Christianity.[851] Thus, even under the Kennedy analysis, many cases of "promotion," "endorsement," or "favoritism" will involve at least the less blatant forms of "coercion"; governmental activities that make nonadherents feel like outsiders may correspondingly generate "proselytization" pressures.[852] Justice Blackmun, in spite of his vigorous attacks on the Kennedy formulation, essentially concedes this point by noting that, if faithfully applied, the Kennedy test should yield many of the same results as *Lemon*.[853]

Suffice it to say, however, that perhaps the verbal formulation of the test is less important than the underlying philosophy of the four justices who propounded it. Those justices are clearly of the mind that official recognition of religion in rites of passage or at holiday times is to be sharply distinguished from the type of permanent intrusion that has longer-lasting psychological effects. Issues such as duration, timing, the vulnerability of the audience, the alternatives available to the audience, the ease in exercising those alternatives - factors that are immaterial under a pure "promotion" test - become highly relevant in assessing the coercive impact of the governmental action under a "proselytization" standard.

In short, while Blackmun's test focuses on the nature of the government's actions, *i.e.*, how would a disinterested observer interpret what the government was doing, Kennedy's test would focus on the *effect* of those actions on the audience exposed to them. Interestingly, Kennedy's analysis has the effect of collapsing the establishment clause into the free exercise one. One would have assumed that the protection of religious autonomy and freedom was the purview of the free exercise clause; historically, at least since *Everson*,[854] the establishment clause had been used to insure government neutrality and separation from religious institutions and influences.[855] Under Kennedy's formulation, the two clauses essentially coalesce into a single focus of concern

---

851. "I doubt not, for example, that the Clause forbids a city to permit the permanent erection of a large Latin cross on the roof of city hall. This is not because government speech about religion is *per se* suspect, as the majority would have it, but because such an obtrusive year-round religious display would place the government's weight behind an obvious effort to proselytize on behalf of a particular religion." *Allegheny* at 661 (opinion of Justice Kennedy).

852. See *supra* text at notes 835-843 (derivation of "endorsement," "promotion," and "favoritism" and the importance of the message conveyed to outsiders).

853. *Allegheny* at 608, 609 note 57 (where he argues that a crèche display should be banned even under a proselytization standard). But *cf. id.* at 602 (Kennedy's arguments are "far reaching in their implications"); 604 ("Justice Kennedy's reading of *Marsh* would gut the core of the Establishment Clause, as this Court understands it."); *id.* at 609 (A "proselytization" test "seems nothing more than an attempt to lower considerably the level of scrutiny in Establishment Clause cases.").

854. See *supra* note 551.

855. This is of course mirrors the famous Jeffersonian "Wall of Separation" metaphor. See *supra* note 551.

directed to the protection of individuals from governmental actions that have the effect, directly or indirectly, of interfering with religious belief.[856] Actions that have no such effects will be permitted under this standard even if they otherwise involve the state in public acknowledgement of the religious beliefs and rituals of its citizenry.

Given the reality that these differing standards will indeed yield different results in at least some cases, what then is the probable test the Court will adopt? While head counting is always a risky predictor, it is significant that two of the five justices (Brennan and Marshall) who would retain *Lemon* scrutiny are no longer on the Court while all four of the justices who would either abandon *Lemon* or emasculate it still are. With respect to the two newest appointees (Souter and Thomas), the recent case of *Lee v. Weisman*[857] indicates

---

856. Query, whether this coalescence renders the establishment clause effectively superfluous? Could not all governmental proselytization activities be equally vulnerable as infringements of free exercise? It should be noted, however, that although a "coercion" test is a departure from establishment clause jurisprudence since the 1947 case of *Everson*, *supra* note 551 (which resurrected the Jeffersonian "Wall of Separation"), it does indeed find solid support in the historical background and genesis of the establishment clause itself. See generally McConnell, *Coercion: The Lost Element of Establishment*, 27 WILLIAM AND MARY LAW REV. 933 (1986).

857. 60 U.S.L.W. 4723 (June 24, 1992). This case involved the constitutional permissibility of nonsectarian prayer at a junior high school graduation ceremony in Providence, Rhode Island. In *Weisman v. Lee* (the original name of the case), 908 F.2d 1090 (1st Cir. 1990), the Court of Appeals affirmed the decision of the District Court to enjoin such prayer. The District Court applied the tripartite test of *Lemon* in a fairly straightforward manner to conclude that the state's sponsorship of a prayer at a public school graduation places its stamp of approval on religion and therefore has the impermissible effect of an endorsement or promotion of religion. Other lower courts had held to the contrary. See, *e.g.*, *Stein v. Plainwell Community Schools*, 822 F.2d 1406 (6th Cir. 1987) (invocation and benedictions in public school graduation ceremonies are not *per se* unconstitutional). The Supreme Court, in yet another 5-4 split, affirmed the decision of the First Circuit that such prayers should be banned. Nevertheless, Justice Kennedy's opinion for the Court scrupulously avoided reliance on the *Lemon* test, prohibiting such prayer on the alternative ground that the school's sponsorship of the prayer, choice of speaker, and formulation of guidelines as to content exercised "subtle, coercive" pressures on impressionable adolescents to participate in religious activities or at least to give the impression of such participation. The student's choice to attend or not to attend cannot be regarded as meaningful in light of the paramount importance that parents and students attach to graduation ceremonies. See 60 U.S.L.W. at 4725 ("psychological coercion" theory; no need to discuss or apply the *Lemon* test). Justice Kennedy's opinion was joined by Justices Blackmun, O'Connor, Souter, and Stevens. Significantly, however, Blackmun and Souter wrote separate concurring opinions which depart from Kennedy's analysis. Blackmun expressly relied on *Lemon's* test, particularly the "promotion and endorsement" prong, noting that it had been employed by the Court numerous times. *Id.* at 4729. Souter, while not utilizing *Lemon per se*, explicitly rejected the idea that an establishment clause violation necessitates

that at least Justice Thomas is prepared to abandon the *Lemon* formula as well.[858] At present, therefore, a majority of the Supreme Court (albeit a bare

---

a finding of coercion and would find the clause implicated whenever the state grants its imprimatur to religious activity. *Id.* at 4723. Both of these concurrences were joined by Justice O'Connor and Stevens.

Justice Scalia, joined by Rehnquist, Thomas, and White, authored a scathing dissent rejecting both the promotion test of *Lemon* and Kennedy's newly-formulated "psychological coercion" standard and took the position that, in the absence of a discernible state penalty or sanction for nonparticipation, accommodating the desires of a majority of parents to have some public expression of religious gratitude at a major milestone in their children's lives cannot be regarded as a violation of the First Amendment. Scalia would differentiate between prayers offered in the elementary school classroom where the potential for coercion and intimidation is greater and the ability to absent oneself is less and those that are offered at a middle or high school graduation where the students are older, attend with their families present, and ultimately have the right to simply not show up, an option not readily available in the classroom setting.

858. Justice Scalia's dissent, joined by Rehnquist, Thomas, and White, notes:

> Our religious clause jurisprudence has become bedeviled (so to speak) by reliance on formulaic abstractions that are not derived from, but positively in conflict with, our long-accepted constitutional traditions. Foremost among those has been the so-called *Lemon* test .... which has received well-earned criticism from many members of this Court. The Court today demonstrates the irrelevance of *Lemon* by essentially ignoring it ... and the interment of that case may be the one happy byproduct of the Court's otherwise lamentable decision. Unfortunately, however, the Court has replaced *Lemon* with its psychological coercion test, which suffers the double disability of having no roots whatever in our people's historic practice and being as infinitely expandable as the reasons for psychotherapy itself.

Lee at 4740.

Rehnquist, Scalia, and White are already on record in calling for the demise of *Lemon*, see *supra* text at note 844, and Thomas' joining the Scalia dissent indicates for the first time that he is of like mind.

It must be emphasized that, insofar as *Lemon* itself is concerned, Kennedy takes a position identical to that of the dissenters. See *supra* text at note 844. Like them, he would limit violations of the establishment clause to instances of state-sponsored coercion or compulsion. Unlike them, Kennedy is willing to consider the psychological elements of peer pressure and intimidation and finds prayer, at least in the school setting, to fall on the other side of the line. (Note, however, that even he would uphold the validity of opening legislative sessions with prayer, see *supra* note 843).

Thus, after *Lee v. Weisman*, the Court falls into three groups: (1) Blackmun, O'Connor, Souter, and Stevens would essentially retain *Lemon*, or at least that prong of *Lemon* that focuses on promotion and endorsement, and would not limit the proscriptions of the establishment clause to instances of compulsion; (2) Rehnquist, Scalia, Thomas, and White would scrap the *Lemon* test entirely and replace it with a test that would focus on the coercive nature

majority of five) have announced their willingness to jettison the *Lemon* test in favor of a far less exacting standard, one that would permit civic acknowledgement of religion in public life as long as the activity does not create an official religion or coerce participation in religious activities. Although to date *Lemon* has not yet been expressly overruled, its demise or emasculation, if not imminent, is at least highly probable.[859]

In sum, the development of establishment law jurisprudence will follow one of three paths: establishment cases will continue to be analyzed under *Lemon*, be judged by a substitute standard that would validate legislation regardless of its "primary effect" as long as its "purpose" is secular, or be judged by an even more liberal standard that would allow legislation or legal practices to stand as long as there are no elements of coercion, intimidation, or the like. Under any of these alternatives, the movement will decidedly not be in the direction of expanding establishment clause claims but of either curtailing them or leaving them where they presently are.

THE IMPACT OF *SMITH*, *ALLEGHENY* AND *LEE* ON THE CONSTITUTIONALITY OF THE *GET* LAWS AND *AVITZUR*

Here the conclusions appear to be relatively simple and straightforward. To the extent that the New York *get* laws can be sustained against free exercise attacks based on the compelling secular state interests that they serve,[860] the laws can certainly survive the far less exacting scrutiny in effect after *Smith*. This result follows for one of two reasons. First, since both statutes are phrased in terms of an obligation to remove "barriers to remarriage" rather than deliver a *get*, they are in themselves laws of general applicability which, under *Smith*, need no longer be justified by reference to a "compelling state interest." Second, even if the *get* laws are viewed as

---

of the government's activity; (3) Kennedy, in essential agreement with the second group, adopts an expanded and expansive definition of "coercion" which may in the future cause him to align himself with the first group (as it did in *Lee*). He is likely to be the "swing vote" in many of the establishment clause cases of the future.

859. For reasons that are not entirely clear and perhaps reflective of the sharp divisions on the Court, the Supreme Court has declined a number of recent opportunities to reexamine the *Lemon* test. See *Doe v. Village of Crestwood*, 917 F.2d 1476 (7th Cir. 1990) (banning the municipal sponsorship of a Catholic Mass as part of an Italian-American festival); *Roberts v. Madigan*, 921 F.2d 1047 (10th Cir. 1990) (upholding the banning of a Bible from a fifth grade classroom); *Cammack v. Waihee*, 932 F.2d 765 (9th Cir. 1991) (upholding a state statute that designates Good Friday as a legal holiday); *Harris v. City of Zion*, 927 F.2d 1401 (7th Cir. 1991), *petition for cert. sub nom. Rolling Meadows v. Kuhn* (upholding the use of Christian symbols as part of a municipal seal). Petitions for *certiorari* (Supreme Court review) were filed in all those cases and *certiorari* was denied. See 60 UNITED STATES LAW WEEK 3878 (June 29, 1992).

860. See *supra* text following note 588. As noted *supra* text at notes 645-655, these arguments (and the ones presented below pertaining to the establishment clause) apply with equal force to the more recent amendment to DRL §236B.

specifically targeted to the problem of the Jewish *agunah* (which is indeed their primary purpose) and thus would not be directly protected under the *Smith* analysis, the "compelling state interests" that they serve as well as the fairly attenuated "free exercise" claims that can be raised in opposition,[861] should continue to immunize the laws from constitutional attack. While *Smith* may have removed the "compelling state interest" test as a basis for evaluating general law, it should not be read to preclude the use of a such a test to validate laws that do not fit the *Smith* rubric. After all, *Smith*'s abandonment of *Sherbert* was designed to curtail free exercise claims, not expand them.

By the same token, to the extent that the laws further legitimate state interests of a secular nature and do not endorse or advance the cause of religion but simply level the playing field by removing a disability that is peculiar to a particular religious class,[862] the statutes pass muster not only under *Lemon* but under any probable alternative test that the Supreme Court is likely to adopt. The same is true for *get* covenants and *Avitzur*-type agreements.[863] If these contractual arrangements were sustainable prior to *Smith* and *Allegheny*, they are even more justifiable afterwards. Thus, as frightening as *Smith* and *Allegheny* may be for the advocates of religious liberty, they pose little threat to the particular religious problems addressed in this book.

---

861. *Id.*

862. These points are addressed *supra* text at notes 574-581.

863. Indeed, it is arguable that the application of Kennedy's proselytization test would even validate a "removal of barrier" tort statute. While such a statute may well constitute a "promotion" or "endorsement" of religion, see *supra* text at notes 734-737, it is difficult to see how a narrowly-tailored legislative initiative, applicable in a relatively-small number of cases, induces any type of psychologically-coercive effect on the citizenry to adhere to the tenets of Judaism. It is a close case, however, for although a "removal of barrier" tort statute may not constitute "proselytization" for Judaism as a whole, it does directly coerce a recalcitrant spouse to comply with a Jewish ceremony or ritual. Thus, the same objections that I raised earlier under the O'Connor test, see *supra* text at notes 734-737, could indeed continue to apply even under the Kennedy formulation.

Conclusion

This book has endeavored to trace the various legal and *halachic* avenues that women unable to obtain *gittin* by conventional means might be able to pursue. Within the exclusive framework of *halacha*, a number of possibilities present themselves. Women have always had access to the *bait din* system in securing a court order directing their husbands to give them a *get* and under certain circumstances this order could be enforced by imprisonment, fines, or corporal punishment. At least some sources would construe women's right of access quite expansively, effectively granting them the right to obtain a divorce at will. Wholly apart from the *halachic* problems inherent in such a position, this approach accomplishes little or nothing in societies like the United States where rabbinical courts possess no coercive powers. The *halachic* power of a *bait din* to incarcerate a husband for his failure to grant a *get* has no meaning under a system where a *bait din* has no power to imprison at all. In a sense, the *agunah* crisis does not stem from any limitations internal to the *halachic* system itself but from the interaction of that system with the non-*halachic* societal structure within which it attempts to operate.

Other "pure" *halachic* responses are even less promising; the conditional marriage, rabbinical annulment, "divorce-in-advance," and reinstitution of concubinage pose social and *halachic* problems of such magnitude that their potential harms exceed the modest benefits they may yield. A possible approach at least in some cases is to dispense with a *get* on the grounds that the underlying marriage is invalid. At best, however, this approach works only in cases of civil or other non-*halachic* marriage and not where the original ceremony complied with all Jewish law requirements. Unfortunately, it is precisely in the latter instance that the *agunah* situation is most prevalent.

On the secular side of the coin, there is ample case law authority that would enforce via an order of specific performance agreements to give a *get* or to submit to the jurisdiction of a rabbinic tribunal. Even those parties not having the foresight to enter into explicit prenuptial agreements may be able to invoke the terms of the traditional *ketubah* to accomplish the same thing. In the absence of contract, aggrieved parties may be able to invoke theories of tort law, though to date that response has not proven very successful. Whether any of these legal solutions are truly adequate depends on an intricate analysis of *halacha* to insure that a resulting *get* is not valid by reason of its being coerced. The divergent opinions among *halachic* schools, the lack of any apparent forum through which *halachic* authorities could provide comprehensive, consistent input to the secular judiciary, and the constitutional limitations of the establishment clause all mean that courts are ill-equipped to engage in this type of comprehensive analysis. In its absence, however, reliance on contract or tort law alone could be fatal to the validity of the *get*. Extreme caution must be employed to insure that judicial solicitude for victimized wives does not engender a "cure" worse than the "illness". Finally, technical devices such as antenuptial support agreements or promissory notes coupled with conditional releases seem to present the fewest *halachic* dilemmas and offer significant and widespread potential for relief, at least for those parties that have the foresight to utilize them. Rabbis should encourage their congregants to employ these expedients and hopefully they will come into common use.

The story of the *agunah* and the responses she elicits is instructive on many levels. From a sociological perspective, it illustrates in a tragic and graphic way the consequences of family breakdown and disintegration so prevalent in the latter-half of the 20th Century, a phenomenon from which even the traditionally strong and cohesive Jewish family has not been immune. It shows us once again the abuses to which religious law can be put. It demonstrates the creative potentialities of *halacha* in dealing with Jewish law in a manner that is faithful to its traditions and sources but at the same time responsive to human suffering and pain, a dual approach that is the hallmark of all outstanding rabbinic decisors. It provides us with a case history of a collaboration between religion and the political process (N.Y. DRL §253 and the more recent amendment to §236B) with all the dangers such collaboration entails and illustrates the possibilities of utilizing the secular legal system to assist religiously-disadvantaged persons. This type of political-legal-religious mixing raises uneasy and disturbing questions about the risks that such interaction poses both for the neutrality of the state and the autonomy and spiritual integrity of the religious system. Enlisting the state on the side of "religion" may be a double-edged sword with short-term victories not necessarily justifying the potential long-term costs. How the legal system responds to the *agunah* problem presents these great issues in a microcosm.

As a final observation, it may be noted that the ability of any legal system to eradicate social evils, particularly those arising in a family setting, is quite limited. A legal or even religious system can cajole, threaten, punish, exhort but cannot really stop antisocial or immoral acts. As long as some people try to wrongfully take advantage of the disabilities, vulnerabilities, and weaknesses of others, there will be women who will be *agunot* just as there will be victims of other blackmailers and extortionists. A long-term resolution of this issue would involve premarital and family counselling, educating couples to constructively deal with tensions and to recognize that even a divorce need not be the occasion for the wanton infliction of pain. Problems arising from dysfunctional human relationships can ultimately be addressed only through attempts to transform those relationships.[864] The Jewish community bears a serious responsibility to do more.

---

864. A recent and pioneering effort to address some of these psychosocial concerns is Bulka, JEWISH DIVORCE ETHICS: THE RIGHT WAY TO SAY GOODBYE (1992). The author is both an ordained rabbi and a clinical psychologist.

Failing the attainment of utopia, however, the legal system can be a useful adjunct to assist Orthodox women in attaining the freedom they need to start their lives anew. Hopefully, religious leaders will have the courage to be willing to enlist it.

Appendixes

*Please note that unless otherwise indicated, all footnote references to prior text, *e.g.*, "see *supra* text at note 45," are to the main body of the text. Cross-references to other parts of the appendixes will so indicate, *e.g.*, "see *supra* Appendix A, text at note 45."

A

The *Ketubah*: Translation, Commentary, and History

TRANSLATION OF STANDARD *KETUBAH*[1] (Orthodox)

The *ketubah* ["writing"] is a standard document written in Aramaic setting out the obligations of a husband towards his wife. It may or may not be accompanied with a translation or a paraphrase. Dating from before the Common Era, its purpose was to create disincentives for the husband's exercising what was originally his unilateral power of divorce. The Conservative movement utilizes a slightly different text while the Reform movement does not use a *ketubah* at all (though the bridal couple may have one if they wish). The *ketubah* is executed and signed by two witnesses immediately before the wedding ceremony and remains property of the wife. Preprinted *ketubot* (Hebrew plural form of *ketubah*) may be obtained at Jewish bookstores with spaces left blank for names, places, and dates. The *ketubah* is also publicly read at the wedding ceremony though usually left untranslated so that few in the audience know what they are hearing. The standard text is as follows:

> On the____[2] day of the week, the ____ day of the month of ____ in the year ____ since the creation of the world according to the manner of reckoning here in the ______, the groom ______[3] the son of ____

1. The translation is based on Horowitz, THE SPIRIT OF JEWISH LAW, pp. 309-310, with significant modifications. The annotations are my own.

2. These blanks indicate time and place. The months used are the lunar months of the Jewish calendar. The years are counted from the traditional date ascribed to the creation of the world. September 1990-Sept. 1991 corresponds to 5751.

3. Historically, the bride and groom were not identified by family name but by parentage, *e.g.*, Paul son of John marries Esther daughter of Henry. Some modern rabbinical authorities favor the use of last names and this innovation will occasionally be encountered though I have not seen it employed in a *get*. See Bleich, I CONTEMPORARY HALAKHIC PROBLEMS, pp.

said to the virgin ___ daughter of _________:

"Be thou my wife in accordance with the law of Moses and Israel and I will work, honor, support, and maintain thee in accordance with the practices of Jewish husbands who work, honor, support, and maintain their wives in faithfulness. And I will give thee 200 *zuz* as alimony for thy virginity which is due to thee under the law of the Torah[4] as well as food, clothing, needs, and cohabitation according to the way of the world."

This virgin _____[5] daughter of ____ consented and became his wife. The dowry that she brought from her father's home in silver, gold, ornaments, clothing, household furnishings, and her clothes amounting in all to the value of _____, the groom has taken upon himself.[6] The groom has also consented to match the above sum by adding the sum of _____[7] making a total in all of _____.[8] Thus, did the groom _____[9] son of _____ declare:

"I hereby accept upon myself and my heirs the responsibility of this *ketubah* document, the dowry, and the addition, that it shall be paid from all my property and possessions, wherever located, that I now possess or that I will acquire in the future. All my property, even the shirt on my shoulders,

---

147-148. The reference to "virgin" tracks the fact that the statutory minimum amount in the *ketubah* depends on whether the woman has been previously married. The term would be deleted and the amounts halved if she were.

4. The amount of 200 *zuz* is the statutory minimum alimony sum that is payable to a wife who was married as a virgin bride in the event of divorce or husband's death. A *zuz* was a small silver coin used in Palestine and Babylonia during the Talmudic period. Its present value is discussed *infra* Appendix A, notes 26-35. If the woman is not a virgin, the minimum amount is halved to 100 *zuz*.

5. See *supra* Appendix A, note 3.

6. In addition to alimony, the groom now agrees to reimburse his bride for the value of all assets she is bringing into the marriage. In theory, this sum should vary with each case and can be the subject of negotiation between parties. In practice, most *ketubot* executed outside of the State of Israel stipulate a standard amount - 100 *zakuk*, a now-defunct currency. Its present value is discussed *infra* Appendix A, notes 26-35. In Israel, *ketubot* often do state the actual value of assets brought in since the stated sum is commonly employed as the basis for a post-dissolution property settlement.

7. In addition to the statutory minimum and dowry, a husband could voluntarily stipulate some additional amount. This amount is called *tosefet*. Again, in theory, the amount of *tosefet*, if any, could vary from case to case. Nevertheless, as a matter of common practice, a standard sum is stipulated - 100 silver *zakuk*, the same as the dowry commitment.

8. The total includes the dowry commitment and the *tosefet* (a total of 200 *zakuk*), which is *in addition* to the earlier stipulated amount of 200 *zuz*. See DERISHA, comments to TUR E.H. 66:3. *Contra*: BAYIT CHADASH, comments to TUR E.H. 66 (sum of 200 *zakuk* includes the 200 *zuz*).

9. See *supra* Appendix A, note 3.

shall be security for and subject to this *ketubah* document, this dowry, and the addition in my lifetime and after my death, forever more."[10]

The responsibility of this *ketubah* document, the dowry, and the addition did the groom take upon himself with the full force and effect of all *ketubah* documents and their additions as is customarily practiced for the benefit of Jewish women and in accordance with the enactments of the Sages (may their memory be a blessing) not as a void penalty nor as a mere form.[11]

And this groom has received in our presence good and valuable consideration[12] to bind himself in accordance with all that is stated above and all is binding and irrevocable.

The words of ____[13]

The words of ____

Additional clause of the Conservative *ketubah* approved by the Rabbinical Assembly in 1954:

We, the bride and groom. . . .hereby agree to recognize the *bait din* of the Rabbinical Assembly and the Jewish Theological Seminary of America or its duly appointed representatives as having authority to counsel us in the light of Jewish tradition which requires husband and wife to give each other complete love and devotion, and to summon either party at the request of the other, in order to enable the party so requesting to live in accordance with the standards of the Jewish law of marriage throughout his or her lifetime. We authorize the *bait din* to impose such terms of compensation as it may see fit for failure to

---

10. To insure the ultimate collectibility of the *ketubah* - the statutory minimum, dowry, and addition - the groom agrees that its obligations constitute a lien and mortgage on all property presently owned or to be acquired in the future. It is generally a first mortgage against the estate.

11. As discussed supra text at notes 306-309, penalty clauses are generally *halachically* invalid. The recital that the *ketubah* is not a penalty clause is a formal declaration of validity, a formula that commonly appeared in all *halachic* business documents.

12. Before the witnesses sign the *ketubah*, they or a third party on behalf of the bride must hand him some object of value, even a handkerchief or a pen. This process is termed *kinyan* ("acquisition"). See *supra* note 343. By receiving even nominal consideration, the groom becomes bound to his commitments.

[While *kinyan* is normally not necessary for obligations incurred by a promissory note, see *supra* note 348, because the obligations of the *ketubah* are conditional (on the husband's death or on his divorcing his wife) rather than absolute, a *kinyan* should be employed. See *supra* note 398. Note, however, that, notwithstanding the conditional nature of the *ketubah*, *kinyan* is *not* needed for the obligation to pay 200 *zuz* since that is an obligation directly imposed by *halacha* irrespective of agreement or consideration. The requirement of *kinyan* would be limited to the additional commitments such as *tosefet* and dowry which are both: (1) voluntary and (2) conditional.]

13. Two witnesses must sign the *ketubah*. The bride and the groom need not sign though they may.

respond to its summons or to carry out its decision.[14]

HISTORICAL EVOLUTION OF THE *KETUBAH*

The custom of a groom's stipulating in advance a sum of money payable to his wife in the event of a divorce is of ancient lineage.[15] The Bible itself mentions the custom of providing the virgin with "*mohar*," a term understood as a form of post-dissolution alimony, though it does not indicate that such provision is mandatory.[16] Indeed, the consensus of most *halachic* authorities is that the obligatory force of the *ketubah* is Talmudic, rather than Biblical in nature, though there are opinions to the contrary.[17]

---

14. As previously discussed, *Avitzur v. Avitzur*, 446 N.E. 2d 136 (N.Y. 1983) held that this portion of the *ketubah* was essentially an enforceable agreement to submit disputes to arbitration. *Supra* text at notes 275-282.

15. See generally Agus, *The Development of the Money Clause in the Ashkenazic Ketubah*, 30 JEWISH QUARTERLY REVIEW 221 (1938-1940) for a superb historical treatment.

16. See GENESIS 34:12 (Shechem son of Chamor, after forcibly seizing Jacob's daughter Dinah, requests Jacob for her hand and states "You may impose upon me "*mohar*" and I shall give it"); EXODUS 22:16 ("If a man entices a virgin to lie with him, he must pay to her father a sum equal to the *virgin's dowry* [*mohar*]". Moreover, DEUTERONOMY 22:29 defines this sum as being 50 shekels which translates to 200 *zuz* or *dinar*, a *zuz* and *dinar* being equivalent. Note that in *none* of these places is the *mohar* spoken as something that *must* be provided; the text simply makes reference to an institution that was commonly employed and uses it to determine other statutory obligations, *i.e.*, the fine payable for raping or enticing a minor.

An even more explicit reference to the *ketubah* appears in the Book of Tobit in the Apocrypha, authored around 130 b.c.e. At the marriage of Tobit and Sarah, "they took paper, wrote a contract and signed it; then they began to eat." BOOK OF TOBIT 7:14. In the original Greek, the word for contract is *syggraphon* which means "that which is written," a literal translation of the word "*ketubah.*" See Kahana, SEFARIM CHITZONIM (Studies in the Apocrypha).

17. Most authorities rule that the obligation of *ketubah* is post-Biblical. See Rambam, MISHNA TORAH, *Hilchot Ishut* 10:7; CHELKAT MECHOKEK E.H. 66:6(26); BAIT SHMUEL E.H. 66:6(14). There are, however, a number of opinions that consider the *ketubah* to be of Biblical origin, at least in the case of a virgin marriage and indeed the very text of the *ketubah* supports this view. See TOSAFOT, T.B. KETUBOT 10a, *s.v. Amar*; TOSAFOT, YEBAMOT 89a, *s.v. Taamah*; SEFER MITZVOT GADOL, Positive Commandment 48. Some maintain that even the *ketubah* of a woman previously widowed is Biblically mandated. See gloss of R. Yaakov Emden to KETUBOT 56b. (The text of the *ketubah*, however, denominates the alimony of a previously-married woman as merely rabbinic.) Yet a fourth school of thought maintains that while *some ketubah* is Biblically required, the exact amount (200 *zuz* or 100 for a nonvirgin) was fixed by rabbinic legislation. See CHIDUSHAI HaRASHBA to T.B. KETUBOT 110b, *s.v. Nasa* and NACHALAT SHIVA 12:32(3).

Whatever the origin of the *ketubah*, it did not originally require a writing nor did its obligations give rise to a lien or mortgage on the husband's assets. The first *ketubot* seem to have involved some sort of prepayment or escrow that would be released to the wife in the event of divorce or widowhood.[18] Since this would afford the wife no protection if the specific property or funds were lost or dissipated, the Sanhedrin under the leadership of Shimon Ben Shetach enacted that the *ketubah* debt created a lien on all of the husband's presently owned and after-acquired property, a lien that is enforceable against the heirs of the estate, subsequent purchasers, and other creditors.[19] According to many opinions, the requirement of a writing dates from this period although the custom of a formal writing existed much earlier.[20] Under Talmudic law, this lien was limited to real estate as is true for virtually all liens[21]; by post-Talmudic enactment, the *ketubah* lien was extended to personal property as well and this is reflected in the text of the *ketubah*.[22]

While the original purpose of the *ketubah* was simply to provide a divorced or widowed wife with some modicum of financial security at a time and in a society where unattached women had few opportunities for economic advancement, it later acquired an additional purpose: to make it more difficult for a man to divorce his wife. By making divorce a costly proposition, the *ketubah* was thought to promote marital stability.[23] Although the later *takkana* of R. Gershom took away the husband's unconditional right to divorce his wife, a *ketubah* is nevertheless required.[24] Indeed, without a *ketubah* a husband and wife are not permitted to cohabit under the same roof and, if the *ketubah* was lost, a new one must be executed immediately.[25]

---

18. See T.B. KETUBOT 82b.

19. Id. This enactment was made in approximately 100 b.c.e., in the waning years of the Second Temple era.

20. See TOSEFTA KETUBOT 12:1.

21. The general rule is stated many times in the Talmud. See, for example, T.B. KIDDUSHIN 26a and KETUBOT 95b. The rule excluding personalty applies only to liens asserted against transferred property, *e.g.*, the debtor died or sold his property to a third party. With respect to enforcing a claim against the debtor himself, personalty and realty are treated alike though Jewish law does recognize some exemptions. See T.B. BABA METZIA 113b and SHULCHAN ARUCH H.M. 97:23.

22. This was a post-Talmudic enactment of the Gaonim. The probable date of the *takkana* was 784 c.e. and the chief promulgator was R. Huna Mar HaLevi son of R. Yitzchok. See IGGERET R. SHERIRA GAON (Levin ed.), p. 105. See also ROSH, KIDDUSHIN 3:14.

23. See T.B. KETUBOT 10a. Note that, in its original form, the *ketubah* could not have served this purpose. To the extent the *ketubah* took the form of an escrow or prepayment, there was no disincentive to divorce since the husband lost the use of the funds as soon as he married. It was only with the advent of Shimon Ben Shetach and the creation of the lien (which replaced the escrow) that the *ketubah* assumed its additional function of deterring divorce.

24. SHULCHAN ARUCH E.H. 66:3 (Rema).

25. See T.B. KETUBOT 56a. The text for a replacement *ketubah* is found in NACHALAT SHIVA, Chapter 13.

THE AMOUNT OF MONEY IN THE *KETUBAH*

The "dowry of the virgins" mentioned in the Bible is stated as fifty *shekels* or 200 *zuz* or *dinar*.[26] This is the sum that is currently stipulated in the standard Orthodox *ketubah*. (The sum is halved if the woman was previously married.) How this amount translates into dollars is uncertain.[27] One method of conversion would be to determine the purchasing power of 200 *zuz* in Talmudic times and ascertain the dollar amount that could buy the same quantity of goods or services today. For a variety of reasons, this method has not been employed.[28] What is done is to take the metallic content of the ancient *zuz* and pay whatever its going market rate happens to be. The *zuz* was a silver coin that contained approximately .2 ounces of pure silver. Two hundred *zuz* therefore equals forty ounces of silver. Irrespective of what such a sum could buy in Talmudic times,[29] the husband need only pay the dollar value of that quantity of silver (whatever it happens to be on the date a demand for payment is made).[30] Since the present value of silver is only around $8 per ounce, the *ketubah* requires only the relatively paltry sum of $320 ($160 for a widow).[31]

---

26. See EXODUS 22:16 (comments of Rashi), DEUTERONOMY 22:29, and *supra* Appendix A, note 16.

27. As will be evident from the following discussion, there is a tremendous diversity of views regarding the appropriate valuation of the *ketubah*. See *infra* Appendix A, notes 31 and 33. This surprising lack of uniformity regarding such a basic question as the value of a *ketubah* may be attributable to three factors: (1) the geographic dispersal of Jewish communities, enabling each community to formulate its own standards, particularly with respect to *tosefet* and dowry; (2) the comparative rarity, at least in modern times, of *ketubot* actually being enforced with the result that, as a practical matter, consensus did not have to emerge; and (3) the existence of explicit prenuptial or separation agreements that spell out with greater specificity (and often to the exclusion of the *ketubah*) what the rights and obligations of the parties are, making a construction of the *ketubah* superfluous. Whether the preemption of a *ketubah* via a subsequent agreement is *halachically* proper is another matter. See *supra* Appendix A, text at note 25.

28. See Benish, MIDOT U'SHIUREI TORAH, pp. 398-405 (who discusses the possibility of conversion based on equivalence of purchasing power but concludes that this is not the generally-accepted *halachic* practice).

29. Evidence indicates this was fairly considerable. See S.R. Hirsch, COMMENTARY ON THE TORAH, Exodus 22:16.

30. See SHULCHAN ARUCH E.H. 100:5 and comment of BAIT SHMUEL E.H. 100:5(25) (discussion concerning in which currency a *ketubah* must be paid where the place of divorce is different than the place of marriage; currency must in all cases be equal to 200 *zuz* on the date of demand).

31. See Kaplan, MADE IN HEAVEN, p. 113. The figure in the text is based on the prevailing Ashkenazic practice; the Sefardic *ketubah*, although containing the same total of 200 *zuz* would be computed at only one-eighth of the amount because of a differing definition of *zuz*.

As noted, the calculation in the text is based on a total silver weight of 40 ounces for 200 *zuz* which is equivalent to .2 ounces of silver per *zuz*. Other authorities calculate the total weight of silver in 200 *zuz* to be as little as

Note, however, that because the *ketubah* does not express its sums in dollars but in *zuz*, it is impossible to know at the time of the marriage what the dollar obligations of the *ketubah* will be.

The *ketubah* mentions additional sums of money for the restoration of property that a wife brought to the marriage ["dowry"] and for a *tosefet* ["additional sum"] on that dowry. Here, however, it speaks not of 200 *zuz* but of 200 *zakuk* (100 for dowry, 100 for *tosefet*; for a woman previously married, these amounts are halved). Unlike the *zuz*, which is a well known Talmudic coin and measure of weight, *zakuk* is not a *halachic* term nor does its usage date from Talmudic times. Rather it was a term used by Jewish communities in Europe at various points in the Middle Ages to describe a certain coin that was in common circulation at the time. Most have identified it with the

---

87.5 grams which is approximately 2.8 ounces (.014 ounce per *zuz*), a weight which translates into a pitiful $20. There are also numerous views in between these extremes though none of these amounts is monetarily significant in this day and age. See generally Adler, NISUIN K'HILCHATAM, p. 306; Reich, MESORET HaSHEKEL, p. 119; Benish, MIDOT U'SHIUREI TORAH, pp. 492-502; and CHAZON ISH E.H. 66:21.

The essence of the dispute focuses on two basic questions, one empirical and one *halachic*. Empirically, there is disagreement concerning the exact weight of the *zuz*. *Halachically*, there is an uncertainty whether the *ketuba* utilizes the *zuz* known as *kesef tzuri* (literally, "Phoenician money") or *kesef medinah* ("standard money"). While both *zuzim* were the same weight, *kesef tzuri* was pure silver while *kesef medinah* contained one part silver to seven parts copper. Thus, the silver content of a *zuz* of *kesef tzuri* was eight times that of *kesef medinah*.

The most lenient view of *ketubah* assumes the weight of a *zuz* to be only .112 ounces and utilizes only the silver content of *kesef medinah*. Per *zuz*, this results in a silver content of only .014 ounces. Multiplied by 200, this yields the paltry quantity of 2.8 ounces of silver. The strictest view calculates the weight of the *zuz* to be .2 ounces and utilizes the 100% silver content of *kesef tzuri*. Multiplied by 200, this yields a total silver content of 40 ounces. Obviously, there can be, and indeed are, any number of permutations in between. One could, for example, assume a high weight for the *zuz* but utilize *kesef medinah*; conversely, one could assume a lower weight for the *zuz* but utilize *kesef tzuri*.

The argument whether *ketubah* is measured in *kesef tzuri* or the less expensive *kesef medinah* depends in turn on whether the *ketubah* obligations are mandated Biblically (in which case higher values must be used) or are later rabbinic enactments. See *supra* Appendix A, note 17. The Sefardic view is that the 200 *zuz* of the *ketubah* is calculated based on the silver content of *kesef medinah* (which is equivalent to only 25 *zuz* of *kesef tzuri*). See Rambam, MISHNA TORAH, *Hilchot Ishut* 10:8 and SHULCHAN ARUCH E.H. 66:6. The Ashkenazic view, however, is that the 200 *zuz* must be *kesef tzuri*, eight times the amount of silver present in *kesef medinah*. See Rema, comment to SHULCHAN ARUCH E.H. 66:6. The calculation in the text follows the Ashkenazic view and utilizes the highest assigned weight for a *zuz*. (Note, however, that although the Sefardic *ketubah*'s statutory minimum is only one-eighth that of the Ashkenazic *ketubah*, the *tosefet* may be considerably greater. See *infra* Appendix A, note 34).

German, French, or British Pound.[32] In light of this uncertainty, one *zakuk* contains between .8 and 1.5 silver ounces of pure silver. Multiplying those figures by 200, we get a total of between 160 and 300 ounces of silver which at $8 an ounce yields between $1280 and $2400. Again, a not very significant amount.[33]

There is nothing, however, that prevents the parties from stipulating much higher amounts and among Sefardic communities adding exorbitant sums in the tens of thousands is fairly common.[34] Ashkenazic communities tend to execute the standard form. As a practical matter, then, in view of the minimal recovery, the *ketubah* is normally not regarded as a significant basis for alimony protection and its enforcement is rarely sought.[35]

---

32. For a discussion of the historical complexities in determining weight and currency conversion, see Reich, MESORET HaSHEKEL especially pp. 17-50; NACHALAT SHIVA 12:49(2); BAIT SHMUEL E.H. 66:6(15); EDUT L'YISRAEL (Henkin), p. 143; BIUR HaGRA, Y.D. 305:1(4) and E.H. 66:6(22).

33. As noted, the *zakuk* was not a coin of Talmudic usage but was a rabbinic term for a coin in use during the Middle Ages. While Kaplan, MADE IN HEAVEN, p. 113, calculates 200 *zakuk* to be no more than 160-300 ounces of silver, other authorities place the figure at a much higher amount. See CHAZON ISH E.H. 61:21 (57,600 grams which is approximately 1858 ounces) and IGROT MOSHE E.H. IV, no. 91 (100 pounds = 1600 ounces). (According to these views, 200 *zakuk* may indeed be a considerable amount of money that may discourage hasty divorce, as the *ketubah* was intended to do.) Still others would calculate it to be as low as 3846 grams (approximately 124 ounces). See Adler, NISUIN K'HILCHATAM, p. 306 who claims that this latter figure is the standard employed by the rabbinical courts in Israel.

The disagreement concerning the valuation of the 200 *zakuk* is *not* based on the same considerations surrounding the valuation of the 200 *zuz*. See *supra* Appendix A, note 31. Since the *zakuk* is not a Talmudic coin, the issue of *kesef tzuri* v. *kesef medinah* - which were two types of currency prevalent during Talmudic times - does not arise. Rather the uncertainty stems, first, from not knowing the precise identity or weight of the coin in question and, second, from not knowing whether the *zakuk* is being employed as weight or as a unit of currency and, if the latter, how it is to be translated into current values. For a superb historical and analytical treatment, see Benish, MIDOT U'SHIUREI TORAH, pp. 471-486 and pp. 492-502. The calculation in the text follows the simpler assumption that the *zakuk* is functioning as weight, obligating the husband to pay a sum of dollars that could purchase the quantity of silver contained in the 200 *zakuk*.

34. One of the reasons this is so stems from the fact that Sefardic communities never formally accepted R. Gershom's ban against unilateral divorce. See *supra* text at note 32. Accordingly, greater precautions had to be taken to insure that the husband would not abuse his preferential position. Interestingly, it is precisely in the Sefardic communities where the statutory minimum of the *ketubah* is lowest, see *supra* Appendix A, note 31.

35. Cognizant of the fact that the sum of money in the *ketubah* is fairly paltry and does not serve its intended purpose of dissuading divorce, the Israeli Chief Rabbinate periodically issues directives to incorporate higher sums in *ketubot*. See, for example, their decree of 1944 (predating the establishment

of the State of Israel) reprinted as Appendix A to Shareshevsky, DINAI MISHPACHA, pp. 427-430 (Rabbis Herzog and Uziel). The impact of these decrees, however, may be fairly minimal. First, these "cost-of-living" raises have not kept up with inflation. Second, these directives are not binding on communities outside of Israel. Finally, many Orthodox Jews even in Israel do not acknowledge the religious authority of the Chief Rabbinate and do not incorporate these larger sums into the *ketubah*. (It is arguable that, for purposes of civil enforcement by Israeli courts, the Rabbinate's stipulated amount would be controlling even if such larger amount were omitted; see paragraph one of the 1944 Decree. Once again, however, many of the most Orthodox Israelis do not utilize the secular court system. See *supra* note 45.)

B

Property Rights of Divorced Spouses under *Halacha*

Under traditional *halacha*, the property rights of married women fell into four categories:

First, earnings that the wife generated during the course of her marriage belong to her husband outright in the event she elects to hold the husband responsible for her support. If she waives her right of marital support, she may keep her earnings. This would normally occur if the wife's earnings exceed whatever support her husband is able to afford.

Second, property that she inherits before or during the marriage or any other premarital assets, whether acquired by gifts or earnings, normally belong to the wife but the husband has the right to use and manage the property for the duration of the marriage. In the terminology of the Talmud, she owns the "principal" but husband gets the "fruits." If, for example, she brings into the marriage a field, husband gets the benefit of the crop; if an apartment building, husband gets rentals; if bank accounts, husband gets interest. If the property is a non-income yielding asset, the husband has the right to convert it into an income-yielding form. In all cases, his managerial decisions must be exercised in a manner that does not impair the value of the principal. Upon termination of the marriage, wife takes the property *in specie*, getting the benefit of appreciation but assuming the risk of loss. Neither party can alienate the property during the marriage without the consent of the other. This property is termed *nichsai melog* ["property of plucking"], by analogy to a chicken where one party owns the chicken but the other may pluck the feathers or get the eggs.

Third, by special agreement, *premarital* property may be assigned a specific monetary value. Husband owns the property outright and may alienate it without the wife's consent but upon termination of the marriage, will pay the designated sum irrespective of the current value of the property. Basically a sale with deferred payment of purchase price, this arrangement leaves the husband with risk of loss but also the benefits of appreciation. This alternative system is termed *nichsai tzon barzel* ["property of iron sheep"] for it gives the wife an "iron-clad" guarantee of a specified sum of money enforceable by a general lien on all the husband's assets. The designation of this sum normally appears in the *ketubah* and, in the standard text, the amount is uniform [100 *zakuk*]. By contrast, a wife's entitlement to *nichsai melog* is *outside* of the *ketubah*.

Finally, gifts of clothing, jewelry, or other items that a husband gives a wife during the course of their marriage are normally the wife's exclusive property.

All of these arrangements may be varied by contrary agreement. Thus, while none of the *halachic* categories enumerated above correspond to joint tenancies or tenancies by the entirety, *halacha* would validate such interests once created by the parties.[36]

36. For additional information concerning marital property rights under Jewish law, see Engel, *Marital Property Rights in Jewish Law: A Survey and Comparison*, 2 NATIONAL JEWISH LAW REVIEW 97 (1987) and Shareshevsky, DINAI MISHPACHA, pp. 152-179. Both authors point out a number of changes introduced by various communities over the years departing from the strict Talmudic model.

C

The *Get* and Its Moslem Analogue

TRANSLATION OF STANDARD *GET* (ORTHODOX) WITH ANNOTATED COMMENTARY

The *get* [a term meaning "document"] is a written bill of divorce that a husband or his agent must physically hand over to his wife or her agent in the presence of witnesses.[37] Unlike the *ketubah*, the entire document must be handwritten for the particular divorce for which it is being used.[38] As a matter of practice, after receipt, the original *get* is normally returned to the *bait din* which keeps it in its records and the wife is simply given a document which states that she is now *halachically* free to remarry. The document, however, is not a *get* but simply evidence of her having received a *get*.[39]

While the Torah requires that a divorce be effected exclusively through a writing, it does not indicate the particular form such writing must take.[40]

---

37. The requirement of witnesses at the time of the *get*'s delivery is totally independent of the separate requirement that the *get* be signed by witnesses *before* it is delivered. The former is generally understood to be Biblical in nature while the latter is a purely rabbinic enactment. See *infra* Appendix C, note 58.

38. See Rambam, MISHNA TORAH, *Hilchot Gerushin* 1:5.

39. The Reform movement does not require a *get* if a civil divorce has been obtained. See Freehof, REFORM JEWISH PRACTICE, pp. 99-110. Many Reform rabbis do encourage their congregants to obtain one to avoid interdenominational complications. See *supra* note 305.

40. See, however, Rambam, MISHNA TORAH, *Hilchot Gerushin* 1:4 who rules, based on Talmudic sources, that while no specific text is mandated, the language must communicate the idea of the woman's being freed of her bond to her husband, rather than vice-versa. Thus, language along the lines of "I am no longer your husband," where the giver of the *get* seems to be removing himself from *her* domain, is invalid as a matter of Torah law. This is based on the Torah's description of divorce as "sending her out of his house" rather than "sending himself out of hers." But see *infra* Appendix C, note 51 (discussing the fact that language in the *get* may not meet this requirement).

Indeed, according to the Mishna,[41] even a one-line statement, "Behold, you are permitted to all men" would suffice and there is no need for the statement to be written in Hebrew.[42] Nevertheless, it has become a universal practice among *halachically*-observant Jews for *gittin* to be written in Aramaic (with a smattering of Hebrew) and to follow a standardized format.[43]

For reasons that are not entirely clear,[44] the style of the *get* differs from that of the *ketubah*. The *ketubah* is a document containing the recitation or testimony of witnesses as to what a third party, *i.e.*, the husband, said or did in their presence. The narrative voice is that of the disinterested outsider. By contrast, the *get* is a first-person direct communication even though its authenticity is verified by the signatures of two witnesses. Thus, while the *ketubah* essentially reads: "We the undersigned witnesses hereby testify that the husband assumed in our presence certain obligations" (and even quotes what the husband said), the *get* is a direct declaration: "I, John Doe, hereby permit my wife to remarry."

The text upon which this translation is based is the one quoted in *Piskai Rosh* at the end of Tractate *Gittin*. Other authorities, *e.g.*, Rambam, have slightly different wordings or sequences.[45] For the most part, these differences do not affect the validity of the *get* one way or the other and the major variations will be noted below. The translation itself is my own. There is actually considerable disagreement among *halachic* authorities as to the exact meaning of the terms in a *get*.[46] In view of this somewhat surprising controversy, the present translation should not be regarded as definitive.

---

41. T.B. GITTIN 85a-85b. The permissive view cited in the text is codified by Rambam, MISHNA TORAH, *Hilchot Gerushin* 1:4 and by SHULCHAN ARUCH E.H. 156:41. There is another opinion in the Mishna that is a bit more restrictive in requiring the insertion of additional terminology indicating that the transfer of the document is the actual mechanism of dissolution and is not merely confirmatory or evidentiary of dissolution taking place. While our standard *get* does indeed incorporate this extra language, its omission will not invalidate the *get*.

42. Rambam, MISHNA TORAH, *Hilchot Gerushin* 4:11.

43. *Id.*

44. Presumably, these stem from the need of the husband to be the one consummating the act of divorce which includes being the active voice behind the document. It is he who effectively writes the *get* even if, as is common, he designates a scribe as his agent. See comment of SHILTAI GIBBORIM to RIF, GITTIN 45b (Vilna ed.).

45. *Cf.* the text at end of PISKAI ROSH with that in Rambam, MISHNA TORAH, *Hilchot Gerushin* 4:11.

46. See, for example, the lengthy symposium in 9 NOAM 1-192 (1966-1967) containing contributions by Rabbis Kasher (1-31); Zevin (32-46); Unterman (47-48); Nissim (49-50); Hutner (51-56); Feinstein (57-60); and others. See also *infra* Appendix C, note 51.

On the _____[47] day of the week, the ____ day of the month ___ in the year ____ since the creation of the world according to the calendar reckoning we are accustomed to count here in the city ____ situated on the River ____, I ____[48] son of _____ [who stands this day in the city ____[49] situated on the River _____] [together with all other

---

47. See *supra* Appendix A, note 2. Because each *get* must be custom-written for the particular occasion, the *Shulchan Aruch* requires that it be extremely specific about the city in which it is being executed; writing "Baltimore", for example, would not be enough for perhaps there are two Baltimores and the *get* that is to be given in Baltimore #1 was in fact written for a couple from Baltimore #2 who fortuitously have the same names (as well as having parents and in-laws with the same names). Thus, some additional identifying information is necessary. Historically, this would be done by specifying the waterway on which the city was located, as in Frankfurt-am-Main or Stratford-on-Avon. The duty for precise specification of location is greater for a *get* than it is for a *ketubah*.

Note that the location to be specified in the *get* is the place at which the witnesses signed, not the place where the scribe composed it. It is conceivable, for example, that a *sofer* (religious scribe) may have composed the *get* in one place but for a variety of reasons the witnesses had to sign the *get* in a different location. According to SHULCHAN ARUCH E.H. 128:1, only the latter location would be included. There is a minority opinion that would require the additional inclusion of the locale at which the *get* was written. To avoid this controversy, it has become customary for the witnesses to be physically present at the writing of the *get* so that the locations of its writing and signing will be identical. *Id.*

According to *all* opinions, there is no need to specify the place of the *get*'s delivery and indeed it is better not to do so since such location may have to be changed subsequent to the *get*'s composition. (In most cases, husband and wife or their agents will in fact be where the *get* is written and delivery will take place immediately after execution. Where spouses are currently residing in different countries, however, it is not uncommon for a *get* to be written and signed in one country and then sent to another.)

48. See *supra* Appendix A, note 3. For the reasons stated in the preceding notes, to insure that the *get* was written specifically for this couple and not for another with an identical name, or at least to prevent the casting of aspersions on such a *get*, the *get* would have to include at this point significant nicknames, diminutives, and the like. Thus, a *get* might read: "Louis who is also known as Lou or Louie son of Robert who is called Bob or Robbie" and Deborah known as Deb or Debbie daughter of Edward known as Teddy, Ted, Ed, or Eddie." Needless to say, ascertaining these variants and transliterating them into Hebrew/Aramaic may be quite a daunting task. Mother's names are commonly not employed in *gittin* or other religio-legal documents.

49. The Mishna in T.B. GITTIN 34b seems on its face to require that the *get* designate not only the place of its execution but also the respective domiciles of the spouses, but *cf.* Rashi, *s.v. Ba'Rishona*. As later interpreted, however, this was taken to refer not to domicile as such but merely to their physical location as of the time of the execution of the *get*. Hence, the wording "who stands this day in the city" rather than "who resides in." See SHULCHAN ARUCH E.H. 128:2. Moreover, this language is included only

names or appellations that I or my place may possess[50]] have desired of my free will, being under no duress, to release [*alt. trans.* - remove, sever], let go, and expel[51] you my wife ____[52] daughter of

---

if the spouses are situated in the same place as the execution of the *get*. *Id*. Thus, the locale filled in at this point will invariably be identical to the locale filled in earlier. If a spouse is not physically present in the city of the *get*, the reference to his/her locale will simply be deleted. The phrase is therefore bracketed.

Interestingly, the text as quoted in Rambam, *Hilchot Gerushin* 4:12 seems to require designation of residence or possibly even place of birth.

50. Rosh, as does Rambam, includes this general catch-all proviso to insure the validity of the *get* in the event some alternative name of the husband or the city was inadvertently omitted. (In point of fact, however, if there is a true omission, such a proviso will often not suffice as it fails to provide the requisite certainty that the *get* was composed for this particular individual, see *supra* Appendix C, note 48.) Rambam at 4:12 adds quite logically "that I or *my father* may possess."

The current custom is not to write such a catch-all phrase but to specify all possible names. See opinion of Rabbeinu Tam, Rambam, and Rashba cited by Rema in SHULCHAN ARUCH E.H. 129:1 as normative. The language is therefore bracketed.

51. The translation of these three verbs which are repeated later in the *get* and utilized as prepositional objects - "book of expulsion," etc. - at the very end (in somewhat different order) has generated a great amount of controversy. See *supra* Appendix C, note 46. The third, *teiruchit* [root- *t'rch*], is the easiest to translate; the root is the Aramaic equivalent of the Hebrew *g'rsh* which means "expel" or "chase away." I have thus translated *sefer teiruchin* as a "book of expulsion."

The first phrase *patrit* [root - *p'tr*] is a bit more difficult. The word *p'tr* is commonly employed in the Talmud in two contexts: one who is exempt from a ritual observance or exonerated in a civil or criminal action is often described as *patur*. The word would therefore suggest a release; discharge; exemption; a freeing of a bond, chain, or restriction. A second usage refers to one who has departed. One who takes leave of his friend is called a *niftar* as is one who dies (and thus, departs from the world.) While people commonly translate *niftar* as one who departs or leaves, the verb form is passive and should be translated as "one who has been removed" or "one who has been discharged." This again suggests that, in the active voice, the verb connotes "removing," "releasing," "discharging." The husband is in effect "releasing" the marital bonds that restrict the freedom of his wife, "exempting" her of all marital responsibilities, and "removing" her from his domain. An alternative interpretation of *patrit* may therefore be "*I remove you*" rather than "*I release you.*" The term *get peturin* at the end of the *get* would correspondingly be rendered either a "document of release" or "document of removal."

It should also be noted that the *Targum Unkelos* to DEUTERONOMY 24:1 translates the Hebrew term "*sefer keritot*" into the Aramaic formula "*get peturin.*" Since *keritot* clearly means "cutting off" or "severing," this suggests yet a third possible meaning for *get peturin*, *i.e.*, a document of severance or cutting-off. In the verb form, *patrit* would mean "I sever" or "I cut you off" (from the marital bond). This too is consistent with the use of the term *p'tr*

> ____ [from the city ____[53] situated on the River____] who has been my wife from time past [together with all other names and appellations that you or your place may possess.[54]] And thus, I release [*alt. trans.* - remove, sever], let go of, and expel you so that you may have permission and authority over yourself to be married to any man you may desire[55] and no one may raise any protest [in my name[56]] against your doing so from this day forward and forever more. Behold, you are permitted to all men. This shall be to you from me a book of expulsion, a letter of letting go, and a document of release [*alt. trans* .- removal, severance][57] in accordance with the law of Moses and Israel.

---

elsewhere. One who is exempt from a ritual commandment is *patur*, cut off or severed, from the obligation. Similarly, one who departs from another's presence may in a sense be viewed as "severed" or "cut-off" from the previously-existing connection. In short, *patrit* can mean: (1) I *release* you; (2) I *remove* you; (3) I *sever* or *cut you off*. While the first translation is the one most commonly employed, the latter two alternatives appear to be *halachically* more acceptable for the reasons stated in the next paragraph.

The second phrase *shavkit* is especially problematical. *Sh'vk* normally connotes abandoning, leaving, forsaking so the natural translation of *shavkit* would be "I leave you." Yet a statement by the husband in a *get* that he is leaving his wife is violative of the *halachic* principle that the man must send his wife away from his domain rather than remove himself from hers. See *supra* Appendix C, note 40. (This is meant, of course, only in a linguistic sense. *Halacha* does not care which one of the parties gets to keep the family residence.) The alternative adopted here, "let go," is somewhat less objectionable as it is essentially synonymous with "release," *i.e.*, removal of a bond. Even this, however, may not be sufficiently active. "Letting" your wife go may not be the same as "sending" her out. *Iggeret shevukin* thus means a "letter of letting go."

Why all three forms are used and why the *get* is referred to by three different names (book, document, and letter) are questions that have not been satisfactorily answered. But see Levinstein, NEFESH HaGER, footnote following comments on DEUTERONOMY 24:1.

52. See *supra* Appendix C, note 48.

53. See *supra* Appendix C, note 49. As noted, current practice omits these words.

54. See *supra* Appendix C, note 50.

55. Interestingly, Rambam at 4:12 has the reading: "to any man that desires you." In any case, the text is surprisingly inaccurate since a divorceé may not marry a *Cohen*, see *supra* text at note 20.

56. Rosh includes these bracketed words presumably on the grounds that the *get* merely severs this particular marital relationship but confers no permanent power to indefinitely enter into new alliances once she remarries again. Other authorities omit these words.

57. See *supra* Appendix C, note 51.

_____[58] son of ____witness
_____ son of ____ witness

As a perusal of the text makes clear, the *get* contains five basic elements: 1) precise and virtually obsessive identification of persons and geographical locale; 2) a statement that the dissolution is volitional on the husband's part; 3) a statement that the wife is now released from her marital bonds and is permitted to remarry; 4) a statement that the transfer of the document is the step that effects such dissolution and is not merely after the fact evidence or confirmation; and 5) the signatures of witnesses who have read the *get* and who are in a position to verify the accuracy of its contents if called upon to do so.

NOTE ON ISLAMIC DIVORCE

Under Islamic law, a wife could be divorced by her husband's reciting a two-word formula "*anti talaq*" ("you are divorced") three times.[59] Once this formula is pronounced, the husband may never remarry her again. The husband's right to divorce his wife was absolute, though if done without justifiable cause, such action was deemed reprehensible.[60] Conversely, there was no provision for a wife to declare *talaq* even if she could establish objective reasons to do so. By contrast, all interpretations of Talmudic law recognized the wife's right to sue for divorce at least under *some* circumstances though there was considerable disagreement as to what those circumstances were. The suggestion that the liberal influence of Islam was a major factor in the *Takkanat HaGaonim* granting women greater access to the *bait din* appears to be incorrect.[61]

---

58. See *supra* Appendix A, note 13. The need for witnesses to affix their signatures to a *get* is generally assumed to be a rabbinic enactment to insure its veracity. See, *e.g.*, Rambam, MISHNA TORAH, *Hilchot Gerushin* 1:15. Note, however, that the entirely-separate requirement that witnesses observe the delivery of the *get* may very well be Biblical in origin. Compare views of ROSH, GITTIN 9:7 and Rabbeinu Tam quoted in TOSAFOT, T.B. GITTIN 4a, *s.v. D'kayma* (*get* invalid unless delivery was witnessed) with Rambam, *Gerushin* 1:16 who rules that although Torah law does indeed require "delivery witnesses" and does not require "signature witnesses," once witnesses have affixed their signatures, this would eliminate the need for subsequent "delivery witnesses." Standard practice, however, is decidedly to the contrary and the view of Rosh and Rabbeinu Tam is universally followed.

59. The facts in this paragraph are taken from IV ENCYCLOPEDIA OF ISLAM, pp. 636-645 and S. Goitien, III THE MEDITERRANEAN SOCIETY, p. 264.

60. *Id.* According to the teachings of the Fikh, such action was described as *makruh* (reprehensible). The Hanafis described such a *talak* as *harum* or forbidden but nonetheless *ex post facto* valid.

61. R. Sherira Gaon, in explaining why the Gaonim enacted that a woman may essentially obtain a *get* upon demand, noted that under the older, more restrictive system, "Jewish women were attaching themselves to the Gentiles to get divorces from their husbands by force and these women were satisfied with a forced divorce not in accordance with the Jewish law." 8 OTZAR HaGAONIM, pp. 191-192. Graetz reads this to mean that dissatisfied Jewish

women could seek the protection of the Islam courts and obtain a divorce under the supposedly more liberal standards of the Koran. See 3 HISTORY OF THE JEWS, p. 92. This is also the position of Weiss and Jacob Mann. See respectively I.H. Weiss, 5 DOR DOR V'DORSHAV, p. 8 and J. Mann, *The Responsa of the Babylonian Geonim as a Source of Jewish History*, 10 JEWISH QUARTERLY REVIEW 121 (1919-1920). This is not borne out by Islamic law. Moreover, the reference to "seeking help from the Gentiles" does not necessarily connote access to legal tribunals but could just as easily mean that women were hiring unscrupulous thugs to coerce their husbands into acting. See Tykocinski, TAKKANOT HaGAONIM, pp. 25-26. Another possibility might be that unsatisfied wives actually converted to Islam. Under Islamic law, this was the *sole* basis by which a woman could obtain a divorce from a nonconverting husband. This would explain R. Natronai's reference to women "coming to a bad end." 8 OTZAR HaGAONIM, p. 189. See Levy, THE SOCIAL STRUCTURE OF ISLAM, pp. 122-123 and Riskin, *supra* note 119, p. 75.

D

Glossary of Technical Terms

1. *Amoraim* [singular: *Amora*] - literally, the "interpreters," traditional term for the rabbis quoted in the Talmud, so called because they were the interpreters of the Mishna although they also added numerous additional material to the corpus of *halacha*.

2. *Asmakhta* - commitments that are vague, contingent, or indeterminate and, by reason of their indefiniteness, do not give rise to *halachically*-binding obligations. What agreements constitute *asmakhta* is the subject of a vast literature. For the most part, however, a standard penalty clause contingent on nonperformance would certainly qualify. Accordingly, as is true under common law, penalty clauses are generally *halachically* unenforceable.

3. *Bait Din* [plural: *Batei Din*] - Hebrew for "House of Justice," it is the term for a rabbinic tribunal, normally comprised of three rabbis. While Biblical and Talmudic law vests *batei din* with extensive enforcement powers, *batei din* in the United States do not possess such authority.

4. *Dina D'Mesivta* - see *Takkanat HaGaonim*.

5. *Gaonim* or *Geonim* [singular: *Gaon*]- term of honor for the post-Talmudic heads of the rabbinical academies in Sura and Pumbpeditha (located in present-day Iraq). For almost 500 years, these academies were accepted as the definitive authorities in Jewish law and Talmudic interpretation by the entire Jewish world. With the rise of the Jewish communities in Europe and persecutions in Babylonia, these academies went into a precipitous decline after the death of R. Hai in the 11th Century from which they never recovered. The assorted responsa of the *Gaonim* are collected in B.M. Levin, *Otzar HaGaonim*.

In a more colloquial sense, *Gaon* is used as a general title of veneration for a distinguished Talmudic scholar. One might refer, for example, to the *Gaon* Rabbi Shlomo Zalman Auerbach who, happily, is still very much with us.

6. *Get* [plural: *gittin*] - a written document of divorce which the husband or his agent must physically deliver to the wife or her agent. See Appendix C.

7. *Get Meusah* - a "coerced *get*," a reference to the principle that any *get* that is executed as a result of duress or compulsion is an invalid *get*.

8. *Halacha* [Hebrew for "way of life"] - the accumulated corpus of Jewish law. Judaism, as traditionally understood and practiced, is not exclusively a religion concerned with liturgical ritual and the like but a complete body of substantive and procedural law that regulates every aspect of human conduct and interaction. Side by side with prescribed rituals such as prayer and the eating of kosher food, the Talmud contains detailed rules and doctrines pertaining to torts, contracts, property rights, and personal status. By and large, even those purely "legal" rules are still binding on observant Jews but there is a subtle ambiguity in the term "binding." In the sense of a set of legally-enforceable rules, Jewish "law" is law virtually nowhere. There is no sovereign state in the world that has either adopted *halacha* or recognized it as legally binding on its Jewish inhabitants. The law of the State of Israel itself is secular in its conception and implementation. This was not always the case. *Halacha* was the national law of the sovereign Judaean state before its destruction in 70 c.e. (though often honored in the breach) and, for hundreds of years, was the officially-recognized law governing the members of Jewish communities at a time when those communities were given a substantial degree of political autonomy. Biblical, Talmudic, and much post-Talmudic law presume the existence of fully functioning court systems capable of enforcing adherence to *halachic* norms just as any other court does with respect to its own domestic law.

Today, *halachic* rules are not enforced. In a sense, they are not "law" at all but a voluminous collection of voluntary norms that people may choose to follow or ignore. On another level, however, the obligatory nature of *halacha* does not stem at all from the coercive backup power of the state and does not lapse when such power disappears but derives from divine revelation and imperative. At least from the perspective of a believer, that is even a higher source of obligation.

Halacha is therefore a legal rather than purely religious system in two distinct respects. Historically, it was in fact a body of legally enforceable norms applicable to certain populations within certain territorial limits. Presently, it is a nonenforceable but morally binding code of law governing the same range of human relationships as does the common law. In topical scope, if not its implementation, *halacha* is law. It should be noted that *halacha* makes its demands on all Jews regardless of where they live and whether they acknowledge its binding effect.

The literature of *halacha* has a well-defined hierarchy of authority. First in rank is the Bible (the Old Testament, particularly the Five Books of Moses), followed by the Talmud. Because the Talmud itself records a wide diversity of opinions and is subject to a wide variety of interpretations, medieval and post-medieval authorities compiled a number of codes and codifications. The most authoritative are those of Rambam (Maimonides) called *Mishna Torah*; Rabbi Yaakov Ben Asher, called *Tur*; and Rabbi Yosef Karo, *Shulchan Aruch*. These codes in turn are the subject of voluminous commentaries and supercommentaries. In addition, new cases and questions constantly arose which were submitted to eminent rabbinical scholars all over the world for decision. This amounted to a huge case law literature and accumulated precedent (known as responsa) construing the Talmud and the Codes. Much of this "case law," however, is not really the product of actual courts with coercive powers but more in the nature of decisions rendered by a eminent authorities whom the parties voluntarily agreed to accept.

Finally, *halacha,* although anchored in fixed immutable principles and a definitive literature, is not a static system. There is considerable flexibility in responding to new situations and much robust debate and disagreement among contemporary scholars and rabbis committed to the discipline. New literature is generated almost daily, sometimes of startling originality. There are also fundamental disagreements among the movements of Judaism whether *halacha* as such is binding, but since the *agunah* crisis is a *halachic* problem, *nonhalachic* responses are essentially irrelevant.

9. *Ketubah* [plural: *ketubot*] - the traditional marriage contract executed immediately prior to the marriage ceremony. See Appendix A. See also *Tosefet*.

10. *Kinyan* ["acquisition"] - a formal ceremony by which ownership of real or personal property is transferred or binding contractual obligations are created. Different types of property require different types of *kinyan*. As used in this work, the term connotes a symbolic barter where an object of (nominal) value (conventionally, a handkerchief) is handed to a promisor by or on behalf of the person to whom the promise is being made. Upon receipt of the object by the promisor, his commitment becomes *halachically* binding. The requirement is similar to, though somewhat less expansive than, the common law doctrine of consideration.

11. *Kofin* ["We force"] and *Yotzee* ["He must divorce"] - two technical terms employed in the formal orders of a *bait din* directing the execution of a *get*. The first term connotes an order that can be enforced by monetary sanctions, incarceration, and corporal punishment. The second can be enforced only by moral suasion or public censure. The Talmud and the codes prescribe the grounds for each type of order. Employment of a *kofin* procedure for a *yotzee* order may invalidate the *get*. See also *Get Meusah*.

12. *K'tav Siruv* - order of contempt issued by a *bait din* after a defendant has failed to appear or has failed to comply with the court's order. Rarely employed, it generally carries no enforceable sanctions other than community opprobrium.

13. *Mamzer* [plural: *Mamzeirim*] - a child born out of an adulterous or incestuous union or the lineal descendant of such a child. (A child born out of wedlock is *not* a *mamzer*.) A *mamzer* may not marry anyone other than a *mamzer* or a convert, but suffers no other civil liability.

14. *Mamzeirut* - the stigma of being a *mamzer*. Children conceived from a marriage following a civil divorce but prior to the granting of a *get* bear the stigma of *mamzeirut*.

15. *Mais Alai* - literally, "he is repulsive to me," the technical claim of a woman who no longer desires to stay married, to be contrasted with the *moredet*.

16. *Moda'ah* - written or oral declaration made in the presence of two witnesses in advance of a transaction indicating that the transaction is occurring under duress.

17. *Moredet* - literally, a "rebellious wife," a woman who refuses to cohabit with her husband out of spite though desires to stay married, to be contrasted with the woman who claims *mais alai*.

18. *Meusah* - compelled or forced. See *Get Meusah*.

19. *Nichsai Melog* ["Property of Plucking"] and *Nichsai Tzon Barzel* ["Property of Iron Sheep"] - types of marital property recognized by Jewish law. See Appendix B.

20. *Rabbeinu Tam* - Rabbi Yaakov Ben Meir, eminent Talmudist of the 12th Century. See Appendix F.

21. *Rambam* - Rabbi Moshe Ben Maimon, also known as Moses

Maimonides. See Appendix E.

22. *Ramban* - Rabbi Moshe Ben Nachman, also known as Nachmanides. See Appendix F.

23. *Rema* - Rabbi Moshe Isserles, author of glosses to *Shulchan Aruch*. See Appendix F.

24. *Saboraim* - literally, the "reasoners." The generation of Babylonian scholars immediately following the *Amoraim*. They are generally credited with final redaction of the Talmud.

25. *Shulchan Aruch* - definitive code of Jewish law, authored by Rabbi Yosef Karo. See Appendix E.

26. *Takkana* [plural: *Takkanot*] - a legislative enactment by competent rabbinical authority to ameliorate the effects of an unduly harsh Biblical or Talmudic law or to promote the general welfare. According to many *halachic* opinions, the power to promulgate *takkanot* was limited to Talmudic authorities or those authorities following the redaction of the Talmud whose views were accepted as binding by the entire Jewish community such as the *Gaonim*. In the absence of a single centralized authoritative body, many submit that the power of *takkana* has lapsed.

27. *Takkanat HaGaonim* - a post-Talmudic enactment that permitted a dissatisfied wife to obtain the order of a *bait din* directing the execution of a *get* without establishing specific grounds. Also known as *Dina D'Mesivta* ["the law of the academy"].

28. *Tenayim* ["Conditions"] - the term for prenuptial agreements that specified dowry obligations, what each party would bring to the marriage, and the like.

29. *Tosefet* ["The Addition"] - a voluntary amount that a husband may stipulate be added on to the *ketubah* obligations.

30. *Yotzee* ["He must divorce"] - see *Kofin*.

31. *ZABLA* ["*Ze Boreir Lo Achad*"] - the constitution of a rabbinical court by each litigant choosing one judge and the two judges choosing a third. Commonly employed in communities where there is no standing *bait din*.

E

Sources of Jewish Law

In order to understand the sources and methodology utilized in this study, it may be helpful to describe the basic structures of Jewish law. The supreme source of authority is of course the Pentateuch, the first five books of the Old Testament which, for *halachically* committed Jews, constitutes not just a source of inspiration but a detailed legal code covering a host of civil and criminal matters as well as those areas that are conventionally regarded as "religious." Along with the written text of the law, there was a received supplementary oral tradition interpreting the text and applying its directives to various situations. For hundreds of years, this tradition though not inaccessible was not committed to writing. Moreover, as new cases arose and the Mosaic legislation had to be creatively applied, the traditions accumulated essentially snowballed. Often, there were major disagreements between courts as to how to apply the law in particular situations. Some of the disagreements were resolved by decision of the Sanhedrin, the seventy-one member supreme court and legislative body established in Jerusalem; other disagreements were allowed to stand with individual courts ruling in different ways.

As the received traditions and the areas of disagreements grew larger and there was a real danger that they would be forgotten, portions of the traditions were committed to writing in the form of outlines or notes. The

---

62. Some useful sources on the evolution of the oral law include Bergman, GATEWAY TO THE TALMUD; Chajes, A STUDENT'S GUIDE TO THE TALMUD; Schimmel, THE ORAL LAW; Steinsaltz, THE ESSENTIAL TALMUD. The classic rabbinic exposition of the composition of the Talmud appears in Rambam, INTRODUCTION TO THE COMMENTARY ON THE MISHNA. This masterful work has appeared in two separate English translations, one by Rosner and a more scholarly effort by Lampel.

earliest authoritative redaction of the oral law was the Mishna ("manual of study") compiled in Palestine by R. Judah the Patriarch (died circa 219 c.e.). Supplementary collections of law dating from around the same period are called "*Baraitot*" ["outside" the authoritative corpus of the Mishna]. While statements in *Baraitot* do not carry the same authority as Mishna, the material contained therein often sheds considerable light on obscure Mishnaic formulations. The Mishna consists of six orders: *Zeraim*, pertaining to agricultural laws; *Moed*, the laws and rituals of the Sabbath and holiday cycles; *Nashim*, laws pertaining to marriage and divorce; *Nezikin*, civil code of torts and contracts, rules of evidence and procedure, and criminal law; *Kodshim*, sacrificial rites of the Temple; *Tohorot*, rules pertaining to ritual purity and impurity. Each order is in turn divided into a number of tractates (a total of sixty-three) or treatises. For example, within the order *Nashim*, there are separate tractates pertaining to marriage, divorce, alimony and property rights, and the procedures to be followed upon suspicion of adultery. Treatises are further subdivided into chapters and paragraphs. For the most part, references to Mishna will mention the tractate, the chapter, and the paragraph without the citation to the larger order. Most, if not all, the discussion in this book draws on the treatises in the order *Nashim*.

The Mishna is not a true code of law. It records many diverse opinions within the tradition and does not attempt to resolve among them. Second, many of its formulations were left deliberately obscure and incomplete so that the bulk of the tradition would remain oral. Moreover, many formulations in the Mishna were stated without accompanying reasons or policies and, in the absence of any statement of reasons, were very difficult to apply as precedent. Finally, the Mishna is occasionally self-contradictory. Mishna was probably intended to serve as a manual or outline to judges, rabbis, and students in their attempts to organize and master a huge corpus of law and application.

The Mishna was the primary text studied in the great academies of learning located primarily in Babylonia where the sages lived under Zoroastrian rule and in Palestine. Questions and contradictions in the text were raised and resolved, new applications were suggested, various obscurities were identified and sources, reasons, and policies were advanced. This intense process of debate, dissection, analysis, and commentary covering a span of almost 400 years was finally incorporated into a work known as the Gemara (Aramaic for "teaching") edited by a college of scholars headed by R. Ashi and Ravina. Technically, therefore, the work known as the Talmud comprises two separate works: the Mishna, a product of 2nd Century Palestine, and the Gemara, containing the accumulated commentary and debate for four centuries on the Mishna. As would be expected, the Gemara is far more voluminous than the Mishna. It is not uncommon for a five-line paragraph of Mishna to be followed by ten or twenty pages of the Gemara.[63] Indeed, the Mishna and Gemara together comprise almost 3000 folio pages.

The Talmud (Mishna and Babylonian Gemara) is the authoritative and definitive source of Jewish law and practice to this very day. Once again, it

---

63. Technically, there are two Gemaras - one a product of the Babylonian academies and the other a product of the Palestinian. For a variety of historical reasons, the Babylonian Gemara is deemed the more authoritative and an unspecified reference to Talmud or Gemara normally means the Babylonian version.

must be emphasized that in no sense of the word is the Talmud a code of law. It is a transcript of debate, discussion, and intense analysis. It records questions, answers, refutations, stories, parables, history, and actual case law. It records a bewildering diversity of opinions and,except in comparatively few instances, makes no attempt to provide final *halachic* decisions. It is above all a shining example of process writ large. As a legal work, it is far more concerned with viewing and presenting all sides of a question than it is with providing a definitive response.

Post-Talmudic *halachic* literature therefore takes on three basic forms. There is a huge literature whose primary focus is commentary explaining and developing the complexities of the Talmudic discussion. The premier works in this genré are the commentaries of *R*abbi *Sh*lomo *B*en *Y*itzchak (Rashi, 1040-1105) of France and the school of the Tosaphists (the "supplementers" to Rashi's commentaries), a number of whom were members of Rashi's own family. These two commentaries are printed side by side with the text of the Talmud itself. There are literally hundreds of other works of commentary of varying degrees of authoritativeness and the process continues to this very day. The literature of commentary, like the Talmud itself, is relatively unconcerned with *halachic* resolution. Obviously, however, one's understanding of the Talmudic dialectic will have a direct impact on the *halachic* decision-making process. By identifying the precise meaning, scope, logic, and policy behind each Talmudic opinion, the rabbinical judge is now in the position of deciding in a *halachically* sound way.

A second strand in the literature consists of codifications and codes, works that attempt to abstract from Talmudic commentary guidelines and principles for practical decision-making. In the absence of a formal legislative body that can enact positive law, the authoritativeness of a code depends on the erudition and prestige of its author and the cogency of its reasoning. Of the many and varied codes that have been compiled, comparatively few have achieved universal recognition. The most prominent of these are described further on. As is true in the common law tradition, many eminent scholars opposed the process of codification as a stifling of the flexibility and creativity needed to apply *halacha* to new situations.[64]

Finally, there is the growing case law or responsa literature. In every generation and in every country where there are observant Jews new issues arise and there is uncertainty as to how the existing principles of *halacha* apply. Questions were addressed to prominent rabbinic leaders and their written responses would often be collected and published in book form. Not all rabbis published their responsa nor are all published works entitled to the same

---

64. See Rabbi Shlomo Luria, Introduction, YAM SHEL SHLOMO to BABA KAMA.

[A parallel debate within Anglo-American law occurred in the mid-19th Century when states began the large-scale codification of areas of law that were previously the exclusive domain of the judiciary. See the collection of papers detailing the controversy surrounding the Field Code in Reppy (ed.), DAVID DUDLEY FIELD: CENTENARY ESSAYS, especially Yntema, *The Jurisprudence of Codification*, p. 251. To some extent, this debate continues even today though our age is commonly termed the "Age of Statutes." See generally Hillman, McDonnell, and Nickles, COMMON LAW AND EQUITY UNDER THE UCC, ¶1.01.]

weight. Nevertheless, over the past 1000 years, a voluminous collection of thousands of volumes from hundreds of authors has been generated covering every conceivable aspect of Jewish law and coming from every part of the globe. This process continues to this day. Until recently, there was no way to index or access any of this literature. At best, scholars could hope to be proficient in only a handful of the more renowned classical authorities. Indeed, even libraries only possessed a small fraction of the published works. With the advent of computer technology, many of these previously inaccessible sources are now available on-line.

There is a symbiotic relationship between codes and responsa. The responsa or living case law take the codes as their source material in formulating new responses to contemporary problems. In turn, codes borrow from the responsa as new *halachic* decisions become crystallized and absorbed into the *halachic* mainstream. Thus, the responsa process precedes, goes on concurrently, and succeeds the codificatory process.

One final word on authority: the designation of responsa literature as case law is somewhat misleading. Many major decisors of Jewish law were not "judges" in the commonly-understood sense of the word. In the absence of a Jewish state and Jewish self-government, all opinions and interpretations of Jewish law are in a sense advisory. Yet parties referring such questions to great authorities clearly intended to abide by their decisions and regarded them as binding in a religious and moral sense. Responsa literature as such does not have any legal precedential value - each decisor must make his own decision - but, depending on the personal reputation and eminence of the author, may be highly persuasive. In the final analysis, however, all decisions of Jewish law must be rooted in principles and concepts found in the Talmud and codified in the major codes.

Major Codes[65]

A. *Mishna Torah* [M.T.] ["Restatement of the Law"] authored by Ra*m*ba*m* (Rabbi *M*oshe *B*en *M*aimon - Moses Maimonides, b. Spain 1135-d. Egypt 1204), a monumental redaction of the entire corpus of Jewish law in a unique organizational scheme. The organization, clarity, and comprehensiveness of Rambam's formulations have never been surpassed though a number of his conclusions were disputed by later authorities. Like the original restatements of the American Law Institute, Rambam provided no sources or derivations for his conclusions, a methodological approach that in itself was subject to criticism by some of his contemporaries. See comment of Ravad to Rambam's introduction.

The M.T. consists of fourteen books which are further subdivided into treatises called *Hilchot* (Laws of). The references in this paper are taken from Book 4: *Nashim* [women], primarily *Hilchot Ishut* (Laws of Marriage) and *Hilchot Gerushin* (Laws of Divorce).

The terse and undocumented formulations of Rambam as well as the many disagreements with his contemporaries spawned a huge literature of annotation and commentary, one that is still growing. The most important commentaries are printed on the same page as Rambam's code and include:

---

65. Other codes - those of Rif, Rosh, Mordechai - are described in Appendix F.

Magid Mishna authored by the 14th Century Spanish scholar R. Vidal De Tulusa; *Kesef Mishna* authored by R. Yosef Karo of 15th Century Palestine (better known for authoring *Shulchan Aruch*); and *Lechem Mishna* of R. Avraham di Boton of Salonika (1548-1588). The standard editions also contain the incisive criticisms of an older contemporary of Rambam, the celebrated Ravad [*R*abbi *A*vrohom *B*en *D*avid] of Posquieres (c. 1120-1197, France).

B. *Arba Turim* ["The Four Rows"] commonly known as *Tur* authored by Rabbi Yaakov Ben Asher (b. Germany c. 1275 - d. Spain c. 1340). Unlike Rambam's approach, *Tur* traces its conclusions back to the Talmudic sources and provides a digest of virtually all opinions on issues of Jewish law. The *Tur* is especially valuable because it incorporates the decisions of German and French schools of thought which Rambam either ignored or was unaware of. Nevertheless, as is true with all subsequent codifications, Rambam looms as a giant presence whose views must be reckoned with. The author of the *Tur* adopted his own plan of arrangement and omits from his code all matters of Jewish law that were merely of historical interest (laws of sacrifice, for example).

Tur comprises four books (hence its title, "Four Rows"):

1. *Orach Hayyim* ("Way of Life") - laws concerning ritual and the holiday cycle.
2. *Yoreh De'ah* [Y.D.] ("The Teacher of Knowledge") - laws concerning kosher food, circumcision, mourning, conversion.
3. *Even HaEzer** [E.H.] ("The Foundation-Rock of Assistance") - laws concerning marriage, divorce, and personal status.
4. *Hoshen Mishpat* [H.M.] ("The Breastplate of Judgment") - the civil code of Judaism governing the court system, contracts, torts, agency, inheritance, partnership, and a host of other interpersonal private law matters.

The bulk of the references in this paper are to *Tur Even HaEzer* [E.H.] particularly *Hilchot Gerushin* (again, as in Rambam's Code, "Laws of Divorce"). While the style of the *Tur* is far more discursive and elaborate than Rambam's, it too has spawned a considerable literature of commentary. These include: *Bait Yosef* [B.Y.], a monumental work authored by R. Yosef Karo which attempts to trace each decision of the *Tur* back to Talmudic sources and to provide a complete digest of all opinions on Jewish law matters including those matters that were decided in the 200 years or so separating R. Karo from *Tur*; *Bayit Chadash* [Bach], commentary by R. Joel Sirkes of 16th Century Poland; and *Perisha* (along with the companion work of extended analysis, *Derisha*), authored by R. Joshua Falk of 16th Century Poland.

C. *Shulchan Aruch* - ("The Prepared Table"), to this day regarded as the definitive code of Jewish law by Orthodox Jewry, the work was authored by R. Yosef Karo (b. 1488 Spain - d. 1575 Palestine). After preparing the monumental *Bait Yosef*, a complete analysis of all source material appearing in and utilized by the *Tur*, as well as later sources and customs, R. Karo prepared what was essentially an abridgement of his masterwork restating his

---

*"Ezer" is the term meaning "assistance"; "Ha" is simply the equivalent of "the."

conclusions. This abridgement, however, soon became accepted as the final word because of the immense personal prestige of the author. As is true of all abridgements or black-letter synopses, however, the rulings cannot truly be understood or applied without a comprehensive mastery of the analyses presented in *Bait Yosef* and the sources that he in turn relied upon.

Rabbi Karo was a Spanish Jew who moved to Turkey as a child following the expulsion of the Jews in 1492 and eventually settled in Palestine where he became Chief Rabbi of Safed, at the time the leading Jewish community in Ottoman-occupied Palestine. Consequently, his decisions are based primarily on the traditions and Talmudic interpretations of the Spanish-North African school, particularly Rambam. Glosses adding the insights and customs of the French-German school were authored by R. Moshe Isserles (1520-1575) of Cracow, Poland in a work he entitled somewhat whimsically the *Mapah* ("Tablecloth"). Although ostensibly an independent work, it is incorporated as an inseparable part of the *Shulchan Aruch* separated only by the word "*Hagah*" ("Note") and a different typeface.

Organizationally, the *Shulchan Aruch*, being an abridgement of the *Tur* and *Bait Yosef*, follows the order of the *Tur* down to the chapter. Thus, for example, E.H., chapter 154 will cover the same material in both *Tur* and *Shulchan Aruch* though the arrangements within chapters differ and the ultimate conclusions may diverge.

Once again, a work that was intended as a simple abridgement generated a huge amount of commentary and gloss, dispelling the cherished belief that the *halachic* system could be cabined within the confines of a simple, short work. Each volume of the *Shulchan Aruch* has its own special commentaries. Since this book draws primarily on Karo's remarks in E.H., the commentaries most utilized are : (1) *Bait Shmuel* authored by R. Samuel Ben Uri (c. 1640-1700, Poland); (2) *Chelkat Mechokek* authored by R. Moshe Lima (c. 1605-1658, Lithuania); (3) *Turai Zahav* authored by R. David HaLevi (1586-1667, Russia); and (4) *Pitchai Teshuva*, an anthology of responsa literature collected by R. Abraham Eisenstadt (19th Century, Lithuania). Mention should also be made of the *Biur HaGra*, a commentary on all four sections of the *Shulchan Aruch* authored by the renowned R. Elijah of Vilna (*Vilna Gaon*) (18th Century, Lithuania) which traces all rulings of the *Shulchan Aruch* back to their Talmudic sources.

The principal commentaries on the other sections of the *Shulchan Aruch* are: for *Orach Hayyim*, the *Magen Avraham* (R. Abraham Gombiner, c. 1634-1682, Poland) and the *Magen David* (R. David HaLevi, author of *Turai Zahav* on E.H.); for *Yore De'ah*, the *Turai Zahav* (again by R. David HaLevi) and the *Siftai Cohen* (R. Shabtai HaCohen, 1622-1663, Lithuania and Moravia); and for *Hoshen Mishpat*, the *Siftai Cohen* (same author), and the *Sefer Meirat Ainayim* (often abbreviated *Sema*) authored by R. Joshua Falk Katz (d. 1614, Poland) who also authored the well-known commentary on the *Tur* entitled *Perisha*.

As noted, despite the codification of the *Shulchan Aruch* and its acceptance as *the* Code of Jewish Law, the creative development of *halacha* continued apace. For one thing, new unresolved questions constantly arose. The status of in-vitro fertilization, for example, is not a subject explicitly discussed in the Talmud or *Shulchan Aruch* though those sources do contain principles that bear on the question. As new issues arise today so it was always. Second, even existing rules were perceived as ambiguous and unclear, necessitating further elucidation based on the fundamental underlying principles found in the Talmud and its commentaries, the theoretical academic basis for all *halachic* development. All of these found expression in the responsa literature as well as in commentaries and glosses to the *Shulchan Aruch* itself. Throughout the years, various digests and indexes were prepared for this literature but these were invariably incomplete. Only the advent of on-line computer technology has finally made it possible to fully access this massive branch of learning.

In any event, insofar as the 20th Century is concerned, four major projects are worthy of special mention:

1. *Aruch HaShulchan* ("Setting of the Table," an inversion of the *Shulchan Aruch*) was an early 20th Century attempt to restate Jewish law in contemporary terms and to show the historical development of the law from Talmud through the present day. Authored by R. Yechiel M. Epstein of Novardok, Poland, this multi-volume work is distinguished by clarity, fine organization, and felicity of expression. While not regarded as a definitive work in the sense of Rambam, *Tur*, and *Shulchan Aruch*, it is nevertheless highly respected and often cited. Its chapter headings are the same as the *Shulchan Aruch* making cross-referencing very easy.
2. *Encyclopedia Talmudit* ("Talmudic Encyclopedia"), a project still in progress that was started more than forty years ago. The work attempts to restate in terse encyclopedic format with full documentation all that has been written about the *halachic* concepts addressed in the Talmud. While not a *halachic* work *per se* since it renders no decisions, the encyclopedia is a goldmine of valuable source material. Twenty volumes to date cover only the first nine letters of the alphabet.
3. *Otzar HaPoskim* ("Encyclopedia of Decisors"), another on-going encyclopedia project designed to collect and summarize all existing responsa in the areas of family law and append them to the text of the *Shulchan Aruch*. As an illustration of how massive a literature this is, the project has been going on for forty years, has produced seventeen volumes, and has only gone through the first sixty or so chapters in E.H., a bit more than one third of the way.
4. Computerization of responsa literature by Bar-Ilan University in Tel Aviv, a project that is still on-going.[66]

This is in addition to a steady spate of academic commentary, monographs, new responsa, practice manuals, and popularizations.

---

66. For a description of the goals of the responsa project, see Slae, *The Responsa Project*, 2 THE JEWISH LAW ANNUAL 84 (1979).

F

Identification of Major Authorities in the Formative Post-Talmudic Era of *Halacha*: 10th-15th Centuries

During this time, the two major schools were the Sefardic based largely in North Africa and Spain and the Ashkenazic based in France and Germany. These schools, both of which considered the Talmud authoritative, developed very different modes of analysis and interpretation and this resulted in divergent practices as well. There were also smaller schools in Provence (Southern France) and Italy which to some degree drew from both the Ashkenazic and Sefardic traditions but often developed original interpretations and rulings of striking originality.

The Sefardic school culminated in the masterwork of R. Yosef Karo in the *Shulchan Aruch* while the Ashkenazic tradition appears in the glosses of Rema. Certain figures "bridged" the two schools drawing creative insights from both, *e.g.*, Ramban and Rosh. As is apparent, these figures are normally identified by acronyms comprising the first letters of each word in their names.[67]

SEFARDIC AUTHORITIES: SPAIN AND NORTH AFRICA

(1) Rabbi Yitzchak Alfasi (Rif or Alfasi)
born Algeria, 1013
died Spain, 1103

Acknowledged leader of North African Jewry, Rif is best known for his monumental code that essentially abridges the Talmud and indicates which view is to be followed in practice. Alfasi's code omits those portions of the Talmud not relevant to the present day, *e.g.*, laws of sacrifice and ritual purity. Rif was a primary, if not dominant, source for Rambam's later rulings and, via the *Mishna Torah*, exercised a profound influence on the *Shulchan Aruch* as well. Rif also established the fundamental principle

---

67. General sources on this area are R. Azulai, SHEM HaGEDOLIM; various entries in ENCYCLOPEDIA JUDAICA; and two works by Goldwurm, THE RISHONIM and THE EARLY ACHARONIM, both of which are published by Mesorah Publications, Ltd.

followed to this very day that in cases of conflict between the Babylonian and Jerusalem Talmud, the former controls.

Because of the great authority Rif enjoyed, many commentaries and critiques were written on his code, including *Sefer HaMaor* by R. Zerachyah HaLevi, *Milchamot HaShem* by Ramban, and works by Ran. Alfasi's code appears in the back of each volume of the standard edition of the Babylonian Talmud.

(2) Rabbi Moshe Ben Maimon [Rambam 1135-1204, Spain and Egypt], author of the monumental *Mishna Torah*. See Appendix E.

(3) Rabbi Moshe Ben Nachman (Ramban, Nachmanides)
born Spain 1194
died Palestine 1270

After Maimonides, Ramban was regarded the supreme *halachic* authority in Spain and was widely respected in other lands as well. He drew from both the Sefardic and Ashkenezic schools due to a three-year sojourn in France. Author of extensive commentaries on the Bible and Talmud, responsa, and various codifications as well as mystical and philosophical writings. Often differs with Maimonides but his influence on the history of *halacha* is profound.

(4) Rabbi Shlomo Ibn Aderet (Rashba)
born Spain 1235
died Spain 1310

Disciple and successor to Ramban, Rashba was acknowledged by the entire Jewish world as the preeminent *halachic* authority of his generation. His literary output was prodigious and took many disparate forms: commentaries on most of the Talmud; responsa numbering in the thousands answering inquiries from Palestine, Italy, Portugal, France, Germany, North Africa, as well as Spain; and guidebooks on particular areas of *halachic* practice. His decisions are cited extensively in the later codes such as *Tur* and *Shulchan Aruch*.

(5) Rabbi Yom Tov Ibn Aseville (Ritva)
14th Century Spain

A disciple of Rashba, Ritva is best known for his voluminous commentaries on the Talmud which are distinguished for their clarity and thoroughness.

(6) Rabbi Nissim Ben Reuven (Ran)
born Spain, c. 1290
died Spain, c. 1375

Successor to the Rashba as Rabbi of the Barcelona community, Ran was also a world-renowned *halachic* authority recognized as such in his lifetime. Author of many responsa, most of which are lost, he is most famous for his commentaries to the Talmud which are distinguished for their clarity, insight, originality, and fine style. He does attempt to distill from his analysis *halachic* conclusions and these are often cited as authoritative. Many of his disciples became outstanding leaders in their own right.

(7) Rabbi Yitzchok Ben Sheshet Perfet (Rivash)
born Spain 1326
died Algiers 1407

A disciple of Ran, Rivash was an outstanding master of *halacha* despite a turbulent life that necessitated fleeing Spain to seek refuge in North Africa. He was the author of a collection of responsa entitled *Teshuvot Rivash*, a collection that weighs heavily in the *halachic* decision-making process.

(8) Rabbi Shimon Ben Tzemach (Rashbatz or Tashbatz)
born Spain 1361
died Algiers 1444

Younger contemporary of and later successor to Rivash as head of the Algerian community. Prolific author of commentaries on the Talmud and Bible, he is best known for his voluminous responsa - over 800 replies - which cover all facets of Jewish law and practice. The work is known as *Tashbatz* (*T*eshuvot *Sh*imon *B*en *Tz*emach - "Responsa of Shimon Ben Tzemach").

ASHKENAZIC AUTHORITIES: FRANCE AND GERMANY

(1) Rabbi Shlomo Ben Yitzchok (Rashi)
born France 1040
died France 1105

Regarded as the greatest commentator in Jewish history, Rashi was not a professional rabbi but earned his living as a vintner. His commentaries on the Talmud explaining the text phrase by phrase are indispensable. They are printed in every edition of the Talmud and without them, the Talmud would have remained a closed book to all but the greatest scholars. His commentary on the Bible has had equal impact and indeed was the first Hebrew book ever printed, a testament to its fundamental importance. His style is brief but matchless in its clarity.

Rashi was also regarded as a great *halachic* authority and authored many responsa. His fame, however, rests primarily on his commentary. As commentator, he rarely indicates a final *halachic* decision but prefers to illuminate the entirety of the Talmudic give-and-take. Rashi's life overlapped with the tragic First Crusade of 1096 when many Jewish communities were destroyed.

(2) Rabbi Shmuel Ben Meir (Rashbam)
born France 1085
died France 1174

A grandson of Rashi, Rashbam was a renowned *halachic* authority in his own right and composed several commentaries to selected tractates of the Talmud. He also wrote a complete commentary to the Pentateuch.

(3) Rabbi Yaakov Ben Meir (Rabbeinu Tam, "Our teacher, the perfect one")
born France 1100
died France 1171

The younger brother of the Rashbam, regarded as the greatest Talmudist of his age. An original, insightful thinker, he proposed many new interpretations of Talmudic passages, pointed out apparent inconsistencies and gaps in Talmudic texts which he then resolved with acuity. The force of his intellect and personality were such that his interpretations often became accepted as definitive even where they represented a sharp break with tradition. His views are recorded in *Tosafot* ("supplement"), a set of glosses to the Talmud which appear side by side with Rashi's commentary and in a work entitled *Sefer HaYashar* ("Book of the Upright").

(4) Rabbi Meir of Rothenberg (Maharam)
born Germany c. 1215
died France 1293

Leading *halachic* authority in Germany and France, he authored commentaries on the Talmud, extensive responsa, and codifications in particular areas of *halacha*. He also established a rabbinical seminary in Rothenberg which produced the religious leadership of France and Germany Jewry for the next generation. His opinions carry great weight in the *halachic* process to this very day. Many of his views are known to us only second-hand (quotations in disciples' works) but a number of his responsa have been published.

Tragically, he spent the last seven years of his life imprisoned by order of Rudolph I who hoped to extort a huge ransom from the Jewish community. Although the sum was raised, Maharam refused to let the community pay it for fear of encouraging other kidnappings in the future. Even after his death, the corpse was not released for burial for fourteen years.

(5) Rabbi Mordechai Ben Hillel
born Germany, c.1240
died Germany, 1298

Author of a major *halachic* compendium arranged according to the order of the Talmud, currently printed as an appendix to the Code of Rif. A major disciple of R. Meir of Rothenberg, he died a martyr's death during the Rindfleish massacres. His code has had enormous influence on the development of *halacha* within Ashkenazic communities and is cited by Rema frequently.

(6) Rabbi Asher Ben Yechiel (Rosh)
born Germany c. 1250
died Spain 1327

The most prominent disciple of Maharam, he succeeded him as spiritual leader and *halachic* authority for Ashkenazic Jewry. Fleeing Germany following the Rindfleish massacres, he spent the last twenty-one years of his life in Spain, where Rashba warmly welcomed him. Following Rashba's death in 1310, Rosh became the acknowledged *halachic* authority in Spain as well. Rosh received inquiries from Germany, France, Spain, and North Africa and his responsa are collected in *Teshuvot Rosh*, a work that is extensively quoted and relied upon in the later codificatory literature. Rosh also composed a *halachic* work which summarized the gist of the Talmudic discussion, outlined the main areas of interpretative disagreement, and indicated his view of the proper resolution. Rosh's code (titled *Piskai Rosh* but often cited as only *Rosh*) unlike the Rambam's *Mishna Torah*, explains the entire process of decision, not just the conclusion. Because of Rosh's German background, he acted as a bridge between the Ashkenazic and Sefardic schools and absorbed and communicated the insights of both.

Rabbi Yaakov, the author of the *Tur*, was the Rosh's son and based his *Tur* on the Rosh's earlier work.

(7) Rabbi Yaakov Ben Asher (author of *Arba Turim*)
born Germany c. 1275
died Spain c. 1340

See description in Appendix E.

(8) Rabbi Yisrael Isserlin
born Germany c. 1390
died Austria 1460

Author of *Terumot HaDeshen*, a work consisting of 354 *halachic* essays on assorted subjects. Although a small work, it was and is very highly regarded and frequently quoted by the later codes and commentaries up to the present day.

(9) Rabbi Yisrael Bruna
born Germany c. 1400
died Prague c. 1480

A disciple of Rabbi Isserlin, Rabbi Bruna was the author of *Sheealot*

U'Teshuvot Mahari Bruna. His rulings are frequently cited by Rema in the *Shulchan Aruch.*

AUTHORITIES OF THE PROVENCAL SCHOOL (SOUTHERN FRANCE)

(1) Rabbi Abraham Ben David (Ravad III)
born France, c. 1120
died France, c. 1197

Scion of illustrious ancestors whose name he bore, Ravad was a prolific and creative writer authoring commentaries, codes, and responsa. He is best known, however, for his comprehensive and incisive critique of Rambam's *Mishna Torah*, a critique which is printed in all editions of Rambam's work. Ravad opposed Rambam's practice of giving rules without citation of sources and, in his own codes, always provided the Talmudic background in support of his rulings.

(2) Rabbi Zerachyah HaLevi (Raza or Baal HaMaor)
born Spain, c. 1125
died France, 1186

A brilliant prodigy who at the young age of nineteen composed the *Sefer HaMaor* ("Book of Enlightenment") containing criticism and arguments against the rulings of the venerable Rif. A younger colleague of Ravad, he and Ravad exchanged considerable correspondence on Talmudic and *halachic* matters, often in quite passionate tones. Ramban wrote *Milchamot HaShem* ("The Wars of G-d") as a defense to R. Zerachyah's criticisms of Rif and, to this very day, the *Sefer HaMaor* and the *Milchamot* appear together in standard editions of Alfasi's code.

(3) Rabbi Menachem HaMeiri (Meiri)
born France, c. 1249
died France, c. 1306

The author of a monumental digest and commentary to most of the Talmud [*Bait HaBechira*], Meiri was virtually forgotten for hundreds of years as many of his writings were lost. Their rediscovery has established his reputation as one of the greatest Talmudic commentators. In the great controversy that erupted concerning alleged heresies in the works of Maimonides, Meiri was a staunch defender of both Maimonides and the study of philosophy and science in general. He also maintained an active correspondence with Rashba.

AUTHORITIES OF THE ITALIAN SCHOOL

(1) Rabbi Nathan Ben Yechiel
born Italy, c. 1035
died Italy, after 1102

Author of the *Aruch*, a compendium of all words found in Talmudic and Midrashic literature along with their meanings. This dictionary was universally accepted as authoritative and is often cited as a *halachic* source. Additional material was added by Dr. Alexander Kohut in the 20th Century and the expanded edition was published under the name *Aruch HaShalem* (*The Complete Aruch*).

(2) Rabbi Yeshaya DiTrani (Rid)
born Italy, c. 1180

died Italy, c. 1260

Recognized leader of Italian Jewry in his generation and author of commentaries to the Talmud that are often startling in their originality and unique perspective. Quoted with great respect by Ashkenazic authorities like R. Meir of Rothenberg and Rosh. Not to be confused with his grandson of the same name (1235-1300) who was also an eminent scholar whose decisions are widely quoted in the work *Shiltai Gibborim* appended to Alfasi's code.

(3) Rabbi Yosef Colon (Maharik)
born France, 1410
died Italy, c. 1480

A leading *halachic* authority in France and Italy, his rulings are frequently quoted by later authorities. Author of *Teshuvot Maharik* ("Responsa of Maharik").

Case Supplement

Case Supplement

The following supplement contains the text of the major decisions concerning the rights of aggrieved spouses to obtain religious divorces by resort to the secular courts. Most of the opinions are reproduced in full; the occasional deletion is indicated by an ellipsis.[1] The cases fall into five major groups (1) those that order the execution of a *get* by construing the *ketubah* as an implied contract that marital termination will be governed by Jewish law; (2) those that enforce, directly or indirectly, express contracts to give or receive a *get*; (3) those that enforce express contracts to submit to the jurisdiction of a *bait din*; (4) those that adjust alimony as an indirect method of compulsion; and (5) those that deny the enforcement of *get* covenants on either statutory or constitutional grounds. As reproduced here, the breakdown of the cases is the following:

---

1. No attempt has been made to secure uniformity of transliteration of Hebrew terms such as *get*, *ketubah*, and *bait din* and I have simply reproduced the spellings that each court employed.

2. Although *Morris* (I) denied enforcement of the *ketubah* and is thus a Class 5 case, it is placed immediately after *Morris* (I) because it is the reversal of that earlier case by a higher tribunal and the two cases must be read together.

It should be noted that *Avitzur*, decided by the New York Court of Appeals, and *Morris* II, decided by the Manitoba Court of Appeal, are the only decisions rendered by the highest court of a jurisdiction. The remainder of the decisions have been rendered by either trial courts (*Minkin*, *Burns*, *Koeppel*, *Rubin*, *Waxstein*[3]) or intermediate level reviewing courts (*Margulies*, *Brett*, *Turner*, *Goldman*) and as such have relatively little precedential weight.

A. *KETUBAH* AS IMPLIED CONTRACT

Re Morris and Morris

36 D.L.R. (3rd) 447
Manitoba Queen's Bench (March 16, 1973)[a]

Wilson, J.: The parties were formerly husband and wife, married at the Hebrew Fraternal Lodge in Winnipeg on October 23, 1955, in accordance with traditional Jewish practices. That union was dissolved by decree pronounced in this Court July 14, 1972, and made absolute October 20th last, which decree, however, while it is recognized by the Jewish religion as a valid exercise of the civil power, is nevertheless ineffective as a divorce in the eyes of the orthodox Jewish community, to which religion the parties claim allegiance.

To perfect their divorce, so that it may have spiritual recognition according to Jewish tradition, the respondent (husband) must take the necessary steps to deliver to the applicant (wife) a "Get" or bill of divorce, which he refuses to do. Hence these proceedings, having for their end a ruling which will compel the respondent to deliver the Get, without which his former wife may not be married in her own faith, and will suffer other disabilities in the eyes of her religious community not least of which is that any children hereafter born to her, and whether within or out of wedlock so far as concerns the civil law, can only be bastards (*mamzerim*) in the eyes of Jewish religion, as will the descendants of such children.

Because a *mamzer* is considered to be less than a whole or complete person in Judaism, and because she foresees the likelihood of further issue, applicant is anxious to avoid the odium she may expect for such children in matters of spiritual concern within her religious community. She has in fact remarried, that ceremony following the perfunctory form prescribed for use by a Judge of the County Court. Her new husband is, again, an orthodox Jew,

---

3. *Waxstein*, however, was affirmed by the Appellate Division in 57 A.D. 2d 863 (1977).

[a]*Edited*. Deletions are indicated by **** and footnotes renumbered.

and while he was not before the Court, I was told that he too would have preferred the traditional Jewish ceremony, and is equally anxious with the applicant that, if and as soon as possible, they repeat their marriage vows in a Jewish congregation before a rabbi.

It may well be that in so remarrying, applicant has not lived up to the laws of her faith, but this should not forever bar her from rectifying the situation, if she so desires.

Their divorce was only the culmination of a series of quarrels and judicial contests between the parties, who have lived apart since July of 1968. Applicant has custody of their three children, aged 15, 12 and 6 years, and respondent has his own application before the Court to reduce the maintenance which he was ordered to pay by the divorce decree. In other proceedings, the parties are at issue touching, *inter alia*, division of the proceeds of sale of certain realty formerly owned by them. Clearly, no (or very little) love is lost between them. Despite their apparent determination to differ, however, I have no reason to believe that applicant is insincere in her protestations to be an orthodox Jewess, and of concern for her own status and, even more, for the status of any children she may bear in her new marriage.

It is, I think, important to note that respondent is not opposed to the notion of divorce, because in answer to his wife's petition he filed his own cross-petition, also praying for dissolution of their union. In granting the decree nisi, the learned trial Judge did not distinguish between them, and simply dissolved the marriage "upon hearing read the pleadings and hearing the evidence adduced."

Although represented by counsel, respondent offered no evidence before me, did not cross-examine applicant on her affidavit, and rests his opposition upon challenge to the Court's jurisdiction to interpret the "Kethubah" or covenant of marriage signed by the parties, or to interfere in any way in which are essentially matters of religion.

And certainly, the civil Courts have steadfastly refused to entertain litigation whose end must depend upon the preferment by the Court of one over another religious opinion, or the duty to observe matters of spiritual belief. So Freedman (then) J.A., giving the decision of our Court of Appeal in *Hofer et al. v. Hofer et al.* (1967), 65 D.L.R. (2d) 607 [affirmed 13 D.L.R. (3d) 1, [1970] S.C.R. 958, 73 W.W.R. 644], said at p. 613:

> Let it be said at once that it is no part of the function of the Court to choose between conflicting religious doctrines and to put its stamp of approval on one and its mark of rejection on the other. This Court has no desire to engage in any such exercise, nor is it qualified to do so.

In *Dunnet v. Fornori* (1877), 25 Gr. 199, Proudfoot, V.C., declined jurisdiction where the plaintiff would-be Anglican communicant sought an order requiring defendant clergyman to allow him to partake of the Lord's Supper, the difference between the parties turning on "a mere abstract question involving religious dogmas" and resulting in no civil consequences which could justify the interposition of a civil Court. Likewise, in A.-G. (*ex rel. Royal College of Organists) v. Dean and Chapter of Ripon Cathedral Church*, [1945] 1 All E.R. 479 (whether full choral service of a Sunday morning required the canticles to be sung in chants or to settings), where Uthwatt, J., at p. 487, saw no "special circumstances pointing to the desirability of the intervention of the court"; *R. v. Chancellor of St. Edmundsbury and Ipswich Diocese*, [1948] 1 K.B. 195 (access to a grave in the churchyard of the parish church); and *Ukrainian Greek Orthodox Church, et al. v. Trustees of Ukrainian Greek*

Orthodox Cathedral et al. (1939), 47 Man. R. 64, where the dispute turned upon the right of a congregation to continue in office a priest ousted by his superiors.

In such matters the attitude of the Court is governed by the view cited in *United States of America v. Seeger* (1964), 326 F.2d 846 at p. 854, that "religion is too personal, too sacred, too holy, to permit its 'unhallowed pervasion' by a civil magistrate" or perhaps for the practical reason given by Wrottesley, L.J., in the *St. Edmundsbury* case, at p. 214, that "it would remove into the King's Bench proceedings not capable of being determined there."

The rule is different whether religious doctrine and civil law conflict, when the significance and sincerity of religious belief will be inquired into; and recently in our own Courts, see *R. v. Chomokowski*, [1973] 2 W.W.R. 75, where the accused's religious discipline, he said, would not permit him to give a breath sample. And, of course, in divorce matters there have been several cases where the decree was not refused as "harsh and oppressive" merely by reason of the respondent's religious objections to divorce; and see Payne's *Digest of Cases and Materials on the Divorce Act* (1968), p. 134.

****

In the instant case, there is no conflict of dogma, nor did respondent advance any argument based upon a personal religious conviction which forbids what is required of him by the applicant. Orthodox Jewish religion itself is not divided upon the subject.

****

Not infrequently, in recent years parties to the Christian marriage are seen to vary the ceremony as it was known to their parents, striking out some of the customary avowals or adding phrases which they feel of particular significance; none of that, however, is of particular legal significance. But in the traditional Jewish marriage, the *Kethubah* and its delivery prior to the actual ceremony is unvarying.

The document signed by the parties in the instant case, apparently prepared by a stationery office in Chicago, I was told follows the standard form. After reciting the place and date of the marriage and the names of the bride and groom, it reads:

The said bridegroom made the following declaration to his bride:

> "Be thou my wife according to the law of Moses and Israel. I faithfully promise, that I will be a true husband unto thee. I will honour and cherish thee, I will work for thee, I will protect and support thee and will provide all that is necessary for thy due sustenance as it Beseemeth a Jewish husband to do. I also take upon myself all such further obligations for thy maintenance, as are prescribed by our religious statute."
> And the said bride has plighted her troth unto him in affection and in sincerity and has thus taken upon herself the fulfillment of all the duties incumbent upon a Jewish wife.
> This covenant of marriage was duly executed and witnessed this day, according to the usage of Israel.

Then follow signatures of the bridegroom and bride and of the two witnesses.

The law recognizes and will give effect to a formal antenuptial marriage contract, to the extent it is not illegal as contrary to public policy or otherwise invalid. And, in the Jewish marriage, execution and delivery of the Kethubah is tantamount to such a prenuptial contract, arguable again as sanctioned by statute by virtue of the *Canadian Bill of Rights*, s. 1(c) of which, in language having retrospective effect, affirms the freedom of religion.

But it is not necessary to pursue the tantalizing question of what indeed is a "ceremony of marriage" under our provincial statute, silent on the point except for the form prescribed for use in the County Court, or to pursue resolution of the seeming conflict (for present purposes) between the federal *Bill of Rights* and s. 92 (12) of the *British North America Act, 1867*, whereby solemnization of marriage is a matter assigned to the Province.

Clearly, upon any reading of the evidence before me, and in answer to her request for a declaration, applicant is entitled as one of her rights under the Kethubah to the preparation and delivery to her, by respondent, of a Jewish bill of divorcement, or *Get*.

In making this declaration, I have not overlooked respondent's objection that the *Kethubah* is not a document of the nature contemplated by Rule 536. It is, however, an instrument in writing, signed by the parties, and intended to have effect, which I think is sufficient to bring it within scope of the Rule. The fact that its reading cannot be divorced for[b] matters of religious belief is not, *per se*, a bar to its interpretation by the Court, particularly where, as here, the parties are agreed upon its explanation or interpretation.

More formidable is respondent's denial of the right of the Court to proceed beyond the mere declaration of the rights of the applicant, and to require that in fact the respondent shall do whatever is necessary to complete their divorce in the eyes of the religious community of which they are both members.

That respondent should refuse this act is no less bewildering when, as already remarked, he filed a counter-petition in answer to applicant's prayer for divorce, not in opposition to the decree, but simply asking that it be pronounced in answer to his grounds rather than hers. To require respondent to finally terminate their marriage, then, would merely oblige him to further perform what he voluntarily set out to do.

What applicant asks is an order of *mandamus*. By the *Queen's Bench Act*, R.S.M. 1970, C280, s. 58:

> 58. A mandamus to command the fulfillment of any duty in the fulfillment of which the party claiming it is personally interested may be granted in any action in which it is claimed by the statement of claim or by the counter-claim; but, notwithstanding anything herein, the court may upon motion, not in an action, in all cases where the prerogative writ of mandamus might at any time formerly have been granted, grant an order of mandamus which shall have the same effect as the writ of mandamus formerly had.

Counsel were unable to refer me to any case in point. In *Brett v. Brett*, [1969] 1 All E.R. 1007, the Court of Appeal recognized the divorced wife's right to a *Get* by reducing the payments due from the former husband conditionally upon his delivery of the *Get*; that case, however, dealt only with the question of maintenance. More to the point was *Koeppel v. Koeppel* (1954), 138 N.Y. Supp. 2d 366, where the Court dismissed the former husband's application to strike out the ex-wife's action for an order requiring him to deliver a *Get*, on the ground the action was academic only, she having remarried in a civil ceremony, as indeed is the case here.

The prerogative writ of *mandamus* was based upon the inherent jurisdiction of the Court of King's Bench as a command, issued in the name of

---

[b]should probably be "from" [*ed.*].

Sovereign, calling upon the person named therein to perform the act specified, being one which it is his duty to do, and which the Court has upon inquiry determined to consonant with right and justice. A history and general account of the writ is set out in Holmested and Gale's *Ontario Judicature Act and Rules of Practice* (1968), vol. 1, s. 16, commencing at p. 75 of the text. In *Re Nathan* (1884), 12 Q.B.D. 461 at pp. 478-9, Bowen, L.J., said:

> A writ of mandamus, as everybody knows, is a high prerogative writ, invented for the purpose of supplying defects of justice. By Magna Charta the Crown is bound neither to deny justice to anybody, nor to delay anybody in obtaining justice. If, therefore, there is no other means of obtaining justice, the writ of mandamus is granted to enable justice to be done.

Beyond its decision to favour the act to be done, the Court must be satisfied the applicant has no other means of compelling its performance, and is not acting *mala fide*, which conditions are satisfied here. Nor is the act in question one which could or ought to offend the conscience of the respondent, whose observation that the Court would refuse to direct the institution of divorce proceedings by one whose religious beliefs exclude the notion of divorce is *nihil ad rem*. The Court is not asked to direct action by the rabbi or other leaders of the synagogue, neither is it asked to direct the respondent to institute proceedings for divorce, the marriage formerly subsisting between the parties being already dissolved by proceedings in this Court in answer to the prayers for its dissolution laid before the Court by each of them.

In *Shaw v. Director of Public Prosecutions*, [1961] 2 All E.R. 446 at p. 452, Viscount Simonds said:

> In the sphere of criminal law, I entertain no doubt that there remains in the courts of law a residual power to enforce the supreme and fundamental purpose of the law, to conserve not only the safety and order but also the moral welfare of the state...The law must be related to the changing standards of life, not yielding to every shifting impulse of the popular will but having regard to fundamental assessments of human values and the purposes of society.

And while the noble Lord confined his remarks to the matters then before him, the ambit of the law is, I think, equally broad in the sphere which would include the request of the applicant, which ought not to be refused on the terse ground that no such order was made heretofore.

In *Re Winnipeg Charter*, [1928] 1 W.W.R. 613 at p. 617, Dysart, J., observed that the granting of a *mandamus* is in the discretion of the Judge, that upon the authorities it appears that this discretion should be exercised liberally, and that no subject should be denied the order on the ground only that his right is doubtful. And here, I am in no doubt.

Allied with the declaratory order earlier pronounced, there will be an order that the respondent do present himself before the Beth Din to institute inquiry whether a bill of divorcement is necessary as between the parties, and to institute proceedings for the same should the Beth Din so determine.

Application granted.

Re Morris and Morris
42 D.L.R. (3d) 550
Manitoba Court of Appeal (December 27, 1973)[a]

Guy, J.A.: This is an appeal from a decision of Wilson, J. It is concerned with the application of Mrs. Morris for an order declaring and determining her right and entitlement to a religious Jewish bill of divorcement ("Get"). The judgment of the learned trial Judge, granting the order, reads in part as follows [36 D.L.R. (3d) 447 at p. 456, [1973] 3 W.W.R. 526, 10 R.F.L. 118]:

> Clearly, upon any reading of the evidence before me, and in answer to her request for a declaration, applicant is entitled as one of her rights under the Kethubah to the preparation and delivery to her, by respondent, of a Jewish bill of divorcement, or Get.
>
> The formal judgment itself reads in part:
>
> > 1. THIS COURT DOTH ORDER that the Applicant is entitled as one of her rights under the Kethubah to the preparation and delivery to her, by the Respondent, of a Jewish Bill of Divorcement ("Get").
> > 2. THIS COURT DOTH FURTHER ORDER that the Respondent do forthwith present himself before the Beth Din (rabbinical court) to institute enquiry whether a Bill of Divorcement ("Get") is necessary as between the Applicant and Respondent, and to institute proceedings for the same should the Beth Din so determine.

In the course of his judgment the learned trial Judge indicated that the premarital covenant of marriage was, in fact, a contract, and should be enforced by any Court having regard to the law relating to contract. In other words, there was a promise, a form, a consideration, a reality of consent, a capacity of the parties to contract, and the legality of the object.

It is with this concept that I take issue with the learned trial Judge, with respect. According to the judgment, which is reported in 36 D.L.R. (3d) 447, the so-called prenuptial statement or *Kethubah* is not all that definite or clear-cut as a contract. It reads [at p. 455]:

> "The said bridegroom made the following declaration to his bride:
>
> 'Be thou my wife according to the law of Moses and Israel. I faithfully promise, that I will be a true husband unto thee. I will honour and cherish thee, I will work for thee, I will protect and support thee and will provide all that is necessary for thy due sustenance as it Beseemeth a Jewish husband to do. I also take upon myself all such further obligations for thy maintenance, as are prescribed by our religious statute.'
>
> "And the said bride has plighted her troth unto him in affection and in sincerity and has thus taken upon herself the fulfillment of all the duties incumbent upon a Jewish wife.
>
> This covenant of marriage was duly executed and witnessed this day, according to the usage of Israel.

---

[a]Edited. Deletions indicated by ***** and footnotes renumbered.

Then follow signatures of the bridegroom and bride and of the two witnesses.

I find very little difference between this wording and the wording of the Anglican marriage ceremony which is also witnessed and signed. The accepted vow in the Anglican Church marriage ceremony is as follows:

> Minister - Wilt thou have this woman to thy wedded wife, to live together after God's ordinance in the holy estate of matrimony? Wilt thou love her, comfort her, honour, and keep her, in sickness and in health; and forsaking all other, keep thee only unto her, so long as ye both shall live?
> Man - I will
> I, (name of man), take thee, (name of woman), to my wedded wife, to have and to hold from this day forward, for better or worse, for richer for poorer, in sickness and in health, to live and to cherish till death us do part, *according to God's holy ordinance*, and thereto I plight thee my troth.

[Emphasis added.]

The United Church of Canada has a similar form of marriage vow or contract which is signed and witnessed following the ceremony. The Roman Catholic Church has similar vows or undertakings.

Each vow is followed by a statement from the presiding priest, minister or clergyman - "Whom, therefore, God hath joined together, let no man put asunder."

I assume that Mohammedans, or Muslims, the adherents of Hinduism, and the Buddhists, have similar forms of marriage vow. I do not know their exact terms, but they are entitled to make whatever extra vows their religious upbringing teaches them to make; and I respect their views.

However, in the context of marriage and divorce, we in Canada, over the past century, have developed our own laws. The British North America Act, 1867 (which is commonly referred to as "Canada's Constitution"), provides as follows:

> 91. It shall be lawful for the Queen, by and with the Advice and Consent of the Senate and House of Commons, to make Laws for the Peace, Order, and good Government of Canada, in relation to all Matters not coming within the Classes of Subjects by this Act assigned exclusively to the Legislatures of the Provinces; and for greater Certainty, but not so as to restrict the generality of the foregoing Terms of this Section, it is hereby declared that (notwithstanding anything in this Act) the exclusive Legislative Authority of the Parliament of Canada extends to all Matters coming within the Classes of Subjects next herein-after enumerated; that is to say,
>
> 26. Marriage and Divorce.

Section 92 of the British North America Act, 1867 provides in part:

> 92. In each Province the Legislature may exclusively make Laws in relation to Matters coming within the Classes of Subjects next herein-after enumerated; that is to say,
> 12. The Solemnization of Marriage in the Province.
> 13. Property and *Civil Rights* in the Province.

[Emphasis added.]

The Marriage Act of the Province of Manitoba which is R.S.M. 1970, c. M50, sets out the essential matters to be included in the marriage ceremony.

The Canadian Divorce Act, which is found in 1967-68 (Can.), c.24 [now R.S.C. 1970, c.D-8], prescribes the essential elements involved in the divorce of two people who are married.

In particular, s.16 of the Divorce Act reads:

> 16. Where a decree of divorce has been made absolute under this Act, either party to the former marriage may marry again.

That is precisely what happened here. The appellant's wife obtained a divorce in the Court of Queen's Bench of Manitoba. She then remarried according to what the learned trial Judge called "the perfunctory form prescribed for use by a Judge of the County Court."

In other words, she is now living with another man, by her own choice, and yet comes before this Court of equity to make her first husband deliver a bill of divorcement or Get so that she will not suffer shame in the eyes of her religious community; and so that any children born to her as a result of this second cohabitation will not be *mamzerim*, or bastards. She feels that she will be looked down upon by the Jewish community, if she cannot remarry in her Jewish faith.

Nothing has been said about how the Jewish community regards her now, when she is living with a second man as a result of her own petition for divorce in a civil rights Court of Canada, and her own remarriage.

Not only is she reluctant to mention this, but she adopts the attitude that the law of Moses and Israel is very important to her in her religious life. According to the statement as to the law of Moses and Israel, as agreed upon by the rabbis who signed the statement (which is included in the judgment of the learned trial Judge) the husband is the only one who can institute proceedings for a bill of divorcement. Yet, forsaking the law of Moses and Israel, the wife herself commenced divorce proceedings in the Canadian civil Court.

Furthermore, this so-called "perfunctory" civil marriage ceremony of hers contains these statements by the bride, pursuant to s. 7 (3) of the Marriage Act:

> Bride - I solemnly declare that I do not know of any lawful impediment why I may not be joined in matrimony to (state name of groom).
>
> Bride - I call upon all persons present to witness that I take (name of groom) to be my lawful wedded husband.

I am of the view that the law relating to marriage and divorce in Canada is a Canadian civil matter and cannot be allowed to become uncertain or schismatic by reference to various sects or religious. I am aware that the Roman Catholic Church does not recognize divorce in any form. It appears that the law of Moses and Israel recognizes a Canadian divorce only as a reason for obtaining a rabbinical court bill of divorcement. In the United States of America, various States have varying rules or standards relating to grounds for divorce - from cruelty, and bestiality to adultery, or mere incompatibility. That is not the concern of a Canadian Court. We are bound to administer the law of Canada as it is written, and the power of the civil Courts of justice should not be extended to assist rabbinical courts or, indeed, any religious sects, to enforce their orders. The administration of justice in Canada, in so far as it relates to divorce, should be concerned solely with civil law, both statute and common. The civil law relating to divorce does not only extend to the final cutting of the conjugal knot, but also to the matter of dower rights, custody of children, adoption of children, maintenance, intestacy, domicile and the

Testators Family Maintenance Act, R.S.M. 1970, c. T50. The rabbinical courts may be concerned with matters such as these, arising out of their bill of divorcement, but they can do nothing about it in the face of authoritative legislation of the Province or the federal Parliament. The religious courts have rules and powers and they enforce them in their own states, but they should not ask this country to depart from its own valid legislative enactments.

But, it is argued, the Canadian law will uphold and enforce a contract. And it will. But one who comes to a Court of equity must come with clean hands, and in the light of the facts we have in the present case, Mrs. Morris does not.

This is not to suggest that even if she had come with clean hands (i.e., no divorce and no remarriage), I would grant this order *mandamus*, because there is another factor to be considered, and that is this; Courts should not ever give judgments that cannot be enforced. As long ago as the case of *Lumley v. Wagner* (1852), 1 De G.M.&G. 604, 42 E.R. 687, it was clearly stated that no Court would order a singer to sing. Orders for specific performance of personal services cannot be enforced. It is true, in the instant case, that Mr. Morris could be fined or imprisoned for contempt if he failed to appear before the rabbinical court. That would not accomplish the performance of the so-called contract. That would simply be a matter of a superior Court in Canada demeaning both itself and the administration of justice by delivering with great solemnity a judgment that nobody can enforce.

With great respect, I would allow the appeal with costs here and below.

Monnin, J.A., concurs with *Guy, J.A.*

Hall, J.A.: The issue, in this appeal, is whether the Court of Queen's Bench of Manitoba has jurisdiction to adjudicate upon and enforce by appropriate order, the right of the respondent, Roberta Morris, to have the appellant, Walter Morris, prepare and deliver to her a Jewish bill of divorcement or Get. Wilson, J., on the application of Mrs. Morris resolved that issue in her favour and accordingly made an order declaring that right and requiring Mr. Morris to present himself before the Beth Din (rabbinical court) to institute inquiry on whether a Get is necessary and to institute proceedings for it should the Beth Din so determine. Mr. Morris appeals from that order.

*****

At the heart of the matter is the refusal of Mr. Morris to prepare and deliver to Mrs. Morris a bill of divorcement or Get, and the inability of the Beth Din to impose any sanction for his refusal. In other words the rabbinical court is unable to provide a remedy for the fulfillment of her undoubted right to a religious divorce.

The question arises of the presence and exercise of jurisdiction by a civil Court in what appears to be uniquely a matter for the Jewish law and its institutions. Mrs. Morris was under no legal disability in marrying a second time. She apparently felt no moral or ethical restraint in remarrying in a civil ceremony before a County Court Judge. Any children of her second marriage will not suffer any legal disability on the grounds of legitimacy or otherwise. But, it is said, she desires to be in a state of grace in the eyes of her religious community. She wishes to have spiritual recognition to her divorce and remarriage. She does not want any children that may hereafter be born to her, to be bastards in the eyes of the Jewish religion. For these reasons, on her behalf stated, the civil Court ought to declare and enforce her right, including by implication appropriate sanction against Mr. Morris if he refuses to obey any order.

In *Ukrainian Greek Orthodox Church et al. v. Trustees of Ukrainian Greek Orthodox Cathedral of St. Mary the Protectress et al.*, [1939] 2 D.L.R. 494, [1939] 1 W.W.R. 481, 47 Man. R. 64, a decision of this Court, Dennistoun, J.A., at p. 498 stated:

> In Canada all religious bodies are considered as voluntary associations. The law recognizes their existence and protects them in their enjoyment of property, but unless civil rights are in question it does not interfere with their organization or with questions of religious faith. *Dunnet v. Fornori* (1877), 25 Gr. 199 at p. 206.

On appeal to the Supreme Court of Canada reported in [1940] 3 D.L.R. 670, [1940] S.C.R. 587, Crockett, J., at p. 671 stated:

> ...it is well settled that, unless some property or civil right is affected thereby, the civil Courts of this country will not allow their process to be used for the enforcement of a purely ecclesiastical decree or order.

While the facts of that case differ from the present case, the principle therein enunciated should not be altered by factual distinction.

In *Dunnet v. Fornori* (1877), 25 Gr. 199, Proudfoot, V.-C., quotes with approval a passage from the judgment of Lord Deas in the *Cardross* case, cited in *Innes' Creeds of Scotland*, 285-298. Lord Deas stated in part [at p. 209]:

> "The interpretation of all contracts belongs to the Civil Courts, to the effect, in the first instance, of ascertaining whether they involve civil rights; and in the next place, if they do, of vindicating or giving redress for the violation of these rights..."

What then are civil rights? In the case of *Hill v. Hill*, [1929] 2 D.L.R. 735 at p. 740, [1929] 2 W.W.R. 41, 24 Atla. L.R. 105, Hyndman, J.A., expressed satisfaction with the definition given by Harrison, C., in *Byers v. Sun Savings Bank* (1914), 52 L.R.A. (N.S.) 320 at p. 323; this definition reads:

> "By the term 'civil rights,' in its broader sense, is meant those rights which are the outgrowth of civilization, which arise from the needs of civil, as distinguished from barbaric, communities, and are given, defined, and circumscribed by such positive laws, enacted by such communities, as are necessary to the maintenance of organized government. The term should not be confounded with, nor distinguished from, the term 'political rights,' as seems to have been done by some authorities. It is a broader and more comprehensive term than the term 'political rights.'
>
> "The word 'civil' is derived from the Latin *civilis*, a citizen, as distinguished from a savage or barbarian, *and the term 'civil rights' comprehends all rights which civilized communities undertake, by the enactment of positive laws, to prescribe, abridge, protect, and enforce.*"

(Italics mine.)

In the present case the right sought to be declared and enforced, in my opinion, affects no civil rights enjoyed by Mrs. Morris. On that ground alone, I would allow the appeal, set aside the order of Wilson, J., and substitute an order dismissing the application with costs here and before him.

Matas, J.A.: Mr. and Mrs. Morris, who are Jews, were married by a rabbi in accordance with traditional Jewish practice which included the execution and delivery of a contract of marriage ("Kethubah").

The parties were divorced by Court of Queen's Bench in 1972. Dissolution of the marriage was accompanied by a series of ancillary acerbic proceedings, some of which have not been settled as yet.

Mrs. Morris (the "applicant" or "wife") has remarried in a civil ceremony. She wants a religious divorce so that she can have a traditional Jewish marriage, one which requires a prior religious divorce to be obtained by the parties. Mr. Morris (the "respondent" or "husband"), whose co-operation is needed for obtaining a Jewish bill of divorcement ("Get"), has refused to be a party to the religious proceedings and has refused to take the action which a husband must initiate under religious law.

Mrs. Morris applied to Court of Queen's Bench for a declaratory order as to her right to a Get and for an order compelling Mr. Morris to institute proceedings for the Get.

A statement of Jewish law (the "statement") was filed in Court by consent. As well, Rabbi Rappaport, chairman of the Winnipeg Council of Rabbis, gave *viva voce* evidence. Also before the Court was a text, "Jews and Divorce," (1968) published by Commission on Synagogue Relations, New York.

Prior to the proceedings in Court of Queen's Bench, applicant had brought the matter to the attention of a rabbinical court ("Beth Din"). That court considered the factual situation, i.e., the existence of a civil divorce, and concluded that under Jewish law there must be a religious divorce. That decision having been made, it would seem to be unnecessary for Mrs. Morris to apply for a confirming order from Court of Queen's Bench. But the Queen's Bench order is necessary as a basis for the additional relief asked for by applicant, i.e., to compel the husband to institute proceedings for a Get. In considering that point, the learned trial Judge said [36 D.L.R. (3d) 447 at pp. 456 and 458, [1973] 3 W.W.R. 526, 10 R.F.L. 118]:

> More formidable is respondent's denial of the right of the Court to proceed beyond the mere declaration of the rights of the applicant, and to require that in fact the respondent shall do whatever is necessary to complete their divorce in the eyes of the religious community of which they are both members.
>
> . . . . .
>
> Allied with the declaratory order earlier pronounced, there will be an order that the respondent do present himself before the Beth Din to institute inquiry whether a bill of divorcement is necessary as between the parties, and to institute proceedings for the same should the Beth Din so determine.

Thus, the real issue between the parties is whether the powers of the civil Court are to be invoked by applicant to enforce her right to a religious divorce.

Wilson, J., held that execution and delivery of the *Kethubah* was tantamount to a pre-nuptial contract and that one of applicant's rights under the *Kethubah* was the preparation and delivery to her, by respondent, of a Get. For the jurisdictional basis of that declaratory order, see the *Queen's Bench Act*, R.S.M. 1970, c. C280, s. 63, Rule 8; 22 Hals., 3rd ed., pp. 746-51. paras. 1610-11; S.A. de Smith, *Judicial Review of Administrative Action*, 3rd ed. (1973), pp. 430-1.

There would seem to be no need, in logic, to order respondent to present himself before the rabbinical court to institute inquiries to determine whether a Get is necessary. That court has decided that it is necessary. But this point is not of crucial importance. The effect of the order of Court of Queen's Bench is to require Mr. Morris to do whatever may be necessary to provide applicant with a Get.

That statement, *supra*, deals with the obligations of the husband and the relationship between civil Courts and the Beth Din as follows:

> The Jewish law states that the man must initiate the divorce proceedings.
>
> Historically and biblically, rabbinical courts had the right to compel the parties to be divorced. The rabbinical courts had the power to impose physical sanctions in the form of imprisonment and beatings to compel the husband to initiate the necessary proceedings for the Jewish divorce. The rabbinical courts no longer have the power to impose physical sanctions and it became acceptable for the rabbinical courts to turn to the civil courts for enforcement of their orders and, in fact, there is authority in Jewish law which permits rabbinical courts to request the assistance of civil courts in enforcing their orders.
>
> . . . . . .
>
> There are no Jewish religious grounds upon which the respondent can refuse to initiate proceedings for a Bill of Divorcement.

Obviously, the application in the case at bar is not made by the Beth Din, for enforcement of one of its orders, but is an application by the wife, based on the implied covenant of the husband, under the *Kethubah*, to grant a bill of divorcement.

Counsel for Mr. Morris argued that this was not a case where the civil Court could safely enter the area of religious belief. Mr. Houston referred to an article by Dr. M.M. Brayer, professor of biblical literature and religious education at Yeshiva University in the text "Jews and Divorce," *supra*. Professor Brayer's article contains a summary of the "Basic Jewish Law of Divorce," which is different in some respects from the Jewish law as delineated in the statement, *supra*, and includes the following comment:

> However, if a non-Jewish court or other methods of compulsion are used, the divorce is invalid, even if it contains rabbinic requirements, because it would be an instrument made out by one who acts not as a free agent.

I do not suggest that the opinion of the learned author, Dr. Brayer, is entitled to the same weight as that of the distinguished rabbis who were instrumental in preparing the statement, *supra*. Nevertheless, the Court is faced with a contrary opinion as to the propriety of intervention by a civil Court. That must be taken into account in considering whether this is a proper case for exercise of the Court's discretion in favour of the applicant: *R. v. Chancellor of St. Edmundsbury and Ipswich Diocese, Ex p. White*, [1948] 1 K.B. 185 at p. 214; *Hofer et al. v. Hofer et al.* (1967), 65 D.L.R. (2d) 607 at p. 613 [affirmed 13 D.L.R. (3d) 1, [1970] S.C.R. 958, 73 W.W.R. 644].

Applicant contends that her civil rights have been infringed. It is contended that she is denied the opportunity of remarriage in a traditional Jewish ceremony; without such a marriage her children (of the second marriage) and their descendants, would be considered illegitimate according to traditional Jewish law. It is not suggested that children of the second marriage would suffer any disability under the civil law.

It should be noted that reform rabbis, those less constrained by orthodox tenets, will officiate at a marriage ceremony notwithstanding absence of a Get.

Under all the circumstances, it appears that allegations by applicant as to infringement of her civil rights are somewhat tenuous. In my view, cases such as *Davis v. Jenkins* (1814), 3 V. & B. 151, 35 E.R. 436; *Gold v. Madaver* (1912), 6 D.L.R. 33, 4 O.W.N. 106, and *Brown v. Cure et Marguilliers de l'Oeuvre et Fabrique de Notre Dame de Montreal* (1874), L.R. 6 P.C. 157, do not assist Mrs. Morris. In the case at bar, in my opinion, there is not such an infringement of civil rights as would warrant intervention by a civil Court.

There is another consideration - the practical result of the order of the Court of Queen's Bench. Presumably, if the husband refuses to present himself to the Beth Din to initiate proceedings for a *Get*, he could be found in contempt of Court and subject to penalties for that conduct. He could thus be gaoled or fined for disobeying, indirectly, an order of a religious court. In my opinion, this result would not be a desirable one.

In view of all the circumstances, I have concluded, with deference to those holding a different opinion, that this is not an appropriate case for exercise of the Court's discretion.

I would allow the appeal with costs here and below.

Appeal allowed.

Freedman, C.J.M. (dissenting): - This appeal confronts the Court with an interesting and important question of public policy. To what extent, if at all, may a Court of law take cognizance of and give effect to a marriage contract entered into between parties of the Jewish faith "according to the law of Moses and Israel"? More specifically, has a Court of law jurisdiction (and, if so, should it exercise such jurisdiction) (1) to declare that the wife is entitled, as one of her rights under such a marriage contract, to receive from her husband a Jewish bill of divorcement (a Get), and (b) to direct the husband to present himself before a rabbinical court in order that the tribunal may make such inquiry and take such action as may be appropriate in the circumstances? Manifestly, these questions raise an issue of the extent to which a civil Court may legitimately concern itself with matters of religion. As such they touch on the relationship of church and state.

The parties were married in Winnipeg on October 23, 1955, by a rabbi in an orthodox Jewish wedding ceremony and in pursuance of the Marriage Act of Manitoba, R.S.M. 1954, c. 154 [now R.S.M. 1970, c. M50]. It is common ground that they entered into the traditional contract of marriage, known as the *Kethubah*. Part of the marriage ceremony consists in the reading aloud of that document by the rabbi. One provision of the *Kethubah* is a declaration made by the groom to the bride as follows: "Be thou my wife according to the law of Moses and Israel." Expert evidence concerning the law of Moses and Israel was adduced. It will be referred to later. For the present, it is enough to say that the *Kethubah*, with the body of law which it incorporated, formed part of the foundation on which this marriage rested.

Following the marriage, the parties lived together as man and wife. Three children were born of the union. The marriage did not prove to be a happy one and ultimately the parties separated. Some years later the wife launched a petition for divorce in the Court of Queen's Bench. The husband cross-petitioned. On July 14, 1972, the Court pronounced a decree *nisi* dissolving the marriage. That decree was made absolute on October 23, 1972.

In all its civil aspects the marriage is accordingly at an end. It is in its religious aspect that a difficulty has arisen. The wife - if I may so refer to her for convenience - is an orthodox Jewess. Under orthodox Jewish law her marriage is not regarded as dissolved until there has been a religious divorce. It is the husband who must initiate the proceedings for such a divorce, and he refuses to do so. Whether his refusal is purely malicious or is based on some reason undisclosed to us does not emerge from the record. No matter. The point is that he refuses. In that situation the wife invoked the assistance of the Court of Queen's Bench. Her application, brought by way of originating notice under Queen's Bench Rules, Rule 536, came on for hearing before Wilson, J. That learned Judge held in favour of the wife, in effect directing the husband to present himself before the rabbinical court for the purpose of a religious divorce. This is an appeal by the husband - I shall so refer to him - against that decision.

*****

I turn now to the central issues of jurisdiction and public policy. Should a civil court adjudicate on and attempt to enforce a contract based on the tenets of a particular religion, in this case the Jewish religion? In seeking the answer to that question it is important to keep in mind that we are here simply concerned with a contract between two parties and the matter of its enforcement.

*****

The contention that the enforcement of the contract herein would be contrary to public policy is sustainable only on the view that the Court should not take cognizance of a contract based on the religious doctrines of a particular faith or ethnic group. To determine whether that contention is valid or not required an examination of the contract, with particular reference to what may be described as its religious aspects.

Against that background of the relevant Jewish law the marriage contract between the parties may be examined to determine whether it is enforceable or whether it offends against public policy. That the contract is deeply affected by religious considerations is not determinative of the issue. That is the beginning and not the end of the matter. Some contracts rooted in the religion of a particular faith may indeed be contrary to public policy. Others may not. Our task is to determine whether the rights and obligations flowing from the marriage contract - specifically, the husband's obligation to give and the wife's right to receive a *Get* - are contrary to public policy.

I find difficulty in pin-pointing the precise aspect of public policy which the present contract may be said to offend. The attack upon it is on more general grounds. It appears that the real basis on which enforcement of the contract is being resisted is simply that it rests on religion, and that on grounds of public policy the Court should keep out of that field. But the law reports contain many instances of Courts dealing with disputes having a religious origin or basis. Wilson, J., in his judgment cites several, including *Gold v. Maldaver* (1912), 6 D.L.R. 333, 4 O.W.N. 106, relating to the sale of pews in a synagogue, and *Hofer et al. v. Hofer et al.* (1970), 13 D.L.R. (3d) 1, [1970] S.C.R. 958, 73 W.W.R. 644, dealing with the dissolution of a Hutterite community. In each case some temporal right confronted the Court, and it did not hesitate to adjudicate thereon.

*****

In the result, I am in agreement with Wilson, J., that the wife is entitled to the declaration and order which she sought. I would dismiss the appeal, with costs.

Minkin v. Minkin

180 N.J. Super. 260, 434 A.2d 665 (1981)
Superior Court of New Jersey, Chancery Div., Bergen County
July 22, 1981

Minushin, J.S.C.:

Plaintiff wife moved post judgment for an order requiring the defendant to obtain and pay for the costs of a Jewish ecclesiastical divorce known as a "get."[1]

The significance if her motion is that only a husband may secure the get and without it the wife cannot remarry under Jewish law.

The issues are:

(1) Whether the parties have entered into a contract enforceable by this court, and

(2) Whether the relief sought by plaintiff would unconstitutionally infringe upon defendant's First Amendment right of exercise of religious freedom.

The parties were married in a Jewish ceremony where they entered into a contract, called a "ketuba," in which they agreed to conform to the provisions of the laws of Moses and Israel.[2] These laws require the husband to give his wife a get when he alleges an act of adultery on his wife's part. In the instant case the husband counterclaimed for divorce on the ground of adultery, giving rise to the wife's claim to require her husband to secure a get. The husband has refused and opposes any order to compel him to do so, claiming that such an order would violate the Establishment of Religion Clause of the First Amendment. The wife asserts that without the get she would be effectively restrained from remarrying in a manner consistent with her religious beliefs.

To compel the husband to secure a get would be to enforce the agreement of the marriage contract (ketuba). A court of equity will enforce a

---

1. Acquisition of a get is unique since it may only be obtained by the husband. See 6 Encyclopedia Judaica, 132 (1971).

> Execution of the Divorce. Divorce is carried into effect by the bill of divorcement being written, signed, and delivered by the husband to his wife. It is written by a scribe upon the husband's instruction to write "for him, for her and for the purpose of a divorce." The materials used in the writing must belong to the husband and the scribe formally presents them as an outright gift to the husband before writing the Get.

2. Every Jewish marriage calls for the execution by the parties of an agreement called the "ketuba." The ketuba obligates the marital partners to comply with the laws of Moses and Israel. Certain rights and privileges as defined in those laws are granted to the wife by the husband. The consideration in the contract is the giving by the wife of her dowry and the husband obligating himself to support and care for his wife during the marriage and to comply with the laws of Moses and Israel. See Encyclopedia Judaica, supra.

contract between husband and wife if it is not unconscionable to do so and if the performance to be compelled is not contrary to public policy. See *Garlinger v. Garlinger*, 128 N.J.Super. 37, 322 A.2d 190 (Ch. Div. 1974); *Schlemm v. Schlemm*, 31 N.J. 557, 158 A.2d 508 (1960); *Equitable Life Assur. Soc. of U.S. v. Huster*, 75 N.J.Super. 492, 183 A.2d 473 (App. Div. 1962).

What constitutes an agreement against public policy was defined in *Garlinger*, supra, where the court said,

> An agreement is against public policy if it is injurious to the interest of the public, contravenes some established interest of society, violates some public statute, is against good morals, tends to interfere with the public welfare or safety, or, as it is sometimes put, if it is at war with the interests of society and is in conflict with public morals. 17 Am.Jur.2d, Contracts, §179 at 541. [129 N.J.Super. at 40, 322 A.2d 190].

In the instant case the ketuba contract requires the participants to comply with certain reciprocal obligations pertaining to the marriage. For example, the wife is to perform the role of homemaker and to supply a dowry; the husband is to support and care for the wife. The ketuba is devoid of any requirement that could be construed to be against public policy. No interest of society is affected or impaired by its provisions, nor does it conflict with public morals. On the contrary, its purpose is obviously to promote a successful marital relationship and its enforcement, therefore, actually advances public policy. The contract simply calls for defendant, in securing a get, to do that which he agreed to do. Without compliance plaintiff cannot remarry in accordance with her religious beliefs. For these reasons the contract should be specifically enforced.

The question of whether an order of this court for specific performance of the ketuba constitutes violation of defendant's First Amendment rights remains to be determined. Authority to permit the issuance of such an order appears in *Koeppel v. Koeppel*, 138 N.Y.S.2d 366 (Sup.Ct. 1954), and *Rubin v. Rubin*, 75 Misc.2d 776, 348 N.Y.S.2d 61 (Family Ct. 1973). In *Koeppel*, where the facts parallel the instant case, the court said:

> Defendant has also contended that a decree of specific performance would interfere with his freedom of religion under the Constitution. Complying with his agreement would not compel the defendant to practice any religion, not even the Jewish faith to which he still admits adherence (paragraph Second of the complaint not denied in the answer). His appearance before the Rabbinate to answer questions and give evidence needed by them to make a decision is not a profession of faith. Specific performance herein would merely require the defendant to do what he voluntarily agreed to do. [at 373]

The *Koeppel* and *Rubin* opinions are within the standards promulgated by the U.S. Supreme Court in its landmark holding of *Committee for Public Education and Religious Liberty v. Nyquist*, 413 U.S. 756, 772-773, 93 S.Ct. 2955, 2965-2966, 37 L.Ed.2d 948, 962-963 (1973). See, also, *Marsa v. Wernik*, 96 N.J. 232, 246, 430 A.2d 888 (1980). The *Nyquist* court set forth a three-prong test for determining whether an act violates the Establishment Clause of the First Amendment.

> ...[T]o pass muster under the Establishment Clause the law[3] in question, first, must reflect a clearly secular legislative purpose, second, must have a primary effect that neither advances nor inhibits religion, and, third, must avoid excessive entanglement with religion. [*Nyquist*, supra 413 U.S. at 773, 93 S.Ct. at 2965.]

To determine whether enforcing the marriage contract would violate the three-prong test, and because "this issue is one of the most sensitive areas in the law," the court on its own motion requested the testimony of several distinguished rabbis[4] well versed in Jewish law, and one of whom (Rabbi Richard Cars) is also a practicing attorney specializing in matrimonial law.

Rabbi Macy Gordon defined the get as a written document of severance, authorized by the husband and delivered to his wife, which states that all marital bonds between them have been severed. He stated that a Jewish couple upon marriage enters into a ketuba, which is essentially a civil contract delineating the obligations of the parties during the marriage. The marriage is severable only by the death of one of the parties or by the acquisition of a get. Failure of the husband to secure the get places the wife in the position of an

---

3. The Establishment Clause bars a state from placing its official support behind a religious belief, while the Free Exercise Clause bars a state from interfering with the practice of religion by its citizens. This prohibition applies to the judiciary as well as the executive and legislative branches of government. See In re Adoption of E., 59 N.J. 36, 51, 279 A.2d 785 (1971).

4. Rabbis:

Rabbi Macy A. Gordon: Master's degree from Columbia University; Ph.D., Yeshiva University, in Jewish Education; ordained rabbi in 1956; on the Religious Studies faculty at Yeshiva University; chairman of the Rabbinical Council of Bergen County; vice-president of the Rabbinical Council of New Jersey; member of the executive board of commission of the Rabbinical Council of America; member of the Beth Din Commission of the Rabbinical Council of America.

Rabbi Judah Washer. Graduate of Yeshiva College; Ph.D. from University of Pittsburg; president of N.Y. Board of Rabbis; rabbi of the Jewish Center of Teaneck, N.J. since 1934.

Rabbi Menahem Meier. B.S. from the City College, New York; Semikha, Yeshiva University; Master's degree, Yeshiva University; Ph.D. from Brandeis University in Jewish Philosophy and Mysticism; past instructor at Yeshiva University High School; present founding principal of The Frisch School; chairman, Yeshiva University High School Principals Council of Greater New York; member, Rabbinical Council of America.

Rabbi Richard J. Cars: Yeshiva Ohelmoshe Elementary School; Yeshiva University (High School), Yeshiva College (received a teaching certificate); licensed teacher and principal of a Hebrew School; B.A. in Philosophy and Literature; postgraduate studies in comparative religion and semitic languages at Hunter College, Columbia and N.Y.U.; J.D. from Brooklyn Law School; rabbi of congregation 12 years; teacher at Yeshiva University; counsel to the Rabbinical Council of America.

"aguna" so that she is precluded from remarrying. He said that the get does not involve a religious ceremony or require a rabbi's presence, and although the husband is required to take the initiative, he does not have to be a believer, state any doctrine or creed, or even acknowledge his Jewishness. Because of this, he concluded that the acquisition of a get is not a religious act, but a severance of a contractual relationship between two parties.

Rabbi Judah Washer agreed that a get is a civil document for the same reasons, adding that the document contains no reference to God's name. In addition, in his opinion, a court order requiring the husband to secure the get would not be an interference with religion since the get does not affect the religious feelings of people, but is only concerned with the right of the wife to remarry.

Rabbi Menahem Meier testified that Jewish law cannot be equated with religious law, but instead is comprised of two components - one regulating a man's relationship with God and the other regulating the relationship between man and man. The get, which has no reference to God but which does affect the relationship between two parties, falls into the latter category and is, therefore, civil and not religious in nature.

Rabbi Richard Cars concurred with Rabbi Meier's opinion that Jewish law is divided into two components and that the get is clearly civil. He described the get as a general release document where the husband releases the wife and frees her to remarry in compliance with the ketuba contract.

Rabbi Dresner, a reform rabbi, was called by defendant and although he concluded that the acquisition of a get was a religious act, he said he would marry the plaintiff. However, the weight to be given to his testimony was weakened when he admitted that the other rabbis called to testify were "far better Jewish scholar[s] than myself."

Relying upon credible expert testimony that the acquisition of a get is not a religious act, the court finds that the entry of an order compelling defendant to secure a get would have the clear secular purpose of completing a dissolution of the marriage. Its primary effect neither advances nor inhibits religion since it does not require the husband to participate in a religious ceremony or to do acts contrary to his religious beliefs. Nor would the order be an excessive entanglement with religion. In addition to testimony to that effect, the court takes judicial notice that the Legislature has seen fit to authorize clergy to perform marriages and, in doing so, permits the use of a religious ceremony. See N.J.S.A. 37:1-13. Such conduct, as sanctioned by the Legislature, has never been considered to be an excessive entanglement with religion. The get procedure is a release document devoid of religious connotation and cannot be construed as any more religious than the marriage ceremony itself. Thus, the three-prong test protecting defendant pursuant to the First Amendment is satisfied. The court concludes that it may, without infringing on his constitutional rights, order defendant to specifically perform his contract.

Order may be entered accordingly.

Burns v. Burns
538 A.2d 438 (1987)
Superior Court of New Jersey, Chancery Div., Camden County
December 4, 1987

Natal, P.J.F.P.:

This matter came before the court on a post-judgment motion by the defendant, Michelle M. Burns, for an order to compel the plaintiff to assist her in securing a Jewish bill of divorcement known as a "get."[1] The plaintiff filed a cross-motion to suppress that portion of the defendant's supporting affidavit relating to his demand for $25,000 to accede to the defendant's request pursuant to Rule 52 of the New Jersey Rules of Evidence.

Background facts in this case are important, as they are not in dispute and they present the basis for the final disposition.

Both the plaintiff and the defendant had been married prior to their marriage to each other in 1969. Since they were of the Jewish religion they felt compelled to secure "gets" from their prior spouses in order to properly enter into a Jewish contract of marriage known as a "ketubbah." Under Jewish law one cannot marry in an Orthodox or Conservative ceremony without securing a "get" from a prior spouse.

At the time the plaintiff and the defendant married, plaintiff willingly proceeded with securing a "get" from his prior spouse and then married the defendant under civil and Jewish law. The marriage did not succeed and a dual judgment of divorce was granted to the parties in 1982. Since that time the plaintiff has remarried, choosing not to proceed with first securing a "get." The defendant now plans to remarry but she believes she is bound by tenet of Jewish law to obtain a "get" terminating her prior marriage before she may marry again.

Defendant's attorney contacted the plaintiff to communicate her desire to have the plaintiff secure the "get."[2] Plaintiff stated his religious beliefs are such that he no longer believed in the necessity of securing a "get." Yet, plaintiff informed defendant's attorney, if the defendant would invest $25,000 in an irrevocable trust for the benefit of their daughter, with the plaintiff and another party of his choosing as joint trustees, he would secure the "get" for the defendant.

I. All of the facts necessary for the court to make its determination were set forth in supporting affidavits. Thus, there were no genuine issues of material fact. The court is not required to take oral testimony and may decide this matter without a plenary hearing. *Skillman v. Skillman*, 136 N.J.Super. 348, 350, 346 A.2d 408 (App.Div. 1975).

---

1. Under Hebraic law, evidence of the granting of a divorce. Black's Law Dictionary Revised 816 (4th Ed. West Publishing Co. 1968).

2. Jewish law requires the husband to actually deliver the "get" to his wife. See 6 Encyclopedia Judaica 125 (MacMillan Co. 1971). "Divorce is carried into effect by the bill of divorcement being written, signed and delivered by the husband to the wife. It is written by a scribe upon the husband's instructions to write 'for him, for her and for the purpose of a divorce'." Id. at 131.

II. Plaintiff's request to suppress and exclude from the court's consideration that part of the defendant's supporting affidavit referring to his request for $25,000 pursuant to Rule 52 is denied. Plaintiff claims the discussion he had with defendant's attorney, wherein he demanded the sum of $25,000 to be placed in trust, was an offer to compromise the current dispute and should be barred from evidence in a court hearing.

Rule 52 provides:

OFFER TO COMPROMISE AND THE LIKE NOT EVIDENCE OF LIABILITY OR CRIMINAL WRONGDOING

(1) Evidence that a person has, in compromise or from humanitarian motives, furnished or offered or promised to furnish money, or any other thing, act or service to another who has sustained or claimed to have sustained loss or damage, is inadmissible to prove his liability for the loss or damage of any part of it. This rule shall not affect the admissibility of evidence (a) of partial satisfaction of an asserted claim, or (b) of a debtor's payment or promise to pay all or part of his pre-existing debt as tending to prove the creation of a new duty on his part, or a revival of his pre-existing duty.

Under this Rule the courts have admitted otherwise excludable evidence, if it relates to some other issue of fact. *Rynar v. Lincoln Transit Co., Inc.*, 129 N.J.L. 525, 30 A.2d 406 (E. & A. 1943); *Leslie Blau Co. v. Alfieri*, 157 N.J.Super. 173, 200, 384 A.2d 859 (App.Div. 1978), cert. den. 77 N.J. 510, 391 A.2d 523 (1978).

Plaintiff's alleged offer to compromise is admissible to demonstrate that his refusal to secure defendant a "get" is not on the basis of his religious beliefs, but instead is an issue of monetary gain. Plaintiff initially claimed that granting the defendant a "get" was not necessary since it was contrary to his current religious beliefs. Plaintiff further asserted that his First Amendment right to practice his religion without interference from the State would be abridged if he were forced to compromise his religious beliefs.

A true religious belief is not compromised as the amount of money offered or demanded is increased. An offer to secure a "get" for $25,000 makes this a question of money not religious belief. This "offer," which is not denied by the plaintiff, takes this issue outside the First Amendment. This so-called "offer" is akin to extortion.

III. This court finds *Minkin v. Minkin*, 180 N.J.Super. 260, 266, 434 A.2d 665 (1981), as the only New Jersey law controlling in this area. Judge Minushin found that "[t]he get procedure is a release document devoid of religious connotation and cannot be construed as any more religious than the marriage ceremony itself."

The court analyzed whether there was a First Amendment entanglement. Judge Minushin found the Establishment Clause of the First Amendment which clearly separates State and religion, is not violated when a party is ordered to secure a "get." The Court applied the standard set by the United States Supreme Court in *Committee for Public Education and Religious Liberty v. Nyquist*, 413 U.S. 756, 772-773, 93 S.Ct. 2955, 2965-66, 37 L.Ed.2d 948 (1973). Under the three-prong test established in *Nyquist*, the *Minkin* court held that ordering a party to secure a "get," (1) reflects a clear secular legislative purpose; (2) has a primary effect that neither advances nor inhibits religion, and (3) avoids excessive entanglement with religion. 190 N.J.Super. 265-66, 434 A.2d 665.

The court in *Minkin* applied the equity powers of the court and enforced the marriage contract or "ketubbah." The "ketubbah" was held as an enforceable agreement entered into by both parties which was not unconscionable nor contrary to public policy. Id. at 262, 434 A.2d 665. The "ketubbah" requires both parties to conform to the provisions of the Law of Moses and of Israel. Under such law the husband is required to give his wife a "get" when the wife commits adultery. Thus, in *Minkin* the court ordered defendant to secure the "get" and deliver it to his wife. Id.

IV. The parties obtained a dual judgment, on the grounds of eighteen months continuous separation without a prospect of reconciliation, commonly referred to as a "no-fault" divorce. The plaintiff argued that *Minkin* was limited to those cases where the wife was divorced on the grounds of adultery. This court rejects plaintiff's argument and thus expands the *Minkin* decision.

Under Rule 9 of the New Jersey Rules of Evidence, this court takes judicial notice of The Bible[3] and of the Encyclopedia Judaica.[4] The court finds both to be learned treatises containing the laws of Moses and Israel and were consulted by the court to decipher the significance of the "ketubbah." Reference is necessary to the laws of Moses and Israel because the parties have signed a written contract, their "ketubbah" (exhibit 1 in evidence), committing themselves to be bound by such law.

In studying the laws of Moses and Israel this court finds there are various circumstances which would require the husband to secure a "get" from his wife. The *Minkin* court found the husband compelled to grant his wife a "get" due to her acts of adultery.

In addition, a husband is compelled to secure a "get" when (1) he unjustifiably refuses conjugal rights; (2) if the husband shows unworthy conduct toward his wife such that the wife cannot be expected to live with him as his wife; (3) if the husband's unjustified refusal to maintain her when he is in the position to do so, or could be if he was willing to work and earn an income; (4) if the husband is unfaithful to his wife, or (5) if the husband habitually assaults or insults her, or is the cause of unceasing quarrels, so she has no choice but to leave the household.[5]

This list is not intended to be exclusive as there are still other circumstances under which a husband is compelled to give a "get," but merely illustrative of the fact that adultery is not the exclusive ground under the laws of Moses and Israel.

The parties no longer live together. Mr. Burns has remarried. He was the plaintiff and sought the divorce. He has chosen another for his wife and married her under civil law, yet under the Jewish law the plaintiff and the defendant are still married. The plaintiff must release the defendant from the ketubbah and put an end to that relationship. The judgment of divorce provided for the parties to "be divorced from the bond of matrimony... and each of them, be freed and discharged from the obligation thereof[.]" For the court to compel the plaintiff to submit to the jurisdiction of the Jewish ecclesiastical court, the "Bet Din," and initiate the procedure to secure a "get" is within the equity powers of this court to do what ought to be done. In doing equity, the

---

3. See Deuteronomy, 24:1, which states, "when a man taketh a wife and marries her, then it comes to pass if she finds no favor in his eyes because he has found some unseemly thing in her that he write her a bill of divorcement and give it in her hand and send her out of the house."

4. 6 Encyclopedia Judaica, (MacMillan Co. 1971).

5. Conduct of husband as a ground for divorce. See 6 Encyclopedia Judaica 128 (MacMillan Co. 1971).

court has power to adapt the equitable remedies to the particular circumstances of each particular case. *Arabia v. Zisman*, 143 N.J.Super. 168, 362 A.2d 1221 (Ch. 1976), aff'd 157 N.J.Super. 335, 384 A.2d 1110 (App.Div. 1978). The ultimate decision of whether a "get" is to be granted is that of the "Bet Din" and not of this court.

Therefore, this court orders the plaintiff to submit to the jurisdiction of the "Bet Din" to initiate the proceedings for a "get." In the alternative, the court will permit the plaintiff to execute the prepared document, (exhibit 2 in evidence), authorizing the preparation and presentation of the "get" to the defendant by an agent on his behalf and forego the actual appearance before the "Bet Din."

An order may be entered accordingly.

In re Marriage of Goldman

554 N.E.2d 1016 (1990)
Appellate Court of Illinois, First District, Fourth Division
March 30, 1990. Rehearing denied May 7, 1990.

Justice Jiganti delivered the opinion of the court:

On March 23, 1989, an order was entered dissolving the marriage of petitioner Kenneth I. Goldman and respondent Annette C. Goldman. The petitioner appeals from a portion of the order compelling specific performance of the parties' antenuptial agreement that in the event the marriage was dissolved, the petitioner would obtain and deliver to the respondent a Jewish bill of divorcement known as a "get." Under Orthodox Jewish law, a get is necessary to dissolve the marriage and permit the woman to remarry. The petitioner also appeals from that portion of the order incorporating a previously entered custody order.

The first issue presented in this appeal concerns the enforceability of the terms of a document, known as a "ketubah," which was entered into as part of the religious marriage ceremony. Annette Goldman contends that the ketubah is a marital contract which requires the husband to obtain a get upon dissolution of the marriage. Kenneth Goldman contends that the ketubah does not constitute a marital contract; that if it is a contract, its terms are too vague to be specifically enforced; and finally that enforcement of the ketubah would violate his constitutional rights under the Establishment and Free Exercise Clauses of the First Amendment (U.S. Const., amend. I) as well as under article I, section 3, of the Illinois Constitution (Ill. Const. 1970, art. I, §3).

The parties were married on May 27, 1979, in a Reconstructionist Jewish ceremony. Neither party was an Orthodox Jew at the time of the marriage; Annette Goldman became an Orthodox Jew during the course of the marriage. Shortly before the marriage ceremony, the parties signed a certificate of marriage called a ketubah. The ketubah is a document written in Aramaic and translated into English. The English translation contains the date and place of the ceremony and the names of the bridegroom and bride, then states as follows:

"The said Bridegroom made the following declaration to his Bride:

> 'Be thou my wife according to the law of Moses and Israel. I faithfully promise that I will be a true husband unto thee; I will honor and cherish thee; I will work for thee; I will protect and support thee, and will provide all that is necessary for thy sustenance, even as it beseemeth a Jewish husband to

do. I also take upon myself all further obligations for thy maintenance, as are prescribed by our religious statute.'

And the said Bride has plighted her troth unto him, in affection and in sincerity, and has thus taken upon herself the fulfillment of all the duties incumbent upon a Jewish wife.

This Covenant of Marriage was duly executed and witnessed this day according to the usage of Israel."

The ketubah was signed immediately before the ceremony while the parties were dressed in their wedding attire. They had not consulted a lawyer about the terms of the ketubah.

In May of 1984, Kenneth Goldman petitioned for dissolution of the marriage and custody of the parties' two children - Shoshana, born in 1980, and Daniel, born in 1982. Annette Goldman and the children were visiting Annette's parents in New Jersey at the time the petition was filed, and Kenneth was awarded temporary custody in an ex parte proceeding. Upon Annette's return to Chicago, she counterpetitioned for dissolution and requested custody of the children. The counterpetition was subsequently amended to include a count requesting specific performance of the ketubah, which Annette alleged constituted a premarital contract between the parties that the status of their marriage would be governed by Orthodox Jewish law. She further alleged that under Jewish law a marriage can be dissolved only upon the transfer from the husband to the wife of a document called a get. The counterpetition also stated that Annette was an Orthodox Jew and that her religion prohibited her from remarrying unless and until Kenneth obtained a get.

A trial was held on the specific performance count between November 18, 1988, and November 23, 1988. No issue was raised concerning the dissolution of the marriage. Annette Goldman testified that before she and Kenneth were married, Kenneth obtained an Orthodox get for his ex-wife, Pauline Gethner, from whom he had been civilly divorced for almost two years. When Annette questioned the need for the get, Kenneth told her that he wanted the divorce to be recognized by everyone, including the State of Israel and every faction of Judaism. He also stated that "when you get married in the Jewish faith you have to get divorced according to the Jewish faith." Annette's testimony concerning these statements was uncontroverted.

Annette further testified that prior to the marriage, she and Kenneth went to a Jewish bookstore to choose a ketubah. Kenneth specifically asked the clerk for an Orthodox ketubah. Annette stated that it was her understanding from conversations with Kenneth and from books and pamphlets given to her by Kenneth that the ketubah was a contract and that the words "[b]e thou my wife according to the law of Moses and Israel" meant that Orthodox Jewish law would govern the status and validity of the marriage. Annette further stated that it was her understanding from the information given to her by Kenneth that if the marriage were to be dissolved, "[t]hat we would have to have a get given in the proper way. That would be important to the Orthodox procedure." Annette admitted, however, that she and Kenneth never specifically discussed whether he would give her a get in the event the marriage was dissolved.

Approximately six months before the wedding, the parties met with Rabbi Rachlis, the rabbi who was to officiate at the marriage ceremony. When he learned that Kenneth had been married before, he asked whether Kenneth had given his first wife a get. Upon learning that he had, Rabbi Rachlis stated, "Good, that eliminates problems." According to Annette, the two witnesses to the signing of the ketubah were Orthodox Jewish males, a requirement under Orthodox Jewish law.

Annette testified that she became an Orthodox Jew after her father died and that it was her understanding that Orthodox law prohibited her from remarrying unless she obtained a get from Kenneth. If she remarried, her marriage would not be recognized by her religion and any children she might have would be considered illegitimate. During the course of the custody trial in 1986, she asked Kenneth for a get. He replied that she was a liar and a cheat and that she was "going to pay" for what she had done to him by being married to him for the rest of her life. He then stated that "everything could be resolved" if Annette would agree to joint custody of the children. Barbara Fox, who at one time served as a court-appointed attorney for the children, testified that Kenneth told her that he "would not be adverse to giving [Annette] a Jewish divorce" if he got his custody terms. Kenneth did not deny making these statements to Annette or to Barbara Fox. According to Annette, Kenneth at no time stated any religious objection to obtaining a get.

Annette then presented expert testimony by two Orthodox Jewish rabbis, Rabbi Gedalia Schwartz and Rabbi Emanuel Rackman. According to the expert witnesses, Judaism is not only a religion but is also a complete body of substantive law. Jewish law contains both religious rules and secular laws, including such matters as contracts, torts, property and family law. Marriage and divorce are secular, contractual undertakings. Although a rabbi is usually present to supervise the marriage ceremony, his presence is not required. Therefore, the religious persuasion of the clergyman officiating at a wedding does not affect the validity of the marriage.

Both expert witnesses testified that the ketubah signed by the parties was a contract. The words "[b]e thou my wife according to the law of Moses and Israel" meant that the status of the marriage would be governed by Orthodox Jewish law. The experts agreed that the termination of the marriage under Orthodox law required the giving of a get. They stated that many non-Orthodox couples followed the get procedure so that the divorce would be recognized by all Jews. A woman who does not receive a get is relegated to the status of an "agunah"; as such, she is prohibited from remarrying or having sexual relations with any man. If she does remarry and has children, the children would be considered illegitimate and would be prohibited from marrying other Jews.

The experts testified that although the get procedure involves several formalities, it is secular rather than religious in nature. A rabbi is ordinarily present but is not necessary to the procedure. The husband obtaining the get need not profess any religious belief or engage in any act of worship. Essentially, a get is a written release from the marriage contract. The husband appoints a scribe to draft the 12 line document in conformance with certain prescribed formalities. The husband then signs the document in the presence of two Orthodox Jewish male witnesses and gives it to the wife stating that she is released from the marriage in accordance with the laws of Moses and Israel. The husband may authorize the get procedure to be done by proxy. Although the witnesses stated that a get must ordinarily be voluntarily given, a certain amount of coercion would be permissible in this case because Kenneth had effectively abandoned Annette. Kenneth did not present any expert witnesses to contradict the testimony of Rabbi Schwartz and Rabbi Rackman.

Kenneth Goldman testified that he considered the ketubah to be poetry or art rather than a contract. In an evidence deposition Rabbi Rachlis, who officiated at the marriage ceremony, stated that from his perspective as a liberal Jew he viewed the ketubah in a symbolic rather than a literal sense. Kenneth testified that he could not read the Aramaic text and the English translation did not contain any reference to divorce or to a get. He stated that neither he nor Annette was an Orthodox Jew at the time of the ceremony and denied discussing the terms of the ketubah or the meaning of the words "[b]e thou my wife according to the law of Moses and Israel" with Annette prior to the marriage. Kenneth then testified at great length as to his dislike for Orthodox Judaism. He stated that Orthodox Jews discriminate against women, and characterized Orthodox Jews as "antimodern" and repulsive.

Following the trial, the court stated its findings in a memorandum opinion. The opinion included findings of fact that the parties' intent at the time they signed the ketubah was to have the marriage recognized by the Orthodox branch of Judaism and that, based on the expert testimony, "the ketubah clearly and unequivocally obligates the husband to proceed with the get procedure." The court also found that although Kenneth had an intense dislike for Orthodox Judaism, his feelings did not rise to the level of a religious belief.

The court then entered an order dissolving the marriage and ordering Kenneth to comply with his contractual obligation to give Annette an Orthodox get, which the order defined as a get recognized by an Orthodox Beth Din (rabbinical tribunal). The order specifically provided that it was not requiring the Beth Din to grant the get and that the court would not supervise the procedure, determine who was a qualified witness or review whether the Beth Din made a correct determination under Jewish law. The order did, however, require Kenneth to truthfully answer all questions put to him and "to participate in the verbal and physical acts necessary to validate the GET." The order then gave Kenneth the following four options for compliance:

"A. Kenneth Goldman may obtain and give Annette Goldman a GET in a manner that is recognized as valid by an Orthodox Beth Din.

B. Kenneth Goldman may appear before an Orthodox Beth Din and give them the information and authorization necessary to proceed with and validate the GET procedure.

C. Kenneth Goldman may execute the necessary documents and provide the necessary information to authorize the giving of a valid Orthodox GET by proxy as determined by an Orthodox Beth Din.

D. Kenneth Goldman may appear before the Chicago Rabbinical Council and give them the information and authorization necessary to proceed with and validate the GET procedure."

The order of dissolution also incorporated a previously entered custody order. The facts relating to the custody order will be detailed later in connection with our discussion of the issues concerning that order.

Kenneth Goldman contends that the trial court erred in ordering him to obtain a get for three reasons. First, he maintains that the ketubah was not a contract but was intended by the parties as mere poetry or art. Second, he argues that if the ketubah was a contract, its terms were too vague to support specific performance. Third, he claims that the order violates his constitutional rights under the Establishment and Free Exercise Clauses of the Federal constitution and article I, section 3, of the Illinois Constitution.

The question of whether the parties intended to enter into a contract is an issue to be decided by the trier of fact. (*Northern Illinois Construction Co. v. Zale* (1985), 136 Ill.App.3d 822, 824, 91 Ill.Dec. 527, 483 N.E.2d 1013). The determination in that regard will not be reversed unless it is contrary to the manifest weight of the evidence. *Howard A. Koop & Associates V. KPK Corp.* (1983), 119 Ill.App.3d 391, 398, 75 Ill.Dec. 276, 457 N.E.2d

66.

Kenneth Goldman maintains that regardless of whether the ketubah, quoted earlier, contains the essential elements of a contract, it was not intended as a contract but merely as poetry or art in connection with the marriage ceremony. To support this claim, Kenneth states that the parties did not negotiate the terms or consult with a lawyer and that the document was signed shortly before the ceremony while the parties were dressed in their wedding attire. On the other hand, Annette Goldman presented testimony, which the trial court accepted as true, that she and Kenneth went to a Jewish bookstore and specifically requested an Orthodox Jewish ketubah. Annette testified that it was her understanding from talking to Kenneth and reading certain materials supplied by him that the ketubah was a contract and the words "[b]e thou my wife according to the law of Moses and Israel" meant that the status and validity of the marriage would be governed by Orthodox Jewish law. Although Kenneth denied these discussions, it was well within the authority of the trial court to determine the credibility of the witnesses and the weight to be given their testimony. Also, the ketubah on its face contains language of consideration and mutual promises. In our view, the court's determination that the parties intended the ketubah as a contract was not against the manifest weight of the evidence.

Kenneth Goldman next argues that even if the ketubah was a contract, the terms of the contract were too vague to support specific performance of the obligation to obtain a get. He maintains that the ketubah contains no reference to divorce or to the obligation to secure a get in the event the marriage was terminated.

In a bench trial, the meaning of the language used by the parties in a contract is to be determined by the trial court as an issue of fact. (*Westminster I Apartments v. Barnard* (1987), 163 Ill.App.3d 36, 37, 114 Ill.Dec. 321, 516 N.E.2d 476.) When the language of the contract leaves the intent of the parties in doubt, extrinsic evidence, is admissible to resolve the conflict. (*Chicago Principals Association v. Board of Education* (1980), 84 Ill.App.3d 1095, 1099, 40 Ill.Dec. 381, 406 N.E.2d 82.) In resolving the conflict, the court will use accepted methods of contract interpretation, including the use of expert testimony, to ascertain the intent of the parties with respect to the contract terms. *Howard A. Koop & Associates v. KPK Corp.* (1983), 119 Ill.App.3d 391, 398, 75 Ill.Dec. 276, 457 N.E.2d 66.

As we have stated, the trial court properly found that the parties intended the ketubah to be a contract that the status and validity of their marriage would be governed by Orthodox Jewish law. The uncontroverted expert testimony presented at trial established that Orthodox Jewish law requires the husband to obtain and deliver to his wife an Orthodox get upon dissolution of the marriage. Rabbi Schwartz testified that although the giving of a get is ordinarily a voluntary act on the part of the husband, a certain degree of compulsion is acceptable under the circumstances presented here, where Kenneth abandoned Annette and refused to cohabit with her and support her according to the terms of the marriage contract. Kenneth Goldman presented no expert testimony to the contrary. Before ordering specific performance of a contract, a court must find that its terms are sufficiently certain and definite that the court can require the specific thing contracted for to be done. (*Kalkounos v. Four K's, Inc.* (1981), 94 Ill.App.3d 1011, 1013, 50 Ill.Dec. 395, 419 N.E.2d 503.) We believe that the court's order of specific performance was justified by the evidence before it.

Finally, Kenneth Goldman claims that enforcement of the ketubah would violate his constitutional rights under the Federal and State constitutions. Specifically, Kenneth relies upon the Establishment and Free Exercise Clauses of the First Amendment and upon article I, section 3, of the Illinois Constitution.[1]

In *Lynch v. Donnelly* (1984), 465 U.S. 668, 104 S.Ct. 1355, 79 L.Ed.2d 604, a case involving the issue of whether a city's inclusion of a Nativity scene in its annual Christmas display violated the Establishment Clause, the Court stated that:

> "Rather than mechanically invalidating all governmental conduct or statutes that confer benefits or give special recognition to religion in general or to one faith - as an absolutist approach would dictate - the Court has scrutinized challenged legislation or official conduct to determine whether, in reality, it establishes a religion or religious faith, or tends to do so." (*Lynch*, 465 U.S. at 678, 104 S.Ct. at 1361-62, 79 L.Ed.2d at 613).

Although it disclaimed a "fixed, per se rule" in conducting analyses under the Establishment Clause, the Court stated that it "often found it useful to inquire whether the challenged law or conduct has a secular purpose, whether its principal or primary effect is to advance or inhibit religion, and whether it creates an excessive entanglement of government with religion." (*Lynch*, 465 U.S. at 679, 104 S.Ct. at 1362, 79 L.Ed.2d at 613, citing *Lemon v. Kurtzman* (1971), 403 U.S. 602, 612-13, 91 S.Ct. 2105, 2111, 29 L.Ed.2d 745, 755). Applying the analysis used in *Lemon v. Kurtzman*, the Court held that the city's action in displaying the Nativity scene did not violate the Establishment Clause.

Using the analysis employed in *Lynch v. Donnelly* and *Lemon v. Kurtzman*, we conclude that the government conduct in question here, i.e., the trial court order, does not violate the Establishment Clause. First, the order has the secular purpose of enforcing a contract between the parties. The right to enter into contracts is recognized by both the Federal and State constitutions. (U.S. Const., art. I, §10; Ill. Const. 1970, art. I, §16). Also, the court order furthers two secular purposes set forth in the Marriage and Dissolution of Marriage Act: "[To] promote the amicable settlement of disputes that have arisen between parties to a marriage; [and to] mitigate the potential harm to the spouses and their children caused by the process of legal dissolution of marriage." (Ill.Rev.Stat. 1987, ch. 40, pars 102(3), 102(4).) The evidence at trial established that under the Orthodox Jewish law, which the parties agreed would govern the status of their marriage, the marriage could be dissolved only by the securing of an Orthodox get. Without the get, Annette was prohibited by her religious beliefs from remarrying. It would have been detrimental to the parties and their children to leave the get issue unresolved.

Second, it is our opinion that the primary effect of the court order was to further the secular purposes stated above and not to advance or inhibit religion. Although the order required Kenneth's participation in an Orthodox Jewish practice, there was ample expert testimony that Judaism contains both

---

1. Briefly, the Establishment Clause bars the State from placing its official support behind a religion, while the Free Exercise Clause bars the State from interfering with the religious practices of its citizens. The Illinois Constitution provides in part that "[n]o person shall be required to attend or support any ministry or place of worship against his consent, nor shall any preference be given by law to any religious denomination or mode of worship."

secular and religious laws and that the get procedure was secular in nature. To comply with the court order, Kenneth need not engage in any act of worship nor profess any religious belief. According to the expert witnesses, the acquisition of a get is a secular act which severs the marriage contract. To the extent that the court order advances Orthodox Judaism by requiring an Orthodox get, it is an incidental effect of the enforcement of the parties' contract that Orthodox Jewish law govern the status of their marriage.

Third, we believe that the court order avoids an excessive entanglement with religion. In resolving disputes involving religion, a court may apply objective, well-established principles of secular law, or "neutral principles of law," which do not entail a consideration of doctrinal matters. (*Jones v. Wolf* (1979), 443 U.S. 545, 602-03, 99 S.Ct. 3020, 61 L.Ed.2d 775, 784.) Here, the trial court merely applied well-established principles of contract law to enforce the agreement made by the parties. The terms of the order were carefully limited to avoid interference with religious doctrine. Our determination that enforcement of the obligation to obtain a get does not violate the establishment clause is in accord with decisions of other courts which have considered the issue. See *Avitzur v. Avitzur* (1983), 58 N.Y.2d 108, 459 N.Y.S.2d 572, 446 N.E.2d 136; *Burns v. Burns* (1987), 223 N.J.Super. 219, 538 A.2d 438; *Minkin v. Minkin* (1981), 180 N.J.Super. 260, 434 A.2d 665.

Kenneth Goldman also contends that the court order violates the Free Exercise Clause. Neither in the trial court nor in his brief on appeal has Kenneth clearly articulated in what manner the court order requiring him to obtain a get prevented the free exercise of his religion. Kenneth testified that he was a liberal Jew and that he abhorred the practices of Orthodox Jews, whom he characterized as discriminatory, repulsive and "antimodern." In its findings of fact, the trial court stated that although Kenneth expressed distaste for many practices of Orthodox Jews, he at no time attacked their religious beliefs. The court accordingly found that Kenneth's dislike for Orthodox Judaism did not rise to the level of religious belief. Only religious as opposed to personal or philosophical beliefs are protected by the Free Exercise Clause. (*Wisconsin v. Yoder* (1972), 406 U.S. 205, 215-16, 92 S.Ct. 1526, 1533, 32 L.Ed.2d 15, 25.) The court's finding in this regard is supported by the fact that Kenneth gave his first wife a get and by testimony that Kenneth was withholding the get as a bargaining tool in the custody dispute. Furthermore, the court order here requires Kenneth to do nothing more than what he promised to do when he signed the ketubah. Expert testimony established that the get procedure was secular in nature and did not require Kenneth to engage in any act of worship or to express any religious belief. Under these circumstances, we find Kenneth's argument involving the Free Exercise Clause to be without merit.

Kenneth then maintains that the order violates article I, section 3, of the Illinois Constitution which provides that:

> "No person shall be required to attend or support any ministry or place of worship against his consent, nor shall any preference be given by law to any religious denomination or mode of worship." (Ill. Const. 1970, art. I, §3).

Kenneth has failed to cite any cases interpreting this provision and has not suggested that it provides greater or different protection than that afforded by the First Amendment of the Federal constitution. The Illinois Supreme Court has stated that provisions of the Illinois Constitution which are similar to provisions of the Federal constitution will be construed as providing similar protection unless there is some indication that the drafters intended otherwise.

(*People v. Porter* (1988), 122 Ill.2d 64, 77, 118 Ill.Dec. 465, 521 N.E.2d 1158.) Because Kenneth has failed to provide any authority that article I, section 3, was intended to provide protection different from that afforded by the Establishment and Free Exercise Clauses of the First Amendment, we must reject this challenge to the trial court's order.

Kenneth Goldman next contends that the trial court erred in incorporating a previously entered custody order into its judgment of dissolution of marriage. Kenneth maintains that the previous order, entered on May 19, 1986, was a temporary custody order and that he was entitled to a trial on custody pursuant to the best interest of the child standard set forth in section 602 of the Marriage and Dissolution of Marriage Act (Act) (Ill.Rev.Stat. 1987, ch. 40, par. 602) before a final custody order was issued. Annette Goldman contends that the May 19. 1986, order was a final custody order which could be modified only upon clear and convincing evidence of changed circumstances as set forth in section 610 of the Act. Ill.Rev.Stat. 1987, ch. 40, par 610.

In February of 1986, Kenneth filed a motion requesting an immediate hearing on the issue of custody. Trial of the custody issue began on May 12, 1986, before Judge Baner and lasted four days. Eleven witnesses, including expert witnesses, testified. On May 19, 1986, the court entered a nine-page order covering all aspects of the children's custody. The order stated that it was "entered as a temporary order which shall, in the absence of any contrary order entered hereafter, become a permanent custody order upon the entry of a Judgment of Dissolution in this cause." The court explained that it did not label the custody order final prior to the judgment of dissolution because of the possibility that the marriage would ultimately not be dissolved.

A custody order is temporary or final according to its substance rather than its form. (*Levy v. Skilling* (1985), 136 Ill.App.3d 727, 729, 91 Ill.Dec. 431, 483 N.E.2d 917; *In re Marriage of Kondos* (1982), 109 Ill.App.3d 615, 618, 65 Ill.Dec. 191, 440 N.E.2d 1046.) In *Kondos*, the court held that an order entered after a full testimonial hearing on all aspects of custody was a final order despite the trial court's characterization of the order as temporary.

Kenneth's main argument is that because the order was not final for purposes of appeal (see *In re Marriage of Leopando* (1983), 96 Ill.2d 114, 70 Ill.Dec. 263, 449 N.E.2d 137), it was merely a temporary custody decision governed by the standards of sections 602 and 603 of the Act. This argument has been previously considered and rejected. (*In re Marriage of Mitchell* (1981), 103 Ill.App.3d 242, 246, 58 Ill.Dec. 684, 430 N.E.2d 716; *Carroll v. Carroll* (1978), 64 Ill.App.3d 925, 21 Ill.Dec. 713, 382 N.E.2d 7.) It is clear from both the substance of the May 19, 1986, order and the comments of Judge Baner that the order was a final custody decision which could be modified only pursuant to the stricter standards set forth in section 610 of the Act.

Kenneth further argues that because certain portions of the order, such as the requirements of enrolling the children in a particular day-care center and using a neutral party to assist in transfers of the children, were either impossible to meet or were ignored by the parties, the order was 'stale" and constituted a "nullity." No authority is cited in support of the argument that situations which were not foreseen by the court and which the parties were able to resolve served to render the custody order a nullity. We find the argument unpersuasive.

Accordingly, the judgment of the circuit court is affirmed

McMorrow, P.J. concurs.

Johnson, J., dissents.

Justice Johnson, dissenting:

I respectfully disagree with the majority. The true issue in this case is whether a civil court has the authority to compel a party to perform terms of a "ketubah," i.e., an antenuptial agreement used by Orthodox Jews, which require interpretation of religious doctrines and religious worship. Petitioner argues that the trial court's order compelling him to perform the terms of the ketubah violate his constitutional rights under the first amendment (U.S. Const., amend. I) and under section 3 of article I of the Illinois Constitution (Ill. Const. 1970, art. I, §3). Petitioner also argues that the terms of the ketubah were too vague to support the specific performance of obtaining a "get," i.e., a Jewish bill of divorcement.

After the trial in this matter the judge ordered specific performance of the ketubah which included the following provision: "Be thou my wife according to the law of Moses and Israel." Expert testimony given by two Orthodox Jewish rabbis and accepted by the trial court established that the provision "meant that [the] status of the marriage would be governed by Orthodox Jewish law." Orthodox law requires the ex-husband to give a "get" to his former wife in order to have the divorce between the parties recognized by all Jewish people. Respondent testified that she believed that Orthodox law requires a get if a divorced woman desires to remarry and have that marriage recognized by the Jewish religion. Otherwise the church refuses to recognize the remarriage as valid and views any issue from the remarriage as illegitimate. Petitioner testified that he did not practice Orthodox Judaism and that he found the beliefs and practices to be "antimodern" and repulsive.

It is a long-standing rule in Illinois that the civil court will not interfere in questions involving religious dogmas unless they have consequences upon civil or property rights. (*Chase v. Cheney* (1871), 58 Ill. 509). In *Chase* our supreme court declined to decide the issue of whether a Protestant episcopal clergyman had breached his employment contract by refusing to recite language prescribed by the religious canons in the ministration of an infant baptism, a church ritual. The court reasoned that the clergyman was a voluntary member to the church association to which he belonged and that he voluntarily adhered to the rules, laws, and canons of the church. No property right had vested under the employment contract so as to authorize the civil court to become involved in a matter which necessarily required the interpretation of religious doctrines and canons of the church.

Religious worship includes performing external acts and observing all ordinances and ceremonies practiced by the religious association to which one belongs. The free exercise and enjoyment of religious worship, or lack thereof, is protected by the constitution. (*Chase*, 58 Ill. at 533-34.) Our "constitution intended to guarantee, from all interference by the State, not only each man's religious faith, but his membership in the church, and the rites and discipline which might be adopted." (*Chase*, 58 Ill. at 537.) There are two exceptions to this uncontrolled liberty, and neither applies here. Any order of the court which requires extensive investigation and evaluation of religious doctrines and tenets is prohibited by the first amendment. *Baumgartner v. First Church of Christ* (1986), 141 Ill.App.3d 898, 906, 96 Ill.Dec. 114, 490 N.E.2d 1319.

Here, determination of whether a civil court can compel specific performance of a form of religious worship does not involve consequences upon petitioner's property rights, nor was there any effect upon petitioner's civil rights before the trial court's order of specific performance. Furthermore, the trial court's construction of the provision, "Be thou my wife according to the law of Moses and Israel" required the court to partake in evaluation, investigation and interpretation of religious dogma. I do not suggest that the trial court was without authority to make a ruling on the contract; rather that the court must not compel petitioner to participate in any performance of a provision within the contract which necessarily required interpretation of a religious doctrine and his involvement in an act of religious worship.

The majority reports that the trial court "found that although Kenneth had an intense dislike for Orthodox Judaism, his feeling did not rise to the level of a religious belief." The inference here is that since petitioner's dislike for Orthodox Judaism did not qualify as a religious belief, his beliefs will not be protected under the Federal or state constitutions and, therefore, he can be compelled to participate in acts which constitute religious worship. I agree that petitioner's dislike of Orthodox Judaism does not qualify as a religious belief; nevertheless, our constitution protects his right to freely choose whether he will participate in acts of religious worship. An individual's participation, even by proxy, in a religious ritual is a form of religious worship. The civil court has no right to dictate one's religion or the form in which one practices the religion of his choice. Our constitutions allow us to make these choices voluntarily. We must remember that one is free to seek such membership and to accept or abandon all of its rules, laws and cannons at his will. Freedom of religious worship cannot be maintained if the civil courts attempt to construe and enforce ecclesiastical laws and doctrines and compel voluntary members to comply with them. This is what the majority attempts to do here. The trial court's order compelling petitioner to engage in the observance of the ordinances and ceremonies of the Orthodox Jewish religion abrogates the very essence of freedom of choice concerning matters of religious worship.

Furthermore, the civil court is limited to dissolving the marriage between the parties in accordance with the Marriage and Dissolution of Marriage Act. (Ill.Rev.Stat. 1983, ch. 40, par. 101 et seq.) There is no reference in that Act to a requirement of a "get" for a valid dissolution of marriage under the civil law. Accordingly, we are prohibited from compelling one to follow religious tenets to fulfill ritualistic requirements of the church. Again, we must leave such a decision to the discretion of the individual.

Additionally, I do not believe that the terms of the ketubah were so definite and certain as to allow the court to require the specific thing contracted for to be performed. The standard for enforcing specific performance of a contract prohibits the court from making a contract for the parties and enforcing it. (*Kalkounos v. Four K's, Inc.* (1981), 94 Ill.App.3d 1011, 1013, 50 Ill.Dec. 395, 419 N.E.2d 503.) Here, the trial court's order, which expressed four specific options for compliance with the ketubah, cannot be distinguished from the court making a contract for the parties. The trial court order, which expresses the four options necessary for petitioner's compliance, would not be necessary had it, indeed, found that the terms of the ketubah were sufficiently certain and definite so as to determine what was specifically contracted for. The expression of the precise options available for compliance with the ketubah should have been left to the parties to determine and include in their agreement. Even if this were the case, this court would be precluded from compelling specific performance of religious rituals in the event of a dispute between the parties concerning the meaning of a contract provision based upon a religious tenet.

I would reverse the judgment of the trial court.

B. EXPRESS CONTRACTS TO GIVE OR RECEIVE A *GET*

Koeppel v. Koeppel
138 N.Y.S. 2d 366 (1954)
Supreme Court, Special Term, Queens County, Part I
December 6, 1954

Hallinan, Justice:

Motion by plaintiff (1) for an order, pursuant to rule 104 of the Rules of Civil Practice, striking out defendant's answer as sham and directing an assessment of damages on the second cause of action, or, in the alternative, (2) for an order, pursuant to rule 103 of the Rules of Civil Practice, striking from defendant's answer paragraphs 1,2,3,4,7,8 and 9 as sham, and (3) for an order, pursuant to rule 109 of Rules of Civil Practice, striking the first and second separate defenses as insufficient.

Cross motion by the defendant (1) for summary judgment dismissing the complaint, pursuant to rule 113 of the Rules of Civil Practice, or, in the alternative, (2) for judgment on the pleadings dismissing the complaint, pursuant to rule 112 of the Rules of Civil Practice, on the ground that it fails to state a cause of action.

The parties hereto were formerly husband and wife. This action was brought by the wife to obtain specific performance of a written agreement made by the parties on January 29, 1954 while they were still married, but were living separate and apart. The complaint contains a second cause of action for money damages for defendant's fraud in inducing the plaintiff to enter into the said agreement. In addition to certain denials, defendant has alleged two separate defenses, the illegality of the contract and a general release.

The parties were married on August 9, 1951 and are both of the Jewish faith. There is no issue of the marriage. On November 20, 1953, while the parties were living separate and apart, plaintiff instituted an action against the defendant (1) for a separation and (2) to impress a trust upon certain monies and household furniture allegedly given to her as wedding gifts by her relatives. Defendant appeared in that action by a firm of attorneys who entered into discussions with plaintiff's attorney with a view to reaching an amicable solution of the problems involved. Before these discussions had ripened into a separation agreement, plaintiff indicated to her attorney that she would prefer to terminate her marriage to the defendant completely and after reviewing the facts again, her attorney advised her that, in his opinion, she had sufficient grounds to justify an action to annul the marriage.

On December 18, 1953 plaintiff commenced an action to annul the marriage by reason of defendant's fraud in the inducement thereof, and the same firm of attorneys appeared for the defendant in that action but interposed no answer on his behalf. That action was noticed for trial for the February 1954 term. Meanwhile, the attorneys for both parties continued discussions to formulate an agreement to become effective if plaintiff's suit for annulment were successful. On January 29, 1954 such an agreement was executed by the parties. It is that agreement which is the basis for this action.

The agreement provided, among other things, for the settlement of the dispute regarding the money, furniture and certain other property, the execution of general releases on both sides and the discontinuance of the separation action. The necessary documents to effectuate these purposes were executed and delivered simultaneously by the parties to their respective attorneys to be held in escrow until the annulment action had been determined. If the plaintiff was successful in said action, the attorneys were authorized to deliver the releases and other papers within 3 days thereafter. If plaintiff's suit was dismissed or resolved in favor of the defendant, the entire agreement was to be null and void.

The agreement expressly provided that the defendant would appear in any action against him for the dissolution of the marriage (he had already appeared) and that he would "take any and all steps which he may deem necessary in defense thereof and nothing herein contained to the contrary notwithstanding shall be considered as limiting or construed as proscribing the rights of the Husband to defend himself in such action." The agreement contained the following provision:

> "5. Upon the successful prosecution of the Wife's action for the dissolution of her marriage, the Husband and Wife covenant and agree that he and she will, whenever called upon, and if and whenever the same shall become necessary, appear before a Rabbi or Rabbinate selected and designated by whomsoever of the parties who shall first demand the same, and execute any and all papers and documents required by and necessary to effectuate a dissolution of their marriage in accordance with the ecclesiastical laws of the Faith and Church of said parties."

On April 6, 1954 plaintiff's action for an annulment came on for trial and an inquest was taken at which defendant was represented by his attorneys. An interlocutory judgment of annulment was granted in favor of the plaintiff on April 13,1954. Said judgment became final on July 14, 1954. No appeal was taken from the judgment nor has defendant attacked it in any way and it remains in full force and effect.

After the annulment decree had become final, repeated demands were made on the defendant to appear before a Rabbi or Rabbinate to execute the papers necessary to effectuate a religious dissolution of the marriage according to the laws of the Jewish faith, but defendant has refused so to appear. Indeed on August 4, 1954, two Rabbis, a Scribe and a Witness called upon the defendant at his father's place of business and requested him to sign the necessary papers, but he again refused. This action was then brought on August 11, 1954 to secure specific performance of defendant's agreement to comply with the necessary procedure to effectuate a religious dissolution in accordance with the laws of his faith, if and when the marriage was dissolved civilly.

There can be no doubt that many of defendant's denials, as well as his affirmative allegations, are sham. Contrary to the defendant's contention, sham denials can be stricken. *Socony-Vacuum Oil Co., Inc., v. City of New York*, 247 App.Div. 163, 168, 287 N.Y.S. 288, 293, affirmed 272 N.Y. 6678, 5 N.E.2d 385. On the other hand, plaintiff has not shown that every denial in the answer is sham. For that reason, plaintiff's motion under rule 104 to strike the entire answer must be denied. The specific paragraphs of the answer attacked under rule 103 will now be considered.

In paragraph Fourth of the complaint, it is alleged that on November 20, 1953 plaintiff instituted an action for an annulment in the Supreme Court, Kings County, based on defendant's fraud; that defendant appeared, but failed to answer the complaint; that an interlocutory judgment was granted and entered on April 13, 1954 and that said judgment became final on July 14,

1954. It appears that the action was commenced on December 18, 1953 instead of November 20, 1953 as alleged in the complaint, but that variance is immaterial. The remaining allegations are either matters of public record or are conceded or, at least, not denied in the affidavits submitted herein. Paragraph 1 of the answer will be stricken.

Similarly the denial of part of paragraph Fifth of the complaint which alleges the execution of the agreement is without substance and paragraph 2 of the answer will be stricken.

Paragraph 3 of the answer categorically denies each and every allegation of paragraphs Sixth and Seventh of the complaint wherein it is alleged that according to the tenets of the Jewish faith, a married woman may not institute a proceeding to obtain a religious dissolution of her marriage; that such a proceeding can be instituted only by the husband; and that the Jewish religion does not recognize a civil dissolution of marriage as having any effect upon the religious bond of matrimony. Neither party has submitted any proof from rabbinical authorities on these points, but plaintiff now claims that they are immaterial and that plaintiff would be entitled to judgment on proof of the agreement, defendant's failure to comply therewith, the insufficiency of money damages as compensation and the absence of any adequate remedy at law. It may well be that defendant should live up to his agreement whether plaintiff needs his cooperation or not, but in order to justify specific performance, there must be proof that defendant's compliance is essential to secure to the plaintiff the benefits of the agreement. Accordingly, the motion to strike paragraph 3 of the answer is denied.

By paragraph 4 of the answer, defendant denies each and every allegation of paragraphs Eighth, Ninth, Tenth and Eleventh of the complaint, except that he admits that he did not appear before a Rabbinate to effectuate a religious dissolution of the marriage. The allegations thus denied are that plaintiff has repeatedly called upon the defendant to appear before the Rabbinate or to permit the Rabbinate to call upon him and to execute the necessary papers to effectuate a religious dissolution of the marriage; that plaintiff has duly performed all the terms and conditions of the agreement on her part to be performed and that plaintiff has no adequate remedy at law. In his opposing affidavit, the defendant contents himself with the statement that paragraph 4 of the answer "is properly pleaded." No evidentiary facts are set forth nor does defendant deny the evidentiary facts contained in the moving affidavit which tend to show that defendant's denial is without substance.

Moreover, a denial that plaintiff has performed the terms and conditions of the contract without alleging specifically and with particularity the terms not performed raises no issue. Rule 92, R.C.P.; *Lourie v. Mishkin*, 279 App.Div. 754, 108 N.Y.S.2d 777; *Klapper v. Greenfield, Sup.*, 100 N.Y.S.2d 921. That plaintiff has no adequate remedy at law is apparent from the pleading itself. (Cf. *Wasserman v. Manson*, 225 App.Div. 342, 233 N.Y.S. 80.) Paragraph 4 of the answer will therefore be stricken.

In passing it might be noted that paragraph 5 of the answer which denies the allegations of paragraph Twelfth of the complaint wherein certain allegations contained in the first cause of action are realleged is unnecessary. Rule 90, R.C.P. Since it has not be challenged on this motion, however, no ruling is made in connection therewith.

Paragraphs 7 and 8 of the answer, constituting the first affirmative defense, allege that the provisions of the agreement of January 29, 1954 had been agreed upon prior to the institution of the action for annulment and that the agreement is, therefore, illegal and contrary to public policy in that its purpose was to procure a dissolution of the marriage. "Not all agreements conditioned on divorce are illegal." *Yates v. Yates*, 183 Misc. 934, 938, 51 N.Y.S.2d 135, 139. Nor is every agreement which is to become effective upon the termination of a marriage necessarily "promotive of divorce." Examples of agreements, whose legality has been upheld although they were to become or to remain effective only if a decree of divorce were subsequently granted, may be found in *Butler v. Marcus*, 264 N.Y. 519, 191 N.E. 544; *Goodman v. Goodman*, 274 App.Div. 287, 83 N.Y.S.2d 62, cf. *Metcalf v. Metcalf*, 274 App.Div. 744, 746, 87 N.Y.S.2d 122, 124, affirmed 302 N.Y.822, 100 N.E.2d 33.

In *Goodman v. Goodman*, supra, 274 App.Div. 287, 83 N.Y.S.2d 62, the court held that since a judgment of annulment had been granted, it was conclusive that grounds for the dissolution existed. Moreover, the court noted the fact that it was the wife who wanted to terminate the marriage and since she was the one receiving the monetary consideration, it could not be said that the husband was buying his freedom.

So in the case at bar. The granting of a judgment in favor of the plaintiff wife must be taken as conclusive that she had just cause for her annulment action. Moreover, since it was the plaintiff wife who wanted the dissolution and who was receiving the major portion of the money and furniture, it cannot be said that the defendant husband was purchasing his freedom or that the agreement was promotive of a dissolution of the marriage. The defense of illegality is sham and paragraphs 7 and 8 of the answer will be stricken.

Paragraph 9 of the answer, constituting the second affirmative defense, alleges that on January 29, 1954 plaintiff executed and delivered a release of the claim set forth in the complaint. Paragraphs 1 and 2 of the agreement provided for the exchange of general releases which were executed simultaneously with the agreement and immediately delivered in escrow to the respective attorneys who were to exchange them along with other documents within 3 days after the dissolution of the marriage. Paragraph 7 of the agreement further provided:

> "7. Upon the successful dissolution of the marriage of the parties, *and except for the rights and obligations herein set forth*, each party hereto waives and releases to the other and forever discharges any and all claims * * * which he or she now has, or * * * may hereafter * * * claim to have * * *."

A mere reading of the underlined phrase shows that the parties expressly excluded from the release the obligations created by the agreement. The defense of release is obviously sham and paragraph 9 of the answer will be stricken.

Since both affirmative defenses have been stricken as sham, it is unnecessary to decide whether they were sufficient as a matter of pleading, and the request for alternative relief under rule 109, being academic, is dismissed.

In his opposing affidavit and brief, defendant has raised several general objections to the entire action which will now be discussed. Defendant claims that the entire action is academic in that plaintiff has already remarried and, in fact, is now on her honeymoon. It is not disclosed, however, whether plaintiff was remarried at a civil ceremony or at a religious ceremony in accordance with the rules of her faith. This action may not be academic to the plaintiff. Nor can it be said that a religious ceremony is of very little importance to the plaintiff if she was willing to marry at a civil ceremony. It may well be that plaintiff has not lived up to the laws of her faith, but this should not forever bar her from rectifying the situation, if she so desires.

Defendant has also contended that a decree of specific performance would interfere with his freedom of religion under the Constitution. Complying with his agreement would not compel the defendant to practice any religion, not even the Jewish faith to which he still admits adherence (paragraph Second of the complaint not denied in the answer). His appearance before the Rabbinate to answer questions and give evidence needed by them to make a decision is not a profession of faith. Specific performance herein would merely require the defendant to do what he voluntarily agreed to so.

Defendant's statement that the ceremony before the Rabbinate takes from two to two and one-half hours is not worthy of discussion. That is not much out of a lifetime, especially if it will bring peace of mind and conscience to one whom defendant must at one time have loved.

Defendant's cross motion for summary judgment, or, in the alternative, for judgment on the pleadings, is denied.

Settle order.

Margulies v. Margulies

344 N.Y.S. 2d 482 (1973)
Supreme Court, Appellate Division, First Department
June 5, 1973

Before *Stevens, P.J.*, and *Markewich, Nunez, Kupferman,* and *Tilzer, JJ.*

Per Curiam:

Order, Supreme Court, New York County, entered March 12, 1973 is modified on the law, the facts and in the exercise of discretion to strike therefrom those provisions directing defendant's civil commitment for contempt of court and to substitute therefor a provision that defendant may purge himself of the contempt by paying a sum of $450, representing the fines previously imposed by the court orders or, in the alternative, by appearing in and participating in a Jewish ritual divorce, and as so modified the order is affirmed, without costs or disbursements.

The parties were divorced in June 1970. Thereafter, certain further disputes developed which were ostensibly settled when the parties stipulated in open court with respect to child visitation rights and the division of certain items of personal property. As part of that stipulation, defendant voluntarily agreed to "appear before a Rabbi to be designated for the purposes of a Jewish religious divorce." Prior to the order appealed from, defendant was on two occasions held in contempt and fined therefor, (orders dated June 23, 1972 and October 2, 1972) subject to the provision that he could purge himself of the contempt upon payment of the fines and by appearing before a Jewish court for the purpose of obtaining the divorce. When defendant continued in his refusal to comply with the court's orders, a further motion for contempt was brought. This time defendant was committed to jail for a period of 15 days, again with the opportunity to purge himself of the contempt if he appeared and participated in a Jewish ritual divorce.

It is argued that the court was without power to direct defendant to participate in a religious divorce, as such is a matter of one's personal convictions and is not subject to the court's interference. We are told further, that since a Jewish divorce can only be granted upon the representation that it is sought by the husband of his own free will, any such divorce, if obtained under compulsion by the court, would in any event be a nullity.

We agree that the defendant may not, under these circumstances, be incarcerated for his failure to honor the stipulations (incorporated into a court order) and accordingly, vacate that portion of the order directing his commitment. However, we believe that the fines imposed upon defendant by the prior orders should stand. Defendant failed to perfect any appeals from the prior orders fining him for his contempt nor did he obtain a stay of the provisions contained in those orders. The initial order was entered upon the parties' open court stipulation concerning the disputes arising after the judgment of divorce, and defendant voluntarily agreed to perform certain acts. The court had jurisdiction over the parties and the subject matter, and even if the orders were erroneous, the defendant was obligated, in the absence of a stay, to obey the court's mandate until vacated or reversed. (See *Burchell v. Cimenti*, 38 A.D.2d 897, 329 N.Y.S.2d 347, 9 N.Y.Jur., Contempt §28.) In any event, there was abundant basis upon which to conclude that defendant's behavior was contumacious. Immediately after the open court stipulation was entered into, defendant, who has remarried, and who accepted the benefits of the agreement, disavowed his representations made in open court. At the time when he agreed to participate in the religious divorce he was well aware of the consequences and nature of the act and that it could only be obtained upon his assertion to the rabbinical court that it was being sought of his own free will. Defendant was also well aware that plaintiff could not enter into a valid remarriage under Jewish law until the "get" had been granted. It is not indicated that any subsequent developments caused defendant to change his mind and upon this record we can only conclude that defendant never intended to carry out the terms of the open court stipulation and that he utilized the court for his own ulterior motives. Such behavior may not be countenanced.

All concur except *Nunez, J.*, who dissents in the following memorandum:

The direction that defendant appear before a Rabbi for the purpose of obtaining a Jewish religious divorce, a "get," contained in the order entered October 28, 1971, is unenforceable. It matters not that defendant consented to its entry. It was for his failure to appear before the appropriate religious authority to obtain the "get" that defendant has been adjudged in contempt three times by the court below. On the first two occasions he was permitted to purge himself by paying fines totalling $450 and submitting to a "get." The order appealed from commits defendant to jail for 15 days without any purge provision.

The Hebrew divorce has no validity unless the husband's consent is given voluntarily and without coercion or duress. See 3 Universal Jewish Encyclopedia, p. 578 and 6 Encyclopedia Judaica 130. Had defendant appeared and given his consent to the "get" under threat of imprisonment, the religious divorce thus obtained would have been a nullity.

Furthermore, while it is true that defendant did not appeal from the two previous orders adjudging him in contempt, and it is for defendant's failure to do so that the majority is upholding the validity of the order appealed from, it should be noted that he was held in contempt solely for his failure to obtain the "get." Religion, as well as religious laws, ceremonies and procedures are matters of individual conscience. The constitutional and traditional complete separation of church and state is most salutary and desirable. No erosion of this basic concept should be permitted. The original order directing the plaintiff to obtain the religious divorce being improper, the subsequent orders did not validate it. I am certain my brethren would not enforce an order directing a litigant to go to confession or to say six Our Fathers and four Hail Marys. I would reverse and deny the motion to punish.

Settle order on notice.

Rubin v. Rubin
348 N.Y.S. 2d 61 (1973)
Family Court, Bronx County
September 17, 1973

Stanley Gartenstein, Judge:

This proceeding pursuant to Article 4 of the Family Court Act for the support of the petitioning former wife brings into focus the interaction between the matrimonial laws of this state and the Jewish religious law of divorce when made relevant by contractual act between parties to an agreement. With the sociological reality of a tremendously increased divorce rate upon us, a phenomenon which cuts across all levels of society, Orthodox Jews find themselves in matrimonial litigation more often and courts are called upon to weigh the import of ecclesiastical laws which are often made crucial by contractual act of the parties. Understandably there is much confusion about these laws and courts often find themselves at a loss when called upon to delve into religious law to which there is no definitive guide in the usual legal sources. A short synopsis, therefore, would appear to be in order.

Petitioner and respondent were married in 1929 and divorced by decree of an Alabama court entered on April 15, 1961 which incorporated by reference but did not merge, a separation agreement executed by the parties on March 10, 1961. By the terms of the agreement, respondent was to pay the sum of $30.00 per week as maintenance for petitioner aside from amounts for the children, now emancipated. Proceedings for enforcement of this decree were brought in this court in 1972 and withdrawn when an agreement in writing was reached between the parties dated and acknowledged on October 4, 1972. In this document, the wife represented that she was self supporting and agreed to accept the lump sum payment of $4,740.00 in full settlement of any past, present or future claims against her former husband. A specific term of the agreement inserted in ink and initialled by the parties provided that each of the parties was to cooperate in securing a Jewish divorce (hereinafter referred to as Get; see footnote 2, infra). Respondent did in fact make tender of the lump sum settlement which was refused. Petitioner also refused to appear at a rabbinical religious court in furtherance of her agreement to cooperate in securing the Get.

Not satisfied with the settlement or with respondent's tender of performance, petitioner commenced a second proceeding by petition dated November 13, 1972, once again seeking enforcement of the Alabama decree in accordance with its original terms, totally ignoring the agreement which was never nullified. This proceeding resulted in a consent order without prejudice providing for the continued payment of $100.00 per month plus arrears of $1000.00, again with the understanding that petitioner cooperate in securing the Get.

Petitioner now seeks enforcement of arrears based upon this latest "settlement." Respondent has paid the lump sum toward arrears and apparently nothing more. He alleges that petitioner has failed to cooperate in securing the Get, a condition precedent upon which the settlement was made contingent. At the first hearing, the wife indeed expressed her refusal to appear at the rabbinical court for the Get but expressed no reservations or opposition to the Get itself. On this basis, the court ruled that inasmuch as the wife's presence was unnecessary at these proceedings if her assent was otherwise manifested, directed compliance with the latest settlement based upon the fact that respondent's factual defense of failure of a condition precedent was unfounded under the very ecclesiastical law upon which he purported to rely. The matter was then adjourned to enable completion of these proceedings and a progress report was directed. On the adjourned date, petitioner, evidently expressing a change of heart, now refused to manifest consent to the Get. She further attacked the agreement which compromised the first enforcement proceeding as being void because she was not represented by counsel during its execution.

Petitioner and respondent both support themselves from Social Security payments. In addition respondent receives a nominal pension and some sporadic income. The court indeed finds petitioner to be self supporting as she represented herself to be in writing.

JEWISH ECCLESIASTICAL LAW OF DIVORCE:

Marriage, which under Anglo-Saxon jurisprudence is a continuing quasi-contractual relationship arising out of the original agreement solemnized in a manner recognized by the state, (Domestic Relations Law Sect. 10) is, under Talmudic law, strictly a contract given validity solely by continued contractual act of the parties, either express or implied (Kiddushin 1A).[1] Indeed, if the Ketubah (marriage contract) leaves the actual or constructive possession of the wife at any time subsequent to the effective commencement date of the marriage contract, further cohabitation is forbidden (Ketubot 7; Even-Ha-Ezer, 66, 1).

Accordingly, given the legal definition of marriage, the Get or divorce is a simple act of release nominally executed by the husband for delivery to the wife "freeing" her for marriage to anyone else, having its Biblical origins in Genesis 21, verses 9-14 and Deuteronomy 22, verses 13-19.[2]

The notion that the Get is a judicial decree requiring appearance and

---

1. In his commentary of the Bible, the late Chief Rabbi Hertz of Great Britain apparently takes issue with this point of view (See, The Hertz Chumash, Soncino, London, 1971, 2nd Edition, Additional notes on Deuteronomy, Section E). However, it is the Rabbi's intention to underscore that the bare expressed terms of the contract do not begin to scratch the surface; that the obligations thus assumed are far more extensive. If one considers these duties as contractual terms outside the four walls of the instrument, imposed by law as part of the contract, the two characterizations are not contradictory.

2. The very name of the marital release, Get, is derived from the statutory formula connected with its execution. Hebrew numbers, being expressed with the same letters which form words, every word has a numerical value. The word Get derives from a combination of letter *gimel* having numerical value of 3 plus *tet*, value 9; total 12 corresponding to statutory formula of twelve-line instrument.

The availability of divorce by consent does not imply Biblical approval thereof. Indeed, to underscore how repugnant the tragedy of divorce is, nowhere in the original Hebrew text of the Bible does the letter *tet* follow the letter *gimel*.

participation by both parties is fallacious. While the formal drafting of the instrument requires the assistance of "those learned in the law" (Kiddushin 60), a Get is Talmudically valid when executed by the husband without the presence of the wife and delivered by his agent (Gittin 1A).

The foregoing is not to imply that the function of the court was nil or that the Get was within the sole province of the husband. Indeed, where grounds existed, the Bet Din (religious court) was convened at the suit of the wife for injunctive relief directing the husband to execute and cause delivery of the Get freeing her. On the other hand, even where proceedings were at the instance of the husband, the staggering minutia of technical details requiring the assistance of experts (Kiddushin 60, supra), gave the rabbinical courts a res upon which to seize in acquiring judicial powers.

Jewish law is framed on the theory that a dead marriage should be dissolved. While divorce by consent (The Talmud recognized no-fault divorce 2000 years ago) is the outgrowth of this attitude, the rabbinical authorities always took great pains to insure that the marriage was really dead and that the parties were afforded every opportunity to turn back. In this spirit, the procedural minutia involved in the execution and delivery of the Get became the vehicle wherein the religious courts assumed their judicial function. For, with the power to lend or withhold that expertise of those "learned in the law" as required by Kiddushin 60, the execution and delivery of a Get became virtually impossible without the help of the rabbinical court which was extended or withheld depending on the existence of specified grounds when mutual consent was not manifested. In the process of exercising this "judicial" function, rabbinical courts developed the principle that no wife was to be divorced against her will unless certain grounds existed. This practice of rabbinical law, in existence for about a thousand years from earliest Talmudic times, was codified by Rabbienu Gershon in the approximate year 1000 of the common calendar.

Obviously, the Get has the same importance today as it has had over the centuries because, in the absence thereof, any re-marriage takes place without capacity to contract. Since the party entering the new liaison is already married under ecclesiastical law, cohabitation with the new spouse is adulterous. Finally, to complete this caveat, even if the first marriage is then dissolved by valid Get, Jewish religious law prohibits marriage to a person with whom adultery has been committed. This can result in a religious prohibition against marrying the very same second spouse with whom a party has in fact been living.

Divorce proceedings under Talmudic Law are maintainable at the suit of the wife on certain enumerated grounds ***** at the suit of the husband under circumstances where the financial emoluments of the Ketubah were forfeited ***** or by the court on its own suit against the wishes of the parties *****. In addition to the foregoing, the rabbinical authorities constituted as courts, had the function of monitoring situations in which a Get was Biblically forbidden (e.g. prior unfounded accusation of unchastity by the husband (Deuteronomy 22, verses 13-19).[3]

---

3. The characterization by both the majority and minority in Margulies v. Margulies, infra, that the Get can only be obtained on consent refers only to so-called "no-fault" decrees without reference to these grounds which when existent, require no consent and which can give rise to a Get against the will of one or even both parties.

Applying these principles to the matter in litigation: at the time the wife indicated her willingness to accept the Get, but her refusal to attend proceedings for that purpose, the husband's contention of non-cooperation was without merit (Gittin 1a, supra). However, with the wife now refusing cooperation, viz., consent, the position of the husband under ecclesiastical law is untenable. At this juncture, respondent's claim that petitioner's failure to cooperate has prejudiced him takes on irresistible merit. Having established this, the court is now faced with issues which may circumscribe its ability to enforce the agreement.

SEPARATION OF CHURCH AND STATE: ENFORCEABILITY OF AGREEMENT

As a general proposition, the fact that parties to an agreement may be married or may be contemplating by agreement, the dissolution thereof, has no bearing on the basic rule of contracts that people are bound by the promises they undertake. Parties to a separation agreement may make alimony or even child support contingent on the express terms thereof (*Callender v. Callender*, 37 A.D.2d 360, 325 N.Y.S.2d 420). And where this agreement survives the entry of a divorce decree, it will be enforced independently even when adherence to any condition precedent therein may have the effect of cutting off support monies (*Callender v. Callender*, supra, citing, *Hettich v. Hettich*, 304 N.Y. 8, 105 N.E.2d 601 and *McMains v. McMains*, 15 N.Y.2d 283, 258 N.Y.S.2d 93, 206 N.E.2d 185).

Constitutionally, it has been held that the separation of church and state mandated by the First Amendment carries with it the obligation of the state to refrain from any act which might interfere with religious disciplines and/or from any act which might interfere with religious tribunal (*Watson v. Jones*, 13 Wall. 679, 20 L.Ed. 666, 1871). The courts of the realm are constitutionally enjoined from entering a dispute with religious implications where the matter has been the subject of litigation in the ecclesiastical courts (*Watson v. Jones*, supra). In this holding, the result was reached even when the subject matter of the dispute was real property, a commodity jealously reserved for the jurisdiction of the local courts.

The courts of this state have recognized the validity of an agreement to obtain a Get. In *Koeppel v. Koeppel*, Sup., 138 N.Y.S.2d 366, the court refused to dismiss an action for specific performance of a defendant husband's agreement to comply with the necessary procedure to effectuate a Jewish Get. On the other hand, *Margulies v. Margulies*, 42 A.D.2d 517, 344 N.Y.S.2d 482, reversed a commitment for contempt based upon failure of a defendant husband to comply with an order directing compliance with an agreement to participate in the Get ritual. This situation is distinguishable from the matter at bar in that this court is not called upon to enforce this religious discipline against a recalcitrant party, but, rather, is being called upon by the defaulting party to enforce other relief in her favor at a time when she refuses to perform a condition precedent thereto, which happens to be an act of religious significance. The condition precedent could well have been anything else made crucial by agreement of the parties. In this latter instance, where one party to an agreement calling for a Get declines to perform, the court will either refuse any relief to the defaulting party, or will hold any application for the same in abeyance pending performance of the obligations assumed pertaining to the Get. (*Pal v. Pal*, N.Y.L.J. July 25, 1973, p. 13, col. 5)

ORDER:

The intent of the parties to make continued support contingent upon the wife's cooperation in securing the Get is clearly set forth. The fact that this clause was written in by hand and initialled give it pre-eminence over any typed portion of the agreement. (*Kratzenstein v. Western Assurance Co.*, 116 N.Y. 54, 22 N.E. 211; *Feldman v. Fiat Estates, Inc.*, 25 A.D.2d 750, 268 N.Y.S.2d 949, 2nd Dept. 1966).

The motion by petitioner to declare the agreement void is denied. The vigor of her participation in its negotiation and the number of initialled amendments show a document signed only after much arm's length give-and-take. Petitioner was not defrauded; was not under undue influence; was certainly aware of the nature and import of the document. Indeed, its execution conforms, in every respect, to the original separation agreement upon which she relies. Its terms are clear and there are no ambiguities, in which event, it is the court's function to enforce it rather than attempt a re-writing thereof based upon some nebulous notion of a better bargain one party thereto feels she might have extracted. (*Churchill Evangelistic Ass'n v. Columbia Broadcasting System*, 236 A.D. 624, 260 N.Y.S. 451; *Textile Capital Building Corp. v. Wendel Foundation*, 253 A.D. 332, 2 N.Y.S.2d 45, affd. 279 N.Y. 769, 18 N.E.2d 8609; *Friedman v. Handelman*, 300 N.Y. 188, 90 N.E.2d 31).

The consent order of February 26, 1973, without prejudice, and conditioned upon petitioner's cooperation in securing the Get, is vacated based upon failure of the one condition made crucial by the parties upon which it was based. Proceedings are therefore rolled back to the next preceding event of significance which is the agreement of Oct. 4, 1972, executed, by its own terms as an amendment to the original separation agreement in accordance with the formalities delineated therein. The court holds the agreement valid and enforceable; it is the law of the case.

Respondent shall, within 10 days from the date of this order, consult a Rabbi of his choice for the purpose of having notice sent to petitioner either to appear or to accept a Get. If the Get is completed within two weeks after notice by the Rabbi, the other terms of the agreement shall be honored and respondent shall pay petitioner the sum of $3,740.00 representing the difference between the amount in the agreement and the $1000.00 heretofore paid. Payment shall be made within 10 days after completion thereof. Failing same, the court, which has before it a petition to enforce a foreign decree and faced with a petitioner who, by her own representation in writing, is self supporting and whose income from Social Security derives from the same source as does respondent's, exercises that discretion vested in it by Family Court Act, Section 466, subd. C and declines to entertain this petition, in which event, this proceeding is dismissed on the merits. The fact that this court unquestionably has jurisdiction does not mean that it is bound to exercise it (*Warden v. Warden*, 68 Misc. 2d 1080, 329 N.Y.S.2d 51). (See also, on the question of support for financially independent former wife, *Kover v. Kover*, 29 N.Y.2d 409, 328 N.Y.S.2d 641, 278 N.E.2d 886).

Waxstein v. Waxstein
395 N.Y.S. 2d 877 (1976)
Supreme Court, Special Term, Kings County, Part V
July 28, 1976

Louis B. Heller, Justice:

In this action for divorce the complaint sets forth seven causes of action wherein the plaintiff seeks the following relief;

1. A judgment of absolute divorce upon the ground of a prior written agreement of separation.[a]

* * * * * * * * * * * *

7. An injunction requiring defendant to commence proceedings for a "Get," i.e., a Jewish religious divorce.

The matter was tried before me without a jury. While both parties were in agreement that the divorce should be granted on the ground of the separation agreement, I reserved decision on the entire case to examine and decide on the basis of factual and legal interpretations of the various provisions of the separation agreement. The parties were given an opportunity to submit memoranda of law, affidavits and an agreed statement of facts.

On the basis of the papers submitted, the court finds the following relevant facts as not being in dispute: The plaintiff and defendant were married on June 7, 1953. They have three children of this marriage, currently ages 18, 19 and 22. On May 29, 1973 the parties duly executed a separation agreement prepared by the plaintiff's attorney. Pursuant to this agreement plaintiff moved out of their marital residence before April 30, 1974 as provided in paragraph Tenth, and the deed transferring her interest in the property to the defendant is held in escrow by her attorneys under the terms of paragraph Thirty-First. Defendant still resides at the former marital home.

The defendant has failed to comply with the separation agreement. He refuses to give the plaintiff a "Get" in accordance with paragraph Seventh. It is appropriate to recite a few general principles concerning separation agreements.

A separation agreement is a contract and if lawful when made will be enforced by the courts like any other contract unless impeached or challenged for some cause recognized by law (*Goldman v. Goldman*, 282 N.Y. 296, 300, 26 N.E.2d 265, 267; *Schmelzel v. Schmelzel*, 287 N.Y. 21, 26, 38 N.E.2d 114, 115). And like other contracts the provisions of a separation agreement may be enforced by specific performance if the remedy at law is inadequate (*Lottridge v. Lottridge*, 73 Misc.2d 614, 617, 342 N.Y.S.2d 251, 255; 2 Foster-Freed, Law and the Family, §28:35). But the court may not modify or alter its provisions as long as the agreement remains unimpeached (*Stoddard v. Stoddard*, 227 N.Y. 13, 20-21, 124 N.E. 91, 93-94; *Goldman v. Goldman*, supra, 282 N.Y. p. 300, 26 N.E.2d p. 267; *Stillman v. Stillman*, 20 A.D.2d 723, 724, 247 N.Y.S.2d 569, 571 [2d Dept.]). Where the terms of the agreement are clear and unambiguous the intent of the parties must be found therein (Matter of Wosnitzer, 47 A.D.2d 402, 404-405, 366 N.Y.S.2d 653, 655-656); any ambiguities will, however, be construed against the party who drafted the contact (*Mars Associates Inc. v. Health & Mental Hygiene Fac.*

---

[a]Ellipsis by Court, [*ed.*]

Impr. Corp., 47 A.D.2d 5, 6, 364 N.Y.S.2d 67, 69).

The burden of establishing an affirmative defense as to the agreement rests with the party asserting such defense and the burden must be met by a fair preponderance of the evidence (*Birnbaum v. Birnbaum*, 70 Misc.2d 462, 464-465, 333 N.Y.S.2d 890, 893-894, affd. 76 Misc.2d 1087, 352 N.Y.S.2d 600). In this connection, the court finds unavailing defendant's affirmative defense that the separation agreement is void under section 5-311 of the General Obligations Law as embracing a provision (viz., paragraph Seventh) which purports to dissolve the marriage between the parties. This paragraph should not be equated to or regarded as "an express provision requiring the dissolution of the marriage" (General Obligations Law §5-311; *Rosen v. Goldberg*. 28 A.D.2d 1051, 283 N.Y.S.2d 804, affd. 23 N.Y.2d 791, 297 N.Y.S.2d 298, 244 N.E.2d 869), nor does the paragraph have a direct tendency to promote a divorce (Matter of Fleischmann, 64 Misc.2d 924, 926, 316 N.Y.S.2d 272, 274, affd. 37 A.D.2d 1044, 326 N.Y.S.2d 376).

1. Judgment of Divorce.

Plaintiff is entitled to a judgment of absolute divorce pursuant to subdivision 6 of section 170 of the Domestic Relations Law as the court finds that the parties "have lived separate and apart pursuant to a written agreement of separation * * * for a period of one or more years after the execution of such agreement and satisfactory proof has been submitted by the plaintiff that she has substantially performed all the terms and conditions of such agreement."

In accordance with the terms of the separation agreement the entire agreement is to be incorporated, but not merged, into the judgment of divorce.

7. Injunction Requiring Defendant to Furnish a "Get" to Plaintiff.

In her last cause of action plaintiff demands judgment enjoining the defendant to institute a proceeding for a "Get," a Jewish religious divorce. In essence plaintiff seeks specific performance of paragraph Seventh of the separation agreement which provides that:

> "Prior to the Wife vacating the premises as hereinbefore set forth, the parties shall obtain a Get from a duly constituted Rabbinical court. The Wife shall, directly or indirectly pay for the Get, and the Husband agrees to the Get provided it is done within the sixty day period prior to the vacation of the marital premises by the Wife."

Defendant urges as an affirmative defense that plaintiff violated this paragraph by vacating the marital premises without obtaining a "Get," thus waiving her right to the "Get." The court rejects this argument. It is the defendant who refuses to give the plaintiff a "Get" in violation of the agreement. Defendant should not thereby benefit because the plaintiff chose to comply with another provision of the agreement requiring her to vacate the marital premises on or before April 1, 1974.

Defendant's second argument is that the court may not enforce a contractual provision requiring a spouse to obtain a "Get." This court does not agree.

The validity of an agreement to obtain a "Get" has been recognized in this state (*Koeppel v. Koeppel*, Sup., 138 N.Y.S.2d 366, 374, affd. 3 A.D.2d 853, 161 N.Y.S.2d 694 [2d Dept.]; *Margulies v. Margulies*, 42 A.D.2d 517, 344 N.Y.S.2d 482, appeal dismissed 33 N.Y.2d 894, 352 N.Y.S.2d 447, 307 N.E.2d 562; *Rubin v. Rubin*, 75 Misc.2d 776, 782, 348 N.Y.S.2d 61, 67).

In *Koeppel v. Koeppel*, supra, the wife brought an action to obtain specific performance of defendant's covenant, pursuant to a separation agreement, to comply with the necessary procedure to effectuate a Jewish religious dissolution of their marriage. Defendant refused to appear before a rabbi or rabbinate to execute the papers necessary to effectuate a religious dissolution in accordance with the laws of the Jewish faith. In denying defendant's cross-motion for summary judgment the court stated:

> "Defendant has also contended that a decree of specific performance would interfere with his freedom of religion under the Constitution. Complying with his agreement would not compel the defendant to practice any religion, not even the Jewish faith to which he still admits adherence (paragraph Second of the complaint not denied in the answer). His appearance before the Rabbinate to answer questions and give evidence needed by them to make a decision is not a profession of faith. Specific performance herein would merely require the defendant to do what he voluntarily agreed to do.
>
> Defendant's statement that the ceremony before the Rabbinate takes from two to two and one-half hours is not worthy of discussion. That is not much out of a lifetime, especially if it will bring peace of mind and conscience to one whom defendant must at one time have loved." (supra, p. 373)

In his memorandum of law defendant omits any reference to the Koeppel decision but instead cites two other cases in support of his position that the court may not enforce the "Get" provision - *Margulies v. Margulies*, 42 A.D.2d 517, 344 N.Y.S.2d 482, appeal dismissed 33 N.Y.2d 894, 352 N.Y.S.2d 447, 307 N.E.2d 562 and *Pal v. Pal* 45 A.D.2d 738, 356 N.Y.S.2d 672.

Margulies v. Margulies, supra, involved a stipulation in open court, subsequent to a judgment of divorce, whereby the defendant-husband voluntarily agreed to "appear before a Rabbi to be designated for the purposes of a Jewish religious divorce." The husband failed to comply with the stipulation and was twice held in contempt and fined therefor, subject to the provision that he could purge himself by paying the fines and appearing before a Jewish court to obtain a religious divorce. The husband refused to comply with the two contempt orders and by a third order was committed to jail for a period of 15 days with the same opportunity to purge himself. On appeal from the third order, the Appellate Division, First Department struck therefrom the provision directing his imprisonment and substituted instead a proviso that he could purge himself by paying the fines imposed under the two prior orders or, alternatively, by appearing and participating in a Jewish divorce. While the court in *Margulies* raised the issue of whether the court was without power to direct defendant to participate in a religious divorce it did not decide the question, except inferentially, when it upheld the underlying orders of contempt and the fines imposed therein and permitted the husband to purge his contempt by paying the fines or by complying with the stipulation.

In *Pal v. Pal*, supra, the parties agreed in a stipulation in open court in a divorce action commenced by plaintiff-husband that they would submit themselves to a rabbinical tribunal as to whether plaintiff should be directed to take the necessary steps to grant a Jewish divorce, a "Get." The stipulation also included provisions with respect to the selection of rabbis to constitute the rabbinical tribunal, which in essence required the court to select a third rabbi in the event the two rabbis chosen by the parties shall fail to select one. In the proceeding before the court, Special Term granted defendant's cross-motion to have the court designate a third rabbi. The Appellate Division, Second Department reversed and held that "Special Term had no authority to, in effect, convene a rabbinical tribunal" (supra, p. 739, 356 N.Y.S.2d p. 673).

However, the court, as in the *Margulies* case, impliedly acknowledged the validity of the parties' stipulation as to the "Get" by denying plaintiff's motion to punish the defendant for contempt for her alleged violation of the divorce judgment concerning visitation. The court said in this regard:

> "Plaintiff's motion to punish defendant for contempt should have been denied, as one who seeks such relief must come into court with clean hands. Plaintiff's conduct in not complying with the terms of a stipulation [i.e., the "Get"] incorporated into the judgment of divorce was such as to preclude the granting of his motion." (supra, p. 739, 356 N.Y.S.2d p. 673.)

On the basis of the above authorities the court concludes that it may grant specific performance of the provision in the separation agreement requiring the parties to obtain a "Get." The *Margulies* and *Pal* decisions do not overrule the *Koeppel* conclusion nor otherwise warrant a contrary result, but they merely preclude enforcement by means of imprisonment or the convening of a rabbinical tribunal.

Accordingly, the defendant is directed to take whatever steps are necessary to secure a "Get" for the plaintiff, be it by his own commencement of and appearance and participation in such a religious proceeding or his consent, appearance and participation in a proceeding begun by the plaintiff (see *Rubin v. Rubin*, 75 Misc.2d 776, 348 N.Y.S.2d 61, 64-66). This court may also condition enforcement of other provisions in the separation agreement upon the defendant's cooperation in securing the "Get" (*"Rubin v. Rubin*, supra, 348 N.Y.S.2d pp. 67-68). Accordingly, the court further holds that the stock and the deed to the marital residence now being held by the plaintiff's attorneys shall not be turned over to the defendant until he has obtained a "Get."

C. EXPRESS CONTRACTS TO SUBMIT TO THE JURISDICTION OF A *BAIT DIN*

Avitzur v. Avitzur

58 N.Y.2d 108, 447 N.E.2d 136, 29 A.L.R. 4th 736 (1983)
Court of Appeals of New York
February 15, 1983

Wachtler, Judge:

This appeal presents for our consideration the question of the proper role of the civil courts in deciding a matter touching upon religious concerns. At issue is the enforceability of the terms of a document, known as a Ketubah, which was entered into as part of the religious marriage ceremony in this case. The Appellate Division, 86 A.D.2d 133, 449 N.Y.S.2d 93, held this to be a religious covenant beyond the jurisdiction of the civil courts. However, we find nothing in law or public policy to prevent judicial recognition and enforcement of the secular terms of such an agreement. There should be a reversal.

Plaintiff and defendant were married on May 22, 1966 in a ceremony conducted in accordance with Jewish tradition. Prior to the marriage ceremony, the parties signed both a Hebrew/Aramaic and an English version of the "Ketubah." According to the English translation, the Ketubah evidences both the bridegroom's intention to cherish and provide for his wife as required by religious law and tradition and the bride's willingness to carry out her obligations to her husband in faithfulness and affection according to Jewish law and tradition. By signing the Ketubah, the parties declared their "desire to ...live in accordance with the Jewish law of marriage throughout [their] lifetime" and further agreed as follows: "[W]e, the bride and bridegroom ...hereby agree to recognize the Beth Din of the Rabbinical Assembly and the Jewish Theological Seminary of America or its duly appointed representatives, as having authority to counsel us in the light of Jewish tradition which requires husband and wife to give each other complete love and devotion, and to summon either party at the request of the other, in order to enable the party so requesting to live in accordance with the standards of the Jewish law of marriage throughout his or her lifetime. We authorize the Beth Din to impose such terms of compensation as it may see fit for failure to respond to its summons or to carry out its decision."

Defendant husband was granted a civil divorce upon the ground of cruel and inhuman treatment on May 16, 1978. Notwithstanding this civil divorce, plaintiff wife is not considered divorced and may not remarry pursuant to Jewish law, until such time as a Jewish divorce decree, known as a "Get," is granted. In order that a Get may be obtained plaintiff and defendant must appear before a "Beth Din," a rabbinical tribunal having authority to advise and pass upon matters of traditional Jewish law. Plaintiff sought to summon defendant before the Beth Din pursuant to the provision of the Ketubah recognizing that body as having authority to counsel the couple in the matters concerning their marriage.

Defendant has refused to appear before the Beth Din, thus preventing plaintiff from obtaining a religious divorce. Plaintiff brought this action, alleging that the Ketubah constitutes a marital contract, which defendant has breached by refusing to appear before the Beth Din, and she seeks relief both in the form of a declaration to that effect and an order compelling defendant's specific performance of the Ketubah's requirement that he appear before the Beth Din. Defendant moved to dismiss the complaint upon the grounds that the court lacked subject matter jurisdiction and the complaint failed to state a cause of action, arguing that resolution of the dispute and any grant of relief to plaintiff would involve the civil court in impermissible consideration of a purely religious matter. Plaintiff, in addition to opposing the motion, cross-moved for summary judgment.

Special Term denied defendant's motion to dismiss, noting that plaintiff sought only to compel defendant to submit to the jurisdiction of the Beth Din, an act which plaintiff had alleged defendant bound himself to do. That being the only object of the lawsuit, Special Term was apparently of the view that the relief sought could be granted without impermissible judicial entanglement in any doctrinal issue. The court also denied plaintiff's motion for summary judgment, concluding that issues concerning the translation, meaning and effect of the Ketubah raised factual questions requiring a plenary trial.

The Appellate Division modified, granting defendant's motion to dismiss. Inasmuch as the Ketubah was entered into as part of a religious ceremony and was executed, by its own terms, in accordance with Jewish law, the court concluded that the document constitutes a liturgical agreement. The Appellate Division held such agreements to be unenforceable where the State, having granted a civil divorce to the parties, has no further interest in their marital status.

Accepting plaintiff's allegations as true, as we must in the context of this motion to dismiss, it appears that plaintiff and defendant, in signing the Ketubah, entered into a contract which formed the basis for their marriage. Plaintiff has alleged that, pursuant to the terms of this marital contract, defendant promised that he would, at plaintiff's request, appear before the Beth Din for the purpose of allowing that tribunal to advise and counsel the parties in matters concerning their marriage, including the granting of a Get. It should be noted that plaintiff is not attempting to compel defendant to obtain a Get or to enforce a religious practice arising solely out of principles of religious law. She merely seeks to enforce an agreement made by defendant to appear before and accept the decision of a designated tribunal.

Viewed in this manner, the provisions of the Ketubah relied upon by plaintiff constitute nothing more than an agreement to refer the matter of a religious divorce to a nonjudicial forum. Thus, the contractual obligation plaintiff seeks to enforce is closely analogous to an antenuptial agreement to arbitrate a dispute in accordance with the law and tradition chosen by the parties. There can be little doubt that a duly executed antenuptial agreement, by which the parties agree in advance of the marriage to the resolution of disputes that may arise after its termination, is valid and enforceable (e.g., *Matter of Sunshine*, 40 N.Y.2d 975, 389 N.Y.S.2d 344, 357 N.E.2d 999, aff'g 51 A.D.2d 326, 381 N.Y.S.2d 260; *Matter of Davis*, 20 N.Y.2d 70, 281 N.Y.S.2d 767, 228 N.E.2d 768). Similarly, an agreement to refer a matter concerning marriage to arbitration suffers no inherent invalidity (*Hirsch v. Hirsch*, 37 N.Y.2d 312, 372 N.Y.S.2d 71, 333 N.E.2d 371; see *Bowmer v. Bowmer*, 50 N.Y.2d 288, 293, 429 N.Y.S.2d 902, 406 N.E.2d 760). This agreement - the Ketubah - should ordinarily be entitled to no less dignity than any other civil contract to submit a dispute to a nonjudicial forum, so long as its enforcement violates neither the law nor the public policy of this State (*Hirsch v. Hirsch*, supra, at p. 315, 372 N.Y.S.2d 71, 333 N.E.2d 371).

Defendant argues, in this connection, that enforcement of the terms of the Ketubah by a civil court would violate the constitutional prohibition against excessive entanglement between church and State, because the court must necessarily intrude upon matters of religious doctrine and practice. It is urged that the obligations imposed by the Ketubah arise solely from Jewish religious law and can be interpreted only with reference to religious dogma. Granting the religious character of the Ketubah, it does not necessarily follow that any recognition of its obligations is foreclosed to the courts.

It is clear that judicial involvement in matters touching upon religious concerns has been constitutionally limited in analogous situations, and courts should not resolve such controversies in a manner requiring consideration of religious doctrine. (*Presbyterian Church v. Hull Church*, 393 U.S. 440, 449, 89 S.Ct. 601, 606, 21 L.Ed.2d 658; *Serbian Orthodox Diocese v. Milivojevich*, 426 U.S. 696, 709, 96 S.Ct. 2372, 2380, 49 L.Ed.2d 151; *Jones v. Wolf*, 443 U.S. 595, 603, 99 S.Ct. 3020, 3025, 61 L.Ed.2d 775; see, e.g., *Reardon v. Lemoyne*, N.H. 454 A.2d 428 [1982]. In its most recent pronouncement on this issue, however, the Supreme Court, in holding that a State may adopt any approach to resolving religious disputes which does not entail consideration of doctrinal matters, specifically approved the use of the "neutral principles of law" approach as consistent with constitutional limitations (*Jones v. Wolf*, supra, 443 U.S. at p. 602, 99 S.Ct. at 3024). This approach contemplates the application of objective, well-established principles of secular law to the dispute (id., at p. 603, 99 S.Ct. at 3025), thus permitting judicial involvement to the extent that it can be accomplished in purely secular terms.

The present case can be decided solely upon the application of neutral principles of contract law, without reference to any religious principle. Consequently, defendant's objections to enforcement of his promise to appear before the Beth Din, based as they are upon the religious origin of the agreement, pose no constitutional barrier to the relief sought by plaintiff. The fact that the agreement was entered into as part of a religious ceremony does not render it unenforceable. Solemnization of the marital relationship often takes place in accordance with the religious beliefs of the participants, and this State has long recognized this religious aspect by permitting duly authorized pastors, rectors, priests, rabbis and other religious officials to perform the ceremony (Domestic Relation Law, §11, subds. 1, 7). Similarly, that the obligations undertaken by the parties to the Ketubah are grounded in religious belief and practice does not preclude enforcement of its secular terms. Nor does the fact that all of the Ketubah's provisions may not be judicially recognized prevent the court from enforcing that portion of the agreement by which the parties promised to refer their disputes to a nonjudicial forum (see *Ferro v. Bologna*, 31 N.Y.2d 30, 36, 334 N.Y.S.2d 856, 286 N.E.2d 244). The courts may properly enforce so much of this agreement as is not in contravention of law or public policy.

In short, the relief sought by plaintiff in this action is simply to compel defendant to perform a secular obligation to which he contractually bound himself. In this regard, no doctrinal issue need be passed upon, no implementation of a religious duty is contemplated, and no interference with religious authority will result. Certainly nothing the Beth Din can do would in any way affect the civil divorce. To the extent that an enforceable promise can be found by the application of neutral principles of contract law, plaintiff will have demonstrated entitlement to the relief sought. Consideration of other substantive issues bearing upon plaintiff's entitlement to a religious divorce, however, is appropriately left to the forum the parties chose for resolving the matter.

Accordingly, the order of the Appellate Division should be reversed, with costs, and defendant's motion to dismiss the complaint denied.

Jones, Judge (dissenting):

We are of the opinion that to grant the relief plaintiff seeks in this action, even to the limited extent contemplated by the majority, would necessarily violate the constitutional prohibition against entanglement of our secular courts in matters of religious and ecclesiastical content. Accordingly, we would affirm the order of the Appellate Division.

We start on common ground. Judicial intervention in disputes with respect to religious and ecclesiastical obligation is constitutionally proscribed, save with respect to a narrow class of issues, as to which, under "neutral principles of law," the secular component of the religious and ecclesiastical rights and obligations may be resolved without impermissible trespass on or even reference to religious dogma and doctrine (pp. 114-115, -N.Y.S.2d -, 446 N.E.2d 138). We depart from the conclusion of the majority that in this case the courts may discern one or more discretely secular obligations which may be fractured out of the "Ketubah," indisputably in its essence a document prepared and executed under Jewish law and tradition.

We are constrained, as is the majority, by the allegations of the complaint. Plaintiff therein alleges: that the parties were married on May 22, 1966 in a religious ceremony in accordance with Jewish law and tradition; that pursuant to the terms and conditions of the religious ceremony they entered into a contract known as a "Ketubah"; that under the Ketubah the husband declared and contracted with the wife to be her husband according to the law of Moses and Israel and to honor and support her, faithfully cherishing her and providing for her needs as Jewish husbands are required to do pursuant to Jewish religious law and tradition; that pursuant to the Ketubah the parties agreed to recognize the Beth Din of the Rabbinical Assembly and the Jewish Theological Seminary of America as having authority to summon either party at the request of the other and further agreed that in the event of any civil divorce decree the husband would grant and the wife accept a Jewish divorce ("Get") in accordance with the authority vested in the Beth Din; that under the law of Moses should the husband arbitrarily refuse to give a "Get" the wife, such as plaintiff in this case, is known and referred to as an "Aguna" which is a state of limbo wherein the wife is considered neither married nor divorced; that a judgment of civil divorce of the parties was entered on May 16, 1978 in the Albany county clerk's office; that the wife has requested and summoned the husband to appear before the Beth Din of the Rabbinical Assembly pursuant to the terms of the Ketubah but that he has willfully and intentionally refused to appear before the assembly in violation of his contractual obligations; that in consequence the wife is consigned to the status of "Aguna" and is barred from remarrying within the context of a Jewish religious ceremony. The wife demands judgment against the husband: declaring "the rights and other legal relation of the plaintiff and defendant in the marriage contract (Ketubah), created by reason of the written instrument"; declaring that the husband specifically perform pursuant to the terms and conditions of the Ketubah in that he appear before the Beth Din of the Rabbinical Assembly and the Jewish Theological Seminary of America or its duly appointed representative pursuant to the wife's request; declaring that failure of the husband so to appear constitutes a breach of contract; and for other incidental relief.

Determination whether judicial relief may be granted the wife without constitutionally impermissible interjection of the court into matters of religious and ecclesiastical content requires examination of the English translation of the Ketubah in the context of the wife's allegation that this document was made and entered into as part of the religious ceremony in accordance with Jewish law and tradition:

"On the First Day of the Week, the 3rd Day of the month Sivan, 5726, corresponding to the 22nd Day of May, 1966, Boaz Avitzur, the bridegroom, and Susan Rose Wieder, the bride, were united in marriage in Old Westbury, N.Y. The bridegroom made the following declaration to his bride: 'Be thou my wife according to the law of Moses and Israel. I shall honor and support thee, faithfully I shall cherish thee and provide for thy needs, even as Jewish husbands are required to do by our religious law and tradition.'

"In turn, the bride took upon herself the duties of a Jewish wife, to honor and cherish her husband, and to carry out all her obligations to him in faithfulness and affection as Jewish law and tradition prescribe.

"And in solemn assent to their mutual responsibilities and love, the bridegroom and bride have declared: As evidence of our desire to enable each other to live in accordance with the Jewish law of marriage throughout our lifetime, we, the bride and bridegroom, attach our signatures to this Ketubah, and thereby agree to recognize the Beth Din of the Rabbinical Assembly and the Jewish Theological Seminary of America, or its duly appointed representative, as having authority to counsel us in the light of Jewish tradition which requires husband and wife to give each other complete love and devotion, and to summon either party at the request of the other, in order to enable the party so requesting to live in accordance with the standards of the Jewish law of marriage throughout his or her lifetime. We authorize the Beth Din to impose such terms of compensation as it may see fit for failure to respond to its summons or to carry out its decision.

"This Ketubah was executed and witnessed this day in accordance with Jewish law and tradition.

"Boaz Avitzur bridegroom Susan Wieder bride Melvin Kieffer rabbi Abraham Weisman witness Melvin Kieffer witness."

At the outset we observe that the complaint contains no allegation that the parties intended that the Ketubah should manifest secular promises or have any civil or secular status or any legal significance independent of the religious ceremony between them of which it was an integral part. Nor is any such assertion advanced in the papers submitted by the wife in support of her cross motion for summary judgment.

Moreover, it appears evident to us that any determination of the content and particulars of the rights of the wife or the obligations of the husband under this document cannot be made without inquiry into and resolution of questions of Jewish religious law and tradition. We think it inaccurate to identify the relief sought by plaintiff, as does the majority, as "simply to compel defendant to perform a secular obligation to which he contractually bound himself." (At p. 115, - N.Y.S.2d - , 446 N.E.2d 139.)

The complaint's first request for relief paints with a broad brush, asking that the court "declare the rights and other legal relations of the plaintiff and defendant in the marriage contract" created by reason of the Ketubah. That such an all-encompassing declaration of rights exceeds the authority of the civil court seems to be implicitly conceded by the majority's attempt to limit its consideration to enforcement of an obligation characterized as "secular" - the alleged obligation of the husband to appear before the Beth Din.

The wife's pleading itself, however, not to mention the affidavits submitted by her, makes it clear that even a definition of the purported "secular obligation" requires an examination into the principles and practice of the Jewish religion. Although the English translation of the Ketubah attached to the complaint recites that the parties "recognize the Beth Din . . . as having authority . . . to summon either party at the request of the other," the complaint seeks a declaration that the husband specifically perform "in that he appear before the Beth Din . . . pursuant to the request of the plaintiff." Thus, the wife tenders her construction of the document, which in turn presumably is predicated on what she contends is tradition in the faith, i.e., that there is an obligation imposed by the agreement to appear before the Beth Din at the summons alone of the other party to the marriage despite the facial reference to a summons by the Beth Din. The husband, tendering his own construction of the document, denies that he is under any obligation to appear before the Beth Din because an earlier request by him for convocation of such a body was refused. Thus, it appears evident that any judicial determination whether the husband is obligated to appear before the Beth Din, or what nature of summons is required to call such obligation into play, necessarily involves reference to substantive religious and ecclesiastical law.*

The unsoundness of the position espoused by the majority to justify judicial action to compel the husband to appear before the Beth Din, is revealed by projection of the course the continuing litigation will take in this case. The motion to dismiss and the cross motion for summary judgment having both been denied, the case will be set down for trial. The evidence which the wife may be expected to introduce is revealed by examination of the affidavits she submitted in opposition to the motion to dismiss and in support of her cross motion for summary judgment. Her affidavit conveys information furnished her by Rabbi Mordecai Kieffer who in his accompanying affidavit describes himself as "qualified to render an expert opinion concerning matters of Jewish laws and custom." She relies on his affidavit to support her claim that there was "good and legal consideration" for the Ketubah and that the Beth Din presently has no authority to compel the husband to submit to its jurisdiction. The rabbi, predicated on what he offers as a more accurate translation of the Ketubah into English, expresses the opinion that "good and legal consideration" is to be found in the document itself. Then, describing in detail the procedures incident to the issuance of a "Get," the rabbi concludes that the husband was obligated to submit to the jurisdiction of the Beth Din without the issuance of any summons by it. Accordingly, it is evident that the wife and her counsel are themselves of the view that substantiation of her position will depend on expert opinion with respect to Jewish law and tradition.

The majority's reference to the fact that marriage relationships solemnized within a religious context are recognized by the civil law is not determinative of the question here presented where what is sought to be enforced is an aspect of the relationship peculiar to the religion within which the ceremony creating it took place. No authority is cited in which a civil court has enforced a concomitant undertaking required by the ecclesiastical authority under which the marriage ceremony was solemnized. That no such civil enforcement of the obligation to appear before the Beth Din was contemplated either by the drafter of the Ketubah or by the parties as its signatories is evident from the inclusion of explicit authorization to the Beth Din "to impose such

---

*The recital in the testimonium clause itself is indicative-"this Ketubah was executed and witnessed this day in accordance with Jewish law and tradition."

terms of compensation as it may see fit for failure to respond to its summons or to carry out is decision." Nothing in the record suggests that it was the intention of the parties when they signed this religious document that the civil courts of the State of New York were to have jurisdiction to determine the substantive rights created thereby or to invoke civil procedures and remedies for the enforcement of such rights. Indeed, any conclusion on the part of our courts that this express provision was not intended by the parties as the exclusive remedy available to them for any breach of their obligations under the Ketubah would itself necessarily entail examination of Jewish law and tradition.

Finally, the evident objective of the present action - as recognized by the majority and irrefutably demonstrated by the complaint - even if procedural jurisdiction were to be assumed, is to obtain a religious divorce, a matter well beyond the authority of any civil court. (Again supplying her own interpretation of the Ketubah, the wife alleges: "That pursuant to the terms of the Ketubah, the plaintiff and defendant agreed that in the event of any civil divorce decree that the husband grant and the wife accept a Jewish divorce decree in accordance with the authority vested in the Beth Din of the Rabbinical Assembly.") As was noted at the Appellate Division, the interest of the civil authorities of the State of New York in the status of the marriage between these parties was concluded when the final judgment of divorce was entered in 1978.

Cooke, C.J., and *Fuchsberg* and *Meyer, JJ.*, concur with *Wachtler, J.*

Jones, J., dissents and votes to affirm in a separate opinion in which *Jasen* and *Simons, JJ.*, concur.

Order reversed, etc.

D. DIFFERENTIAL ALIMONY AWARDS AS A REMEDY FOR RECALCITRANCE

Brett v. Brett[a]

[1969] 1 All Eng. Rep. 1006 (C.A.)
Court of Appeal, Civil Division
December 2-5, 1968

Willmer, L.J.: We have before us an appeal and cross-appeal from an order made by Baker, J., on 5th July 1968, varying a previous order made by the senior registrar on 14th June 1968, awarding to a successful wife petitioner maintenance consisting partly of a lump sum payment and partly of annual payments, including a nominal order for secured maintenance. The case has raised interesting questions as to the considerations affecting the award of a lump sum payment and the proper balance to be maintained between any such lump sum payment and an award of annual payments.

The order appealed from was made in pursuance of s.16(1) of the Matrimonial Causes Act 1965, the effect of which was substantially to re-enact s. 5(1) of the Matrimonial Causes Act 1963. The subsection reads as follows:

> "On granting a decree of divorce or at any time thereafter (whether before or after the decree is made absolute), the court may, if it thinks fit and subject to subsection (3) of this section, make one or more of the following orders--(a) an order requiring the husband to secure to the wife, to the satisfaction of the court, such lump or annual sum for any term not exceeding her life as the court thinks reasonable having regard to her fortune (if any), his ability and the conduct of the parties; (b) an order requiring the husband to pay to the wife during their joint lives such monthly or weekly sum for the maintenance as the court thinks reasonable; (c) an order requiring the husband to pay to the wife such lump sum as the court thinks reasonable."

It has been held by this court in *Davis v. Davis*[1] that the word "reasonable" in para. (b) and para. (c) is governed by the same considerations as are applicable to para. (a); i.e., "reasonable" means "reasonable having regard to the wife's fortune, the husband's ability and the conduct of the parties."

The history of the marriage, since it lasted only some 5 1/2 months, can be briefly stated. The marriage took place on 11th December 1966. The parties lived together until 1st June 1967, when the wife left the husband. She complained that during that period of 5 1/2 months' cohabitation the husband had horrified her by his revolting sexual demands and practices. She obtained leave to file a petition forthwith, notwithstanding that three years had not elapsed since the marriage, obtaining that order on the grounds of exceptional depravity and exceptional hardship. The petition was not defended by the husband, and it resulted in a decree nisi being granted to the wife on the ground of cruelty on 10th October 1967. On the wife's application leave was granted

---

[a] *Edited.* Deletions are indicated by **** and footnotes renumbered.

1. [1967] 1 All E.R. 123; [1967] P. 185.

to expedite the decree absolute, and the decree was in fact made absolute on 26th October 1967.

At the time of the marriage the wife had just been admitted as a solicitor, and she had in fact worked for a month or so for her father, but had not taken out a practicing certificate. As a result of the husband's treatment of the wife, her health was adversely affected. According to the doctors, whose affidavits we have seen, she was reduced to a severe anxiety state which appeared likely, if she went on, to lead to a complete breakdown in her health. We are informed that even now she is not fully recovered and has not yet been able to resume work as a solicitor. In the meantime, since the breakdown of the marriage, she has lived mostly with her parents.

It is common ground that the husband is an extremely wealthy man. Exactly how wealthy he is is not really known because of his persistent failure to afford proper discovery of documents. The case proceeded before the senior registrar and before the learned judge on the basis that in relation to any facts which were in dispute the court was entitled to draw inferences in favour of the wife and against the husband, as was done in *J. v. J.*[2]

In this court it was at first submitted on behalf of the wife that the husband was not entitled to be heard at all on his appeal, having regard to his contempt in failing to comply with the order of the court; but when it appeared that the court might be disposed to order an adjournment, so as to enable the husband to purge his contempt and give proper discovery, counsel for the wife on instructions elected to waive his objection so as to enable the court to achieve finality on this hearing. The case, therefore, proceeded before us on the same basis as it had proceeded in the court below. I should state that there was an order for interim maintenance made by the learned registrar on 19th December 1967, which was varied by Baker, J., on 16th February 1968. But I do not think that anything now turns on the provisions of this order.

****

Both parties have now appealed to this court. On behalf of the husband it has been contended that there should, in the circumstances of this case, be no lump figure other than that ordered by the learned judge. It is conceded on his behalf that if the lump sum awarded is set aside or reduced, then the annual payments should be correspondingly increased. But it is also contended that if, on the other hand, the lump sum payment is to stand as ordered, then the annual payments should be decreased. On the other side, on behalf of the wife, it has been contended that both the lump sum payment and the annual payments should be increased.

I turn now to consider the provisions of s. 16(1) of the Act of 1965. In the present case the wife's fortune consists substantially of her ability to earn about 11,150 per annum as soon as she is well enough to resume work. The husband's ability is obviously very large indeed. I do not think I need say more about it than that it is certainly large enough to provide for any payment to the wife that could conceivably be justified.

With regard to the conduct of the parties, that of the wife does not appear to be open to any criticism whatsoever. In that respect this case is to be contrasted with *Davis v. Davis*[3], to which I have already referred, in which case the wife had been guilty of adultery in respect of which she had to pray

2. [1955] 2 All E.R. 617; [1955] P. 215.
3. [1967] 1 All E.R. 123; [1967] P. 185.

for the exercise of the court's discretion in her favour. As to the conduct of the husband, perhaps the less said the better. It is, I think, sufficient to remark that the charges made against him by the wife have never been denied. The question was raised, however, as to the relevance in the circumstances of this case of the husband's conduct when it comes to assessing the maintenance due to the wife. It has been conceded on her behalf that an award of maintenance cannot be used as a means of punishing the husband for the misbehaviour. But it has been submitted--and I think rightly submitted--that the husband's conduct is, at any rate, relevant in two ways. First, in view of his conduct, which had the effect of driving the wife out, it is submitted that he can hardly be heard to use the argument that this marriage only lasted a very short time. In that respect also this case is to be contrasted with that of *Davis v. Davis*[3], where the marriage had lasted for something over ten years. Secondly, it is said that the conduct of the husband is relevant in relation to his refusal or failure to grant a Get, thereby precluding the possibility of the wife remarrying and thus finding some other man to support her in the event of her wishing to do so.

****

Finally, I am disposed to accept the submission put forward on behalf of the wife that, in the circumstances of this case, it would be right to make provision in the award for the possibility of the husband persisting in his refusal to grant the Get which would make it possible for the wife to remarry if she wants to.

In all the circumstances, I have come to the conclusion that the proper award to make in this case is, first, a lump sum award of 130,000, payable in two installments, 125,000 within 14 days and the balance of 15,000 three months from today, if by that time the husband has not granted a Get. With regard to the annual payments, I think the proper award is 12,000 per annum less tax, with this further addition: that in the event of the husband granting a Get, so that the L5,000 lump sum amount does not become payable, then the annual payment should be increased by 1250 to 12,250 per annum less tax; i.e., the sum at which the learned registrar originally arrived. That, as it seems to me, involves the dismissal of the husband's appeal and allowing the wife's gross-appeal to the extent which I have stated.

Danckwerts, L.J.: I agree with the judgment which has been delivered by Willmer, L.J., and I do not wish to add anything.

Phillimore, L.J.: ****

So far as the 15,000 to be paid if no Get has been granted, it is perhaps material to observe that this man, as we are informed--and I do not think he has disputed it--is not an orthodox Jew, whereas his wife is an orthodox Jewess. For all practical purposes, therefore, the position at the moment is this: that since only the husband can apply for the Get, he is in a position to remarry, whereas the wife being an orthodox Jewess is not. I have not the slightest doubt that his failure to apply for a Get has been due to the reason which the learned judge concluded; viz., the hope that he could use his power to bargain and avoid payment of part of any maintenance award by the court. Apparently, it costs 25 guineas to obtain a Get, and the procedure involved only occupies a few days. By his failure to apply for a Get he is preventing this woman from obtaining other support, and in addition, as I have said, I have no doubt that he is seeking to obtain an advantage in bargaining with her.

For these reason, I entirely agree with the order as proposed by my Lords, and I would dismiss the husband's appeal and allow the wife's cross-appeal accordingly.

E. DENIAL OF ENFORCEMENT

Turner v. Turner

192 So.2d 787 (Fla. 1967)
District Court of Appeal of Florida, Third District
December 13, 1966. Rehearing denied January 4, 1967.

Per Curiam:

The appellant has appealed a final decree of divorce. She has assigned and argued error on each of the financial provisions of the decree. The appellee has cross assigned each provision which he deems adverse to him. The question presented in each instance is whether the record supports the finding of the chancellor.

While we cannot say that the record is without error, we hold that, with the exception of one particular hereafter discussed, it does not present reversible error. The essential holding of the chancellor is that because of devious and deceptive dealings of the parties he was unable, upon the evidence before him, to trace the equitable interest of the parties in the various assets acquired by the parties during their marriage.[1] This holding is fully substantiated by the record. We therefore affirm the decree as to the attacks upon its financial provisions upon authority of *Picchi v. Picchi*, Fla. 1958, 100 So.2d 627.

One of the cross assignments of error argued by the appellee urges that the following portion of the decree is unenforceable:

> "(j) The defendant is ordered to cooperate with plaintiff in obtaining a Jewish divorce, any expense therefor shall be paid by the plaintiff."

It is apparent that the thrust of the order by the chancellor to the appellee is that the appellee must submit to a religious ceremony in which he will be required to take an active part. If allowed to stand, this order would be enforceable by contempt proceedings and possibly by confinement of the appellee in jail.

---

1. "Plaintiff brought to this marriage certain property consisting of an apartment house in Chicago, Illinois. This property was sold after the marriage for approximately seventy thousand dollars. She had other assets of about thirty thousand dollars. These monies were invested in a home, in business and cannot be traced with accuracy because of the devious, hidden and deceptive business dealings of the parties."

"At present, the assets of this matrimonial estate consist of the matrimonial home and furnishings, two retail tie shops and stocks and bonds totalling several thousand dollars in value. These assets are held jointly except for the said two stores which bear a corporate name with both parties hereto owning equal shares therein."

"This court has searched the record to be able to make some specific conclusions and findings as to the large sums of money frequently referred to in the testimony. It is impossible to do so because of the eccentric, unconventional conduct of the parties. This includes the seven thousand five hundred dollar under the table transaction. There is scant evidence to make any legally supported conclusion, and it is 'next to impossible' to determine their true financial status."

The statutes of the State of Florida (see Ch. 65) provide for only one kind of divorce; that is, a civil divorce "from the bonds of matrimony." An examination of the statute reveals that there is no authorization for a chancellor to require the parties to secure a religious divorce.

We have not considered the appellee's contentions that requiring him to participate in a religious ceremony is a violation of his civil rights and the principle of the separation of church and state.

We hold that the circuit judge had no authority to order the appellee to participate in a religious ceremony. We amend the final decree by striking the reference to a religious divorce (paragraph "j" quoted above). See Fla.Stat. 1965, §59.34, F.S.A. As amended, the final decree is affirmed.

Affirmed.

****

See also *Morris v. Morris*, 42 D.L.R. (3d) 550, Manitoba Court of Appeal, reproduced earlier on pp. 329-337. [*ed.*]

Bibliography and Tables

Selected Bibliography

The following listing enumerates works that were utilized in the preparation of this book. The listings fall into ten categories: (1) primary sources in Jewish law; (2) secondary sources in Jewish law; (3) constitutional law; (4) contract and tort law; (5) comparative and international law; (6) jurisprudence; (7) legal procedure; (8) domestic relations law; (9) history; and (10) fiction. As a convenience to the general reader, I've tried to list English translations of Jewish law works when available although such translations were not necessarily consulted by this author. The reader should also refer to Appendixes E and F for additional structural and biographical information pertaining to many of the works and authors listed here, particularly those in Part I of this bibliography. Finally, the fact that a reference is listed under one particular heading or sub-heading does not preclude its containing information pertaining to another heading. Articles exploring the constitutionality of a *get* law, for example, will obviously contain at least a rudimentary exposition of Jewish famiy law as well. For bibliographical purposes, however, such articles are listed exclusively under the heading corresponding to their dominant subject matters. Please note the following abbreviations: b. = born, d. = died, R. = Rabbi.

I. PRIMARY SOURCES: JEWISH LAW

A. Bible and Commentaries

MIKRAOT GEDOLOT (Hebrew text of the Bible with standard rabbinic commentaries included, reprinted in many editions). Commentaries include Rashi (R.Shlomo Ben Yitzchok, France, d.1105); Ibn Ezra (Spain, d.1167); Rashbam (R. Shmuel Ben Meir, France, d.1174); Ramban (Nachmanides, Spain and Palestine, d.1270); Sforno (Italy, d.1550) and Baal HaTurim (R. Yaakov Ben Asher, Spain, d.1343).

The commentaries of Rashi and Ramban are also available in English translation, the former published by Feldheim and the latter by Ktav.

Abarbanel, Isaac. COMMENTARY OF ABARBANEL ON THE BIBLE (Spain, Italy, d.1508).

Chavel, Charles (ed.). COMMENTARY OF RAMBAN ON THE TORAH (Jerusalem: Mosad HaRav Kook, 1962).

Hertz, Joseph (ed.). THE PENTATEUCH AND HAFTORAS (London: Soncino Press, 1965).

Hirsch, Samson Raphael. COMMENTARY ON THE TORAH (New York: Judaica Press, 1989).

B. Talmud and Commentaries

BABYLONIAN TALMUD or TALMUD BAVLI with commentaries of Rashi and Tosafot (many editions). The standard edition of the Babylonian Talmud is a photo offset of the 1895 Vilna-Romm edition containing the basic commentaries of Rashi and Tosafot as well as many other commentaries, cross-reference notes, and finding aids. All page references are to the Vilna edition and its later offsets. The entire Talmud (without, however, the commentaries) has been translated into English and published by the Soncino Press under the editorship of Isidore Epstein. More recently, newer translations have begun to appear by Adin Steinsaltz (Random House, 1989) and the staff of Artscroll (Mesorah Publications, Ltd.), respectively. To date, however, the Steinsaltz-Random House project has produced only a few chapters within two tractates and the Artscroll somewhat more. Note should also be taken of the multivolume Steinsaltz edition of the Talmud translated into modern Hebrew (Israel Institute for Talmudic Publications), a project that is approximately 50% complete.

JERUSALEM TALMUD or TALMUD YERUSHALMI - The standard edition of the Jerusalem Talmud is also an offset of the Vilna-Romm edition, containing the standard commentaries of *P'nai Moshe* (R. Moshe Margolis, 18th Century) and *Korban Eidah* (R. David Frankel, 18th Century)

Professor Jacob Neusner is in the process of translating the Jerusalem Talmud into English. THE TALMUD OF THE LAND OF ISRAEL, trans. by Jacob Neusner (Chicago: University of Chicago Press, 1982 - ongoing).

Commentaries on the Talmud utilized in this work include, in addition to those appearing with the text, the works of Ramban, Rashba, Ritva, Ran, Meiri, and Rid, none of which has been translated into English. For a discussion of these authorities, see Appendix F.

C. Codes (Chronological Order)

CODE OF ALFASI (Rif) - printed in back of standard Vilna edition of the Babylonian Talmud along with commentaries of *Sefer HaMaor* (R. Zerachyah HaLevi) and *Milchamot HaShem* (Nachmanides). No translation has been made.

MISHNA TORAH or YAD HaCHAZAKA, (Moses Maimonides) - containing the standard commentaries of *Kesef Mishna*, *Magid Mishna*, *Mishna L'Melech*. Once again, the standard editions are offsets from those of Vilna. A new edition is currently in progress under the editorship of Shabsai Frankel. To date, the project is approximately 50% complete. The exemplary quality of the Frankel edition in terms of asthetics, textual accuracy, and finding aids assures that it will become the new standard. Maimonides' lucid prose and gift for organization lend themselves to translations. The Yale University Press, as part of its Judaica series, has translated the entire Mishna Torah and a new translation is currently being authored by Rabbi Eliyahu Tougher and published under the imprint of Moznaim.

CODE OF ASHERI or PISKAI ROSH - authored by R. Asher Ben Yechiel, printed in back of the standard Vilna edition of the Babylonian Talmud. No translation has been made. See Appendix F.

CODE OF MORDECHAI - authored by R. Mordechai Ben Hillel, printed in the back of the standard Vilna edition of the Babylonian Talmud. No translation has been made. See Appendix F.

ARBA TURIM or TUR - authored by R. Yaakov Ben Asher with commentaries of *Bait Yosef*, *Bayit Chadash*, and *Perisha*. No translation available. See Appendix E.

SHULCHAN ARUCH - R. Yosef Karo. No translation available. See Appendix E.

ARUCH HaSHULCHAN - R. Yechiel M. Epstein. No translation available. See Appendix E.

D. Responsa

Gaonim (7th-10th Century)

Harkavy (ed.). TESHUVOT HaGAONIM (Jerusalem: 1949)

Levin (ed.). OTZAR HaGAONIM (Jerusalem: 1938)

Rishonim (11th - 15th Century, by title)

TASHBATZ (R. Shimon Ben Tzemach Duran, Spain and North Africa, d.1444).

TERUMOT HaDESHEN (R. Israel Isserlin, Austria, d. 1460).

TESHUVOT MAHARIK (R. Yosef Colon, France and Italy, d. 1480).

TESHUVOT MEYUCHOSOT L'RAMBAN (attributed to Ramban but mostly by Rashba).

TESHUVOT RASHBA (R. Shlomo Ben Aderet, Spain, d. 1310).

TESHUVOT RITVA (R. Yom Tov Ibn Aseville, Spain, 14th Century).

TESHUVOT RIVASH (R. Isaac Ben Sheshet Perfet, Spain and North Africa, d. 1408).

TESHUVOT ROSH (R. Asher Ben Yechiel, Germany and Spain, d.1327).

Acharonim (16th Century to present, by title)

BAIT AVI (R. Yitzchok Liebes, United States, Contemporary).

BAIT MEIR (R. Meir Posner, Germany, 19th Century).

B'EER YITZCHOK (R. Yitzchok Elchonon Spector, Russia, 19th Century).

CHAIM SHE'AL (R. Yosef Chaim David Azulai, Palestine, d. 1806).

CHAIM V'SHALOM (R. Chaim Palaggi, Morocco, d. 1869).

CHATAM SOFER (R. Moshe Sofer, Germany and Hungary, d. 1839).

CHELKAT YAAKOV (R. Mordechai Yaakov Breisch, Switzerland, 20th Century).
CHIKREI LEV (R. Rafael Chazan, Morocco, d. 1820).
HaELEF L'CHA SHLOMO (R. Shlomo Kluger, Poland, d. 1868).
HAICHAL YITZCHOK (R. Yitzchok Herzog, Ashkenazic Chief Rabbi of Israel, d. 1959).
IGROT MOSHE (R. Moshe Feinstein, Russia and United States, d. 1986).
IMREI AISH (R. Meir Eisenstadt, Hungary, d. 1851).
MISHKENOT YAAKOV (R. Yaakov Karliner, Lithuania, 19th Century).
MISHNE HALACHOT (R. Menashe Klein, Hungary and United States, Contemporary).
MISHPATEI UZIEL (R. Meir BenZion Chai Uziel, Sefardic Chief Rabbi of Israel, d. 1953).
NODA B'YEHUDA (R. Ezekiel Landau, Prague, d. 1793).
NOFET TZUFIM (R. Psachya Birdigo, Morocco, 19th Century).
OTZAR HaCHAIM (Anthology of responsa, edited by Rabbi C. Ehrenreich 1930-1931).
RAV PO'ALIM (R. Yosef Chaim, Baghdad, d. 1909).
SHAAREI SHOMAYIM (R. Menachem Risikoff, Russia and United States, 20th Century).
SHEEALAT YAAVETZ (R. Yaakov Emden, Germany, d. 1776). See also TESHUVOT CHACHAM TZVI.
SHEEALOT U'TESHUVOT HaRIM (R. Yitzchok Meir Alter, Poland, d. 1865).
SHEEALOT U'TESHUVOT MISHPATIM YESHARIM (R. Raphael Birdigo, Morocco, d. 1821).
SHEEALOT U'TESHUVOT YAM HaGADOL (R. Yaakov Moshe Toledano, Palestine, 20th Century)
SHVUT YAAKOV (R. Yaakov Reisher, Prague, d. 1733)
SHEVET M'YEHUDA (R. Isser Yehuda Unterman, Ashkenazic Chief Rabbi of Israel, 20th Century).
SIMCHAT COHEN (R. Rachamim Chai HaCohen, Tunisia, 20th Century).
TESHUVOT BACH HaCHADASHOT (R. Joel Sirkes, Poland, 16th Century).
TESHUVOT CHACHAM TZVI (R. Tzvi

Ashkenazy, Germany and Poland, 17th Century, father of R. Yaakov Emdin, see SHEEALAT YAAVETZ).
TESHUVOT MABIT (R. Moshe Ben Yosef Trani, Greece and Palestine, d. 1580). See also TESHUVOT MAHARIT.
TESHUVOT MAHARAM ALSHAKER (R. Moshe Alshaker, Egypt, d. *circa* 1542).
TESHUVOT MAHARAM LUBLIN (R. Meir of Lublin, Poland, d. 1615).
TESHUVOT MAHARIT (R. Yosef Trani, son of Mabit, Palestine and Turkey, d. 1639).
TESHUVOT RABBI AKIVA EIGER (R. Akiva Eiger, Germany, d. 1837).
TESHUVOT RANACH (R. Eliyahu Ibn Chaim, Turkey, d. 1610).
TZITZ ELIEZER (R. Eliezer Waldenberg, Israel, Contemporary).
TZOFNAT PA'ANEACH (R. Yosef Rosen, Latvia, d. 1936).
YECHAVE DA'AT (R. Tzvi Makovsky, Russia and U.S., 20th Century).
YECHAVE DA'AT (R. Ovadiah Yosef, former Sefardic Chief Rabbi of Israel, Contemporary)

E. Other Primary Sources

ARUCH HaSHALEM - Dictionary of Talmudic and Midrashic literature, originally compiled by R. Nathan of Rome (11th Century) with additional etymological and philological material added by Dr. Alexander Kohut (Hungary and United States, d. 1894).

CHAZON ISH - Compendium of interpretations and rulings on the Talmud and Shulchan Aruch authored by R. Abraham Yeshaya Karelitz (Lithuania and Israel, 1878-1953).

CHELKAT YOAB - Commentary on topics in Talmud and *halacha* authored by R. Yoab Yehoshua (Lithuania, 19th century).

EDUT L'YISROEL and PERUSHAI IBRA - Two collections of essays on *halachic* topics by R. Yosef E. Henkin (Russia and U.S., 20th Century), reprinted together in KOL KITVAI Ha'GRIYA.

GEVUROT ANASHIM - A treatise on the Jewish laws of divorce, authored by R. Shabtai HaCohen, famed author of *Siftai Cohen* (Lithuania and Moravia, 1622-1663).

HAGAHOT MAIMONIYOT - An anonymous compendium of comments on Rambam's MISHNA TORAH, printed in all standard editions. Sometimes attributed to R. Moshe HaCohen (France, 12th Century).

HALAKHOT GEDOLOT - Early Gaonic compendium of *halachic* rulings, authorship has been attributed to either R. Yehudai Gaon or R. Shimon Kaira.

IGGERET R. SHERIRA GAON - An account of the composition of the Talmud along with the history of the Gaonate, authored by R. Sherira (10-11th Century).

INTRODUCTION TO THE COMMENTARY ON THE MISHNA - (Moses Maimonides - reprinted in the back of Volume One, standard edition of the Babylonian Talmud). An excellent annotated translation is provided by Zvi Lampel, MAIMONIDES' INTRODUCTION TO THE TALMUD (New York: Judaica Press, 1972).

KOL BO - *Halachic* work by an unknown authority thought to be of Spanish origin, circa 13th Century.

KNESSET HaGEDOLAH - *Halachic* anthology compiled by R. Chaim Beneviste (Turkey, d. 1673).

LEVUSH - *Halachic* work authored by R. Mordechai Jaffe (Czechoslovakia and Poland, c. 1535-1612).

NACHALAT SHIVA - Comprehensive form book containing the *halachic* requirements for the execution of legal documents, authored by R. Shmuel Ben David HaLevi (Poland and Germany, 17th Century).

OR ZARUA - Code of law and assorted responsa authored by R. Isaac of Vienna (13th Century). Major influence on Ashkenazic Jewry.

SEFARIM CHITZONIM - The apocryphal works that were excluded from the canonical literature. Mostly dating from the Second Commonwealth Era, these works occasionally shed light on various customs and practices prevalent in the Jewish community of the time. The standard edition is the one edited by A. Kahana (Tel Aviv: 1937).

SEFER HaCHINUCH (Book of Instruction) - Medieval work of anonymous authorship explaining the commandments found in the Torah, based primarily though not exclusively on the works of Rambam and Ramban. A good translation is Wengrov, THE BOOK OF THE COMMANDMENTS (New York: Feldheim, 1978).

SEFER HaYASHAR - Commentaries on the Talmud and responsa authored by R. Yaakov Ben Meir known as Rabbeinu Tam (France, 12th Century).

SEFER MITZVOT GADOL - A major compendium of laws organized according to the traditional 613 mitzvot of the Torah. Authored by R. Moshe of Coucy (France, 13th Century).

SHILTAI GIBBORIM - Commentary and annotations on the Code of Alfasi, authored by R. Joshua Boaz (Italy, d. 1555).

TESHUVOT MAIMONIYOT - Anthology of responsa by various authors organized according to the sequence of Rambam's Code. Printed at end of standard editions of MISHNA TORAH.

TORAT GITTIN - Commentary on the Jewish laws of divorce, authored by R. Yaakov Loerborbaum (Poland, 18th Century).

URIM Ve'TUMIM - Commentary on Jewish civil law authored by R. Yonatan Eibeshutz (Prague, 18th Century).

YAM SHEL SHLOMO - Code and commentary on large portions of the Talmud, authored by R. Shlomo Luria (Poland, 16th Century).

II. SECONDARY SOURCES: JEWISH LAW

A. Books

Adler, Benjamin. NISUIN K'HILCHATAM (Jerusalem: Mesorah, 1984).
Agudas, HaRabbonim. L'DOR ACHARON (New York: 1937).

Amram, David. THE JEWISH LAW OF DIVORCE ACCORDING TO THE BIBLE AND THE TALMUD (2nd Ed. New York: Hermon Press, 1968).
Assaf, Simcha. HaONSHIN ACHAR CHATIMAT HaTALMUD [Punishments After the Completion of the Talmud] (Jerusalem: 1922).
Benish, Chaim. MIDOT U'SHIUREI TORAH (Benai Brak, Israel: 1987).
Bergman, Meir. GATEWAY TO THE TALMUD (New York: Mesorah Publications, 1985).
Berkovitz, Eliezer. T'NAI B'NISUIN V'GET (Jerusalem: Mosad HaRav Kook, 1967), critically reviewed by Kasher, 11 NOAM 346 (1968).
Bleich, J. David. CONTEMPORARY HALAKHIC PROBLEMS, 3 vol. (Hoboken, New Jersey: Ktav, 1977-1989).
Bulka, Reuven. JEWISH DIVORCE ETHICS: THE RIGHT WAY TO SAY GOODBYE (Ogdensburg, New York: Ivy League Press, 1992).
Chajes, T. A STUDENT'S GUIDE TO THE TALMUD [translated from Hebrew by J. Schachter] (New York: Feldheim, 1960).
Chigier, Moshe. ISH V'ISHA B'DINAI YISRAEL (Jerusalem: Harry Fischel Institute, 1984).*
Elon, Menachem (ed.). THE PRINCIPLES OF JEWISH LAW (Jerusalem: Encyclopedia Judaica, 1975).
ENCYCLOPEDIA TALMUDIT (Jerusalem: Yad HaRav Herzog, ongoing)
Epstein, Louis. HATZA'AH L'MAAN TAKKANAT AGUNOT (New York: 1930).
-------------------. L'SHEELAT HaAGUNAH (New York: 1940).
Epstein, Mendel. A WOMAN'S GUIDE TO THE GET PROCESS (New York: Moznaim, 1989).
Ellinson, Getzel. NISUIN SHELO K'DAT MOSHE V'YISRAEL (Jerusalem: Alumim, 1980).
Freehof, Solomon. REFORM JEWISH PRACTICE (Cincinnati: Hebrew Union College Press, 1952).
Freiman, Abraham. SEDER KIDDUSHIN V'NISUIN ACHAR CHATIMAT HaTALMUD (Jerusalem: Mosad HaRav Kook, 1944).
Haut,Irwin. DIVORCE IN JEWISH LAW AND LIFE (New York: Hermon Press, 1983).
Herzog,Isaac. THE MAIN INSTITUTIONS OF JEWISH LAW, 2 vol. (London: Soncino Press, 1966-1967).
Horowitz, George. THE SPIRIT OF JEWISH LAW (New York: Central Book Co., 1953).
Kaplan, Aryeh. MADE IN HEAVEN (New York: Moznaim, 1983).
Klein, Isaac. A GUIDE TO JEWISH RELIGIOUS PRACTICE (New York: Jewish Theological Seminary Press, 1979).
Lamm, Maurice. BECOMING A JEW (Middle Valley, New York: Jonathan David, 1992).
Levin, A. Leo and Meyer Kramer. NEW PROVISIONS IN THE KETUBAH (New York: Yeshiva University Press, 1955).
Levinstein, Mordechai. NEFESH HaGER (Jerusalem: Mekor, 1972)
Lubetsky, Yehuda (ed.). EIN T'NAI B'NISUIN (Vilna: 1930).

---

*Chigier's work has also appeared in a revised English edition entitled HUSBAND AND WIFE IN ISRAELI LAW (Jerusalem: Harry Fischel Institute, 1985). Notably, the English edition contains a chapter on *agunah* problems (pp. 256-278) that does not appear in the Hebrew.

Meiselman, Moshe. JEWISH WOMEN AND JEWISH LAW (Hoboken, New Jersey: Ktav, 1978)
OTZAR HaPOSKIM (Jerusalem: Yad HaRav Herzog, ongoing).
Quint, Emmanuel. A RESTATEMENT OF JEWISH CIVIL LAW, Vol. One (Northvale, New Jersey: Jason Aronson, 1990).
Rabbinical Assembly. PROCEEDINGS (1932, 1938, 1968); BULLETIN (1939).
Reich, Shmuel. MESORET HaSHEKEL (Jerusalem: Feldheim, 1988).
Riskin, Shlomo. WOMEN AND JEWISH DIVORCE: THE REBELLIOUS WIFE, THE AGUNAH, AND THE RIGHT OF WOMEN TO INITIATE DIVORCE IN JEWISH LAW: A HALAKHIC SOLUTION (Hoboken, New Jersey: Ktav 1989).
Schimmel, Harry. THE ORAL LAW (New York: Feldheim, 1971).
Schreiber, Aaron. JEWISH LAW AND DECISION MAKING: A STUDY THROUGH TIME (Philadelphia: Temple University Press, 1979).
Shareshevsky, Ben Zion. DINAI MISHPACHA [Family Law in Israel] (2nd Ed. Jerusalem: Rubin Mass, 1967).
Shilo, Shmuel. DINA D'MALCHUTA DINA (Jerusalem: Jerusalem Academic Press, 1974).
Steinsaltz, Adin. THE ESSENTIAL TALMUD (New York: Basic Books, 1976).
Tykocinski, Chaim. TAKKANOT HaGAONIM (Jerusalem: 1959).
Werdyger, Jacob. EDUT L'YISRAEL (Tel Aviv: A. Gitler, n.d.).

B. Articles

Agus, Irving. *The Development of the Money Clause in the Ashkenazic Ketubah*, 30 JEWISH QUARTERLY REVIEW 221 (1939-1940).
Bleich, J. David. *A Suggested Antenuptial Agreement: A Proposal in the Wake of Avitzur*, 7 JOURNAL OF HALACHA AND CONTEMPORARY SOCIETY 25 (Spring 1984)
-------------------. *The Prohibition Against Intermarriage*, 1 JOURNAL OF HALACHA AND CONTEMPORARY SOCIETY 5 (Spring 1981).
-------------------. *The Conversion Crisis: A Halakhic Analysis*, 11 TRADITION 16 (1971).
Breitowitz, Irving. *Book Review of Quint, A Restatement of Jewish Civil Law*, 51 JEWISH ACTION 78 (Summer 1991).
Broyde, Michael. *On the Practice of Law According to Halacha*, 20 JOURNAL OF HALACHA AND CONTEMPORARY SOCIETY 5 (Fall 1990).
Chigier, Moshe. *Rabbinical Courts in Israel*, 2 ISRAEL LAW REVIEW 147 (1967).
Dick, Judah. *Is an Agreement to Deliver or Accept a Get in the Event of a Civil Divorce Halakhically Feasible*? 21 TRADITION 91 (1983).
Dichovsky, Shlomo. *Kifiyat Get* (Heb.), *Compelling a Get: A Proposal for Reduction of Sentence*, I TECHUMIN 248 (1980).
Ellinson, Getzel. *Civil Marriage in Israel: Halakhic and Social Implications*, 13 TRADITION 24 (1972).
-------------------. *Siruv Latet Get*, 69 SINAI 135 (1971).
Engel, Diane. *Marital Property Rights in Jewish Law: A Survey and Comparison*, 2 NATIONAL JEWISH LAW REVIEW 97 (1987).
Falk, Ze'ev. *Al Nisuin Shel Cohen U'Gerusha*, 27 DAOT 35 (1965).
Friedman, David. *The Status of Non-Halachic Marriages*, 8 JOURNAL

OF HALACHA and CONTEMPORARY SOCIETY 118 (Fall 1984).
Frimer, Dov. *The Role of the Lawyer in Jewish Law*, 1 JOURNAL OF LAW AND RELIGION 297 (1983).
------------------. *Selected English Bibliography on the Enforcement of Jewish Divorce in the Secular Courts; Selected Relevant Contemporary Halakhic literature in Hebrew*, 10/11 DINE ISRAEL 127-29 (1981-1983).
Frimer, Norman and Dov Frimer. *Reform Marriages in Contemporary Halakhic Responsa*, 21 TRADITION 7 (1984).
Gartner, Tzvi. *Problems of a Forced Get*, 9 JOURNAL OF HALACHA AND CONTEMPORARY SOCIETY 118 (Spring 1985).
------------------. *L'Takkanat Agunot* (Heb.), *For the Benefit of Agunahs*, 16 MORIAH 79 (Iyar 5748/1988)
------------------. *Book Review*, 50 JEWISH ACTION 70 (Spring 1990).
Gordis, Robert, *et al*. *The Issue of Patrilineal Descent: A Symposium*, 34 JUDAISM 3 (1985).
Jakobovitz, Immanuel. *Preserving the Oneness of the Jewish People: Can a Permanent Schism Be Avoided*? 24 TRADITION 78 (1989).
Kahan, Linda. *Jewish Divorce and Secular Courts: The Promise of Avitzur*, 73 GEORGETOWN LAW JOURNAL 193 (1984).
Kasher, Menachem, *et al*. *Symposium on the Meaning of Get*, 9 NOAM 1 (1966-1967).
Kirsh, Harvey. *Conflict Resolution and the Legal Culture: A Study of the Rabbinical Court* , 9 OSGOODE HALL LAW JOURNAL 335 (1971).
Kirschenbaum, Aaron. *Representation in Litigation in Jewish Law*, 6 DINE ISRAEL XV (1975).
Lamm, Norman. *Recent Additions to the Ketubah*, 2 TRADITION 93 (1959).
Lichtenstein, Aaron. *On Conversion*, 23 TRADITION 1 (1988).
Lieberman, Elizabeth. *Avitzur v. Avitzur: The Constitutional Implications of Judicially Enforcing Religious Agreements*, 33 CATHOLIC UNIVERSITY LAW REVIEW 219 (1983).
Lubling, Aaron. *Conversion in Jewish Law*, 9 JOURNAL OF HALACHA AND CONTEMPORARY SOCIETY 76 (Spring 1985).
Mann, Jacob. *The Responsa of the Babylonian Geonim as a Source of Jewish History*, 10 JEWISH QUARTERLY REVIEW (1919-1920) 121, 309.
Note. *Rabbinical Courts: Modern Day Solomons*, 6 COLUMBIA JOURNAL OF LAW AND SOCIAL PROBLEMS 49 (1970).
Novak, David. *The Marital Status of Jews Married Under Non-Jewish Auspices*, 1 JEWISH LAW ASSOCIATION STUDIES (Touro Conference) 61 (1985).
Rabbinowitz-Teumim, Benjamin. *Self-Imposed Constraints in Divorce* (Heb.), 1 NOAM 287 (5718/1958-1959).
Schachter, Hershel. *"Dina De'Malchusa Dina": Secular Law as a Religious Obligation*, 1 JOURNAL OF HALACHA AND CONTEMPORARY SOCIETY 103 (Spring 1981).
Schaffer, Sylvan. *Child Custody: Halacha and the Secular Approach*, 6 JOURNAL OF HALACHA AND CONTEMPORARY SOCIETY 33 (Fall 1983).
Schwartz, Gedaliah. *Heter Meah Rabbanim*, 11 JOURNAL OF HALACHA AND CONTEMPORARY SOCIETY 33 (Spring 1986).
------------------. *Book Review*, 25 TRADITION 94 (Winter 1990).

Slae, Menachem. *The Responsa Project*, 2 THE JEWISH LAW ANNUAL 84 (1979).
Warburg, Ronnie. *Child Custody: A Comparative Analysis*, 14 ISRAEL LAW REVIEW 480 (1981).
Yaron, Reuven. *Biblical Law: Prolegomena*, JEWISH LAW IN LEGAL HISTORY AND THE MODERN WORLD (B. Jackson, ed.) 27 (1980).
Zaks, Nissan. *Kiddushin Al T'nai*, 1 NOAM 52 (5718/1958-1959).

III. CONSTITUTIONAL LAW

A. Books

Gobert, James and Neil Cohen. RIGHTS OF PRISONERS (Colorado Springs, Colorado: Shepard's-McGraw Hill, 1981, 1991 Supplement).
Legislative Drafting Research Fund. CONSTITUTIONS OF THE UNITED STATES: NATIONAL AND STATE (Dobbs Ferry, New York: Oceana Publications, 1982, 1992).
Nowak, John, Ronald Rotunda, Nelson Young. CONSTITUTIONAL LAW: SUBSTANCE AND PROCEDURE (3rd ed. St. Paul: West, 1986).
Tribe, Laurence. AMERICAN CONSTITUTIONAL LAW (2nd ed. Mineola, New York: Foundation Press, 1988).

B. Articles

Brennan, William. *The Bill of Rights and the States: The Revival of State Constitution as Guardians of Individual Rights*, 61 NEW YORK UNIVERSITY LAW REVIEW 535 (1986).
-------------------. *State Constitutions and the Protection of Individual Rights*, 90 HARVARD LAW REVIEW 489 (1977).
Choper, Jesse. *The Religion Clauses of the First Amendement - Reconciling the Conflict*, 41 UNIVERSITY OF PITTSBURGH LAW REVIEW 673 (1980).
-------------------. *The Establishment Clause and Aid to Parochial Schools*, 56 CALIFORNIA LAW REVIEW 260 (1969); 75 CALIFORNIA LAW REVIEW 5 (1977).
Comment. *Jewish Divorce and the Civil Law*, 12 DE PAUL LAW REVIEW 295 (1962).
Freund, Paul. *Public Aid to Parochial Schools*, 82 HARVARD LAW REVIEW 1680 (1969).
Friedell, Steven. *The First Amendment and Jewish Divorce: A Comment on Stern v. Stern*, 18 JOURNAL OF FAMILY LAW 525 (1979-1980).
Johnson, Phillip. *Concepts and Compromise in First Amendment Religious Doctrine*, 72 CALIFORNIA LAW REVIEW 817 (1984).
Kurland, Philip. *The Irrelevance of the Constitution: The Religion Clauses of the First Amendment and the Supreme Court*, 24 VILLANOVA LAW REVIEW 3 (1978).
-------------------. *Of Church and State and the Supreme Court*, 29 UNIVERSITY OF CHICAGO LAW REVIEW 1 (1961).
Lupu, Ira. *Where Rights Begin: The Problem of Burdens on the Free Exercise of Religion*, 102 HARVARD LAW REVIEW 933 (1989).

McConnell, Michael. *Coercion: The Last Element of Establishment*, 27 WILLIAM AND MARY LAW REVIEW 933 (1986).

------------------. *Accommodation of Religion*, 1985 SUPREME COURT REVIEW 1.

Note. *Civil Religion and the Establishment Clause*, 95 YALE LAW JOURNAL 1237 (1986).

Note. *Lynch v. Donnelly: Has the Lemon Test Soured?* 19 LOYOLA OF LOS ANGELES LAW REVIEW 133 (1985).

Note. *Prisoners' Religious Free Exercise Rights*, 37 AMERICAN UNIVERSITY LAW REVIEW 453 (1988).

Pollack, Stewart. *State Courts As Separate Sources of Fundamental Rights*, 35 RUTGERS LAW REVIEW 707 (1983).

Rostain, Tanina. *Permissible Accommodation of Religion: Reconsidering the New York Get Statute*, 96 YALE LAW JOURNAL 1147 (1987).

Schwartz, David. *Larkin v. Grendel's Inn, Inc.: The Burger Court and the Establishment Problem*, 21 HOUSTON LAW REVIEW 179 (1984).

Sullivan, Kathleen. *Unconstitutional Conditions*, 102 HARVARD LAW REVIEW 1413 (1989).

Williams, Robert. *In the Supreme Court's Shadow: Legitimacy of State Rejection of Supreme Court Reasoning and Result*, 35 SOUTH CAROLINA LAW REVIEW 353 (1984).

IV. CONTRACT AND TORT LAW

A. Books

Corbin, Arthur. CONTRACTS (St. Paul: West, 1950).

Farnsworth, E. Allan. CONTRACTS (2nd ed. Boston: Little, Brown, 1990).

Hillman, Robert A., Julian McDonnell, Steve Nickles. COMMON LAW AND EQUITY UNDER THE UNIFORM COMMERCIAL CODE (Boston: Warren, Gorham and Lamont, 1985).

Keeton, W. Page, Dan Dobbs, Robert Keeton, David Owen. PROSSER AND KEETON ON THE LAW OF TORTS (5th ed. St. Paul: West, 1984) (revision of the classic treatise authored by the late William Prosser).

McCormick, Charles. HANDBOOK OF THE LAW OF DAMAGES (St. Paul: West, 1935).

RESTATEMENT OF CONTRACTS (Second) (Philadelphia: American Law Institute, 1981 with annual supplements).

RESTATEMENT OF TORTS (Second) (Philadelphia: American Law Institute, 1965 with annual supplements).

B. Articles

Annotation. *Modern Status of International Infliction of Mental Distress as Independent Tort; "Outrage"*, 38 AMERICAN LAW REPORTS (4th Series) 998 (1985, 1990 Supp.).

Annotation. *Right to Recover Damages in Negligence for Fear of Injury to Another or Shock or Mental Anguish at Witnessing Such Injury*, 29 AMERICAN LAW REPORTS (2nd Series) 1337 (1970, 1990 Supp.).

Brown, Jack. *The Rise and Threatened Demise of the Prima Facie Tort Principle*, 54 NORTHWESTERN LAW REVIEW 563 (1959).

Cobin, David. *Jewish Divorce and the Recalcitrant Husband - Refusal to Give a Get as Intentional Infliction of Emotional Distress*, 4 JOURNAL OF LAW AND RELIGION 405 (1986).
Dawson, John. *Duress Through Civil Litigation*, 45 MICHIGAN LAW REVIEW 571 (1947).
Dobbs, Dan. *Tortious Interference with Contractual Relations*, 34 ARKANSAS LAW REVIEW 335 (1980).
Farnsworth, E. Allan. *Meaning in the Law of Contracts*, 76 YALE LAW JOURNAL 939 (1967).
Feinsinger, Nathan. *Legislative Attack on Heart Balm*, 33 MICHIGAN LAW REVIEW 979 (1935)
------------------. *Current Legislation Affecting Breach of Promise to Marry, Alienation of Affection, and Related Actions*, 10 WISCONSIN LAW REVIEW 417 (1935).
Forkosch, Morris. *An Analysis of the Prima Facie Tort Action*, 42 CORNELL LAW QUARTERLY 465 (1957).
Lloyd, William. *Penalties and Forfeitures*, 29 HARVARD LAW REVIEW 117 (1915).
Magruder, Calvert. *Mental and Emotional Disturbance in the Law of Torts*, 49 HARVARD LAW REVIEW 1033 (1936).
MacNeill, Ian. *Power of Contract and Agreed Remedies*, 47 CORNELL LAW QUARTERLY 495 (1962).
Redman, Barbara. *Jewish Divorce: What Can Be Done in Secular Courts to Aid the Jewish Women?* 19 GEORGIA LAW REVIEW 389 (1985) (primarily an analysis of tort law).

V. COMPARATIVE AND INTERNATIONAL LAW

A. Books

Blaustein, Albert and Gisbert Flanz. CONSTITUTIONS OF THE COUNTRIES OF THE WORLD (London, Rome, New York: Oceana, 1984 with periodic supplementation).
South African Law Commission, WORKING PAPER 45: JEWISH DIVORCE (1992) (primarily a comparative study of how different jurisdictions deal with the *agunah* problem).

B. Articles

Glenn, H. Patrick. *Where Heavens Meet: The Compelling of Religious Divorces*, 28 AMERICAN JOURNAL OF COMPARATIVE LAW 1 (1980).
Kisch, Guido. *Relations Between Jewish and Christian Courts in the Middle Ages*, LOUIS GINZBERG JUBILEE VOLUME 201 (1945).
Maidment, Susan. *The Legal Effect of Religious Divorces*, 37 MODERN LAW REVIEW 611 (1974).
Note. *Civil Enforcement of Religious Antenuptial Agreements*, 23 UNIVERSITY OF CHICAGO LAW REVIEW 122 (1955).

VI. JURISPRUDENCE

Hohfeld, Wesley. FUNDAMENTAL LEGAL CONCEPTIONS AS APPLIED IN JUDICIAL REASONING AND OTHER LEGAL ESSAYS (New Haven: Yale University Press, 1923).
Holmes, Oliver Wendell. COLLECTED LEGAL PAPERS (New York: Harcourt, Brace, 1920).
Pound, Roscoe. JURISPRUDENCE (St. Paul: West, 1959).

VII. LEGAL PROCEDURE*

A. Books

Crandall, Thomas, Richard Hagedorn, Frank Smith, Jr. THE LAW OF DEBTORS AND CREDITORS (Rev. ed. Boston and New York: Warren, Gorham and Lamont, 1991).
Domke, Martin. COMMERCIAL ARBITRATION (Rev. ed. Deerfield, Illinois: Callaghan, 1984).
James, Fleming and Geoffrey Hazard. CIVIL PROCEDURE (2nd ed. Boston: Little, Brown, 1977).
King, Lawrence (ed.). COLLIER ON BANKRUPTCY (15th ed. New York: Matthew Bender, 1981 with annual supplements).
Newberg, Herbert. ATTORNEY FEE AWARDS (Colorado Springs, Colorado: Shepard's/McGraw-Hill, 1986, 1991 Supp.).
Reppy, Alison (ed.). DAVID DUDLEY FIELD: CELEBRATING ONE HUNDRED YEARS OF LEGAL REFORM (New York: NYU School of Law, 1949).
RESTATEMENT OF JUDGMENTS (Second) (Philadelphia: American Law Institute, 1982).
Scoles, Eugene and Peter Hay. CONFLICT OF LAWS (St. Paul: West, 1982, 1986 Supp.).

B. Article

Vukowich, George. *Debtors' Exemption Rights*, 62 GEORGETOWN LAW JOURNAL 779 (1974).

VIII. DOMESTIC RELATIONS

Blake, Nelson. THE ROAD TO RENO: A HISTORY OF DIVORCE IN THE UNITED STATES (Westport: Greenwood Press, 1977).
Clark, Homer. THE LAW OF DOMESTIC RELATIONS IN THE UNITED STATES (Practicioner's ed. St. Paul: West, 1987).
Golden, Lawrence. EQUITABLE DISTRIBUTION OF PROPERTY (Colorado Springs, Colorado: Shepard's/McGraw Hill, 1983 with 1990 Supp.).
Melli, Marygold, Ann Stanton, Margaret Haynes, *et al.* ALIMONY, CHILD SUPPORT AND COUNSEL FEES - AWARD, MODIFICATION AND ENFORCEMENT, 3 vol. (New York:

---

*This includes creditors' rights and bankruptcy.

Matthew Bender, 1991).
Rutkin, Arnold (ed.). FAMILY LAW AND PRACTICE, 4 vol. (New York: Matthew Bender, 1991).

IX. HISTORY

Azulai, Chaim. SHEM HaGEDOLIM (Brooklyn: 1982).
ENCYCLOPEDIA JUDAICA (Jerusalem: Keter, 1971).
ENCYCLOPEDIA OF ISLAM (Leiden and London: 1913, rev. ed. 1960).
Finkelman, Shimon. REB MOSHE: THE LIFE AND IDEALS OF HAGAON RABBI MOSHE FEINSTEIN (New York: Mesorah Publications, 1986).
Goitein, S.D. A MEDITERRANEAN SOCIETY: THE JEWISH COMMUNITIES OF THE ARAB WORLD AS PORTRAYED IN THE DOCUMENTS OF THE CAIRO GENIZAH, 5 vol. (Berkeley: University of California, 1967-1988).
Goldwurm, Hersh. THE RISHONIM (New York: Mesorah Publications, 1982).
Goldwurm, Hersh. THE EARLY ACHARONIM (New York: Mesorah Publications, 1989).
Graetz, Heinrich. HISTORY OF THE JEWS (Philadelphia: Jewish Publication Society, 1891-1898).
Grayzel, Solomon. HISTORY OF THE JEWS (New York: New American Library, 1968).
Grossman, Aryeh. THE EARLY SAGES OF ASHKENAZ [Heb.] (Jerusalem: Magnes Press, 1981).
Hertzberg, Arthur. THE FRENCH ENLIGHTENMENT AND THE JEWS (New York: Columbia University Press, 1968 and 1990).
Holder, Meir. HISTORY OF THE JEWISH PEOPLE: FROM YAVNEH TO PUMBEDISA (New York and Jerusalem: Mesorah Publications and Hillel Press, 1986).
Levy, Reuben. THE SOCIAL STRUCTURE OF ISLAM (London: Cambridge University Press, 1957).
Weiss, Isaac. DOR DOR V'DORSHAV (Berlin: 1923).

X. FICTION

Grade, Chaim. THE AGUNAH (Indianapolis: Bobbs, 1974).
Kritch, Rochelle. TIL DEATH DO US PART (New York: Avon, 1992).

Table of References to Bible, Talmud, Codes, and Responsa

*The following abbreviations are used in this table: BACH - *Bayit Chadash*; BS - *Bait Shmuel*; BY - *Bait Yosef*; CM - *Chelkat Mechokek*; DER - *Derisha*; GRA - *Biur HaGra*; PT - *Pitchai Teshuva*; SEMA - *Sefer Meirat Ainayim*; TG - *Torat Gittin*.

*Responsa that are central to the analysis in this book are highlighted in bold type.

**Responsa and other works that are central to the analysis in this book are highlighted in bold type.

Table of Cases

A

B

*Cases brought by the United States are listed under the name of the opposing party. Thus, *United States v. Lee* is listed as *Lee*, *United States* v. Also, for the benefit of the general reader, it should be pointed out that the New York Supreme Court is a trial court of general jurisdiction. The highest court in that state is the Court of Appeals.

Cases discussed extensively in the text or reproduced in full are indicated in boldface.

G

H

I

J

R

S

T

Table of Statutes and Regulations

Index

---

*This index does not reference authors and works cited in the footnotes without comment. Such works and their authors may be found in the Bibliography. There are also separate tables for case law, statutes and regulations, and Biblical and Talmudic passages, none of which are indexed here.

About the Author

IRVING A. BREITOWITZ is Associate Professor of Law at the University of Maryland School of Law, as well as a Rabbi and an attorney.

www.ingramcontent.com/pod-product-compliance
Ingram Content Group UK Ltd.
Pitfield, Milton Keynes, MK11 3LW, UK
UKHW020228290926
15470UKWH00001B/423